Conten

Plan Your Trip

This is Japan.................6

Japan Map.................8

Japan's Top 25
Highlights.................10

Japan's Top
Itineraries.................32

Japan Month
by Month.................42

What's New.................46

Get Inspired.................47

Need to Know.................48

Discover Japan

Tokyo 51

Highlights.................54

Best....................56

Strolling Yanaka
Walking Tour.................58

Itineraries.................59

Tokyo.................60

Around Tokyo.................120

Mt Fuji Area.................120

Nikkō.................129

Minakami &
Takaragawa Onsen....133

Hakone.................135

Kamakura.................139

Central Honshū 143

Highlights.................146

Best.....................148

Itineraries.................150

Hida District.................152

Takayama.................152

Northern
Japan Alps.................160

Kamikōchi.................161

Shin-Hotaka Onsen....163

Nagano Prefecture 165

Shiga Kōgen.................166

Nozawa Onsen.................167

Hakuba.................170

Matsumoto.................172

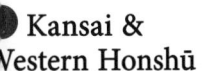

Kansai &
Western Honshū

ighlights............................256

Nara-kōen

Kinosaki Onsen

Hiroshima

Benesse Art Site
aoshima

Miyajima

Contents

Discover Japan

Kiso Valley Nakasendō 176

Ishikawa Prefecture **181**

Kanazawa 181

Noto Peninsula 189

Kaga Onsen 191

Kyoto **193**

Highlights **196**

Best... .... **198**

Southern Higashiyama Walking Tour **200**

Itineraries **201**

Kyoto **202**

Takao 233

Manshu-in 234

Kansai & Western Honshū **253**

Highlights **256**

Best... .... **258**

Itineraries **260**

Osaka **262**

Nara **276**

Kōya-san **287**

Kinosaki **292**

Kōbe **295**

Himeji **299**

Naoshima **301**

Hiroshima **306**

Miyajima **312**

The Best of the Rest **317**

Niseko **318**

Daisetsuzan National Park **320**

Asahidake Onsen 321

Iya Valley **322**

Ōboke & Koboke 323

Chiiori 324

Nagasaki **325**

Southwest Islands **330**

Yakushima 330

Okinawa-hontō 332

Kerama Islands 336

Discover
Japan

Experience the best of Japan

This edition written and researched by

Chris Rowthorn,
Laura Crawford, Trent Holden,
Craig McLachlan, Rebecca Milner, Kate Morgan,
Benedict Walker, Wendy Yanagihara

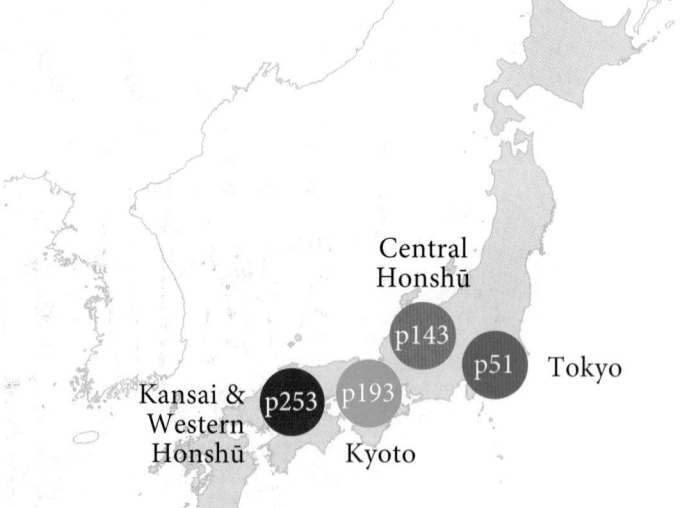

Central
Honshū

p143

p51

Tokyo

Kansai &
Western
Honshū

p253

p193

Kyoto

● Tokyo

Highlights............................54

o Meiji-jingū
o Shibuya
o Tsukiji Fish Market
o Nikkō
o Kamakura

● Central Honshū

Highlights..........................146

o Kanazawa
o Tateyama-Kurobe Alpen Route
o Takayama
o Kamikōchi
o Tsumago & Magome

● Kyoto

Highlights..........................196

o Arashiyama
o Nanzen-ji
o Kiyomizu-dera
o Kinkaku-ji
o Fushimi Inari-taisha

In Focus

Japan Today 340

History 342

The People of Japan .. 350

Food & Drink 354

Arts & Architecture .. 362

Onsen 367

Ryokan 369

Family Travel 371

Survival Guide

Directory 374

Accommodation 374

Customs Regulations .. 374

Electricity 375

Embassies &
Consulates 375

Gay & Lesbian
Travellers 376

Health 377

Insurance 377

Internet Access 377

Climate 377

Left Luggage 379

Maps 379

Money 379

Opening Hours 381

Public Holidays 381

Solo Travellers 382

Telephone 382

Time 383

Toilets 383

Tourist Information ... 383

Travellers with
Disabilities 383

Visas 384

Women Travellers 384

Transport 385

Getting There &
Away 385

Getting Around 386

Language 394

Behind the Scenes ... 395

Index 396

How to Use
This Book 406

Our Writers 408

This Is Japan

Japan is a world apart – a wonderful little planet floating off the coast of China. It is a kind of cultural Galápagos, a place where a unique civilisation has been allowed to grow and unfold on its own, unmolested by invading powers.

Japan's ancient culture is a bounty of riches.
From the retina-burning splendour of a Kyoto geisha dance to the spare beauty of a Zen rock garden, Japan has the power to enthral even the most jaded traveller.

Japan is a place to leave your comfort zone without suffering any real discomfort.
Whether it's staying in a ryokan (traditional Japanese inn), soaking in a bubbling onsen (hot spring) or gazing at the apparition of a geisha, Japan offers regular doses of 'Wow!' against a backdrop of ultramodern comfort.

Savouring the delights of Japanese cuisine is half the reason to come to Japan.
Indeed, many travellers come to Japan solely to sample the delights of Japanese food on its home turf. Eat just one meal in a top-flight Tokyo sushi restaurant and you'll see why: the Japanese attention to detail, genius for presentation and insistence on the finest ingredients result in food that can change your perception of what is possible in the culinary arena.

The wonders of Japan's natural world are a well-kept secret.
The hiking in the Japan Alps and Hokkaidō is world class, and with an extensive hut system you can do multiday hikes with just a day pack. Down south, the coral reefs of Okinawa will have you wondering if you've somehow been transported to Thailand. And you never have to travel far in Japan to get out in nature: in cities like Kyoto, a few minutes of travel will get you into forested mountains.

> 66
>
> Japan has the power to enthral even the most jaded traveller
>
> 99

Geisha in Kyoto (p192)
WIBOWO RUSLI / GETTY IMAGES ©

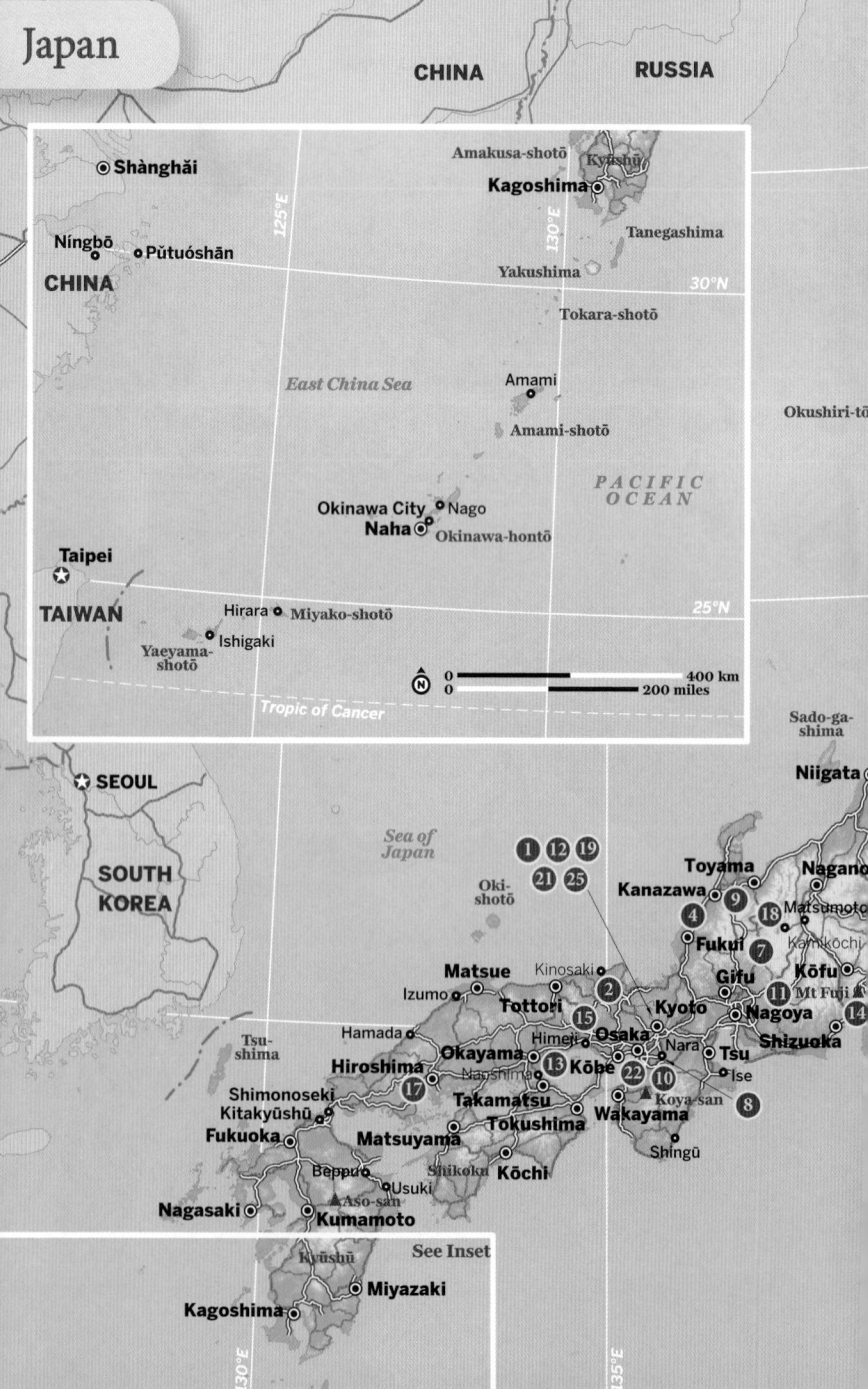

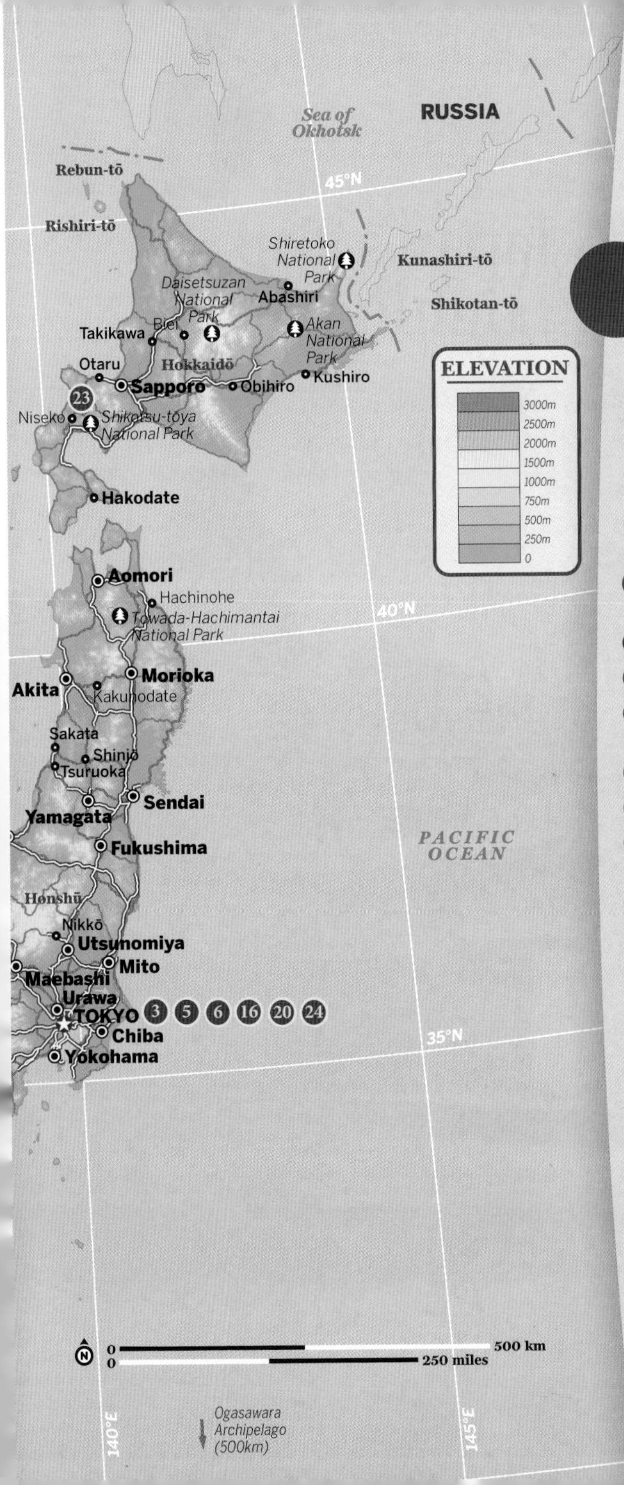

Sea of Okhotsk

RUSSIA

45°N

Rebun-tō

Rishiri-tō

Shiretoko National Park

Kunashiri-tō

Daisetsuzan National Park

Abashiri

Shikotan-tō

Takikawa · Biei

Akan National Park

Otaru

Hokkaidō

Sapporo · Obihiro · Kushiro

Niseko · 23 *Shikotsu-tōya National Park*

Hakodate

ELEVATION

	3000m
	2500m
	2000m
	1500m
	1000m
	750m
	500m
	250m
	0

Aomori

Hachinohe

Towada-Hachimantai National Park

40°N

Morioka

Akita · Kakunodate

Sakata · Shinjō

Tsuruoka

Yamagata · **Sendai**

Fukushima

Honshū

Nikkō

Utsunomiya

Maebashi · **Mito**

Urawa

TOKYO · ③ ⑤ ⑥ ⑯ ⑳ ㉔

Chiba

Yokohama

PACIFIC OCEAN

35°N

N

0		500 km
0		250 miles

Ogasawara Archipelago (500km)

140°E · 145°E

25
Top Highlights

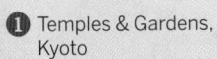

1 Temples & Gardens, Kyoto

2 Onsen, Kinosaki

3 Japanese Cuisine, Tokyo

4 Staying in a Ryokan, Kayōtei

5 Cherry-Blossom Viewing, Tokyo

6 Tokyo's Tsukiji Fish Market

7 Hiking in the Japan Alps

8 Nara's Tōdai-ji & Daibutsu (Great Buddha)

9 Kenroku-en, Kanazawa

10 Kōya-san

11 Hiking, Magome to Tsumago

12 Geisha Dances, Kyoto

13 Naoshima

14 Mt Fuji

15 Castle, Himeji

16 Sumō, Tokyo

17 Hiroshima

18 Kamikōchi

19 Nishiki Market, Kyoto

20 Tokyo's Modern Architecture

21 Kabuki, Kyoto

22 Dōtombori, Osaka

23 Skiing, Niseko

24 Shopping in Tokyo

25 Arashiyama Bamboo Grove, Kyoto

25 Japan's Top Highlights

Temples & Gardens, Kyoto

With over 1000 temples to choose from, you're spoiled for choice in Kyoto. Spend your time finding one that suits your taste. If you like things gaudy and grand, you'll love the retina-burning splendour of Kinkaku-ji (p223). If you prefer *wabi-sabi* to rococo, then you'll find the tranquility of Hōnen-in (p218) or Shōren-in (p212) more to your liking. And don't forget that temples are where you find the best gardens: you'll find some of the finest at Ginkaku-ji (p218), Ryōan-ji (p223) and Tōfuku-ji (p229). Below: Ginkaku-ji

Onsen

There's nothing like lowering yourself into the tub at a Japanese onsen (natural hot spring bath). The 'ahhh' that you emit is just a simple way of saying 'Damn, I'm glad I came to Japan!'. If you're lucky, the tub is outside and there's a nice stream running nearby. The Japanese have turned the simple act of bathing into a folk religion and the country is dotted with temples and shrines to this most relaxing of faiths. For the classic onsen experience, head to Kinosaki (p292).

Japanese Cuisine

Japan is a food-lover's paradise and the cuisine (p354) is incredibly varied, running the gamut from impossibly fresh sushi around Tsukiji Fish Market to grilled skewers of chicken under the train tracks in Yūrakuchō. In a city like Tokyo, you could eat a different Japanese specialty cuisine every night for a month without repeating yourself. There's no doubt that a food tour of Japan will be memorable, but there's just one problem: once you try the real thing in Japan, the restaurants back home will pale in comparison. The only solution is another trip to Japan!

3

The Best...
Onsen (Hot Springs)

KINOSAKI
Japan's classic onsen town is everything an onsen town ought to be: quaint, friendly and packed with good ryokan. (p292)

KAYŌTEI
Kayōtei is a first-class onsen ryokan in Ishikawa Prefecture, an easy three-hour train ride from Kyoto. (p191)

SHIN-HOTAKA ONSEN
Shin-Hotaka Onsen is a superb onsen resort located at the base of the northern Japan Alps. (p163)

KURAMA ONSEN
Located less than an hour north of Kyoto by train, this quaint onsen feels worlds away. (p231)

The Best...
Ryokan (Traditional Inns)

TAWARAYA
Kyoto's Tawaraya is a secret world all of its own – once you enter, you may never want to leave. (p235)

HIIRAGIYA
Hiiragiya gives Tawaraya stiff competition for the title of 'Kyoto's best ryokan'. (p235)

KAYŌTEI
A ryokan with its own private onsen (hot spring bath) is the ultimate in relaxation. (p191)

NISHIMURAYA HONKAN
As soon as you enter the elegant courtyard of Nishimuraya Honkan, you'll know you're in for something special. (p294)

LONELY PLANET / GETTY IMAGES ©

④ Staying in a Ryokan

Eat in your bedroom. Spend the day lounging in a robe. Soak in a bath while looking at a garden. Don't lift a finger except to eat. Sounds relaxing? Then we highly recommend a night in a top-flight ryokan (traditional Japanese inn) such as Ishikawa Prefecture's Kayōtei (p191). The Japanese had this whole spa thing figured out long before they even heard the word 'spa'. If your finances don't run to a first-class place, even the most humble ryokan will give you a taste of how the Japanese used to live.

TOM BONAVENTURE / LONELY PLANET / GETTY IMAGES ©

⑤ Cherry-Blossom Viewing

If you think of the Japanese as a sober, staid and serious people, then you owe it to yourself to join them under a cherry tree in the springtime for a *hanami* (blossom viewing) party (p75) in a place such as Tokyo's Ueno-kōen.

Tokyo's Tsukiji Fish Market

If it swims in the sea, it's probably on sale in Tokyo's Tsukiji Fish Market (p68). The mother of all fish markets, Tsukiji is a sprawling monument to the Japanese love of seafood. It's a must for sushi fans and anyone who loves a good market tour. Even if you don't want to wake up early to see the tuna auction, if Tokyo is in your Japan itinerary, you've gotta make the pilgrimage to Tsukiji.

Hiking in the Japan Alps

Close your eyes and picture Japan. If all you see are geisha, Zen gardens, bullet trains and hyper-modern cities, then you might be in for a surprise when you get to the Japan Alps (p152). Hike right into the heart of the high peaks here and you might think you're in New Zealand or the Rockies. You can go hut to hut here among the peaks for a week with nothing but a solid day pack.

Nara's Tōdai-ji & Daibutsu (Great Buddha)

Here's the drill: go to the temple of Tōdai-ji (p279) in Nara and stop for a moment outside the main hall. Then, without looking up, step into the hall. Calm your thoughts. Now raise your eyes to behold the Great Buddha. This is probably the closest one can come to enlightenment without years of meditation. Perhaps no other sight in Japan has as much impact as this cosmic Buddha – you can almost feel the energy radiating out from its vast bulk.

The Best...
Places to Eat

TOKYO
With more Michelin stars than any city on earth, Tokyo is the best eating city on earth. (p97)

KYOTO
Kyoto is *the* place to sample traditional Japanese cuisine, known as *kaiseki* (Japanese haute cuisine). (p238)

NAGASAKI
Nagasaki has always been Japan's gateway to the rest of Asia and its cuisine is redolent of mainland flavours. (p325)

OSAKA
The motto of this city is '*kuidaore*' (eat until you drop), so, naturally, it's a food-lover's paradise. (p267)

Kenroku-en, Kanazawa

This is one of the country's top three gardens. Developed over 200 years by the Maeda clan as part of Kanazawa-jō castle, Kenroku-en (p185) is said to incorporate the six attributes of a perfect landscape. Stroll the meandering paths along arching bridges, gurgling fountains and plum and pine groves, and savour the garden's highlights – the unique Kenroku-en Kikuzakura cherry tree, and the iconic Kotoji-tōrō stone lantern by Kasumiga-ike pond. A visit to Kenroku-en is best capped off with a cup of green powdered tea at the Shigure-tei Teahouse.

The Best...
Cities for Temples, Shrines and Gardens

KYOTO
You could spend a month in Kyoto and see a different garden, temple and shrine each day. (p202)

NARA
Nara is a compact wonder of a city that some consider the birthplace of Japanese culture. (p276)

KANAZAWA
Kanazawa is thick with traditional culture and home to one of Japan's finest gardens: Kenroku-en. (p185)

TOKYO
That's right: amid all that concrete and neon there are some wonderful hints of traditional Japan. (p60)

Kōya-san

10

Riding the funicular up to the sacred Buddhist monastic complex of Kōya-san (p287), you almost feel like you're ascending to another world. The place is permeated with a kind of august spiritual grandeur and nowhere is this feeling stronger than in the vast Oku-no-in cemetery. Trails weave their way among towering cryptomeria trees and by the time you arrive at the main hall, a sudden appearance by a Buddha would seem like the most natural thing in the world. Left: Stone figures in Kōya-san

Hiking, Magome to Tsumago

11

A beautifully preserved post town in southern Nagano-ken, Tsumago is home to traditional wooden inns including Tsumago Honjin (p178). From Tsumago follow the old Nakasendō post road (p176) up through sleepy alpine hamlets, old-growth cedar forests and waterfalls to Magome-tōge pass before continuing to Magome. The 8km hike winds past farmhouses, waterwheels and rice paddies that time seems to have passed by.
Right: Nakasendō post road

JUDY BELLAH / GETTY IMAGES ©

Geisha Dances, Kyoto

12

We can't stress this enough: if you find yourself in Kyoto (p244) when the geisha dances are on (usually in the spring), then do everything in your power to see one. It's hard to think of a more colourful, charming and absorbing stage spectacle. If you're like us, you might find that the whole thing takes on the appearance of a particularly vivid dream. When the curtain falls after the final burst of colour and song, the geisha might just continue to dance in your mind for hours afterward.

Naoshima

13

What would happen if you took a whole island and turned it into an art museum? Japan's Benesse Corporation decided to find out and the result is the Inland Sea art-lover's paradise of Naoshima (p301). The island is dotted with art museums, galleries and installations, and even the local *sentō* (public bath) has been turned into an art project of sorts. You can stay here in a yurt, a quaint local inn, or in one of the art museums. It is, simply put, one of Japan's most interesting attractions.

'Red Pumpkin' by Yayoi Kusama

ALISON WRIGHT / CORBIS ©

Mt Fuji

Even from a distance Mt Fuji (p121) will take your breath away. Close-up, the perfectly symmetrical cone of Japan's tallest peak is nothing short of awesome. Dawn from the summit? Pure magic. Fuji-san is Japan's most revered and timeless attraction. Hundreds of thousands of people climb it every year, continuing a centuries-old tradition of pilgrimages up this sacred volcano. Those who'd rather search for picture-perfect views from the less-daunting peaks nearby can follow in the steps of Japan's most famous painters and poets.

The Best...
Places to Hike

KAMIKŌCHI
Kamikōchi is a pristine alpine sanctuary in the heart of the Northern Japan Alps. (p161)

TSUMAGO & MAGOME
The mountainous Nakasendō used to be one of the main highways between Tokyo and Kyoto. (p176)

TATEYAMA
If you want to get high in the Japan Alps without hiking, take the Tateyama-Kurobe Alpen Route. (p180)

KYOTO
Surrounded by mountains on three sides, Kyoto happens to be one of the best places in Japan for hiking. (p202)

The Best...
Only in Japan Experiences

KARAOKE IN TOKYO
There's nothing like grabbing the mic to 'entertain' your friends in the land where they invented the pastime. (p109)

RIDING THE *SHINKANSEN* (BULLET TRAIN)
Train freaks will love Japan's famed *shinkansen*. (p392)

JOINING A *HANAMI* (CHERRY-BLOSSOM VIEWING) PARTY
When the *sakura* (cherry trees) burst into bloom, Japan goes wild. (p75)

SPOTTING A GEISHA IN KYOTO
The sight of a geisha shuffling to an appointment is a moment of pure magic. (p217)

CLIMBING MT FUJI
Whether it's from a speeding *shinkansen* or from one of the lakes at the base of the mountain, the sight of Mt Fuji is unforgettable. (p121)

15

Castles

Japan's castles have about as much in common with their European counterparts as kimono have in common with Western dinner dresses. Their graceful contours belie the grim military realities that lay behind their construction. Towering above the plains, they seem designed more to please the eye than to protect their lords. If you've got an interest in the world of samurai, shōguns and military history, you'll love Japan's castles. Himeji-jō (p299) is arguably Japan's finest castle, although it's presently under wraps while it's being restored to its former glory. Left: Himeji-jō; Above: Corridor inside Himeji-jō

LEFT: VIN FRATES / GETTY IMAGES © ABOVE: DAVID CLAPP / GETTY IMAGES ©

Sumō

Sitting ringside at Ryōgoku Kokugikan (p112) when two *yokozuna* (sumō grand champions) clash is like watching two mountains get into a shoving match. You can just about feel the earth shake. Even if you're up in the nosebleed seats, catching a sumō match is a highlight of any Japan trip. It's just so different from any other sport we know of: the salt-throwing ritual, the other-worldly calls of the referee, the drawn-out staring matches before the bout, the whole thing just screams 'only in Japan!'

16

17

Hiroshima

Seeing the city's leafy boulevards, it's hard to picture Hiroshima (p306) as a devastated victim of an atomic bomb. Monuments in the Peace Memorial Park hint at the story, but it's not until you walk through the Memorial Museum that the terrible reality becomes clear. But outside the quiet of the park, energetic Hiroshima rolls on. A visit here is a heartbreaking, important, history lesson, but the city and its people ensure that's not the only memory you leave with. Left: Atomic Bomb Dome, Hiroshima

R CREATION / GETTY IMAGES ©

Kamikōchi

One of the most stunning natural vistas in Japan, Kamikōchi (p161) is a highland valley surrounded by the eye-popping summits of the Northern Japan Alps. Trails start from the photogenic Kappa-bashi bridge and follow the pristine Azusa-gawa river through tranquil forests. The birthplace of Japanese alpinism, Kamikōchi can be the gateway for ascending Yariga-take (3180m) or for a simple 1-hour stroll along the river to the local hot spring baths. In winter, you can trek in through the access tunnel and have the entire valley to yourself for a snowshoe jaunt.

18

The Best...
Places to Learn About Japanese History

KYOTO
Capital of Japan for more than 1000 years, Kyoto is the stage where much of Japanese history played out. (p202)

NARA
Nara was the first permanent, long-term capital of Japan and it remains a storehouse of Japanese tradition. (p276)

TOKYO
In historical terms, Tokyo is a mere upstart compared to Kyoto or Nara, but it's still packed with interesting historical sites. (p60)

HIROSHIMA
Hiroshima, the scene of Japan's greatest tragedy, manages to leave the visitor with a feeling of hope for the future. (p306)

Nishiki Market, Kyoto

There's something strangely enjoyable about touring a food market where over half of the goods on display are utterly baffling (is it a food, a spice or some sort of Christmas tree decoration?). Even after years in Japan, we're not sure about some of the things on sale here, but we love wandering Kyoto's Nishiki Market (p206). The place positively oozes 'old Japan' atmosphere and you can imagine what it was like here before some decided to attach the word 'super' to the word 'market'.

LONELY PLANET / GETTY IMAGES ©

The Best...
Places for Kids

TOKYO
If your kids are not fans of traditional Japanese culture, then Tokyo is the best city in Japan to keep them happy. (p60)

NARA
Nara is one of those rare Japanese cities where parents can indulge their interest in traditional culture without the kids going bonkers from boredom. (p276)

KYOTO
Sure, your kids might not appreciate the Zen gardens, but there are heaps of things they will enjoy in Kyoto. (p202)

OKINAWA
If your kids are the outdoors types, then a trip down to Okinawa is sure to please. (p332)

Tokyo's Modern Architecture

20

Japan may be known for its traditional temples, but Tokyo's cityscape is a veritable open-air museum of contemporary structures. The capital has come a long way from copying the Eiffel Tower – these days you'll find dozens of inspired and original works by a pantheon of the world's greatest designers. Fill up on such architectural eye-candy at the chic boutiques in Omote-sandō (p73), the quirky postmodern projects on Odaiba (p87), or even the new army of office towers in Marunouchi (p60). Left: Tokyo International Forum building (p64; architect Rafael Viñoly)

TIM HUGHES / GETTY IMAGES ©

Kabuki

21

For sheer other-worldly bizarreness, few theatrical spectacles come close to kabuki. It's better not to understand the words, for this really amps up the 'alien beings who've come down to earth to flummox and mind-boggle the earthlings' factor that makes kabuki one of the most entertaining ways to lose yourself in Japan. Probably the most atmospheric place to catch a performance of kabuki is at Kyoto's venerable Minami-za Theatre (p245).

22

Dōtombori, Osaka

Osaka's Dōtombori district (p270) is what Lady Gaga would look like if she was a city. It's an over-the-top neon madhouse where human peacocks prowl beneath giant plastic crabs and *fugu* the size of small airships (don't worry, we're not hallucinating – you'll see what we mean when you get there). Allow yourself to be carried along by the human tide that rushes through the endless arcades here and be sure to stop for some octopus balls or automatic sushi.

Skiing

Travellers the world over are finally savvy to one of Japan's greatest secrets: skiing. From the Japan Alps in Central Honshū (p160) to the Hokkaidō highlands (p318), this is one country where it pays to pack a few extra layers. Well-priced equipment rental shops will have you on the slopes in no time, while onsen are waiting to receive you for a unique après-ski experience. Indeed, there is nothing quite like a hot bath and a cold sake after a day of black diamonds.

The Best...
Pop Culture Paradises

SHIBUYA
Shibuya is the shopping paradise at the centre of Tokyo's youth universe. (p71)

AKIHABARA
Tokyo's Akihabara (or 'Akiba' to the locals) is electronics and geek heaven. (p78)

HARAJUKU
If you've ever seen a photo of a Tokyo Goth Girl, you can be pretty sure it was snapped in Tokyo's Harajuku district. (p73)

KYOTO INTERNATIONAL MANGA MUSEUM
If you're an anime *otaku* (comic freak), then you'll be in heaven at Kyoto's wonderful International Manga Museum. (p207)

Shopping in Tokyo

If you want to see some incredible shops, you've got to come to a country that's been running a multibillion-dollar trade surplus for the last several decades. If it's available to humanity, you can buy it in Japan. Whether it's US$100 melons or curios from Y100 shops (where everything goes for about US$1), you'll be amazed at the sheer variety of the goods on offer in Tokyo. Head to the boutiques of Ginza (p113) to see the glitterati do their shopping or join the mere mortals in Shibuya (p115) and Shinjuku (p116). Below: Shibuya at dusk

The Best...
Places to Shop

TOKYO
If it can't be found in a store somewhere in Tokyo, it probably doesn't exist. (p112)

KYOTO
Kyoto has everything from traditional shops and trendy boutiques to treasure-filled flea markets. (p245)

OSAKA
Osaka is a city of merchants and you better believe the shopping's good here. (p272)

NAOSHIMA
The island-turned-art museum of Naoshima, in Japan's Inland Sea, is a good place to find quirky souvenirs. (p301)

25

Arashiyama Bamboo Grove, Kyoto

Western Kyoto is home to one of the most magical places in all Japan: the famed bamboo grove (p225) in Arashiyama. The visual effect of the seemingly infinite stalks of bamboo is quite different from any forest we've ever encountered – there's a palpable presence to the place that is utterly impossible to capture in pictures, but don't let that stop you from trying. If you've seen *Crouching Tiger, Hidden Dragon*, then you have some idea of what this place is about.

Japan's
Top Itineraries

Tokyo & Around
Capital Sights & Day Trips

5 DAYS

If your time in Japan is limited, consider spending the whole time in Tokyo and making a few day trips outside the city. Fly into Narita or Haneda airport (the latter is closer to the city).

PACIFIC OCEAN

① Tokyo (p51)

Base yourself in a convenient transport hub like Shinjuku, Shibuya, Ginza or the Tokyo Station area. Visit Tsukiji Fish Market on your first morning (a good idea if you've got jet lag). Next, head up to Asakusa to visit the temple of Sensō-ji, then over to nearby Ueno for the Tokyo National Museum. The next day, take the loop line to Harajuku and walk to Meiji-jingū, the city's finest Shintō shrine, then take a stroll down chic Omote-sandō. From there, head up to Shibuya to soak up some of modern Tokyo. Make sure you spend an evening wandering east Shin-juku to experience Tokyo's neon madness.

TOKYO ➡ NIKKŌ

🚇 **One hour 45 minutes** Tōbu Nikkō line *tokkyū* (limited express) from Tokyo's Asakusa Station to Nikko.

② Nikkō (p129)

Nikkō, a World Heritage Site, is one of the most rewarding day trips out of Tokyo. It's a collection of spectacular and gaudy (at least by Japanese standards) temples and shrines surrounded by towering evergreens.

TOKYO ➡ KAMAKURA

🚇 **One hour** JR Yokosuka line from Tokyo Station or Shōnan Shinjuku line from Shinjuku, Shibuya or Ikebukuro.

③ Kamakura (p139)

While you can certainly see temples in Tokyo (for example, Asakusa's Sensō-ji), if you really want to soak up the ambience of Buddhist Japan, head south to the coastal town of Kamakura to see the Daibutsu (Great Buddha), as well as lots of small Buddhist temples.

TOKYO ➡ MT FUJI

🚇 **One hour 45 minutes** Direct bus from the Shinjuku Highway Bus Terminal in Tokyo to Kawaguchi-ko and Fuji-Yoshida (Mt Fuji Station), at the base of Mt Fuji.

④ Mt Fuji (p121)

The symbol of Japan, Mt Fuji is occasionally visible from skyscrapers in Tokyo on really clear days, but to maximise your chances of seeing the mountain, head to the towns at its base (but don't bother going on a cloudy day – the mountain will not be visible).

View over Tokyo from the Sky Deck (p65)

33

5
DAYS

Tokyo to Kyoto
Something Old & Something New

If you've got a week to spend in Japan, you should see Tokyo and Kyoto. These two cities will give you a taste of the two faces of Japan: hypermodern and charmingly traditional. Spend two days in each city and add one day in Nara (very near Kyoto) to round things out.

1 TOKYO
KYOTO
2
3 NARA
PACIFIC OCEAN

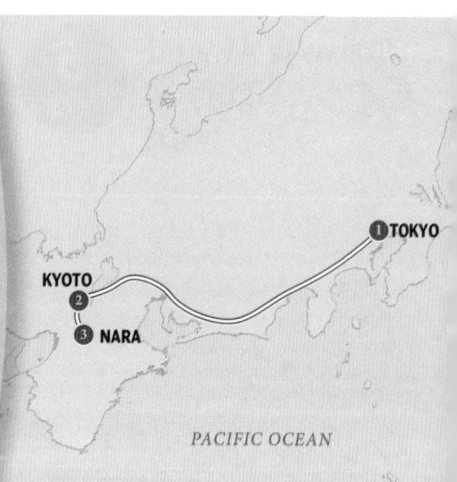

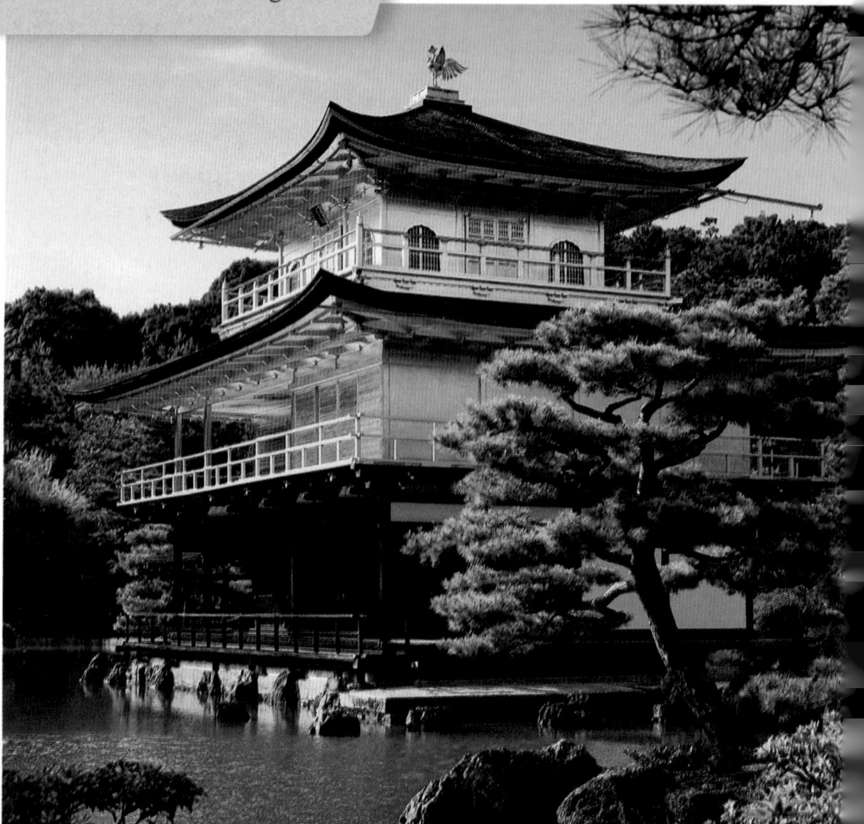

① Tokyo (p51)

You'll probably fly into either Narita or Haneda airport (if you have a choice, opt for the latter, since it's closer to the city). It's a good idea to choose a hotel or ryokan (traditional Japanese inn) in an area with plenty of nightlife, shopping, dining and transport options. Shinuku, Shibuya, Roppongi, Ginza and the Tokyo Station area all fit this bill. Wake early on your first day to check out Tsukiji Fish Market. Then head to Shibuya or Shinjuku to soak up the modern side of Tokyo. On the following day, go to Asakusa to enter the spiritual hub of Tokyo: Sensō-ji, and, if time permits, cross town and visit Meiji-jingū (the city's most important shrine). From Meiji-jingū, it's a short walk to Harajuku and the ultrafashionable arcade known as Omote-sandō, which is where many Japanese fashion trends first see the light of day. Other areas to check out include the electronics district of Akihabara, the high-end shopping district of Ginza and the nightlife zone of Roppongi.

- -

TOKYO ⊙ KYOTO

🚊 **Two hours and 45 minutes** *Shinkansen* (bullet train) between Tokyo Station and Kyoto Station (leaving Tokyo, sit on the north/right side of the train and keep your eyes peeled for Mt Fuji soon after passing Yokohama).

- -

② Kyoto (p193)

Spend your first day in the Southern Higashiyama district checking out some of Japan's most amazing sights: Kiyomizu-dera, Maruyama-kōen, Chion-in and Shōren-in. The next day, visit the Northern Higashiyama district, walking from Nanzen-ji to Ginkaku-ji via the Tetsugaku-no-Michi (Path of Philosophy). Spend one day downtown exploring Nishiki Market and the nearby shopping streets. Spend at least one evening strolling the Gion entertainment area, and if you're lucky, you might catch sight of a geisha. Finally, if time allows, head to the west side of town to visit the Arashiyama & Sagano district, where you'll find some of the city's most impressive sights, including the famous bamboo grove and Tenryū-ji.

- -

KYOTO ⊙ NARA

🚊 **45 minutes** JR Nara line or Kintetsu *tokkyū*

- -

③ Nara (p276)

If you've got more than two days in Kansai, then consider making a day trip to Nara from Kyoto (there's little need to spend the night in Nara, since it's so close to Kyoto). First, relax for a while in the superb Isui-en, then check out the awe-inspiring Daibutsu (Great Buddha) at Tōdai-ji. If time permits, continue to explore Nara-kōen, making your way all the way up to Kasuga Taisha, an incredibly atmospheric shrine.

Kinkaku-ji (p223), Kyoto

10 DAYS

Kansai in Depth
Japan's Cultural Heartland

Kansai contains the highest concentration of must-see sights in all of Japan. If you want to see a lot of traditional Japanese sights without spending a lot of time in transit, then spending your entire trip in Kansai is a great idea.

Sea of Japan

5 KANAZAWA

KINOSAKI
6

1 KYOTO

OSAKA **2** **3** NARA

Osaka-wan

4 KŌYA-SAN

PACIFIC OCEAN

① Kyoto (p193)

Kyoto is the obvious place to base your-self: it's central and it's got a wide range of excellent accommodation, not to mention the nation's finest temples, gardens and shrines. If possible, fly into Kansai International Airport (KIX). Spend a day in Kyoto exploring the Higashiyama area (both southern and northern), followed by another day strolling through the bamboo groves of Arashiyama & Sagano.

KYOTO ➲ OSAKA

🚃 **About 45 minutes** Take a limited express *shinkaisoku* on the JR line from Kyoto Station to Osaka Station (or, if you have a Japan Rail Pass, you can take the *shinkansen*, which takes 15 minutes). The private Hankyū and Keihan lines also connect Kyoto and Osaka.

② Osaka (p262)

Since you won't be going to Tokyo on this trip, you'll want to check out the urban Japan experience in Osaka, a very short train ride from Kyoto. The Minami district is the best place to explore for those with limited time.

KYOTO ➲ NARA

🚃 **About 45 minutes** Take the JR Nara line from Kyoto Station or Nara Station. If you want to go in more comfort, take a *tokkyū* on the Kintetsu line from Kintetsu Kyoto Station to Kintetsu Nara Station (it takes just over half an hour).

③ Nara (p276)

Nara is the most rewarding day trip out of Kyoto. Spend your day exploring the attractions of Nara-kōen, the park that contains all the must-sees of the city.

KYOTO ➲ KŌYA-SAN

🚃 **About two and a half hours** Take a limited express *shinkaisoku* on the JR line from Kyoto Station to Osaka Station (about 45 minutes, or, if you have a Japan Rail Pass, you can take the *shinkansen*, which takes 15 minutes). Then, take the Midōsuji subway line to Nankai Namba Station and get on the Nankai-Dentetsu line *kyūkō* (express) to Kōya-san (one hour and 40 minutes).

④ Kōya-san (p287)

Spend a night at a Buddhist monastery in the Buddhist centre of Kōya-san, high in the mountains of Wakayama, south of Kyoto.

KYOTO ➲ KANAZAWA

🚃 **About two hours and 15 minutes** Take the *tokkyū* Thunderbird from Tokyo Station to Kanazawa Station.

⑤ Kanazawa (p181)

While not technically part of Kansai, Kanazawa is so close, both in spatial and spiritual terms, that it may as well be. Take the comfortable express train up here from Kyoto and enjoy one of Japan's best gardens – Kenroku-en – as well as a fantastic preserved district (not to mention great seafood and friendly people).

KYOTO ➲ KINOSAKI

🚃 **About two and a half hours** Take a *tokkyū* train from Kyoto Station to Kinosaki Station.

⑥ Kinosaki (p292)

Kinosaki, a charming onsen (hot spring) resort on the Sea of Japan coast, is a great way to wind up your stay in Kansai. You can soak away in the baths and relax in a ryokan before heading home.

Deer in Nara-kōen (p277), Nara
SUNNYWINDS / GETTY IMAGES ©

Tokyo to Kyoto via the Japan Alps
Japan's Classic Route

The classic Tokyo–Japan Alps–Kyoto route is the best way to get a quick taste of the country. You'll experience three faces of Japan: the modern wonders of Tokyo, the traditional culture of Kyoto and the natural beauty of the Japan Alps.

Sea of Japan

TAKAYAMA ② ═ ③ KAMIKŌCHI

TOKYO ①

KYOTO ④ ○ NAGOYA

⑤ NARA

PACIFIC OCEAN

1 Tokyo (p51)

Spend two or three days in the capital soaking up the modern side of Japan before heading west to discover a completely different Japan.

TOKYO ○ TAKAYAMA

🚄 **Four hours** Take a *shinkansen* from Tokyo Station to Nagoya Station (one hour and 45 minutes), then take a *tokkyū* from Nagoya Station to Takayama Station (two hours and 15 minutes).

2 Takayama (p152)

Takayama is the gateway to the Northern Japan Alps and a fine destination in its own right. Explore the Sanmachi-suji district and check out the thatched-roof houses in Hida-no-Sato.

TAKAYAMA ○ KAMIKŌCHI

🚌 **One hour and 15 minutes** Take a bus from Takayama to Hirayu Onsen (one hour) and then another to Kamikōchi (15 minutes).

3 Kamikōchi (p161)

Kamikōchi offers the finest alpine panorama in the Northern Alps (at least the finest panorama accessible without having to hike). Stay at least a night to soak up the mountain air and scenery. If you're a hiker, hike up the Azusa-gawa, a beautiful stream that runs through the valley.

KAMIKŌCHI ○ KYOTO

🚌 **One hour and 15 minutes** Take a bus from Kamikōchi to Hirayu Onsen (15 minutes) then another to Takayama (one hour). 🚄 **About three hours and 15 minutes** Take a *tokkyū* from Takayama Station to Nagoya Station (two hours and 15 minutes), followed by a *shinkansen* from Nagoya Station to Kyoto Station (about one hour).

4 Kyoto (p193)

Spend three or four days in the old capital enjoying some of Japan's finest temples, gardens and shrines. At the very least, check out both the Higashiyama area (north and south) and the Arashiyama & Sagano area.

KYOTO ○ NARA

🚄 **About 45 minutes** Take the JR Nara line from Kyoto Station or Nara Station. If you want to go in more comfort, take a *tokkyū* on the Kintetsu line from Kintetsu Kyoto Station to Kintetsu Nara Station (it takes just over a half an hour).

5 Nara (p276)

With an enormous Buddha, hoards of deer, plenty of greenery and lots for the kids to do, Nara is one of Japan's most rewarding destinations.

Arashiyama (p224), Kyoto
KYLE LIN / GETTY IMAGES ©

Tokyo to Hiroshima via Kyoto
From the Capital to the Inland Sea

Start in the capital, then hop on the bullet train to sample the traditional delights of Kyoto. Then head west along the Inland Sea, stopping at the art island of Naoshima, then continue on to Hiroshima and Miyajima.

① Tokyo (p51)

You'll want to spend about two or three days in Tokyo before heading west. Visit Tsukiji Fish Market your first morning, for a truly sensory experience first up. Next, head to Asakusa to visit the temple of Sensō-ji, followed by a trip to Tokyo National Museum, in nearby Ueno. The next day, take the loop line to Harajuku and walk to Meiji-jingū, the city's finest Shintō shrine, then take a stroll down chic Omote-sandō. From there, head up to Shibuya to soak up some of modern Tokyo. Make sure you spend an evening wandering east Shinjuku, since this is where you'll get full experience of Tokyo's neon madness.

TOKYO ➲ KYOTO

🚄 **Two hours and 45 minutes** Take a *shinkansen* between Tokyo Station and Kyoto Station. Keep your eyes peeled soon after leaving Tokyo and you just might catch a glimpse of Mt Fuji if the weather is really clear.

② Kyoto (p193)

Spend a day in Kyoto exploring the Higashi-yama area, followed by another day strolling through the bamboo groves of Arashiyama & Sagano. If possible, spend three or four days in Kyoto and consider a day trip to Nara if time allows. Nara is an easy trip from Kyoto, but spending a night is also a good option if you really want to slow down.

KYOTO ➲ NAOSHIMA

🚄 **One hour and 50 minutes** Take a *shinkansen* from Kyoto Station to Okayama Station (one hour), then a train to Uno Station (50 minutes). ⛴ **20 minutes** Take a ferry from Uno Port to Naoshima.

③ Naoshima (p301)

Naoshima is easily one of Japan's most interesting attractions; it's a small island in the Inland Sea that has been converted into one giant art museum (well, there are several museums, installations and galleries dotted all around the place). It's worth spending at least one night here to get the most out of the experience.

NAOSHIMA ➲ HIROSHIMA

⛴ **20 minutes** Take a ferry from Naoshima to Uno Port. 🚄 **One hour and 35 minutes** Take a train from Uno Station to Okayama Station (50 minutes) and then a *shinkansen* from Okayama Station to Hiroshima Station (45 minutes).

Floating torii (p313), Miyajima
CHRIS RENNIE / GETTY IMAGES ©

MIYAJIMA ➡ TOKYO

🛳 **45 minutes** Take a ferry from Miyajima back to Hiroshima Station. 🚈 **About four hours** Take a *shinkansen* from Hiroshima Station to Tokyo Station.

⑥ Tokyo (p60)

After returning to Tokyo, you might want to pack in some last-minute souvenir shopping and dining in the capital before catching your flight home.

④ Hiroshima (p306)

A few hours west from Naoshima, Hiroshima is an essential stop for anyone with an interest in Japanese history. The displays at the Peace Park are both sobering and saddening, but the vitality of the modern city will give you faith in the ability of the human spirit to bounce back from tragedy. You can stay overnight in Hiroshima, or on the nearby island of Miyajima.

HIROSHIMA ➡ MIYAJIMA

🛳 **45 minutes** Take a ferry from Hiroshima Peace Park direct to Miyajima.

⑤ Miyajima (p312)

You've probably seen pictures of the famous floating torii (shrine gate) at Miyajima (well, just offshore). In addition to this superb sight, there is plenty to do on this green and mountainous island.

Japan Month by Month

Top Events

- **Gion Matsuri**, July
- **Cherry-Blossom Viewing**, April
- **Takayama Matsuri**, April
- **Tenjin Matsuri**, July
- **Shōgatsu (New Year)**, 31 December to 3 January

January

Japan comes to life after the lull of the New Year holiday. Winter grips the country in the mountains and in the north, but travel is still possible in most places.

⊛ Shōgatsu (New Year)

New Year (31 December to 3 January) is one of the most important celebrations in Japan and includes plenty of eating and drinking. The central ritual, *hatsu-mōde*, involves the first visit to the local shrine to pray for health, happiness and prosperity during the coming year. Keep in mind that a lot of businesses and attractions shut down during this period and transport can be busy as people head back to their hometowns.

⊛ Skiing

While many ski areas open in December, the ski season really gets rolling in January.

February

It's still cold in February in most of Japan (with the exception of Okinawa). Skiing is in full swing and this is a good time to soak in onsen (hot springs).

⊛ Setsubun Matsuri

On 2, 3 or 4 February, to celebrate the end of winter and drive out evil spirits, the Japanese engage in throwing roasted beans while chanting *'oni wa soto, fuku wa uchi'* (meaning 'out with the demons, in with good luck'). Check local shrines for events.

⊛ Yuki Matsuri

Drawing over two million annual visitors, Sapporo's famous snow festival really warms up winter in Hokkaidō in early February. Teams from around the world compete to

April Geisha at cherry-blossom viewing celebrations, Kyoto
CLAIRE TAKACS / GETTY IMAGES ©

create the most impressive ice and snow sculptures. After touring the sculptures, head to one of the city's friendly pubs and eateries to warm up with sake and great local food.

March

By March it's starting to warm up on the main islands of Japan. Plums start the annual procession of blossoms across the archipelago. This is a pleasant time to travel in Honshū, Kyūshū and Shikoku.

Plum-Blossom Viewing

Not as famous as the cherries, but quite lovely in their own right, Japan's plum trees bloom from late February into early March. Strolling among the plum groves at places like Kyoto's Kitano Tenman-gū is a fine way to spend an early spring day in Japan.

April

Spring is in full swing by April. The cherry blossoms usually peak early in April in most of Honshū. Japan is beautiful at this time, but places like Kyoto can be crowded.

Cherry-Blossom Viewing

When the cherry blossoms burst into bloom, the Japanese hold rollicking *hanami* (cherry-blossom viewing) parties. It's hard to time viewing the blossoms: to hit them at their peak in Tokyo or Kyoto, you have to be in the country from around 25 March to 5 April.

Takayama Matsuri

The first part of this festival, the Sannō Matsuri, is held on 14 and 15 April. The festival floats here are truly spectacular. Book well in advance if you want to spend the night or come back in October for the second part, the Hachiman Matsuri.

 May

May is one of the best months to visit Japan. It's warm and sunny in most of the country. Book accommodation well in advance during the April/May Golden Week holidays.

Golden Week

Most Japanese are on holiday from 29 April to 5 May, when a series of national holidays coincide. This is one of the busiest times for domestic travel, so be prepared for crowded transport and accommodation.

Sanja Matsuri

The grandest of all Tokyo festivals is held on the third weekend in May. It features hundreds of *mikoshi* (portable shrines) paraded through Asakusa, starting from Asakusa-jinja.

June

June is generally a lovely time to travel in Japan – it's warm but not sweltering. Keep in mind that the rainy season generally starts in Kyūshū and Honshū sometime in June. It doesn't rain every day but it can be humid.

Japan Alps Hiking Season

Most of the snow has melted off the high peaks of the Japan Alps by June and hikers flock to the trails. You should check conditions before going, however, as big snow years can mean difficult conditions for hikers and skiers.

July

The rainy season ends in Honshū sometime in July and, once it does, the heat cranks up and it can be very hot and humid. Head to Hokkaidō or the Japan Alps to escape the heat.

# August

August is hot and humid across most of Japan. Once again, Hokkaidō and the Japan Alps can provide some relief. Several of the year's best festivals and events happen in August.

❀ Matsumoto Bonbon

Matsumoto's biggest event takes place on the first Saturday in August, when hoards people perform the 'bonbon' dance through the city streets.

❀ O-Bon

This Buddhist observance, which honours the spirits of the dead, occurs in mid-August (it is one of the high-season travel periods). This is a time when ancestors return to earth to visit their descendants. Lanterns are lit and floated on rivers, lakes or the sea to help guide them on their journey. See also Daimon-ji Gozan Okuribi.

❀ Daimon-ji Gozan Okuribi

Huge fires in the shape of Chinese characters and other symbols are set alight in Kyoto during this festival, which forms part of O-Bon (Festival of the Dead). It's one of Japan's most impressive spectacles.

🏃 Mt Fuji Climbing Season

Mt Fuji officially opens to climbing on 1 July, and the months of July and August are ideal for climbing the peak.

❀ Gion Matsuri

Held on 17 July, this is the mother of all Japanese festivals. Dozens of huge floats are pulled through the streets of Kyoto by teams of chanting citizens. On the three evenings preceding the parade, people stroll through Shijō-dōri's street stalls dressed in beautiful *yukata* (light cotton kimonos).

❀ Tenjin Matsuri

Held on 24 and 25 July, this is your chance to see the city of Osaka let its hair down. Try to make the second day of the festival, when huge crowds carry *mikoshi* through the city.

September

Sometime in early to mid-September, the heat breaks and temperatures become very pleasant in the main islands. Skies are generally clear at this time, making it a great time to travel.

❀ Kishiwada Danjiri Matsuri

Huge *danjiri* (festival floats) are pulled through the narrow streets in the south of Osaka during this lively festival on 14 and 15 September. Much

alcohol is consumed and occasionally the *danjiri* go off course and crash into houses.

October

October is one of the best months to visit Japan: the weather can be warm or cool and it's usually sunny. The autumn foliage peaks in the Japan Alps at this time.

 ### Kurama-no-hi Matsuri

On 22 October, huge flaming torches are carried through the streets of the tiny hamlet of Kurama in the mountains north of Kyoto. This is one of Japan's more primeval festivals.

November

November is also beautiful for travel in most of Japan. Skies are reliably clear and temperatures are pleasantly cool. Snow starts to fall in the mountains and foliage peaks in places like Kyoto and Nara. Expect crowds.

 ### Shichi-Go-San (7-5-3 Festival)

This is a festival in honour of girls aged three and seven and boys aged five. On 15 November, children are dressed in their finest clothes and taken to shrines or temples, where prayers are offered for good fortune.

December

December is cool to cold across most of Japan. The Japanese are busy preparing for the New Year. Most things shut down from 29 or 30 December, making travel difficult (but transport runs and accommodation is open).

Far left: February Yuki Matsuri, Sapporo
Below: May Portable shrine, Sanja Matsuri festival

What's New

For this new edition of Discover Japan, our authors hunted down the fresh, the transformed, the hot and the happening. Here are a few of our favourites. For up-to-the-minute recommendations, see lonelyplanet.com/japan

1 EXTENDED *SHINKANSEN* LINES
Shinkansen (bullet train) lines have been extended northeast to the city of Aomori, at the northern tip of Honshū, and south to the city of Kagoshima, in Kyūshū, so that it's now possible to cross almost all of Kyūshū and Honshū by bullet train. The Hokuriku *shinkansen* is also slated to start an extended service in the spring of 2015 to the city of Toyama (great for access to the Japan Alps and the Tateyama–Kurobe Alpen Route; p180). The line will eventually be extended as far as the culturally important city of Kanazawa.

2 A NEW HOME FOR KABUKI IN TOKYO
Tokyo's new kabuki venue, Kabuki-za, reopened in Ginza (Tokyo) in spring 2013. (p111)

3 CHEAP AIRFARES TO HOKKAIDŌ
Budget airlines are proliferating in Japan and several offer incredibly reasonable fares to Hokkaidō, bringing this once distant destination within easy and inexpensive reach of budget travellers.

4 CRAFT BEER & BREWPUB BOOM
Microbrews are all the rage across the archipelago. Beer lovers will find the widest pickings in Hokkaidō and Kyūshū.

5 D.T. SUZUKI MUSEUM
The new D.T. Suzuki Museum in Kanazawa honours Japan's best-known proponent of Zen Buddhism, and the garden here is an eloquent lesson in Zen aesthetics. (p184)

6 HIP CAPSULE HOTELS
Capsule hotels used to be the refuge of sozzled salarymen who missed the last train home. Not anymore. A wave of cool designer capsule hotels has swept the country; a good example of this is the Capsule Ryokan Kyoto. (p232)

7 SKY TREE BLOOMS IN TOKYO
Opened in 2012, the Tokyo Sky Tree soars to 634m and features two observation decks. (p85)

8 JR SCMAGLEV AND RAILWAY PARK
This fantastic new museum on the outskirts of Nagoya features a real Maglev train, *shinkansen* and classic trains. It's a must-see for train lovers. (JR リニア・鉄道館; ☎050-3772-3910; www.museum.jr-central.co.jp/en; Kinjofuto 3-2-2; adult/child ¥1000/500; ⊙10am-5.30pm Wed-Mon; 🚉JR Aonami line, Kinjofuto Station)

9 FREE WI-FI IN KYOTO
The city of Kyoto has recently launched a free wi-fi access program (p378) for foreign travellers, with hot spots across the city.

Get Inspired

Books

o **The Roads to Sata** (nonfiction; 1985; Alan Booth) An account of a four-month walk from Hokkaidō to Kyūshū.

o **Inventing Japan: 1853–1964** (nonfiction; 2004; Ian Buruma) A brilliant and concise history of Japan as it went from a closed country to a First World nation.

o **Dogs and Demons** (nonfiction; 2002; Alex Kerr) A clear-eyed look at the state of modern Japan by one of the ultimate Japan insiders.

Films

o **Tampopo** (1985) Itami Jūzō's film about *rāmen* (egg noodles) is told in the manner of a spaghetti Western.

o **Osōshiki** (The Funeral; 1984) A penetrating look at Japanese society through the lens of a funeral – a classic from Itami Jūzō.

o **My Neighbor Totoro** (1988) This touching children's story is the perfect introduction to the work of Miyazaki Hayao, the master of Japanese anime.

Music

o **The New Best of Shoukichi Kina & Champloose** (Shoukichi Kina & Champloose) A mix of mellow and upbeat Okinawan-style music.

o **Okinawa Jyoka** (Tokiko Kato) Mellow tunes with an Okinawan vibe.

o **World Order** (Sudo Genki) Check out the video of this song online (the one shot in Japan is best).

Websites

o **Hyperdia Japan** (www.hyperdia.com) Get Japan transport information (fares, times etc) in English.

o **Japan Ministry of Foreign Affairs** (MOFA; www.mofa.go.jp) Useful visa info and embassy/consulate locations.

o **Japan Rail** (www.japanrailpass.net) Information on rail travel in Japan, with details on the Japan Rail Pass.

Short on time?

This list will give you an instant insight into Japan.

Read *Memoirs of a Geisha*, by Arthur Golden, is the classic tale of a Kyoto geisha.

Watch The story of emotional near misses in Tokyo, *Lost in Translation* is a great pretrip look at Japan.

Listen Female vocalist Moto Chitose's album, *Hainumikaze*, is head and shoulders above the standard J-pop offerings.

Log on Japan National Tourism Organization (JNTO; www.jnto.go.jp) provides information on all aspects of travel in Japan.

Women practising calligraphy
MICHAEL HITOSHI / GETTY IMAGES ©

Need to Know

Currency
Yen (¥)

Language
Japanese

Visas
Issued on arrival for most
nationalities for stays of up
to 90 days.

Money
ATMs are available in
post offices and some
convenience stores. Credit
cards are accepted in most
hotels and department
stores, but only some
restaurants and ryokan.

Mobile Phones
Only 3G phones work
in Japan. SIM cards for
phones are not available,
but data-only SIM cards are
available for smartphones
and tablets.

Wi-Fi
Wi-fi, particularly free wi-fi, is
less common in Japan than
in some other countries.
Available in some cafes,
restaurants, bars and hotels.

Internet Access
Internet cafes are common in
big cities. Many hotels have
LAN cable access and some
also have wi-fi.

Tipping
Tipping is not practiced in Japan.

When to Go

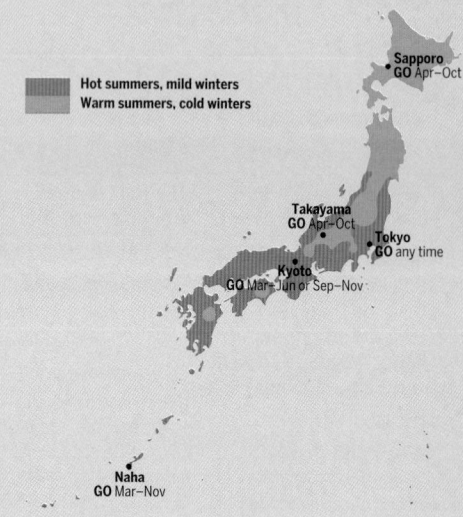

Hot summers, mild winters
Warm summers, cold winters

Sapporo
GO Apr–Oct

Takayama
GO Apr–Oct

Tokyo
GO any time

Kyoto
GO Mar–Jun or Sep–Nov

Naha
GO Mar–Nov

High Season
(Apr–early
May, mid-Aug,
New Year)
o Kyoto, Nara and
other Honshū
tourist cities are
crowded during the
cherry-blossom
season (late March
into early April)
and autumn foliage
season.

Shoulder
(Jun–Jul,
Sep–mid-Dec)
o June and July
is rainy season
in most of Japan
(Hokkaidō
excepted). While it
doesn't rain every
day, it can be pretty
humid.

Low Season
(Jan–Mar)
o Winter is cool
or cold in most of
Honshū, but it's fine
for travel. Be ready
for snow in the
mountains.

Advance Planning

o **Several months before** Make accommodation reservations
several months in advance if you are travelling in cherry-blossom
season (March and April) and the autumn foliage season in Honshū
(October and November).

o **One month before** Buy a Japan Rail Pass. This pass, which is only
available for purchase outside of Japan, can save you a lot of money
if you are planning to travel extensively by rail within Japan.

Daily Costs

Budget Less than ¥8000
- Guest house accommodation: ¥2800
- Two simple restaurant meals: ¥2000
- Train/bus transport: ¥1500
- One temple/museum admission: ¥500
- Snacks, drinks, sundries: ¥1000

Midrange ¥15,000–¥20,000
- Business hotel accommodation: ¥9000
- Two midrange restaurant meals: ¥4000
- Train/bus transport: ¥1500
- Two temple/museum admissions: ¥1000
- Snacks, drinks, sundries: ¥2000

Top End More than ¥20,000
- First-class hotel accommodation: ¥20,000
- Two good restaurant meals: ¥6000
- Two taxi rides: ¥3000
- Two temple/museum admissions: ¥1000
- Snacks, drinks, sundries: ¥2000

Exchange Rates

Australia	A$1	¥87
Canada	C$1	¥86
Europe	€1	¥117
New Zealand	NZ$1	¥65
UK	£1	¥134
US	US$1	¥83

For current exchange rates see www.xe.com

What to Bring

- **International licence** If you plan to rent a car in Japan, get an international licence from your country's automobile association.
- **Japan Rail Pass** You must purchase this pass before arriving in Japan.
- **Slip-on shoes** You'll be taking off your shoes a lot, especially in Kyoto.

Arriving in Japan

Narita International Airport (Tokyo; p118)

Trains Narita Express (N'EX) to Tokyo Station; 53 minutes; ¥2940

Limousine buses 90 minutes; ¥3000

Taxis 90 minutes; ¥20,000 to 30,000

Haneda Airport (Tokyo; p119)

Monorail 25 minutes; ¥470

Limousine buses 45 minutes; around ¥1000

Taxis around ¥6000

Kansai International Airport (Kyoto; p250)

Trains 78 minutes; ¥2980

Limousine buses 90 minutes; ¥2500

Taxis 90 minutes; ¥3500

Getting Around

- **Air** Japan's domestic flight network is efficient, reasonably priced and comfortable.
- **Bus** Long-distance and local buses are comfortable and widely available.
- **Car** Driving in Japan is surprisingly easy, but you'll need an international licence. Avoid driving in big cities like Tokyo.
- **Taxi** These are found everywhere and can be cheap for groups, especially in Kyoto.
- **Train** Japan has one of the best train systems in the world, including the famous *shinkansen* (bullet trains).

Sleeping

- **Hotels** From cheap 'business' hotels to first-class international-standard ones.
- **Guest houses** Traveller-friendly and cheap.
- **Ryokan** Traditional Japanese inns.
- **Youth hostels** Plentiful and cheap.

Be Forewarned

- **Crowds** Kyoto and Nara can be very crowded in cherry-blossom season (late March to early April).
- **Heat** Most of Japan is very hot and humid in July and August.
- **New Year holiday** Most businesses and many sights shut down from 27 December to 3 January.

Tokyo

Tokyo is like 10 normal cities crammed into one megacity.
Chaotic yet organised, hypermodern yet utterly classic, garish yet demure, unique yet unquestionably Japanese, Tokyo is a paradox that – like a pop star – seems smug in its greatness yet obsessed with reinvention.

It's a city bent on collecting superlatives, and since the early days of Edo, Tokyo's done everything in its power to stay ahead of the pack, from reclaiming miles of swampland to transforming war-torn moonscapes into shimmering skyscraper districts.

Today, that constant hunger for improvement and change has created a tapestry of sensorial madness unlike anywhere else in the world. In sheer size and scope alone, Tokyo far outweighs other major global centres.

Simply put, Tokyo is a city that everyone should visit at least once in their lifetime.

Shibuya Crossing (p71)

Tokyo Sky Tree (p85)
FRANK DEIM / GETTY IMAGES ©

Tokyo

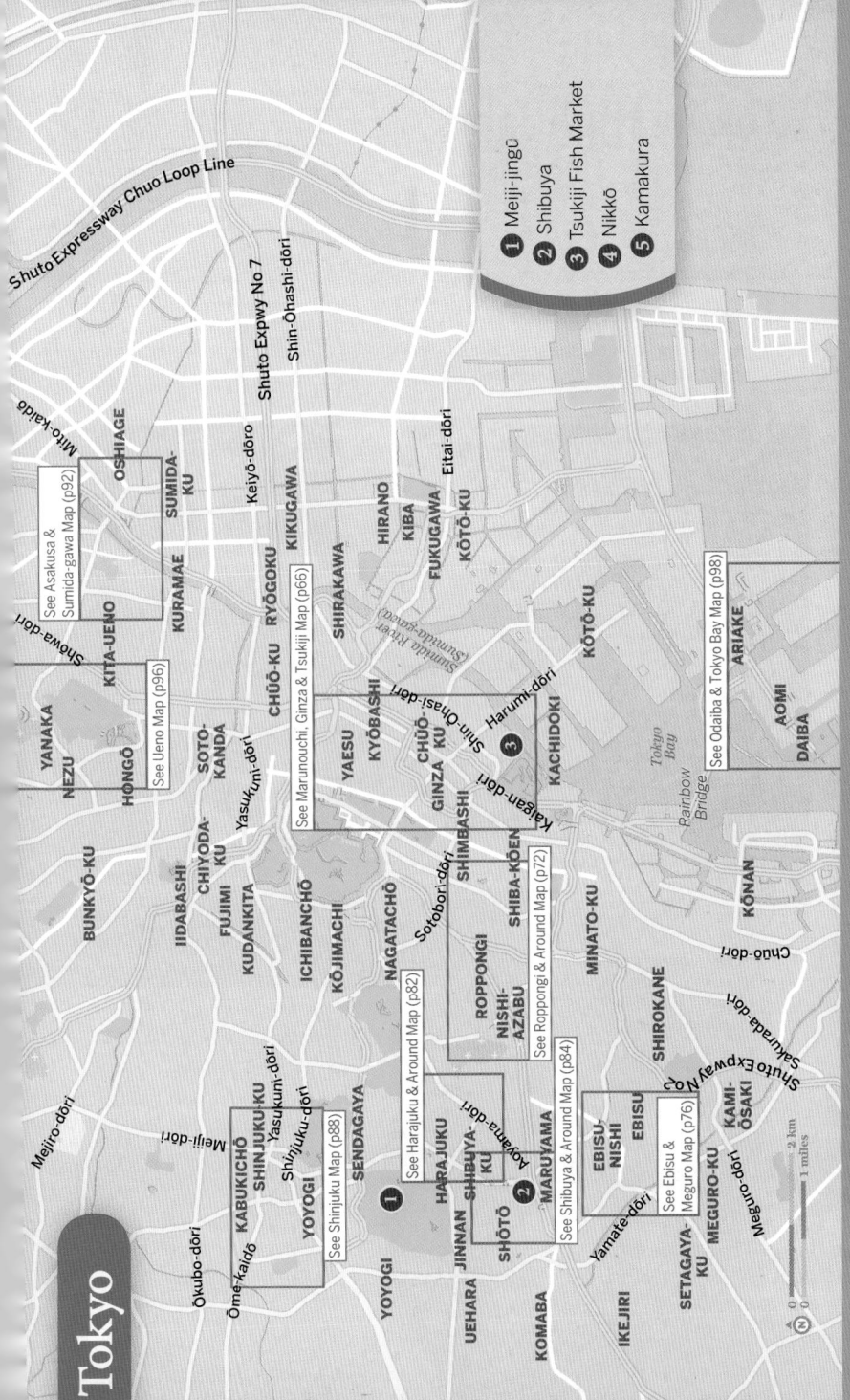

1 Meiji-jingū
2 Shibuya
3 Tsukiji Fish Market
4 Nikkō
5 Kamakura

Shuto Expressway Chuo Loop Line

Mito-kaidō

Shuto Expwy No 7

Shin-Ōhashi-dōri

Showa-dōri

Keiyō-dōro

Eitai-dōri

Harumi-dōri

Shin-Ōhashi-dōri

Kaigan-dōri

Sotobori-dōri

Yasukuni-dōri

Yasukuni-dōri

Shinjuku-dōri

Meiji-dōri

Meiji-dōri

Ōme-kaidō

Ōkubo-dōri

Aoyama-dōri

Yamate-dōri

Meguro-dōri

Shuto Expwy No 2

Sakurada-dōri

Chūō-dōri

OSHIAGE
SUMIDA-KU
KURAMAE
KITA-UENO
RYŌGOKU
CHŪŌ-KU
KIKUGAWA
SHIRAKAWA
HIRANO
KIBA
FUKUGAWA
KŌTŌ-KU
KŌTŌ-KU
ARIAKE
AOMI
DAIBA
KONAN
KAMI-ŌSAKI
SHIROKANE
MINATO-KU
MEGURO-KU
SETAGAYA-KU
IKEJIRI
KOMABA
UEHARA
YOYOGI
YOYOGI
SENDAGAYA
HARAJUKU
JINNAN
SHŌTŌ
SHIBUYA-KU
MARUYAMA
EBISU
EBISU-NISHI
NAGATACHŌ
KŌJIMACHI
ICHIBANCHŌ
KUDANKITA
FUJIMI
CHIYODA-KU
IIDABASHI
BUNKYŌ-KU
HONGŌ
NEZU
YANAKA
SOTO-KANDA
KABUKICHŌ
SHINJUKU-KU
NISHI-AZABU
ROPPONGI
SHIBA-KŌEN
SHIMBASHI
GINZA
CHŪŌ-KU
KYŌBASHI
YAESU
NIHOMBASHI
KACHIDOKI

Sumida River (Sumida-gawa)

Tokyo Bay

Rainbow Bridge

See Asakusa & Sumida-gawa Map (p92)
See Ueno Map (p96)
See Marunouchi, Ginza & Tsukiji Map (p66)
See Odaiba & Tokyo Bay Map (p98)
See Roppongi & Around Map (p72)
See Harajuku & Around Map (p82)
See Shinjuku Map (p88)
See Shibuya & Around Map (p84)
See Ebisu & Meguro Map (p76)

0 ——— 2 km
0 ——— 1 mile

Tokyo Highlights

Meiji-jingū

For a break from Tokyo's seemingly endless concrete and neon, head to Meiji-jingū (p74). Sitting amid a rolling expanse of forest, this shrine serves as a retreat for harried Tokyoites. A walk down any of the tree-lined avenues is the perfect way to spend a few peaceful hours in the city. Buy an *omikuji* (paper fortune) at the shrine to check your luck and keep your eyes peeled for a traditional Japanese wedding.

Shibuya

Shibuya (p71) is Tokyo at its most Tokyoesque: throngs of people, huge neon signs, busy overhead train lines and an almost infinite number of shops and restaurants. If you've seen *Lost in Translation*, you've seen Shibuya: many of the city scenes were shot here. The people-watching here is the best anywhere and the shopping is among the best in the city. Shibuya Crossing (p71)

DAVID KOITER / GETTY IMAGES ©

Tsukiji Fish Market

The mother of all fish markets, Tsukiji (p68) is far more than just the tuna auction for which it's famed. It's aisle upon aisle of weird and wonderful things pulled from the sea, at least half of which you might not even recognise as edible food products. Red octopus

Nikkō

In a country where the default colour for temples is bare wood, Nikkō (p129) stands out like a peacock among pigeons. This shrine/temple complex three hours north of Tokyo is the closest Japan has ever gotten to the riotous exuberance of rococo. Nikkō vies with Kamakura as the Tokyo area's most rewarding day trip. If you're not going to Kyoto, this is highly recommended. Tōshō-gū (p129)

Kamakura

Only about an hour away from Tokyo by express train, Kamakura (p139) feels like a different world. This seaside collection of temples and shrines, and one giant bronze Buddha statue, makes a fine day trip out of the city, especially if you need a break from the big city. Like Nikkō, this is highly recommended if you're not heading to Kyoto.

Tokyo's Best...

Experiences

○ **Shibuya Crossing** When the lights turn green here, a human tide steps off the curb. (p71)

○ **Roppongi** A cosmopolitan interzone where the world comes to drink. (p106)

○ **Tokyo Metropolitan Government Offices** There's no finer view of the city. (p75)

○ **Tsukiji Fish Market** Sensory overload at dawn. (p68)

Places to Stay

○ **Park Hyatt Tokyo** An oasis of calm and beauty in the sky above Tokyo. (p95)

○ **The Peninsula Tokyo** A polished princess in a brilliant location. (p91)

○ **Claska** A designer's dream in Meguro. (p93)

○ **Hōshi Onsen Chōjūkan** A brilliant choice for the classic onsen (hot springs) ryokan (traditional Japanese inn) experience. (p134)

Places to Shop

○ **Ginza** Head to Ginza to check out where the old money shops for international luxury items. (p113)

○ **Shinjuku** Start at Takashimaya Times Sq and go from there. (p116)

○ **Harajuku** The wide boulevard known as Omote-sandō here is the closest Japan will ever get to Paris. (p115)

○ **Shibuya** More department stores, boutiques and record stores than anywhere on earth. (p115)

Need to Know

Escapes

○ **Nikkō** Phantasmagorical temples and shrines among towering trees. (p129)

○ **Kamakura** A great Buddha and quiet temples by the sea. (p139)

○ **Hakone** Onsen, Fuji views and a lovely lake in the mountains. (p135)

○ **Minakami & Takaragawa Onsen** Classic riverside onsen within easy reach of Tokyo. (p133)

RESOURCES

○ **JNTO Tourist Information Center** (www.jnto.go.jp) The best English-speaking Tourist Information Centre in the city.

○ **Metropolis** (http://metropolis.co.jp) This free English-language magazine is another good source of info. Available at big bookshops and foreigner-friendly businesses.

○ **Tokyo Tourist Information** (www.tourism.metro.tokyo.jp) Municipally run website detailing what to see, do and eat in greater Tokyo. Walking-tour ideas are also on offer.

○ **Tokyo Art Beat** (www.tokyoartbeat.com) Bilingual art and design guide with a regularly updated list of events.

○ **Grutt Pass** (www.rekibun.or.jp/grutto) If you're planning on sticking around Tokyo for a week or more, then consider investing in a Grutt Pass – a booklet of discount coupons to over 70 museums in greater Tokyo.

GETTING AROUND

○ **Walk** Explore the urban hubs of Tokyo on foot.

○ **Taxi** Only catch one if you miss the last train (Tokyo taxi prices are high).

○ **Subway** Unless the loop line is more direct, the subway will get you around all parts of the city.

○ **JR Yamanote loop line** From one Tokyo hub to the next (except places off the line, like Roppongi).

○ **Private train lines** For day trips to places like Nikkō and Kamakura.

BE FOREWARNED

○ **Rush hour** Huge crowds on subways and trains in and around Tokyo from 7am–9am and 4.30pm–7pm. Travel outside these hours is much more comfortable.

○ **Summer (July and August)** Can be very hot and humid in Tokyo. Be prepared to sweat if you come during these months. Winter can be chilly, but not too cold.

Left: Shopping in Harajuku (p115);
Above: Stone statues in Nikkō

Strolling Yanaka

This walk takes you through the neighbourhood of Yanaka, one of the few areas of Tokyo that retains buildings from before WWII – quite a contrast to the urban hubs of the city. Don't start out too late as many temples close their doors by 5pm.

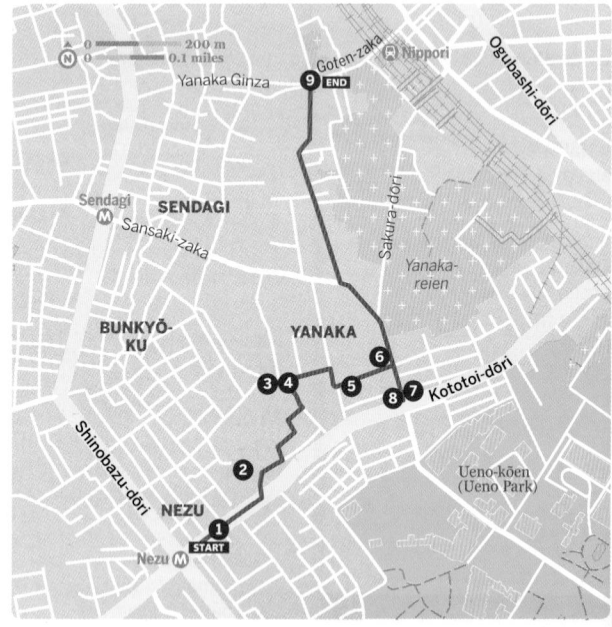

WALK FACTS

- **Start** Nezu Station
- **Finish** Yanaka Ginza
- **Distance** About 2km
- **Duration** About two hours

❶ Kototoi-dōri

From exit 1 of Nezu Station head up Kototoi-dōri. Here, a handful of traditional, wooden two-storey merchants' houses – with a shop on the ground floor and the living quarters above – remain alongside the mid-20th-century concrete buildings with colourful awnings. Don't miss the shops selling *sembei* (rice crackers) and *wagashi* (Japanese sweets).

❷ Gyokurin-ji

Pay a visit to the temple Gyokurin-ji. Just inside the grounds, on your right, a stone wall guards a narrow alley: follow it. This twisting path takes you deep into Yanaka's most atmospheric quarters.

❸ Enju-ji

When you emerge from the back alleys, head left and you'll soon spot a pretty cluster of temples, including Enju-ji, which has some fantastic gnarled trees.

❹ Himalayan Cedar Tree

Double back towards the fork in the road marked by an ancient, thick-trunked Himalayan cedar tree. On the left side of the tree is a classic, old-school corner shop.

❺ Allan West Studio

Continue past the shop to the studio of painter Allan West.

⑥ SCAI the Bathhouse

The next landmark is SCAI the Bathhouse, a centuries-old public bathhouse that became a contemporary-art gallery in 1993.

⑦ Shitamachi Museum Annex

One block over, the Shitamachi Museum Annex preserves an old liquor shop built in 1910; it's free to enter.

⑧ Kayaba Coffee

If you're in need of a break, you can soak up more local atmosphere over coffee at Kayaba Coffee. From here, double back, taking a left at the fork and then heading down the narrow road to the left of the Yamazaki shop. You can safely put away the guidebook – it's a straight shot up to Yanaka Ginza – and enjoy the stroll past temples, tiny galleries and craft shops.

⑨ Yanaka Ginza

When you reach an intersection with lively vendors – that's Yanaka Ginza. Join the locals as they shop and snack their way up and down the lane. Walk west and you can pick up the subway at Sendagi Station; to the east is Nippori Station, where you can hop on the JR Yamanote line.

Tokyo in...

TWO DAYS

Start the day with a pilgrimage to **Meiji-jingū** (p74) in Harajuku, followed by a stroll through the pop-culture bazaar along **Takeshita-dōri** (p115). Take a lunch break at **Harajuku Gyōza Rō** (p102), then check out the architecture along Omote-sandō. Head to Shinjuku in the evening for a dose of neon and a drink in one of the watering holes of Golden Gai. The next day, visit the old side of town for some sightseeing in Asakusa and Ueno, and then spend the afternoon taking our walking tour through Yanaka. Finish up with dinner at **Hantei** (p104).

FOUR DAYS

On day three, take a taxi at dawn to the **Tsukiji Fish Market** (p68), followed by sushi breakfast at **Daiwa Sushi** (p99). Walk to nearby **Hama-rikyū Onshi-teien** (p64), then scoot over to Ginza and its delectable *depachika* (basement food hall). Catch an exhibition at the **Mori Art Museum** (p65) in Roppongi, followed by a nightcap in one of the neighbourhood's myriad watering holes. Spend your last afternoon exploring anime-mad Akihabara.

Girl in Takeshita-dōri (p73), Harajuku
LLUÍS VINAGRE - WORLD PHOTOGRAPHY / GETTY IMAGES ©

Discover Tokyo

🎵 03 / POP 13.24 MILLION

At a Glance

● **Ginza** (p64) The first 'modern' district in the city, this is still where the old money shops.

● **Roppongi** (p65) The cosmopolitan dining and nightlife hub that's boomed in recent years.

● **Shibuya** (p71) The centre of Tokyo's youth and fashion worlds.

● **Shinjuku** (p75) The most Tokyoesque part of Tokyo – neon, skyscrapers and masses of people.

● **Ueno** (p78) Home of the city's best park and many of its museums.

● **Asakusa** (p84) Old-school Tokyo with the city's most popular Buddhist temple.

👁 Sights & Activities

Tokyo is endless in size and scope and can feel more like a collection of cities than one cohesive one. In Edo times, the city was divided into Yamanote ('uptown' or 'high city') and Shitamachi ('downtown' or the 'low city'). On the elevated plain west of the castle (now the Imperial Palace), Yamanote was where the feudal elite built their estates. In the east, along the banks of the Sumida-gawa, Shitamachi was home to the working classes, merchants and artisans.

Even today, remnants of this distinction exist: the east side of the city is still a tangle of alleys and tightly packed quarters. Neighbourhoods such as Asakusa and Ueno retain a down-to-earth vibe, more traditional architecture and an artisan tradition – the closest approximation to old Edo that remains. This is one of the best places to put the guidebook away and just explore. Yamanote developed into the moneyed commercial and business districts. Further west, newer neighbourhoods such as Shinjuku and Shibuya came to life after WWII – this is the hypermodern Tokyo of riotous neon and giant video screens.

·····························

Marunouchi (Tokyo Station area) 丸の内 (東京駅)

The Imperial Palace marks the centre of the city and just to the east you'll find the bustling business district of Marunouchi. The **Marunouchi Building** (丸の内ビル; Maru Biru; Map p66; www.marunouchi.com/marubiru; 2-4-1 Marunouchi, Chiyoda-ku; 🕐11am-9pm Mon-Sat, to 8pm Sun, restaurants 11am-11pm Mon-Sat, to 10pm

Imperial Palace
FRANK DEIM / GETTY IMAGES ©

Sun; 🚉 JR Yamanote line to Tokyo, Marunouchi north exit), towers above the city and offers restaurants, shopping and privileged views of the imperial grounds. Its sister structure, the **Shin-Marunouchi Building** (新丸の内ビル; Shin-Maru Biru; Map p66; www.marunouchi.com/shinmaru; 1-5-1 Marunouchi, Chiyoda-ku; 🕐11am-9pm Mon-Sat, to 8pm Sun, restaurants 11am-11pm Mon-Sat, to 10pm Sun; 🚉 JR Yamanote line to Tokyo, Marunouchi north exit), soars over the skyline next door.

Naka-dōri, which runs parallel to the palace between Hibiya and Ōtemachi Stations, is a pretty, tree-lined avenue with upscale boutiques and patio cafes.

At the heart of the neighbourhood is **Tokyo Station**, which turns 100 in 2014. The elegant red-brick building was heavily damaged during WWII and hastily rebuilt shortly after. A lengthy renovation project, completed in 2012, saw it returned to its former height and glory and its ornate domes restored.

Imperial Palace   Palace

(皇居; Kōkyo; Map p62; 📞3213-1111; http://sankan.kunaicho.go.jp/english/index.html; 1 Chiyoda, Chiyoda-ku; dMarunouchi Line to Ōtemachi, exits C13b or C8b) FREE
The residence of Japan's emperor occupies the site of Edo-jō, the Tokugawa shōgunate's castle. In its heyday the castle was the largest in the world, though little remains of it apart from the moat and walls. The present palace, structurally modern, but traditional in style, was completed in 1968, replacing the one built in 1888 and destroyed during WWII. The palace itself is closed to the public for all but two days of the year – 2 January and 23 December (the Emperor's birthday). It is possible, however, to take a tour of the imperial grounds, but you must book ahead through the Imperial Household Agency's website. Reserve well in advance – slots become available on the 1st day of the month preceding the month you intend to visit. Tours, leaving from Kikyō-mon (桔梗門; Map p62), run twice daily from Monday to Friday, but only in the mornings from late July through to the end of August.

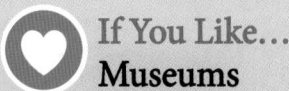

If You Like…
Museums

If you enjoyed the artistic offerings at the Tokyo National Museum, you'll probably enjoy a visit to the following museums:

1 BRIDGESTONE MUSEUM OF ART
(ブリヂストン美術館; Map p66; www.bridgestone-museum.gr.jp; 1-10-1 Kyōbashi, Chūō-ku; adult/student ¥800/500; 🕐10am-6pm, closed Mon; 🚉Ginza line to Nihombashi, Takashimaya exit) The Bridgestone Tyre Company's collection, which was previously kept as a private collection by Bridgestone founder Ishibashi Shōjiro, features all the big names and an interesting selection of works by Japanese Impressionists as well.

2 IDEMITSU MUSEUM OF ARTS
(出光美術館; Map p66; www.idemitsu.co.jp/museum; 9th fl, Teigeki Bldg, 3-1-1 Marunouchi, Chiyoda-ku; adult/student/child ¥1000/700/free; 🕐10am-5pm, closed Mon; 🚉Hibiya line to Hibiya, exit B3) This museum's collection includes Japanese and Chinese art and artefacts – most notably the works of Zen monk Sengai. It's next door to the Imperial Theatre and affords excellent views of the imperial grounds.

3 NATIONAL ART CENTER TOKYO
(国立新美術館; Map p72; 📞5777-8600; www.nact.jp; 7-22-1 Roppongi, Minato-ku; admission varies by exhibition; 🕐10am-6pm Wed, Thu & Sat-Mon, to 8pm Fri; 🚉Chiyoda line to Nogizaka, exit 6, 🚉Roppongi line, exits 4a & 7) With 42 gallery spaces, this is one of the largest museums in Japan. And there are no permanent collections, which makes it the go-to spot for many of the world's most engaging exhibitions.

4 JAPAN FOLK CRAFTS MUSEUM
(日本民藝館; Mingeikan; http://mingeikan.x0.com; 4-3-33 Komaba; admission ¥1000; 🕐10am-5pm Tue-Sun; 🚉Keiō Inokashira line to Komaba-Todaimae, West exit) Set in an old mansion from the early Showa era, this museum is dedicated to the nameless artists in Japanese history who produced publicly consumed items including everything from kitchenware to dolls.

TOKYO

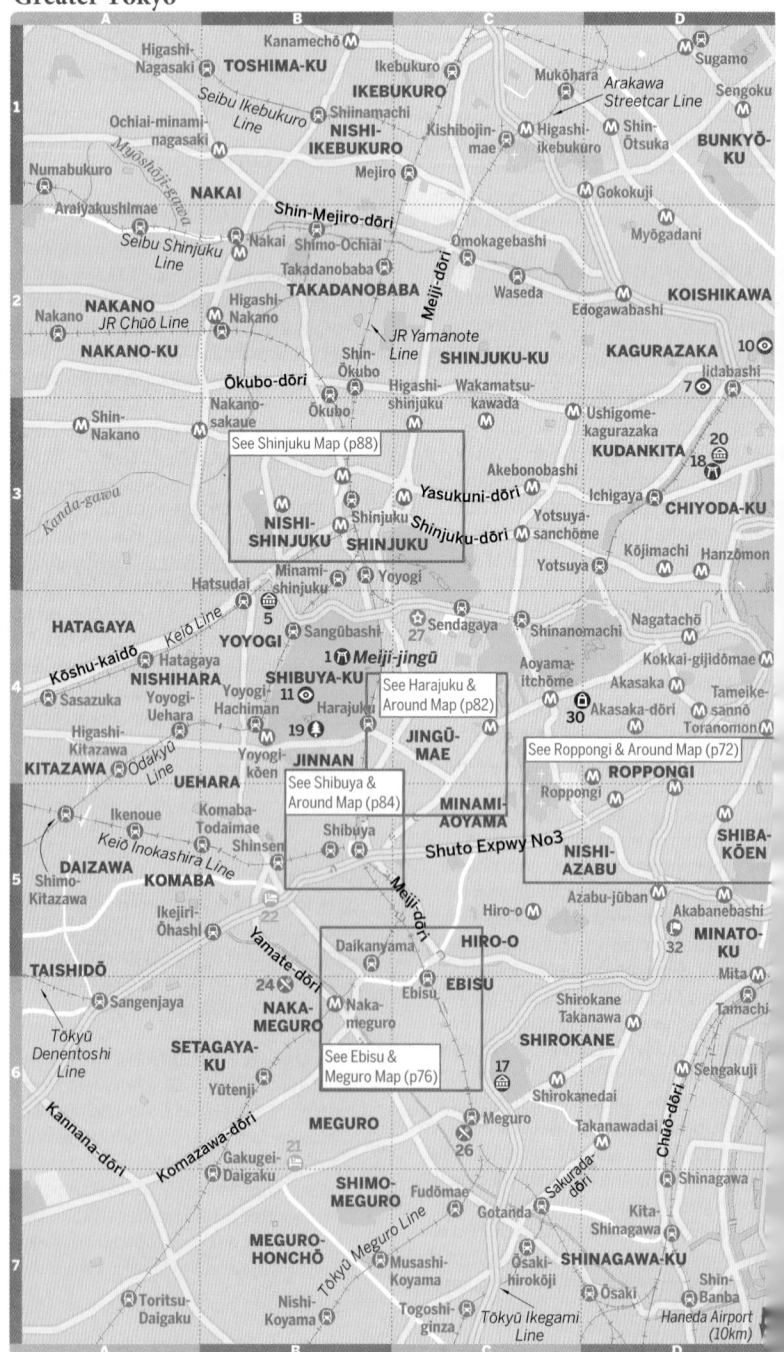

0 — 2 km
0 — 1 miles

NISHI-NIPPORI

Nishi Nippori

ARAKAWA-KU

Minowa

Minami-senju

Yotsugi

Sendagi

Nippori

Tōbu Isesaki Line

Mito-kaidō

Yahiro

Arakawa

YANAKA

NEZU

Uguisudani

TAITŌ-KU

Kokusai-dōri

Sumida River (Sumida-gawa)

Higashi-Mukōjima

Tōbu Oshiage Line

Todai-mae

Nezu

Iriya

See Asakusa & Sumida-gawa Map (p92)

Tokyo Sky Tree Station

Hikifune

OSHIAGE

Tōbu Kameido Line

UENO

Ueno

Keisei Ueno

Inarichō

Asakusa

Tawaramachi

Oshiage

Omurai

Kasuga

See Ueno Map (p96)

Shin-okachimachi

KURAMAE

Kuramae

SUMIDA-KU

Kameido

Kōrakuen

Suidōbashi

Suehirochō

JR Chūō Line

AKIHABARA

Asakusabashi

Asakusabashi

JR Sōbu Line

Ochanomizu

Jimbōchō

Akihabara

Bakuroyokoyama

Ryōgoku

Keiyō-dōro

Kinshichō

Kanda

RYŌGOKU

Shuto Expwy No 7

Narita Airport (58km)

Takebashi

Higashi-nihombashi

Hamachō

Kikukawa

Sumiyoshi

Shin-Ōhashi-dōri

Nishi-Ojika

Ojima

Ōtemachi

Ningyōchō

Morishita

SHIRAKAWA

CHŪŌ-KU

MARUNOUCHI

Tokyo

KYŌBASHI

Kayabachō

Kiyosumi-shirakawa

KIBA

Sakuradamon

Yūrakuchō

KIYOSUMI

KŌTŌ-KU

Hibiya

Ginza

Hatchōbori

Monzen-nakachō

FUKUGAWA

Eitai-dōri

GINZA

Shimbashi

Tsukiji

Etchujima

Kiba

Shiodome

Tsukiji-shijō

Tsukishima

TSUKIJI

See Marunouchi, Ginza & Tsukiji Map (p66)

Daimon

Hamamatsucho

KACHIDOKI

Toyosu

Hinode Pier

Hinode

KŌTŌ-KU

Shin-Toyosu

Tokyo Disney Resort (4km)

SHINKIBA

Shibaura Futō

Shijo-maé

Ariake Tennis-no-mori

Tatsumi

Bayshore Line Expwy

Shin-kiba

Shinonome

Kokusai Tenjijō

Ariake Tennis-no-mori

Ariake

See Odaiba & Tokyo Bay Map (p98)

ARIAKE

Kokusai-tenjijō Seimon

Odaiba Kaihin-kōen

Daiba

Tokyo Teleport

Aomi

AOMI

Tokyo Bay

Fune-no-Kagakukan

Telecom Center

Greater Tokyo

⊙ Don't Miss Sights
1 Meiji-jingū B4

⊙ Sights
2 Arashio Stable F3
3 Edo-Tokyo Museum G3
4 Imperial Palace E4
5 Japanese Sword Museum B4
6 Jimbōchō E3
7 Kagurazaka D2
8 Kitanomaru-kōen (Kitanomaru Park) E3
9 Kiyosumi-teien F4
10 Koishikawa Kōrakuen D2
11 Meiji-jingū-gyoen B4
12 Museum of Contemporary Art, Tokyo (MOT) G4
13 National Museum of Modern Art (MOMAT) E3
14 National Shōwa Memorial Museum E3
15 Sumō Museum F3
16 Tokyo Anime Center Akiba Info F3
17 Tokyo Metropolitan Teien Art Museum C6
18 Yasukuni-jinja D3
19 Yoyogi-kōen B4
20 Yūshū-kan D3

⊖ Sleeping
21 Claska B6
22 Hotel Fukudaya B5
23 Nui F2

⊗ Eating
24 Higashi-Yama B6
25 Kikanbō F3
26 Tonki C6

⊗ Entertainment
27 National Nō Theatre C4
Ryōgoku Kokugikan .... (see 15)
28 Tokyo Dome E2

⊖ Shopping
29 2k540 Aki-Oka Artisan F2
30 Japan Traditional Crafts C4
31 Yodobashi Akiba F3

ⓘ Information
32 Australian Embassy D5
33 Japanese Red Cross Language Service Volunteers E5

Ginza & Tsukiji
銀座 ●築地

Ginza is Tokyo's answer to New York's Fifth Ave or London's Oxford St. In the 1870s the area was the first neighbourhood in Tokyo to modernise, welcoming Western-style brick buildings, the city's first department stores, gas lamps and other harbingers of globalisation.

It's a superb place to window-shop and people-watch. Ginza is also Tokyo's original gallery district, and there are still many in the neighbourhood.

The heart of Ginza is the 4-chōme crossing, where Chūō-dōri and Harumi-dōri intersect. Narrow Namiki-dōri is Tokyo's most exclusive nightlife strip, where elegant women in kimono wait on company execs and politicians in members-only bars and clubs. Stroll down here in the evening and you might catch a glimpse of this secretive world.

A short walk to the southeast is a luxury commercial centre of a different sort: Tsukiji Fish Market.

Hama-rikyū Onshi-teien　Gardens
(浜離宮恩賜庭園; Detached Palace Garden; Map p66; www.tokyo-park.or.jp/park/format/index028.html; 1-1 Hama-rikyū-teien, Chūō-ku; adult/child ¥300/free; ◷9am-5pm; ☒Ōedo line to Shiodome, exit A1) Once the horse stables and hunting ground of the Tokugawas, this gorgeous garden features perfectly manicured hills set below the imposing towers of Shiodome next door. The park is accessible via Tokyo Cruise (p119) water buses from Asakusa.

Tokyo International Forum　Architecture
(東京国際フォーラム; Map p66; 3-5-1 Marunouchi, Chiyoda-ku; ☒JR Yamanote line to Yūrakuchō, central exit) FREE Looking like a glass ship plying the urban waters, this is one of Tokyo's architectural marvels. Architect Rafael Viñoly won Japan's first

international architecture competition with his design; the building was completed in 1996. Although it's used mainly for its meeting halls, casual visitors are free to wander its courtyard-cum-sculpture garden and the glass eastern wing.

Roppongi & Around
六本木

Once primarily known for its debauched nightlife, Roppongi has reinvented itself over the last decade and now has an air of sophistication (at least during the day).

The transformation started with the opening in 2003 of **Roppongi Hills** (六本木ヒルズ; Map p72; www.roppongihills.com/en; Roppongi 6-chōme, Minato-ku; ⏰11am-11pm; 🚉Hibiya line to Roppongi, exit 1), an enormous complex with shops, offices, restaurants and an art museum. It took developer Mori Minoru no fewer than 17 years to acquire the land and construct his labyrinthine kingdom. He envisioned improving the quality of urban life by centralising home, work and leisure into a utopian microcity.

A grand vision realised? It's a matter of opinion, but similar structures, such as **Tokyo Midtown** (東京ミッドタウン; Map p72; www.tokyo-midtown.com/en; 9-7 Akasaka, Minato-ku; ⏰11am-11pm; 🚉Ōedo line to Roppongi, exit 8), followed.

Mori Art Museum   Museum
(森美術館; Map p72; www.mori.art.museum; 52nd fl, Mori Tower, Roppongi Hills, 6-10-1 Roppongi, Minato-ku; adult/student/child ¥1500/1000/500, Sky Deck additional ¥300; ⏰10am-10pm Wed-Mon, to 5pm Tue, Sky Deck 10am-10pm; 🚉Hibiya line to Roppongi, exit 1) When this museum, perched on the 52nd and 53rd floors of Mori Tower in the Roppongi Hills complex, opened in 2003 it was a watershed moment for the Tokyo art scene. Previously scattered, contemporary art now had a home with the space to stage large-scale exhibitions. Every three years, an exhibition called Roppongi Crossing (next up in autumn 2013) focuses on up-and-coming Japanese artists and has emerged as a barometer of current trends.

Admission to the museum includes entry to **Tokyo City View**, the observatory on the 52nd floor, which has some of the best views in central Tokyo. Weather permitting, the rooftop **Sky Deck** has open-air views.

Tokyo City View

Marunouchi, Ginza & Tsukiji

0 — 400 m
0 — 0.2 miles

National Museum of Modern Art (MOMAT) (1km)

Imperial Palace (400m)

7

5

Wadakura Sq

Ōtemachi

Ōtemachi

Ōtemachi

Nihombashi

Eitai-dōri

Sotobori-dōri

13

11

Naka-dōri

Marunouchi Central Exit

Tokyo

Babasaki Moat

Imperial Palace Outer Garden

8

CHIYODA-KU

MARUNOUCHI

22

37

Tokyo

YAESU

32

JP Tower

19

Nijūbashimae

CHŪŌ-KU

2

35

31

12

Yūrakuchō

Kyōbashi

Takarachō

Harumi-dōri

Uchibori-dōri

Hibiya-dōri

Hibiya

16

Yūrakuchō

23 **30**

Hibiya-kōen (Hibiya Park)

YŪRAKUCHŌ

20

26 **24**

Ginza-itchōme

15

GINZA

28

Ginza

Mitsukoshi

29

Ginza-yonchōme Crossing

Ginza

Shōwa-dōri

CHŪŌ-KU

SHINTOMI

Shintomi-chō

Shin-Ōhashi-dōri

UCHISAIWAI-CHŌ

Miyuki-dōri

Namiki-dōri

Chūō-dōri

34

Higashi-Ginza

25

Kokkai-dōri

33

27 **21**

Shimbashi

Shimbashi

Tsukiji

TSUKIJI

HIGASHI-SHIMBASHI

Shimbashi

Caretta Shiodome

Tsukijishijō

9

36

Shiodome

18

Kachidoki-bashi

SHIODOME

14

10

Tsukiji Fish Market

1

Tokyo Cruise Pier

MINATO-KU

Tokyo Cruise Route

3

Shiori-no-Ike

Sumida-gawa

66

Marunouchi, Ginza & Tsukiji

◉ Don't Miss Sights
1 Tsukiji Fish Market.................................C7

◎ Sights
2 Bridgestone Museum of Art.................D3
3 Hama-rikyū Onshi-teien.......................B7
4 Idemitsu Museum of Arts.....................A3
5 Imperial Palace East Garden................A2
6 Kachidoki-mon......................................D6
7 Kikyō-mon...A1
8 Marunouchi Building.............................B2
9 Outer Market...C6
10 Seafood Intermediate Wholesalers
   Area...C6
11 Shin-Marunouchi Building...................B2
12 Tokyo International Forum...................B3

◎ Sleeping
13 Hotel Ryumeikan Tokyo.......................C1
14 Hotel Villa Fontaine Shiodome...........A6
15 Mercure Hotel Ginza Tokyo................C4
16 The Peninsula Tokyo............................A3
17 Tokyo Station Hotel.............................B2

◎ Eating
18 Daiwa Sushi..C6
   Ishii...(see 11)
19 Marunouchi Brick Square....................B2
20 Robata Honten......................................A4

21 Sushi Kanesaka.....................................B5
22 Tokyo Rāmen Street.............................C2
23 Yakitori stands.....................................B3

◎ Drinking & Nightlife
24 Aux Amis Des Vins................................C4

◎ Entertainment
25 Kabuki-za..C5

◎ Shopping
26 Ginza Hands..B4
27 Hakuhinkan...A5
28 Itōya..C4
29 Mitsukoshi..B4
30 Muji...B3
31 Ōedo Antique Market..........................B3
32 Takashimaya...D2
33 Takumi..A5
34 Uniqlo...B5

◎ Information
Fish Information Center.................(see 6)
35 JNTO Tourist Information Center.........B3
36 Tourist Information Center..................C6

◎ Transport
37 Heiwa Kōtsū..C2

Musée Tomo
Museum

(智美術館; Map p72; ☎5733-5131; www.musee-tomo.or.jp; 4-1-35 Toranomon, Minato-ku; admission varies; ⏰11am-6pm Tue-Sun; ☒Hibiya line to Kamiyachō, exit 4B) Perhaps Tokyo's most elegant museum, Musée Tomo is named for Kikuchi Tomo, whose collection of contemporary Japanese ceramics wowed them in Washington and London before finally being exhibited in Tokyo. Exhibitions change every few months; the displays are always beautifully laid out, with informative exhibition notes. The museum is behind the Hotel Ōkura.

Tokyo Tower
Tower

(東京タワー; Map p72; www.tokyotower.co.jp/english; 4-2-8 Shiba-kōen, Minato-ku; adult/child main observation deck ¥820/460, special observation deck ¥600/400; ⏰observation deck 9am-10pm; ☒; ☒Ōedo line to Akabanebashi,

Akabanebashi exit) It might look like a garish Eiffel Tower rip-off, but to Tokyoites, Tokyo Tower remains a powerful symbol of the city's post-WWII rebirth. At 333m, Tokyo Tower, finished in 1958, is 13m taller than the French tower that inspired its design. Lifts whisk visitors up to the main **observation deck** at 150m; there's another **'special' deck** at 250m.

Roughly a third of the steel used to build the tower came from scrap metal salvaged at the end of the war.

While the view from the top can't compete with Tokyo Sky Tree (p85), it's still not too shabby. However, Tokyo Tower is best appreciated when you catch a glimpse of it peeking out from between skyscrapers – like Mt Fuji appearing through the clouds – especially when it's lit up at night.

Don't Miss
Tsukiji Fish Market

Tsukiji Fish Market is the world's biggest seafood market, moving an astounding 2400 tonnes of seafood a day. All manner of creatures pass through the market, but it's the *maguro* (bluefin tuna) that has emerged as the star. The tuna auction starts at 5am. The market is slated for a controversial move to Toyosu in the spring of 2015.

築地市場; Tsukiji Shijō

Map p66

☎3542-1111

www.tsukiji-market.or.jp

5-2 Tsukiji, Chūō-ku

⊙closed Sun & most Wed

🚇Ōedo line to Tsukijishijō, exits A1 & A2

Working Market

Even if you don't arrive at dawn, you can still get a flavour of the frenetic atmosphere of the other parts of the market. Tsukiji is very much a working market, where handcarts and forklifts perform a perfect high-speed choreography not accounting for the odd tourist, and you'll have to exercise caution to avoid getting in the way. Don't come in large groups, with small children or in nice shoes and, by all means, don't touch anything you don't plan to buy.

Seafood Intermediate Wholesalers Area

Tsukiji isn't just the tuna auction, though. The **Seafood Intermediate Wholesalers Area** (水産仲卸業者売場; ⊘9-11am), which opens to the public from 9am, is arguably more interesting – it is certainly more colourful. Here you can see a truly global haul of sea creatures, from gloriously magenta octopuses to gnarled turban shells. All are laid out for buyers in styrofoam crates – it's a photographer's paradise, though again you'll need to be careful. It's also advisable to get here as early as possible; by 11am the crowds have dwindled and the sprinkler trucks plough through to prep the empty market for tomorrow's sale.

Outer Market

The **Outer Market** (場外市場; Jōgai Shijō; ⊘5am-2pm) is where rows of vendors hawk related goods, such as dried fish and seaweed, rubber boots and crockery – it's far more pedestrian friendly. Of particular note is Uogashi-yokochō, a cluster of tiny sushi restaurants inside the market, where you can sink your teeth into some ultrafresh fish. There's also the market's Shintō shrine, Namiyoke-jinja, whose deity protects seafarers.

There's a **Tourist Information Center** (TIC; 5-2 Tsukiji, Chūō-ku; ⊘8am-2pm) in the outer Market with maps and English-speaking staff.

Local Knowledge

Tsukiji Fish Market

BY KONO KIYOMI,
TOKYO RESIDENT AND
PROFESSIONAL GUIDE

1 EXPLORING THE MARKET

The famous tuna auction takes place around 5am, but you don't have to go that early to enjoy the other parts of the market. If you make it by 9am or so, you'll see plenty of stalls open. Just wander the alleyways and check out all the weird and wonderful things for sale.

2 SUSHI ZAMMAI

I often go to the restaurant Sushi Zammai in the outer market. It serves sushi on a conveyer belt and it's the freshest fish straight from the market. The colour of the plate indicates the price of sushi, so it's easy to pick whatever appeals to you.

3 HAMA-RIKYŪ ONSHI-TEIEN

If you walk for seven minutes west from the market, you'll find a traditional stone wall to your left. This is the wall of Hama-Rikyū Onshi-teien which used to be the shōgun's villa in the 17th century. Go inside and take a pleasant stroll among the greenery.

4 NAMIYOKE-JINJA

One of the market's hidden treasures is Namiyoke-jinja, a shrine located south of the outer market and east of the inner market – look for the torii (Shintō shrine gate). On the left side of the shrine you'll find small gravestones. These are dedicated to fish, shrimp and eggs to give thanks for their role in Japanese food. You can get a sense of the Japanese appreciation of seafood here.

5 DENTSU OBSERVATORY

Another secret spot is the free observatory on the 46th floor of the Dentsu building, across from the market. You can take an elevator from the B1 floor which takes you straight up to the 46th floor for free. From the observatory you can look down on Tsukiji Fish Market and Hama-Rikyū Onshi-teien, as well as the Sumida-gawa, Tokyo Bay, the Rainbow Bridge, and the man-made island of Odaiba.

Zōjō-ji
Buddhist Temple

(増上寺; Map p72; www.zojoji.or.jp/en/index.html; Shiba-kōen, Minato-ku; ☉dawn-dusk; 🚇Ōedo line to Akabanebashi, Akabanebashi exit) **FREE** One of the most important temples of the Jōdō (Pure Land) sect of Buddhism, this is also the former funerary temple of the Tokugawa regime, and the tombs of six shōgun stand out back. Zōjō-ji is most dramatic at dusk when Tokyo Tower lights the grounds from behind.

The temple dates from 1393, but its original structures have been relocated and were subject to war, fire and natural disasters. It has been rebuilt several times in recent history, the last time in 1974. The main gate, Sangedatsu-mon, was constructed in 1622. The giant bell (1673; 15 tonnes) is considered one of the great three bells of the Edo period.

Ebisu & Meguro
恵比寿・目黒

Named for the prominent beer manufacturer that once provided a lifeline for most of the neighbourhood's residents, Ebisu has morphed into a hip neighbourhood with a generous smattering of excellent restaurants and bars.

A short zip along the 'Skywalk' from Ebisu Station takes you to **Yebisu Garden Place** (恵比寿ガーデンプレイス; Map p76; www.gardenplace.jp; 4-20 Ebisu, Shibuya-ku; 🚇JR Yamanote line to Ebisu, east exit), another one of Tokyo's 'microcities' with a string of shops and restaurants, office buildings and two museums.

Meguro, just one stop south of Ebisu on the JR Yamanote line, is synonymous with its main drag, Meguro-dōri, which is lined with fantastic interior and antique shops (otherwise known as MISC – Meguro Interior Shops Community).

Tokyo Metropolitan Museum of Photography
Museum

(東京都写真美術館; Map p76; ☎3280-0099; www.syabi.com; 1-13-3 Mita, Meguro-ku; admission ¥500-1650; ☉10am-6pm Tue, Wed, Sat & Sun, to 8pm Thu & Fri; 🚇JR Yamanote line to Ebisu, east exit) This is the city's top photography museum, with excellent changing exhibitions of both international and Japanese photographers. There are usually several exhibitions going on at once and ticket prices are based on how many you see. Take the Skywalk from Ebisu Station to Yebisu Garden Place; the five-storey museum is on the right towards the back.

Visiting the Tuna Auction

Tsukiji's famous tuna auction is without a doubt one of Tokyo's highlights, but it's only for the hardy. Up to 120 visitors a day are allowed to watch from a gallery between 5.25am and 6.15am. You must be at the **Fish Information Center** (おさかな普及センター; 6-20-5 Tsukiji, Chūō-ku), by the market's **Kachidoki-mon** (勝どき門; Map p66), at 5am to register as a visitor, though the queue begins to form up to an hour earlier.

It's first come, first served, so to ensure you make the cut, it's a good idea to arrive even earlier (especially on a Saturday morning). Public transportation doesn't start up early enough to get you here on time, so you'll have to take a taxi or hang out nearby all night.

The market is closed on Sundays, most Wednesdays and public holidays; it also closes to visitors during busy periods (like December and January). Check the calendar here: www.tsukiji-market.or.jp/tukiji_e.htm.

The market has banned visitors to the tuna auction in the past, so please be on your best behavior so as not to give the authorities any reason to do so again.

Detour:
Ghibli Museum

Master animator Hayao Miyazaki, whose Studio Ghibli ('jiburi') produced
Princess Mononoke and *Spirited Away*, designed this museum himself. Fans
will enjoy the original sketches; kids, even if they're not familiar with the
movies, will fall in love with the fairy-tale atmosphere and the climbable Cat
Bus. Don't miss the original 20-minute animated short playing on the 1st floor.

Getting to the **Ghibli Museum** (ジブリ美術館; www.ghibli-museum.jp; 1-1-83 Shimo-
Renjaku, Mitaka-shi; adult ¥1000, child ¥100-700; ☻10am-6pm Wed-Mon; 🚻; 🚊JR Chūō line
to Mitaka, south exit) is all part of the adventure. Tickets must be purchased in
advance, and you must also choose the exact time and date of your visit. You
can do this online through a travel agent before you arrive in Japan (the easy
option) or from a kiosk at any Lawson convenience store in Tokyo (the difficult
option, as it will require some Japanese-language ability to navigate the ticket
machine). Both options are explained in detail on the website, where you will
also find a useful map.

A minibus (return trip/one way ¥300/200) leaves for the museum
approximately every 20 minutes from the south exit of Mitaka Station (bus stop
9). Alternatively, you can walk there in about 15 minutes by following the canal
and turning right when you reach a park. The museum is actually on the western
edge of Inokashira-kōen and you can walk there through the park from Kichijōji
Station in about 30 minutes.

Tokyo Metropolitan Teien Art Museum
Museum

(東京都庭園美術館; www.teien-art-museum.
ne.jp; 5-21-9 Shirokanedai, Minato-ku; admission
varies; ☻10am-6pm, closed 2nd & 4th Wed each
month; 🚊Namboku line to Shirokanedai, exit
1) Inside a beautiful art-deco structure
that was once a princely estate, the Teien
museum hosts mostly exhibitions of
decorative arts. It began a comprehensive renovation project in 2011 and plans
to reopen sometime in 2014; check the
website for updates.

Shibuya & Around
渋谷

Shibuya is the centre of the city's
teen culture, and its brightly dressed,
bleached-hair denizens aren't shy about
living loud.

If a local friend asks to meet you
at Shibuya, you'll probably gather at
Hachikō (ハチ公) plaza in front of the
station. The always-buzzing Shibuya
Crossing leads from the station to the
pedestrian street **Center-gai** (センター
街; Sentā-gai; Map p84; 🚊JR Yamanote line to
Shibuya, Hachikō exit), Shibuya's main artery,
with plenty of shops, restaurants and
bars.

Beyond is Dōgenzaka, also known
as **Love Hotel Hill** (ラヴホテルヒル; Map
p84; 🚊JR Yamanote line to Shibuya, Hachikō
exit), home to nightclubs and by-the-hour
hotels.

The newest landmark, opened in 2012,
is the 34-floor **Shibuya Hikarie** (渋谷ヒカ
リエ; Map p84; 🕿5468-5892; www.hikarie.jp;
2-21-1 Shibuya, Shibuya-ku; ☻10am-9pm; 🚊JR
Yamanote line to Shibuya, east exit) building. Its
upmarket shops and restaurants threaten
to attract grown-up sophisticates to
Shibuya.

Shibuya Crossing
Street

(渋谷交差点; 🚊JR Yamanote line to Shibuya,
Hachikō exit) Rumoured to be the world's
busiest, this intersection in front of
Shibuya Station is famously known as
'The Scramble'. It's an awesome spec-
tacle of giant video screens and neon.

Roppongi & Around

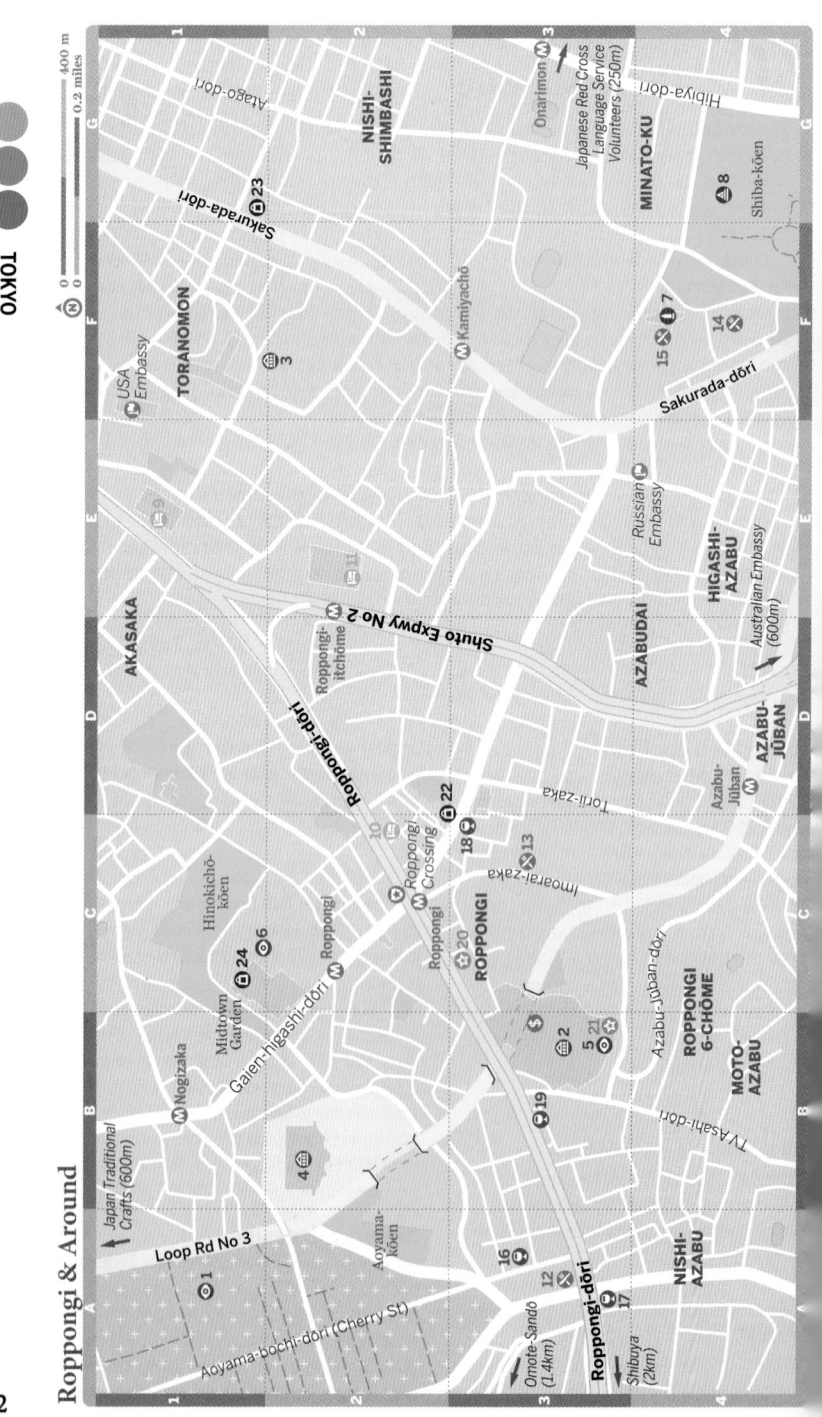

N
0   400 m
0   0.2 miles

Japan Traditional Crafts (600m)

Loop Rd No 3

Aoyama-bochi-dōri (Cherry St)

Omote-Sandō
(1.4km)

Shibuya
(2km)

Roppongi-dōri

NISHI-AZABU

Aoyama-kōen

Nogizaka

Midtown Garden

Hinokichō-kōen

AKASAKA

Gaien-higashi-dōri

Roppongi

Roppongi-dōri

Roppongi Crossing

ROPPONGI

ROPPONGI 6-CHŌME

MOTO-AZABU

TV Asahi-dōri

Azabu-Jūban-dōri

Azabu-Jūban

AZABU-JŪBAN

Imoarai-zaka

Torii-zaka

Roppongi-itchōme

Shuto Expwy No 2

USA Embassy

TORANOMON

Sakurada-dōri

Atago-dōri

NISHI-SHIMBASHI

Kamiyachō

Russian Embassy

AZABUDAI

HIGASHI-AZABU

Australian Embassy
(600m)

Onarimon

Japanese Red Cross
Language Service
Volunteers (250m)

MINATO-KU

Shiba-kōen

Hibiya-dōri

Sakurada-dōri

1
3
2
4
5
6
7
8
9
10
11
12
13
14
15
16
17
18
19
20
21
22
23
24

Roppongi & Around

◎ Sights
1	Aoyama Rei-en	A1
2	Mori Art Museum	B3
3	Musée Tomo	F2
4	National Art Center Tokyo	B2
5	Roppongi Hills	B3
6	Tokyo Midtown	C1
7	Tokyo Tower	F4
8	Zōjō-ji	G4

⊜ Sleeping
9	ANA Intercontinental Tokyo	E1
10	B Roppongi	C2
11	Villa Fontaine Roppongi	E2

⊗ Eating
12	Gonpachi	A3
13	Jōmon	C3
14	Tofuya-Ukai	F4
15	Tokyo Curry Lab	F4

◎ Drinking & Nightlife
16	Eleven	A3
17	Muse	A3
18	Pink Cow	B3
19	SuperDeluxe	B3

⊗ Entertainment
| 20 | Alfie | C3 |
| 21 | Toho Cinemas Roppongi Hills | B3 |

🛍 Shopping
22	Don Quijote	D2
23	Japan Sword	G1
24	Muji	C1

People come from all directions at once – sometimes over a thousand with every light change – yet still manage to dodge each other with a practiced, nonchalant agility.

It's worth pausing for a moment to take in a bird's-eye view of the crowds from the **Starbucks** (Map p84; 1st & 2nd fl, QFront Bldg, 21-6 Udagawa-chō, Shibuya-ku; ⊘6.30am-4am; 🛜; 🚃JR Yamanote line to Harajuku, Hachikō exit) perched above the easily spotted Tsutaya bookshop, adjacent the station.

Hachikō Statue · Monument

ハチ公像; Map p84; Hachikō Plaza; 🚃JR Yamanote line to Shibuya, Hachikō exit) Hachikō, an Akita dog, belonged to a professor who lived near Shibuya Station. The professor died in 1925, but the dog continued to show up and wait at the station for his master until his own death 10 years later. The story became legend and a small statue was erected at the station plaza in the dog's memory.

Harajuku & Around · 原宿

Harajuku is Tokyo's catwalk, where the city's fashionistas go to shop and show off. **Takeshita-dōri** is the neighbourhood's famous subculture bazaar, a pilgrimmage site for teens from all over Japan and particularly famous for its *goth-loli* girls (think zombie Little Bo Peep).

Fans of contemporary architecture will want to check out Omote-sandō – the regal boulevard that connects Harajuku and Aoyama – where the designer boutiques come in designer buildings.

Yoyogi-kōen · Park

(代々木公園; Map p62; 🚃JR Yamanote line to Harajuku, Omote-sandō exit) If it's a sunny and warm weekend afternoon you can count on there being a crowd lazing around the large grassy expanse that is Yoyogi-kōen. You can also usually find revellers and noisemakers of all stripes, from hula-hoopers to African drum circles to a group of retro greasers dancing around a boom box.

It's an excellent place for a picnic and probably the only place in the city where you can reasonably toss a frisbee without fear of hitting someone. While you're there, check out the nearby Yoyogi National Stadium, an early masterpiece by architect Tange Kenzō, built for the 1964 Olympics.

Ukiyo-e Ōta Memorial Museum of Art · Museum

(浮世絵太田記念美術館; Map p82; ☎3403-0880; www.ukiyoe-ota-muse.jp; 1-10-10 Jingūmae, Shibuya-ku; adult ¥700-1000, child free; ⊘10.30am-5.30pm Tue-Sun, closed 27th to end of month; 🚃JR Yamanote line to Harajuku, Omote-sandō exit) Pad quietly in slippers through this museum to view the collection of *ukiyo-e* (woodblock prints) amassed by Ōta Seizo, the former head

EIGHTFISH / GETTY IMAGES ©

⭐ Don't Miss
Meiji-jingū

Tokyo's grandest Shintō shrine is dedicated to the Emperor Meiji and Empress Shōken. Constructed in 1920, the shrine was destroyed in WWII air raids and rebuilt in 1958; however, unlike so many of Japan's postwar reconstructions, Meiji-jingū has an authentic feel. The towering 12m wooden torii (shrine gate) that marks the entrance was created from a 1500-year-old Taiwanese cyprus.

The shrine itself ocupies only a small fraction of the sprawling forested grounds. **Meiji-jingū-gyoen** (明治神宮御苑; Inner Garden; admission ¥500; ⊘9am-4.30pm) was once imperial land; the Meiji emperor himself designed the iris garden here to please the empress. The garden is most impressive when the irises bloom in June.

NEED TO KNOW
明治神宮; Map p62; www.meijijingu.or.jp; 1-1 Yoyogi Kamizono-chō, Shibuya-ku; ⊘dawn-dusk; 🚃JR Yamanote line to Harajuku, Omote-sandō exit

of the Toho Life Insurance Company. A small selection of the collection, which numbers more than 10,000 prints and includes works by masters such as Hokusai and Hiroshige, is arranged in changing, thematic exhibitions.

Downstairs from the museum is a branch of the shop **Kamawanu** (かまわ ぬ; www.kamawanu.co.jp; 23-1 Sarugaku-chō, Shibuya-ku; ⊘11am-7pm; 🚃Tōkyū Tōyoko line to Daikanyama), which specialises in beautifully printed *tenugui* (traditional hand-dyed thin cotton towels).

Nezu Museum
Museum

(根津美術館; Map p82; ☎3400-2536; www.nezu-muse.or.jp; 6-5-1 Minami-Aoyama, Minato-ku; adult/student/child/¥1000/800/free, special exhibitions extra ¥200; ⊘10am-5pm Tue-Sun; 🚃Ginza line to Omote-sandō, exit A5) This recently renovated museum offers a striking blend of old and new: a renowned collection of Japanese, Chinese and Korean antiquities in a gallery space designed by contemporary architect Kuma Kengō. Select items from the extensive collection are displayed in manageable monthly exhibitions. Behind the galleries there's a woodsy strolling garden studded with teahouses and sculptures.

Shinjuku & West Tokyo
新宿

Here in Shinjuku, much of what makes Tokyo tick is crammed into one busy district: upscale department stores, anachronistic shanty bars, buttoned-up government offices, swarming crowds, streetside video screens, hostess clubs, hidden shrines and soaring skyscrapers.

At the heart of Shinjuku is the sprawling train station, which acts as a nexus for over three million commuters each day, making it one of the busiest in the world. The west side of the station (Nishi-Shinjuku) is a perfectly planned expanse of gridded streets and soaring corporate towers. Tokyo's municipal government moved here in 1991 from Yūrakuchō. Also worth a look is the

photogenic **Mode Gakuen Cocoon Tower** (Map p88; 1-7-3 Nishi-shinjuku, Shinjuku-ku; JR Yamanote line to Shinjuku, west exit).

The east side of Shinjuku is one of Tokyo's largest – and liveliest – entertainment districts.

Tokyo Metropolitan Government Offices   Building

(東京都庁; Map p88; Tokyo Tochō; www.metro.tokyo.jp/ENGLISH/TMG/observat.htm; 2-8-1 Nishi-Shinjuku, Shinjuku-ku; observatories 9.30am-11pm; Ōedo line to Tochōmae, exit A4) **FREE** Tokyo's seat of power is a grey granite complex designed by Tange Kenzō. It has stunning, distinctive architecture and great views from the 202m-high **observatories** on the 45th floors of the twin towers of Building 1 (the views are virtually the same from either tower). On a clear day, look west for a glimpse of Mt Fuji.

Japanese Sword Museum   Museum

(刀剣博物館; Map p62; www.touken.or.jp; 4-25-10 Yoyogi, Shibuya-ku; adult/student/child ¥600/300/free; 9am-4.30pm Tue-Sun; Keiō New line to Hatsudai, east exit) In 1948, after American forces returned the *katana* (Japanese swords) they'd confiscated during the postwar occupation, the national Ministry of Education established a society to preserve the feudal art of Japanese

Cherry-Blossom Viewing

When it comes to cherry-blossom viewing, parks such as Ueno-kōen (p82), Yoyogi-kōen (p73), **Inokashira-kōen** (井の頭公園; www.kensetsu.metro.tokyo.jp/seibuk/inokashira/index.html; 1-18-31 Gotenyama, Musashino-shi; Keiō Inokashira line to Kichijōji, Kōen exit) and Shinjuku-gyoen (p90) are obvious choices. Here are two spots known only by locals that blissfully fly under the radar in spring:

Meguro-gawa (目黒川; Map p76; Hibiya line to Naka-Meguro) Naka-Meguro's canal is lined with *sakura* (cherry trees) that form an awesome pale pink canopy. Local restaurants set up food stalls and, rather than staking out a seat, visitors stroll under the blossoms, hot wine in hand.

Aoyama Rei-en (青山霊園; Map p72; 2-32-2 Minami-Aoyama, Minato-ku; Ginza line to Gaienmae, exit 1B) This sprawling cemetery, with many famous inhabitants, comes alive with cherry blossoms blanketing the tombs and statues. It's a pretty, if not unusual, *hanami* (blossom-viewing) spot. Why should the living have all the fun?

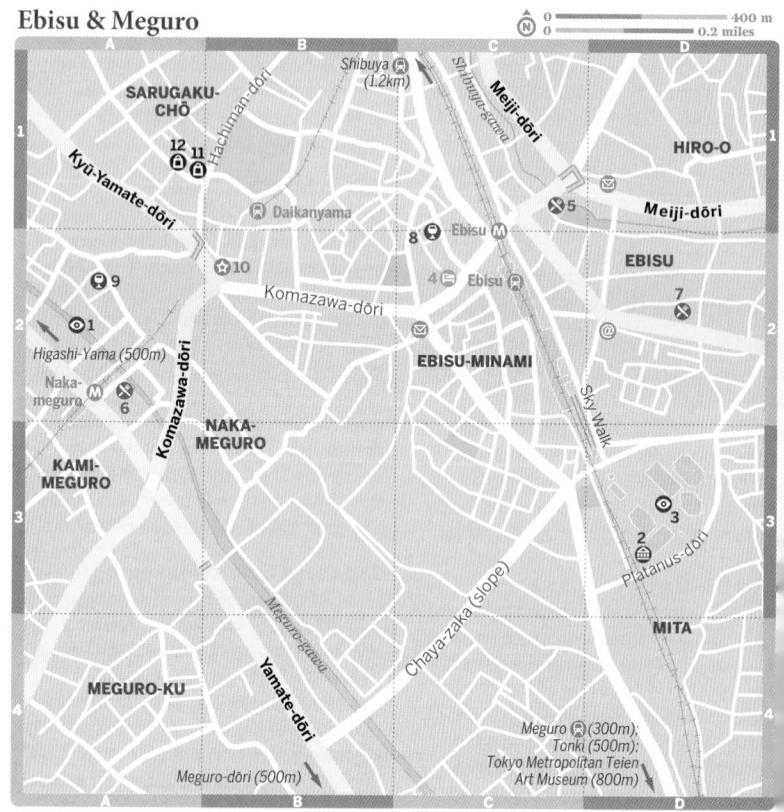

sword-making. There are about 120 swords with their fittings in the collection, of which about one-third are on exhibition at any one time, with English explanations throughout.

The museum's location, in a residential neighbourhood, is not obvious. Head down Kōshū-kaidō to the Park Hyatt and make a left, then the second right under the highway, followed by another quick right and left in succession. There's a map on the website.

Iidabashi & Northwest Tokyo 飯田橋

Iidabashi and its surrounds formed part of the Edo-era Yamanote district of villas belonging to the governing elite.

Kitanomaru-kōen, the leafy expanse north of the Imperial Palace grounds, is home to several museums. The stretch along the moat explodes with cherry blossoms (and flower photographers) in spring.

Yasukuni-jinja   Shintō Shrine
(靖国神社; Map p62; ☎ 3261-8326; www.yasukuni.or.jp; 3-1-1 Kudan-kita, Chiyoda-ku; 🚊 Hanzōmon line to Kudanshita, exit 1) Literally 'For the Peace of the Country Shrine', Yasukuni is the memorial shrine to Japan's war dead, around 2.5 million souls. It's a beautiful shrine, completed in 1869 and with torii gates made, unusually, out of steel and bronze. It is also incredibly controversial: in 1979 14 class-A war criminals, including WWII general Hideki Tōjō, were enshrined here.

Ebisu & Meguro

⊙ Sights
1 Meguro-gawa A2
2 Tokyo Metropolitan Museum of
   Photography.....................................D3
3 Yebisu Garden Place D3

⊜ Sleeping
4 Hotel Excellent Ebisu.........................C2

⊗ Eating
5 Afuri C1
6 Chano-ma A2
7 Ippo D2

⊖ Drinking & Nightlife
8 Buri C2
9 Kinfolk Lounge A2

⊛ Entertainment
10 Unit B2

⊝ Shopping
11 Kamawanu..A1
12 Okura A1

The annual decision by leading politicians whether or not to visit the shrine on 15 August, the anniversary of Japan's defeat in WWII, is closely watched by neighbouring Asian countries and can result in sharp rebukes from their political leaders.

Yūshū-kan   Museum
(遊就館; Map p62; ☎3261-8326; www.yasukuni. or.jp; 3-1-1 Kudankita , Chiyoda-ku; adult/student ¥800/500; ☉9am-4pm; ℝHanzōmon line to Kudanshita, exit 1) This contentious museum, on the ground of Yasukuni-jinja, begins with Japan's samurai tradition and ends with its imperialist aggressions in the first half of the 20th century. While the text has been purportedly toned down over the years, it's still known to boil the blood of some visitors with its particular view of history.

There are also some emotionally harrowing exhibits, such as the messages (translated into English) of kamikaze pilots written to their families before their final missions.

Koishikawa Kōrakuen   Gardens
(小石川後楽園; Map p62; 1-6-6 Kōraku, Bunkyō-ku; adult/child ¥300/free; ☉9am-5pm; ℝJR Sōbu line to Iidabashi, exit C3) Established in the mid-17th century as the property of the Tokugawa clan, this 7-hectare formal garden incorporates elements of Chinese and Japanese landscaping, although nowadays the *shakkei* (borrowed scenery) includes Tokyo Dome stadium. The garden is famed for plum trees in February, irises in June and autumn colours. Don't miss the Engetsu-kyō (Full-Moon Bridge), which dates from the early Edo period.

National Shōwa Memorial Museum   Museum
(昭和館; Shōwa-kan; Map p62; ☎3222-2577; www.showakan.go.jp; 1-6-1 Kudan-minami, Chiyoda-ku; adult/student/child ¥300/150/80; ☉10am-5.30pm; ℝHanzōmon line to Kudanshita, exit 4) This museum of WWII-era Tokyo gives a sense of everyday life for the common people: how they ate, slept, dressed, studied, prepared for war and endured martial law, famine and loss of loved ones. An English audio guide (free) fills in a lot. On the 5th floor, media consoles show film footage shot during the war.

Kagurazaka   Neighbourhood
(神楽坂; Map p62; ℝJR Sōbu line to Iidabashi, west exit) Kagurazaka is an old geisha quarter with winding cobblestone streets and some of Tokyo's most exclusive restaurants. Though short on sights, this neighbourhood is heavy on atmosphere, at times feeling like a Tokyo of a hundred years ago. To reach the more ambient area, cross Sotobori-dōri, head up Kagurazaka Hill and turn right at the Royal Host restaurant.

National Museum of Modern Art (MOMAT)   Museum
(国立近代美術館; Kokuritsu Kindai Bijutsukan; Map p62; ☎5777-8600; www.momat.go.jp/ english; 3-1 Kitanomaru-kōen, Chiyoda-ku; adult/ student ¥420/130, special exhibitions extra; ☉10am-5pm Tue-Thu, Sat & Sun, to 8pm Fri; ℝTozai line to Takebashi, exit 1B) Picking up from the Meiji period, this excellent museum traces the evolution of Japanese art following the introduction of Western-style techniques in the late 19th century through to the mid-20th century.

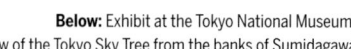

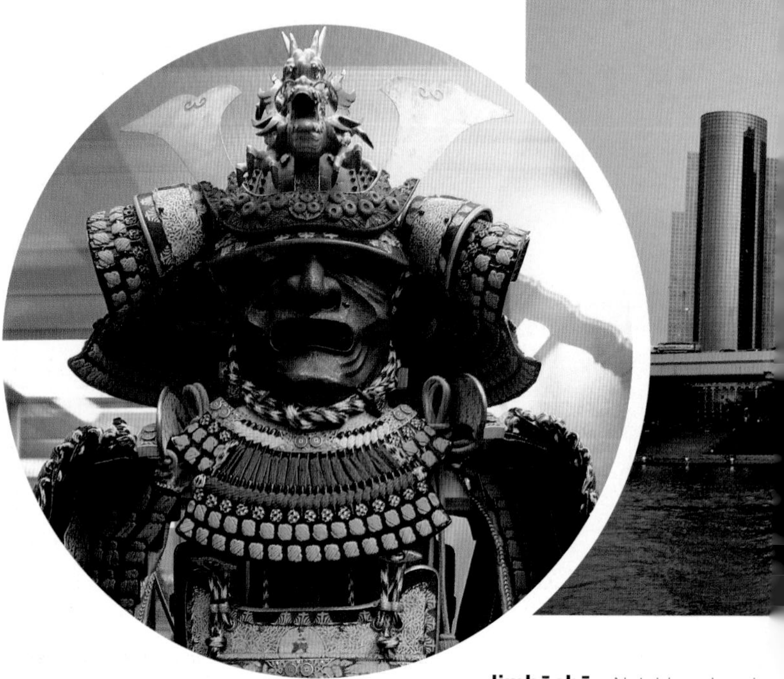

Akihabara & Around
秋葉原

Akihabara began its evolution into **Electric Town** (秋葉原電気街; Denki-Gai; 🚇JR Yamanote line to Akihabara, Denki-gai exit) post-WWII, when the area around the station became a black market for radio parts. In more recent decades, Akihabara has been widely known as *the* place to hunt for bargains on new and used electronics. Nowadays, Akiba, as the neighbourhood is called, is also the centre of the *otaku* (geek) universe, catching manga and anime fans in its gravitational pull.

Pick up a map at **Tokyo Anime Center Akiba Info** (東京アニメセンターAkiba Info; Map p62; www.animecenter.jp; 2nd fl, Akihabara UDX Bldg, 4-14-1 Soto-Kanda, Chiyoda-ku; 🕙11am-7pm Tue-Sun; 🚇JR Yamanote line to Akihabara, Electric Town exit); the helpful staff here speak English.

Jimbōchō   Neighbourhood
(神保町; Map p62; 🚇Hanzōmon line to Jimbōchō) Bibliophiles take note: there are literally over a hundred secondhand book-sellers here, concentrated along a stretch of Yasukuni-dōri. While naturally most books are in Japanese, this a good place to trawl for art tomes, vintage manga and other collectibles. Suzuran-dōri, one block behind Yasukuni-dōri, has a retro vibe to go with the books on sale here.

Ueno   上野

Ueno, revolving around its sprawling park, has been one of Tokyo's top draws since the Edo period. Ueno Hill, where **Kanei-ji** (寛永寺; Map p96; 1-14-11 Ueno-sakuragi, Taitō-ku; 🚇JR Yamanote line to Uguisudani, north exit) stands, is also known as the site of a last-ditch defence of the Tokugawa shōgunate by 2000 loyalists in 1868. They were duly dispatched by the imperial army, and the new Meiji government set about turning

the newly christened Ueno-kōen into a shining example of its 'civilization and enlightenment' campaign. Grand museums modeled after those in Europe were added, starting with the Tokyo National Museum.

To the north is **Yanaka** (谷中; Yanaka, Taitō-ku ; ◻JR Yamanote line to Nippori, west **exit)**, where not just the spirit, but also the actual structures, that define the old Shitamachi still exist. The neighbourhood miraculously survived the Great Kantō Earthquake of 1923, the allied firebombing of WWII and the slash-and-burn modernization of the postwar years. But that's not the only thing that makes Yanaka unique: there are more than a hundred temples here, relocated from around Tokyo during an Edo-period episode of urban restructuring. It's a magical area, the kind of scene that visitors come hoping to see in Japan but often miss.

Tokyo National Museum   Museum

(東京国立博物館; Tokyo Kokuritsu Hakubutsukan; Map p96; www.tnm.jp; 13-9 Ueno-kōen, Taitō-ku; adult/student/child ¥600/400/free;

⏱9:30am-5pm Tue-Sun, open later some weekends in summer; ◻JR Yamanote line to Ueno, **Ueno-kōen exit)** If you visit only one museum in Tokyo, make it this one. The world's largest collection of Japanese art covers ancient pottery, religious sculpture, samurai swords, *ukiyo-e* (woodblock prints), exquisite kimono and much, much more. There are several buildings, the most important of which is the **Honkan** (Main Gallery), built in the imperial style, fusing Western and Japanese architectural motifs.

Another must-see is the **Gallery of Hōryū-ji Treasures**, which displays masks, scrolls and gilt Buddhas from Hōryū-ji – located in Nara Prefecture, and said to be the first Buddhist temple in Japan (founded in 607) – in a spare, elegant box of a contemporary building (1999) by Taniguchi Yoshio, who also designed New York's Museum of Modern Art (MoMA).

The **Heiseikan** (Heisei Hall), which opened in 1993 to commemorate the marriage of Crown Prince Naruhito, houses the Japanese Archaeology Gallery as well as special exhibits.

Tokyo National Museum

Historic Highlights

It would be a challenge to take in everything the sprawling Tokyo National Museum has to offer in a day. Fortunately, the Honkan (Main Gallery) is designed to give visitors a crash course in Japanese art history from the Jōmon era (13,000–300 BC) to the Edo era (AD 1603–1868). The works on display here are rotated regularly, to protect fragile ones and to create seasonal exhibitions – you're always guaranteed to see something new.

Buy your ticket from outside the main gate then head straight to the Honkan with its sloping tile roof. Stow your coat in a locker and take the central staircase up to the 2nd floor, where the exhibitions are arranged chronologically. Allow two hours for this tour of the highlights.

The first room on your right starts from the beginning with **ancient Japanese art** ❶. Be sure to pick up a copy of the brochure *Highlights of Japanese Art* at the entrance.

Continue to the **National Treasure Gallery** ❷. 'National Treasure' is the highest distinction awarded to a work of art in Japan. Keep an eye out for more National Treasures, labelled in red, on display in other rooms throughout the museum.

Moving on, stop to admire the **art of the Imperial court** ❸, the **samurai armour and swords** ❹ and the **ukiyo-e and kimono** ❺.

Next, take the stairs down to the 1st floor, where each room is dedicated to a different craft, such as lacquerware or ceramics. Don't miss the excellent examples of **religious sculpture** ❻ and **folk art** ❼.

Finish your visit with a look inside the enchanting **Gallery of Hōryū-ji Treasures** ❽.

REBECCA MILNER ©

Ukiyo-e & Kimono (Room 10)
Chic silken kimono and lushly coloured *ukiyo-e* (woodblock prints) are two icons of the Edo era (AD 1603–1868) *ukiyo* – the 'floating world', or world of fleeting beauty and pleasure.

Museum Garden
Don't miss the garden if you visit during the few weeks it's open to the public in spring and autumn.

Japanese Sculpture (Room 11)
Many of Japan's most famous sculptures, religious in nature, are locked away in temple reliquaries. This is a rare chance to see them up close.

Heiseikan & Japanese Archaeology Gallery

Research & Information Centre

Hyōkeikan

Kuro-mon

Main Gate

Gallery of Hōryū-ji Treasures
Surround yourself with miniature gilt Buddhas from Hōryū-ji, said to be one of Japan's oldest Buddhist temples, founded in 607. Don't miss the graceful Pitcher with Dragon Head, a National Treasure.

REBECCA MILNER ©

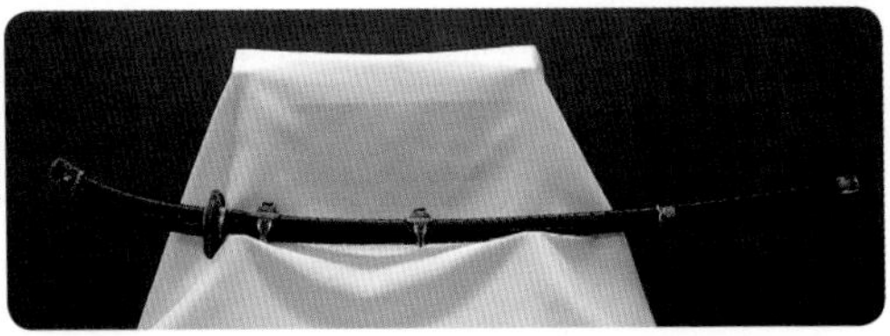

Samurai Armour & Swords (Rooms 5 & 6)

Glistening swords, finely stitched armour and imposing helmets bring to life the samurai, those iconic warriors of Japan's medieval age.

Art of the Imperial Court (Room 3-2)

Literature works, calligraphy and narrative picture scrolls are displayed alongside decorative art objects, which allude to the life of elegance led by courtesans a thousand years ago.

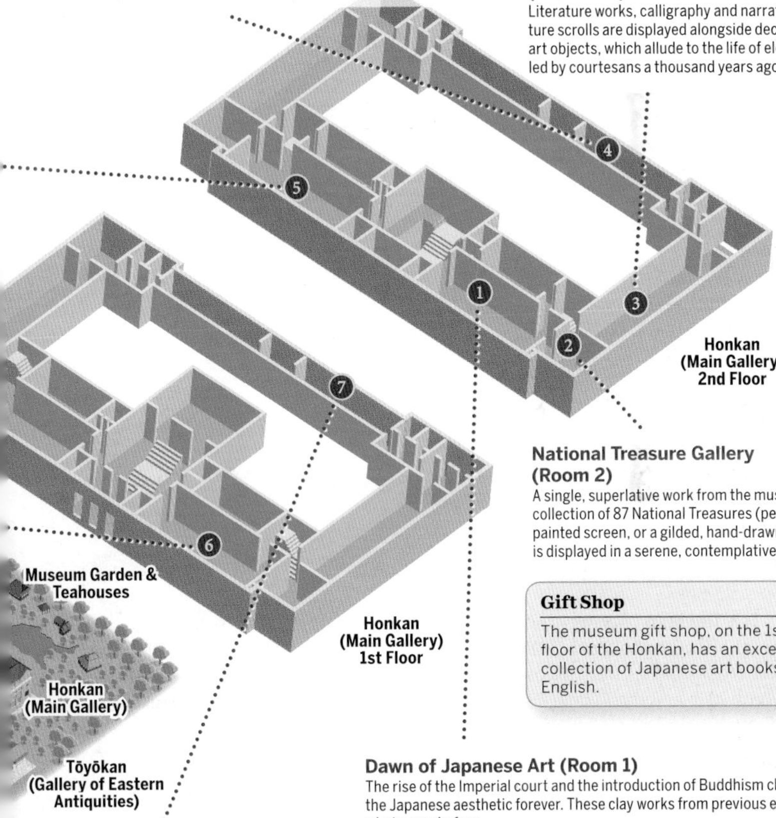

Honkan (Main Gallery) 2nd Floor

National Treasure Gallery (Room 2)

A single, superlative work from the museum's collection of 87 National Treasures (perhaps a painted screen, or a gilded, hand-drawn sutra) is displayed in a serene, contemplative setting.

Gift Shop

The museum gift shop, on the 1st floor of the Honkan, has an excellent collection of Japanese art books in English.

Honkan (Main Gallery) 1st Floor

Museum Garden & Teahouses

Honkan (Main Gallery)

Tōyōkan (Gallery of Eastern Antiquities)

Dawn of Japanese Art (Room 1)

The rise of the Imperial court and the introduction of Buddhism changed the Japanese aesthetic forever. These clay works from previous eras show what came before.

Folk Culture (Room 15)

See artefacts from Japan's historical minorities – the indigenous Ainu of Hokkaidō, the Kirishitan (persecuted Christians of the middle ages) and the former Ryūkyū Empire, now Okinawa.

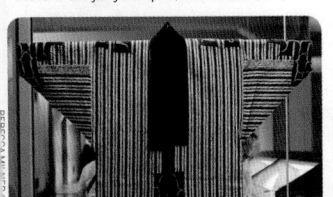

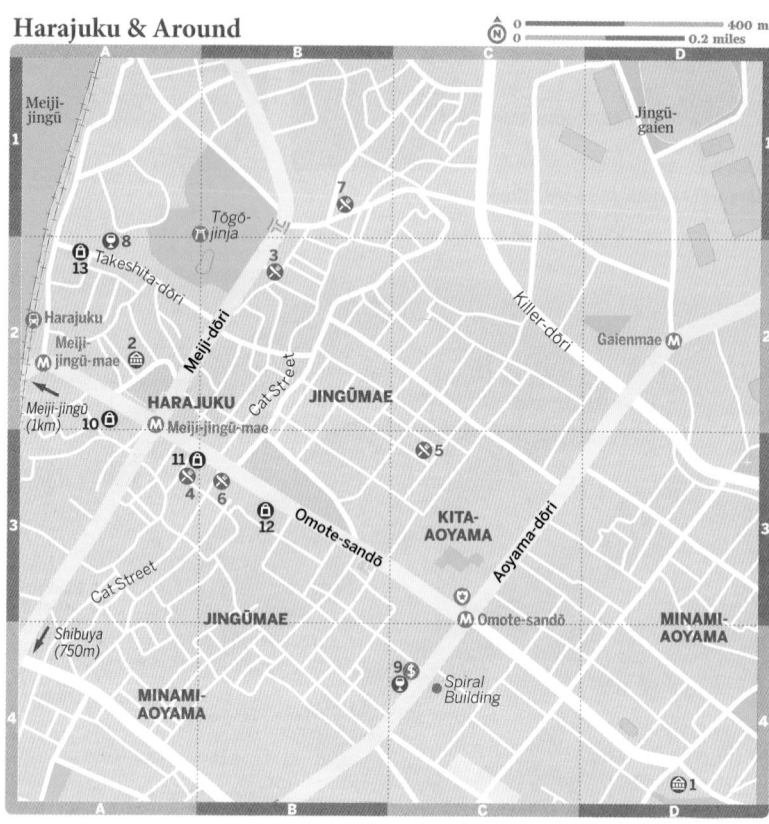

The **Tōyōkan** (Gallery of Eastern Antiquities), reopened in 2013, showcases pieces from across East and South Asia and the Middle East. The **Hyōkeikan** (Hyōkei Hall) was built in 1909, with Western-style architecture that is reminiscent of a museum you might find in Paris, but is closed for earthquake retrofitting.

Ueno-kōen   Park

(上野公園; Map p96; ⏰5am-11pm; 🚃JR Yamanote line to Ueno, Ueno-kōen & Shinobazu exits) Established in 1873, Ueno-kōen is known as Japan's first public park (in the Western sense), but it's much older than that. Structures here date as far back as the 17th century. There's a **Kiyōmizu Kannon-dō** (清水観音堂; 1-29 Ueno-kōen, Taitō-ku; ⏰9am-4pm; 🚃JR Yamanote line to Ueno, Shinobazu exit) FREE, modeled after

the landmark temple in Kyoto, and a **Tōshōgū** (東照宮; Map p96; admission ¥200; ⏰9.30am-4.30pm; 🚃JR Yamanote line to Ueno, Shinobazu exit) like the shrine in Nikkō (under reconstruction until January 2014).

Shinobazu Pond (不忍池), where couples now paddle swan-shaped boats, was likened to the country's central Lake Biwa and Ueno-kōen was billed as a mini-Japan – a sort of prototypical Disney World. During the Edo period, when travel was heavily restricted, Tokyoites could 'see' the country without having to leave home. The park's reputation as the most famous *hanami* (cherry-blossom viewing) spot in the city dates to this era.

Shitamachi Museum   Museum

(下町風俗資料館; Map p96; 📞3823-7451; www.taitocity.net/taito/shitamachi; 2-1 Ueno-kōen, Taitō-ku; adult/child ¥300/100;

Harajuku & Around

◎ Sights
1	Nezu Museum	D4
2	Ukiyo-e Ōta Memorial Museum of Art	A2

✪ Eating
3	Agaru Sagaru Nishi Iru Higashi Iru	B2
4	Harajuku Gyōza Rō	A3
5	Maisen	C3
6	Marukaku	B3
7	Mominoki House	B1

◎ Drinking & Nightlife
8	Harajuku Taproom	A2
9	Two Rooms	C4

◎ Shopping
10	Chicago Thrift Store	A2
11	KiddyLand	A3
12	Oriental Bazaar	B3
13	Takeshita-dōri	A2

9.30am-4.30pm Tue-Sun; 🚻; 🚉 JR Yamanote line to Ueno, Shinobazu exit) This museum re-creates life in the plebeian quarters of Tokyo during the Meiji and Taishō periods (1868–1926) through an exhibition of typical wooden buildings from that era. Take off your shoes and look inside an old tenement house or around an old sweet shop while soaking up the atmosphere of Shitamachi. Ask for an English-language leaflet; English-speaking guides are available, too.

National Science Museum   Museum

(国立科学博物館; Map p96; Kokuritsu Kagaku Hakubutsukan; www.kahaku.go.jp; 7-20 Ueno-kōen, Taitō-ku; adult/child ¥600/free; 9am-5pm Tue-Thu, Sat & Sun, to 8pm Fri; 🚻; 🚉 JR Yamanote line to Ueno, Ueno-kōen exit) Of particular interest here is the Japan Gallery, which showcases the rich and varied wildlife of the Japanese archipelago, from the bears of Hokkaidō to the giant beetles of Okinawa. Also: a rocket launcher, a giant squid, an Edo-era mummy and a digital seismograph that charts earthquakes in real time. There's English signage throughout, plus an English-language audio guide (¥300).

Yanaka-reien   Cemetery

(谷中霊園; Map p96; 7-5-24 Yanaka, Taitō-ku; 🚉 JR Yamanote line to Nippori, west exit) One of Tokyo's largest graveyards, Yanaka-reien is the final resting place of more than 7000 souls, many of whom were quite well known in their day, such as Japan's most famous female novelist of the modern era, Higuchi Ichiyō (you'll find her portrait on ¥5000 bills). It's also where you'll find the **tomb of Yoshinobu Tokugawa** (徳川慶喜の墓), the last shōgun.

Asakura Chōso Museum   Museum

(朝倉彫塑館; Map p96; www.taitocity.net/taito/asakura; 7-16-10 Yanaka, Taitō-ku; adult/student ¥400/150; 9.30am-4.30pm Tue-Thu, Sat & Sun; 🚉 JR Yamanote line to Nippori, north exit) Sculptor Asakura Fumio (artist name Chōso; 1883–1964) designed this fanciful house and studio himself; it's now a museum with a number of the artist's signature realist works, mostly of people and cats, on display. At the time of research this museum was still closed for renovation, but was set to reopen in autumn 2013.

National Museum of Western Art   Museum

(国立西洋美術館; Kokuritsu Seiyō Bijutsukan; Map p96; www.nmwa.go.jp; 7-7 Ueno-kōen, Taitō-ku; adult/student ¥420/130, permanent collection 2nd & 4th Sat free; 9.30am-5.30pm Tue-Thu, Sat & Sun, to 8pm Fri; 🚉 JR Yamanote line to Ueno, Ueno-kōen exit) The permanent collection here runs from medieval Madonna and Child images to 20th-century abstract expressionism, but is strongest in French Impressionism, including a whole gallery of Monet. The main building was designed by Le Corbusier in the late 1950s and is now on Unesco's World Heritage list.

Tokyo Metropolitan Museum of Art   Museum

(東京都美術館; www.tobikan.jp; 8-36 Ueno-kōen, Taitō-ku; admission varies; 9am-5pm Tue-Sun; 🚉 JR Yamanote line to Ueno, Ueno-kōen exit) Newly reopened after a long renovation, this museum, established in 1926, is back to staging wildly popular temporary exhibits from leading international museums (such as New York's Metropolitan Museum of Art).

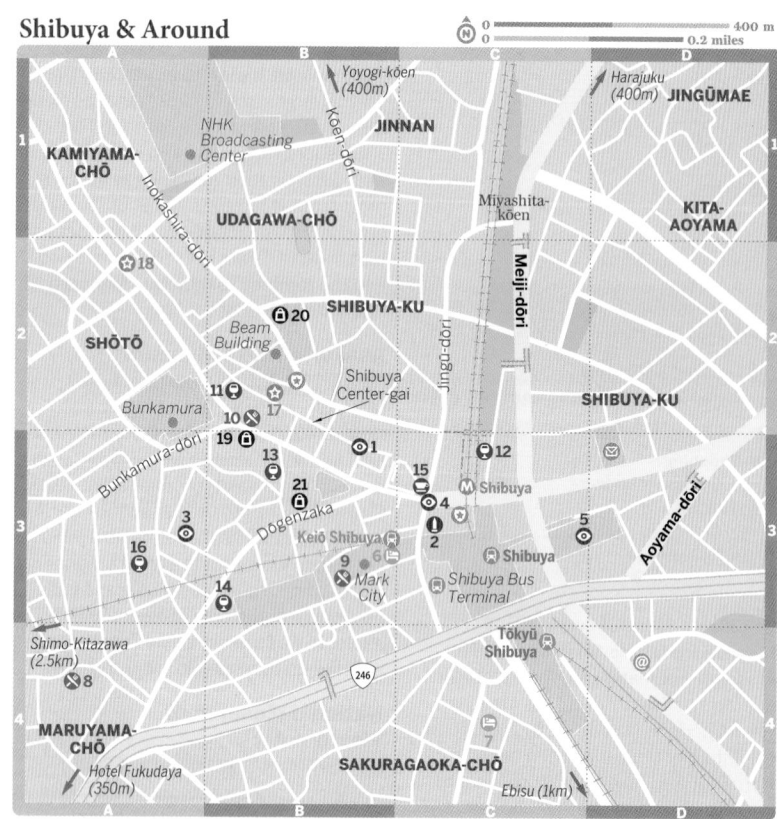

Ueno Zoo
Zoo

(上野動物園; Map p96; Ueno Dōbutsu-en; www.
tokyo-zoo.net; 9-83 Ueno-kōen, Taitō-ku; adult/
child ¥600/free; ⏰9.30am-5pm Tue-Sun; ⓘ;
ⓇJR Yamanote line to Ueno, Ueno-kōen exit) Japan's oldest zoo was established in 1882,
and is home to animals from around the
globe, but the biggest attractions are two
giant pandas that arrived from China in
2011 – Rī Rī and Shin Shin. Ueno Zoo is
larger than you'd think, given the obvious
space constraints of Tokyo.

Asakusa & Sumida-gawa
浅草・隅田川

Asakusa, with its ancient temple, retains
a lot of that old Shitamachi spirit. At the
turn of the last century, the neighbour-

hood was a pleasure district likened to
Montmartre in Paris, though hardly any of
that old bawdiness remains today.

The neighbourhoods across the
Sumida-gawa, too, look much like they
have for decades, having experienced
little of the development seen elsewhere
in the city – save for Tokyo Sky Tree. Given
its location, among low-lying residential
buildings and unburied electrical wires,
Tokyo's newest landmark looks as though
it were dropped here by aliens.

Ryōgoku, also east of the Sumida-
gawa, is home to the national sumō
stadium Kokugikan – you'll often see
chubby wrestlers waddling around
Ryōguku Station.

Edo-Tokyo Museum
Museum

(江戸東京博物館; Map p62; ☎3626-9974;
www.edo-tokyo-museum.or.jp; 1-4-1 Yokoami,

Shibuya & Around

◎ Sights
1	Center-gai	B3
2	Hachikō Statue	C3
3	Love Hotel Hill	A3
4	Shibuya Crossing	C3
5	Shibuya Hikarie	C3

◎ Sleeping
6	Excel Hotel Tōkyū	B3
7	Shibuya Granbell Hotel	C4

◎ Eating
8	Kaikaya	A4
9	Sushi-no-Midori	B3
10	Viron	B2

◎ Drinking & Nightlife
11	Beat Cafe	B2
12	Nonbei-yokochō	C3
13	Ruby Room	B3
14	Sound Museum Vision	B3
15	Starbucks	C3
16	Womb	A3

◎ Entertainment
17	Club Quattro	B2
18	Uplink	A2

◎ Shopping
19	Don Quijote	B3
20	Tōkyū Hands	B2
21	Uniqlo	B3

Sumida-ku; adult/child ¥600/free; ⊙9.30am-5.30pm Tue-Sun, to 7.30pm Sat; 🚃JR Sōbu line to Ryōgoku, west exit) In addition to looking like a retro-future space station, this city history museum is among the best we've seen. Exhibitions document Tokyo's epic transition from Edo to its modern avatar with heaps of interesting facts. Highlights include a replica of the original Nihon-bashi bridge, real examples of Edo-era infrastructure and impeccably detailed scale models of markets and shops.

You could easily spend half a day here if you want to take a thorough look at things. There are often special exhibits, but the permanent collection is enough to overwhelm most visitors. English signage goes a long way, but the museum really comes to life with the help of a volunteer guide (free). There is usually an English-speaking guide on hand, but if you want to be extra sure there's one when you visit, contact the museum two weeks in advance.

Tokyo Sky Tree
Tower

(東京スカイツリー; Map p96; www.tokyo-skytree.jp; 1 Oshiage, Sumida-ku; admission to 350m/450m observation decks ¥2000/3000; ⊙8am-10pm; 🚃Hanzōmon line to Oshiage, Sky Tree exit) Even if you don't go in for heights, Tokyo Sky Tree is an engineering marvel. It opened in May 2012 as the world's tallest 'free-standing communication tower' at 634m. Its silvery exterior of steel mesh morphs from a triangle at the base to a circle at 300m. There are two observation decks, one at 350m and another at 450m.

The panorama from the lower deck, the Tembō Deck, is plenty spectacular; at peak visibility you can see up to 70km away. To increase your chances of spotting Mt Fuji, go in the early morning or during the winter months. Don't miss the small section of glass floor panels, where you can see – dizzyingly – all the way to the ground.

The upper deck, the Tembō Galleria, beneath the digital broadcasting antennas, features a circular glass corridor for more vertiginous thrills.

The ticket counter is on the 4th floor. Try to avoid visiting on the weekend, when you might have to wait in line.

Museum of Contemporary Art, Tokyo (MOT)
Museum

(東京都現代美術館; Map p62; www.mot-art-museum.jp; 4-1-1 Miyoshi, Kōtō-ku; adult/child ¥500/free; ⊙10am-6pm Tue-Sun; 🚃Ōedo line to Kiyosumi-Shirakawa, exit B2) For a primer in the major movements of post-WWII Japanese art, a visit to the permanent collection gallery here should do the trick. The building's stone, steel and wood architecture by Yanagisawa Takahiko is a work of art in its own right. The museum is on the edge of Kiba-kōen, a well-signposted 10-minute walk from the subway station.

TRAVEL IMAGES / UIG / GETTY IMAGES ©

⭐ Don't Miss
Sensō-ji

Tokyo's most visited temple enshrines a golden image of Kannon (the Buddhist Goddess of Mercy), which, according to legend, was miraculously pulled out of the nearby Sumida-gawa by two fishermen in AD 628. The image has remained on the spot ever since; the present structure dates from 1950. Entrance to the temple complex is via the fantastic, red **Kaminari-mon** (雷門; Thunder Gate).

Through the gate, protected by Fūjin (the god of wind) and Raijin (the god of thunder) is **Nakamise-dōri**, the temple precinct's shopping street. Here everything from tourist trinkets to genuine Edo-style crafts is sold.

At the end of Nakamise-dōri is the temple itself, and to your left you'll spot the 55m **Five-storey Pagoda** (五重塔). It's a 1973 reconstruction of a pagoda built by Tokugawa Iemitsu and is even more picturesque at night, all lit up.

NEED TO KNOW

浅草寺; Map p96; http://www.senso-ji.jp/about/index_e.html; 2-3-1 Asakusa, Taitō-ku; ⏰24hr; 🚇Ginza line to Asakusa, exit 1

Kiyosumi-teien   Garden
(清澄庭園; Map p62; 3-3-9 Kiyosumi, Kōtō-ku; adult/child ¥150/free; ⏰9am-5pm; 🚇Ōedo line to Kiyosumi-Shirakawa, exit A3) Kiyosumi-teien started out in 1721 as the villa of a *daimyō* (domain lord). After the villa was destroyed in the 1923 earthquake, Iwasaki Yatarō, founder of the Mitsubishi Corporation,

purchased the property. He used company ships to transport prize stones here from all over Japan, which are set around a pond ringed with Japanese black pine, hydrangeas and Taiwanese cherry trees.

Sumō Museum   Museum
(相撲博物館; Map p62; www.sumo.or.jp/museum; 1-3-28 Yokoami, Sumida-ku; ⏰10am-4.30pm

Mon-Fri; JR Sōbu line to Ryōgoku, west exit)

FREE On the ground floor of the national sumō stadium, Ryōgoku Kokugikan (p112), this museum displays the photos of all the past *yokozuna* (top-ranking sumō wrestlers), or for those who lived before the era of photography, *ukiyo-e*. During tournaments, it is only open to ticket holders.

Odaiba & Tokyo Bay
お台場・東京湾

Developed mostly in the '90s on reclaimed land, Odaiba is a bubble-era vision of urban planning, where the buildings are large, the streets are wide and the waterfront is the main attraction. Love it or hate it, you'll definitely feel like you're in an alternate Tokyo.

Viewed from the promenades and elevated walkways of **Odaiba Kaihin-kōen** (お台場海浜公園; Map p98; Odaiba Seaside Park; 1-4-1 Daiba, Minato-ku; 24hr; Yurikamome line to Odaiba Kaihin-kōen), the city looks less sinister than it does downtown, pretty even – especially at night.

There's some interesting architecture here too, notably the **Fuji TV Building** (フジテレビ; Map p98; tel, info 5500-8888; 2-4-8 Daiba, Minato-ku; observation deck adult/child ¥500/¥300; 10am-6pm Tue-Sun; Yurikamome line to Daiba), with its giant suspended orb (which holds an observatory).

At the time of writing, an 18m-tall 1:1 scale model of **Gundam** (ガンダム), the robotic 'mobile suit' from the immensely popular anime series of the same name, was stationed in front of the Diver City mall – though it was planned as a limited-time only installation.

Travelling to Odaiba is most fun on the driverless Yurikamome monorail, which departs from Shimbashi Station and snakes through skyscrapers before crossing the Rainbow Bridge.

Ōedo Onsen Monogatari Onsen
(大江戸温泉物語; Map p98; www.ooedoonsen. jp/higaeri/english; 2-6-3 Aomi, Kōtō-ku; adult/child from ¥1980/900, after 6pm from ¥1480/900; 11am-8am; ; Yurikamome line to Telecom Centre, Rinkai line to Tokyo Teleport with free shuttle bus) This honest-to-goodness onsen

Tokyo for Children

In many ways, Tokyo is a parent's dream: hyperclean, safe and with every mod con. The downside is that most of the top attractions aren't that appealing to little ones.

Older kids and teens, however, should get a kick out of Tokyo's pop culture and neon streetscapes. **Shibuya** and **Harajuku** in particular are packed with the shops, restaurants and arcades that local teens love.

Odaiba is a popular destination for local families. Here, kids can meet Asimo the humanoid robot at the National Museum of Emerging Science & Innovation (p89) and run loose at virtual-reality arcade Tokyo Joypolis (p89).

Tokyo Disney Resort (p89) has all the classic rides and is another top draw. There's also the Ghibli Museum (p71), which honours Japan's own animation genius, Miyazaki Hayao *(Princess Mononoke, Spirited Away)*. If your kids have caught the Japanese character bug, reward good behaviour with a trip to toy emporium KiddyLand (p115).

Japanese kids are wild about **trains** – chances are yours will be too. The southern terrace at Shinjuku Station overlooks the multiple tracks that feed the world's busiest train station. Another treat is a ride on the driverless Yurikamome line that weaves in between skyscrapers.

Shinjuku

400 m
0.2 miles

Wakamatsu-Kawada Station (500m)

Ichigaya (2km)

Yasukuni-dōri

SHINJUKU-NICHŌME

Meiji-dōri

Gyoen-dōri

Shinjuku-gyoenmae

2

Golden Gai

13
10

Kuyakusho-dōri

17 Shinjuku-sanchōme

15
12
11

Shinjuku-sanchōme

Kōshū-kaidō

Meiji-dōri

19 18

Bunka Senta-dōri

KABUKICHŌ

16

Central Rd

Seibu Shinjuku

Shinjuku

Shinjuku-nishiguchi

Shinjuku

Narita Limousine Bus Stop

Shinjuku

9
8

Shinjuku

5

Shin-Ōkubo (500m)

14

Shinjuku West Exit Bus Terminal

Haneda Limousine Bus Stop

YOYOGI

$

Ōme-kaidō

SHINJUKU-KU

20

1

6

NISHI-SHINJUKU

Season Rd

Gijido-dōri

Kōshū-kaidō

Japanese Sword Museum (500m)

KITA-SHINJUKU

Nishi-shinjuku

Kita-dōri

Tochō-dōri

Tochōmae

21

3

One Day's St

7

Kōen-dōri

Shinjuku Chūō-Kōen

Ōme-kaidō

Kanda-gawa

Shinjuku

◎ Sights
1 Mode Gakuen Cocoon Tower...............C2
2 Shinjuku-Gyoen (Shinjuku Park)...F4
3 Tokyo Metropolitan Government Offices.........................B3

ⓘ Sleeping
4 Citadines...G3
5 Hotel Century Southern Tower.........D4
6 Kadoya Hotel.....................................C3
7 Park Hyatt Tokyo..............................B4

⊗ Eating
8 Lumine...D3
9 Mylord...D3
10 Nagi...E2
11 Nakajima..E3
12 Tsunahachi..E3

◎ Drinking & Nightlife
13 Araku...E2
Champion................................(see 10)
New York Bar............................(see 7)
14 Zoetrope..D1

◎ Shopping
15 Disk Union...E3
16 Don Quijote.......................................E2
17 Isetan..E2
18 Kinokuniya...E4
19 Tōkyū Hands.....................................E4
20 Yodobashi Camera...........................D3

ⓘ Information
21 Tokyo Tourist Information Center..B3

actually pipes in hot-spring water from 1400m below Tokyo Bay. Billed as an 'on-sen theme park', the interior is done up like a Disneyland-style version of an Edo-era town, with games and food stalls. Visitors change their clothes for colourful *yukata* (light cotton summer kimono).

There are a variety of baths, including *rotemburo* (outdoor baths). Some, like the *iwashioyoku* (hot stone bath) and *tsunaburo* (hot sand bath), cost extra and require reservations. Only the baths themselves are divided by gender, so couples and families can enjoy the rest of the complex, including the outdoor foot-bath, together.

There's an overnight surcharge of ¥1700 per person between 2am and 5am. Note that visitors with tattoos will be denied admission.

National Museum of Emerging Science & Innovation (Mirai-kan) Museum

(未来館; Map p98; www.miraikan.jst.go.jp; 2-3-6 Aomi, Kōtō-ku; adult/child ¥600/200; ◷10am-5pm Wed-Mon; ♿; ☒Yurikamome line to Telecom Centre) *Miraikan* means 'hall of the future', and exhibits here present the science and technology that will likely shape the years to come. Lots of hands-on displays make this a great place for kids. Don't miss the demonstration of the humanoid robot ASIMO. The popular Gaia dome theatre/planetarium has an English audio option; reserve your seats as soon as you arrive.

Tokyo Joypolis Amusement Park

(東京ジョイポリス; Map p98; http://tokyo-joypolis.com; 3rd-5th fl, Decks Tokyo, 1-6-1 Daiba, Minato-ku; passport adult/child ¥3900/2900, after 5pm ¥2900/1900; ◷10am-11pm; ♿; ☒Yurikamome line to Odaiba Kaihin-kōen) Unleash your inner child at this three-storey indoor amusement park, operated by game-maker Sega. You'll find a mix of virtual-reality and action rides, including a roller coaster where you can simultaneously shoot zombies (Veil of Dark) and a driving game using real cars (Initial D Arcade Stage 4). Lines are shortest on weekdays when kids are in school.

Separate admission and individual ride tickets (from ¥500) are available, but if you plan to go on more than six attractions the unlimited 'passport' makes sense.

Tokyo Disney Resort Amusement Park

(東京ディズニーリゾート; www.tokyodis-neyresort.co.jp; 1-1 Maihama, Urayasu-shi; 1-day ticket adult/child ¥6200/4100, after 6pm ¥3300; ◷hours vary by season; ♿; ☒JR Keiyō line to Maihama) Pop quiz: what's the most visited sight in Japan? Kyoto's temples? Nope, it's Tokyo Disney Resort. There are actually two parks here: Tokyo Disney, modelled after the California original, and Tokyo DisneySea, which has shows

If You Like...
Gardens

If you like the greenery on offer in the Hama-Rikyū Onshi-teien, you might like these gardens:

1 **IMPERIAL PALACE EAST GARDEN**
(皇居東御苑; Kōkyo Higashi-gyoen; ⏱9am-4.30pm Tue-Thu; ⊠Maranouchi line to Ōtemachi, exit C10) This section of the Imperial Palace is open to the public and is good for a bit of fresh air in the city centre.

2 **SHINJUKU-GYOEN (SHINJUKU PARK)**
(新宿御苑; ☎3350-0151; www.env.go.jp/garden/shinjukugyoen; 11 Naito-chō; adult/6-15yr/under 6yr ¥200/50/free; ⏱9am-4.30pm Tue-Sun; underground rail Marunouchi line to Shinjuku-gyōenmae, exit 1) One of the city's best escapes and top cherry-blossom-viewing spots, Shinjuku-gyoen is also one of Tokyo's largest parks at 57.6 hectares (144 acres).

3 **KITANOMARU-KŌEN (KITANOMARU PARK)**
(北の丸公園; ⊠Hanzōmon line to Kudanshita, exit 2, ⊠Tozai line toTakebashi, exit 1a) Rounding out the northern edge of the Imperial Palace grounds, Kitanomaru-kōen makes a pleasant picnicking locale and is good for a leisurely stroll.

and international pavilions that are popular with adults. Invest in a Fast Pass to cut down on time lost waiting in lines.

Festivals & Events

Tokyo has hundreds of annual festivals, with the biggest ones happening during the warmer months. Here are some of the major ones; see **Go Tokyo** (www.gotokyo.org/en/index.html) for month by month listings.

Hanami   Cherry Blossom Festival
(花見) In late March to early April, cherry-blossom-viewing obsession takes over as locals gather in the city's parks for rare public displays of euphoria.

Sanja Matsuri   Parade
(三社祭) The grandest of all Tokyo festivals features hundreds of *mikoshi* (portable shrines) paraded through Asakusa, starting from **Asakusa-jinja** (浅草神社; Map p92; ☎3844-1575; www.asakusajinja.jp/english/; 2-3-1 Asakusa, Taitō-ku; ⏱9am-4.30pm; ⊠Ginza line to Asakusa, exit 1). On the third weekend in May.

Sumida-gawa Fireworks Fireworks
(隅田川花火大会; Sumida-gawa Hanabi Taikai) The largest of the summer firework shows sees 20,000 pyrotechnic wonders explode over Asakusa on the last Saturday of July.

Sleeping

Tokyo accomodation runs the gamut from over-the-top luxury hotels to cheap dorm rooms in converted warehouses. While boutique hotels haven't really taken off here, ryokan (traditional inns) fill the need for small-scale sleeping spaces with a personal touch. Prices are higher than elsewhere in Japan, but even backpackers can find a comfortable place to nest, especially on the east side of the city.

Wherever you decide to stay, advanced booking is highly recommended. Not only will you get a better price at most hotels, but even at hostels walk-ins can fluster staff.

Hotel rates can fluctuate wildly; compare prices for your travel dates at hotels around the city with **Japanican** (www.japanican.com), which also does online bookings.

It should be noted that some midrange and budget options do not accept credit cards – come prepared with cash.

Marunouchi (Tokyo Station area) 丸の内 (東京駅)

Central and convenient for travel in and out of Tokyo, Marunouchi makes sense as a base, though rates here are among the highest in the city.

The Peninsula Tokyo
Luxury Hotel ¥¥¥

(ザ・ペニンシュラ東京; Map p66; 6270-2288; www.peninsula.com/tokyo; 1-8-1 Yūrakuchō, Chiyoda-ku; r from ¥69,300; JR Yamanote line to Yūrakuchō, Hibiya exit) One almost gets a feeling of guilty extravagance when sprawling out in the Peninsula's vast rooms (starting at 51 sq metres), which overlook the Imperial Palace and Hibiya Moat and have floor-to-ceiling windows. Latticed caramel woodwork, sumptuous marble bathrooms and a dark central atrium unite in a delicious symphony of design.

Hotel Ryumeikan Tokyo
Hotel ¥¥¥

(ホテル龍名館東京; Map p66; 3271-0971; www.ryumeikan-tokyo.jp; 1-3-22 Yaesu, Chūō-ku; s/d ¥17,000/30,000; JR Yamanote line to Tokyo, Yaesu north exit) Three minutes on foot from Tokyo Station, Ryumeikan strikes the right balance between comfortable amenities, polite service and winning location. The decor is stylish and modern, with subtle Japanese touches. Bicycle and mobile-phone rentals are available too.

Tokyo Station Hotel
Luxury Hotel ¥¥¥

(東京ステーションホテル; Map p66; 5220-1112; www.tokyostationhotel.jp; 1-9-1 Marunouchi, Chiyoda-ku; d from ¥30,030; JR Yamanote line to Tokyo, Marunouchi south exit) Part of the newly renovated Tokyo Station, this is the city's newest luxury hotel. Rooms are spacious and decorated in an opulent European fashion, with tall ceilings, marble counters and dripping chandeliers; some have views of the Imperial Palace. It's supremely located for those catching an early *shinkansen* (bullet train).

Ginza & Tsukiji
銀座 ●築地

In Ginza, you'll have excellent shopping, cafes and restaurants at your doorstep, not to mention the Imperial Palace and Tsukiji Fish Market. This, of course, comes with a price.

Hotel Villa Fontaine Shiodome
Business Hotel ¥¥

(ホテルヴィラフォンテーヌ汐留; Map p66; 3569-2220; www.hvf.jp/eng; 1-9-2 Higashi-Shimbashi, Minato-ku; s/d incl breakfast from ¥14,000/16,000; @ ; Ōedo line to Shiodome, exit 10) Stylish, if not compact, rooms, and a location that puts you within easy striking distance of Tsukiji Fish Market make this a solid choice.

Mercure Hotel Ginza Tokyo
Business Hotel ¥¥¥

(メルキュールホテル銀座; Map p66; 4335-1111; www.mercure.com; 2-9-4 Ginza, Chūō-ku; s/d from ¥17,000/21,000; @ ; Yūrakuchō line to Ginza-itchōme, exit 11) With chinoiserie

Cherry blossom trees in Shinjuku-gyoen
JOHN W BANAGAN / GETTY IMAGES ©

Asakusa & Sumida-gawa

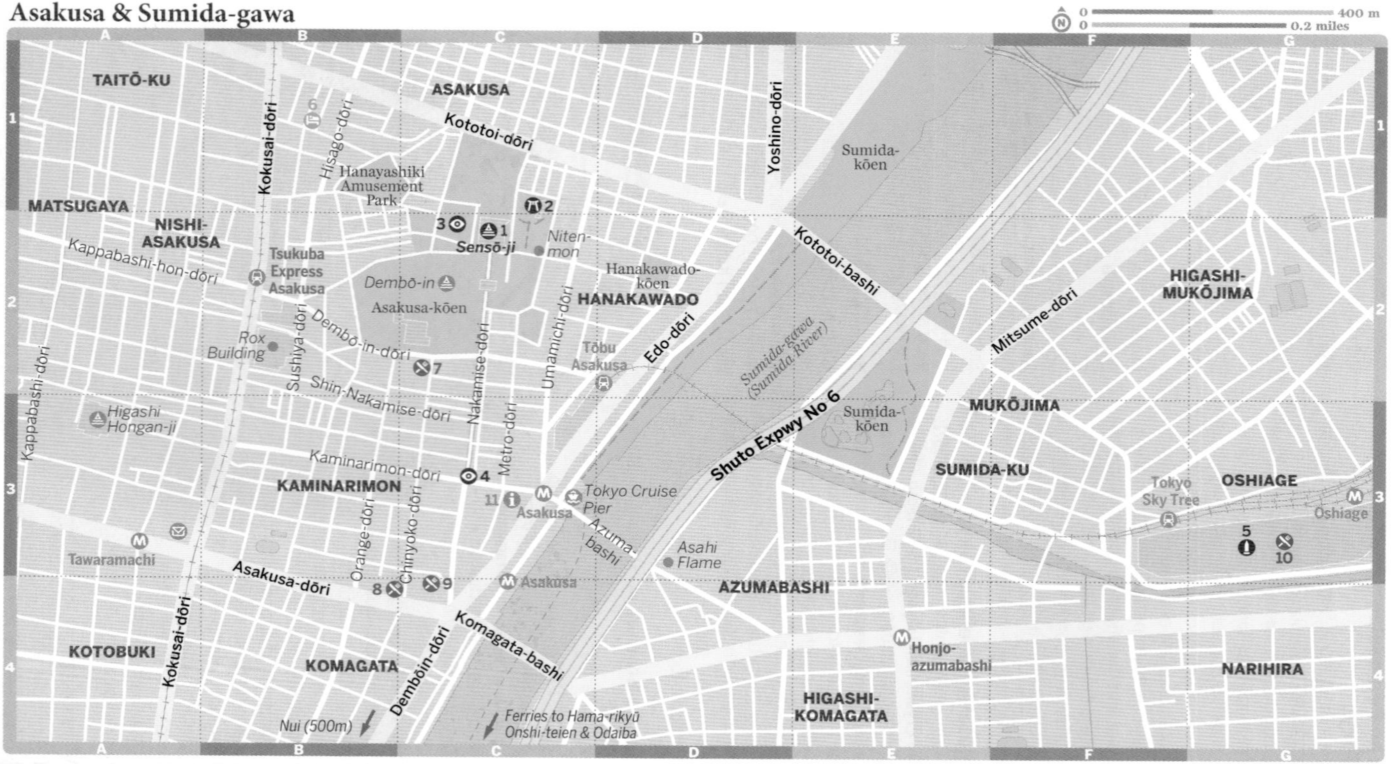

0 400 m
0 0.2 miles

TAITŌ-KU

MATSUGAYA

NISHI-ASAKUSA

ASAKUSA

HANAKAWADO

HIGASHI-MUKŌJIMA

MUKŌJIMA

SUMIDA-KU

OSHIAGE

NARIHIRA

AZUMABASHI

HIGASHI-KOMAGATA

KOMAGATA

KAMINARIMON

KOTOBUKI

Kappabashi-hon-dōri
Kappabashi-dōri
Kokusai-dōri
Hisago-dōri
Kototoi-dōri
Tsukuba Express Asakusa
Rox Building
Higashi Hongan-ji
Tawaramachi
Dembo-in-dōri
Shin-Nakamise-dōri
Sushiya-dōri
Asakusa-kōen
Dembo-in
Sensō-ji
Niten-mon
Hanakawado-kōen
Edo-dōri
Umamichi-dōri
Nakamise-dōri
Metro-dōri
Tōbu Asakusa
Asakusa
Asakusa
Tokyo Cruise Pier
Azuma-bashi
Asahi Flame
Kaminarimon-dōri
Chiyoko-dōri
Orange-dōri
Asakusa-dōri
Dembōin-dōri
Komagata bashi
Kokusai-dōri
Yoshino-dōri
Kototoi-bashi
Sumida-kōen
Sumida-gawa (Sumida River)
Shuto Expwy No 6
Sumida-kōen
Mitsume-dōri
Tokyo Sky Tree
Oshiage
Oshiage
Honjo-azumabashi
Ferries to Hama-rikyū Onshi-teien & Odaiba
Hanayashiki Amusement Park
Nui (500m)

1
2
3
4
5
6
7
8
9
10
11

Asakusa & Sumida-gawa

◎ Don't Miss Sights
1 Sensō-ji C2

◎ Sights
2 Asakusa-jinja C1
3 Five-Storey Pagoda C2
4 Kaminari-mon C3
5 Tokyo Sky Tree G3

⊜ Sleeping
6 Sukeroku No Yado Sadachiyo B1

⊗ Eating
7 Daikokuya C2
8 Irokawa B4
9 Namiki Yabu Soba C4
10 Rokurinsha G3

ℹ Information
11 Asakusa Tourist Information
Center... C3

prints and sprays of orchids, this hotel has more style than other cookie-cutter options in the same price range. It's a short walk from here to Ginza's department-store-lined main boulevards.

Roppongi & Around
六本木

If nightlife features prominently on your agenda, Roppongi is a good place to hang your hat. Akasaka, with its embassies and multinational headquarters, is known for its luxury hotels.

B Roppongi   Business Hotel ¥¥
(ザ・ビー六本木; Map p72; ☎5412-0451; www.theb-hotels.com/the-b-roppongi/en/index.html; 3-9-8 Roppongi, Minato-ku; s/d incl breakfast from ¥10,000/12,000; ☒@☎; ⓡHibiya line to Roppongi, exit 5) The B Roppongi has slick, white-brown rooms ranging in size from 10 to 31 sq metres. Atmosphere is business-casual and the location is perfect for Roppongi's nocturnal attractions, though light sleepers should request a quiet room. A light breakfast is included.

Villa Fontaine Roppongi   Hotel ¥¥
(ヴィラフォンテーヌ六本木; Map p72; ☎3560-1110; www.hvf.jp; 1-6-2 Roppongi,

Minato-ku; s/d incl breakfast ¥15,000/17,000; ☒@☎; ⓡNamboku line to Roppongi-itchōme, exit 2) Stylish, modern and reasonably priced, Villa Fontaine offers 160cm-wide beds and a complimentary buffet breakfast. It's close enough to Roppongi's centre to experience its madness, but far enough away for a quiet sleep.

ANA Intercontinental Tokyo   Luxury Hotel ¥¥¥
(ANAインターコンチネンタルホテル東京; Map p72; ☎3505-1111; www.anaintercontinental-tokyo.jp/e; 1-12-33 Akasaka, Minato-ku; s/d from ¥26,200/36,750; ☒@☎☒; ⓡGinza line to Tameike-sannō, exit 13) The spacious rooms here have fantastic night-time views and a sophisticated contemporary design. There's a gym too. Considering the location – within walking distance of Roppongi – and the prices at neighbouring establishments, it's a pretty good deal.

Ebisu & Meguro
恵比寿・目黒

Not a conventional area to bed down, but Ebisu and Meguro are both fairly central and close to scores of excellent bars and restaurants.

Claska   Boutique Hotel ¥¥
(クラスカ; Map p62; ☎3719-8121; www.claska.com/en/hotel; 1-3-18 Chūō-chō, Meguro-ku; s/d from ¥12,600/19,950, weekly per night s ¥7875; @; ⓡJR Yamanote line to Meguro, west exit) The Claska is hands down Tokyo's most stylish hotel; its handful of rooms have been done up by local designers. Some have tatami and floor cushions; others have terraces and glass-walled bathrooms. The hotel is smack in the middle of the city's interior design district, along Meguro-dōri. It's a 10-minute (about ¥1000) taxi ride from Meguro Station, 2km away. Book early.

Hotel Excellent Ebisu   Business Hotel ¥¥
(ホテルエクセレント恵比寿; Map p76; ☎5458-0087; www.soeikikaku.co.jp/english/index.html; 1-9-5 Ebisu-nishi, Shibuya-ku; s/d from ¥9150/11,550; ☒@; ⓡJR Yamanote line

Below Young women in Harajuku; **Right:** National Art Center Tokyo
(BELOW) LONELY PLANET / GETTY IMAGES ©; (RIGHT) TRAVELASIA / GETTY IMAGES ©

to Ebisu, west exit) Though the rooms here are utterly ordinary, and rather small, this is a solid choice if you want to take advantage of the excellent bars and restaurants in and around Ebisu. The hotel is situated right in front of the train station.

Shibuya & Around　渋谷

Staying in Shibuya puts you right in the thick of things, and the rail access is excellent. Though if you're not planning on taking advantage of the local nightlife, you might want to pick somewhere a little more peaceful.

Hotel Fukudaya　　Ryokan ¥¥
(ホテル福田屋; ☎3467-5833; www2.gol.com/users/ryokan-fukudaya/index.html; 4-5-9 Aobadai, Meguro-ku; s/d from ¥6300/10,500; ⊝@🛜; 🚃JR Yamanote line to Shibuya, south exit) Hotel Fukudaya is pretty classy for its price, with well-tended tatami rooms both with and without private bathrooms. It's located near the upscale residential neighbourhoods of Daikan-yama and Ikejiri-Ōhashi. While Shibuya is technically the closest station, it's still a 20-minute walk (or about a ¥1000 taxi ride) away.

Shibuya
Granbell Hotel　Boutique Hotel ¥¥¥
(渋谷グランベルホテル; Map p84; ☎5457-2681; www.granbellhotel.jp; 15-17 Sakuragaoka-chō, Shibuya-ku; s/d from ¥13,000/22,000; ⊝@🛜; 🚃JR Yamanote line to Shibuya, south exit) One of the city's few boutique hotels, the Granbell is a step up from a business hotel, but priced about the same. Stylish rooms have glass-enclosed bathrooms, Simmons beds and pop-art curtains. Only a few minutes' walk from Shibuya Station, on a narrow lane, the Granbell is the best place to hole up in Shibuya. Try to book early.

Excel Hotel Tōkyū
Hotel ¥¥¥

(エクセルホテル東急; Map p84; ☎ 5457-0109; www.tokyuhotelsjapan.com/en/; 1-12-2 Dōgenzaka, Shibuya-ku; s/d from ¥22,500/30,000; ☺ @; ☒ JR Yamanote line to Shibuya, Shibuya Mark City exit) This tower, connected to Shibuya Station, boasts excellent night views from the upper floors. Rooms are spacious though ordinary, but at least you're right on top of the action.

Shinjuku & West Tokyo
新宿

As a major transportation hub on the west side of the city, Shinjuku makes for a convenient base, though it's mostly big-name hotels here.

Citadines
Hotel ¥¥

(シタディーン; Map p88; ☎ 5379-7208; www. citadines.com; 1-28-13 Shinjuku, Shinjuku-ku; r from ¥13,800; ☺ @ ☎; ☒ Marunouchi line to Shinjuku-gyoenmae, exit 2) Rooms at the recently opened Citadines are bright and modern, if not compact, and include a small kitchenette. The hotel is a bit far from the Shinjuku action, though travellers staying for more than a few days will likely come to appreciate the relative quiet. Weekly rates available too.

Kadoya Hotel
Business Hotel ¥¥

(かどやホテル; Map p88; ☎ 3346-2561; www.kadoya-hotel.co.jp; 1-23-1 Nishi-Shinjuku, Shinjuku-ku; s/d from ¥7560/13,650; ☺ @; ☒ JR Yamanote line to Shinjuku, west exit) A steal for its Nishi-Shinjuku address, this family-run hotel has simple, clean rooms and friendly service. The newer 'comfort' rooms have Simmons beds and better decor. Check online for packages that include breakfast, early check-in, or mobile-phone rental.

Park Hyatt Tokyo
Luxury Hotel ¥¥¥

(パークハイアット東京; Map p88; ☎ 5322-1234; http://tokyo.park.hyatt.com; 3-7-1-2 Nishi-Shinjuku, Shinjuku-ku; r from ¥52,175; ☺ @ ☎ ☒; ☒ Ōedo line to Tochōmae, exit A4)

Ueno

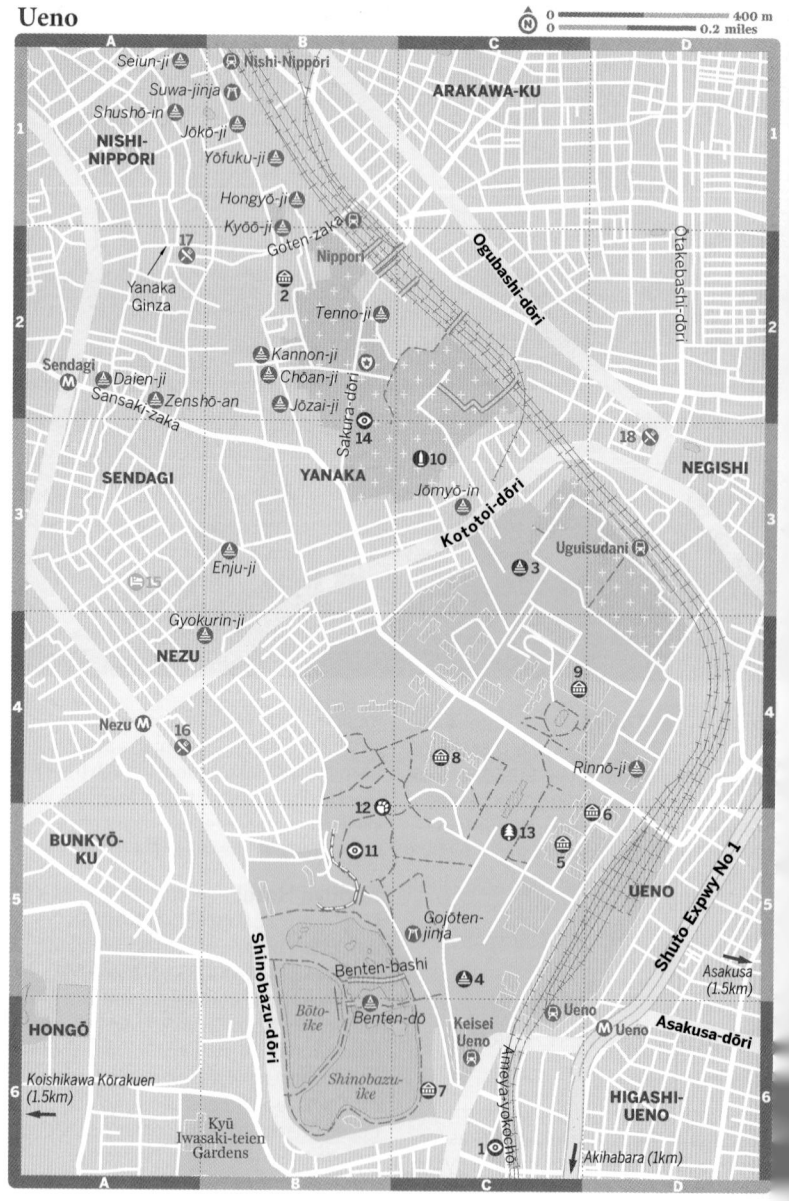

Tokyo's most famous hotel has 177 rooms spread out over a dozen floors of a Tange Kenzō–designed skyscraper in Nishi-Shinjuku. The hotel starts from the 41st floor, meaning even the entry-level rooms have otherworldly views. The service here is gracious and above all accommodating: perks for guests include complimentary mobile-phone rentals.

Ueno

◎ Sights

1 Ameya-yokochō C6
2 Asakura Choso Museum B2
3 Kanei-ji C3
4 Kiyōmizu Kannon-dō C5
5 National Museum of Western
   Art C5
6 National Science Museum D5
7 Shitamachi Museum C6
8 Tokyo Metropolitan Museum of
   Art C4
9 Tokyo National Museum C4
10 Tomb of Yoshinobu Tokugawa C3
11 Tōshōgū B5
12 Ueno Zoo B5
13 Ueno-kōen C5
14 Yanaka-reien B3

⏟ Sleeping

15 Sawanoya Ryokan A3

⊗ Eating

16 Hantei A4
17 Nagomi A2
18 Sasa-no-Yuki D3

Hotel Century Southern Tower
Hotel ¥¥¥

(ホテルセンチュリーサザンタワー;
Map p88; ☏ 5354-0111; www.southerntower.
co.jp/english; 2-2-1 Yoyogi, Shibuya-ku; s/d
¥18,480/27,720; ☺@☏; ☒JR Yamanote line
to Shinjuku, south exit) The location – just
outside Shinjuku Station's south exit – is
the big draw here. Rooms are comfortable
but not splashy, with winter views of Mt
Fuji possible from one side and the green
space of Shinjuku-gyoen on the other.
Rates may decrease for longer stays.

Ueno
上野

If you'd like to immerse yourself in historic
Tokyo, then Ueno, with its welcoming,
inexpensive ryokan, is an excellent choice.
A direct train connects Ueno with Narita
Airport.

Sawanoya Ryokan
Ryokan ¥¥

旅館澤の屋; Map p96; ☏ 3822-2251; www.
sawanoya.com; 2-3-11 Yanaka, Taitō-ku; s/d from
¥5040/10,080; @☏⏧; ☒Chiyoda line to

Nezu, exit 1) Sawanoya is a gem in quiet
Yanaka, with very friendly staff and all the
traditional hospitality you would expect of
a ryokan – even origami cranes perched
on your pillow. The shared cypress and
earthenware baths are the perfect balm
after a long day. The lobby overflows with
information about travel options in Japan
and bicycles are available for rent.

Asakusa & Sumida-gawa
浅草 ● 隅田川

While not central, Asakusa has an attractive, unpretentious, traditional atmosphere and the city's best hostels.

Nui
Hostel ¥

(ヌイ; Map p62; ☏ 6240-9854; http://backpack-
ersjapan.co.jp/nui_en; 2-14-13 Kuramae, Taitō-ku;
dm/d from ¥2700/6500; ☺@☏; ☒Ōedo line
to Kuramae, exit A7) In a former warehouse,
this brand-new hostel raises the bar for
stylish budget digs in Tokyo. High ceilings
means bunks you can comfortably sit up
in and there's an enormous kitchen and
workspace. Best of all is the ground-floor
bar and lounge, with its glass front, grand
piano and furniture handmade from
salvaged timber.

Sukeroku No Yado Sadachiyo
Ryokan ¥¥¥

(助六の宿貞千代; Map p92; ☏ 3842-6431;
www.sadachiyo.co.jp; 2-20-1 Asakusa, Taitō-ku;
s/d from ¥14,000/19,000; @☏; ☒Ginza line
to Asakusa, exit 1) This gorgeous traditional
ryokan virtually transports its guests to old
Edo. The well-maintained tatami rooms are
spacious for two people, and all come with
modern, Western-style bathrooms. Splurge
on an exquisite meal here, and make time
for the o-furo (traditional Japanese baths),
one made of fragrant Japanese cypress
and the other of black granite. Look for the
rickshaw parked outside.

✖ Eating

When it comes to Tokyo superlatives,
the city's eating scene takes the cake.
There are more restaurants in this pulsing
megalopolis than in any other city in the

Odaiba & Tokyo Bay

⊙ **Sights**
1 Fuji TV...B2
2 Gundam..B2
3 National Museum of Emerging
   Science & Innovation
   (Mirai-kan).......................................B3
4 Odaiba Kaihin-kōen B1
5 Ōedo Onsen Monogatari..................B3

⊕ **Activities, Courses & Tours**
6 Tokyo Joypolis B1

world. Tokyo's victual vocabulary extends far beyond fish and noodles: the cosmopolitan city boasts some of the best international cuisine on the planet. And the quality is unparalleled, too – you're rarely more than 500m from a good, if not great, restaurant.

Best of all, you can eat well on any budget in pretty much every neighbourhood. Lunch is usually excellent value, with many pricier restaurants offering cheaper courses during the noontime hours. Reservations are necessary only at upmarket restaurants, though they're a good idea at midrange places (especially on Friday and Saturday evenings) if you have a party larger than two.

Marunouchi (Tokyo Station area) 丸の内 (東京駅)

Marunouchi is experiencing a dining renaissance along with its redevelopment. The 5th floor of the Shin-Marunouchi Building (p61) has dozens of restaurants and is popular with the young, after-work crowd. Nearby **Marunouchi Brick Square** (丸の内ブリックスクエア; Map p66; www.marunouchi.com/brick; 2-6-1 Marunouchi, Chiyoda-ku; ⊙11am-11pm; ⒭Chiyoda line to Nijūbashimae, exit 1) has several upscale alfresco options.

There are also plenty of places to eat within Tokyo Station.

Tokyo Rāmen Street   Rāmen ¥
(東京ラーメンストリート; Map p66; www.tokyoeki-1bangai.co.jp/ramenstreet; basement fl, Tokyo Station; rāmen from ¥750; ⊙7.30am-10.30pm; ⒭JR Yamanote line to Tokyo Station,

Yaesu south exit) Eight of Japan's famous *rāmen-ya* (*rāmen* – egg noodle – shops) operate minibranches out of a corner of Tokyo Station (in the basement on the Yaesu side). All of the major styles are covered, from *shōyu* (soy sauce base) to *tsukemen* (noodles served on the side). Good luck picking just one!

Ishii   Kushiyaki ¥

(い志井; Map p66; 5th fl, Shin-Marunouchi Bldg, 1-5-1 Marunouchi, Chiyoda-ku; skewers from ¥140; 🕐11am-2pm, 4pm-2am Mon-Sat, 11am-10pm Sun; 🖳; 🚇JR Yamanote line to Tokyo, Marunouchi north exit) *Yakiton* (grilled pork skewers) – rather than the more common *yakitori* (grilled chicken skewers) – is the speciality here. Trendy Ishii is done up like a retro, post-WWII food stand and is notorious for using all of the pig (and we mean *all* of it). Look for the lanterns.

Ginza & Tsukiji   銀座

Sushi breakfast at Tsukiji is a classic Tokyo experience. In the evening the day's catch is sliced up by expert hands in Ginza's sushi restaurants, which are among the most highly regarded in the world. But budget diners needn't fear Ginza; look instead to the inexpensive **yakitori stands** (Map p66; skewers from ¥120; 🕐5pm-11pm) crammed under the JR tracks around Yūrakuchō Station.

Robata Honten   Izakaya ¥

(炉端本店; Map p66; 🕿3591-9905; 1-3-8 Yūrakuchō, Chiyoda-ku; dishes ¥1000-1500; 🕐5-11pm Mon-Sat; 🚇Ginza line to Hibiya, exit A4) Alongside the train tracks and inside an old wooden building blackened by the years, this *izakaya* (pub-eatery) has enough ambience that it needn't worry about the food. Fortunately, it

does: filling, home-style dishes, a mix of Japanese and Western, are served family-style, piled high in bowls along the counter – just point to what you want.

Daiwa Sushi   Sushi ¥¥

(大和寿司; Map p66; 🕿3547-6807; Bldg 6, 5-2-1 Tsukiji, Chūō-ku; sushi sets ¥3500; 🕐5am-1.30pm Mon-Sat, closed occasional Wed; 🖳; 🚇Ōedo line to Tsukijishijō, exit A2) This is one of Tsukiji's most famous sushi counters and waits of over an hour are commonplace. Trust us, it's worth it. The standard set is a solid bet and includes *chū-toro* (medium-grade tuna) and *uni* (sea urchin roe). Though the staff may be too polite to say so, you're expected to eat and run.

Sushi Kanesaka   Sushi ¥¥¥

(鮨かねさか; Map p66; 🕿5568-4411; www.sushi-kanesaka.com; basement fl, 8-10-3 Ginza, Chūō-ku; lunch/dinner courses from ¥5000/20,000; 🕐11.30am-1pm, 5-10pm Mon-Fri, to 9pm Sat & Sun; 🖳; 🚇JR Yamanote line to Shimbashi, Ginza exit) Tucked away below street level, this sushi superstar is the workshop of the eponymous master chef

Restaurant near Yūrakuchō Station
OLIVER STREWE / GETTY IMAGES ©

who slices through premium pieces of fresh fish with a surgeon's precision. If you're contemplating a sushi splurge during your time in Tokyo, this is the place to do it. But book ahead – there are only 20 seats.A small square lantern marks the entrance.

Roppongi & Around
六本木

It's only logical that there's an abundance of international options in Tokyo's capital of *gaijin*-dom, and you can find everything from a classic eggs Benedict brunch to late-night kebab stands here. Roppongi, a playground for those with expense accounts, is also known for high-end dining and ambitious concept restaurants.

The basement of Tokyo Midtown (p65) has dozens of reasonably priced options as well as takeaway counters – perfect for a picnic lunch in the garden out back.

Tokyo Curry Lab   Curry ¥
(東京カレーラボ; Map p72; 2nd fl, Tokyo Tower, 4-2-8 Shiba-kōen, Minato-ku; meals ¥1000-1350; ⏰11am-10pm; 📖; 🚇Hibiya line to Kamiyachō,

exit 1) Under Tokyo Tower, this space-station-like restaurant specializes in the curiously addicting Japanese dish *kare-raisu* (curry-rice). There are personal TVs at each bar stool and hilariously illustrated place mats (you'll see).

Gonpachi   Izakaya ¥
(権八; Map p72; 📞5771-0170; www.gonpachi. jp/nishiazabu; 1-13-11 Nishi-Azabu, Minato-ku; skewers ¥180-1500, lunch sets weekday/weekend from ¥800/2050; ⏰11.30am-3.30am; 😊 📖; 🚇Hibiya line to Roppongi, exit 1) Gonpachi is a Tokyo institution, serving charcoal-grilled skewers plus tempura, noodles etc. Cavernous by local standards, it looks like an Edo-era night market on the inside and a feudal villa on the outside. (And if it looks vaguely familiar, that's because the restaurant inspired the set for one of the epic fight scenes in the movie *Kill Bill*).

Jōmon   Izakaya ¥¥
(ジョウモン; Map p72; 📞3405-2585; www. teyandei.com; 5-9-17 Roppongi, Minato-ku; skewers ¥150-1600; ⏰6pm-5am; 📖; 🚇Hibiya line to Roppongi, exit 3) Slide the wooden door open to find a cosy kitchen with bar seating and rows of ornate *shochū* (liquor)

Tempura and rice

OLIVIER CIRENDINI / GETTY IMAGE

jugs lining the wall. Skewers of grilled meat and vegetables are the speciality here, from straight up divine (top-grade beef) to ingeniously delicious (bacon-wrapped quail eggs). The restaurant is almost directly across from the Family Mart; book ahead on weekends.

Tofuya-Ukai
Kaiseki ¥¥¥

(とうふ屋うかい; Map p72; ☎3436-1028; www.ukai.co.jp; 4-4-13 Shiba-kōen, Minato-ku; lunch/dinner courses from ¥5500/8400; ☺11am-10pm; ✈📖; 🚇Toei Ōedo line to Akabanebashi, exit 8) One of the city's most impressive restaurants, Tofuya-Ukai has only private rooms, all of which overlook a beautiful, manicured garden. The *kaiseki* (Japanese haute cuisine) courses feature delicate, handmade tofu served a variety of ways, but may also include sashimi and grilled fish; considering the spread, it's excellent value. Enquire when booking about vegetarian meals; reserve well in advance.

Ebisu & Meguro
恵比寿・目黒

Ebisu is one of the best places in the city for eating out: there are scores of unpretentious restaurants that serve just plain good food. There are some creative, stylish places too, especially as you move further out to Daikanyama and Naka-meguro.

Tonki
Tonkatsu ¥

(とんき; 1-2-1 Shimo-Meguro, Meguro-ku; meals ¥1800; ☺4-11pm Wed-Mon, closed 3rd Mon of month; ➡📖; 🚇JR Yamanote line to Meguro, west exit) There are only two things on the menu here – *rosu-katsu* (fatty loin cutlet) and *hire-katsu* (lean fillet cutlet) – but Tonki's loyal customers never tire of it. Sit at the counter to watch the perfectly choreographed chefs breading, frying and garnishing the tender cutlets. Look for a white sign and *noren* (doorway curtains) across the sliding doors.

From Meguro Station, walk down Meguro-dōri and take the first left in front of the Pachinko parlour.

Afuri
Rāmen ¥

(あふり; Map p76; 1-1-7 Ebisu, Shibuya-ku; noodles from ¥750; ☺11am-5am; ➡📖; 🚇JR Yamanote line to Ebisu, east exit) Hardly your typical, surly *rāmen-ya*, Afuri has upbeat young cooks and a hip industrial interior. The unorthodox menu might draw eye-rolls from purists, but house specialities such as *yuzu-shio* (a light, salty broth flavoured with *yuzu* – a type of citrus – peel) draw lines at lunchtime.

Chano-ma
Japanese ¥

(チャノマ; Map p76; 1-22-4 Kami-Meguro, Meguro-ku; lunch set & mains from ¥880; ☺noon-2am Sun-Thu, to 4am Fri & Sat; ✈📖; 🚇Hibiya line to Naka-Meguro) By day, Chano-ma is a laid-back cafe with a popular 'deli lunch' special of healthy Japanese food. By night, it's a chilled-out lounge where you can sip cocktails by candlelight on a row of raised mattresses. It's in an impossibly narrow building across the street from Naka-Meguro Station.

Ippo
Izakaya ¥¥

(一歩; Map p76; ☎3445-8418; 2nd fl, 1-22-10 Ebisu, Shibuya-ku; mains from ¥800-1500; ☺6pm-3am; 🚇JR Yamanote line to Ebisu, east exit) This mellow joint specialises in simple pleasures: fish and sake (there's an English sign out front that says just that). There's only a counter and a few small tables, so groups should call ahead; staff speak English. Follow the wooden stairs under the sage ball.

Higashi-Yama
Japanese ¥¥

(ヒガシヤマ; Map p62; ☎5720-1300; www.higashiyama-tokyo.jp; 1-21-25 Higashi-yama, Meguro-ku; lunch/dinner courses from ¥2100/4000; ☺11.30am-2pm, 6pm-1am Mon-Sat; ➡; 🚇Hibiya line to Naka-Meguro) Chic, starkly minimalist, and all but completely hidden, Higashi-Yama serves set courses of seasonal, all-natural, modern Japanese cuisine on gorgeous crockery. The basement lounge – an even better-kept secret – is perfect for an after-dinner drink. From Naka-Meguro Station, walk 10 minutes down Yamate-dōri towards Shibuya, turning left in front of the Family Mart; Hagashi-Yama will be on your left. Reservations recommended.

Shibuya & Around　渋谷

Shibuya is chock-a-block with fast-food joints and cheap *izakaya* catering to the youthful crowd who hang out here. Shibuya Hikarie (p71) has some more sophisticated, yet still reasonably priced, restaurants on the 6th and 7th floors that stay open until 4am Friday and Saturday nights, and a basement (level 3) food-court with good takeaway options.

For more eccentric eateries hop on the train and head to Shimo-Kitazawa.

Viron　Bakery ¥
(Map p84; ☎5458-1770; 33-8 Udagawa-chō, Shibuya-ku; sandwiches ¥525-1050; ⊙9am-10pm; ☒JR Yamanote line to Shibuya, Hachikō exit) A fantastic French bakery (it apparently imports the flour from the motherland), Viron serves up sandwiches and quiches to take away.

Kaikaya　Seafood ¥¥
(開花屋; Map p84; ☎3770-0878; www.kaikaya.com; 23-7 Maruyama-chō, Shibuya-ku; lunch from ¥780, dishes ¥680-2500; ⊙11.30am-2pm, 5.30-11.30pm Mon-Fri, 5.30-11.30pm Sat & Sun; ☻⏷; ☒Yamanote line to Shibuya, Hachikō exit) Everything on the menu here is caught in nearby Sagami Bay. It's a boisterous, popular place; reservations are recommended. From Dōgenzaka, turn right after the police box and the restaurant, with a red awning, will be on your right.

Sushi-no-Midori　Sushi ¥¥
(寿司の美登利; Map p84; 4th fl, Mark City, 1-12-3 Dōgenzaka, Shibuya-ku; sets from ¥2100; ⊙11am-10pm Mon-Fri, to 9pm Sat & Sun; ☻⏷; ☒JR Yamanote line to Shibuya, Hachikō exit) Sushi-no-midori, famed for being excellent value, almost always has a line. Don't let the wait put you off; service is quick and the generous sushi sets are worth it. Look for the signs to the Mark City complex inside Shibuya Station, near the Inokashira line.

Harajuku　原宿

Sticky sweet crepes are the official food of Takeshita-dōri. Elsewhere you'll find plenty of fashionable restaurants and cafes.

Harajuku Gyōza Rō　Gyōza ¥
(原宿餃子楼; Map p82; 6-4-2 Jingūmae, Shibuya-ku; 6 gyōza ¥290; ⊙11.30am-4.30am; ⏷; ☒JR Yamanote line to Harajuku, Omote-sandō exit) *Gyōza* (dumplings) are the only thing on the menu here, but you won't hear any complaints from the regulars who queue up to get their fix. Have them *sui* (boiled) or *yaki* (pan-fried), with or without *niniku* (garlic) or *nira* (chives) – they're all delicious. Expect to wait on weekends.

Maisen　Tonkatsu ¥
(まい泉; Map p82; http://mai-sen.com; 4-8-5 Jingūmae, Shibuya-ku; lunch/dinner from ¥995/1680; ⊙11am-10pm; ☻⏷; ☒Ginza line to Omote-sandō, exit A2) You could order something else, but pretty much everyone is here for the famous *tonkatsu* (breaded, deep-fried pork cutlets). Price is determined by grade of meat: you can splurge on the prized *kurobuta* (black pig), but even the cheapest is melt-in-your-mouth divine. The restaurant is housed in an old public bathhouse. A takeaway window serves delicious *tonkatsu sando* (sandwich).

Marukaku　Japanese ¥
(丸角; Map p82; 4th fl, Gyre Bldg, 5-10-1 Jingūmae, Shibuya-ku; lunch set ¥900, small dishes ¥380-700; ⊙11.30am-11pm; ⏷; ☒JR Yamanote line to Harajuku, Omote-sandō exit) The lunchtime *sakana teishoku* (fish set meal) here has a loyal following; it's fresh, filling and a steal – especially considering the location on top of Chanel. Options change daily, depending on what's in season. The dinner menu expands to include sashimi, small dishes and skewers of grilled meat and vegetables. Look for the white *noren*.

Agaru Sagaru Nishi Iru Higashi Iru　Kaiseki ¥¥
(上ル下ル西入ル東入ル; Map p82; ☎3403-6968; www.agarusagaru.com; Basement fl, 3-25-8 Jingūmae, Shibuya-ku; course ¥3990; ⊙5.30-10pm Mon-Sat; ☒JR Yamanote line to Harajuku, Takeshita exit) The young, unpretentious chefs here serve up a procession of artful dishes that are Kyoto-inspired but tweaked for Tokyoites' been-there-done-that tastes. Also, the restaurant looks like a cave – even from the street.

A chef prepares *oden*

GREG ELMS / GETTY IMAGES ©

There's only a counter and a few tables, so call ahead on weekends. Sitting at the counter is more fun.

Mominoki House Organic ¥¥
(もみの木ハウス; Map p82; http://omotesando. mominokihouse.net; 2-18-5 Jingūmae, Shibuya-ku; lunch/dinner sets from ¥800/3200; 11.30am-10pm; ; JR Yamanote line to Harajuku, Takeshita exit) Boho Tokyoites have been coming here for tasty and nourishing macrobiotic fare since 1976. The casual, cosy dining room has seen some famous visitors too, like Paul McCartney. Chef Yamada's menu is heavily vegetarian, but also includes free-range chicken and *Ezo shika* (Hokkaidō venison; ¥4800).

Shinjuku & West Tokyo 新宿

Shinjuku has an overwhelming number of restaurants in all styles and budgets. If you want to narrow down your choices – or grab a quick bite without having to brave the crowds – head to one of the *resutoran-gai* (restaurant 'towns') found on the top floor of most department

stores; both **Lumine** (ルミネ; Map p88; 11am-11pm) and **Mylord** (ミロード; Map p88; 11am-11pm), inside Shinjuku Station near the south exit, have reasonably priced options.

One stop north of Shinjuku on the Yamanote line, **Shin-Ōkubo** is Tokyo's Little Seoul, home to many authentic Korean restaurants.

Nagi Rāmen ¥
(凪; Map p88; www.n-nagi.com; 2nd fl, Golden Gai G2, 1-1-10 Kabukichō, Shinjuku-ku; rāmen from ¥750; 11:30am-3pm, 6pm-5am Mon-Sat, to 2am Sun; JR Yamanote line to Shinjuku, east exit) The excellent noodles at this tiny Golden Gai joint, up a treacherous flight of stairs, are served in a dark broth deeply flavoured with *niboshi* (dried sardines). There is almost always a wait; first purchase your order from the vending machine inside, then claim your spot at the end of the line. Look for the sign with a red circle.

Nakajima Kaiseki ¥
(中嶋; Map p88; 3356-4534; www.shinjyuku-nakajima.com; Basement fl, 3-32-5 Shinjuku, Shinjuku-ku; lunch/dinner from ¥800/8400; 11.30am-2pm, 5.30pm-10pm Mon-Sat;

Marunouchi line to Shinjuku-sanchōme, exit A1) In the evening, this Michelin-starred restaurant serves exquisite *kaiseki* dinners. On weekdays it does a set lunch of humble *iwashi* (sardines) for one-tenth the price. In the hands of Nakajima's chefs they're divine; get yours sashimi or *yanagawa nabe* (stewed with egg). The line for lunch starts to form shortly before the restaurant opens. Reservations are necessary for dinner.

A tiny sign marks the stairs leading down to the restaurant, which has white door curtains out front.

Tsunahachi
Tempura ¥¥

(つな八; Map p88; ☎ 3352-1012; www.tunahachi.co.jp; 3-31-8 Shinjuku, Shinjuku-ku; sets ¥1995-3990; ⏱11am-10pm; 🚇 ⏐ ; 🚉 JR Yamanote line to Shinjuku, east exit) Tsunahachi has been expertly frying prawns and seasonal vegetables for nearly 90 years. The sets are served in courses so each dish comes piping hot. Sit at the counter for the added pleasure of watching the chefs at work. Indigo *noren* mark the entrance.

Akihabara & Around
秋葉原

Akihabara and nearby Jimbōchō are good places to sample *b-kyū gurume* (b-grade gourmet) – the term used to describe comfort food done well. Think *tonkatsu*, *rāmen* and all those other stick-to-your-ribs dishes that defy the generally healthy image of Japanese food.

Kikanbō
Rāmen ¥

(鬼金棒; Map p62; http://karashibi.com; 2-10-8 Kaji-chō, Chiyoda-ku; rāmen from ¥780; ⏱11am-9.30pm Mon-Sat, to 4pm Sun; 🚉 JR Yamanote line to Kanda, north exit) The *'karashibi'* (カラシビ) spicy miso *rāmen* here has a cult following. You can choose the level of *kara* (spice) and *shibi* (strange mouth-numbing sensation created by Japanese *sanshō* pepper). We recommend *futsū-futsū* (regular for both) for first-timers; *oni* (devil) level costs an extra ¥100. Look for the red door curtains and purchase your order from the vending machine.

Ueno
上野

Ueno has some wonderful traditional restaurants. In and around the Ameya-yokochō shopping street there are dozens of places for a quick bite.

Hantei
Japanese ¥¥

(はん亭; Map p96; ☎ 3828-1440; www.hantei.co.jp/nedu.html; 2-12-15 Nezu, Bunkyō-ku; lunch/dinner courses from ¥3150/2835; ⏱noon-3pm & 5-10pm Tue-Sun; 🚉 Chiyoda line to Nezu, exit 2) Housed in a beautifully maintained, nearly 100-year-old traditional wooden building, Hantei is a local landmark. Delectable skewers of seasonal *kushiage* (fried meat, fish and vegetables) are served with small, refresh-

Soba (buckwheat noodle) dish
GREG ELMS / GETTY IMAGES ©

ing side dishes. Lunch courses include eight sticks and dinner courses start with six, after which you'll continue to receive additional rounds (¥210 per skewer) until you say stop.

Sasa-no-Yuki   Tofu ¥¥

(笹乃雪; ☎ 3873-1145; 2-15-10 Negishi, Taitō-ku; dishes ¥350-1000, set meals ¥2600-4500; ⏰ 11.30am-8pm Tue-Sun; ⚶ 🗐 ; 🚃 JR Yamanote line to Uguisudani, north exit) 🍂 Sasa-no-Yuki opened its doors in the Edo period, and continues to serve its signature dishes, with tofu made fresh every morning with water from the shop's own well. The best seats overlook a tiny garden with a koi pond. Vegetarians should not assume every thing is purely veggie – ask before ordering. There is bamboo and a bench out front.

Nagomi   Yakitori ¥¥

(和味; Map p96; ☎ 3821-5972; 3-11-11 Yanaka, Taitō-ku; skewers from ¥180; ⏰ 5pm-midnight; 🗐 ; 🚃 JR Yamanote line to Nippori, north exit) On Yanaka Ginza, Nagomi deals in juicy skewers of *ji-dori* (free-range chicken). There are plenty of grilled veggie options, too. Wash it all down with a bowl of chicken soup *rāmen*. Look for the sake bottles in the window.

Asakusa & Sumida-gawa
浅草・隅田川

Down-home, unpretentious fare is an Asakusa speciality. Don't miss the snack vendors on Nakamise-dōri, dishing out traditional treats such as *mochi* (sticky-rice cakes) stuffed with sweet bean paste.

Daikokuya   Tempura ¥

(大黒家; Map p92; www.tempura.co.jp/english/index.html; 1-38-10 Asakusa, Taitō-ku; meals ¥1500-2050; ⏰ 11am-8.30pm Mon-Fri, to 9pm Sat; 🗐 ; 🚃 Ginza line to Asakusa, exit 6) Near Nakamise-dōri, this is the place to get old-fashioned tempura fried in pure sesame oil, an Asakusa specialty. It's in a white building with a tile roof. If there's a queue (and there often is), you can try your luck at the annexe one block over.

Rokurinsha   Rāmen ¥

(六厘舎; Map p92; www.rokurinsha.com; 6th fl, Solamachi, 1-1-2 Oshiage, Sumida-ku; rāmen from ¥850; ⏰ 11am-11pm; 🚃 Hanzōmon line to Oshiage, Sky Tree exit) Rokurinsha's speciality is *tsukemen* – *rāmen* noodles served on the side with a bowl of concentrated soup for dipping. The noodles here are thick and perfectly al dente, the soup is a rich *tonkotsu* (pork bone) base topped with pork, hard-boiled egg and bamboo shoots. It's an addicting combination.

Namiki Yabu Soba   Soba ¥

(並木藪蕎麦; Map p92; ☎ 3841-1340; 2-11-9 Kaminarimon, Taitō-ku; noodles ¥700-1800; ⏰ 11am-7.30pm Fri-Wed; 😀 🗐 ; 🚃 Ginza line to Asakusa, exit 2) Delicate, handmade noodles draw locals and tourists alike to this timeless, classy *soba* (buckwheat noodle) shop, in business since 1913. Seating is on tatami mats or at communal tables. There's a raised white vertical sign out front.

Irokawa   Unagi ¥¥

(色川; Map p92; ☎ 3844-1187; 2-6-11 Kaminarimon, Taitō-ku; sets from ¥2500; ⏰ 11.30am-1.30pm, 5-8.30pm Mon-Sat; 😀 🗐 ; 🚃 Ginza line to Asakusa, exit 2) This tiny restaurant has a real old Edo flavour and is one of the best, unpretentious *unagi* (eel) restaurants in town. The menu is simple: a 'small' gets you two slices of charcoal-grilled eel over rice, a 'large' gets you three. The chef grills everything right behind the counter. Look for the light green building.

🍷 Drinking & Nightlife

Tokyo's nightlife is undoubtably one of the city's highlights. Whatever stereotypes you may have held about Japanese people being quiet and reserved will fall to pieces after dark. Tokyo is a 'work hard, play hard' kind of place and you'll find people out any night of the week.

There is truly something for everyone here, from sky-high lounges to grungy holes-in-the-wall. In the last few years, the craft-beer scene has exploded. Another trend is *tachinomi-ya* ('standing bars') – small, lively joints where patrons crowd around the bar.

Tokyo has a healthy club scene, centred mostly on Shibuya and Roppongi. Check out **Clubberia** (www.clubberia.com) and **iFlyer** (www.iflyer.tv) to find out what's going on when you're in town. Most of the big clubs have discount flyers that can be printed or downloaded from their websites. Be prepared to show photo ID at the door.

Ginza & Tsukiji
銀座 ● 築地

Ginza is where people dress to the nines to go out and splurge, though not every bar here charges a premium. Towards Shimbashi, there are many salaryman (male white-collar worker) joints, where workday warriors go to let off steam.

Aux Amis Des Vins — Wine Bar
(オザミデヴァン; Map p66; ☎ 3567-4120; 2-5-6 Ginza, Chūō-ku; ☺ 5.30pm-2am Mon-Fri, noon-midnight Sat; ☒ Yūrakuchō line to Ginza-itchōme, exits 5 & 8) Even when it rains, the plastic tarp comes down over the small terrace and good wine is drunk alleyside. The enclosed upstairs seating area is warm and informal, and you can order snacks or full *prix-fixe* dinners. A solid selection of wine, mostly French, comes by the glass (from ¥800) or by the bottle.

Roppongi & Around
六本木

Exiting the subway station at Roppongi Crossing at night can feel like entering the world of *Bladerunner* or *Star Wars,* where throngs of the galaxy's most unscrupulous citizens gather to engage in a host of unsavoury activities under the sizzling neon lights. Club music thumps, and the streets are filled with catcalls and other shady offers.

Here, *gaijin* (foreigners) and locals mix it up and boozily schmooze until the first trains at dawn. There are loads of shot bars and cheap dives for getting wasted, but also plenty of spots that offer style as well as stiff drinks.

SuperDeluxe — Lounge
(スーパー・デラックス; Map p72; ☎ 5412-0515; www.super-deluxe.com; Basement fl, 3-1-25 Nishi-Azabu, Minato-ku; admission varies; ☒ Hibiya line to Roppongi, exit 1B) This basement bunker morphs from lounge to gallery to club to performance space from night to night; check the website for event details. Whatever is happening you're guaranteed to run into an interesting mix of creative types from Tokyo and beyond. It's in an otherwise unremarkable building; look for the tiny sign and the staircase leading down.

Pink Cow — Bar
(ピンクカウ; Map p72; www.thepinkcow. com; Basement fl, Roi Bldg, 5-5-1 Roppongi, Minato-ku; ☺ 5pm-late Tue-Sun; ☒ Hibiya line to Roppongi, exit 3) The Pink Cow is a funky, friendly place to hang out, with excellent California-style food and yummy, reasonably priced wines by the glass. It's a hub for the artsy expat community – with events such as indie film screenings, writers' salons and burlesque nights – and a good bet if you're in the mood to mix with a creative crowd.

Muse — Club
(ミューズ; Map p72; ☎ 5467-1188; www.muse-web.com; B1 fl, 4-1-1 Nishi-Azabu, Minato-ku; admission women/men incl 2 drinks free/¥3000; ☺ 9pm-late Mon-Fri, 10pm-late Sat & Sun; ☒ Hibiya line to Roppongi, exit 3) Muse is a catacomb-like underground space that looks like something out of a Tim Burton film. There's something for everyone here: two dance floors playing house and hip hop, plenty of sofas and a billiard table. Muse draws a mix of locals and foreigners and really picks up after midnight. The cover charge is usually less on weekday nights; ID required.

Eleven — Club
(イレブン; Map p72; ☎ 5775-6206; www.go-to-eleven.com; Basement fl, 1-10-11 Nishi-Azabu, Minato-ku; admission ¥3000-4000; ☺ from 10pm Wed-Sat; ☒ Hibiya line to Roppongi, exit 2) The reincarnation of notorious party box 'Yellow', Eleven is as hot, and as stylish, as ever. Dive down to the lower basement and dance the night away to electro, dub and house music.

LONELY PLANET / GETTY IMAGES ©

Ebisu & Meguro
恵比寿・目黒

Ebisu is known for its lively *tachinomi-ya* (standing bars), Naka-Meguro for its riverside cafes and hard-to-find lounges.

Buri   Bar

(ぶり; Map p76; ☎ 3496-7744; www.buri-group.com; 1-14-1 Ebisu-nishi, Shibuya-ku; ◷ 5pm-3am; 🚇 JR Yamanote line to Ebisu, west exit) The name means 'super' in Hiroshima dialect and the lively crowd that packs in on weekends certainly seems to agree. Generous quantities of sake (more than 50 varieties; ¥750) are served semifrozen – like slushies! – in colourful jars. Although there are some stools around the horseshoe-shaped counter, Buri is a *tachinomi-ya* at heart.

Kinfolk Lounge   Lounge

(キンフォーク; Map p76; ☎ 5499-8683; http://www.kinfolklife.com/tokyo/; 2nd fl, 1-11-1 Kami-Meguro, Meguro-ku; ◷ 6pm-midnight; 🚇 Hibiya line to Naka-Meguro) Sip mojitos under wooden rafters in this dim, moody lounge run by custom bicycle-makers Kinfolk. From Naka-Meguro Station, cross Yamate-dōri and the river, then take the first left. It's a few minutes' walk on the left, up a rickety metal staircase above a cafe.

Shibuya & Around   渋谷

Shibuya is Tokyo's most musically inclined neighbourhood: some of the best clubs are here, along with live-music houses and bars where the soundtrack *is* the atmosphere. There are lots of bars here in general; most – but not all – are cheap joints catering to 20-somethings. **Nonbei-yokochō** (のんべえ横丁), northeast of Shibuya Station near the JR tracks, is a gaggle of cramped bars each seating but a handful of people.

Womb   Club

(ウーム; Map p84; ☎ 5459-0039; www.womb.co.jp; 2-16 Maruyama-chō, Shibuya-ku; admission varies; ◷ 11pm-late; 🚇 JR Yamanote line to Shibuya, Hachikō exit) Womb's state-of-the art sound system, mirror ball and laser lighting go perfectly with the house and techno music played here. Though it draws more diehard music fans than scene chasers, Womb's four floors still get jammed at weekends. Photo ID is required.

Beat Cafe
Bar

(Map p84; www.facebook.com/beatcafe; 3rd fl, 33-13 Udagawa-chō, Shibuya-ku; ⏰7pm-5am; 🚉JR Yamanote line to Shibuya, Hachikō exit) It's all about the music at this shabby bar on Center Gai. Join an eclectic mix of local and international regulars who swig beers (¥650) and chat beats under the watchful eyes of taxidermic elk. Sister club Echo downstairs has a small dance floor and a groovy yard-sale decor.

Sound Museum Vision
Club

(Map p84; ☎5728-2824; www.vision-tokyo. com; Basement fl, 2-10-7 Dōgenzaka, Shibuya-ku; admission ¥3000-4000; ⏰Events from 10pm; 🚉JR Yamanote line to Shibuya, Hachikō exit) One of Tokyo's newer clubs, Sound Museum Vision is a cavernous space with four dance floors. With a sleek modern interior and not so much of a cruisy vibe, Vision is downright classy for this side of Shibuya. A solid line-up of international DJs plays mostly house and techno. Bring ID.

Ruby Room
Club

(ルビールーム; Map p84; ☎3780-3022; www. rubyroomtokyo.com; 2nd fl, 2-25-17 Dōgenzaka, Shibuya-ku; admission incl 1 drink ¥1500; ⏰8pm-late; 🚉JR Yamanote line to Shibuya, Hachikō exit) This tiny, sparkly gem of a club hosts both DJ and live-music events. It's an appealing spot for older kids hanging out in Shibuya. Tuesday is open mic night (free entry with two-drink minimum); if you're musically inclined, you're welcome to join the stage.

Harajuku 原宿

Harajuku has a handful of hidden gems, but feels pretty quiet after the shops close. Scoot down to Aoyama to hang out with the fashion crowd.

Two Rooms
Bar

(トゥールームス; Map p82; ☎3498-0002; www.tworooms.jp; 5th fl, AO Bldg, 3-11-7 Kita-Aoyama, Minato-ku; ⏰11.30am-2am Mon-Sat, to 10pm Sun; 🚉Ginza line to Omote-sandō, exit B2) With its sleek contemporary design, this restaurant and bar, popular with expats, could be anywhere – save for the sweeping view towards the Shinjuku skyline from the terrace. Expect a crowd dressed like they don't care that wine by the glass starts at ¥1400. You can eat here too, but the real scene is at night by the bar.

Izakaya in Asakusa

Harajuku Taproom   Pub

(原宿タップルーム; Map p82; http://baird-beer.com/en/taproom; 2nd fl, 1-20-13 Jingūmae, Shibuya-ku; ⏰5pm-midnight Mon-Fri, noon-midnight Sat & Sun; 🚉JR Yamanote line to Harajuku, Takeshita exit) Come here to sample more than a dozen different beers on tap from respected local craft brewer Baird's Brewery. Heading down Takeshita-dōri, take a left after Cafe Solare and the bar will be at the end of the lane on the right.

Shinjuku & West Tokyo
新宿

The main drag on the east side of Shinjuku Station, Yasukuni-dōri, is wall-to-wall *izakaya*. The most ambient watering holes can be found further down in Golden Gai, a cluster of eccentric, closet-sized bars in what was originally a post-WWII black market. It's known to be a haunt for writers and artists. Though most establishments are likely to give tourists a cool reception, there are a few friendly places. Cover charges (of ¥500 and up) are standard at bars in Golden Gai.

Kabukichō is Tokyo's most notorious red-light district, full of cabarets, hostess (and host!) clubs, love hotels and fetish bars. If you're curious to take a peek, it's generally safe to stroll through, though it's wise not to go alone. Note that if you follow a tout to a bar or club here you will likely end up with a hefty bill.

Zoetrope   Bar

(ゾートロープ; Map p88; http://homepage2.nifty.com/zoetrope; 3rd fl, 7-10-14 Nishi-Shinjuku, Shinjuku-ku; ⏰7pm-4am Mon-Sat; 🚉JR Yamanote line to Shinjuku, west exit) Behind the small counter are more than 300 varieties of Japanese whisky – more than you'll find anywhere else in the world. If you tell the bar staff what you like, they'll help you narrow down some choices from the menu. Meanwhile silent films are screened on the wall.

Araku   Bar

(亜楽; Map p88; www.facebook.com/bar.araku; 2nd fl, G2-dōri, 1-1-9 Kabukichō, Shinjuku-ku;

cover charge ¥500; ⏰8pm-5am Mon-Sat; 🚉JR Yamanote line to Shinjuku, east exit) If you're looking for a welcoming place to hole up in Golden Gai, this is it. There's a sofa, Australian wines by the glass and a groovy atmosphere. Look for the steps carpeted with red shag.

New York Bar   Bar

(ニューヨークバー; Map p88; ☎5323-3458; http://tokyo.park.hyatt.com; 52nd fl, Park Hyatt, 3-7-1-2 Nishi-Shinjuku, Shinjuku-ku; ⏰5pm-midnight Sun-Wed, to 1am Thu-Sat; 🚉Ōedo line to Tochōmae, exit A4) You may not be lodging at the Park Hyatt, but you can still ascend to the 52nd floor to swoon over the sweeping nightscape. Live music plays nightly at this bar famed for its appearance in the movie *Lost in Translation*. There's a cover charge of ¥2200 after 8pm (7pm Sunday) and a dress code (no shorts or sandals).

Champion   Bar

(チャンピオン; Map p88; G2-dōri, 1-1-10 Kabukichō, Shinjuku-ku; ⏰6pm-5am; 🚉JR Yamanote line to Shinjuku, east exit) At the entrance to Golden Gai, Champion isn't exactly representative of the district, but it's fun just the same. There's no cover charge, drinks are just ¥500 a pop and the karaoke is loud – you can't miss it.

⭐ Entertainment
CINEMAS
Uplink   Cinema

(アップリンク; Map p84; www.uplink.co.jp; 2nd fl, 37-18 Udagawa-chō, Shibuya-ku; 🚉JR Yamanote line to Shibuya, Hachikō exit) Day and night Uplink screens quirky independent films (domestic and foreign) in a tiny art-house cinema with comfy armchairs.

Toho Cinemas
Roppongi Hills   Cinema

(TOHOシネマズ六本木ヒルズ; Map p72; https://hlo.tohotheater.jp/net/schedule/009/TNPI2000J01.do; 6-10-2 Roppongi, Minato-ku; adult ¥1800-3000, child ¥1000, 1st day of month & women on Wed ¥1000; ⏰10am-midnight Sun-Wed, to 5am Thu-Sat; 🚉Hibiya line to Roppongi, exit 1C) Toho's nine-screen multiplex has luxurious reclining seats and internet

Below: A kabuki actor; **Right:** Baseball fans at Tokyo Dome (p112)

booking up to two days in advance for re-served seats. Look for all-night screenings on nights before holidays.

LIVE MUSIC

Tokyo's home-grown live-music scene has turned out some good acts, often found playing around Shibuya and Ebisu. If you wander a bit further, the tiny underground bars and clubs in Shimo-Kitazawa, Kōenji and Kichijōji are where the local talent cuts their teeth.

Check out **Tokyo Gig Guide** (www. tokyogigguide.com) for a directory of venues and recommended shows.

Unit
Live Music

(ユニット; Map p76; ☎5459-8630; www. unit-tokyo.com; 1-34-17 Ebisu-nishi, Shibuya-ku; admission ¥2500-5000; ☒Tōkyū Tōyoko line to Daikanyama) This subterranean club often has two shows: live music in the evening and a DJ-hosted event after hours. It's an excellent place to catch Japanese indie bands or overseas artists making their Japan debut. In stylish Daikanyama, Unit isn't as grungy as other Tokyo live-music houses, but the bookings are solid.

Club Quattro
Live Music

(クラブクアトロ; Map p84; ☎3477-8750; www.club-quattro.com; 32-13-4 Udagawa-chō, Shibuya-ku; admission ¥3000-4000; ☒JR Yamanote line to Shibuya, Hachikō exit) This venue feels like a concert hall, but it's actually more along the lines of a slick club. Though there's no explicit musical focus, emphasis is on rock and roll and world music, and the quality is generally high. Expect a more varied, artsy crowd than the club's location – near Sentā-gai in Shibuya – might lead you to expect.

Alfie
Jazz

(アルフィー; Map p72; ☎3479-2037; http:// homepage1.nifty.com/live/alfie; 5th fl, 6-2-35 Roppongi, Minato-ku; admission ¥3000-4000; ⏰shows 8pm Mon-Sat, 7pm Sun; ☒Hibiya line

to Roppongi, exit 1) This is Roppongi's classi-
est jazz venue, where soft amber lighting
melts over the lounge singers as patrons
nurse their cocktails.

THEATRE & DANCE

Intensely visual kabuki developed in Edo
during the 18th and 19th centuries and
an afternoon at the theatre has been a
favourite local pastime ever since.

A full kabuki performance lasts
several hours and comprises several
acts (usually from different plays), with
long intervals in between. Get tickets for
Tokyo performances via www.kabuki-
bito.jp/eng.

You can also catch other forms of
traditional theatre, such as nō (stylised
dance-drama) and bunraku (classic
puppet theatre), throughout the year,
though performances are irregular.

Kabuki-za   Traditional Theatre
(歌舞伎座; Map p66; 3545-6800; www.
kabuki-bito.jp/eng; 4-12-15 Ginza, Chūō-ku;
tickets ¥4000-20,000, single-act tickets ¥800-
2000; Hibiya line to Higashi-Ginza, exit 3)
Tokyo's premier kabuki theatre reopened
after a lengthy renovation in spring
2013. While many are still mourning the
historic old building (there wasn't always
a skyscraper sticking out the back),
there's no doubt that this is the place to
catch a show. Rent a headset for blow-
by-blow explanations in English (¥700,
plus ¥1000 deposit), and pick up a bentō
(boxed meal) for the long intermission.

It may be possible to buy same-day,
single act 'makumi' tickets (availability-
pending), though only for seats in the
upper tiers.

**National
Nō Theatre**   Traditional Theatre
(国立能楽堂; Map p62; Kokuritsu Nō-gakudō;
3423-1331; www.ntj.jac.go.jp/english; 4-18-1
Sendagaya, Shibuya-ku; tickets from ¥2600;
JR Sōbu line to Sendagaya) This theatre
stages the traditional music, poetry and
dances that nō is famous for, as well as the
interludes of kyōgen (short, lively comic
farces) that serve as comic relief. Each

111

Getting Tickets

Found a show or event that strikes your fancy? **Ticket Pia** (チケット ぴあ; ☎0570-02-9111; http://t.pia.jp/; ◷10am-8pm) handles just about everything, including concerts and theatre performances major and minor. Tickets (when not sold out) can be purchased up to three days before the show. There are convenient branches on the 4th floor of Shibuya Hikarie (p71) and inside the **Asakusa Tourist Information Center** (浅草文化観光 センター; Map p92; http://taitonavi.jp; 2-18-9 Kaminarimon, Taitō-ku; ◷9am-8pm; @ ⊚; ⏻Ginza line to Asakusa, exit 2).

seat has a small screen that can display an English translation of the dialogue. It's a five-minute walk west of the station; tickets go fast.

SPORT

Sumō is fascinating, highly ritualised and steeped in Shintō tradition. It's also the only traditional Japanese sport that still has enough clout to draw big crowds and dominate prime-time TV.

Tournaments take place in Tokyo at Ryōgoku Kokugikan in January, May and September. Other times of year you can drop in on an early-morning practice session at one of the stables, like **Arashio Stable** (荒汐部屋; Map p62; Arashio-beya; ☎3666-7646; www.arashio.net; 2-47-2 Hama-chō, Nihombashi, Chūō-ku; ◷7.30-10am; ⏻Toei Shinjuku line to Hamachō, exit A2) FREE.

Baseball is more of an obsession than a sport in Japan, and it's worth getting tickets to a game if only to see the fans go wild at each play and to witness the perfectly choreographed 7th-inning stretch. Within Tokyo, the Yomiuri Giants and Yakult Swallows are cross-town rivals.

Baseball season runs from April through October. Check the schedules on the stadium websites.

Ryōgoku Kokugikan　　　Sumō
(両国国技館; Ryōgoku Sumō Stadium; Map p62; ☎3623-5111; www.sumo.or.jp/eng/ticket/index. html; 1-3-28 Yokoami, Sumida-ku; ◷tournaments Jan, May & Sep; ⏻JR Sōbu line to Ryōgoku, west exit) If you're in town when a tournament is on, don't miss the chance to catch a match at Japan's largest sumō stadium. Doors open at 8am, but the action doesn't really heat up until the senior wrestlers hit the ring around 2pm. You can rent a radio (¥100 fee, plus ¥2000 deposit) to listen to commentary in English.

Ringside tickets cost ¥14,300, boxes cost between ¥9200 and ¥11,300 per person, and arena tickets will set you back between ¥2100 and ¥8200. Tickets can be purchased online in English (for a ¥1000 handling fee) up to a month in advance. You can usually turn up on the day and get an arena ticket (but you'll have to arrive very early, say 6am, to snag seats during the last days of a tournament).

Tokyo Dome　　　Baseball
(東京ドーム; Map p62; ☎5800-9999; www. tokyo-dome.co.jp/e/dome; 1-3-61 Kōraku, Bunkyō-ku; ⏻JR Chūō line to Suidōbashi, west exit) The 'Big Egg' is home to Japan's favourite baseball team, the Yomiuri Giants. Tickets often sell out in advance; get them online at www.e-tix.jp/ticket_giants/en/ticket_ pc_en.php.

🔒 Shopping

Tokyo is the trendsetter for the rest of Japan, and its residents shop – economy be damned – with an infectious enthusiasm. Merchandise is generally of excellent quality, and not as wildly expensive as you might think.

Marunouchi (Tokyo Station area) 丸の内 (東京駅)

Takashimaya　　　Department Store
(高島屋; Map p66; 2-4-1 Nihombashi, Chūō-ku; ◷10am-8pm; ⏻Ginza line to Nihombashi, Takashimaya exit) Takashimaya's branch on New York's Fifth Ave is renowned for its

cutting-edge Japanese-inspired interior, but the design of the Tokyo flagship store (1933) tips its pillbox hat to New York's Gilded Age. Uniformed female elevator operators still announce each floor in high-pitched sing-song voices.

Muji
Clothing, Homewares

(無印良品; Map p66; www.mujiyurakucho.com; 3-8-3 Marunouchi, Chiyoda-ku; ⏰10am-9pm; 🚃JR Yamanote line to Yūrakuchō, Kyōbashi exit) Muji (short for Mujirushi) means 'no brand', though by now the label's simple, functional aesthetic is just as iconic as any brand. This Yūrakuchō outpost is one of the largest in Tokyo and carries clothes for men and women, housewares and Muji's unbeatable line of travel accessories. There's another sizeable branch in **Tokyo Midtown** (無印良品; Map p72; Basement fl, Tokyo Midtown, 9-7 Akasaka, Minato-ku; ⏰11am-9pm; 🚃Ōedo line to Roppongi, exit 8).

Ōedo Antique Market
Antiques

(大江戸骨董市; Map p66; 🕿6407-6011; www.antique-market.jp; 3-5-1 Marunouchi, Chiyoda-ku; ⏰9am-4pm 1st & 3rd Sun of month; 🚃JR Yamanote line to Yūrakuchō, central exit) You can find all sorts of treasures, from vintage kimono and delicate sake cups to Buddhist

statuary at Japan's largest outdoor antique market. Held in the courtyard at the Tokyo International Forum (p64), the market has around 250 vendors and is the largest in the country.

Ginza
銀座

Ginza is Tokyo's original shopping neighbourhood, and although other areas have risen in power, it is still the benchmark to which the other boutique-filled districts are compared. Don't miss the grandiose department stores, vestiges of the 1950s and '60s when ceremony and much ado were wrapped up in the shopping experience.

Mitsukoshi
Department Store

(三越; Map p66; www.mitsukoshi.co.jp; 4-6-16 Ginza, Chūō-ku; ⏰10am-8pm; 🚃Ginza line to Ginza, exits A7 & A11) One of Ginza's grande dames, Mitsukoshi is the quintessential Tokyo department store, and it gleams after a recent renovation. The housewares department on the 8th floor has beautiful made-in-Japan crockery and chopsticks and the basement food court is peerless. The tax-refund counter is on the 2nd-floor mezzanine.

Ginza shopping district

Uniqlo
Clothing

(ユニクロ; Map p66; www.uniqlo.com; 5-7-7 Ginza, Chūō-ku; 🕐11am-9pm; 🚇Ginza line to Ginza, exit A2) Uniqlo made its name with inexpensive, well-made basics that are tweaked with style – designers such as Jil Sander and Takahashi Jun have participated in recent capsule collections. This enormous, 12-storey outpost offers everything in the Uniqlo canon, from socks to coats. Check out the T-shirts on the 11th floor and the limited-edition items on the 12th floor.

There are Uniqlo all over the city, including another fairly big – though not nearly 12-storey – branch in **Shibuya** (Map p84; 2-29-5 Dōgenzaka, Shibuya-ku; 🕐11am-9pm Mon-Fri, from 10am Sat & Sun; 🚇JR Yamanote line to Shibuya, Hachikō exit).

Itōya
Arts & Crafts

(伊東屋; Map p66; 2-7-15 Ginza, Chūō-ku; 🕐10.30am-8pm Mon-Sat, to 7pm Sun; 🚇Ginza line to Ginza, exit A13) Nine floors of stationery-shop love await visitors to this century-old purveyor of fountain pens and paper-bound luxuries. The 6th floor offers more traditional Japanese wares including *washi* (fine Japanese handmade paper) and *furoshiki* (wrapping cloths).

Takumi
Craft

(たくみ; Map p66; 📞3571-2017; www.ginza-takumi.co.jp; 8-4-2 Ginza, Chūō-ku; 🕐11am-7pm Mon-Sat; 🚇Ginza line to Shimbashi, exit 5) Takumi has been around for more than 60 years and has acquired an elegant selection of toys, textiles, ceramics and other traditional folk crafts from around Japan.

Hakuhinkan
Children

(博品館; Map p66; www.hakuhinkan.co.jp; 8-8-11 Ginza, Chūō-ku; 🕐11am-8pm; 🚇JR Yamanote line to Shimbashi, Ginza exit) This toy store is crammed with plush toys, character goods and novelty items. There's another branch at Narita Airport (Terminal 1) that opens at 7.30am for last-chance purchases.

Roppongi 六本木

A worthwhile place to check out is the 3rd floor of Tokyo Midtown (p65), which has a cluster of homewares shops.

Japan Sword
Antiques

(日本刀剣; Map p72; 📞3434-4324; www.japansword.co.jp; 3-8-1 Toranomon, Minato-ku; 🕐9.30am-6pm Mon-Fri, to 5pm Sat; 🚇Ginza line to Toranomon, exit 2) Japan Sword sells the genuine article: antique swords and samurai helmets dating from the Edo period and modern creations from 'living treasure' artisans. The 2nd-floor gallery is one of the few places you can see real swords that aren't behind glass. The staff speak English and can arrange the necessary paperwork for export. Convincing replicas are sold here too.

Japan Traditional Crafts
Craft

(全国伝統的工芸品センター; http://kougeihin.jp/en/top; 8-1-22 Akasaka, Minato-ku; 🕐11am-7pm Mon-Sat; 🚇Ginza line to Aoyama-itchōme, exit 4) Supported by the Japanese Ministry of Economy, Trade and Industry, this shop showcases crafts from around Japan, ranging from lacquerwork boxes to earthy pottery. The emphasis is on high-end goods, but you can find beautiful things in all price ranges here.

Ebisu & Meguro 恵比寿・目黒

Daikanyama and Naka-Meguro are two good places to hunt for one-of-a-kind fashion finds. In Daikanyama, look for boutiques wedged in the space between main drags Kyū-Yamate-dōri and Hachiman-dōri. In Naka-Meguro check the riverside and the narrow streets behind it.

Okura
Fashion, Accessories

(オクラ; 20-11 Sarugaku-chō, Shibuya-ku; 🕐11.30am-8pm Mon- Fri, 11am-8.30pm Sat & Sun; 🚇Tōkyū Tōyoko line to Daikanyama) Almost everything in this enchanting shop is dyed a deep indigo blue – from sweatshirts to scarves. There are some beautiful, original items, though unfortunately most aren't cheap. The shop itself looks like a rural house, with worn wooden floorboards and whitewashed walls. Note: there's no sign out the front, but look for the traditional building.

Shibuya & Around 渋谷

Shibuya is the stomping ground of fashion-conscious *joshikōsei* (high school girls), though you'll find more grown-up clothes in the new Shibuya Hikarie (p71) building. It's also an excellent place to hunt for *zakka* (miscellaneous goods) – cute stationery, lifestyle gadgets and bizarre beauty products all fall into this category.

Tōkyū Hands — Souvenirs

(東急ハンズ; Map p84; http://shibuya.tokyu-hands.co.jp; 12-18 Udagawa-chō, Shibuya-ku; ⏰10am-8.30pm; 🚉JR Yamanote line to Shibuya, Hachikō exit) This DIY and *zakka* (miscellaneous goods) store has eight fascinating floors of everything you didn't know you needed. It's perfect for souvenir hunting – surely someone you know needs reflexology slippers, right?

There's another branch in **Shinjuku** (新宿ハンズ; Map p88; Takashimaya Times Sq, 5-24-2 Sendagaya, Shibuya-ku; ⏰10am-8.30pm; 🚉JR Yamanote line to Shinjuku, new south exit) and an upscale version in Ginza, **Ginza Hands** (銀座ハンズ; Map p66; 📞3538-0109; http://ginza.tokyu-hands.co.jp/; 5th-9th fl, Marronnier Gate, 2-2-14 Ginza, Chūō-ku; ⏰11am-9pm; 🚉JR Yamanote line to Yūrakuchō, Kyōbashi exit).

Harajuku 原宿

Omote-sandō is lined with upscale boutiques. Narrow, meandering Cat St, which intersects it, offers a more chilled-out shopping experience. The web of alleys surrounding the two, known as Ura-Hara (literally 'behind Harajuku'), is where you'll find the small boutiques and vintage shops that keep the neighbourhood's indie spirit alive.

Takeshita-dōri — Variety

(竹下通り; 🚉JR Yamanote line to Harajuku, Takeshita exit) This teaming alley is where aspiring goths, Lolitas and punks come to shop, and you'll spot some pretty wild stuff. Even if you're not in the market for a dress inspired by the Victorian era, there is still plenty to pull out your wallet for here, like funky tights and mobile-phone charms.

KiddyLand — Children

(キデイランド; Map p82; www.kiddyland.co.jp/en/index.html; 6-1-9 Jingūmae, Shibuya-ku; ⏰10am-9pm; 🚉JR Yamanote line to Harajuku, Omote-sandō exit) This multistorey toy emporium is packed to the rafters with character goods, from Hello Kitty to Studio Ghibli. It's not just for kids either; you'll spot plenty of teens and even adults indulging their love of *kawaii* (cute).

Oriental Bazaar — Souvenirs

(オリエンタルバザー; Map p82; www.orientalbazaar.co.jp; 5-9-13 Jingūmae, Shibuya-ku; ⏰10am-6pm Mon-Wed & Fri, to 7pm Sat & Sun; 🚉JR Yamanote line to Harajuku, Omote-sandō

Takeshita-dōri in Harajuku
FRANK DEIM / GETTY IMAGES ©

WILL ROBB / GETTY IMAGES ©

exit) Stocking a wide selection of souvenirs at very reasonable prices, Oriental Bazaar is an easy one-stop destination. Items to be found here include fans, pottery, *yukata* and T-shirts, some made in Japan, some not (check the labels).

Chicago Thrift Store   Vintage
(シカゴ; Map p82; 6-31-21 Jingūmae, Shibuya-ku; ⊙10am-8pm; ®JR Yamanote line to Harajuku, Omote-sandō exit) Stuffed to the rafters with funky hats, ties and coats, Chicago is a treasure trove of vintage clothing. Don't miss the collection of used kimono and *yukata* in the back corner.

Shinjuku & West Tokyo
新宿

Shinjuku is a major shopping hub. You'll find branches of most major fashion retailers in the department stores attached to the train station. Nearby are several electronics outfitters, such as **Yodobashi Camera** (ヨドバシカメラ; Map p88; 1-11-1 Nishi-Shinjuku, Shinjuku-ku; ⊙9.30am-10pm; ®JR Yamanote line to Shinjuku, west exit).

Don Quijote   Variety
(ドン・キホーテ; Map p88; ☎5291-9211; www.donki.com; 1-16-5 Kabukichō, Shinjuku-ku; ⊙24hr; ®JR Yamanote line to Shinjuku, east exit) In Kabukichō, this fluorescent-lit bargain castle is filled to the brink with weird loot. Chaotic piles of knock-off electronics and designer goods sit alongside sex toys, fetish costumes and packaged foods.

Look for other branches in **Roppongi** (Map p72; 3-14-10 Roppongi, Minato-ku; ⊙24hr; ®Hibiya line to Roppongi, exit 3) and **Shibuya** (Map p84; 2-25-8 Dōgenzaka, Shibuya-ku; ⊙10am-4.30am; ®JR Yamanote line to Shibuya, Hachikō exit).

Disk Union   Music
(ディスクユニオン; Map p88; 3-31-4 Shinjuku, Shinjuku-ku; ⊙11am-9pm; ®JR Yamanote line to Shinjuku, east exit) Scruffy Disk Union is known by local audiophiles as Tokyo's best used-CD and vinyl store. Eight storeys carry a variety of musical styles; if you still can't find what you're looking for, there are several other branches in Shinjuku that stock more obscure genres (pick up a map here).

Isetan
Department Store

(伊勢丹; Map p88; www.isetan.co.jp; 3-14-1 Shinjuku, Shinjuku-ku; ⏱10am-8pm; 🚇Marunouchi line to Shinjuku-sanchōme, exits B3, B4 & B5) Most department stores play to conservative tastes, but this one is an exception. The recently redone 3rd floor has some edgy womenswear, including collections from famous and not-yet-famous Japanese designers. Men get a whole building of their own (connected by a passageway). The basement food hall here is tops too.

Kinokuniya
Books

(紀伊國屋書店; Map p88; www.kinokuniya. co.jp; Takashimaya Times Sq, 5-24-2 Sendagaya, Shibuya-ku; ⏱10am-8pm; 🚇JR Yamanote line to Shinjuku, south exit) A broad selection of foreign-language books and magazines, including English-teaching texts.

Akihabara & Around
秋葉原

Akihabara's Electric Town (p78) is crowded with stores hawking gadgets and *otaku* paraphenalia (anime, manga, figures etc). Many of the big electronics retailers have tax-exemption counters, so make sure to have your passport on you. Nearby Jimbōchō (p78) is famous for its secondhand bookshops.

2k540 Aki-Oka Artisan
Craft

(アキオカアルチザン; Map p62; www.jrtk. jp/2k540; 5-9 Ueno, Taitō-ku; ⏱hours vary; 🚇Ginza line to Suehirochō, exit 2) *Monozukuri* (the art of making things) is the focus of the few dozen shops gathered in this minimalist arcade under the JR tracks. This is the place to find fans in cool geometric patterns and mobile-phone cases carved from wood.

Yodobashi Akiba
Electronics

(ヨドバシカメラ Akiba; Map p62; www. yodobashi-akiba.com; 1-1 Kanda Hanaoka-chō, Chiyoda-ku; ⏱9.30am-10pm; 🚇JR Yamanote line to Akihabara, Shōwa-tōriguchi exit) Inside this complex are six monster floors of electronics, cameras, toys and appliances – if you can plug it in, it's probably here. For all the modern convenience that it hawks, Yodobashi Camera feels like an old-time bazaar with all the sights and sounds clamouring for your attention.

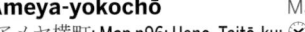
Ueno
上野

Ameya-yokochō
Market

(アメヤ横町; Map p96; Ueno, Taitō-ku; ⏱10am-7pm; 🚇JR Yamanote line to Ueno, Ueno-kōen exit) The gravelly *irasshai* ('welcome') of the fishmongers and clothing vendors at this old-fashioned open-air market couldn't be further from Ginza or Shibuya. Ameya Yokochō got its start as a black market after WWII when American goods were sold here, and you can still find the blue jeans and Hawaiian shirts that were in vogue at the time.

ℹ Information

Money

Getting cash is easier in Tokyo than elsewhere in Japan, and even though most places take credit cards, it's still a good idea to have some cash as back-up.

7-Eleven (セブン・イレブン; www.sevenbank. co.jp/english) Have 24-hour cash dispensers that routinely work with overseas ATM cards; you'll find one in most neighbourhoods.

Citibank (シティバンク; www.citibank.co.jp/ en) The only bank with ATMs that accept cards from every country; its ATMs are 24-hour, though locations are few and far between.

Post offices (ゆうちょ銀行; www.jp-bank. japanpost.jp/en/ias/en_ias_index.html) Have English-language ATMs, though they often close early in the evenings and on weekends.

Tourist Information

There are tourist information centres at both terminals at Narita Airport with English-speaking staff who can help you get oriented.

JNTO Tourist Information Center (TIC; Map p66; ☎3201-3331; www.jnto.go.jp; 1st fl, Shin-Tokyo Bldg, 3-3-1 Marunouchi, Chiyoda-ku; ⏱9am-5pm; 🚇JR Yamanote line to Yūrakuchō, Tokyo International Forum exit) This main TIC operated by the Japan National Tourism Organisation (JNTO) has the most comprehensive information on travel in Tokyo and Japan, and knowledgable, English-speaking staff.

Tokyo Tourist Information Center (東京観光情報センター; Map p88; ☎5321-3077;

117

Suica Cards & Discount Packages

Transferring between multiple lines and calculating fares becomes a no-brainer with this prepaid train pass kitted out with an electromagnetic chip. Simply swipe the card over the reader on the ticket gates. Suica is good on all subway, rail and bus lines in greater Tokyo and can be charged at most electronic ticket machines. The cards require a ¥500 deposit, refundable when you return it to a JR window.

Pick up a Suica charged with ¥2000 and get a deal on airport transport with the Suica & N'EX (from Narita) or Suica & Monorail (from Haneda) packages, available from JR East Travel Service Centers at either airport. A round-trip package from Narita to Tokyo Station costs ¥5880 (saving you ¥2000).

www.gotokyo.org/en/index.html; 1st fl, Tokyo Metropolitan Government Bldg 1, 2-8-1 Nishi-Shinjuku, Shinjuku-ku; ⏰9.30am-6.30pm; 🚇Ōedo line to Tochōmae, exit A4) Run by the municipal government, this TIC has local info, but can't make bookings.

There's also a branch at Keisei Ueno Station (☎3836-3471; ⏰9.30am-6.30pm) and at the international terminal in Haneda Airport.

ℹ Getting There & Away

Air

Tokyo has two major airports: Narita Airport (成田空港; ☎0476-34-8000; www.narita-airport.jp/en; Narita-shi, Chiba-ken) and Haneda Airport (羽田空港; ☎5757-8111, international terminal 6428-0888; www.tokyo-airport-bldg.co.jp/en; Ōta-ku). Most international flights operate through the former while domestic travel is usually through the latter. However, Haneda opened an international wing in October 2010. In general, flights to Narita are cheaper, but it is considerably further from the city centre than Haneda.

Immigration and customs procedures are usually straightforward, but they can be time-consuming. Note that Japanese customs officials can be very scrupulous; backpackers arriving from anywhere even remotely exotic (the Philippines, Thailand etc) can expect some questions and perhaps a thorough search.

It is important to note that there are two distinct terminals at Narita, separated by a five-minute train ride. Be sure to check which terminal your flight departs from. Airport officials recommend leaving at least four hours before your flight.

ℹ Getting Around

To/From Narita Airport

Narita Airport is 66km from central Tokyo. With the exception of very early morning flights, public transportation can usually meet all arrival and departure times.

Depending on where you're headed, it's generally cheaper and faster to travel into Tokyo by train than by limousine bus. However, rail users will probably need to change trains somewhere, and this can be frustrating on a jetlagged first visit.

Bus services provide a hassle-free direct route to many major hotels, and you don't have to be a hotel guest to use them; a short taxi ride (and there are always taxis waiting in front of big hotels) can take you the rest of the way.

We don't recommend taking a taxi from Narita – it'll set you back around ¥30,000. Figure one to two hours into your itinerary to get to/from Narita.

Bus

Heiwa Kōtsū (平和交通; http://heiwakotsu.com/na_top_english.htm#3) Discount buses run between Ginza, Tokyo Station and Narita Airport (¥1000, one to 1¼ hours); however, you'll have to reserve online (in Japanese) or take your chances on there being a spare seat.

Limousine Bus (リムジンバス; www.limousinebus.co.jp/en) Convenient, hourly shuttle buses connect Narita to major hotels and train stations, such as Shinjuku (¥3000, 1½ hours to two hours). Buses also run between Narita and Haneda airport (¥3000, one to 1½ hours).

Train

The local JR 'Airport Narita' train costs ¥1280 and takes 1½ hours to or from Tokyo Station.

Keisei Skyliner (京成スカイライナー; www.keisei.co.jp) Zips between the airport and Ueno Station (¥2400, 45 minutes), also stopping at Nippori Station. The economical Keisei Limited Express (¥1000, 1½ hours) is its main-line (read: turtle speed) counterpart. If you're transferring to/from the JR Yamanote line, access the train from Nippori Station; subway passengers should use Ueno Station.

Narita Express (**N'EX**; 成田エクスプレス; www.jreast.co.jp/e/nex/index.html) Runs approximately every half-hour, linking the airport to Tokyo Station (¥2940, 53 minutes) before branching off to either Shinjuku, Shibuya or Shinagawa Stations (all ¥3110, 1½ hours). Seats are reserved, but tickets can be bought immediately before departure if they are available from the ticket counters in either airport terminal. Japan Rail Pass holders can ride for free.

To/From Haneda Airport

From downtown Tokyo, it takes far less time to reach Haneda Airport than Narita. Taxis to the city centre cost around ¥6000; this will be your only option if your flight gets in before dawn.

Keikyu Line (京急線; www.haneda-tokyo-access.com/en/transport/) 'Airport Express' trains run between Shinagawa Station and Keikyu Haneda Station (¥400, 16 minutes).

Limousine Bus Coach buses connect Haneda with major centres such as Shibuya (¥1000), Shinjuku (¥1200) and Tokyo Station (¥900), as well as Narita Airport (¥3000, one to 1½ hours).

Travel time depends on traffic, but averages about 45 minutes to most points in the city centre. The last bus of the evening from Haneda leaves for Shibuya Station at 12.30am; buses start up again around 5am.

Tokyo Monorail (東京モノレール; www.tokyo-monorail.co.jp/english) A direct link to Haneda from Hamamatsuchō Station on the JR Yamanote line (¥470, 25 minutes).

Taxi

It rarely makes economic sense to take a taxi, unless you've got a group of four. The meter starts at a steep ¥710, which gives you 2km of travel. After that, the meter starts to clock an additional ¥100 for every 350m (and up to ¥100 for every two minutes you sit idly in traffic). Figure around ¥2500 for a ride from Roppongi to Ginza. It's best to have cash on you, as not all taxis take credit cards.

While it's possible to hail a cab from the street, your best bet is a taxi stand in front of a train station. Taxis with their indicator in red are free; green means taken.

Even in Tokyo, most cabbies don't speak English and have trouble finding all but the most well-known spots. Fortunately many have GPS systems, so have an address or a business card for your destination handy.

Taxi

Train

Tokyo's train network includes JR lines, a subway system, and private commuter lines. It's so thorough, especially in the city centre, that you rarely have to walk more than 10 minutes from a station to your destination. Stations have English signage.

Riverboat Cruise

Riverboats were once a primary means of transportation in Tokyo, and the Sumida-gawa was the main 'highway.' You can experience this centuries-old tradition (and happily combine sightseeing and transport) by hopping on one of the water buses run by **Tokyo Cruise** (水上バス; Suijō Bus; http://suijobus.co.jp).

Of the four routes, the Sumida-gawa line is the most popular, which runs from Asakusa to Hama-rikyū-teien (¥720, 35 minutes) and terminates at **Hinode Pier** (日の出桟橋; [R] Yurikamome line to Hinode, east exit) on Tokyo Bay.

The Asakusa–Odaiba Direct Line connects Asakusa with Odaiba Kaihin-kōen (¥1520, 50 minutes), also via the Sumida-gawa. If you're planning to take this route, try to catch one of the two spaceshiplike boats, *Himiko* and *Hotaluna,* designed by famous manga artist Leiji Matsumoto.

Train Tips

As far as public transport networks go, no city can touch Tokyo's awesome network of trains and subway lines. It's clean, quick, efficient and convenient, but it does have its quirks. Some tips:

○ Avoid rush hour (around 8am to 9.30am and 5pm to 8pm), when 'packed in like sardines' is an understatement.

○ Note your last train. The whole system shuts down from approximately midnight to 5am. The last train of the night can also be especially crowded (often with swaying drunks).

○ If you can't work out how much to pay, one easy trick is to buy a ticket at the cheapest fare (¥130 for JR; ¥160 for Tokyo Metro; ¥170 for Toei) and use one of the 'fare adjustment' machines, near the exit gates, to settle the difference at the end of your journey.

○ Tokyo's competing rail lines can make getting from point A to point B – in the cheapest, most economical way – a little confusing. Jorudan (www.jorudan.co.jp/english/norikae), also available as an iPhone app, is a lifesaver: it calculates routes by speed and fare.

○ Most train stations have multiple exits – make sure you get the right one (which can save you a lot of time and confusion above ground). There are usually maps in the station that show which exits are closest to major area landmarks.

Tickets are sold from vending machines near the automated ticket gates. Look for the newer touch-screen ones that have an English option. Fares are determined by how far you ride; there should be a fare chart above the ticket machines. You'll need a valid train ticket to exit the station.

Day Passes

Day passes can save you money, though only if you plan to cover a lot of ground in one day. You'll need to get one that covers the rail lines you'll be using, and purchase it from one of the station windows on those lines.

Tokyo Metro 1-Day Open Ticket Costs ¥710 (child ¥360) and covers Tokyo Metro subway lines.

Common 1-Day Ticket Costs ¥1000 (child ¥500) and covers both Tokyo Metro and Toei subway lines.

Tokyo Combination Ticket Costs ¥1580 (child ¥790) and covers JR trains in Tokyo, all subway lines and Toei buses.

Subway Lines

There are a total of 13 colour-coded subway lines zigzagging through Tokyo. Four are operated by Toei; nine belong to Tokyo Metro. Transfers between lines within the same group are seamless; if you plan to switch between TOEI trains and Tokyo Metro trains, you'll need to purchase a transfer ticket at the start of your journey.

AROUND TOKYO

Mt Fuji Area

Mt Fuji (富士山周辺; Fuji-san; 3776m), Japan's highest and most famous peak, is obviously this region's natural draw. In addition to climbing Fuji-san, visitors can hunt for precious views of the sacred volcano, and get outdoorsy around the Fuji Five Lakes (Fuji go-ko) with plenty of camping, hiking and lake activities.

 # Tours

Discover Japan Tours Guided Tour
(www.discover-japan-tours.com/en) Reputable
tour company running guided group tours
of Mt Fuji from Tokyo (¥10,000 per person
for groups of two or more), specialising in
less frequented routes. Private tours also
available.

ℹ️ Information

All of the following have English-speaking staff
and brochures on climbing and sights.
Fuji-Yoshida Tourist Information Center
(📞0555-22-7000; 🕐9am-5pm) Inside Fujisan
(Mt Fuji) Station, has all the info on climbing, and
brochures and maps of the area.
Kawaguchi-ko Tourist Information Center
(📞0555-72-6700; 🕐8.30am-5.30pm Sun-Fri,
till 7pm Sat) At Kawaguchi-ko Station, with maps
and brochures.
Shin-Fuji Station Tourist Information Center
(📞0545-64-2430; 🕐8.45am-5.30pm) On the 1st
floor of the *shinkansen* (bullet train) station in Tokyo.

ℹ️ Getting There & Away

The Mt Fuji area is most easily reached from Tokyo
by bus or train. The two main towns on the north
side of the mountain, Fuji-Yoshida and Kawaguchi-
ko, are the principal gateways. It's also possible to
bus in from Tokyo straight to the Kawaguchi-ko
Fifth Station on the mountain during the
official climbing season.

Coming from western Japan
(Kyoto, Osaka), you can take an
overnight bus to Kawaguchi-ko.

Bus

Frequent **Keiō Dentetsu**
(📞03-5376-2222;
www.highwaybus.com)
and **Fujikyū Express**
(📞0555-72-2922; http://
transportation.fujikyu.co.jp)
buses (¥1700, one hour and
50 minutes) operate directly
to Kawaguchi-ko Station,
and Fujisan Station in Fuji-
Yoshida, from the **Shinjuku
Highway Bus Terminal**
(📞03-5376-2222).

Coming from western Japan, the overnight bus
departs from Osaka's Higashi-Umeda Subway
Station (¥8500, 10.15pm) via Kyoto Station
(¥8000, 11.18pm) to Kawaguchi-ko Station
(arrives 8.32am).

Train

JR Chūō line trains go from Shinjuku to Ōtsuki
(*tokkyū* ¥2980, one hour; *futsū* ¥1280, 1½ hours),
where you transfer to the Fuji Kyūkō line for
Fujisan (¥990, 45 minutes) and Kawaguchi-ko
(¥1110, 50 minutes).

MT FUJI 富士山

Of all the iconic images of Japan,
Mt Fuji is the real deal. Admiration
for the mountain appears in Japan's
earliest recorded literature, dating
from the 8th century. Back then the
now dormant volcano was prone to
spewing smoke, making it all the
more revered. Mt Fuji continues to
captivate both Japanese and international visitors; in 2012, some 318,000
people climbed it. It's currently under
consideration to become a
World Heritage Site.

Snow-capped Mt Fuji
TAKESHI.K / GETTY IMAGES ©

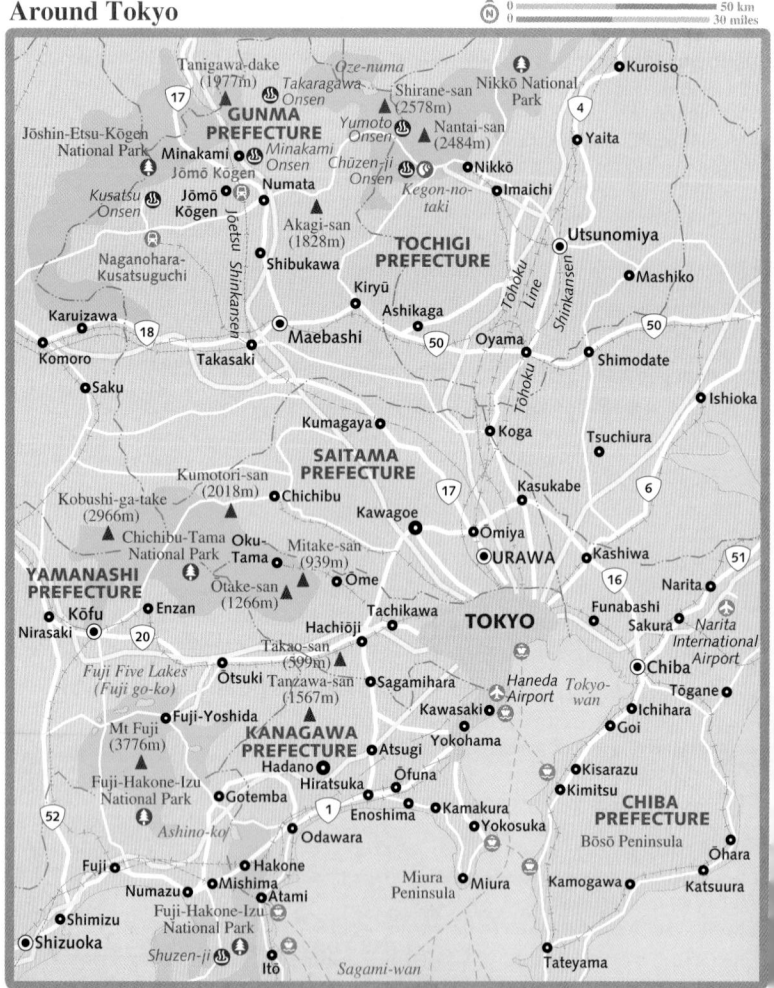

At the summit, the crater has circumference of 4km. As expected, views are spectacular, but be prepared for it to be clouded over. The highest point (3776m) is on the opposite side of the crater, and there's a post office if you want to send a postcard back home.

Mt Fuji Climbing Guide (www.mountfujiguide.com) and **Climbing Mt Fuji** (www17.plala.or.jp/climb_fujiyama/index.html) are both excellent online resources with all info needed by climbers. The *Climbing Mt Fuji* brochure, available at the Fuji-Yoshida Tourist Information Center, is also worth picking up.

When to Go

The official climbing season is from 1 July to 31 August. It's a busy mountain during these two months, with occasional queues for the rush to see sunrise. To get around the crowds, consider heading up on a weekday or starting earlier during the day to avoid the afternoon rush, and spend a night in a mountain hut.

Authorities strongly caution against climbing outside the regular season, when the weather is highly unpredictable and first-aid stations on the mountain are closed. Despite this, many people do climb out of season, as it's the best time to avoid the crowds. During this time, climbers generally head off at dawn, and return early afternoon – however, mountain huts on the Kawaguchi-ko Trail stay open through mid-September when weather conditions may still be good; none open before July, when snow still blankets the upper stations.

Outside of the climbing season, check weather conditions carefully before setting out (see www.snow-forecast.com/resorts/Mount-Fuji/6day/top), bring appropriate equipment, do not climb alone, and be prepared to retreat at any time. A guide can be invaluable.

Once snow or ice is on the mountain, Fuji becomes a very serious and dangerous undertaking and should only be attempted by those with winter mountaineering equipment and plenty of experience. It's highly advised that off-season climbers register with the local police department for safety reasons; fill out the form at the Kawaguchi-ko or Fuji-Yoshida Tourist Information Center.

Trails

The mountain is divided into 10 'stations' from base (First Station) to summit (Tenth). From the base station is the original pilgrim trail, but these days most climbers start from the halfway point at one of the four Fifth Stations, which is accessed via bus. All the routes converge at the Eighth Station, so be sure you take the right path on the way down.

To time your arrival for dawn you can either start up in the afternoon, stay overnight in a mountain hut and continue early in the morning, or climb the whole way at night. You do not want to arrive on the top too long before dawn, as it's likely to be very cold and windy.

Fifth Station Routes

There are four Fifth Station trails for climbing Mt Fuji: Kawaguchi-ko, also known as Yoshida (2305m); Subashiri (1980m); Fujinomiya (2380m); and

Climbing Mt Fuji: Know Before You Go

Although children and grandparents regularly reach the summit of Mt Fuji, this is a serious mountain. It's high enough for altitude sickness, and on the summit it can go from sunny and warm to wet, windy and cold remarkably quickly. Even if conditions are fine, you can count on it being close to freezing in the morning, even in summer. Also be aware that visibility can rapidly disappear with a blanket of mist rolling in suddenly. At a minimum, bring clothing appropriate for cold and wet weather, including a hat and gloves. You should also bring water, a map and light snacks. If you're climbing at night, bring a torch (flashlight) or headlamp, and spare batteries.

Descending the mountain is much harder on the knees than ascending; hiking poles can help. To avoid altitude sickness, be sure to take it slowly and take regular breaks. If you're suffering severe symptoms, you'll need to make an immediate descent.

The *Shobunsha Yama-to-kōgen Mt Fuji Map* (山と高原地図・富士山; in Japanese), available at major bookshops, is the most comprehensive map of the area.

For summit weather conditions, see www.snow-forecast.com/resorts/Mount-Fuji/6day/top.

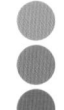
Gotemba (1440m). Allow five to six hours to reach the top (though some climb it in half the time) and about three hours to descend, plus 1½ hours for circling the crater at the top.

The **Kawaguchi-ko Trail** is by far and away the most popular route. It's accessed from Kawaguchi-ko Fifth Station (aka Mt Fuji Fifth Station), and has the most modern facilities and is easiest to reach from Kawaguchi-ko town.

Sleeping

From the Fifth Stations and up, dozens of mountain huts offer hikers simple hot meals and a place to sleep (with/without meals from ¥7350/5250). Though much maligned for their spartan conditions (a blanket on the floor sandwiched between other climbers), they can fill up fast – reservations are recommended and are essential on weekends. **Taishikan** (太子館; ☎22-1947) and **Fujisan Hotel** (富士山ホテル; ☎0555-22-0237; www. fujisanhotel.com; per person with 2 meals/ without from ¥7900/5700) at the Eighth Station (Kawaguchi-ko trail) usually

have an English-speaker on hand. Most huts allow you to rest inside as long as you order something. Camping on the mountain is not permitted, other than at the designated campsite near the Kawaguchi-ko Fifth Station.

The Subashiri Fifth Station has the atmospheric **Higashi Fuji Lodge** (☎75-2113; r ¥5000), which is very convenient for the off-season trekkers, and cooks up steaming *soba* with mushrooms and Fuji herbs.

Getting There & Around

For those wanting to start trekking as soon as they arrive from Tokyo, Keiō Dentetsu Bus (p121) runs direct buses (¥2600, 2½ hours; reservations necessary) from the Shinjuku Highway Bus Terminal to Kawaguchi-ko Fifth Station (does not operate in winter).

Buses run from both Kawaguchi-ko Station and Fujisan Station to the starting point at Kawaguchi-ko Fifth Station (one way/return ¥1500/2000, 50 minutes) roughly mid-April to early December. In the trekking season, buses depart hourly from around 7am until 8pm (ideal for climbers intending to make an overnight ascent). Returning from Fifth Station, buses head back to town from 8am to 9pm.

View from Mt Fuji's Seventh Station

In the off season, the first bus inconveniently leaves Kawaguchi-ko and Fujisan Stations at 9.30am, and the last bus returns at 3.30pm (around ¥12,000, plus tolls), meaning most trekkers will need to get a taxi in the morning to have enough time, before getting the bus back. The bus schedule is highly seasonal; call Fujikyū Yamanashi bus (p121) or your hotel for details.

In the low season you should be able to find other trekkers to share a taxi at K's House (☎83-5556; http://kshouse.jp/fuji-e/index. html; 6713-108 Funatsu; dm from ¥2500, d with/ without bathroom ¥7800/6800; ☺@☏). Car hire is another option (particularly if there's a group), costing around ¥6800 per day, plus ¥2000 in tolls.

To get to the Subashiri Fifth Station trail, you can catch a train from Kawaguchi-ko to Gotemba (¥1470), from where regular buses head to the Subashiri access point. Check timetables carefully before heading off.

FUJI FIVE LAKES   富士五湖
☎555

The Fuji Five Lakes (Fuji go-ko) region is a postcardlike area around Fuji's northern foothills; its lakes act as natural reflecting pools for the mountain's perfect cone. Yamanaka-ko is the easternmost lake, followed by Kawaguchi-ko, Sai-ko, Shōji-ko and Motosu-ko. Particularly during the autumn *kōyō* (foliage) season, the lakes make a good overnight trip out of Tokyo, for leisurely strolling, lake activities and for hiking in the nearby mountains.

Fuji-Yoshida and Kawaguchi-ko are the most accessible and developed areas. Kawaguchi-ko is the most popular place to stay, with best range of accommodation, but both make good bases if you plan on climbing Mt Fuji and don't intend on overnighting in a mountain hut.

Fuji-Yoshida   富士吉田

Not actually a lake, Fuji-Yoshida is one of the main gateway towns for the Fuji Five Lakes area. The central district, Gekkō-ji, feels like the little town that time forgot, with original mid-20th-century facades. The Fujisan Station is in the centre of Fuji-Yoshida.

Fujisan Train Station

In 2011, Fuji-Yoshida Station changed its name to Fujisan Station. It's also commonly referred to as Mt Fuji Station in English. This is not to be confused with the Kawaguchi-ko Fifth Station which is also commonly referred to as Mt Fuji Fifth Station. It's not a train station but a climbing access point (and bus stop) on the mountain, the starting point for the Kawaguchi-ko Trail to the summit. Confused yet?

⊙ Sights & Activities

Fuji Sengen-jinja   Shintō Shrine

(富士浅間神社; ☎0555-22-0221; http://sengen-jinja.jp/index.html; 5558 Kami-Yoshida, Fuji-Yoshida; ⏰grounds 24hr, staffed 9am-5pm) A necessary preliminary to the Mt Fuji ascent was a visit to this deeply wooded, atmospheric temple, built in 1615 but thought to have been the site of a shrine as early as 788. It's worth a visit for its 1000-year-old cedar; its main gate, which is rebuilt every 60 years (slightly larger each time); and its two 1-tonne *mikoshi* used in the annual Yoshida no Himatsuri (Yoshida Fire Festival). From Fujisan Station it's a 15-minute walk, or take a bus to Sengen-jinja-mae (¥150, five minutes).

Togawa-ke Oshi-no-ie Restored Pilgrim's Inn   Historic Building

(御師旧外川家住宅; 3-14-8 Kami-Yoshida; adult/child ¥100/50; ⏰9.30am-4.30pm, closed Tue) Fuji-Yoshida's *oshi-no-ie* (pilgrims' inns) have served visitors to the mountain since the days when climbing Mt Fuji was a pilgrimage rather than a tourist event. Very few still function as inns but Togawa-ke Oshi-no-ie offers some insight into the fascinating Edo-era practice of Mt Fuji worship.

Below: Climbers on Mt Fuji; **Right** Kawaguchi-ko in the Fuji Five Lakes region
(BELOW) ANDREW PEACOCK / GETTY IMAGES ©; (RIGHT) PRASIT CHANSAREEKORN / GETTY IMAGES ©

Kawaguchi-ko   河口湖

Easily the most popular place to stay in Fuji Five Lakes, Kawaguchi-ko is the closest town to four of the five lakes and departure points for climbing Mt Fuji. Even if you have no intention of climbing, this is a great spot to hang out and enjoy what the Fuji Five Lakes region has to offer, along with great Mt Fuji views.

◉ Sights & Activities

Kachi Kachi Yama
Ropeway   Ropeway

(カチカチ山ロープウェイ; 1163-1 Azagawa; 1 way/return adult ¥400/700, child ¥200/350; ◷9am-5pm) Around 600m north of Kawaguchi-ko Station, on the lower eastern edge of the lake, this ropeway runs to the **Fuji Viewing Platform** (1104m). If you have time, there is a 3½-hour hike from here to **Mitsutōge-yama** (三つ峠

山; 1785m); it's an old trail with excellent Fuji views. Ask at Kawaguchi-ko Tourist Information Center for a map.

Fuji Visitor Center   Visitor Centre

(富士ビジターセンター; 📞72-0259; 6663-1 Funatsu; ◷8.30am-5pm) **FREE** Worth dropping in before your climb to get up to speed on Mt Fuji at this well-presented visitor centre. An English video (12 minutes) with blockbuster-movie soundtrack is a little cheesy but gives a good summary of the mountain and its geological history. There's also an observation deck.

Tensui Onsen   Onsen

(天水; http://tensui-kawaguchiko.com; admission ¥1000; ◷10am-10pm) A 10-minute walk uphill behind the Itchiku Kubota Museum, this onsen has a large indoor bath and rocky *rotemburo* with mountain views, although none of Fuji unfortunately. Towel rental is ¥200.

Onsen-ji
Onsen

(☎72-6111; www.onsenji.net; ⏰11am-10pm Mon-Fri, 10am-10pm Sat & Sun) Just the place to soothe those aching legs, the waters of this popular *rotemburo* will feel like heaven for those returning from a day's trekking.

 Sleeping

Tominoko Hotel
Hotel ¥¥

(☎72-5080; www.tominoko.net; 55 Asakawa; r per person with 2 meals ¥12,000) Most lodgings on the lake with these views come with hefty price tags, but this place is a steal. Rooms are modern, smart Western-style twins. Ask for one on an upper level to score a balcony and take in the spectacular view of Mt Fuji across the lake. Also has a *rotemburo*.

Fuji Lake Hotel
Hotel ¥¥

(☎72-2209; www.fujilake.co.jp; 1 Funatsu; r per person with 2 meals from ¥15,750; @🛜) Near the Kawaguchi-ko town centre, and right on the shores of the lake, this historic 1935 hotel offers either Mt Fuji or lake views from its Japanese-Western combo rooms. Some rooms have private *rotemburo,* otherwise there's a common onsen.

Sunnide Resort
Hotel ¥¥¥

(サニーデリゾート; ☎76-6004; www.sunnide. com; 2549-1 Ōishi; d/cottages ¥21,000, 16,000 ; @🛜) Offering views of Mt Fuji from the far side of Kawaguchi-ko, friendly Sunnide has hotel rooms and cottages with a delicious outdoor bath. You can splash out in the stylish suites or the discounted 'backpacker' rates (¥4200, no views), if same-day rooms are available. Breakfast/dinner costs ¥1500/1575.

Kozantei Ubuya
Ryokan ¥¥¥

(湖山亭うぶや; ☎72-1145; www.ubuya.co.jp; Asakawa; r per person with 2 meals from ¥20,100) Elegant and ultrastylish, Ubuya offers some of the best views we've seen from any hotel room. The unobstructed panoramic view of Mt Fuji reflected in Kawaguchi-ko is simply unbeatable, especially when soaking in an outdoor tub on your balcony. One for the honeymooners.

127

Top Views of Mt Fuji

Mt Fuji has many different personalities depending on the season. Winter and spring months are your best bet for seeing it in all its clichéd glory; however, even during these times the snowcapped peak may be visible only in the morning before it retreats behind its cloud curtain. Its elusiveness, however, is part of the appeal, making sightings all the more special. Here are some of our top spots for viewing, both in the immediate and greater area:

Kawaguchi-ko On the north side of the lake, where Fuji looms large over its shimmering reflection.

Motosu-ko The famous view depicted on the ¥1000 bill can be seen from the northwest side of the lake.

Panorama-dai The end of this **hiking trail** (パノラマ台) rewards you with a magnificent front-on view of the mountain.

Kōyō-dai From this lookout Mt Fuji is particularly stunning in the autumn colours.

🍴 Eating

Kawaguchi-ko's local noodles are *hōtō*, hand-cut and served in a thick miso stew with pumpkin, sweet potato and other vegetables.

Akai
Izakaya ¥

(mains from ¥525; ⊙6-11pm, closed Thu; 📖) Great little *izakaya*, popular with the locals, serving sensational whole grilled fish and *ika yakisoba* (fried noodles with squid). It's off Rte 137, down an alleyway next to the petrol station near the Ogino supermarket.

Hōtō Fudō
Noodles ¥¥

(ほうとう不動; 707 Kawaguchi; hōtō ¥1050; ⊙11am-7pm) Four branches around town serve this massive hearty stew, bubbling in its own cast-iron pot, but certainly the most interesting is this one. South of the lake, this architecturally designed igloo-like concrete building sits against the Mt Fuji backdrop.

Sanrokuen
Teppanyaki ¥¥

(3370-1 Funatsu; set meals ¥2100-4200; ⊙10am-7.30pm Fri-Wed; 📖) Here diners sit on the floor around traditional *irori* charcoal pits

grilling their own meals – skewers of fish, meat, tofu and vegies. From Kawaguchi-ko Station, turn left, left again after the 7-Eleven and after 600m you'll see the thatched roof on the right.

ℹ Getting Around

City buses run from Kawaguchi-ko to Fujinomiya Fifth Station (¥2040, 75 minutes), via the three smaller lakes.

From Fujisan Station it's an eight-minute bus ride (¥230) or five-minute train (¥210) to Kawaguchi-ko Station.

The Retro-bus has hop-on-hop-off service from Kawaguchi-ko Station to all of the sightseeing spots around the western lakes. One route (two-day passes adult/child ¥1000/500) follows Kawaguchi-ko's northern shore, and the other (¥1300/650) heads south and around Sai-ko and Aokigahara.

There is a Toyota Rent-a-Car (☎72-1100, in English 0800-7000-815) a few minutes' walk from Kawaguchi-ko Station; head right from the station, turning right at the next intersection. Sazanami (⊙7am-5pm summer, 9am-5pm winter), on Kawaguchi-ko's southeast shore, rents regular bicycles (¥400/1500 per hour/day), electric pedal-assisting bicycles (¥600/2600 per hour/day) and row boats (¥1000 per hour/day).

Nikkō 日光

🎵0288 / POP 90,000

Ancient moss clinging to a stone wall; rows of perfectly aligned stone lanterns; vermilion gates; and towering cedars: this is only a pathway in Nikkō, a sanctuary that enshrines the glories of the Edo period (1600–1868). Scattered among hilly woodlands, Nikkō is one of Japan's major attractions. The drawback is that plenty of other people have discovered it too; high season (summer and autumn) and weekends can be extremely crowded and the spirituality of the area can feel a little lost.

Nikkō is certainly possible as a day trip from Tokyo, though spending at least one night allows for an early start before the crowds arrive. And a couple of nights gives you time to explore the gorgeous natural scenery in the surrounding area.

 Sights

The World Heritage Sites around Tōshō-gū are Nikkō's centrepiece. A ¥1000 combination ticket, valid for two days and available at booths in the area, covers entry to Rinnō-ji, Tōshō-gū and Futarasan-jinja. The Nemuri-Neko (Sleeping Cat) and Ieyasu's tomb in Tōshō-gū require a separate admission ticket (¥520).

Most sites are open from 8am to 4.30pm (until 3.30pm from November to March). To avoid the hordes, visit early on a weekday. Be sure to pick up a map from the tourist information office, as finding the English signposts to the shrines and temples can be tricky.

Tōshō-gū Shintō Shrine
(東照宮) The entrance to the main shrine is through the torii at **Omote-mon** (表門), a gate protected on either side by Deva kings.

Just inside are the **Sanjinko** (三神庫; Three Sacred Storehouses). On the upper storey of the last storehouse are imaginative relief carvings of elephants by an artist who famously had never seen the real thing. To the left of the entrance is **Shinkyūsha** (神厩舎; Sacred Stable), adorned with allegorical relief carvings of monkeys. The famous 'hear no evil, see no evil, speak no evil' monkeys demonstrate three principles of Tendai Buddhism.

Tōshō-gū, Nikkō

DARYL BENSON / GETTY IMAGES ©

Pass through another torii, climb another flight of stairs, and on the left and right are a drum tower and a belfry. To the left of the drum tower is **Honji-dō** (本地堂). This hall is best known for the painting on its ceiling of the Nakiryū (Crying Dragon). Monks demonstrate the acoustical properties of this hall by clapping two sticks together. The dragon 'roars' (a bit of a stretch) when the sticks are clapped beneath the dragon's mouth, but not elsewhere.

Next comes **Yōmei-mon** (陽明門; Sunset Gate), dazzlingly decorated with glimmering gold leaf and intricate, coloured carvings and paintings of flowers, dancing girls, mythical beasts and Chinese sages. Worrying that its perfection might arouse envy in the gods, those responsible for its construction had the final supporting pillar placed upside down as a deliberate error. Although the style is more Chinese than Japanese and some critics deride it as gaudy, it's a grand spectacle.

To the left of Yōmei-mon is **Jin-yōsha** (神輿舎), the storage for the *mikoshi* used during festivals.

Tōshō-gū's **Honden** (本殿; Main Hall) and **Haiden** (拝殿; Hall of Worship) are across the enclosure. Inside – open only to *daimyō* during the Edo period – are paintings of the 36 immortal poets of Kyoto, and a ceiling-painting pattern from the Momoyama period; note the 100 dragons, each different. *Fusuma* (sliding door) paintings depict a *kirin* (a mythical beast that's part giraffe and part dragon). It's said that the creature will appear only when the world is at peace.

Through Yōmei-mon and to the right is **Nemuri-Neko** (眠り猫), a small wooden sculpture of a sleeping cat that's famous throughout Japan for its lifelike appearance (though admittedly the attraction is lost on some visitors). From here, **Sakashita-mon** (坂下門) opens onto an uphill path through towering cedars to the appropriately solemn **tomb of Ieyasu** (奥社 (徳川家康の墓)).

Rinnō-ji
Buddhist Temple

(輪王寺) This Tendai-sect temple was founded 1200 years ago by Shōdō Shōnin. The **Sambutsu-dō** (三仏堂; Three-Buddha Hall) is constructed from some 360m of zelkova trees and is the main attraction. Inside are three 8m gilded wooden Buddha statues. The central image is Amida Nyorai (one of the primal deities in the Mahayana Buddhist canon), flanked by Senjū (1000-armed Kannon, deity of mercy and compassion) and Batō (a horse-headed Kannon), whose special domain is the animal kingdom.

Rinnō-ji's **Hōmotsu-den** (宝物殿 **Treasure Hall; admission ¥300**) houses some 6000 treasures associated with the temple; the separate admission ticket includes entrance to the **Shōyō-en** strolling garden.

Taiyūin-byō Shintō Shrine

(大猷院廟) Enshrining Ieyasu's grandson Iemitsu (1604–51) is Taiyūin-byō. Though it houses many of the same elements as Tōshō-gū, its smaller, more intimate scale and setting in a cryptomeria forest make it very appealing.

Among Taiyūin-byō's many structures, look for dozens of lanterns donated by *daimyō*, and the gate Niō-mon, the guardian deities of which have a hand up (to welcome those with pure hearts) and a hand down (to suppress those with impure hearts). Inside the main hall, 140 dragons painted on the ceiling are said to carry prayers to the heavens; those holding pearls are on their way up, and those without are returning to gather more prayers.

Futarasan-jinja Shintō Shrine

(二荒山神社) Shōdō Shōnin founded this shrine; the current building dates from 1619, making it Nikkō's oldest. Set among cypress trees, it's very atmospheric. It's the protector shrine of Nikkō itself, dedicated to the nearby mountain, Nantai-san (2484m), the mountain's consort, Nyotai-san, and their mountainous progeny, Tarō. There are other shrine branches on Nantai-san and by Chūzenji-ko.

Eating & Drinking

A local speciality is *yuba* (the skin that forms when making tofu) cut into strips; better than it sounds, it's a staple of *shōjin ryōri* (Buddhist vegetarian cuisine). You'll see it all over town, in everything from *yuba soba* (noodles) to *age yuba manju* (fried bean buns).

Hi no Kuruma Okonomiyaki ¥

(ひの車; 597-2 Gokō-machi; mains ¥500-1500; ⏰noon-3pm & 6-9pm Thu-Tue; 📖) A popular choice for cheap and easy grill-your-own meals. Look for the small parking lot and red, black, green and white Japanese sign.

Yuba Yūzen Kaiseki ¥¥

(日光ゆば遊膳; 1-22 Yasukawachō; sets ¥2700-3200; ⏰11am-2pm Thu-Tue) A *yuba*-speciality restaurant that serves it sashimi-style, with tofu and soy milk, and with the addition of a variety of seasonal

Under Restoration

A few of Nikkō's temples have been undergoing restoration work for the past few years and this is set to continue. At Rinnō-ji, the Sanbutsudo Hall, the temple's main hall, is undergoing major renovation works and is due for completion in 2020. At Tōshō-gū, the Yomeimon Gate was scheduled for renovation at the time of writing and scaffolding may still shroud the gate so visitors will be unable to fully view the shrine. Haiden Hall and Taiyūin-byō's Nitennmon Gate (second gate) were also being restored at time of writing.

While this does mean you might only get partial exterior views of some temples, this shouldn't put you off visiting. The interiors are completely on display and the temples remain impressive sights. You can check with the tourist information office for an update before you visit.

Detour:
Chūzen-ji Onsen

This highland area 11.5km west of Nikkō offers some natural seclusion and striking views of Nantai-san from Chūzen-ji's lake, Chuzenji-ko. The lake itself is 161m deep and a fabulous shade of deep blue in good weather with the usual flotilla of sightseeing boats.

Buses run from Tōbu Nikkō Station to Chūzen-ji Onsen (¥1100, 45 minutes) or use the economical Tōbu Nikkō Bus Free Pass, available at Tōbu Nikkō Station.

side dishes. There's no English menu, but there are only two choices for sets: ¥2700 if you're hungry and ¥3200 if you're really hungry. Look for the two-storey tan building across from the first left turn after Shin-kyō.

Gyōshintei   Kaiseki ¥¥¥

(尭心亭; ✆53-3751; www.meiji-yakata.com/gyoushin; 2339-1 Sannai; set courses ¥3465-8400; ⏰11am-7pm; ✈🔲) Splurge here on deluxe spreads of *shōjin ryōri*, featuring local bean curd and vegetables served half a dozen delectable ways. The elegant tatami dining room overlooks a carefully tended garden. It's directly north of the Shin-kyō bridge (about 250m) and there's a three-peaked emblem on the door curtain.

Nikko Park Lodge Cafe   Cafe

(11-6 Matsubaracho; ⏰10am-7pm; @🔲) Across the street from the Tōbu Station, this guest house cafe serves a good brew, cheap beer and has free wi-fi and internet. A good place to meet fellow travellers.

❶ Information

Kyōdo Center Tourist Information Office (✆54-2496; www.nikko-jp.org; 591 Gokomachi; internet per 15min ¥50, wi-fi for 20min free; ⏰9am-5pm) The main tourist information office with English-speakers (guaranteed between 10am and 2pm) and maps for sightseeing and hiking. Has internet access.

Post office (日光郵便局; ✆54-0101; 896-1 Nakahatsuishi-chō) On the main road, three blocks past the Kyōdo Center. There's another office across the street from Tōbu Nikkō Station on Rte 119; both have international ATMs.

Tōbu Nikkō Station Tourist Information Desk (✆53-4511; ⏰8.30am-5pm) At the Nikkō Station, there's a small information desk where you can pick up a town map and get help in English to find buses, restaurants and hotels.

Tochigi Volunteer Interpreters & Guides Association (NikkoTVIGA@hotmail.co.jp) Offers free guided tours. Contact in advance.

❶ Getting There & Away

Nikkō is best reached from Tokyo via the Tōbu Nikkō line from Asakusa Station. You can usually get last-minute seats on the hourly reserved *tokkyū* (limited-express) trains (¥2620, 1¾ hours). *Kaisoku* (rapid) trains (¥1320, 2½ hours, hourly from 6.20am to 4.50pm) require no reservation. For the *tokkyū*, you may have to change at Shimo-imaichi. Be sure to ride in the last two cars to reach Nikkō (some cars may separate at an intermediate stop).

JR Pass holders can take the Tohoku *shinkansen* from Tokyo to Utsunomiya (¥4800, 54 minutes) and change there for an ordinary train to Nikkō (¥740, 45 minutes).

Both JR Nikkō Station (designed by Frank Lloyd Wright) and the nearby Tōbu Nikkō Station lie southeast of the shrine area within a block of Nikkō's main road (Rte 119, the old Nikkō-kaidō).

From the station, follow this road uphill for 20 minutes to reach the shrine area, past restaurants, souvenir shops and the main tourist information centre, or take a bus to the Shin-kyō bus stop (¥190).

Bus stops are announced in English. Buses leave from both JR and Tōbu Nikkō Station; buses bound for both Chūzen-ji Onsen and Yumoto Onsen stop at Shin-kyō and other stops around the World Heritage Sites.

Train/Bus Passes

Tōbu Railway (www.tobu.co.jp/foreign; ⏰Sightseeing Service Center 7.45am-5pm) Offers two passes covering rail transport from Asakusa to Nikkō (though not the *tokkyū* surcharge, from ¥1040) and unlimited hop-on hop-off bus services around Nikkō. Purchase these passes at the Tōbu Sightseeing Service Center in Asakusa Station.

All Nikko Pass (adult/child ¥4400/2210) Valid for four days and includes buses to Chūzen-ji Onsen and Yumoto Onsen.

World Heritage Pass (adult/child ¥3600/1700) Valid for two days and includes buses to the World Heritage Sites, plus admission to Tōshō-gū, Rinnō-ji and Futarasan-jinja.

Tōbu Nikkō Bus Free Pass If you've already got your rail ticket, two-day bus-only passes allow unlimited rides between Nikkō and Chūzen-ji Onsen (adult/child ¥2000/1000) or Yumoto Onsen (adult/child ¥3000/1500), including the World Heritage Site area. The **Sekai-isan-meguri** (World Heritage Bus Pass; adult/child ¥500/250) covers the area between the stations and the shrine precincts. Buy these at Tōbu Nikkō Station.

Minakami & Takaragawa Onsen
水上温泉・宝川温泉

📞 0278 / POP 21,000

In the northern region of the Gunma Prefecture is the sprawling onsen town of Minakami, an all-year-round destination and mecca for outdoor-adventure sports, hiking and skiing. When the spring snow melts between April and June, the Tone Gawa (利根 川) is the source of some of the best **white-water rafting** and **kayaking** in Japan. It's also home to Takaragawa Onsen (about 30 minutes away by road), a riverside spa ranked among the nation's best.

The train station is in the village of Minakami.

Activities

Takaragawa Onsen
Onsen
(www.takaragawa.com; admission ¥1500; ⊙9am-5pm) This stunning outdoor onsen is idyllic. All of the bathing pools – save one just for women – are mixed and will appeal more to the exhibitionists out there. Women can take modesty towels (rental is ¥100) into the mixed baths. The curious junk and gems you'll pass on your way to the baths are decades' worth of gifts from local villagers. The bears in cages are the only downside here. Buses run hourly between Minakami Station and Takaragawa Onsen (¥1100, 40 minutes) or Takaragawa Iriguchi (¥1000, 30 minutes), from where it's a short walk to the onsen.

Hōshi Onsen Chōjūkan
Onsen
(法師温泉長寿館; www.houshi-onsen.jp; 650 Nagai; admission for daytrippers ¥1000; ⊙10.30am-1.30pm) The main bathhouse at this ryokan is a stunning wooden structure from 1896, with rows of individual bathing pools and a unique style of water

Rafting on Tone Gawa, Minakami
DAJ / GETTY IMAGES ©

bubbling up from below. It's mixed bathing, with an additional modern bathhouse just for women and *rotemburo*.

Sleeping

Tenjin Lodge
Lodge ¥

(天神・ロッジ; ☎25-3540; www.tenjinlodge.com; 220-4 Yubiso; r per person from ¥5000; 🛜) Across from a waterfall and nearby swimming holes, this Australian/Korean-run lodge offers comfy, spacious Japanese and Western rooms; ask for a riverside one. Kieran and Bo are welcoming hosts and offer home-cooked meals (¥1000), and BBQs in the warmer months; they also lead guided hiking and snowshoeing tours. There are plans for backpacker dorms. Located at the foot of Tanigawadake. Take the Joetsu *shinkansen* from Tokyo Station to Jōmō Kōgen Station (70 minutes, ¥5750), from where it's free pick-up.

Hōshi Onsen Chōjūkan
Ryokan ¥¥

(法師温泉長寿館; ☎66-0005; www.houshi-onsen.jp; 650 Nagai; r per person incl 2 meals from ¥13,800) Perfectly rustic and supremely photogenic, this lodging is one of Japan's finest onsen ryokan on the southwestern fringes of Minakami. Its onsen (p133) is a stunner. To get here, take a bus from Gokan Station (two stops before Minakami on the Jōetsu line) or from the Jōmō Kōgen *shinkansen* station to Sarugakyō (40 minutes); at the last stop, take another bus for Hōshi Onsen (15 minutes).

Ōsenkaku
Ryokan ¥¥

(汪泉閣; ☎75-2121; www.takaragawa.com; 1899 Fujiwara; r per person ¥10,000) Adjacent to Takaragawa Onsen, this inn has gorgeous riverfront rooms over several buildings and an old-style feel. It also has 24-hour use of the Takaragawa baths. Prices rise steeply for nicer rooms with better views and private baths, but aim for the 1930s-vintage No 1 annexe. Note that dinner includes bear-meat soup; if you'd prefer not to eat this, ask for *no kuma-jiru* (熊汁) when reserving.

Eating

Kadoya
Soba ¥¥

(そば処角弥; www.kadoya-soba.com; soba for 2 from ¥2700; ⏱11am-2.30pm) Expect to queue at this popular 'local' specialising

Takaragawa Onsen (p133)

in *hegi soba* (soba flavoured with seaweed and served on a special plate, a *hegi*). The noodles are hand-rolled fresh every day and staff close up shop once they sell out. It's a five-minute walk from Canyon's Alpine Lodge on the main street; look for the back-and-white building.

La Biere Pizza ¥¥
(pizzas from ¥800; ⏰11am-2.30pm & 5-8.30pm, closed Tue; 📖) Simple and tasty wood-fired pizzas in this cute pizzeria with pot plants and umbrella-covered decking out the front. Takeway is also available. It's in Minakami Village, a short walk from the station.

🛈 Information

Minakami Tourist Information Center (水上観光協会; 📞62-0401; www.enjoy-minakami.jp/eng; ⏰8.30am-5.30pm) Across from the station, this office has very helpful English-speaking staff, brochures and bus schedules.

🛈 Getting There & Away

From Ueno, take the Joetsu *shinkansen* (¥4600, 50 minutes) or JR Takasaki line (¥1890, two hours) to Takasaki and transfer to the Jōetsu line (¥950, one hour). You can also catch the Joetsu *shinkansen* to Jōmō Kōgen from Tokyo/Ueno (¥5750/5550, 1¼ hours), from where buses run to Minakami (¥600, 25 minutes).

....

Hakone 箱根

📞0460 / POP 13,500

If you only have a day or two outside Tokyo, Hakone can give you almost everything you could desire from the Japanese countryside – spectacular mountain scenery crowned by Mt Fuji, onsen and traditional inns. It's also home to world-class art museums. Ashino-ko is in the centre of it all and provides the foreground for the iconic image of Mt Fuji with the torii gate of the Hakone-jinja rising from the lake.

During holidays, Hakone can be quite busy and feel highly packaged. To beat the crowds, plan your trip during the week. For more information, try www.hakone.or.jp/english.

🛈 Getting There & Away

The private **Odakyū line** (www.odakyu.jp) from Shinjuku Station goes directly into Hakone-Yumoto, the region's transit hub. Use either the convenient Romance Car (¥2020, 90 minutes) or *kyūkō* (regular-express) service (¥1150, two hours); the latter may require a transfer at Odawara. The last trains from Hakone-Yumoto to Shinjuku run at 7.45pm weekdays and 8.50pm Saturday and Sunday for the Romance Car, and 10.30pm weekdays and 11pm Saturday and Sunday for the Odakyu line.

JR Pass holders can take the Kodama *shinkansen* (¥3840, 50 minutes) or the JR Tōkaidō line (*futsū* ¥1750, one hour; *tokkyū* ¥2350, one hour) from Tokyo Station or the Shōnan-Shinjuku line from Shinjuku (¥1450, 80 minutes) to Odawara and change there for trains or buses for Hakone-Yumoto.

The narrow-gauge, switchback Hakone-Tōzan line runs from Odawara via Hakone-Yumoto to Gōra (¥650, one hour).

Odakyū's Hakone Freepass (箱根フリーパス), available at Odakyū stations and Odakyū Travel branches, is an excellent deal, covering the return fare to Hakone and unlimited use of most modes of transport within the region, plus other discounts. It's available as a two-day pass (adult/child from Shinjuku ¥5000/1500, from Odawara if you're not planning on returning to Shinjuku, ¥3900/1000) or a three-day pass (adult/child from Shinjuku ¥5500/1750, from Odawara ¥4400/1250). Freepass holders need to pay an additional limited-express surcharge (¥870 each way) to ride the Romance Car.

For those wanting to combine Hakone with Mt Fuji on their itinerary, there is the Fuji Hakone Pass (¥7200), a three-day pass offering discount round-trip travel from Shinjuku as well as unlimited use of most transportation in the Hakone and Fuji areas.

🛈 Getting Around

Part of Hakone's popularity comes from the chance to ride assorted *norimono* (modes of transport): switchback train (from Hakone-Yumoto to Gōra), cable car (funicular), ropeway (gondola), ship and bus. Check out www.odakyu.jp, which describes this circuit.

Boat

From Tōgendai, sightseeing boats criss-cross Ashino-ko to Hakone-machi and Moto-Hakone (¥970, 30 minutes).

Bus

The Hakone-Tōzan and Izu Hakone bus companies service the Hakone area, linking most of the sights. Hakone-Tōzan buses, included in the Hakone Freepass, run between Hakone-machi and Odawara (¥1150, 55 minutes) and between Moto-Hakone and Hakone-Yumoto (¥930, 35 minutes).

Cable Car & Ropeway

Gōra is the terminus of the Hakone-Tōzan railway and the beginning of the cable car to Sōun-zan, from where you can catch the Hakone Ropeway line to Ōwakudani and Tōgendai.

Luggage Forwarding

At Hakone-Yumoto Station, deposit your luggage with **Hakone Baggage Service** (箱根キャリーサービス; ☎86-4140; per piece from ¥700; ⏱8.30am-7pm) by noon, and it will be delivered to your inn within Hakone from 3pm. Hakone Freepass holders get a discount of ¥100 per bag.

HAKONE-YUMOTO ONSEN
箱根湯元温泉

Hakone-Yumoto is the starting point for most visits to Hakone. Though heavily visited, it's an ambient riverside resort town with a high concentration of onsen, the main attraction here.

Activities

Tenzan Tōji-kyō   Onsen
(天山湯治郷; www.tenzan.jp; 208 Yumoto-chaya; admission ¥1200; ⏱9am-10pm) Soak in *rotemburo* of varying temperatures and designs (one is constructed to resemble a natural cave) at this large, popular bath 2km southwest of town; weekends and holidays can be busy. To get here, take the 'B' Course shuttle bus from the bridge outside the Hakone-Yumoto Station (¥100).

Furasato   Onsen
(ふるさと; ☎85-5559; www.hakone-furusato.com; admission ¥850; ⏱9am-6pm Mon-Fri, to 8pm Sat & Sun) A popular ryokan with atmospheric *rotemburo* and indoor onsen, open to day trippers.

Yu-No-Sato   Onsen
(湯の里; www.yunosato-y.jp; 191 Yumotochaya; admission ¥1400; ⏱11am-11pm) A spa complex with several baths, including a *rotemburo* amid the fresh mountain air, jet bubble bath, plasma bath and private onsen for two, available by reservation. Towel rental is ¥200.

Sleeping

Hakone-no-Mori Okada   Hotel ¥
(箱根の森おかだ; ☎85-6711; www.hakonenomori-okada.jp; 191 Yumoto-chaya; r per person from ¥5930) Adjacent to the Hotel Okada, includes access to the onsen at Yu-no-Sato.

Omiya Ryokan   Ryokan ¥¥
(☎85-7345; www.o-miya.com; 116 Yumotochaya; r from ¥6150, weekends with meals ¥13,000; 🛜) This ryokan has well-priced midweek tatami rooms; some with mountain views. There's a small indoor onsen, but it offers 50% discount to a more attractive *rotemburo*, a short walk away. To get here, take the 'B' course bus from Hakone-Yumoto Station.

Fukuzumirō   Ryokan ¥¥¥
(福住楼; ☎85-5301; www.fukuzumi-ro.com; 74 Tōnozawa; r per person incl 2 meals from ¥18,000) No two rooms are alike at this 100-year-old inn, though all have exquisite original woodwork. Most have sun terraces that rub up against the Haya-kawa; the small, quiet room overlooking the garden was a favourite of author Kawabata Yasunori. There are onsen baths but no private facilities. The inn is just below Tōnozawa Station on the Hakone-Tōzan railway, on the river side of the road, or a short taxi ride from Hakone-Yumoto.

Hotel Okada   Hotel ¥¥¥
(ホテルおかだ; ☎85-6000; www.hotel-okada.co.jp; 191 Yumoto-chaya; r per person from ¥15,000; 🚭🛜♿) This rambling hotel on the edge of the Sukumo-gawa has excellent Japanese- and Western-style rooms and baths including direct entry to the large Yu-no-Sato complex nearby. Take bus A from the train station (¥100, 10 minutes).

Ship sailing on Ashino-ko (p138)

PETER WILSON / GETTY IMAGES ©

ℹ️ Information

Tourist Information Center (📞85-8911; www.hakone.or.jp; ⏰9am-5.45pm)ourist Information Center (📞85-8911; www.hakone.or.jp; ⏰9am-5.45pm) Pick up maps and info at the excellent Tourist Information Center with English-speakers. By the bus stop across the main road from the train station. There are large coin lockers for luggage storage at the station (¥500).

MIYANOSHITA 宮ノ下

The first worthwhile stop on the Hakone-Tōzan railway towards Gōra, this village has antique shops along the main road, some splendid ryokan, and a pleasant **hiking** trail skirting up 800m Sengen-yama (浅間山). The trailhead is just below Fujiya Hotel, marked by a shrine.

🛏️ Sleeping

Fujiya Hotel Hotel ¥¥¥
(富士屋ホテル; 📞82-2211; www.fujiyahotel.jp; 359 Miyanoshita; d from ¥19,830; ❄️@🛜🏊) One of Japan's finest Western-heritage hotels. It opened in 1878 and played host to Charlie Chaplin back in the day (Room 45). Now sprawled across several wings, it remains dreamily elegant due to its old-world lounge areas and hillside garden. It's worth a visit to soak up the atmosphere and have tea in the lounge.

CHŌKOKU-NO-MORI & GŌRA 彫刻の森・強羅

Gōra, one stop after Chōkoku-no-mori, is the terminus of the Hakone-Tōzan line and the starting point for the funicular and cable-car trip to Tōgendai on Ashino-ko.

◎ Sights & Activities

Hakone Open-Air Museum Museum
(彫刻の森美術館; www.hakone-oam.or.jp; 1121 Ninotaira; adult/child ¥1600/500; ⏰9am-4.30pm; 👶) On a rolling hillside setting, this museum is a safari for art lovers, with an impressive selection of 19th- and 20th-century Japanese and Western sculptures (including works by Henry Moore, Rodin and Miró) found among the foliage. It also has an excellent Picasso Pavilion with more than 300 works ranging from paintings, glass art and tapestry. Kids will love the giant crochet

137

artwork/playground with its Jenga-like exterior walls. End the day by soaking your feet in the outdoor footbath. Located two stops beyond Miyanoshita, uphill from the Chōkoku-no-Mori Station. Hakone Freepass holders get ¥200 off the admission price.

POLA Museum of Art   Museum

(www.polamuseum.or.jp; 1285 Kozukayama; adult/child ¥1800/700; ⏰9am-5pm) Showcasing the impressive private collection of the late Suzuki Tsuneshi, son of the founder of the Pola Orbis Group (cosmetics company), this quality museum is located in an equally impressive architecturally designed building. Artworks in the collection include those from such famous names as Van Gogh, Cézanne, Renoir, Matisse, Picasso and Rodin.

Hakone Museum of Art   Museum

(箱根美術館; www.moaart.or.jp; 1300 Gōra; adult/child ¥900/free; ⏰9.30am-4.30pm, closed Thu) Sharing grounds with a lovely velvety moss garden and teahouse (¥700 matcha green tea and sweet), this museum has a collection of Japanese pottery dating from as far back as the Jōmon period (ie some 5000 years ago).

SŌUN-ZAN & ŌWAKUDANI
早雲山・大桶谷

From Gōra, continue to near the 1153m-high summit of Sōun-zan by cable car (¥410, 10 minutes).

From Sōun-zan, there are several **hiking trails** including one to Kami-yama (1¾ hours) and another up to Ōwakudani (1¼ hours). The latter is sometimes closed due to the mountain's toxic gases. Check at the tourist information office.

Sōun-zan is the starting point for the **Hakone Ropeway**, a 30-minute, 4km gondola ride to Tōgendai (one way/return ¥1330/2340), stopping at Ōwakudani en route. In fine weather Mt Fuji looks fabulous from here.

Ōwakudani is a volcanic cauldron of steam, bubbling mud and mysterious smells where you can buy onsen tamago, eggs boiled and blackened in the sulphurous waters. Don't linger, as the gases are poisonous. From here you can take the **Ōwakudani-Togendai Nature Trail**, a one hour hike.

ASHINO-KO   芦ノ湖

Between Tōgendai, Hakone-machi and Moto-Hakone, this lake is touted as the primary attraction of the Hakone region; but it's Mt Fuji, with its snow-clad slopes glimmering in reflection on the water, that lends the lake its poetry.

HAKONE-MACHI & MOTO-HAKONE
箱根町・元箱根

The sightseeing boats across Ashino-ko deposit you at either of these two towns, both well touristed and with sights of historical interest.

Cable car at Mt Fuji
JONATHAN P. ELLGEN / GETTY IMAGES ©

 Sights

Hakone Sekisho   Museum

(箱根関所; Hakone Checkpoint Museum; 1 Hakone-machi; adult/child ¥500/250; ⏰9am-4.30pm Mar-Nov, to 4pm Dec-Feb) A recent reconstruction of the feudal-era checkpoint on the Old Tōkaidō Hwy, this museum has Darth Vader–like armour and grisly implements used on lawbreakers. Unfortunately only has basic English explanations on some displays.

Narukawa Art Museum   Museum

(www.narukawamuseum.co.jp; 570 Moto Hakone; adult/child ¥1200/800; ⏰9am-5pm) Art comes in two forms here – the exquisite Japanese-style paintings, *nihonga*, on display, and the stunning Mt Fuji views from the panorama lounge looking across the lake. Don't miss the kaleidoscope displays.

Hakone-jinja   Shintō Shrine

(箱根神社; ⏰9am-4pm) A pleasant stroll around the lake follows a cedar lined path to this shrine set in a wooded grove, in Moto-Hakone. Its signature red torii rises from the lake; get your camera ready for that picture-postcard shot.

Kamakura   鎌倉

☎0467 / POP 174,000

An hour from Tokyo, Kamakura was Japan's first feudal capital, between 1185 and 1333, and its glory days coincided with the spread of populist Buddhism in Japan. This legacy is reflected in the area's high concentration of stunning temples. The town has a laid-back, earthy vibe complete with organic restaurants and summer beach shacks – which can be added to sunrise meditation and hillside hikes as reasons to visit. Kamakura does tend to get packed on weekends and in holiday periods, so plan accordingly.

Sights & Activities

Kenchō-ji   Buddhist Temple

(建長寺; 8 Yamanouchi; adult/child ¥300/100; ⏰8.30am-4.30pm) Established in 1253, Kenchō-ji is Japan's oldest Zen monastery and is still active today. It once comprised seven buildings and 49 subtemples, most of which were destroyed in the fires of the 14th and 15th centuries. However, the 17th and 18th centuries saw its restoration, and you can still get a sense of its splendour. The central Butsuden (Buddha Hall) was brought piece by piece from Tokyo in 1647. Its Jizō Bosatsu statue, unusual for a Zen temple, reflects the valley's ancient function as an execution ground – Jizō consoles lost souls. Other highlights include a bell cast in 1253 and the juniper grove, believed to have sprouted from seeds brought from China by Kenchō-ji's founder some seven centuries ago.

Engaku-ji   Buddhist Temple

(円覚寺; 409 Yamanouchi; adult/child ¥300/100; ⏰8am-5pm Apr-Oct, to 4pm Nov-Mar) Engaku-ji, one of the five major Rinzai Zen temples in Kamakura, is on the left as you exit Kita-Kamakura Station. It was founded in 1282, allegedly as a place where Zen monks might pray for soldiers who lost their lives defending Japan against Kublai Khan. Engaku-ji remains an important temple, and a number of notable priests have trained here. All of the temple structures have been rebuilt over the centuries; the Shariden, a Song-style reliquary, is the oldest structure, last rebuilt in the 16th century. At the top of the long flight of stairs is the Engaku-ji bell, the largest bell in Kamakura, cast in 1301.

Tsurugaoka Hachiman-gū   Shintō Shrine

(鶴岡八幡宮; 2-1-31 Yukinoshita; treasure hall adult/child ¥200/100; ⏰9am-4pm) Kamakura's most important shrine is, naturally, dedicated to Hachiman, the god of war. Minamoto Yoritomo (see Domination through Military Rule, p344) ordered its construction in 1191 and designed the pine-flanked central promenade that leads to the coast. The sprawling grounds are ripe with historical symbolism: the Gempei Pond, bisected by bridges, is said to depict the rift between the Minamoto (Genji) and Taira (Heike) clans. Behind the pond is the **Kamakura National**

Treasure Museum (鎌倉国宝館; ☎22-0753; 2-1-1 Yukinoshita, Kamakura Kokuhōkan; admission ¥300; ⏰9am-4.30pm Tue-Sun), housing remarkable Buddhist sculptures from the 12th to 16th centuries.

Daibutsu Monument

(大仏; 4-2-28 Hase, Great Buddha; adult/child ¥200/150; ⏰8am-5.30pm Apr-Sep, to 5pm Oct-Nov) Kamakura's most iconic sight, an 11.4m bronze statue of Amida Buddha (*amitābha* in Sanskrit), is in Kōtoku-in, a Jōdo sect temple. Completed in 1252, it's said to have been inspired by Yoritomo's visit to Nara (where Japan's biggest Daibutsu holds court) after the Minamoto clan's victory over the Taira clan. Once housed in a huge hall, today the statue sits in the open, the hall having been washed away by a tsunami in 1495. For an extra ¥20, you can duck inside to see how the sculptors pieced the 850-tonne statue together.

Buses from stops 1 and 6 in front of Kamakura Station run to the Daibutsu-mae stop. Alternatively, take the Enoden Enoshima line to Hase Station and walk north for about five minutes. Better yet, take the **Daibutsu Hiking Course**.

Hase-dera Buddhist Temple

(長谷寺; Hase Kannon; 3-11-2 Hase; adult/child ¥300/100; ⏰8am-4.30pm) About 10 minutes' walk from the Daibutsu, Hase-dera (Jōdo sect) is one of the most popular temples in the Kantō region. The focal point of the temple's main hall is a 9m-high carved wooden *jūichimen* (11-faced) Kannon statue. Kannon (*avalokiteshvara* in Sanskrit) is the bodhisattva of infinite compassion and, along with Jizō, is one of Japan's most popular Buddhist deities. According to legend, the temple dates back to AD 736, when the statue is said to have washed up on the shore near Kamakura.

Eating

Vegetarians can eat well in Kamakura; pick up the free, bilingual *Vegetarian Culture Map* at the Tourist Information Center.

Bowls Donburi Café Japanese ¥

(鎌倉どんぶりカフェbowls; 2-14-7 Komachi; meals from ¥880-1680; ⏰11am-3pm & 5-10pm; ☺@📶🖊📖) The humble *donburi* (rice bowl) gets a hip, healthy remake at this modern bright cafe, with toppings

Daibutsu in Kamakura

such as roasted tuna, soy sauce and sesame oil. You get a discount if you discover the word *atari* at the bottom of the bowl. Also serves excellent coffee and has free wi-fi and computer terminals with internet.

Matsubara-an Noodles ¥¥
(松原庵; 4-10-3 Yuiga-hama; mains from ¥550-1800; ⏰11am-9pm; 📶) In a former residence tucked in a quiet backstreet is this upscale *soba* restaurant capturing the feel of early-20th-century Kamakura. You can't go wrong with the tempura *goma seiro soba* (al dente noodles served cold with sesame dipping sauce). Dine alfresco or indoors where you can watch noodles being hand-made. From Yuiga-hama Station (on the Enoden line) head towards the beach and then take the first right. Look for the blue sign; the entrance is just to the left.

Bonzo Soba ¥¥
(📞73-7315; http://bonzokamakura.com; 3-17-33 Zaimokuza; dishes ¥300-1700; ⏰11.30am-3pm & 6-9pm, closed Thu; 📶) Intimate and suave Michelin-star restaurant that specialises in handmade *ju-wari* (100% soba), including *kamo seiro* (cold soba in hot broth) with wild duck imported from France. The homemade sesame tofu is incredibly creamy and not to be missed. Catch bus 12, 40 or 41 to Kuhonj.

ℹ️ Information

For information about Kamakura, see www.city.kamakura.kana gawa.jp/english.
Kamakura Post Office (郵便局; 📞22-1200; 1-10-3 Komachi; ⏰9am-7pm Mon-Fri, to 3pm Sat) Has ATMs inside.
Kamakura Welcome Guides (www1.kamakuranet.ne.jp/kwga) Offers half-day tours on Fridays with volunteer guides in English for a nominal fee; five days' notice is required.

Tourist Information Center (鎌倉市観光協会観光総合案内所; 📞22-3350; ⏰9am-5.30pm Apr-Sep, to 5pm Oct-Mar) Just outside the east exit of Kamakura Station, the English-speaking staff are helpful and can book accommodation. Pick up a guide to Kamakura's temples (¥1575), as well as free brochures and maps for the area.

ℹ️ Getting There & Away

JR Yokosuka-line trains run to Kamakura from Tokyo (¥890, 56 minutes) and Shinagawa (¥690, 46 minutes), via Yokohama (¥330, 27 minutes). Alternatively, the Shōnan Shinjuku line runs from the west side of Tokyo (Shibuya, Shinjuku and Ikebukuro, all ¥890) in about one hour, though some trains require a transfer at Ōfuna, one stop before Kita-Kamakura. The last train from Kamakura back to Tokyo Station is 11.28pm and Shinjuku 9.15pm.

JR Kamakura-Enoshima Free Pass (from Tokyo/Yokohama ¥1970/1130) Valid for two days; covers the trip to and from Tokyo/Yokohama and unlimited use of JR trains around Kamakura, the Shōnan monorail between Ōfuna and Enoshima, and the Enoden Enoshima line.

Odakyū Enoshima/Kamakura Free Pass (from Shinjuku/Machida ¥1430/990) Valid for one day; includes transport to Fujisawa Station (where it meets the Enoden Enoshima line), plus use of the Enoden.

ℹ️ Getting Around

You can walk to most temples and shrines from Kamakura or Kita-Kamakura Stations. Sites in the west, like the Daibutsu, can be reached via the Enoden line from Kamakura Station to Hase (¥190) or by bus from Kamakura Station stops 1 and 6. **Kamakura Rent-a-Cycle** (レンタサイクル; per hour/day ¥600/1600; ⏰8.30am-5pm) is outside the east exit of Kamakura Station, and right up the incline.

Central Honshū

Central Honshū is the place for hot springs, hiking and history. The main island of Japan is neatly bisected by the Japan Alps, which form the rocky spine of the country. The northern end of the Alps, between Kamikōchi and Tateyama, is the most popular area in Japan for hiking and mountain climbing in the summer months. The cities of Matsumoto and Takayama serve as gateways to the Japan Alps and each is a worthy destination in its own right: Takayama has a wonderfully preserved historical district and Matsumoto is home to a lovely castle.

To the west, on the Japan Sea coast, you'll find Kanazawa, a sort of miniature version of Kyoto that is packed with temples, museums and traditional houses.

Cental Honshū can easily be visited en route from Tokyo to Kyoto, or vice versa, and a stop at one of the area's fine onsen (hot springs) is the perfect way to recover from travel fatigue.

Hiking in the Japan Alps

Cable car, Tateyama (p180)

Central Honshū

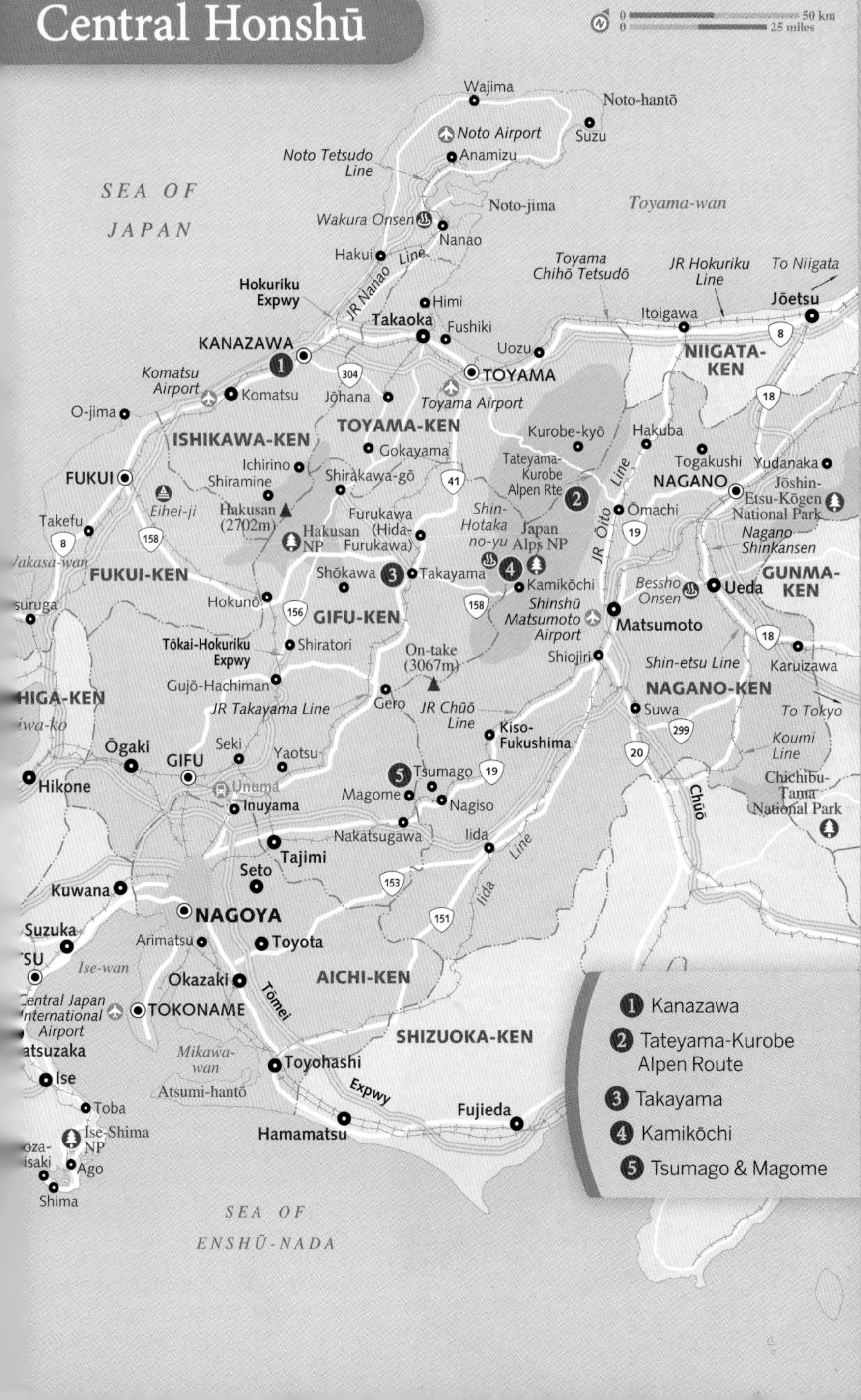

0 _____ 50 km
0 _____ 25 miles

SEA OF JAPAN

Wajima
Noto-hantō
Noto Airport
Anamizu
Suzu

Noto Tetsudo Line

Toyama-wan

Wakura Onsen
Noto-jima
Nanao

Hakui
JR Nanao Line
Toyama Chihō Tetsudō

Hokuriku Expwy

Himi
Takaoka
Fushiki
Uozu
Itoigawa
JR Hokuriku Line
To Niigata
Jōetsu

KANAZAWA
JR Hokuriku Line

❶

TOYAMA

NIIGATA-KEN

Komatsu Airport
Komatsu
Jōhana
Toyama Airport
Kurobe-kyō
Hakuba

ISHIKAWA-KEN

O-jima

Ichirino
Shiramine
TOYAMA-KEN
Gokayama
Shirakawa-gō
Tateyama-Kurobe Alpen Rte
Togakushi
Yudanaka

FUKUI

Eihei-ji
Hakusan (2702m)
Furukawa
Shin-Hotaka no-yu
Japan Alps NP
Ōmachi
NAGANO
Jōshin-Etsu-Kōgen National Park

Takefu
Hakusan (Hida-Furukawa) NP
❷
JR Ōito Line
Nagano Shinkansen

8

Wakasa-wan

Hokunō
Shōkawa
❸ Takayama
Kamikōchi
GIFU-KEN
Bessho Onsen
Ueda
GUNMA-KEN

FUKUI-KEN

❹
Shinshū Matsumoto Airport
Matsumoto

156

SHIGA-KEN
Tōkai-Hokuriku Expwy
Shiratori
On-take (3067m)
Shiojiri
Karuizawa

Biwa-ko

Gujō-Hachiman
Gero
Suwa
Shin-etsu Line
18

Ōgaki
JR Takayama Line
JR Chūō Line
Kiso-Fukushima
NAGANO-KEN
To Tokyo

Hikone
GIFU
Seki
Yaotsu
❺ Tsumago
299
Koumi Line

Inuyama
Unuma
Magome
Nagiso
20
Chūō
Chichibu-Tama National Park

Kuwana
Nakatsugawa
Iida

Tajimi
Seto
Iida Line

Arimatsu
NAGOYA
153

Suzuka
Toyota

Okazaki
151
AICHI-KEN

TSU
Ise-wan

Central Japan International Airport
TOKONAME
SHIZUOKA-KEN

Matsuzaka
Mikawa-wan
Toyohashi
Fujieda

Ise
Atsumi-hantō
Tomei Expwy

Toba
Hamamatsu

Ise-Shima NP
Ago
Shima
Daiō-zaki

SEA OF ENSHŪ-NADA

❶ Kanazawa
❷ Tateyama-Kurobe Alpen Route
❸ Takayama
❹ Kamikōchi
❺ Tsumago & Magome

Central Honshū Highlights

Kanazawa

Sometimes called 'Little Kyoto', Kanazawa (p181) is a small city packed with worthwhile attractions. It's got one of Japan's best gardens, attractive traditional streetscapes, some fine temples and a handful of museums. Located in Ishikawa-ken with regular express train services to Kyoto, Kanazawa is a nice addition to the usual Kyoto–Tokyo itinerary. It can also be easily paired with excursions to Noto-hantō, the Japan Alps and Takayama. Geisha houses

Tateyama-Kurobe Alpen Route

A testament to Japanese engineering skills, the Tateyama-Kurobe Alpen Rou (p180) is a series of lifts, buses and tro leys that works its way up and over (ar sometimes through) the Northern Jap Alps. For those who want to get among the peaks without breaking a sweat, th is the way to go. The eastern and weste gateways to the route are Matsumoto a Toyama, respectively. Kurobe-dam

TAKASHI TSUJINAKA / GETTY IMAGES ©

Takayama

3

In view of the Japan Alps and rich in history, the city of Takayama (p152) makes the perfect side trip between Tokyo and Kyoto. It's just a bit over two hours north of Nagoya by direct express, but it feels worlds away. The wonderfully preserved Sanmachi-suji (p153) district has some incredible old merchants' houses and nearby Hida-no-Sato (p156) has a collection of thatched-roof houses brought from across the region. Traditional house, Hida-no-Sato

4

Kamikōchi

A pristine sanctuary surrounded by high mountains walls, Kamikōchi (p161) is arguably the most scenic spot in the entire Japan Alps. With several lodges and hotels scattered along the banks of the crystal-clear Azusa-gawa, it makes a great base for hiking. You can choose from gentle day hikes along the mostly flat river valley, or set off for multiday treks among the high peaks. Footbridge over the Azusa-gawa

5

Tsumago & Magome

If you crave a taste of old Japan and some excellent natural scenery, the walk from Magome (p176) to Tsumago (p178) is sure to please. These two preserved towns on the old Nakasendō route, which connected Tokyo (then known as Edo) and Kyoto, via the Japan Alps, are about as picturesque as Japan gets. This is a great way to enjoy some traditional scenery while giving the legs a good workout. Tsumago

Central Honshū's Best...

Hiking Areas

○ **Kamikōchi** An alpine sanctuary with comfortable lodges and fantastic hiking. (p161)

○ **Shin-hotaka Onsen** Take the ropeway (tramway) to the ridge and keep on climbing. (p163)

○ **Tateyama-Murodō Plateau** Take the Alpen Route to this plateau high in the Alps and set out on an adventure. (p163)

○ **Kiso Valley Region** Hike from Tsumago to Magome along the old Nakasendō way. (p176)

Onsen (Hot Springs)

○ **Shin-hotaka Onsen** This riverside onsen is one of Japan's most scenic. Ryokan (traditional Japanese inns) nearby have great private baths. (p163)

○ **Takama-ga-hara Onsen** You'll have to walk for two or three days to find this hidden onsen south of the Murodō-daira. (p161)

○ **Utsukushi-ga-hara Onsen** Spend an evening soaking at this quaint onsen in Matsumoto. (p174)

○ **Kayōtei** Simply put: one of the best onsen ryokan in Japan. (p191)

Overnight Getaways

○ **Takayama** From Nagoya, take an express train to this fine old town on the doorstep of the Japan Alps. (p152)

○ **Kanazawa** This culture-rich city on the Sea of Japan is just an express train ride from Kyoto. (p181)

○ **Matsumoto** At the foot of the Japan Alps, this castle town is easily reached by train from either Tokyo or Nagoya. (p172)

○ **Yarimikan** An easy journey from Takayama brings you to this magical riverside onsen ryokan. (p164)

Need to Know

Experiences

○ **Kenroku-en** The Japanese consider this one of the finest gardens in their land. (p185)

○ **Yuki-no-Ōtani** It's like walking through the middle of a glacier. (163)

○ **Azusa-gawa** The crystal-clear waters of this stream in Kamikōchi might remind you of New Zealand. (p161)

○ **Takayama Matsuri** Central Honshū's best festival features awesome parade floats. (p153)

ADVANCE PLANNING

○ **Three months before** Get in shape if you plan to do serious hiking or climbing in the Japan Alps.

○ **Three months before** Make accommodation bookings early if you plan to stay in or near the Japan Alps during foliage season (October in most of the Japan Alps).

○ **One month before** Get an international driver's licence if you plan to explore Central Honshū by car (which is a good way to cover a lot of ground in this area).

○ **One week before** Check snow conditions if you are hiking early or late in the Japan Alps hiking season (this means any time before early June or after 1 October).

GETTING AROUND

○ **Walk** Around Takayama, Kanazawa and the Japan Alps.

○ **Tateyama-Kurobe Alpen Route** Across the Japan Alps.

○ **Train or bus** Between cities and towns.

○ **Rent a car** Around Central Honshū if you want more freedom than trains or buses allow.

BE FOREWARNED

○ **Winter (December to March)** Can be very cold in Central Honshū, particularly in the mountains. Hiking is not possible at higher elevations between late October and late May (unless you are an experienced winter mountaineer).

○ **Conditions** Can change quickly in the Japan Alps, even during the normal hiking months of July and August.

○ **Japan Alps** Can be very crowded on summer weekends, particularly in the mid-August O-Bon holiday period.

ild monkeys, often spotted in Kamikōchi (p161);
Above: Tateyama-Kurobe Alpen Route (p180)

Central Honshū Itineraries

By adding the traditional attractions of Takayama or Kanazawa and the scenic wonders of the Japan Alps to your standard Tokyo–Kyoto itinerary, your Japan trip is set to gain a lot of depth and variety.

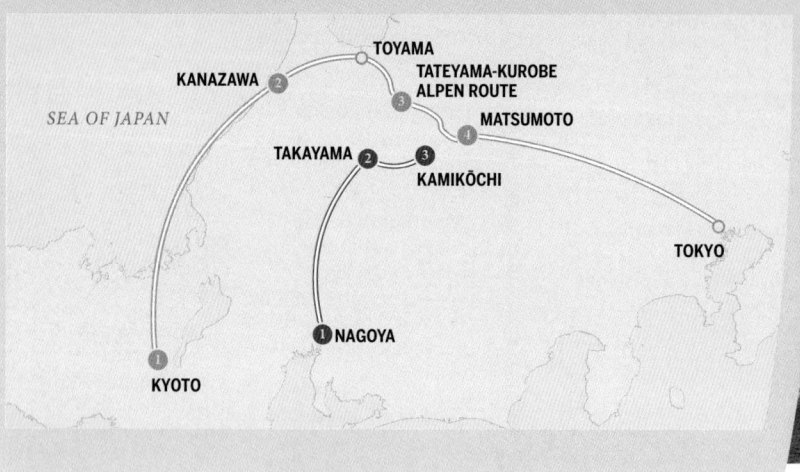

3 DAYS

TOKYO TO KYOTO VIA THE JAPAN ALPS
Takayama & The Japan Alps

If you've only got limited time in Japan but would like to see a little bit more than just Tokyo and Kyoto, this jaunt is the perfect add-on. A bit over two hours north of Nagoya, which is on the Tōkaidō *shinkansen* (bullet train) line that runs between Tokyo and Kyoto, Takayama is the perfect place to base yourself for this itinerary. Takayama is a historical city with a well-preserved traditional district and a variety of foreigner-friendly ryokan and restaurants. It also serves as the gateway to the Northern Japan Alps.

Take a *shinkansen* from Kyoto or Tokyo to ❶**Nagoya** and switch to an express train north to ❷**Takayama** (p152). Spend your first day exploring Takayama itself. Check out the traditional wooden houses in the Sanmachi-suji area, walk over to the Takayama Yatai Kaikan, which houses the festival floats used in the Takayama Matsuri, and take a bus, taxi or bicycle over to Hida-no-Sato, a collection of thatched-roof houses from the region. Then, take the bus (actually, two buses) to ❸**Kamikōchi** (p161), do some hiking, spend the night and then make your way back to Kyoto or Tokyo via Takayama (or Matsumoto). Note that it's also possible to get to Kanazawa by bus or train from Takayama, and then continue south to Kyoto by train.

5 DAYS

KYOTO TO TOKYO VIA TATEYAMA

Kanazawa & the Alpen Route

If you start in Tokyo and travel to Kyoto by *shinkansen*, this itinerary allows you to return to Tokyo without retracing your steps. This is a good trip for hikers and you should budget a night or two up in the mountains (in a mountain lodge or tent) to enjoy the brilliant hiking of the Northern Japan Alps. Note that this route is only possible from mid-April to mid-November (and sometimes the route opens later and closes earlier due to snowfall).

Start in ❶**Kyoto** (p193), where you can catch a direct express train to ❷**Kanazawa** (p181). Spend a day in Kanazawa enjoying Kenroku-en and the city's temples. Then,

take an express train to Toyama and switch to local trains for the journey to the western terminus of the ❸**Tateyama-Kurobe Alpen Route** (p180), which will bring you by a funicular and bus to the Murodō-daira. Consider spending a night here in one of the hiking lodges, which will allow you to do some hiking – maybe you can bag the 3015m peak of Tateyama. Then, continue east along the Alpen Route to the JR Oito line, which will bring you to the city of ❹**Matsumoto** (p172), where you can catch an express train to Tokyo.

Matsumoto-jō (p172), Matsumoto
NORBERTO CUENCA / GETTY IMAGES ©

151

Discover
Central Honshū

At a Glance

○ **Takayama** The gateway to the Japan Alps, Takayama contains a lovely preserved traditional centre.

○ **Northern Japan Alps** (p160) The rooftop of Japan draws skiers and hikers from all over the world.

○ **Matsumoto** (p172) This ancient castle town is one of central Japan's most worthwhile destinations.

○ **Kanazawa** (p181) One of Japan's most culturally rich cities and home to Kenroku-en, one of Japan's best gardens.

Sakurayama Hachiman-gū, Takayama
FRÃ©DÃ©RIC SOREAU / GETTY IMAGES ©

HIDA DISTRICT
飛騨地域

Takayama 高山

☎0577 / POP 92,750

A working city that has retained its traditional charm, Takayama boasts one of Japan's most atmospheric townscapes and best-loved festivals. Its present layout dates from the late 17th century and includes a wealth of museums, galleries and temples for a city of this size.

Takayama should be considered a high priority on any visit to Central Honshū. Meiji-era inns, hillside shrines and temples and a pretty riverside setting beckon you. Excellent infrastructure and friendly, welcoming locals seal the deal. Give yourself two or three days to enjoy it all, if you can. Takayama is easily explored on foot or by bicycle and is the perfect start or end point for trips into Hida and the Northern Japan Alps.

Almost all of the main sights are clearly signposted in English and within walking distance of the station, which sits between the main streets of Kokubunji-dōri and Hirokōji-dōri. Both run east and cross the Miya-gawa (river) where they become Yasugawa-dōri and Sanmachi-dōri, respectively. Once across the river (about 10 minutes' walk), you're in the middle of the infinitely photogenic Sanmachi-suji (district) of sake breweries, cafes, retailers and immaculately preserved old private houses (古い町並み; *furui machinami*).

◎ Sights & Activities

Sanmachi-suji Neighbourhood

(三町筋) This original district of three main streets (Ichino-machi, Nino-machi and Sanno-machi) of merchants has been immaculately preserved. Sake breweries are designated by spheres of cedar fronds hanging above their doors; some open to the public in January and early February, but year-round, most just sell their brews. Day or night, photographic opportunities abound.

Fujii Folk Museum Museum

(藤井美術民芸館; Fujii Bijutsu Mingeikan; 69 Kamisanno-machi; adult/child ¥700/350; ⊙9am-5pm, often closed Tue-Fri early Dec-early Mar) A private collection in an old merchant's house, with folk craft and ceramics from the Muromachi and Edo periods.

Hida Folk Archaeological Museum Museum

(飛騨民族考古館; Hida Minzoku Kōkō-kan; 82 Kamisanno-machi; adult/child ¥500/200; ⊙7am-5pm Mar-Nov, 9.30am-4pm Nov-Feb) A former samurai house boasting interesting secret passageways and an old well in the courtyard.

Yoshijima Heritage House Historic Building

(吉島家; Yoshijima-ke; 1-51 Ōjin-machi; adult/child ¥500/300; ⊙9am-5pm Mar-Nov, to 4.30pm Wed-Sun Dec-Feb) Design buffs shouldn't miss Yoshijima-ke, which is well covered in architectural publications. Its lack of ornamentation allows you to focus on the spare lines, soaring roof and skylight. Admission includes a cup of delicious shiitake tea, which you can also purchase for ¥600 per can.

Takayama-jinya Historic Building

(高山陣屋; ☎32-0643; 1-5 Hachiken-machi; adult/child ¥420/free; ⊙8.45am-4.30pm, to 5pm Aug) These sprawling grounds south of Sanmachi-suji house the only remaining prefectural office building of the Tokugawa shōgunate, originally the administrative centre for the Kanamori clan. The present main building dates back to 1816 and was used as local government offices until

Takayama Matsuri

One of Japan's great festivals, the Takayama Matsuri is in two parts. On 14 and 15 April is the Sannō Matsuri; a dozen *yatai* (floats), decorated with carvings, dolls, colourful curtains and blinds, are paraded through the town. In the evening the floats are decked out with lanterns and the procession is accompanied by sacred music. Hachiman Matsuri, on 9 and 10 October, is a slightly smaller version. Book accommodation months in advance.

1969. There's also a rice granary, garden and a torture chamber with explanatory detail. Free guided tours in English are available (reservations advised).

Kusakabe Folk Crafts Museum Museum

(日下部民藝館; Kusakabe Mingeikan; 1-52 Ōjin-machi; adult/child ¥500/300; ⊙9am-4.30pm Mar-Nov, to 4pm Wed-Mon Dec-Feb) This building dating from the 1890s showcases the striking craftsmanship of traditional Takayama carpenters. Inside is a collection of folk art.

Takayama Festival Floats Exhibition Hall Museum

(高山屋台会館; Takayama Yatai-kaikan; 178 Sakura-machi; adult/child ¥820/410; ⊙8.30am-5pm Mar-Nov, 9am-4.30pm Dec-Feb) A rotating selection of four of the 23 multitiered *yatai* (floats) used in the Takayama Matsuri can be appreciated here. These spectacular creations, some dating from the 17th century, are prized for their flamboyant carvings, metalwork and lacquerwork. Some floats feature *karakuri ningyō* (marionettes) that perform amazing feats courtesy of eight accomplished puppeteers manipulating 36 strings. The museum is on the grounds of the stately **Sakurayama Hachiman-gū** (shrine), which presides over the festival and is dedicated to the protection of Takayama.

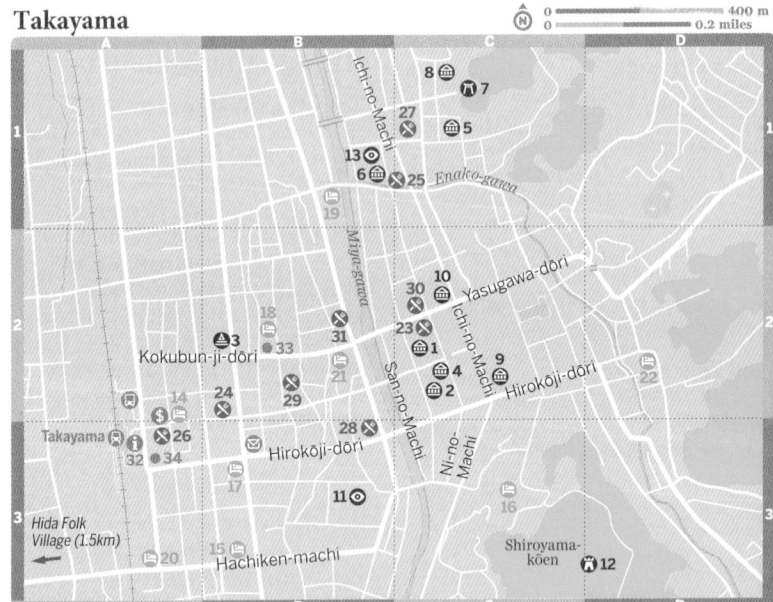

Takayama

Karakuri Museum   Museum

((飛騨高山獅子会館)からくりミュージアム; ☎32-0881; 53-1 Sakura-machi; adult/child ¥600/400; ⏰9am-4.30pm) On display are over 800 *shishi* (lion) masks, instruments and drums related to festival dances. The main draws are the twice-hourly puppet shows where you can see the mechanical *karakuri ningyō* in action.

Hida Kokubun-ji   Buddhist Temple

(飛騨国分寺; 1-83 Sōwa-chō; treasure hall adult/child ¥300/250; ⏰9am-4pm) The original buildings of this, Takayama's oldest temple, were constructed in the 8th century, but later destroyed by fire. The oldest of the present buildings dates from the 16th century. The temple's treasure hall houses some Important Cultural Properties, and the courtyard boasts a three-storey pagoda and an impressively gnarled gingko tree believed to be 1200 years old.

Takayama Shōwa-kan   Museum

(高山昭和館; 6 Shimoichino-machi; adult/child ¥500/300; ⏰9am-5pm) We love this nostalgia bonanza from the Shōwa era

(1926–1989), concentrating on the period between 1955 and 1965, a time of great optimism between Japan's postwar malaise and pre-Titan boom. Lose yourself among the delightful mishmash of endless objects, from movie posters to cars and everything between, haphazardly arranged in a series of themed rooms.

Teramachi & Shiroyama-kōen   Neighbourhood

(寺町・城山公園) These lovely, hilly districts to the east are linked by a well-signposted walking path. Teramachi has over a dozen temples and shrines you can wander around before taking in the greenery of Shiroyama-kōen. Various trails lead through the park and up the mountainside to the ruins of the castle, **Takayama-jō** (高山城跡; Shiroyama-kōen).

Takayama Museum of History & Art   Museum

(飛騨高山まちの博物館; Hida-Takayama Machi no Hakubutsukan; ☎32-1205; 75 Kamiichino-machi; ⏰museum 9am-7pm, garden 7am-9pm) **FREE** Not to be confused with the Hida Takayama Museum of Art, this free

Takayama

⊙ Sights

1	Fujii Folk Museum	C2
2	Hida Folk Archaeological Museum	C2
3	Hida Kokubun-ji	B2
4	Hirata Folk Art Museum	C2
5	Karakuri Museum	C1
6	Kusakabe Folk Crafts Museum	B1
7	Sakurayama Hachiman-gū	C1
8	Takayama Festival Floats Exhibition Hall	C1
9	Takayama Museum of History & Art	C2
10	Takayama Shōwa-kan	C2
11	Takayama-jinya	B3
12	Takayama-jō	D3
13	Yoshijima Heritage House	B1

⊜ Sleeping

14	Best Western Hotel	A2
15	Hida Takayama Temple Inn Zenkō-ji	B3
16	Hōshōkaku	C3
17	K's House Takayama	B3
18	Rickshaw Inn	B2
	Spa Hotel Alpina	(see 17)
19	Sumiyoshi Ryokan	B1
20	Takayama Ouan	A3
21	Tanabe Ryokan	B2
22	Yamakyū	D2

⊗ Eating

23	Ebisu-Honten	C2
24	Kotarō	B2
25	Kyōya	C1
26	Myōgaya	A3
27	Rakuda	C1
28	Restaurant Le Midi	B3
29	Suzuya	B2
30	Takumi-ya	C2
31	Tenaga Ashinaga	B2

ⓘ Information

32	Tourist Information Office	A3

ⓘ Transport

33	Hara Cycle	B2
34	Toyota Rent-a-Car	A3

museum is situated around pretty gardens and features 14 themed exhibition rooms relating to local history, culture, literature and the arts.

Hirata Folk Art Museum   Museum

(平田記念館; Hirata Kinenkan; ☎33-1354; 39 Kaminino-machi; ☺9am-5pm) Hirata Folk Art Museum dates from the turn of the 20th century and displays items from everyday rural Japanese life.

 **Sleeping**

One of Takayama's pleasures is its variety of high-quality accommodation, both Japanese and Western, for all budgets. If visiting during festival times, book accommodation months in advance and expect to pay a 20% premium. The Ryokan Hotel Association can further assist with lodging enquiries: www.takayamaryokan.jp/english.

Hida Takayama Temple Inn Zenkō-ji   Hostel ¥

飛騨高山善光寺宿坊; ☎32-8470; www.takayamahostelzenkoji.com; 4-3 Tenman-chō;

dm/s per person ¥2500/3000; **P**🚭🛜) Good karma washes over this branch of Nagano's famous Zenkō-ji (temple), where donations are accepted in return for accommodation. Private rooms are generously proportioned around a courtyard garden. Even the dorms have temple charm. There's a shared kitchen and no curfew for respectful guests.

K's House Takayama   Hostel ¥

(☎34-4410; www.kshouse.jp/takayama-e; 4-45-1 Tenman-cho; dm/s/d/tr per person from ¥2800/4500/3900/3600; 🛜) Opened in October 2012, this sparkly hostel is likely to cause a stir on the Takayama hostel scene. All rooms, including dorms, have private bathroom, TV and wi-fi. There's a kitchen and common area, and bicycle rentals are available.

Rickshaw Inn   Hotel ¥

(力車イン; ☎32-2890; www.rickshawinn.com; 54 Suehiro-chō; s without bathroom from ¥4900, tw with/without bathroom from ¥11,900/10,200; 🚭@) Well positioned on the fringe of Takayama's entertainment district, this travellers' favourite is great value. There's

155

PETER OSHKAI / GETTY IMAGES ©

Don't Miss
Hida Folk Village

The sprawling, open-air Hida-no-Sato is a highly recommended half-day trip. It features dozens of traditional houses and buildings which were dismantled at their original sites throughout the region and rebuilt here. Well-presented displays offer the opportunity to envision rural life in previous centuries. During clear weather, there are good views of the Japan Alps. To get here, hire a bicycle, or catch a bus from Takayama bus station (¥200, 10 minutes). The *Hida-no-Sato setto ken* ticket combines return fare and admission to the park for ¥900. Be sure to check return times for the bus.

NEED TO KNOW

飛騨の里; Hida-no-sato; www.hidanosato-tpo.jp/english12; 1-590 Kamiokamoto-chō; adult/child ¥700/200; ⊗8.30am-5pm

a range of room types, a small kitchen, laundry facilities and a cosy lounge. Friendly English-speaking owners are founts of information about Takayama.

Yamakyū   Ryokan ¥¥
(山久; ☎32-3756; www.takayama-yamakyu.com; 58 Tenshōji-machi; r without bathroom with/without meals ¥7980/5880; ℙ@⏺) Occupying a lovely hillside spot opposite Hokke-ji, Yamakyū is a 20-minute walk from the station. Inside, antique-filled curio

cabinets, clocks and lamps line the red-carpeted corridors. All 20 tatami rooms (wooden floor matted room) have a sink and toilet and the common baths are of a high standard. Some English is spoken. This is an excellent choice for a ryokan experience without the expense.

Takayama Ouan   Hotel ¥¥
(高山桜庵; ☎37-2230; www.hotespa.net/ hotels/takayama; 4-126 Hanasato; s/d from ¥9000/20,000; ℙ@) Although the popu-

larity of this hulking recent addition to the Takayama hotel scene is evident in wear and tear, we love how East meets West and new meets old here. Reasonable rates are appropriate for well-proportioned Western style rooms with big comfortable beds and traditional design elements; dark woods, tatami and moody lighting set the scene. The rooftop *rotemburo* (outdoor baths), including free private *kazoku-buro* (family baths) will make your friends jealous. There's a lot of tatami, so you'll be leaving your shoes in a locked box in the lobby. As you leave the station, look to your right – it's the tallest building in sight.

Tanabe Ryokan
Ryokan ¥¥

(旅館田邊; ☎ 32-0529; www.tanabe-ryokan.jp; 58 Aioi-chō; r per person with 2 meals from ¥12,600; ☺ @) This elegant, atmospheric inn has a premium, central location and friendly, welcoming staff who speak some English. Tatami rooms are stylish and spacious – each has an en suite bath, although the lovely common baths with their beamed ceilings are worth enjoying. A sumptuous dinner of Hida *kaiseki* (Japanese haute cuisine) completes the experience.

Sumiyoshi Ryokan
Ryokan ¥¥

(寿美吉旅館; ☎ 32-0228; www.sumiyoshi-ryokan.com; 4-21 Hon-machi; r per person with/without meals from ¥10,500/6300; P @) The kind owners of this delightfully antique-y inn, set in a Meiji-era merchant's house, have been welcoming guests from abroad for years. Some rooms have river views through panes of antique glass, and the common baths are made of wood and slate tiles. One room has a private bath.

Spa Hotel Alpina
Hotel ¥¥

(スパホテルアルピナ; ☎ 33-0033; www.spa-hotel-alpina.com; 5-41 Nada-cho; s/tw from ¥7200/13,000; P ☺ @) This glorified business hotel has a slightly clinical feel for a 'spa hotel', but offers comfortable beds, bright rooms and a fantastic rooftop onsen with views across the city. Discounted rates can be secured online.

Best Western Hotel
Hotel ¥¥

(ベストウェスタンホテル高山; ☎ 37-2000; www.bestwestern.co.jp; 6-6 Hanasato-machi; s/d/tw from ¥7000/11,000/13,000; ☺ 🛜) Popular with overseas guests, this tourist hotel's refurbished rooms have a splash

Gasshō-zukuri Architecture

Hida winters are unforgiving. Inhabitants braved the elements long before the advent of propane heaters and 4WD vehicles. The most visible symbol of their adaptability is *gasshō-zukuri* architecture; steeply slanted straw-roofed homes that dot the regional landscape.

Sharply angled roofs prevent snow accumulation, a serious concern in an area where most mountain roads close from December to April. The name *gasshō* comes from the Japanese word for prayer, because the shape of the roofs was thought to resemble hands clasped together. *Gasshō* buildings often featured pillars crafted from stout cedars to lend extra support. The attic areas were ideal for silk cultivation. Larger *gasshō-zukuri* buildings were inhabited by wealthy families, with up to 30 people under one roof. Peasant families lived in huts so small that today they'd only be considered fit for tool sheds.

The art of *gasshō-zukuri* construction is dying out. Most remaining examples have been relocated to folk villages, including Hida-no-Sato, Ogimachi, Suganuma and Ainokura. Homes that are now neighbours may once have been separated by several days of travel on foot or sled. These cultural preservation efforts have made it possible to imagine a bygone life in the Hida hills.

If You Like…
Takayama

If you like Takayama we think you'll like these other less-visited but wonderful Central Honshū destinations:

1 INUYAMA
About 30 minutes northwest of Nagoya by train (Meitetsu Inuyama line, ¥540, 30 minutes), this castle town has some quaint streets and nearby rivers.

2 HIDA-FURUKAWA
About 15 minutes north of Takayama by train (JR line, ¥230, 15 minutes) this town has some fine carp-filled canals lined by old *kura* (storehouses).

3 BESSHO ONSEN
With some fine temples, this mountain hot-spring resort makes a relaxing getaway. Take the Nagano *shinkansen* (bullet train) to Ueda, then the Ueda Dentetsu line to Bessho Onsen.

of colour. Good-value rates can be found online and usually include the decent breakfast buffet.

Hōshōkaku Ryokan ¥¥¥
(宝生閣; ☎34-0700; www.hoshokaku.co.jp; 1-88 Baba-machi; r per person with 2 meals from ¥15,750; P) Surrounded by the greenery of Shiroyama-kōen park, this upscale hillside ryokan on the edge of town has outdoor hot springs with city views and sumptuous *kaiseki* cuisine. It's easiest to grab a taxi when you arrive.

Eating

Takayama's specialities include *soba* (buckwheat noodles), *hoba-miso* (sweet miso paste grilled at the table on a magnolia leaf), *sansai* (mountain vegetables) and *Hida-gyū* (Hida beef). Street foods include *mitarashi-dango* (skewers of grilled riceballs seasoned with soy sauce) and *shio-sembei* (salty rice crackers). *Hida-gyū* turns up on *kushiyaki* (skewers),

in *korokke* (croquettes) and *niku-man* (steamed buns). If you're on a budget, keep an eye out for the numerous bakeries around town where you can stock up on delicious, inexpensive fresh breads and sandwiches.

Rakuda Cafe ¥
(らくだ; ☎34-5574; 1-94 Ōjin-machi; lunch from ¥850; ◷10am-6pm Wed-Mon; 🖥) As laid-back as its namesake ('camel'), comfy and sunny Rakuda has curry lunches, open sandwiches topped with omelette and veggies, and daily homemade cakes. It's in a small square beside a mini parking lot.

Ebisu-Honten Noodles ¥
(恵比寿本店; ☎32-0209; 46 Kami-Ni-no-machi; soba dishes ¥830-1530; ◷10am-5pm Thu-Tue; 🍴) This Sanmachi shop has been making *teuchi* (handmade) *soba* since 1898. The menu explains the *soba*-making process. Try cold *zaru soba* (¥830) for the real flavour of the buckwheat, or delicious tempura *soba* (¥1350). It has an interesting red-glass sign with white characters and a little roof on it.

Kotarō Tonkatsu ¥¥
(小太郎; ☎32-7353; 6-1 Tenmanmachi; meals ¥1050-2100; ◷11.30am-2pm & 5pm-9pm Thu-Tue; 🖥) Expect satisfaction from this compact workmanlike eatery the chef of which has spent over 25 years mastering the art of *tonkatsu* (deep-fried pork cutlets) and other fried goodies. Generous *teishoku* (set menu; from ¥1050) feature crispy, crunchy katsu, cooked to perfection, accompanied by perfectly balanced sides; fluffy rice, rich miso soup, fruit, salad and pickles. Try the cheese katsu (¥1350) for something different.

Kyōya Shokudō ¥¥
(京や; ☎34-7660; 1-77 Ōjin-machi; mains ¥600-5000; ◷11am-10pm Wed-Mon; 🖥) This traditional eatery specialises in regional dishes such as *hoba-miso* and *Hida-gyū soba*. Seating is on tatami mats around long charcoal grills, under a cathedral ceiling. It's on a corner, by a bridge over the canal. Look for the sacks of rice over the door.

Suzuya
Shokudō ¥¥

(寿々や; ☎ 32-2484; 24 Hanakawa-chō; sets ¥1155-4200; ⏰ 11am-3pm & 5-9pm Wed-Mon; 🍴 🅿) In the centre of town, Suzuya is one of Takayama's long-standing favourites, serving local specialities such as *Hida-gyū*, *hoba-miso* and various stews. There's plenty of signage to direct you.

Takumi-ya
Beef ¥¥

(匠家; ☎ 36-2989; 2 Shimo-Ni-no-Machi; mains downstairs ¥680-980, upstairs from ¥1500; ⏰ 11am-3pm & 5-9pm Thu-Tue; 🅿) Hida beef on a burger budget. Adjacent to Takumi-ya's butcher shop is a casual restaurant specialising in *rāmen* (egg noodles) in Hida-beef broth and Hida *gyū-don* (beef and onion over rice). The pricier upstairs restaurant serves *yakiniku* (Korean-style barbecue).

Myōgaya
Vegan ¥¥

(茗荷舎; ☎ 32-0426; 5-15 Hanasato-chō; mains around ¥1000; ⏰ lunch Wed-Sun; 🍴 🅿) Healthy and delicious go hand in hand at this cosy vegan eatery. Look for tasty veggie curry with brown rice, samosas, juices and dandelion tea. Reservations requested on Saturdays.

Tenaga Ashinaga
Shokudō ¥¥

(てながあしなが; ☎ 34-5855; 3-58-11 Honmachi; small plates from ¥180, meals ¥650-3450; ⏰ lunch & dinner; 🅿) If you're looking for a tasty, uncomplicated meal, this large, well-positioned eatery, near Kaji-bashi, is a good choice. A diverse English and Japanese photo menu has most of your favourites, such as *udon*, *rāmen* and *donburi* (rice bowls), as well as gristlier, meatier choices. The location attracts many foreign clientele whose smiling faces line the photo wall.

Restaurant Le Midi
French ¥¥¥

(☎ 36-6386; www.le-midi.jp/english; 2-85 Honmachi; appetisers ¥650-3400, hida beef dishes ¥2400-7500; ⏰ 11.30am-2pm & 6pm-9pm Fri-Wed; 🅿) One street back from the river, this upscale restaurant serves traditional French cuisine with a Japanese twist. Mouthwatering appetisers include Hida beef carpaccio and onion gratin soup. Lunch sets range from ¥1800 to 4800 and course dinners including hors d'oeuvres, mains, soup, salad and coffee start at ¥4800. For dessert, the local *sukune kabocha* (pumpkin) pudding is a must. If you're feeling French and fancy, you're unlikely to be disappointed.

Rickshaws, Takayama

Detour:
Shirakawa-gō

The Shirakawa-gō region's central settlement has some 600 residents and the largest concentration of *gasshō-zukuri* (p157) buildings – over 110. It's also the most accessible. Pick up a free English-language map at the **Tourist Information Office** (観光案内所; ☏6-1013; 2495-3 Ogimachi; ☺9am-5pm), by the main bus stop outside the Folk Village. Be sure to bring enough cash – there are no ATMs and credit cards are not accepted.

❶ Information

Jūroku Bank (十六銀行) Can change cash or travellers cheques. For the rest of us ATM users, **Takayama Post Office** (高山郵便局; ☏32-0540; 5-95-1 Nada-machi) A few blocks east of the station.

Tourist Information Office (飛騨高山観光案内所; ☏32-5328; www.hida.jp/english; ☺8.30am-5pm Nov-Mar, to 6.30pm Apr-Oct) Directly in front of JR Takayama Station, knowledgeable English-speaking staff dispense English-language maps and a wealth of pamphlets on sights, accommodation, special events and regional transit. Staff are unable to assist with accommodation reservations.

❶ Getting There & Away

From Tokyo or Kansai, the most efficient way to reach Takayama is via Nagoya on the JR Takayama line (Hida *tokkyū*, ¥5360, 2¼ hours); the mountainous train ride along the Hida-gawa is *gorge*-ous. Some trains continue on to Toyama (¥2770, 90 minutes), where you can connect to Kanazawa (¥2100, 40 minutes).

Nōhi Bus (濃飛バス; ☏32-1688; www.nouhibus.co.jp/english) Operates highway bus services between Takayama and Tokyo's Shinjuku station (¥6500, 5½ hours, several daily, reservations required) and Matsumoto (¥3100, 2½ hours). Takayama's bus station is adjacent to the train station. Schedules vary seasonally and some routes don't run at all during winter, when many roads are closed.

Toyota Rent-a-Car (トヨタレンタカー; ☏36-6110) Opposite the station, to the right.

❶ Getting Around

Most sights in Takayama can be covered easily on foot. You can amble from the train station to Teramachi in about 20 minutes. Takayama is bicycle friendly. Some lodgings lend bikes, or you can hire one from **Hara Cycle** (ハラサイクル; ☏32-1657; 61 Suehiro-cho; 1st hour ¥300, each additional hour ¥200, per day ¥1300; ☺9am-8pm Wed-Mon).

NORTHERN JAPAN ALPS　北日本アルプス

Boasting some of Japan's most dramatic scenery, the Northern Japan Alps of Gifu, Toyama and Nagano Prefectures contain stunning peaks above 3000m, accessible even to amateur hikers. Also called the Hida Ranges, the most spectacular scenery is protected within the 174,323-hectare Chūbu-Sangaku National Park (中部山岳国立公園). Highlights include hiking the valleys and peaks of Kamikōchi, doing it easy on the Shin-Hotaka Ropeway and soaking up the splendour of Hida's many mountain *rotemburo*. The northern part of the park extends to the Tateyama-Kurobe Alpen Route.

❶ Getting There & Around

Matsumoto and Takayama are the gateway cities into the peaks, while the main transit hubs when you're up there are Hirayu Onsen and Kamikōchi. Buses make the journey from Takayama. From Matsumoto, it's a ride on the private Matsumoto Dentetsu train to Shin-Shimashima, then a bus. Either way, the journey is breathtaking.

Hiring a car is a good option if windy roads don't bother you, and you're not overnighting in Kamikōchi – the road between Naka-no-yu and Kamikōchi is open only to buses and taxis.

Kamikōchi　上高地

0260

Some of Japan's most spectacular scenery is found here – majestic snowcapped peaks, bubbling crystal brooks, wild monkeys, wildflowers and ancient forests. That said, it wouldn't be Japan without the crowds. Timing is everything.

Kamikōchi is closed from 15 November to 22 April, and in peak times (late July to late August, and during the foliage season in October) can seem busier than Shinjuku Station – plan to arrive early in the day. June to July is rainy season. It's perfectly feasible to visit as a day trip but you'll miss out on the pleasures of staying in the mountains and taking uncrowded early-morning or late-afternoon walks.

Visitors arrive at Kamikōchi's sprawling bus station, surrounded by visitor facilities. A 10-minute walk along the Azusa-gawa takes you to *Kappa-bashi,* a bridge named after a legendary water sprite. Hiking trails begin here.

◉ Activities

ONSEN

Kamikōchi Onsen Hotel　Onsen
(www.kamikouchi-onsen-spa.com; admission ¥800; ⏰7-9am & 12.30-3pm) Open to non-hotel guests during limited off-hours, the baths here are a refreshing respite, especially on drizzly days.

Bokuden-no-yu　Onsen
(admission ¥700; ⏰noon-5pm) Not for the claustrophobic, the area's most unusual onsen – a tiny cave bath dripping with minerals – is found near the Naka-no-yu bus stop, right before the bus-only tunnel towards Kamikōchi proper. Pay at the small shop for the key to the little mountain hut housing the onsen. It's yours privately for up to 30 minutes.

Hiking & Climbing in Kamikōchi

The river valley offers mostly level, short-distance, signposted walks.

A four-hour round trip starts east of Kappa-bashi past Myōjin-bashi (one hour) to Tokusawa (another hour) before returning. By Myōjin-bashi, the idyllic Myōjin-ike (pond) marks the innermost shrine of Hotaka-jinja (admission ¥300). West of Kappa-bashi, you can amble alongside the river to Weston Relief (monument to Walter Weston; 15 minutes) or to Taishō-ike (40 minutes).

Other popular hikes include the mountain hut at Dakesawa (2½ hours up) and fiery Yakedake (four hours up, starting about 20 minutes west of the Weston Relief, at Hotaka-bashi). From the peaks, it's possible to see all the way to Mt Fuji in clear weather – it's a breathtaking view.

Numerous long-distance hikes vary in duration from a few days to a week. Japanese-language maps of the area show routes and average hiking times between huts, major peaks and landmarks. Favourite hikes and climbs (which can mean human traffic jams during peak seasons) include Yariga-take (3180m) and Hotaka-dake (3190m).

A steep but worthwhile hike connects Kamikōchi and Shin-Hotaka. From Kappa-bashi, the trail crosses the ridge below Nishi-Hotaka-dake (2909m) at Nishi-Hotaka San-sō (cottage; three hours) and continues to Nishi-Hotaka-guchi, the top station of the Shin-Hotaka Ropeway. The hike takes nearly four hours in this direction but is far easier in reverse. To reach the ropeway, take a bus from Takayama or Hirayu Onsen.

Sleeping & Eating

Accommodation in Kamikōchi is expensive and advance reservations are essential. Except for camping, rates quoted here include two meals. Some lodgings shut down power in the middle of the night (emergency lighting stays on).

Dotted along the trails and around the mountains are dozens of spartan *yama-goya* (mountain huts), which provide two meals and a futon from around ¥8000 per person; some also serve simple lunches. Enquire before setting out to make sure there's one on your intended route.

The bus station has a very limited range of eateries and retailers. Depending on your length of stay, bring essential munchies and take your rubbish with you.

Kamikōchi Gosenjaku Hotel and Lodge — Hotel ¥¥

(上高地五千尺ホテル・ロッヂ; [☎] hotel 95-2111, lodge 95-2221; www.gosenjaku.co.jp/english; 4468 Kamikōchi; lodge skier's bed per person ¥10,500, s/tw without bath ¥23,805/17,850, hotel per person d/tw from ¥28,000) By Kappa-bashi, this compact lodge recently expanded to include a small hotel. The lodge has 34 Japanese-style rooms and some 'skier's beds'; basically curtained-off bunks. Rooms all have sink and toilet, but baths are shared. The hotel is more upscale with a combination of comfortable Western and Japanese rooms, some with balconies.

Kamikōchi Nishiitoya San-sō — Inn ¥¥

(上高地西糸屋山荘; [☎] 95-2206; www.nishiitoya.com; 4469-1 Kamikōchi; dm from ¥8000, d per person from ¥10,500; [→][@][⚲]) This friendly lodge, west of Kappa-bashi, has a cosy lounge and dates from the early 20th century. Rooms are a mix of Japanese and Western styles, all with toilet. The shared bath is a large onsen facing the Hotaka mountains.

Tokusawa-en — Campground ¥¥

(徳澤園; [☎] 95-2508; www.tokusawaen.com/english; campsite/dm ¥500/9500, s-tw per person 13,900-15,900) A marvellously secluded place in a wooded dell about 7km northeast of Kappa-bashi. It's both a camping ground and a lodge, and has Japanese-style rooms (shared facilities) and hearty meals served in a dining hall. Access is by walking only, and takes about two hours.

Kamikōchi Imperial Hotel — Hotel ¥¥¥

(上高地帝国ホテル; [☎] 95-2001; www.imperialhotel.co.jp/j/kamikochi; Azumino Kamikochi; s/tw without meals from ¥29,400; [@]) Expect exceptional service and rustic, European Alps styled rooms in this historic red-gabled lodge, completed in 1933. Prices are elevated, but a wide range of stay plans are available and the hotel occasionally offers excellent packages including French haute cuisine.

Azusa-gawa, Kamikōchi (p161)

ℹ️ Information

Kamikōchi is entirely closed from 16 November to 22 April. Serious hikers should consider insurance (保険; *hoken*; from ¥1000 per day), available at Kamikōchi bus station.

Kamikōchi Information Centre (上高地インフォメーションセンター; ☎95-2433; ⊙8am-5pm) This invaluable resource at the bus station complex provides information on hiking and weather conditions and distributes the English-language *Kamikōchi Pocket Guide* with a map of the main walking tracks.

Kamikōchi Visitor Centre (上高地ビジターセンター; ☎95-2606; ⊙8am-5pm) Ten minutes' walk from Kamikōchi bus station along the main trail; this is the place for information on Kamikōchi's flora, fauna, geology and history. You can also book guided walks to destinations including Taishō-ike and Myōjin-ike (from ¥500 per person). Nature guides (from ¥2000/hour) and climbing guides (approx ¥30,000/day) may be available. English-speakers may be offered but cannot be guaranteed.

ℹ️ Getting Around

Private vehicles are prohibited between Naka-no-yu and Kamikōchi; access is only by bus or taxi as far as the Kamikōchi bus station. Those with private cars can use car parks en route to Naka-no-yu in the hamlet of Sawando for ¥500 per day; shuttle buses (¥1800 return) run a few times per hour.

Buses run via Naka-no-yu and Taishō-ike to the bus station. Hiking trails commence at Kappa-bashi, which is a short walk from the bus station.

Shin-Hotaka Onsen
新穂高温泉

☎ 0578

The main reason people visit Shin-Hotaka Onsen, an otherwise sleepy hollow north of Fukuchi Onsen, is the Shin-Hotaka Ropeway, Japan's longest.

◎ Sights & Activities

Shin-Hotaka Ropeway   Ropeway
新穂高ロープウェイ; www.okuhi.jp/rop/ top; Shin-Hotaka; 1 way/return ¥1500/2800; ⊙8.30am-4.30pm) A few minutes' walk

1 TSURUGI-DAKE CLIMB
The 2999m peak of Tsurugi-dake is one of Japan's most impressive sights: the jagged ridges leading to the summit will tempt any serious hiker or mountain climber. The standard route is from Murodō-daira via Tsurugi-sawa-goya hut and back to Murodō. You can also start at Murodō, cross the summit and descend right into the Tsurugi-sawa valley or do this in reverse. Keep in mind that this climb is fairly serious and is only for experienced climbers comfortable with heights and exposed routes.

2 MURODŌ TO TARŌBEI DAIRA TRAVERSE
This is the classic North Alps traverse. Start by taking the Tateyama-Kurobe Alpen Route from Toyama up to the Murodō-daira and spend the night there – don't miss the onsen (hot springs). Then, climb off the plateau and traverse the long mountain ridge to the south, stopping for the night en route at the huts at Goshiki-ga-hara and Tarōbei-daira, before exiting at Oritate or continuing south in the direction of Shin-Hotaka Onsen or even Kamikōchi.

3 ABOVE KAMIKŌCHI: YARI-GA-TAKE AND THE HODAKAS
Kamikōchi is an alpine sanctuary surrounded by high mountains on all sides. Unlike Murodō-daira, Kamikōchi sits at the base of the mountains. You can enjoy gentle hikes along the Azusa-gawa in the valley or climb the peaks that loom over the valley. The route over the Hodaka Range to the Matterhorn-like spire of 3180m Yari-ga-take is a classic.

uphill from the Shin-Hotaka Onsen bus terminus, the ropeway celebrated its 40th anniversary in 2010. From a starting elevation of 1308m, two cable cars whisk you to 2156m towards the peak of Nishi Hotaka-dake (2909m). Views from the top are spectacular, from observation decks and walking trails – in winter, snows can be shoulder deep. In season, properly equipped hikers with ample time can choose longer options from the top cable-car station, Nishi Hotaka-guchi, including hiking over to Kamikōchi (three hours), which is much easier than going the other way.

Nakazaki Sansou Okuhida-no-yu
Onsen

(中崎山荘奥飛騨の湯; adult/child ¥800/400; ⏰8am-8pm) Over 50 years old but completely rebuilt in 2010, the facility still commands a spectacular vista of the mountains. The milky waters of its large indoor baths and *rotemburo* do wonders for dry skin. There's a small dining room. It's next to Hotel Hotaka.

Sleeping & Eating

Yarimikan
Ryokan ¥¥

(槍見舘; ☎89-2808; www.yarimikan.com; Okuhida Onsen-gun Kansaka; r per person with meals from ¥15,900; P) Yarimikan is a wonderfully traditional onsen ryokan on the Kamata-gawa, with two indoor baths, eight riverside *rotemburo* (some available for private use) and only 15 rooms. Guests can bathe 24 hours a day (it's stunning by moonlight) and day visitors are accepted between 10am and 2pm for

Sample Bus Routes & Discounts: Northern Japan Alps

Within the Alps, bus schedules change seasonally. A number of discount passes are available.

Alpico's '3-day Free Kippu' (¥6400) offers unlimited rides between Matsumoto, Takayama and within the Chūbu-Sangaku National Park. The 'Alps-wide Free Passport' (¥10,000) gives you an extra day and also includes Shirakawa-gō.

Meitetsu's 'Marugoto value kippu' (¥5000) includes two days' travel anywhere between Takayama and Shin-Hotaka, a ride on the Shin-Hotaka Ropeway and a soak in the *rotemburo* (outdoor baths) at Hirayu Onsen bus station.

Tourist Information Offices should direct you to the latest schedules and fares.

BUS FARES

FROM	TO	FARE (¥; ONE WAY/RETURN)	DURATION (MIN; ONE WAY)
Takayama	Hirayu Onsen	1530	55
	Kamikōchi	2660/4900	80
	Shin-Hotaka	2100	90
Matsumoto	Shin-Shimashima	680 (train)	30
	Kamikōchi	2400/4400	95
Shin-Shimashima	Naka-no-yu	1550	50
	Kamikōchi	1900/3300	70
	Shirahone Onsen	1400/2300	75
Kamikōchi	Naka-no-yu	600	15
	Hirayu Onsen	1130/2000	25
	Shirahone Onsen	1350	35
Hirayu Onsen	Naka-no-yu	540	10
	Shin-Hotaka	870	30

LIGHTROCKET / GETTY IMAGES ©

Don't Miss
Shin-Hotaka-no-yu

Exhibitionists will love this bare bones *konyoku* (mixed bathing) *rotemburo* (outdoor bath), by the Kamata-gawa, visible from the bridge which passes over it. Entry is free (or by donation). Enter through segregated change rooms and emerge into a single large pool.

NEED TO KNOW

新穂高の湯; ☎89-2458; Okuhida Onsengo Kansaka; ⏱8am-9pm May-Oct (closed Nov-Apr)

¥500. Cuisine features local Hida beef and grilled freshwater fish. It's just off Route 475, a few kilometres before the Shin-Hotaka Ropeway.

Nonohana Sansō   Inn ¥¥
野の花山荘; ☎89-0030; www.nono87.jp; per person with 2 meals from ¥13,800, day guests adult/child ¥800/500; ⏱day guests 0am-5pm; P) Along a road that ascends from Rte 475, Nonohana Sansō opened its doors in 2010. All tatami guestrooms are traditionally styled and have private facilities, although the lobby and lounge are refreshingly contemporary. There's an open kitchen preparing local specialties and the large *rotemburo* have a fantastic outlook – they're open to visitors.

NAGANO PREFECTURE   長野県

Formerly known as Shinshū and often referred to as the 'Roof of Japan', Nagano Prefecture is a wonderful place to visit for its regal mountains, rich cultural history, fine architecture and cuisine.

In addition to a hefty chunk of the Japan Alps National Park, Nagano boasts several quasi-national parks that attract skiers, mountaineers and onsen aficionados.

Nagano, the prefectural capital and past host of the Olympic Games is home to Zenkō-ji, a spectacular temple of national significance. Ever-lovable Matsumoto, Nagano Prefecture's other main city, makes the most of its wonderful geography, vibrant city centre and photogenic original castle.

....

Shiga Kōgen 志賀高原

♪ 0269

The site of several events in the 1998 Nagano Olympics and the 2005 Special Olympics World Winter Games, Shiga Kōgen is Japan's largest ski resort and one of the largest in the world: there are 21 linked areas covering 80 runs. One lift ticket gives access to all areas as well as the shuttle bus between the various base lodges. There is a huge variety of terrain for all skill levels, as well as ski-only areas.

Outside winter, the mountains' lakes and ponds make an excellent destination for hikers. Otherwise, there's no compelling reason to visit. If you're a skier, read on...

If time is limited, base yourself somewhere central like the Ichinose Family Ski Area, which has a central location and wide variety of accommodation and restaurants. The Nishitateyama area has good wide runs and generally ungroomed terrain. The Terakoya area is a little hard to get to but it is generally uncrowded and has good short runs and a pleasant atmosphere.

 Sleeping & Eating

Hotel Shirakabasō   Hotel ¥¥

(ホテル白樺荘; ♪ 34-3311; www.shirakaba. co.jp/english; 7148 Hirao; r per person with 2 meals from ¥11,700; P 🛜) Close to the cable-car base station and the Sun Valley ski area is this pleasant little hotel with a variety of rooms and its own indoor and outdoor onsen baths.

Hotel Heights Shiga Kōgen   Hotel ¥¥

(ホテルハイツ志賀高原; ♪ 34-3030; www.shigakogen.jp/heights; r per person with 2 meals from ¥8300; P) Near the base of the Kumanoyu ski area, the large Hotel Heights boasts clean Japanese- and Western-style rooms and its own onsen.

Hotel Sunroute Shiga Kōgen   Hotel ¥¥

(ホテルサンルート志賀高原; ♪ 34-2020; r per person with 2 meals from ¥10,500; P) Popular with a Western crowd, this hotel is a three-minute walk from the Ichinose Diamond ski lift, with great access to other ski areas. The rooms are Western style with en suite baths; some have mountain views.

Villa Ichinose   Inn ¥¥

(ヴィラ・一の瀬; ♪ 34-2704; www.villa101. biz/english; 7149 Hirao; r per person from ¥6000; P 🛜) With a great location in front of the Ichinose bus stop, English-speaking staff and a friendly atmosphere, this inn is popular with overseas guests. Japanese-style rooms have toilet only and Western-style rooms have their own bathroom. There's wi-fi in the lobby and a 24-hour public bath on the 2nd floor.

Chalet Shiga   Inn ¥¥

(シャレー志賀; ♪ 34-2235; www.shigakogen. jp/chalet; r per person with 2 meals from ¥10,500; P) Chalet Shiga is convenient to the slopes and has a popular sports bar on-site. Both Western- and Japanese-style rooms are available.

ℹ Information

Shiga Kōgen Ropeway Association (志賀高原索道協会; ♪ 34-2404; www.shigakogen.gr.jp; 1-day lift ticket ¥4800; ⏰ 8.30am-4.30pm Dec-Apr) The conglomeration of hills are managed by this central body – limited information in English can be found on their website. Lift passes are available in a variety of durations and a wide range of equipment can be rented from numerous outlets. In the Hasuike area, in front of the Shiga Kōgen ropeway station, its office has English speaking staff.

ⓘ Getting There & Away

Direct buses run between Nagano Station and Shiga Kōgen, with frequent departures in ski season (¥1600, 70 minutes). You can also take a train from Nagano to Yudanaka and continue to Shiga Kōgen by bus – take a Hase-ike-bound bus and get off at the last stop (¥760, approximately 40 minutes).

Nozawa Onsen
野沢温泉

☎0269 / POP 3800

This wonderful working village tucked in a picturesque corner of the eastern Japan Alps is both a humming ski resort winterlong and a year-round onsen town – worth visiting any time of year.

Settled as early as the 8th century, it's compact and quaint, though the maze of narrow streets will challenge even the best of drivers. Dotted throughout are 13 free public onsen and a range of excellent accommodation. Outside the busy ski season, it's possible to briefly escape modernity and get a sense of life in an ancient mountain village.

◎ Activities

Nozawa Onsen
Snow Resort   Snow Sports
(野沢温泉スキー場; www.nozawaski.com/winter/en/; 1-day lift ticket ¥4600; ⏰8.30am-4.30pm, Dec-Apr;) Nozawa Onsen Ski Resort, one of Honshū's best, dominates the 'upper' village. The relatively compact ski face is easy to navigate and enjoy with a variety of terrain at all levels. The main base is around the Higake gondola station, where there are beginner and kid-friendly runs. Snowboarders should try the Karasawa terrain park or the half-pipe at Uenotaira and advanced skiers will enjoy the steep and often mogulled Schneider Course.

Onsen   Onsen
(⏰6am-11pm) Onsen water is still wisely used by many villagers for laundry, cooking and heating, and there are 13

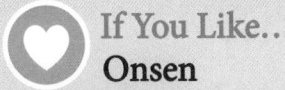

If You Like...
Onsen

If you like Shin-Hotaka Onsen, we think you'll enjoy a soak in these other nearby onsen:

1 HIRAYU ONSEN
Hirayu is a transport hub just south of Kamikōchi. It's also home to a few nice onsen that make for a good soak after hiking in the Northern Japan Alps. To get here, take the bus from Takayama (¥1530, 55 minutes).

2 FUKUCHI ONSEN
This quiet onsen village is located near the more popular resort of Hirayu. Take the bus from Hirayu Onsen to get here.

3 SHIRAHONE ONSEN
This wonderful onsen village, in a gorge near the entrance to Kamikōchi, is a must for onsen lovers. It's a bus ride from Hirayu Onsen.

free onsen (for bathing) dotted about the town, each with a history. Our favourite is **Ō-yu**, with its fine wooden building, followed by the scalding-hot **Shin-yu**, and the atmospheric old **Kuma-no-tearai** (Bear's Bathroom). The waters here are *hot* and full of minerals - if you have silver jewellery, leave it in your room unless you don't mind it temporarily turning black. Some baths are cordoned off because they are so hot that only hardened locals are permitted to enter them!

🛏 Sleeping & Eating

Pension Schnee   Inn ¥
(ペンションシュネー; ☎85-2012; www.pensionschnee.com; 8276 Hikage-sukī-jō; r per person with meals from ¥8400; @) Near the Higake gondola base, you can ski in and out of this super friendly, family-run chalet, popular with Western clientele, who appreciate its premium location.

Below: Cable car, Nagano mountains; **Right:** An onsen in Matsumoto (p172)

(BELOW) ALAN NEE / GETTY IMAGES ©; (RIGHT) TANUKI PHOTOGRAPHY / GETTY IMAGES ©

European pension-style rooms are spacious and there's a woody dining room/bar.

Lodge Nagano   Inn ¥
(ロッジながの; 📞090-8670-9597; www. lodgenagano.com; 6846-1 Toyosato; r per person with breakfast from ¥4000, r in summer from ¥2500; 🛜) This popular foreign-run guesthouse attracts lots of Aussies – there's Vegemite in the dining room. It's a friendly, fun place with bunk dorm and tatami rooms, some with private bath.

Address Nozawa   Apartment ¥¥
(アドレス野沢; 📞67-0360; www.address-nozawa.com; 9535 Nozawa Onsen; studios s/d from ¥12,750/17,000; @ 🛜 ♿) We love this innovative, boutique property, opened in 2011. Formerly a traditional inn, its new owners sought to re-create a space which combined Japanese and European design elements and have done just that. Large Western-style rooms with tatami floors feature fresh colours, soft downy beds, bright bathrooms and a full kitchen stocked with breakfast provisions. There's an on-site onsen bath, kids' room, ski storage and plenty of high technology.

Kiriya Ryokan   Ryokan ¥¥
(桐屋旅館; 📞85-2020; www.kiriya.jp; 8714-2 Nozawa Onsen; r per person with meals from ¥12,000; P 🛜 ♿) This friendly ryokan has been in the family for generations. The owner's attentive service and excellent English ensure its abiding popularity with overseas guests. All rooms have private toilets. Some have their own baths in addition to the large communal onsen baths. There's a guest laundry and a wonderful garden.

Mura-no-hoteru Sumiyoshi-ya   Ryokan ¥¥
(村のホテル住吉屋; 📞85-2005; www. sumiyoshiya.co.jp; 8713 Toyosato; r per person with meals from ¥18,900; @) This wonderful ryokan, the oldest in town, has a wide

range of inviting traditional room types, many with private bathrooms and great views. The communal onsen baths with stained-glass windows are dreamy. Limited English is spoken but the friendly staff are committed to excellence in service.

Haus St Anton   Inn ¥¥
(サンアントンの家; ☎85-3597; www. nozawa.com/stanton; 9515 Nozawa Onsen; r per person with meals with/without bathroom from ¥14,000/11,550; **P** **@**) Owned by a two-time former Olympian, this comfortable Austrian-themed inn has helpful staff and is close to the village's main street. There are six handsome Western-style bedrooms and a dining area/bar with a woody, warm atmosphere.

Lodge Matsuya   Inn ¥¥
(ロッヂまつや; ☎85-2082; www2u.biglobe. ne.jp/~onotaka; 9553 Nozawa Onsen; r per person with breakfast from ¥6500, with 2 meals from ¥8500; **@**) In the centre of town,

this large, family-run ski lodge has both Western- and Japanese-style rooms.

Pasta di Pasta   Italian ¥
(パスタディパスタ; ☎85-5055; www.pastadi-pasta.net; 8376-145 Toyosato; dishes ¥500-1200; ⏱lunch & dinner, hours vary seasonally) Freshly cooked pasta, pizza and appetisers are order of the day in this cosy upstairs eatery. The not-too-creamy *wafū sanshū no kinoko* pasta (three kinds of mushroom) is delicious.

Tōyō Rāmen   Noodles ¥
(東洋ラーメン; ☎85-3363; 9347 Toyosato; ⏱lunch & dinner) Chunky *rāmen* bowls and mouthwatering *tezukuri* (handmade) *gyōza* (dumplings) are dished out year-round in this 30-seat Chinese eatery.

 Drinking

Main Street Bar Foot   Bar
(マインストリトバーフット; **@**) A casual place on the main street, with free internet (with drink purchase) and fussball.

169

Stay
Bar

(ステイ; www.seisenso.com) Stay is a cosy basement bar that's open late and run by a music-loving Japanese man who has lived abroad.

Minato Bar
Izakaya

(みなと) On the slopes near the base of the gondola, Minato appeals to an older crowd. It's a Japanese-style place that seats 50 and offers karaoke next door.

ⓘ Information

Nozawa Onsen Visitor Centre (野沢温泉ビジターセンター; ☑85-3155; www.nozawakanko.jp/english; 9780-4 Toyosato; ⓧ8.30am-6pm) In the centre of the village. Has English-speaking staff who can assist with accommodation and tour bookings.

ⓘ Getting There & Away

There are direct buses between Nagano Station's east exit and Nozawa Onsen (¥1400, 90 minutes, seven buses per day in winter, three buses per day in summer). Alternatively, take a JR Iiyama-line train between Nagano and Togari Nozawa Onsen Station (¥740, 55 minutes). Regular buses connect Togari Nozawa Onsen Station and Nozawa Onsen (¥300, 20 minutes, nine per day). The bus station/ticket office is about 200m from the main bus stop, which is directly in the middle of town. This can be a little confusing, but there are staff around to help get people where they need to be.

Hakuba
白馬

☑0261

At the base of one of the highest sections of the Northern Japan Alps, Hakuba is one of Japan's main skiing and hiking centres. In winter, skiers from across Japan and increasingly overseas flock to Hakuba's seven ski resorts. In summer, the region draws hikers attracted by easy access to the high peaks. There are many onsen in and around Hakuba-mura, the main village, and a long soak after a day of action is the perfect way to ease your muscles.

🏃 Activities

Happō-One Ski Resort
Skiing

(八方尾根スキー所; www.happo-one.jp/english; 1-day lift ticket ¥4600; ⓧDec-Apr) Host of the downhill races at the 1998 Winter

Skiing, Hakuba

Olympics, Happō-One is one of Japan's best ski areas, with superb mountain views and beginner, intermediate and advanced runs catering to skiers and snowboarders. For the low-down, check the excellent English-language home page.

Most runs go right down the face of the mountain, with several good burners descending from Usagidaira 109, the mountain's centre-point. Above this, two chairlifts run to the top. On busy days, avoid lift bottlenecks by heading to areas like the Skyline 2.

The rest house at Usagidaira 109 is the largest eating establishment with a selection of vendors. There are plenty of hire places in the streets around the base of the mountain, some with boots up to 31cm. All have roughly the same selection and prices (¥2500 to ¥3000 per day for skis/board and boots).

From Hakuba Station, a five-minute bus ride (¥260) takes you into the middle of Hakuba-mura; from there it's a 10-minute walk to the base of Happō-One and the main 'Adam' gondola base station. In winter, a shuttle bus makes the rounds of the village, lodges and ski base.

Mimizuku-no-yu — Onsen
(みみずくの湯; 5480 Ō-aza Hokujō; adult/child ¥500/250; ⏱10am-9.30pm, enter by 9pm) One of Hakuba's many onsen. Many contend this has the best mountain views from the tub.

HIKING

In summer you can take the gondola and the two upper chairlifts, then hike along a trail for an hour or so to Happō-ike (pond) on a ridge below Karamatsu-dake (唐松岳; 2695m). From here, follow a trail another hour up to Maru-yama, continue for 1½ hours to the Karamatsu-dake San-sō (mountain hut) and then climb to the peak of Karamatsu-dake in about 30 minutes. The return fare is ¥2340 if purchased at the Hakuba tourist office, ¥2600 otherwise.

 **Sleeping & Eating**

Hakuba Panorama Hotel — Inn ¥¥
(白馬パノラマホテル; ☎85-4031; www. hakuba-panorama.com; 3322-1 Hokujō; s/d incl breakfast from ¥10,900/16,900; 🅿🛜) About 300m from one of the lifts at Happō-One, this Australian-run outfit has bilingual Japanese staff, an on-site travel agency and a variety of room types with en suite bathrooms. There's a guest laundry and a wonderful onsen.

Hakuba Highland Hotel — Hotel ¥¥
(白馬ハイランドホテル; ☎72-3450; www.hakuba-highland.net; 1582 Hokujō; r per person with meals from ¥9680; 🅿) This older hotel has sensational views over the Hakuba range and a great indoor-outdoor onsen, but it's away from the action. In winter there's a free shuttle bus to the main resorts, each about 20 minutes drive.

Ridge Hotel & Apartments — Hotel ¥¥¥
(☎85-4301; www.theridge.jp; 4608 Hakuba; s/d from ¥16,350/10,900, apt r from ¥36,000; 🅿@🛜) Sophisticated, sexy and stylish, this stunning property has it all, year-round: location, amenities, views. A variety of room types range from the sublime (Western rooms with Japanese elements) to the ridiculous (gorgeous loft balcony suite in the shadow of the slopes). Obliging, attentive staff speak English well. Splurge if you can.

Hakuba Tokyu Hotel — Hotel ¥¥¥
(白馬東急ホテル; ☎72-3001; www.tokyuhotelsjapan.com/en/; Happō-wadanomori; s/d incl breakfast from ¥18,400/25,400; 🅿🛜) This elegant year-round hotel has large rooms with great views and a wonderful garden, popular for weddings. The Grand Spa boasts the highest alkaline content in the area, and there's both French and Japanese restaurants.

Bamboo Coffee Bar — Cafe ¥
(☎090-7017-5331; ⏱8am-6pm; 🛜📷) On the left as you exit Hakuba Staion, this wonderful modern cafe serves delicious speciality coffees, sweet treats and panini

sandwiches. The mellow tunes, friendly staff and free wi-fi (with purchases) make it a great place to log on and get your bearings.

 Drinking & Entertainment

Tanuki's
Sports Bar

(タヌキ; 📞090-7202-9809; 6350-3 Hokujo; 🕐noon-late Thu-Tue) This neat little bar to your right as you exit the station serves juicy original burgers and your favourite fast foods in a welcoming environment with free pool, darts and fussball on the 2nd floor.

Tracks Bar
Bar

(📞75-4366) Located between Kamishiro Station and Goryū, this is one of the favourite night spots for the younger, foreign crowd, with live music, pool tables, woodburner stoves and sports on a huge screen.

The Pub
Pub

(📞72-4453; www.thepubhakuba.com; 🕐4.30pm-late; @ 📶) The only English pub in the village is found in a Swiss-style chalet on the grounds of the Momonoki hotel. By Japanese standards, it's huge and happening. There's a daily happy hour and free internet and wi-fi.

ℹ Information

Hakuba Accomodation Information Centre (白馬宿泊情報センター; Hakuba Shukuhaku Jōhō Sentā; 📞72-6900; www.hakuba1.com; 🕐7am-6pm) For information, maps and lodging assistance. Located to the right of Hakuba station.

Hakuba Tourist Information Office (白馬村観光案内所; 📞72-3232; www.vill.hakuba.nagano.jp/english; 🕐8.30am-5.30pm) Provides maps and leaflets relating to tourism in the area. In addition to all things winter, the website has detailed information on summer gondola operating schedules and fares. It's just outside Hakuba station.

ℹ Getting There & Away

Hakuba is connected with Matsumoto by the JR Ōito line: tokkyū (limited express) ¥2260, one hour; futsū (local) ¥1110, 1½ hours). Continuing north, change trains at Minami Otari to meet the JR Hokuriku line at Itoigawa, with connections to Niigata, Toyama and Kanazawa.

Alpico group operates buses from Nagano station (¥1500, approximately 70 minutes) and Shinjuku Nishi-guchi, in Tokyo (¥4700, 4½ hours).

....

Matsumoto 松本

📞0263 / POP 243,000

Embraced by seven great peaks to the west (including Yariga-take, Hotaka-dake and Norikura-dake, each above 3000m) and three smaller sentinels to the east (including beautiful Utsukushi-ga-hara-kōgen), Matsumoto occupies a protected position in a fertile valley no more than 20km across at its widest. Views of the regal Alps are never far away and sunsets are breathtaking.

Formerly known as Fukashi, Nagano prefecture's second-largest city has been here since the 8th century. In the 14th and 15th centuries, it was the castle town of the Ogasawara clan and continued to prosper through the Edo period, to the present.

Today, Matsumoto is one of Japan's finest cities – an attractive, cosmopolitan place loved by its residents. Admirers from around the world come to enjoy its superb castle, pretty streets, galleries, cafes and endearing vistas. With plenty of well-priced, quality accommodation and excellent access to/from and around the town, Matsumoto is the perfect base for exploring the Japan Alps and the Kiso and Azumino Valleys.

◎ Sights & Activities

Matsumoto-jō
Castle

(松本城; 4-1 Marunōchi; adult/child ¥600/300; 🕐8.30am-6pm mid-Jul–Aug, to 5.30pm early-Sep–mid-Jul) Magnificent, must-see Matsumoto-jō is Japan's oldest wooden castle and one of four castles designated National Treasures – the others are Hikone, Himeji and Inuyama. The magnificent three-turreted donjon (main keep) was completed around 1595, in contrasting black and white, leading to the nickname Karasu-jō (Crow Castle).

JASON WEDDINGTON / GETTY IMAGES ©

Steep steps lead up six storeys, with impressive views from each level. Lower floors display guns, bombs and gadgets with which to storm castles, and a delightful *tsukimi yagura* (moon-viewing pavilion). It has a tranquil moat full of carp, with the occasional swan gliding beneath the red bridges. The basics are explained over loudspeakers in English and Japanese. You can also ask at the entrance about a free tour in English (subject to availability), or call the **Goodwill Guide Group** (☎32-7140), which gives free one-hour tours.

Nakamachi   Neighbourhood
(中町) This charming former merchant district by the Metoba-gawa, with its *namako-kabe kura* (lattice walled storehouses) and Edo-period streetscapes, makes for a wonderful stroll. Many buildings have been preserved and transformed into cafes, galleries and craft shops specialising in wood, glass, fabric, ceramics and antiques.

Matsumoto City Museum of Art   Museum
(松本市美術館; Matsumoto-shi Bijutsukan; 4-2-22 Chūō; adult/child ¥400/free; ⏲9am-5pm Tue-Sun) This sleek museum has a good collection of Japanese artists, many of whom hail from Matsumoto or depict scenes of the surrounding countryside. Highlights include the striking avant-garde works of Kusama Yayoi (look for the 'Infinity Mirrored Room').

Japan Ukiyo-e Museum   Museum
(日本浮世絵美術館; 2206-1 Koshiba; adult/child ¥1050/530; ⏲10am-5pm Tue-Sun) Housing more than 100,000 wood-block prints, paintings, screens and old books, this renowned museum exhibits a minuscule fraction of its collection. The museum is approximately 3km from Matsumoto Station, 15 minutes' walk from Ōniwa Station on the Matsumoto Dentetsu line (¥170, six minutes), or about ¥2000 by taxi.

Matsumoto Open-Air Architectural Museum   Museum
(松本市歴史の里; Matsumoto-shi Rekishi-no-sato; ☎47-4515; 2196-1 Shimadachi; admission ¥400; ⏲9am-4.30pm Tue-Sun) Adjacent to the better known Japan Ukiyo-e Museum, amid fields and rice paddies, 'neath the gaze of the Alps stand these five examples of striking late-Edo- and early-Showa-era architecture for you to explore.

173

Utsukushi-ga-hara Onsen & Asama Onsen
Onsen

(美ヶ原温泉・浅間温泉) Northeast of downtown, Utsukushi-ga-hara Onsen (not to be confused with Utsukushi-ga-hara-kōgen) is the prettier of these spa villages, with a quaint main street and views across the valley. Asama Onsen's history is said to date back to the 10th century and includes writers and poets, though it looks quite generic now. Both areas are easily reached by bus from Matsumoto's bus terminal (Utsukushi-ga-hara Onsen ¥330, 18 minutes, twice hourly; Asama Onsen ¥350, 23 minutes, hourly).

Utsukushi-ga-hara-kōgen
Plateau

(美ヶ原高原) This stunning alpine plateau (2000m) boasts over 200 varieties of flora which come alive in the summer. It's a great day trip from Matsumoto (612m), reached via an ooh-and-ahh drive on twisty mountain roads called Azalea Line and Venus Line (open late April to early November). A car will give you freedom to explore the beauty, but there's also a bus, in season (¥1500 one way, 1½ hours).

Utsukushi-ga-hara Open Air Museum
Museum

(美ヶ原美術館; Utsukushi-ga-hara Bijutsukan; adult/child/student ¥1000/700/800; ⏰9am-5pm late Apr-early Nov) Atop Utsukushi-ga-hara-kōgen you'll find this seemingly random sculpture garden with some 350 pieces, mostly by Japanese sculptors. The surrounding countryside provides an inspiring backdrop. Nearby are pleasant walks and the opportunity to see cows in pasture (a constant source of fascination in Japan). **Furusato-kan** (ふ る里館), the shop at the hilltop farm, sells ice cream made from local *kokemomo* (lingonberries). Buses (¥1500, 1½ hours) run several times daily during the warmer months, athough a rental car is good option if windy roads don't phase you.

 Festivals & Events

Locals love to celebrate – you're never far from a festival here.

Matsumoto Bonbon
Parade

Matsumoto's biggest event takes place on the first Saturday in August, when over 25,000 people of all ages perform the 'bonbon' dance through the streets, well into the hot summer's night. Be prepared to be drawn into the action.

Sleeping

Matsumoto is compact enough that you can stay anywhere downtown and get around easily. Most business hotels are by the station, but there are some great traditional options in picturesque Nakamachi.

Nunoya
Inn ¥

(ぬのや旅館; ☎32-0545; www.mcci.or.jp/www/ nunoya/en; 3-5-7 Chūō; r per person from ¥4500) Few inns have more heart

Cherry blossoms, Matsumoto-jō (p172), Matsumoto
HUAYANG / GETTY IMAGES ©

than this simple, traditional charmer, meticulously kept by its friendly owner. The spotless inn has shiny dark-wood floors and atmospheric tatami rooms. No meals are served, but you're right in the heart of the best part of town. If you don't mind sharing a bathroom, the rate is wonderful for this much character.

Richmond Hotel   Hotel ¥
(リッチモンドホテル松本; ☎37-5000; www.richmondhotel.jp/en/matsumoto; 1-10-7 Chūō; s/d from ¥5200/8500; ⌨@) A few minutes' walk from JR Matsumoto Station, this 204-room business hotel is in great shape and a great location. The deluxe double rooms are large by Japanese standards, and reasonably priced. There's a Gusto family restaurant (with picture menu) downstairs.

Marumo   Ryokan ¥
(まるも; ☎32-0115; 3-3-10 Chūō; r per person ¥5250, with breakfast ¥6300) Between Nakamachi and the river, this creaky wooden ryokan dates from 1868 and has lots of traditional charm, including a bamboo garden and coffee shop. Although the rooms aren't huge and don't have private facilities, it's quite popular, so book ahead.

Seifūsō   Ryokan ¥
(静風荘; ☎46-0639; www.ryokanseifuso.jp/english; 634-5 Minami-asama; r per person from ¥4700; P@) Free pick-up (arrange in advance) and free bicycles make up for the fact that this inn is closer to Asama Onsen than Matsumoto. Otherwise, it's run by a friendly family who love to welcome overseas guests. Japanese-style rooms are clean and bright, have a nice outlook and shared baths. Once you're there, take bus 2 to get back into town.

Hotel Buena Vista   Hotel ¥¥
(ホテルブエナビスタ; ☎37-0111; www.buena-vista.co.jp/english; 1-2-1 Honjo; s/tw from ¥9240/17,640; ⌨@) An oldie but a goodie, Matsumoto's sharpest Western hotel recently received a makeover in its public spaces and rooms, leaving it looking quite the part. The executive rooms and suites are the way to go, if you're going to do it. Many rooms have exceptional views.

Dormy Inn Matsumoto   Hotel ¥¥
(ドーミーイン松本; ☎33-5489; www.hotespa.net/hotels/matsumoto; 2-2-1 Fukashi; s/d from ¥8000/10,500; P@) This newer property has compact, well-designed rooms with pleasant, neutral decor. There's an onsen featuring a sunny *rotemburo* and the breakfast buffet is decent. Otherwise, there's all the things travellers need, including a laundry. Deals can be found online (in Japanese).

Sugimoto   Ryokan ¥¥¥
(旅館すぎもと; ☎32-3379; 451-7 Satoyamabe; r per person from ¥15,000; ☒Utsukushigahara Onsen line/Town Sneaker North Course) The lack of English spoken at this upscale ryokan in Utsukushigahara Onsen may be its only downfall for non-Japanese-speakers. With some fascinating elements, such as the art collection, underground passageway and bar full of single malts, this is a unique property. Rooms range in size and decor (Japanese, Western and mixed), but all are ineffably stylish.

Eating & Drinking

For a quick coffee and cake, cafes line the banks of the Metoba-gawa and Nawate-dōri.

Kura   Shokudō ¥
(蔵; ☎33-6444; 1-10-22 Chūō; dishes from ¥300, teishoku ¥945-2100; ⏰lunch & dinner Thu-Tue) Located near Nakamachi, Kura serves meticulously prepared sushi and tempura for lunch and dinner in a stylish former warehouse. For the daring: *basashi* (raw horse meat).

Nomugi   Noodles ¥
(野麦; ☎36-3753; 2-9-11 Chūō; soba ¥1100; ⏰lunch Thu-Mon; 🖋) In Nakamachi, this is one of central Japan's finest *soba* shops. Its owner used to run a French restaurant in Tokyo before returning to his home town. Keeping things Zen, there are two dishes: *zaru-soba* and *kake-soba*. Oh, and beer.

Robata Shōya   Grill ¥
(炉ばた庄屋; ☎37-1000; 11-1 Chūō; dishes ¥300-900; ⏰lunch & dinner) Close to the station you'll find this lively *robatayaki*

(grill) house, doing it before your eyes to a wide range of seafood, chicken, meats and mountain delights. Order lots of small plates.

Shizuka
Izakaya ¥¥

(しづか; ☎ 32-0547; 4-10-8 Ōte; dishes ¥480-4410; ☺ lunch & dinner Mon-Sat; 🏠) This wonderfully traditional *izakaya* (pub-eatery) serving favourites like *oden* (a stew of fishcakes, tofu, vegetables and eggs simmered in a kelp-flavoured broth) and *yakitori* (skewers of grilled chicken) as well as some more challenging specialities.

Old Rock
Pub

(オールドロック; ☎ 38-0069; 2-30-20 Chūō; mains from ¥750; ☺ lunch & dinner) In the perfect spot, a block south of the river, across from Nakamachi, you'll find this popular pub with good lunch specials and, appropriately, a wide range of beers.

ℹ Information

Although small streets radiate somewhat confusingly from the train station, soon you're on a grid.

On the web, visit: www.city.matsumoto.nagano.jp.

Main Post Office (Honmachi-dōri)

Tourist Information Office (松本市観光案内所; ☎ 32-2814; 1-1-1 Fukashi; ☺ 9.30am-5.45pm) This excellent Tourist Information Office inside Matsumoto Station has friendly English-speaking staff and a wide range of well-produced English-language materials on the area.

ℹ Getting There & Away

Air

Shinshū Matsumoto airport has flights to Fukuoka, Osaka and Sapporo.

Bus

Alpico runs buses between Matsumoto and Shinjuku in Tokyo (¥3400, 3¼ hours, 18 daily), Osaka (¥5700, 5¾ hours, two daily, and one longer overnight service), and Nagoya (¥3460, 3½ hours, eight daily). Nohi Bus services Takayama (¥3100, 2½ hours, six daily). Reservations are advised. The Matsumoto bus station is in the basement of the Espa building across from the train station.

Car

Renting a car is a great way to explore the beauty outside town, but expect narrow, windy roads. There are several agencies around the station. Rates are generally around ¥6500 per day.

Train

'Matsumotooo... Matsumotooo...' is connected with Tokyo's Shinjuku Station (*tokkyū*, ¥6200, 2¾ hours, hourly), Nagoya (*tokkyū*, ¥5360, two hours) and Nagano (Shinano *tokkyū*, ¥2260, 50 minutes; Chūō *futsū*, ¥1110, 1¼ hours).

ℹ Getting Around

An airport shuttle bus connects Shinshū Matsumoto airport with downtown (¥540, 25 minutes) wheras a taxi costs around ¥4500.

Matsumoto-jō and the city centre are easily covered on foot and free bicycles are available for loan – enquire at the Tourist Information Office. Three 'town sneaker' loop bus routes operate between 9am and 5.30pm for ¥190/500 per ride/day; the blue and orange routes cover the castle and Nakamachi.

Kiso Valley Nakasendō
木曽谷中仙道

☎ 0264

The Nakasendō was one of the five highways of the Edo period connecting Edo (now Tokyo) with Kyoto. Much of the route is now followed by National Roads, however, in this thickly forested section of the Kiso Valley, there are several sections of the twisty, craggy post road which have been carefully restored, the most impressive being the 7.8km stretch between Magome and Tsumago, two of the most attractive Nakasendō towns. Walking this route is one of Japan's most rewarding tourist experiences.

It's worth a stay in any or all of these special towns to have them to yourself once the day trippers clear out. For street foods, look for *gohei-mochi* (skewered rice dumplings coated with sesame-walnut sauce) and in autumn you can't miss *kuri-kinton* (chestnut dumplings).

Magome
馬篭

In Gifu-ken, pretty Magome is the furthest south of the Kiso Valley post towns.

DAISUKE OKA / GETTY IMAGES ©

Its buildings line a steep, cobblestone pedestrian road which is unfriendly to heavy wheelie suitcases, but its rustic shopfronts and mountain views will keep your finger on the shutter.

 Activities

From Magome, the 7.8km hike to Tsumago follows a steep, largely paved road until it reaches its peak at the top of Magome-tōge (pass); elevation 801m. After the pass, the trail meanders by waterfalls, forest and farmland. The route is easiest in this direction, from Magome (elevation 600m) to Tsumago (elevation 420m). The route is clearly signposted in English; allow three to six hours to enjoy it.

If fitness or a disability might prevent you from appreciating this amazing walk, there is an easier way. The Magome–Tsumago bus (¥600, 30 minutes, two to three daily in each direction) also stops at Magome-tōge. If you alight and begin the walk here, it's a picturesque 5.2km downhill run through to Tsumago.

If you do the hike, both towns offer a handy baggage forwarding service from either Tourist Information Office to the other. Deposit your bags between 8.30am and 11.30am, for delivery by 1pm.

Sleeping & Eating

Minshuku Tajimaya   Inn ¥
(民宿但馬屋; ☑ 69-2048; www.kiso-taji-maya.com; 4266 Magome; s/d incl 2 meals ¥8925/16,800; ❷ ☎) This inn has compact rooms and friendly staff, although the location of the bathrooms can be inconvenient. The array of local specialities served in the common dining area is impressive, as are the *hinoki* (cypress) baths.

Magome-Chaya   Inn ¥¥
(馬籠茶屋; ☑ 59-2038; www.magomechaya.com; r per person incl 2 meals from ¥9450) This popular *minshuku* (guest house) is almost halfway up the hill, near the water wheel. Room-only plans are available.

Information

Tourist Information Office (観光案内館; ☑ 59-2336; ☺ 9am-5pm) Inconveniently halfway up the hill to the right. You can pick up maps here and staff can book accommodation.

177

Tsumago 妻籠

Tsumago feels like an open-air museum, about 15 minutes' walk from end to end. It was designated by the government as a protected area for the preservation of traditional buildings, where modern developments such as telephone poles aren't allowed. The dark-wood glory of its lattice-fronted buildings is particularly beautiful at dawn and dusk. Film and TV crews are often spotted here.

On 23 November, the **Fūzoku Emaki** parade is held along the Nakasendō, featuring townsfolk in Edo-period costume.

Sights & Activities

Waki-honjin (Okuya) & Local History Museum _Museum_
(脇本陣（奥谷）・歴史資料館 Rekishi Shiryōkan; adult/child ¥600/300; ⊙9am-5pm) The former rest stop for the retainers of the _daimyō (domain lords)_, this Waki-honjin was reconstructed in 1877 by a former castle builder under special dispensation from Emperor Meiji. It contains a lovely moss garden and a special toilet built in case Meiji happened to show up. He never did. The adjacent Local History Museum houses elegant exhibitions about Kiso and the Nakasendō, with some English signage.

Tsumago-honjin _Historic Building_
(妻籠本陣; adult/child ¥300/150; ⊙9am-5pm) Here is where _daimyō_ themselves would spend the night, although the building's architecture is more noteworthy than its exhibits. A combined ticket (¥700/350) also gives you admission to Waki-honjin and the Local History Museum, opposite.

Kisoji Resort _Onsen_
(木曽路館 Kisoji-kan; ☎58-2046; 2278 Azuma; baths ¥700; ⊙9am-7pm) A few kilometres above Tsumago, you'll find this _rotemburo_ with panoramic mountain vistas, a sprawling dining room and a souvenir shop.

Sleeping & Eating

Oyado Daikichi _Inn ¥_
(御宿大吉; ☎57-2595; www17.plala.or.jp/daiki-ti/english; r per person with 2 meals from ¥9,000; ⊖@) Popular with foreign visitors, this traditional-looking inn benefits from modern construction and has a prime top-of-the-hill location – all rooms have a lovely outlook. It's at the very edge of town.

Restaurant in Tsumago

JUDY BELLAH / GETTY IMAGES

Fujioto
Ryokan ¥¥

(藤乙; ☎57-3009; www.takenet.or.jp/~fujioto; r per person from ¥10,500; ⊖ 🛜) The owner of this unpretentious, welcoming inn has ability in English, French, Italian and Spanish. It's a great place to have your first ryokan experience as most staff are able to communicate well, especially over the wonderful *kaiseki* dinner, served in the dining room. Corner upstairs rooms have lovely views. You can also stop by for lunch – try the Kiso Valley trout (*teishoku* – set-course meal ¥1350).

Yoshimura-ya
Noodles ¥

(吉村屋; ☎57-3265; dishes ¥700-1500; ⏱lunch, closed Thu; 🖉📖) If you're hungry after a long walk, this handmade *soba* will fill you up.

🛈 Information

Tourist Information Office (観光案内館; ☎57-3123; fax 57-4036; ⏱8.30am-5pm) Tsumago's Tourist Information Office is in the centre of town, by the antique phone booth. Some English is spoken and there's English-language literature. Ask here for any directions.

🛈 Getting There & Away

Nakatsugawa and Nagiso Stations on the JR Chūō line serve Magome and Tsumago respectively, though both are still at some distance. Nakatsugawa is connected with Nagoya (*tokkyū*, ¥2430, 57 minutes) and Matsumoto (*tokkyū*, ¥3670, 1¼ hours). A few *tokkyū* daily stop in Nagiso (from Nagoya ¥2770, one hour); otherwise change at Nakatsugawa (*futsū* ¥320, 20 minutes).

Buses leave hourly from Nakatsugawa Station for Magome (¥540, 30 minutes). There's also an infrequent bus service between Magome and Tsumago (¥600, 25 minutes), via Magome-tōge.

Buses run between Tsumago and Nagiso Station (¥270, 10 minutes, eight per day), or it's an hour's walk.

Meitetsu operates highway buses that connect Tokyo's Shinjuku Station with Magome (¥4500, 4½ hours). Note that the stop is at the highway interchange, from where it's a 1.3km uphill walk, unless timed with the bus from Nakatsugawa.

Kiso-Fukushima
木曽福島

North of Tsumago and Magome, Kiso-Fukushima is larger and considerably more developed, but its historical significance as an important checkpoint on the Nakasendō and its riverside position make it a pleasant lunch stop en route to (or from) Matsumoto.

From Kiso-Fukushima Station, turn right and head downhill towards the town centre and the Kiso-gawa. Sights are well signposted. Look for **Ue-no-dan** (上の段), the historic district of atmospheric houses, many of which are now retailers.

◎ Sights

Fukushima Checkpoint Site
Museum

(福島関所跡; Fukushima Sekisho-ato; adult/child ¥300/150; ⏱8am-5pm Apr-Oct, 8.30am-4pm Nov-Mar) This is a reconstruction of one of the most significant checkpoints on the Edo-period trunk roads. From its perch above the river valley, it's easy to see the barrier's strategic importance. Displays show the implements used to maintain order, including weaponry and *tegata* (wooden travel passes), as well as the special treatment women travellers received.

🍴 Eating

Kurumaya Honten
Noodles ¥

(くるまや本店; ☎22-2200; 5367-2 Kiso-machi Fukushima; mains ¥630-1575; ⏱10am-5pm Thu-Tue; 🖉📖) One of Japan's most renowned *soba* shops. The classic presentation is cold *mori* (plain) or *zaru* (with strips of nori seaweed) with a sweetish dipping sauce. Near the first bridge at the bottom of the hill.

🛈 Information

Tourist Office (木曽町観光協会; Kiso-machi Kankō Kyōkai; ☎22-4000; 2012-10 Kiso-machi Fukushima; ⏱9am-4.45pm) Across from the station, these friendly ladies have some English maps, but appreciate some Japanese ability.

🛈 Getting There & Away

Kiso-Fukushima is on the JR Chūō line (Shinano *tokkyū*), easily reached from Matsumoto (¥2100, 38 minutes), Nakatsugawa (¥2100, 34 minutes) and Nagoya (¥4500, 1½ hours).

Tateyama-Kurobe Alpen Route
立山黒部アルペンルート

Open from mid-April to mid-November, this popular seasonal 90km route connects Shinano-ōmachi in Nagano-ken with Tateyama (Toyama-ken).

Travel is possible in either direction; instructions here are from Shinano-ōmachi. Full details are online at: www.alpen-route.com/english.

The fare for the entire route is ¥10,560/17,730 one way/return; tickets for individual sections are available. It takes *at least* six hours, one way. If you're starting in Toyama, you may find a return trip to Murodō (¥6530), the route's highest point, sufficient.

Setting off in the morning from Matsumoto, take a local train to Shinano-ōmachi station. Buses depart in front of the station for **Ogizawa** (¥1330, 40 minutes), where you'll board the trolleybuses that take you through a 5.8km tunnel to the colossal **Kurobe-dam** (¥1500, 16 minutes). From here, it's a 15-minute walk across the dam to **Kurobeko**, then an underground cable car to **Kurobe-daira** (¥840, five minutes). From here, the Tateyama Ropeway whisks you 488m up to **Daikanbō** (¥1260, seven minutes). Next, board another trolleybus – this one tunnelling through Mt Tateyama for 3.7km, to **Murodō** (¥2100, 10 minutes).

At 2450m, Murodō is the route's highest point. Ten minutes' walk north is the pond **Mikuri-ga-ike** (みくりが池), home to an inn of the same name that houses a small restaurant and Japan's highest onsen.

The trek down continues with a bus to **Bijodaira** (美女平; ¥1660, 50 minutes) via the spectacular alpine plateau of **Midagahara Kōgen**.

The last stage of the route is the cable car down to **Tateyama** (立山; ¥700, seven minutes).

Narai 奈良井

A less known, but equally important example of a Nakasendō post town, Narai is one of our favourites, tucked away in the folds of a narrow valley. Once called 'Narai of a thousand houses', it flourished in the Edo period when its proximity to the highest pass on the Nakasendō made it a popular resting place for travelers. Today, it's a conservation area with a preserved main street showcasing some wonderful examples of Edo-period architecture.

Narai is famed for *shikki* (lacquerware). Plenty of quality souvenir shops line the street, many with reasonable prices.

 Sights

Nakamura House   Historic Building
(中村邸; ☎34-2655; adult/child ¥300/free; ☉9am-4pm) This wonderfully preserved former merchant's house and garden looks as if it has stood still while time passed by.

Sleeping & Eating

Echigo-ya   Ryokan ¥¥
(ゑちごや旅館; ☎34-3011; www.naraijyuku-echigoya.jp; 493 Narai; r per person incl 2 meals from ¥13,650) In business for over 220 years, this charming family-run ryokan is one of a kind. With only two guestrooms, this is a unique opportunity to experience the Japanese art of hospitality in its most undiluted form. Expect to feel like you've stepped back in time. Some Japanese ability will help make the most of the experience. Book well in advance. Cash only

Oyado Iseya   Inn ¥¥
(御宿伊勢屋; ☎34-3051; www.oyado-iseya.jp; 388 Narai; r per person incl 2 meals from ¥9000)

The streetfront of this former merchant house built in 1818 has been beautifully preserved. Now a pleasant 10-room inn, guest rooms are in the main house and a newer building out back.

Matsunami Shokudō ¥
(松波; ☎ 34-3750; 397-1 Narai; meals ¥850; ⏱11.30am-8pm Wed-Mon) This delightful little eatery on a corner serves simple favourites such as special-sauce *tonkatsu-don*.

ℹ Information

Tourist Information Office (奈良井宿観光協会; ☎ 54-2001; www.naraijuku.com) Inside Narai station, it has some English-language leaflets and a map. Little English is spoken.

ℹ Getting There & Away

Only *futsū* trains stop at Narai, which is on the JR Chūō line. It takes no more than an hour or three to see the sights, making a neat daytrip from Matsumoto (¥560, 50 minutes), but you could easily pass a peaceful evening here. From Nagoya, change trains at Nakatsugawa (¥1280, 1½ hours) or Kiso-Fukushima (¥400, 20 minutes).

villages. Hakusan National Park, near the southern tip of the prefecture, offers great hiking. You can find good overviews at www.hot-ishikawa.jp.

Kanazawa 金沢

☎076 / POP 462,360
Kanazawa's array of cultural attractions makes it the drawcard of the Hokuriku region. Best known for Kenroku-en, a castle garden dating from the 17th century, it also boasts beautifully preserved samurai and geisha districts, attractive temples and a wealth of museums. We recommend a two- or three-day stay to take it all in.

◉ Sights & Activities

Kanazawa is a sprawling city, but unfortunately public transport isn't the best. You'll orient yourself soon enough; a plethora of city maps are available from the Tourist Information Office in JR Kanazawa Station.

ISHIKAWA PREFECTURE

Ishikawa Prefecture (石川県; Ishikawa-ken), made up of the former Kaga and Noto fiefs, offers a blend of cultural and historical sights and natural beauty. Kanazawa, the Kaga capital and power base of the feudal Maeda clan, boasts traditional architecture and one of Japan's most famous gardens. To the north, the peninsula, Noto-hantō, has sweeping seascapes and quiet fishing

Higashi-chaya-gai, Kanazawa
PETER PTSCHEL / GETTY IMAGES ©

Kanazawa

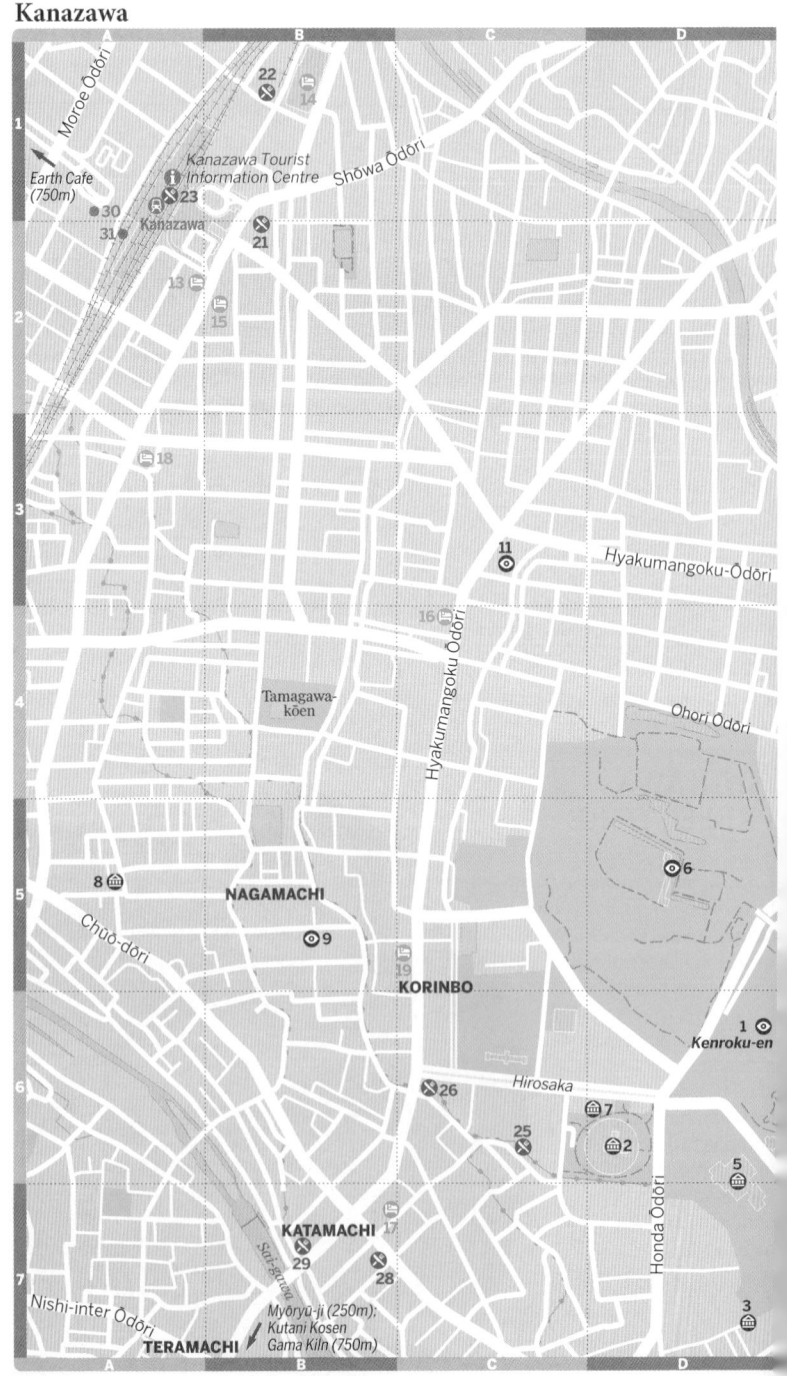

Moroe-Ōdōri

Earth Cafe
(750m)

22

14

Kanazawa Tourist
Information Centre

Shōwa-Ōdōri

30

23

31

Kanazawa

21

13

15

18

11

Hyakumangoku-Ōdōri

16

Tamagawa-
kōen

Hyakumangoku-Ōdōri

Ōhori-Ōdōri

8

NAGAMACHI

9

Chūō-dōri

19

KORINBO

6

1

Kenroku-en

26

Hirosaka

7

25

2

Honda-Ōdōri

5

17

KATAMACHI

29

28

Suji-dōri

3

Nishi-inter-Ōdōri

TERAMACHI

Myōryū-ji (250m);
Kutani Kosen
Gama Kiln (750m)

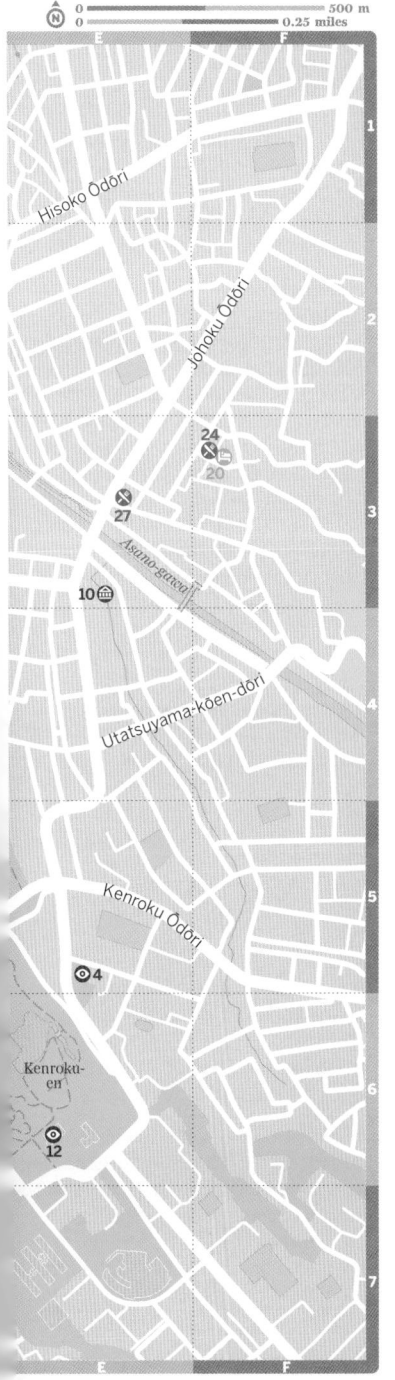

Kanazawa

◎ **Don't Miss Sights**
1 Kenroku-en D6

◎ **Sights**
2 21st Century Museum of
    Contemporary Art D6
3 D.T. Suzuki Museum D7
4 Gyokusen-en E5
5 Ishikawa Prefectural Art
    Museum D6
6 Kanazawa Castle Park D5
7 Kanazawa Noh Museum D6
8 Nagamachi Yūzen-kan A5
9 Nomura Samurai House B5
10 Ōhi Pottery Museum E3
11 Ōmichō Market C3
12 Seison-kaku E6

⊜ Sleeping
13 ANA Crowne Plaza Kanazawa A2
14 Hotel Dormy Inn Kanazawa B1
15 Hotel Nikkō Kanazawa B2
16 Hotel Resol Trinity C4
17 Murataya Ryokan B7
18 Pongyi A3
19 Tōyoko Inn Kanazawa
    Kenroku-en Kōrinbō C5
20 Yōgetsu F3

✖ **Eating**
21 Daiba Kanazawa Ekimae B2
22 Forus Department Store B1
23 Fureai-kan A1
24 Hotaruya F3
25 Itaru Honten C6
26 Janome-sushi Honten C6
27 Kanazawa Todoroki-tei E3
28 Oden Miyuki Honten B7
29 Tamazushi B7

ⓘ **Transport**
30 Hokutetsu Bicycle Rental A1
31 JR Kanazawa Station Rent-a-
    Cycle A2

The station area has its own vibe, but is set back from most of the action. Heading south of the station along Hyakumangoku-dōri, you'll first reach Kōrinbō, the shopping and business district, before arriving in Katamachi, by the banks of the Sai-gawa; this is where to eat, drink and be merry. If you're staying near the station, note that buses stop early evening. Taxis back from the area's countless bars and restaurants will set you back at least ¥1300.

Tera-machi and Nishi-chaya-gai are just over the bridge from Kata-machi, but the big-name sights are to its east: Kenroku-en, Castle Park and many museums are here. To their north, across the Asano-gawa, lies pretty Higashi-chaya-gai in the shadow of hilly Utatsuyama's many temples. Heading west will loop you back to the station, passing Ōmichō Market.

Nagamachi District   Neighbourhood

(長町) Once inhabited by samurai, this attractive, well-preserved district (Nagamachi Buke Yashiki) framed by two canals features winding streets lined with tile-roofed mud walls.

Nagamachi Yūzen-kan   Museum

(長町友禅館; 2-6-16 Nagamachi; admission ¥350; ⏰9am-noon & 1-4.30pm Fri-Wed) In a nontraditional building at the edge of the district, the Nagamachi Yūzen-kan displays some splendid examples of Kaga yūzen kimono-dyeing and demonstrates the process. Enquire ahead about trying the silk-dyeing process yourself (¥4000).

Nomura Samurai House   Historic Building

(武家屋敷跡 野村家; 1-3-32 Nagamachi; adult/child/student ¥500/250/400; ⏰8.30am-5.30pm Apr-Sep, to 4.30pm Oct-Mar) Nomura Samurai House, though partly transplanted from outside Kanazawa, is worth a visit for its decorative garden.

21st Century Museum of Contemporary Art   Museum

(金沢21世紀美術館; www.kanazawa21.jp; 1-2-1 Hirosaka; adult/child ¥350/free; ⏰10am-6pm Tue-Thu & Sun, to 8pm Fri & Sat) A low-slung glass cylinder, 113m in diameter, forms the perimeter of this 2004 'it' building. Inside, galleries are arranged like boxes on a tray, showcasing works by leading contemporary artists from Japan and abroad, with occasional music and dance performances. Check the website for events; admission fees may vary for special exhibitions.

Kanazawa Noh Museum   Museum

(金沢能楽美術館; 1-2-25 Hirosaka; adult/child ¥300/free; ⏰10am-6pm Tue-Sun) Come here for a basic introduction to the ancient art of nō (noh), one of the world's oldest continuously performed theatre forms. With special emphasis on Kaga-style performance, changing exhibits complement permanent displays. The ground floor is marked with the outline of a nō stage.

Kanazawa Castle Park   Historic Building

(金沢城公園 Kanazawa-jō Kōen; 1-1 Marunouchi; grounds/Bldg free/¥300; ⏰grounds 5am-6pm Mar-15 Oct, 6am-4.30pm 16 Oct-Feb, castle 9am-4.30pm) Originally built in 1580, this massive structure was called the 'castle of 1000 tatami' and housed the Maeda clan for 14 generations until it was ultimately destroyed by fire in 1881. What remains is the elegant gate **Ishikawa-mon** (石川門), rebuilt in 1788, providing a dramatic entry from Kenroku-en; holes in its turret were designed for ishi-otoshi (hurling rocks at invaders). Two additional buildings, the **Hishi-yagura** (菱櫓; diamond-shaped turret) and **Gojikken-Nagaya** (五十間長屋; armoury), were reconstructed in 2001, offering a glimpse of the castle's unique wood-frame construction. Restoration and archaeological work continues.

Seison-kaku   Historic Building

(☎221-0580; 2-1 Dewa-machi; adult/student ¥700/300; ⏰9am-5pm Thu-Tue) Inside the Castle Park, Seison-kaku is a retirement villa built by a Maeda lord for his mother in 1863. Elegant chambers named for trees and animals are filled with furniture, clothing and furnishings. A detailed English-language pamphlet is available.

D.T. Suzuki Museum   Museum

(鈴木大拙館; ☎221-8011; www.kanazawa-museum.jp/daisetz/english; 3-4-20 Honda-machi; adult/senior/child 300/200/free; ⏰9.30am-4.30pm Tue-Sun) Opened in 2012, this wonderful new museum is a tribute to Daisetsu Teitaro Suzuki, one of the foremost Buddhist philosophers and writers (in both Japanese and English) of our time largely credited for introducing Zen to the West. This stunning concrete complex

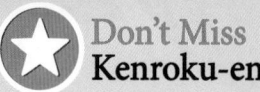

DIANE COOK AND LEN JENSHEL / GETTY IMAGES ©

⭐ Don't Miss
Kenroku-en

Ranked as one of the top three gardens in Japan (the other two are Kairaku-en in Mito, and Kōraku-en in Okayama), this Edo-period garden draws its name (*kenroku*; 'combined six') from a renowned Sung-dynasty garden in China that dictated six attributes for perfection: seclusion, spaciousness, artificiality, antiquity, abundant water and broad views. Kenroku-en has them all. The garden, originally belonging to an outer villa of Kanazawa-jō, began in 1876 but was later enlarged to serve the castle itself. It was 'completed' in the early 19th century and opened to the public in 1871.

In winter the branches of Kenroku-en's trees are famously suspended with ropes via a post at each tree's centre, forming elegant conical shapes that protect the trees from breaking under Kanazawa's heavy snows. In spring irises turn Kenroku-en's waterways into rivers of purple. Arrive before the crowds to increase potential for silent contemplation.

NEED TO KNOW

兼六園; 1-1 Marunouchi; adult/child ¥300/100; ⊘7am-6pm Mar-15 Oct, 8am-4.30pm 16 Oct-Feb

---

embodies the heart of Zen. Come to learn about the man and contemplate by the immaculate water mirror garden.

shikawa Prefectural
Art Museum   Museum

石川県立美術館; 2-1 Dewa-machi; adult/child ¥350/free; ⊘9.30am-5pm) All the local pecialities are covered here with an

emphasis on Kutani porcelain, Japanese painting and *Kaga yūzen* (silk-dyed) fabrics and costumes. Admission prices vary during special exhibitions.

Gyokusen-en   Garden

(玉泉園; 1-1 Marunouchi; adult/child ¥500/350; ⊘9am-4pm Mar–mid-Nov) For more intimacy and fewer crowds than Kenroku-en, this

Below: Carp streamers, Noto Peninsula (p189);
Right: Ishikawa-mon (p184), Kanazawa

(BELOW) FRANK CARTER / GETTY IMAGES ©; (RIGHT) SENICHI TAWARA / GETTY IMAGES ©

Edo-period garden rises up a steep slope. Enjoy a cup of tea here for an additional ¥700, while contemplating the tranquil setting.

Ōhi Pottery Museum Museum
(大樋美術館; Hashiba-chō; adult/child ¥700/500; ⊙9am-5pm) Established by the Chōzaemon family and now in its 10th generation. The first Chōzaemon developed this pottery style in nearby Ōhi village, using a slow-fired amber glaze, specifically for use in *chanoyu* (tea ceremonies).

Teramachi District Neighbourhood
(寺町) This hilly neighbourhood across Sai-gawa, southwest of the centre, was established as a first line of defence and contains dozens of temples.

Myōryū-ji Temple
(妙立寺; ☏241-0888; 1-2-12 Nomachi; admission ¥800; ⊙9am-4.30pm Mar-Nov, to 4pm Dec-Feb, reservations required) In Teramachi, fascinating Myōryū-ji (aka Ninja-dera), completed in 1643, was designed to protect its lord in case of attack. It contains hidden stairways, escape routes, secret chambers, concealed tunnels and trick doors. Contrary to popular belief, this ancient temple has nothing to do with ninja. Admission is by tour only (in Japanese with an English guidebook). Phone for reservations (in English).

Kutani Kosen Gama Kiln Gallery
(九谷光仙窯; 5-3-3 Nomachi; ⊙9am-5pm) **FREE** The Kutani Kosen Gama Kiln is a must for pottery lovers. Short tours give visitors a glimpse of the process and history of this fine craft. You can decorate porcelain yourself.

Ōmichō Market Market
(近江町市場; 35 Ōmichō; ⊙9am-5pm) Between Kanazawa Station and Katamachi, this market, reminiscent of Tokyo's Tsukiji, is a bustling warren of fishmongers, buyers and restaurants. It's a great place

to watch everyday people in action or indulge in the freshest of sashimi. The nearest bus stop is Musashi-ga-tsuji.

🛏 Sleeping

Pongyi Guesthouse ¥
(ポンギー; ☎225-7369; www.pongyi.com; 2-22 Rokumai-machi; dm, r per person from ¥2600; @) Run by a friendly Japanese man who did a stint in Southeast Asia as a monk, Pongyi is a charmingly renovated old shop alongside a canal. Cosy dorms are located in the attached vintage *kura* warehouse. Private rooms are available from ¥6000.

Tōyoko Inn Kanazawa Kenroku-en Kōrinbō Hotel ¥
東横イン金沢兼六園香林坊; ☎232-1045; www.toyoko-inn.com; 2-4-28 Korinbo; s/d from ¥4980/5980) In Kōrinbō, this business hotel has clean, cheap and cheerful little rooms and a free shuttle to the train station. It's about 15 minutes' walk from both Katamachi and JR Kanazawa Station, in either direction.

Yōgetsu Minshuku ¥
(陽月; ☎252-0497; 1-13-22 Higashiyama; r per person with/without breakfast from ¥5000/4500) This beautifully renovated 200-year-old geisha teahouse has only three rooms and features a circular *goemonburo* bath. It's located right in the picturesque Higashi-chaya district. No English is spoken.

Murataya Ryokan Ryokan ¥
(村田屋; ☎263-0455; www.murataya-ryokan. com; 1-5-2 Katamachi; s/tw ¥4700/ 9000; ➗ @) Eleven well-kept rooms around a lovely courtyard and friendly hosts await at this travellers' favourite in Katamachi. It's central to nightlife and restaurants, but that can also make things noisy.

Hotel Resol Trinity Hotel ¥¥
(ホテルレソルトリニティ; ☎221-9629; www.trinity-kanazawa.com; 1-18 Musashi-machi; r from s/d ¥5000/7000; @) This lovely niche hotel is a breath of fresh air. Rooms have a splash of colour and have been designed to make you feel comfortable in a compact

187

space. Its location is central to everything; you can walk to the station, Katamachi and Kenroku-en in about 15 minutes.

Hotel Dormy Inn Kanazawa
Hotel ¥¥

(ドーミーイン金沢; ☎263-9888; www.hotespa.net/hotels/kanazawa; 2-25 Horikawa-shinmachi; s/d/tw ¥8500/12,000/15,000; 🚭@) Around the corner from the station, this popular, modern tourist hotel has well-designed, functional rooms, a terrarium and a calcium-rich onsen *rotemburo* on the top floor, and a coin laundry.

ANA Crowne Plaza Kanazawa
Hotel ¥¥

(☎224-6111; www.anacrowneplaza-kanazawa.jp; 16-3 Showa-machi; s/d/tw from ¥9945/10,115/12,415; 🅿@) By the station, most of the Crowne Plaza's almost 250 rooms could be considered small for an international hotel, but they are well furnished and many have great views. Recommended if you want to be by the station and can get a deal online in your home country.

Hotel Nikkō Kanazawa
Hotel ¥¥¥

(ホテル日航金沢; ☎234-1111; www.hnkanazawa.jp; 2-15-1 Hon-machi; s/d from ¥26,250) Kanazawa's most luxurious hotel, near the station, has a wide range of room types from singles to lavish suites and an impressive selection of on-site restaurants and bars. Most rooms have exceptional views. The 'Luxe Style' and 'Stylish' rooms are the most recently refurbished and worthy of the extra coin.

🍴 Eating

Seafood is the staple of Kanazawa's *Kaga ryōri* (Kaga cuisine); even the most humble train-station *bentō* (boxed meal) usually features some type of fish. *Oshi-zushi,* a thin layer of fish pressed atop vinegared rice, is said to be the precursor to modern sushi. Another favourite is *jibuni,* which is flour-coated duck or chicken stewed with shiitake and green vegetables.

The JR Kanazawa Station building has plenty of food outlets in its Fureai-kan (ふれあい館), otherwise, the neighbouring

Forus department store has the 'Kuugo Dining Resort' on its 6th floor, with over 15 restaurants. Otherwise, head to Katamachi. Closer by, Ōmichō Market (p186) has fresh-from-the-boat eateries; both are great for browsing.

Itaru Honten
Seafood, Izakaya ¥¥

(いたる本店; ☎252-5755; 3-8 Kakinokibatake; ⏰dinner Mon-Sat; 📱) Here you'll find some of the best sushi and sashimi in Japan, including regional specialties *hotaru-ika* and *shiro-ebi*. The Kanazawa Omakase (leave it to the chef) course is ¥3000. Otherwise, you can try *jibuni*.

Oden Miyuki Honten
Izakaya ¥

(三幸本店; ☎222-6117; 1-10-3 Katamachi; oden ¥100-400, most other dishes ¥400-600; ⏰dinner Mon-Sat) For fish in another form (ground and pressed into cakes and served in broth), *oden* is very satisfying, especially on chilly nights. Some of the staff are English-speaking.

Daiba Kanazawa Ekimae
Izakaya ¥¥

(台場金沢駅前店 ; ☎263-9191; 6-10 Konohana-machi, Kanazawa Miyako Hotel 1F; items from ¥420; ⏰lunch & dinner; 📱) This trendy spot in the Kanazawa Miyako hotel building has a comprehensive Japanese menu and a limited English one with all the Western favourites and some local specialities. It's a great place for your first *izakaya* experience.

Earth Cafe
Vegan ¥¥

(☎233-0722; www.earth-p.net/cafe/; 2-12-30 Ekinishi-honmachi; items ¥550-1480; ⏰11am-6pm Mon-Sat; 🍴) Vegans (and those feeling the need for healthy food) will rejoice at this wholesome, airy cafe. It's a little pricey for what you get, but, there's no comparison in town. Keeping it simple, we rate both the veggie burgers and the curries. It's about 1km northwest of the station, on Rte 60.

Tamazushi
Sushi ¥¥

(玉寿司; ☎221-2644; 2-21-18 Katamachi; mains ¥1300-3300; ⏰dinner Mon-Sat) Near the river in Katamachi, this classic sushi counter is one of Kanazawa's best. There's no

Detour:
Noto Peninsula

With rugged seascapes, traditional rural life, fresh seafood and a light diet of cultural sights, Noto Peninsula (Noto-hantō) atop Ishikawa-ken is a picturesque escape from the Hokuriku region's urban sprawl. The lacquer-making town of Wajima is the hub of the rugged north, known as Oku-Noto, and the best place to stay overnight. Famous products include Wajima-nuri lacquerware, renowned for its durability and rich colours, Suzu-style pottery and locally harvested sea salt and *iwanori* seaweed.

In the centre of Oku-Noto, Noto airport connects the peninsula with Tokyo. **Furusato Taxi** (☏ 0768-22-7411) is a van service to locations around the peninsula. Fares start at ¥700 to nearby communities including Wajima (about 30 minutes).

Although there are trains, most sights can be reached by road only. For the west Noto coast, take the JR Nanao line from Kanazawa to Hakui (*tokkyū*, ¥1370; *futsū*, ¥740) and connect to buses. For Oku-Noto, trains continue to Wakura Onsen, connecting to less frequent buses. **Hokutetsu** (☏ 076-234-0123) runs buses between Kanazawa and Wajima (¥2200, two hours, 10 daily).

Self-driving is easily the best way to see the peninsula. The 83km Noto Yūryo (能登有料; Noto Toll Rd) speeds you as far as Anamizu (toll ¥1180). Noto's mostly flat west coast also appeals to cyclists. However, cycling is not recommended on the Noto-kongō coast and east because of steep, blind curves.

English, but a picture menu. It's a brown-white building on your right as you enter from the main street.

Janome-sushi Honten   Sushi ¥¥
(蛇之目寿司本店; ☏ 231-0093; 1-1-12 Kōrinbō; mains ¥1000-3400, Kaga ryōri sets from ¥4000; ⏰ lunch & dinner Thu-Tue; 📖) Regarded for sashimi and Kaga cuisine since 1931. One of our Japanese friends says that when he eats here, he knows he's really in Kanazawa. You can't go wrong with the lunch of the day (¥1000).

Kanazawa Todoroki-tei   Bistro ¥¥
金沢とどろき亭; ☏ 252-5755; 1-2-1 Higashi-yama; plates from ¥1200; ⏰ lunch & dinner) In a wonderful Taisho-era (1912–26) building with vaulted ceilings, near Higashi-chaya-gai, you'll find this atmospheric Western restaurant. Think art deco, wooden tables and candlelight. It's looking a little rough around the edges, but that's part of its charm – not too snooty. Romantic eight-course dinners for two are good value at ¥3675 per person.

Hotaruya   Kaiseki ¥¥¥
(蛍屋; ☏ 251-8585; 1-13-24 Higashiyama; lunch/dinner courses from ¥3675/6300) To splurge on *Kaga ryōri* and step back in time, visit this shop in Higashi-Chaya-gai; it's on the corner in a little square. You'll be rewarded with wood-beam and tatami room surroundings, and understated, standard-setting course meals. For lunch, try the *hanamachi kaiseki* set, ¥6300.

ℹ Information

Kanazawa Tourist Information Centre (石川県金沢観光情報センター; KGGN; ☏ 232-6200, 232-3933; http://kggn.sakura.ne.jp; 1 Hirooka-machi; ⏰ 9am-7pm) This excellent office inside Kanazawa Station has incredibly helpful staff and a plethora of well-made English-language maps, pamphlets and magazines, including *Eye on Kanazawa*. The friendly folk from the Goodwill Guide Network (KGGN) are also here to assist with hotel recommendations and free guiding in English – two weeks' notice is requested.

ⓘ Getting There & Away

Air

Nearby **Komatsu airport** (KMQ; www.komatsuairport.jp) has air connections with major Japanese cities, as well as Seoul, Shanghai and Taipei.

Bus

JR Highway Bus operates express buses from in front of Kanazawa Station's east exit, to Tokyo's Shinjuku Station (¥7840, 7½ hours) and Kyoto (¥4060, 4¼ hours). Hokutetsu buses serve Nagoya (¥4060, four hours). Nōhi Bus Company services Takayama, via Shirakawa-go (¥3300, 2½ hours).

Train

The JR Hokuriku line links Kanazawa with Fukui (*tokkyū*, ¥2430, 50 minutes; *futsū*, ¥1280, 80 minutes), Kyoto (*tokkyū*, ¥6200, 2¼ hours), Osaka (*tokkyū*, ¥6930, 2¾ hours) and Toyama (*tokkyū*, ¥2100, 35 minutes), with connections to Takayama (total ¥4870, additional 90 minutes).

From Tokyo take the Jōetsu *shinkansen* and change at Echigo-Yuzawa in Northern Honshū (¥11,840, four hours), until spring 2015, when the Hokuriku *shinkansen* makes its bold entry into Kanazawa, slashing travel times and increasing visitor numbers dramatically.

ⓘ Getting Around

JR Kanazawa Station is the hub for transit to/from and around Kanazawa.

Full-size bikes can be rented from **JR Kanazawa Station Rent-a-Cycle** (駅レンタサイクル; ☏ 261-1721; per hour/day ¥200/1200; ⏰ 8am-8.30pm) and **Hokutetsu Bicycle Rental** (北鉄レンタルサイクル; ☏ 263-0919; per 4hr/day ¥630/1050; ⏰ 8am-5.30pm), in the offices of Nippon Rentacar. Both are by the West exit.

The city recently introduced a pay-as-you-go bicycle-rental system called 'Machi-nori'. The bikes are a bit dinky, but with a bit of planning, the system functions well. For the low-down on how it works, in English, go to: www.machi-nori.jp/pdf/machinoriEnglishmap.pdf.

Buses depart from the circular terminus in front of the station's East exit. Any bus from station stop 7, 8 or 9 will take you to the city centre (¥200, day pass ¥900). The Kanazawa Loop Bus (single ride/day pass ¥200/500, every 15 minutes from 8.30am to 6pm) circles the major tourist attractions in 45 minutes. On Saturday, Sunday and holidays, the Machi-bus goes to Kōrinbō for ¥100.

Airport buses (¥1100, 40 minutes) depart from station stop 6. Some services are via Katamachi and Kōrinbō 109, but take one hour to reach the airport.

Numerous car-rental agencies are dotted around the station's west exit.

Korogi-bashi, Yamanaka Onsen

MIXA / GETTY IMAGE

Kaga Onsen 加賀温泉

0761

This broad area consisting of three hot-spring villages, **Katayamazu Onsen**, **Yamashiro Onsen** and **Yamanaka Onsen**, is centred on Kaga Onsen and Daishōji Stations along the JR Hokuriku line and is famed for its onsen-ryokan, lacquerware and porcelain. Of the three villages, Yamanaka Onsen is the most scenic.

Sights & Activities

Kutaniyaki Art Museum　Museum
(石川県九谷焼美術館; 1-10-13 Jikata-machi; admission ¥500; ◷9am-5pm, closed Mon) Stunning examples of bright and colourful local porcelain are on display here, an eight-minute walk from Daishōji Station.

Zenshō-ji　Buddhist Temple
(全昌寺; 1 Daishōji Shinmei-chō; admission ¥500; ◷9am-5pm) The Daishōji Station area is crammed with temples including Zenshō-ji, which houses over 500 amusingly carved Buddhist arhat sculptures.

Yamanaka Onsen　Onsen
In lovely Yamanaka Onsen, the 17th-century haiku poet Basho rhapsodised on the chrysanthemum fragrance of the local mineral springs. It's still an ideal spot for chilling at the bathhouse **Kiku no Yu** (菊の湯; admission ¥420; ◷6.45am-10.30pm), and for river walks by the Kokusenkei gorge, spanned by the elegant **Korogi-bashi** (Cricket bridge) and the whimsical, modern-art **Ayatori-hashi** (Cat's Cradle bridge). Yamanaka Onsen is accessible by bus (¥410, 30 minutes) from Kaga Onsen Station.

Yamashiro Onsen　Onsen
(総湯) A few kilometres closer to Kaga Onsen Station, Yamashiro Onsen is a sleepy town centred on a magnificent wooden bathhouse that was recently rebuilt. **Kosōyu** (古総湯; admission ¥500, Sōyu combined ticket ¥700; ◷6am-10pm) has beautiful stained-glass windows and a rest area on the top floor; neighbouring **Sōyu** is a larger, more modern bathhouse.

 Sleeping

The friendly folk at the **Yamanaka Onsen Tourism Association** (山中温泉観光協会; ☑78-0330; www.yamanaka-spa.or.jp/english; Yamanaka Onsen Bunka Kaikan, 5-1 Yamanaka Onsen) can help with the difficult task of picking the right ryokan for your budget and tastes – there are many in this region. Our two favourites are below.

Beniya Mukayū　Ryokan ¥¥¥
(べにや無何有; ☑77-1340; www.mukayu.com; 55-1-3 Yamashiro Onsen; per person with meals from ¥47,400; P@) The friendly staff at this award-winning ryokan are committed to upholding the Japanese art of hospitality. Gorgeously minimalist, with an interior designed by renowned architect Kiyoshi Sey Takayama, this ryokan has a quiet, Zen-like philosophy that pervades every aspect of the guest experience, from a welcoming private tea ceremony to the gentle morning yoga classes. Rooms are a beautiful coming together of traditional and contemporary – all feature private outdoor cypress baths and elements of understated luxury. Spa treatments are out of this world. Mukayū's cuisine features only the best and freshest local seasonal ingredients, exquisitely prepared. This is truly a special place.

Kayōtei　Ryokan ¥¥¥
(かよう亭; ☑78-1410; www.kayotei.jp; 1-20 Higashi-machi; per person with meals from ¥39,000; P@) This delightful, opulent ryokan along the scenic Kokusenkei gorge has only 10 rooms, giving it an intimate feel. Some rooms have private outdoor baths facing the inn's own mountain.

Getting There & Away

The JR Hokuriku line links Kaga Onsen with Kanazawa (*tokkyū*, ¥1470, 25 minutes; *futsū*, ¥740, 44 minutes) and Fukui (*tokkyū*, ¥1300, 20 minutes; *futsū*, ¥570, 48 minutes). A bus (¥700, 45 minutes, one daily April to November) links Yamanaka Onsen with Fukui-ken's famous Eihei-ji.

Kyoto

For much of its history, Kyoto *was* Japan. Even today, Kyoto is *the* place to go to see what Japan is all about. Here is where you'll find all those things you associate with Japan: ancient temples, colourful shrines and sublime gardens. Indeed, Kyoto is the storehouse of Japan's traditional culture, and it's the place where even Japanese go to learn about their own culture.

With 17 Unesco World Heritage Sites, more than 1600 Buddhist temples and over 400 Shintō shrines, Kyoto is one of the world's most culturally rich cities. It is fair to say that Kyoto ranks with Paris, London and Rome as one of those cities that everyone should see at least once in their lives. And, needless to say, it should rank at the top of any Japan itinerary.

Geisha at Setsubun Matsuri (p231)
FRANK CARTER / GETTY IMAGES ©

Autumn in Kyoto

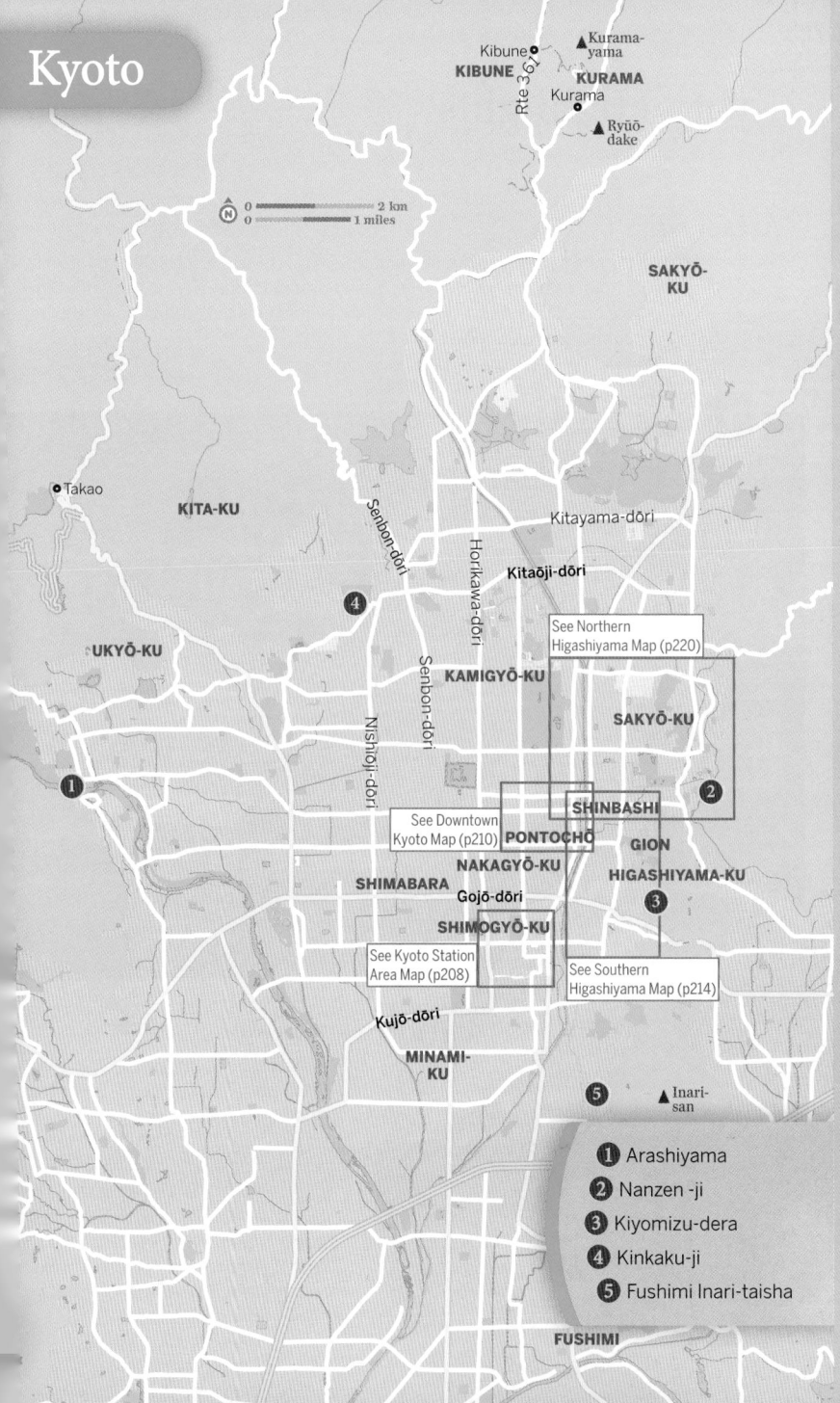

Kyoto

Kibune
Kurama-yama
KIBUNE
Rte 36
KURAMA
Kurama
Ryūō-dake

SAKYŌ-KU

0 — 2 km
0 — 1 miles

Takao
KITA-KU
Kitayama-dōri

Senbon-dōri

Horikawa-dōri
Kitaōji-dōri

❹

See Northern
Higashiyama Map (p220)

UKYŌ-KU

Senbon-dōri

KAMIGYŌ-KU

SAKYŌ-KU

Nishiōji-dōri

❶

❷

See Downtown
Kyoto Map (p210)

SHINBASHI

PONTOCHŌ

GION

NAKAGYŌ-KU

HIGASHIYAMA-KU

SHIMABARA

Gojō-dōri

❸

SHIMOGYŌ-KU

See Kyoto Station
Area Map (p208)

See Southern
Higashiyama Map (p214)

Kujō-dōri

MINAMI-KU

❺

Inari-san

FUSHIMI

❶ Arashiyama
❷ Nanzen-ji
❸ Kiyomizu-dera
❹ Kinkaku-ji
❺ Fushimi Inari-taisha

Kyoto Highlights

Arashiyama

Located 8km west of the city centre, Arashiyama (p224) is the romantic side of Kyoto. Here you can enjoy cool breezes by the river against a backdrop of mountains, with colours that change with the seasons. The area was originally developed as a detached villa for the imperial family to escape the heat of summer.

Nanzen-ji

This stately Zen temple (p219) in the Higashiyama area is the perfect introduction to the world of Japanese temples. It's got everything from the classic dry landscape garden (sometimes called a 'Zen garden') to a soaring *san-mon* gate and several intimate subtemples scattered around its spacious ground. Most of the precinct can be entered fr of charge and an evening stroll here is nothing short of magical.

FRANK CARTER / GETTY IMAGES ©

Kiyomizu-dera

3

If you only see one temple in Kyoto, make it Kiyomizu-dera (p213). This flamboyant complex overlooking Kyoto is everything a temple shouldn't be: noisy, crowded and overtly mercantile. But we're willing to forgive these failings because it's an awful lot of fun, it's gorgeous in the spring and autumn, and it's got a holy spring that bestows longevity and health.

DAVID CLAPP / GETTY IMAGES ©

4

Kinkaku-ji

Talk about eye candy: the gold-plated main hall of this immensely popular temple (p223) in northwest Kyoto is probably the most impressive sight in all Kyoto – especially if your tastes run to the grand and gaudy. If you are lucky enough to be there on a bright, sunny day, you almost need sunglasses to look at it. Go early on a weekday morning to avoid the crush of people that descend on the temple each day.

5

Fushimi Inari-taisha

There are thousands of vermillion torii (Shintō shrine gates) spread all across the mountain here at this shrine (p226) in southeast Kyoto. Visit the main hall and then head up the hill through the hypnotic arcades of torii. Be prepared to be utterly mesmerized – it's quite unlike anything else on earth. If you have time, climb all the way to the summit and enjoy the views.

Kyoto's Best...

Places to Contemplate

∘ **Nanzen-ji** A world of Zen temples and subtemples scattered amid the trees. (p219)

∘ **Chion-in** A vast Pure Land Buddhist temple – the Vatican of Japanese Buddhism. (p216)

∘ **Ginkaku-ji** The famed 'Silver Pavilion' boasts one of Kyoto's finest gardens. (p218)

∘ **Hōnen-in** A secluded retreat only a short walk from perpetually crowded Ginkaku-ji. (p218)

Places to Stay

∘ **Tawaraya** Some rank this sublime Kyoto ryokan (traditional Japanese inn) among the world's best accommodation. (p235)

∘ **Hyatt Regency Kyoto** The slick, smooth and efficient Hyatt is Kyoto's best hotel. (p236)

∘ **Hiiragiya Ryokan** Both the classic old wing and the pristine new wing are superb at this downtown Kyoto ryokan. (p235)

∘ **Westin Miyako Kyoto** This sprawling hotel claims one of Kyoto's best locations for sightseeing. (p237)

Places for a Walk

∘ **Tetsugaku-no-Michi (Path of Philosophy)** Running along a canal in the Higashiyama district, this path is picturesque in any season. (p218)

∘ **Kyoto Imperial Palace Park** Kyoto's central park, surrounding the palace, is a vast expanse of paths, fields and trees. (p209)

∘ **Maruyama-kōen** Mobbed in the cherry-blossom season, this pleasant tree-studded park is usually peaceful. (p215)

∘ **Gion** Stroll through the floating world and keep your eyes peeled for geisha. (p217)

Need to Know

Festivals

○ **Daimon-ji Gozan Okuribi** Five giant characters are set alight on mountains around Kyoto during this awesome summer ritual. (p232)

○ **Gion Matsuri** Considered the most important festival in Japan; the real fun is wandering downtown Kyoto in the nights leading up to the main event. (p231)

○ **Aoi Matsuri** Watch fabulously costumed participants process from the Gosho to Shimogamo-jinja. (p231)

○ **Kurama-no-hi Matsuri** Make your way into the mountains to witness this primeval event. (p232)

○ **Kyoto Tourist Information Center** (p248) Conveniently located in Kyoto Station, this should be your first stop in Kyoto. Note that it's known as 'Kyo Navi' in Japanese. It's not far from either the *shinkansen* (bullet train) or the regular train entrance/exit.

○ **Kyoto Visitor's Guide** Pick up a copy of this useful magazine at any major hotel in Kyoto; it's the best source of information on what's on while you're in town.

○ **Walk or cycle** These are the best ways of seeing Kyoto.

○ **Taxi** Catch one from Kyoto Station to your hotel or ryokan.

○ **Subway** This is helpful if you have to move quickly across the city: if travelling between north and south, catch the Karasuma Subway line, which stops at Kyoto Station; between east and west, the Tōzai Subway line runs from Higashiyama and the west side of Kyoto.

○ **Shinkansen** For rapid travel to/from Nagoya, Tokyo and Hiroshima.

○ **Seasonal festivals** Cherry-blossom season and autumn foliage season draw huge crowds to Kyoto: escape them by going to lesser-known temples and shrines.

○ **Summer (July and August)** These months are very hot and humid in Kyoto. You might consider doing your sightseeing in the early morning or late afternoon.

○ **Slip-on shoes** These are very useful for exploring the temples of Kyoto (you have to slip off your shoes to enter most temple buildings). You'll also find them useful if you stay in a ryokan.

Left: *Geiko* at a teahouse in Gion;
e: Cherry blossom trees near Ginkaku-ji (p218)

RE CIKAJLO / GETTY IMAGES ©; (ABOVE) AJ1008 / GETTY IMAGES ©

199

Southern Higashiyama Walking Tour

The southern Higashiyama area contains Kyoto's thickest concentration of first-class sights. A walk through this area is the perfect way to spend your first full day in the city. Note that this is also a pleasant route for an evening stroll.

WALK FACTS

- **Start** Gojō-zaka bus stop, Higashiōji-dōri
- **Finish** Jingū-michi bus stop, Sanjō-dōri; Higashiyama Station
- **Distance** 5km
- **Duration** Four hours

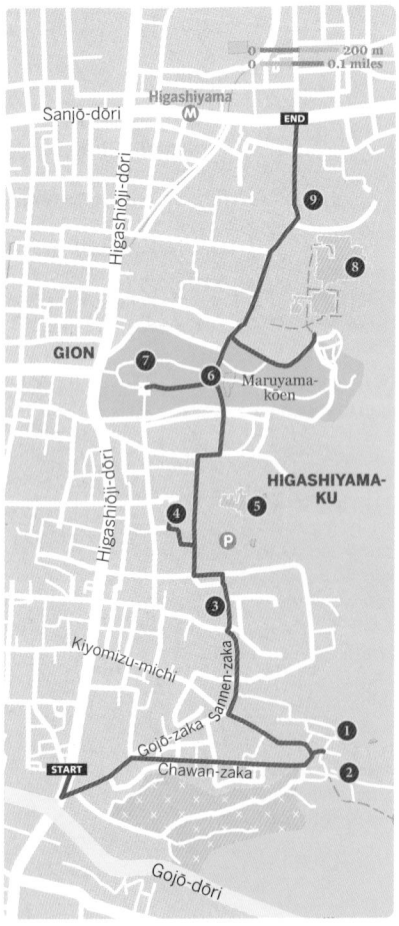

❶ Tainai-meguri

Just to the left of the ticket window of Kiyomizu-dera, this small subterranean walk through the darkness easily qualifies as Kyoto's most unusual attraction. We won't say too much about it– just try it.

❷ Kiyomizu-dera

At the top of Chawan-zaka, this grande dame of Kyoto temples commands an impressive view over the city. While you're visiting Kiyomizu-dera (p213), be sure to check out Jishu-jinga, home of the famous 'Love Stone', and take a sip of the holy water from the spring below the main hall.

❸ Kasagi-ya

On the left just after you start down Sannen-zaka, Kasagi-ya (p241) is a charming little teahouse and the ideal place to stop for a cup of hot *matcha* (powdered green tea) in winter or an *uji kintoki* (shaved ice with sweetened green tea) in summer. Be prepared to ask a local shop owner to point it out.

❹ Ishibei-kōji

After you descend Sannen-zaka and Ninen-zaka and start along Nene-no-Michi (just past the public toilet), you will find the entrance to this atmospheric pedestrian-only lane on your left. There is no English sign, so be prepared to ask someone. This is Kyoto's single-most attractive street.

❺ Kōdai-ji

At the top of a flight of steps on the right of Nene-no-Michi, you will find Kōdai-ji (p215), a temple famous for interesting evening illuminations of its gardens. At night the bamboo forest here is surreal.

6 Maruyama-kōen

This fine park (p215) is wonderful for an al-fresco lunch along this route, or just a quick can of coffee or tea (yes, a can). If you are at Maruyama-kōen during cherry-blossom season, be prepared for a rollicking scene.

7 Yasaka-jinja

Below (west) of Maruyama-kōen, you will find this attractive open-plan shrine (p216). Yasaka-jinja is usually busy with passing worshippers. If you are here on New Year's Eve or the first three days of the New Year, be ready for throngs of people.

8 Chion-in

An immense Pure Land Buddhist Temple, Chion-in (p216) is one of the great centres of Japanese Buddhism and it's grand in every way. Take off your shoes, enter the main hall and spend some time soaking up the atmosphere. It's free.

9 Shōren-in

A nice counterpoint to Chion-in, Shōren-in (p212) is a fine little Tendai sect temple with a wonderful garden and a lovely bamboo forest. You can sip a cup of *matcha* while gazing over the garden. Look for the giant camphor trees out front.

Kyoto in...

THREE DAYS

Spend your first day in the **southern Higashiyama** (p212) district checking out some of Japan's most amazing sights: Kiyomizu-dera, Maruyama-kōen, Chion-in and Shōren-in. If time allows, continue to the **northern Higashiyama** (p218) district to visit Nanzen-ji and the Tetsugaku-no-Michi. On the second day, head west to visit **Arashiyama and Sagano** (p224) and visit iconic sights such as the famous bamboo grove and Tenryū-ji. On your last day in town, check out Fushimi Inari-taisha and then visit the sights downtown, like Nishiki Market and the department stores' food floors. Don't forget to do an evening walk in Gion or Ponto-chō while you're in Kyoto.

ONE WEEK

On your first three or four days, follow the preceding itinerary. Then, on the following days, head north to **Kurama and Kibune** (p229); check out **Kinkaku-ji** (p223), the Zen garden at **Ryōan-ji** (p223), stroll the many subtemples of **Daitoku-ji** (p209), drop into **Tōfuku-ji** (p229) and consider a day trip to **Nara** (p276).

Above: Nishiki Market (p206)

AWL IMAGES / GETTY IMAGES ©

Discover Kyoto

🎵 075 / POP 1.47 MILLION

At a Glance

○ **Downtown Kyoto** (p206)
Here's where you'll do a lot of your eating, dining, partying and maybe sleeping.

○ **Southern Higashiyama** (p212)
This is Kyoto's premier sightseeing district – major sights are thick on the ground.

○ **Northern Higashiyama** (p218)
Another major sightseeing district, but with a bit more greenery and breathing room.

○ **Arashiyama & Sagano** (p224)
A seething tourist circus that quickly gives way to soothing bamboo groves and temples.

◉ Sights

Kyoto is laid out in a grid pattern and is extremely easy to navigate. Kyoto Station, the city's main station, is located at the southern end of the city, and the JR and Kintetsu lines operate from here. The real centre of Kyoto is located around Shijō-dōri, about 2km north of Kyoto Station via Karasuma-dōri. The commercial and nightlife centres are between Shijō-dōri to the south and Sanjō-dōri to the north, and between Kawaramachi-dōri to the east and Karasuma-dōri to the west.

Although some of Kyoto's major sights are in the city centre, Kyoto's best sightseeing is on the outskirts of the city, along the base of the eastern and western mountains (known as Higashiyama and Arashiyama, respectively). Sights on the east side are best reached by bus, bicycle or the Tōzai subway line. Sights on the west side (Arashiyama etc) are best reached by bus or train (or by bicycle if you're very keen). Outside the city itself, the mountain villages of Ōhara, Kurama and Takao make wonderful day trips and are easily accessible by public transport.

The Kyoto Tourist Information Centre (TIC) stocks the following maps: the *Kyoto City Map*, a useful map with decent insets of the main tourist districts; the oddly named *Kyoto Map for Tourist*, which is fairly detailed; the *Kyoto City Bus Sightseeing Map*, the most useful guide to city buses; and the leaflet *Kyoto Walks*, which has detailed walking maps for major sightseeing areas in and around Kyoto (Higashiyama, Arashiyama, northwestern Kyoto and Ōhara).

Nishi Hongan-ji
STEVE VIDLER / GETTY IMAGES ©

Kyoto Station Area

Although most of Kyoto's attractions are further north, there are a few attractions within walking distance of the station. The most impressive sight in this area is the vast Higashi Hongan-ji, but don't forget the station building itself – it's an attraction in its own right.

Higashi Hongan-ji   Temple

(東本願寺; Karasuma-dōri, Shichijō agaru; Map p208; ⏱5.50am-5.30pm Mar-Oct, 6.20am-4.30pm Nov-Feb; 🚇JR Tōkaidō main line, JR Tōkaidō shinkansen line, Sanyō shinkansen line, Kintetsu Kyoto line) FREE A short walk north of Kyoto Station, this temple is the last word in all things grand and gaudy. Considering the proximity to the station, the free admission, the awesome structures and the dazzling interiors, this temple is an obvious spot to visit if you find yourself near the station.

In 1602, when Tokugawa Ieyasu engineered the rift in the Jōdo Shin-shū school, he founded this temple as a competitor to Nishi Hongan-ji. Rebuilt in 1895 after a series of fires destroyed all of the original structures, the temple is now the headquarters of the Ōtani branch of Jōdo Shin-shū.

In the corridor between the two main buildings you'll find a curious item encased in glass: a tremendous coil of rope made from human hair. Following the destruction of the temple in the 1880s, an eager group of female temple devotees donated their locks to make the ropes that hauled the massive timbers used for reconstruction.

The enormous Goei-dō (main hall) is one of the world's largest wooden structures, standing 38m high, 76m long and 58m wide.

Nishi Hongan-ji   Temple

(西本願寺; Horikawa-dōri, Hanaya-chō sagaru; Map p208; ⏱5.30am-6pm May-Aug, to 5.30pm Mar, Apr, Sep & Oct, 6am-5pm Nov-Feb; 🚇JR Tōkaidō main line, JR Tōkaidō shinkansen line, Sanyō shinkansen line, Kintetsu Kyoto line) FREE This temple contains five buildings, featuring some of the finest examples of architecture and artistic achievement from the Azuchi-Momoyama period (1568–1600). The **Goei-dō** is a marvellous sight and the **Daisho-in Hall** has sumptuous paintings, carvings and metal ornamentation. A small garden and two nō (stylised Japanese dance-drama) stages are connected with the hall. The dazzling **Kara-mon** has intricate ornamental carvings.

In 1591 Toyotomi Hideyoshi built this temple, known as Hongan-ji, as the new headquarters for the Jōdo Shin-shū (True Pure Land) school of Buddhism, which had accumulated immense power. Later, Tokugawa Ieyasu saw this power as a threat and sought to weaken it by encouraging a breakaway faction of this school to found Higashi Hongan-ji (higashi means 'east') in 1602. The original Hongan-ji then became known as Nishi Hongan-ji (nishi means 'west'). It now functions as the headquarters of the Hongan-ji branch of the Jōdo Shin-shū school, with over 10,000 temples and 12 million followers worldwide.

Tō-ji   Buddhist Temple

(東寺; Map p204; 1 Kujō-chō; admission to grounds free, Kondō, Kōdō & Treasure Hall each ¥500, pagoda, Kondō & Kōdō ¥800; ⏱8.30am-5.30pm, to 4.30pm Sep-Mar; 🚇JR Tōkaidō main line, JR Tōkaidō shinkansen line, Sanyō shinkansen line, Kintetsu Kyoto line) This temple was established in 794 by imperial decree to protect the city. In 818 the emperor handed the temple over to Kūkai, the founder of the Shingon school of Buddhism. Many of the buildings were destroyed by fire or fighting during the 15th century; most of those that remain date from the 17th century.

The Kōdō (Lecture Hall) contains 21 images representing a Mikkyō (Esoteric Buddhism) mandala. The Kondō (Main Hall) contains statues depicting the Yakushi (Healing Buddha) trinity. In the southern part of the garden stands the five-storey pagoda, which burnt down five times. It was rebuilt in 1643 and is now the highest pagoda in Japan, standing 57m tall.

Greater Kyoto

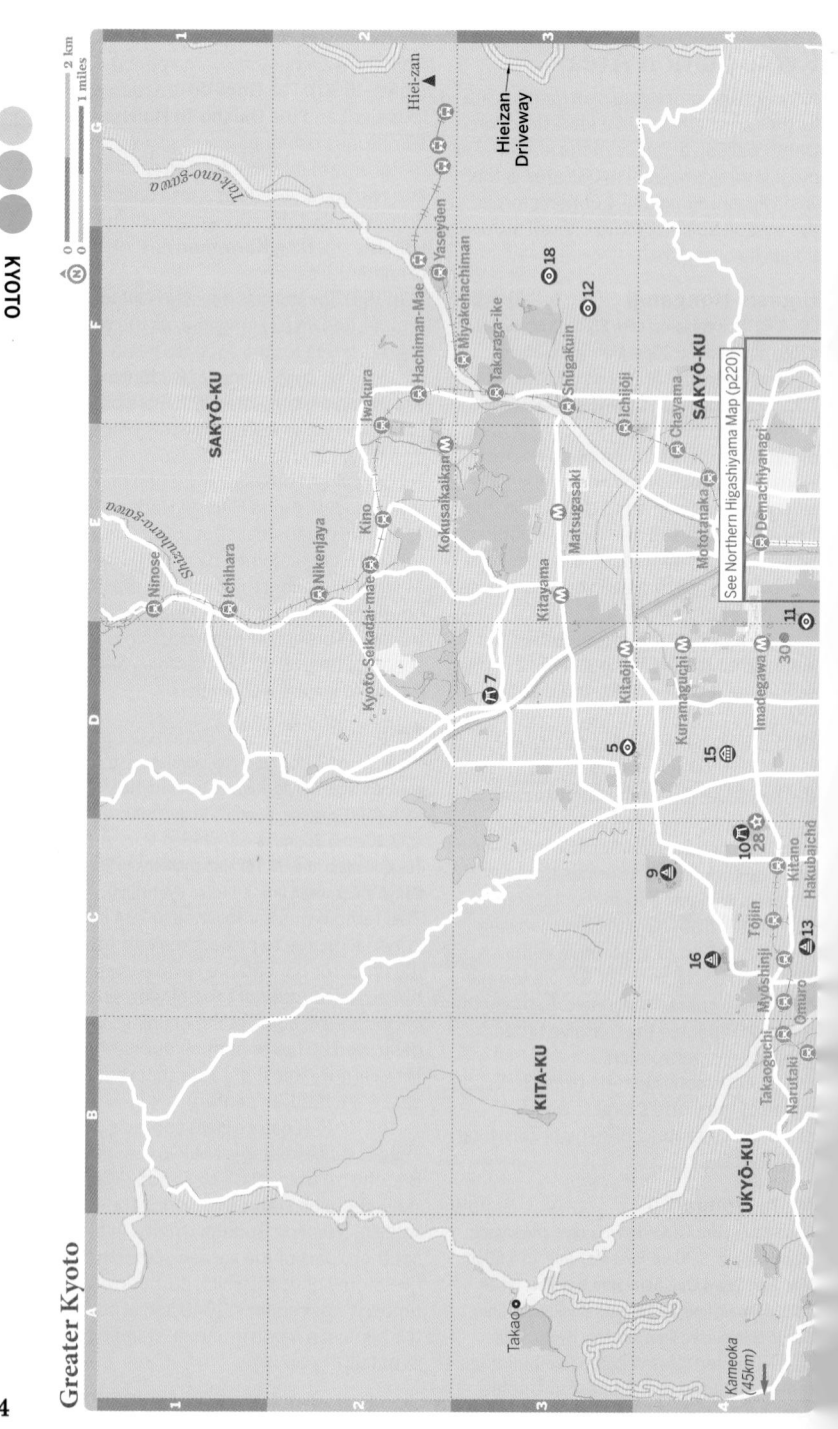

N
0 — 2 km
0 — 1 miles

KITA-KU

UKYŌ-KU

SAKYŌ-KU

SAKYŌ-KU

Takao

Kameoka (45km)

Takaoguchi
Narutaki
Omuro
Myōshinji
Tōjiin

Hakubaichō
Kitano

16

9

13

Hieizan
Driveway

Hiei-zan

Yaseyūen

Hachiman-mae

Miyakehachiman

Takaraga-ike

Shūgakuin

Ichijōji

18

12

Ōtoyama

Mototanaka

Demachiyanagi

See Northern Higashiyama Map (p220)

11

30

Imadegawa

Kuramaguchi

Kitaōji

Kitayama

Matsugasaki

Kokusaikaikan

Kino

Nikenjaya

Iwakura

Ichihara

Ninose

Kyoto-Seikadai-mae

7

5

15

10

28

Takano-gawa

Kurama-gawa

Shizuhara-gawa

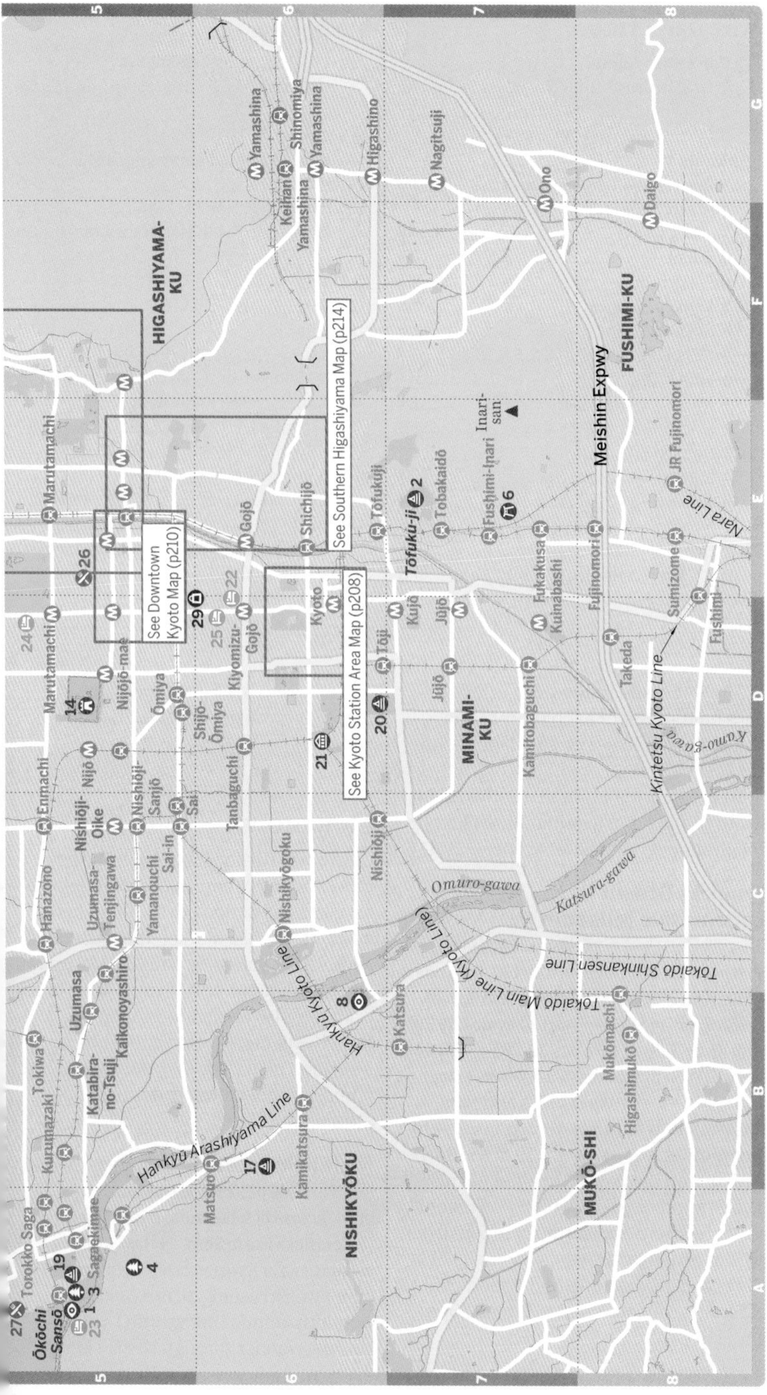

HIGASHIYAMA-KU

FUSHIMI-KU

MINAMI-KU

NISHIKYŌKU

MUKŌ-SHI

Meishin Expwy

See Southern Higashiyama Map (p214)

See Downtown Kyoto Map (p210)

See Kyoto Station Area Map (p208)

Tōfuku-ji 🔺 2

Nara Line

Kintetsu Kyoto Line

Kamo-gawa

Tōkaidō Shinkansen Line

Tōkaidō Main Line (Kyoto Line)

Katsura-gawa

Omuro-gawa

Hankyū Kyoto Line

Hankyū Arashiyama Line

Ōkōchi Sansō

Stations / labels:

Yamashina, Shinomiya, Keihan Yamashina, Higashino, Nagitsuji, Ono, Daigo, JR Fujinomori, Fujinomori, Fukakusa, Inari-san, Fushimi-Inari, Tobakaidō, Kuinabashi, Takeda, Fushimi, Sumizome, Tōfukuji, Shichijō, Gojō, Kujō, Jūjō, Kyoto, Tōji, Nishikyō, Kamitobaguchi, Marutamachi, Nijō-mae, Ōmiya, Shijō-Ōmiya, Nishijin, Tanbaguchi, Nishiōji-Oike, Nishiōji-Sanjō, Sai, Sai-in, Nishikyōgoku, Nishioji, Enmachi, Hanazono, Tenjingawa, Uzumasa Tenjingawa, Yamanouchi, Katsura, Kamikatsura, Mukōmachi, Higashimukō, Matsuo, Kurumazaki, Katabira-no-Tsuji, Kaikonoyashiro, Tokiwa, Uzumasa, Arashiyama, Torokko Saga, Sagano, Sageekimae, Saga Arashiyama

24, 26, 29, 25, 22, 14, 21, 20, 17, 8, 4, 6, 27, 19, 23, 1, 3

Greater Kyoto

⊙ Don't Miss Sights
1 Ōkōchi Sansō A5
2 Tōfuku-ji E7

⊙ Sights
3 Arashiyama Bamboo Grove A5
4 Arashiyama Monkey Park
   Iwatayama A5
5 Daitoku-ji D3
6 Fushimi Inari-taisha E7
7 Kamigamo-jinja D3
8 Katsura Rikyū B6
9 Kinkaku-ji C4
10 Kitano Tenman-gū C4
11 Kyoto Imperial Palace (Gosho) E4
12 Manshu-in F3
13 Myōshin-ji C4
14 Nijō-jō D5
15 Orinasu-kan D4
16 Ryōan-ji C4
17 Saihō-ji B6
18 Shūgaku-in Rikyū F3
19 Tenryū-ji A5
20 Tō-ji D6

21 Umekōji Steam Locomotive
   Museum D6

⊙ Sleeping
22 Citadines Kyoto Karasuma Gojō D6
23 Hoshinoya A5
24 Palace Side Hotel D5
25 Tōyoko Inn Kyoto Gojō Karasuma D6

⊗ Eating
26 Café Bibliotec HELLO! E5
27 Komichi A5

⊕ Entertainment
28 Kamishichiken Kaburen-jō
   Theatre C4

⊙ Shopping
Kōbō-san Market .... (see 20)
29 Morita Washi D6
Tenjin-san Market .... (see 10)

⊙ Information
30 Imperial Household Agency D4

The Kōbō-san market-fair is held here on the 21st of each month. The fairs held in December and January are particularly lively.

Tō-ji is a 15-minute walk southwest of Kyoto Station or a five-minute walk from Tōji Station on the Kintetsu line.

Umekōji Steam Locomotive Museum   Museum

(梅小路蒸気機関車館; Map p204; Kankiji-chō, Shimogyō-ku; adult/child ¥400/100; train ride ¥200/100; ☉10am-5pm, closed Mon, except 25 Mar-7 Apr and 21 Jul-7 Aug; 🚌Kyoto City Bus from Kyoto Station, take bus 33, 205 or 208 from Kyoto Station to the Umekō-ji Kōen-mae stop) A hit with steam-train buffs and kids, this museum features 18 vintage steam locomotives (dating from 1914 to 1948) and related displays. It's in the former Nijō Station building, which was recently relocated here and carefully reconstructed. For an extra few yen, you can take a 10-minute ride on one of the fabulous old trains (departures at 11am, 1.30pm and 3.30pm).

If catching the bus to the museum, make sure you get on a westbound service.

Downtown Kyoto

Downtown Kyoto looks much like any other Japanese city, but there are some excellent attractions to be found here, including Nishiki Market, the Museum of Kyoto, the Kyoto International Manga Museum and Ponto-chō. If you'd like a break from temples and shrines, then downtown Kyoto can be a welcome change. It's also good on a rainy day, because of the number of covered arcades and indoor attractions.

Nishiki Market   Market

(錦市場; Map p210; Nishikikōji-dōri, btwn Teramachi & Takakura; ☉9am-5pm; 🚇Karasuma line to Shijō, 🚇Hankyū line to Karasuma or Kawaramachi) If you are interested in seeing all the weird and wonderful foods that go into Kyoto cuisine, wander through Nishiki Market.

It's in the centre of town, one block north of (and parallel to) Shijō-dōri, running west off Teramachi Shopping arcade and ending shortly before Daimaru department store.

This market is a great place to visit on a rainy day or if you need a break from temple-hopping (note that some stalls are closed on Wednesdays). The variety of foods on display is staggering, and the frequent cries of *irasshaimase!* (welcome!) are heart-warming.

Kyoto International Manga Museum   Museum

(京都国際マンガミュージアム; Map p210; www.kyotomm.com/english; Karasuma-dōri, Oike agaru; adult/child ¥800/300; ⊙10am-6pm, closed Wed; S Karasuma or Tōzai lines to Karasuma-Oike) This fine museum has a collection of some 300,000 manga (Japanese comic books). Located in an old elementary school building, the museum is the perfect introduction to the art of manga. While most of the manga and displays are in Japanese, the collection of translated works is growing.

In addition to the galleries that show both the historical development of manga and original artwork done in manga style, there are beginners' workshops and portrait drawings on weekends. Visitors with children will appreciate the children's library and the occasional performances of *kami-shibai* (humorous traditional Japanese sliding-picture shows), not to mention the Astroturf lawn where the kids can run free. The museum hosts six month-long special exhibits yearly: check the website for details.

It's a short walk from the Karasuma-Oike Station on the Karuma line subway or the Tōzai line subway.

Ponto-chō   Neighbourhood

(先斗町; Map p210; Ponto-chō, Nakagyō-ku; ℞Keihan line to Sanjo, S Tōzai line to Sanjo-Keihan or Kyoto Shiyakusho-mae stations, ℞Hankyū line to Kawaramachi) A traditional nightlife district and one of Kyoto's five geisha districts, Ponto-chō is a narrow alley running between Sanjō-dōri and Shijō-dōri, just west of Kamo-gawa. It's best visited in the evening, when the traditional wooden buildings and hanging lanterns create a wonderful atmosphere of old Japan, perhaps combined with a walk in nearby Gion.

Geisha district, Ponto-chō

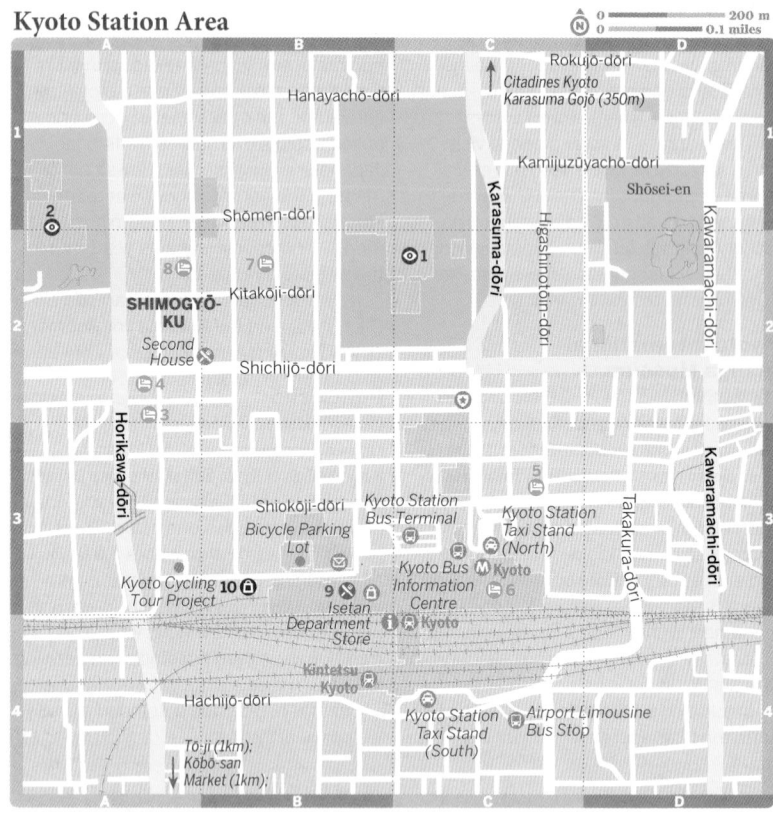

Kyoto Station Area

◎ **Sights**
| 1 Higashi Hongan-ji | C2 |
| 2 Nishi Hongan-ji | A1 |

🛏 **Sleeping**
3 Budget Inn	A2
4 Capsule Ryokan Kyoto	A2
5 Dormy Inn Premium Kyoto	
Ekimae	C3
6 Hotel Granvia Kyoto	C3
7 Ryokan Shimizu	B2
8 Tour Club	A2

⊗ **Eating**
9 Cube	B3
Eat Paradise	(see 9)
Kyoto Rāmen Koji	(see 9)

🛍 **Shopping**
| 10 Bic Camera | B3 |

Central Kyoto

The area we refer to as Central Kyoto includes the Kyoto Imperial Palace Park, Nijō-jō, a couple of important shrines and the Nishijin weaving district, among other sights. It's flat and easy to explore by bicycle or on foot.

Kyoto Imperial Palace (Gosho)   Historic Building

(京都御所; Map p204; Kyoto Gosho; Kyoto-gosho, Nakagyō-ku; **S** Karasuma line to Maru-tamachi or Imadegawa) The original imperial palace was built in 794 and was replaced numerous times after destruction by fire. The present building, on a different site and smaller than the original, was constructed in 1855. Enthronement of a new emperor and other ceremonies are still held here.

The Gosho does not rate highly in comparison with other attractions in Kyoto and you must apply for permission to visit at the Imperial Household Agency. However, you shouldn't miss the park surrounding the Gosho.

To get there, take the Karasuma line subway to Imadegawa or a bus to the Karasuma-Imadegawa stop and walk 600m southeast.

Imperial Household Agency — Booking Office

(宮内庁京都事務所; Map p204; ☎ 211-1215; ⏰ 8.45am-noon & 1-5pm Mon-Fri; S Karasuma line to Imadegawa) The Imperial Household Agency is the place to make advance reservations to see the Sentō Gosho, Katsura Rikyū and Shūgaku-in Rikyū.

Permission to visit the Gosho is granted by the Kunaichō, the Imperial Household Agency, which is inside the walled park surrounding the palace, a short walk from Imadegawa Station on the Karasuma line. You have to fill out an application form and show your passport. Children can visit if accompanied by adults over 20 years of age (but are forbidden entry to the other three imperial properties of Katsura Rikyū, Sentō Gosho and Shūgaku-in Rikyū). Permission to tour the palace is usually granted the same day (try to arrive at the office at least 30 minutes before the start of the tour you'd like to join). Guided tours, sometimes in English, are given at 10am and 2pm from Monday to Friday. The tour lasts about 50 minutes.

The Gosho can be visited without reservation during two periods each year, once in spring and once in autumn. The dates vary each year, but as a general guide, the spring opening is around the last week of April and the autumn opening is in the middle of November. Check with the TIC for exact dates.

Sentō Gosho Palace — Historic Building

(仙洞御所; Map p220; ☎ 211-1215; Kyoto gyōen, Nakagyō-ku; S Karasuma line to Marutamachi or Imadegawa) This palace is a few hundred metres southeast of the main Kyoto Gosho. It was originally built in 1630 during the reign of Emperor Go-Mizunō as a residence for retired emperors. The palace was repeatedly destroyed by fire and reconstructed but served its purpose until a final blaze in 1854 (it was never rebuilt).

The gardens, which were laid out in 1630 by Kobori Enshū, are superb. The route takes you past lovely ponds and pathways, and in many ways, a visit here is more enjoyable than a visit to the Gosho, especially if you are a fan of Japanese gardens. Visitors must obtain advance permission from the Imperial Household Agency and be over 20 years old. Tours (in Japanese) start at 11am and 1.30pm.

Kyoto Imperial Palace Park — Park

(京都御苑; Map p220; Kyoto gyōen, Nakagyō-ku; ⏰ dawn to dusk; S Karasuma line to Marutamachi or Imadegawa) FREE The Kyoto Gosho and Sentō Gosho are surrounded by the spacious Kyoto Imperial Palace Park, which is planted with a huge variety of flowering trees and open fields. It's perfect for picnics, strolls and just about any sport you can think of. Take some time to visit the pond at the park's southern end, which contains gorgeous carp.

The park is most beautiful in the plum- and cherry-blossom seasons (late February and late March, respectively). The plum arbour is located about midway along the park on the west side. There are several large *shidarezakura* ('weeping' cherry trees) at the north end of the park, making it a great cherry-blossom destination. The park is between Teramachi-dōri and Karasuma-dōri (to the east and west) and Imadegawa-dōri and Marutamachi-dōri (to the north and south).

Daitoku-ji — Temple

(大徳寺; Map p204; 53 Daitokuji-chō, Murasakino; ⏰ dawn-dusk; S Karasuma line to Kitaōji) FREE Daitoku-ji is a separate world within Kyoto – a collection of Zen temples, raked gravel gardens and wandering lanes. It is one of the most rewarding destinations in

Downtown Kyoto

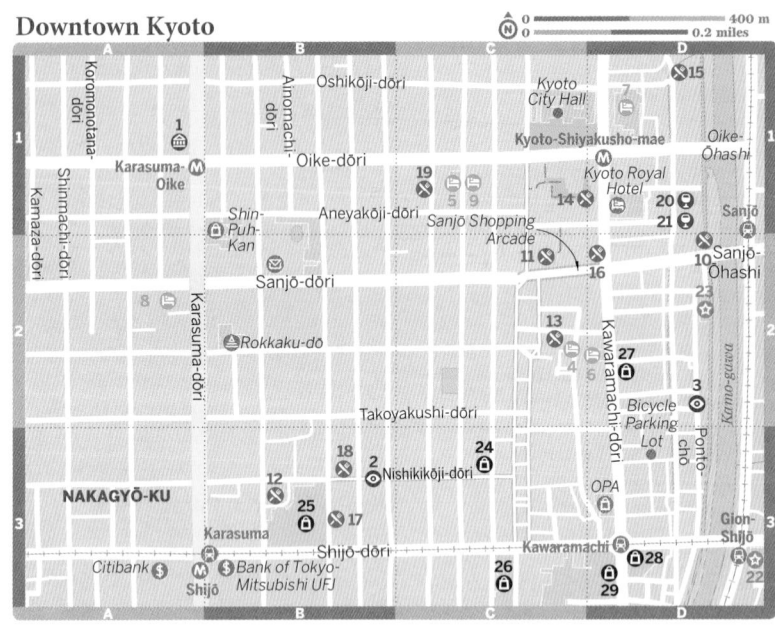

Downtown Kyoto

⊙ Sights
1 Kyoto International Manga
  Museum A1
2 Nishiki Market B3
3 Ponto-chō D2

🛏 Sleeping
4 Best Western Hotel Kyoto C2
5 Hiiragiya Ryokan C1
6 Hotel Unizo D2
7 Kyoto Hotel Ōkura D1
8 Mitsui Garden Hotel Kyoto Sanjō A2
9 Tawaraya C1

❌ Eating
10 Ganko Zushi.. D2
11 Honke Tagoto C2
12 Ippūdō B3
13 Kane-yo C2
14 Kerala C1
15 Kiyamachi Sakuragawa D1

16 Musashi Sushi...................................... D2
17 Tsukiji Sushisei B3
18 Warai B3
19 Yoshikawa C1

🍸 Drinking & Nightlife
20 McLoughlin's Irish Bar &
  Restaurant... D1
21 Sama Sama... D1

🎭 Entertainment
22 Minami-za Theatre............................. D3
23 Ponto-chō Kaburen-jō Theatre D2

🛍 Shopping
24 Aritsugu C3
25 Daimaru Department Store.................. B3
26 Fujii Daimaru Department Store...........C3
27 Junkudō D2
28 Marui D3
29 Takashimaya Department Store...........D3

this part of the city, particularly for those with an interest in Japanese gardens.

The name Daitoku-ji confusingly refers to both the main temple here and the entire complex, which contains a total of 24 temples and subtemples. We discuss three of them here, but another five are open to the public.

The eponymous Daitoku-ji is on the eastern side of the grounds. It was founded in 1319, burnt down in the next century and rebuilt in the 16th century. The San-mon contains an image of the famous tea master, Sen-no-Rikyū, on the 2nd storey. If you enter via the main gate on the east side of the complex, Daitoku-ji will be on your right, a short walk north.

Just north of Daitoku-ji, Daisen-in is famous for its two small gardens. At the western edge of the complex, Kōtō-in is famous for its stunning bamboo-lined approach and the maple trees in its main garden (try to visit in the foliage season).

The temple bus stop is Daitoku-ji-mae and convenient buses from Kyoto Station are buses 205 and 206. Daitoku-ji is also a short walk west of Kitaō-ji subway station on the Karasuma line.

Nijō-jō　　　　　　　　　Castle
(二条城; Map p204; 541 Nijōjō-chō, Nijō-dōri, Horikawa Nishi iru; admission ¥600; ⏰8.45am-5pm, closed Tue in Dec, Jan, Jul & Aug; Ｓ Tōzai line to Nijō-jō-mae) This castle was built in 1603 as the official Kyoto residence of the first Tokugawa shōgun, Ieyasu. The ostentatious style of its construction was intended as a demonstration of Ieyasu's prestige and also to signal the demise of the emperor's power. As a safeguard against treachery, Ieyasu had the interior fitted with 'nightingale' floors (that sings and squeaks at every move, making it difficult for intruders to move about quietly), as well as concealed chambers where bodyguards could keep watch.

After passing through the grand Kara-mon gate, you enter Ninomaru Palace, which is divided into five buildings with numerous chambers. The Ohiroma Yon-no-Ma (Fourth Chamber) has spectacular screen paintings. Don't miss the

excellent Ninomaru Palace Garden, which was designed by the tea master and landscape architect Kobori Enshū.

Nishijin　　　　　　Neighbourhood
(西陣; Nishijin; 🚌 Kyoto City Bus 9 to the Horikawa-Imadegawa stop) The Nishijin district is the home of Kyoto's textile industry, the source of the fantastically ornate kimonos and obi (ornamental kimono belts) for which the city is famous. It's one of Kyoto's more traditional districts, and there are still lots of good old *machiya* (traditional town houses) scattered about.

Orinasu-kan　　　　　　Museum
(織成館; Map p204; 693 Daikoku-chō; adult/child ¥500/350; ⏰10am-4pm, closed Mon; 🚌 Kyoto City Bus 9 to the Horikawa-Imadegawa stop) This museum, housed in a Nishijin weaving factory, has impressive exhibits of Nishijin textiles. It's more atmospheric and usually quieter than the Nishijin Textile Center. The Susamei-sha building across the street is also open to the public and worth a look. It's a short walk north of the Nishijin Textile Center.

Cherry blossoms, Kyoto Imperial Palace (p208)
FRANK DEIM / GETTY IMAGES ©

Southern Higashiyama

The Higashiyama district, which runs along the base of the Higashiyama mountains (Eastern Mountains), is the main sightseeing district in Kyoto and it should be at the top of your Kyoto itinerary. It is thick with impressive sights: fine temples, shrines, gardens, museums, traditional neighbourhoods and parks.

Shōren-in   Buddhist Temple

(青蓮院; Map p214; 69-1 Sanjōbō-chō, Awataguchi, Higashiyama-ku; admission ¥500; ⏰9am-5pm; [S]Tōzai line to Higashiyama) This temple is hard to miss, with the giant camphor trees growing just outside its walls. Shōren-in was originally the residence of the chief abbot of the Tendai school of Buddhism. The present building dates from 1895, but the main hall has sliding screens with paintings from the 16th and 17th centuries.

Often overlooked by the crowds that descend on other Higashiyama temples, this is a pleasant place to sit and think while gazing out over the beautiful gardens.

The temple is a five-minute walk north of Chion-in.

Sanjūsangen-dō   Buddhist Temple

(三十三間堂; Map p214; 657 Sanjūsangendōmawari-chō, Higashiyama-ku; admission ¥600; ⏰8am-4.30pm Apr-Oct, 9am-3.30pm Nov-Mar; [S]Keihan line to Shichijō, 🚌Kyoto City Bus 206 or 208 to the Sanjūsangen-dō-mae stop) The original Sanjūsangen-dō was built in 1164 at the request of the retired emperor Go-shirakawa. The temple's name refers to the 33 (sanjūsan) bays between the pillars of this long, narrow building, which houses 1001 statues of the 1000-armed Kannon (the Buddhist goddess of mercy). The largest Kannon is flanked on either side by 500 smaller Kannon images, neatly lined up in rows.

Kyoto National Museum   Museum

(京都国立博物館; Map p214; www.kyohaku.go.jp; 527 Chaya-machi, Higashiyama-ku; adult/student ¥500/250; ⏰9.30am-6pm, to 8pm Fri, closed Mon; 🚆Keihan line to Shichijō, 🚌Kyoto City Bus 206 or 208 to the Sanjūsangen-dō-mae stop) The Kyoto National Museum is housed in two buildings opposite Sanjūsangen-dō. It was founded in 1895 as an imperial repository for art and treasures from local temples and shrines.

Tea room at Nijō-jō (p211)

Kyoto Tips

Common sense varies from place to place. In Kyoto, even if you dispense with common sense, you don't run the risk of serious trouble, but there are a few things to keep in mind to make everything easier and perhaps a little safer:

◦ Look both ways when exiting a shop or hotel onto a footpath, especially if you have young ones in tow: Kyoto is a city of cyclists and there is almost always someone on a bicycle tearing in your direction.

◦ Bring a pair of slip-on shoes to save you from tying and untying your shoes each time you visit a temple.

◦ Don't take a taxi in the main Higashiyama sightseeing district during cherry-blossom season – the streets will be so crowded that it will be faster to walk or cycle.

◦ Head for the hills to find the most beautiful sights. Yes, the middle of the city has some great sights, but as a general rule, the closer you get to the mountains, the more attractive the city gets.

There are 17 rooms with displays of over 1000 artworks, historical artefacts and handicrafts.

The permanent collection is excellent but somewhat poorly displayed; unless you have a particular interest in Japanese traditional arts, we recommend visiting this museum only when a special exhibition is on. Note that at the time of writing, the museum was undergoing a partial reconstruction; you can still enter the museum but construction will be going on until late 2013.

Kiyomizu-dera   Buddhist Temple
(清水寺; Map p214; 1-294 Kiyomizu, Higashiya-ma-ku; admission ¥300; ◷6am-6pm; 🚍Kyoto City Bus 206 to the Kiyōmizu-michi or Gojō-zaka stops, 🚃Keihan line to Kiyomizu-Gojō) This ancient temple was first built in 798, but the present buildings are reconstructions dating from 1633. As an affiliate of the Hossō school of Buddhism, which origi-nated in Nara, it has successfully survived the many intrigues of local Kyoto schools of Buddhism through the centuries and is now one of the most famous landmarks of the city (it can get crowded during spring and autumn).

The main hall has a huge verandah that is supported by pillars and juts out over the hillside. Just below this hall is the waterfall Otowa-no-taki, where visitors drink sacred waters believed to bestow health and longevity. Dotted around the precincts are other halls and shrines. At Jishu-jinja, the shrine up the steps above the main hall, visitors try to ensure success in love by closing their eyes and walking about 18m between a pair of stones – if you miss the stone, your desire for love won't be fulfilled! Note that you can ask someone to guide you, but if you do, you'll need someone's assistance to find your true love.

Before you enter the actual temple precincts, check out the Tainai-meguri, the entrance to which is just to the left (north) of the pagoda that is located in front of the main entrance to the temple (there is no English sign). We won't tell you too much about it as it will ruin the experience. Suffice to say that by entering the Tainai-meguri, you are symbolically entering the womb of a female bodhi-sattva. When you get to the rock in the darkness, spin it in either direction to make a wish.

Southern Higashiyama

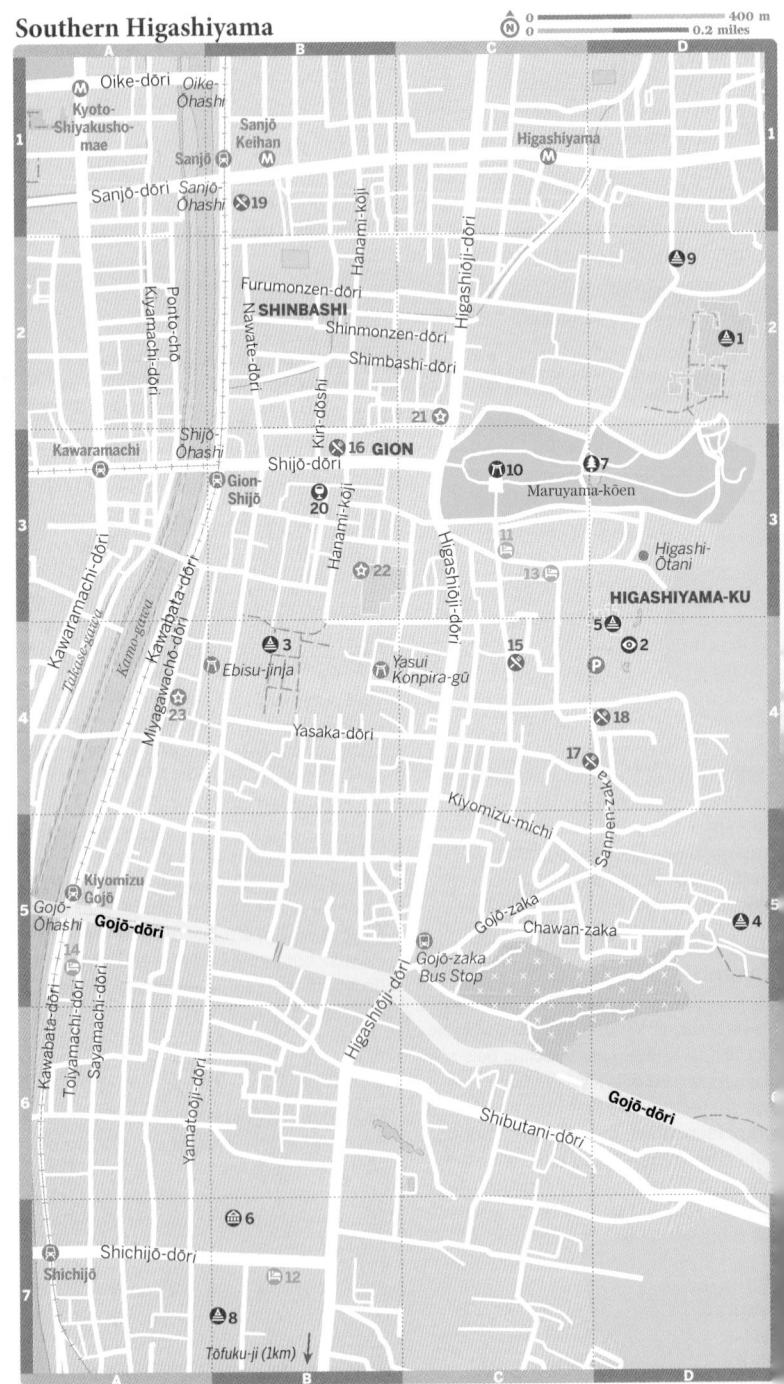

0 — 400 m
0 — 0.2 miles

Oike-dōri
Oike-Ōhashi
Kyoto-Shiyakusho-mae
Sanjō Keihan
Sanjō
Sanjō-Ōhashi
Higashiyama
Sanjō-dōri
19

Furumonzen-dōri
SHINBASHI
Nawate-dōri
Shinmonzen-dōri
Hanami-kōji
Higashiōji-dōri
Shimbashi-dōri
9
1

Kawaramachi
Shijō-Ōhashi
Gion-Shijō
Kiri-dōshi
21
Shijō-dōri
16 GION
20
10
7
Maruyama-kōen
11
Higashi-Ōtani
13
HIGASHIYAMA-KU

Kawaramachi-dōri
Ponto-chō
Kiyamachi-dōri
Kamo-gawa
Takase-gawa
Kawabata-dōri
Miyagawachō-dōri
3
Ebisu-jinja
23
22
Hanami-kōji
Higashiōji-dōri
Yasui Konpira-gū
15
5
2
P
18
17
Yasaka-dōri
Sannen-zaka
Kiyomizu-michi

Kiyomizu Gojō
Gojō-Ōhashi
Gojō-dōri
14
Kawabata-dōri
Toiyamachi-dōri
Sayamachi-dōri
Yamatoōji-dōri
Gojō-zaka
Chawan-zaka
4
Gojō-zaka
Bus Stop
Higashiōji-dōri
Shibutani-dōri
Gojō-dōri

6
Shichijō-dōri
Shichijō
12
8
Tōfuku-ji (1km)

KYOTO

Southern Higashiyama

◎ Sights
1 Chion-in	D2
2 Gion	D4
3 Kenin-ji Temple	B4
4 Kiyomizu-dera	D5
5 Kōdai-ji	D4
6 Kyoto National Museum	B7
7 Maruyama-kōen	D3
8 Sanjūsangen-dō Temple	B7
9 Shōren-in	D2
10 Yasaka-jinja	C3

◎ Sleeping
11 Gion Hatanaka	C3
12 Hyatt Regency Kyoto	B7
13 Ryokan Motonago	C3
14 Seikōrō Ryokan	A5

⊗ Eating
15 Hisago	C4
16 Kagizen Yoshifusa	B3
17 Kasagi-ya	C4
18 Omen Kodai-ji	D4
19 Santōka	B1

◎ Drinking & Nightlife
20 Gion Finlandia Bar	B3
Tōzan Bar	(see 12)

⊕ Entertainment
21 Gion Kaikan Theatre	C2
22 Gion Kōbu Kaburen-jō Theatre	B3
Kyoto Cuisine & Maiko Evening	(see 11)
23 Miyagawa-chō Kaburen-jō Theatre	A4

The steep approach to the temple is known as Chawan-zaka (Teapot Lane) and is lined with shops selling Kyoto handicrafts, local snacks and souvenirs.

Check at the TIC for the scheduling of special night-time illuminations of the temple held in the spring and autumn.

It's about 10 minutes' walk uphill from the Kiyōmizu-michi or Gojō-zaka bus stops or 20 minutes walk uphill from the Keihan Line's Kiyomizu-Gojō Station.

Ninen-zaka & Sannen-zaka   Neighbourhood

(二年坂・三年坂; Higashiyama-ku; 🚌 Kyoto City Bus 206 to the Kiyomizu-michi or Gojō-zaka stops, 🚃 Keihan line to Kiyomizu-Gojō)

Just below and slightly to the north of Kiyomizu-dera, you will find one of Kyoto's loveliest restored neighbourhoods, the Ninen-zaka-Sannen-zaka area. The name refers to the two main streets of the area: Ninen-zaka and Sannen-zaka, literally 'Two-Year Hill' and 'Three-Year Hill' (the years referring to the ancient imperial years when they were first laid out).

These two charming streets are lined with old wooden houses, traditional shops and restaurants. If you fancy a break, there are many teahouses and cafes along these lanes.

Kōdai-ji   Buddhist Temple

(高台寺; Map p214; 526 Shimokawara-chō, Kōdai-ji, Higashiyama-ku; admission ¥600; ⊙9am-5pm; 🚇 Tōzai Line to Higashiyama, 🚌 Kyoto City Bus 206 to the Yasui stop) This temple was founded in 1605 by Kita-no-Mandokoro in memory of her late husband, Toyotomi Hideyoshi. The extensive grounds include gardens that were designed by the famed landscape architect Kobori Enshū, and teahouses designed by the renowned master of the tea ceremony Sen-no-Rikyū.

The temple is a 10-minute walk north of Kiyomizu-dera or a 10-minute walk south of Maruyama-kōen. The easiest access is probably from the Tōzai subway line's Higashiyama Station. Check at the TIC for the scheduling of special night-time illuminations of the temple (when the gardens are lit by multicoloured spotlights).

Maruyama-kōen   Park

(円山公園; Map p214; Maruyama-chō, Higashiyama-ku; 🚇 Tōzai Line to Higashiyama) This park is a great place to escape the bustle of the city centre and amble around gardens, ponds, souvenir shops and restaurants. Peaceful paths meander through the trees and carp glide through the waters of a small pond in the centre of the park.

For two weeks in late March/early April, when the park's many cherry trees come into bloom, the calm atmosphere of the park is shattered by hordes of revellers

enjoying *hanami* (blossom-viewing). For those who don't mind crowds, this is a good place to observe the Japanese at their most uninhibited.

The park is a five-minute walk east of the Shijō-Higashiōji intersection. To get there from Kyoto Station, take bus 206 and get off at the Gion stop. Alternatively, take the Tōzai subway line to the Higashiyama stop and walk south for about 10 minutes.

Yasaka-jinja
Shinto Shrine

(八坂神社; Map p214; 625 Gion-machi Kitagawa, Higashiyama-ku; ⏰24hr; **S** Tōzai line to Higashiyama) **FREE** This colourful shrine is just down the hill from Maruyama-kōen. It's considered to be the guardian shrine of neighbouring Gion and is sometimes endearingly referred to as 'Gion-san'. This shrine is particularly popular as a spot for *hatsu-mōde* (the first shrine visit of the new year).

If you don't mind a stampede, come here around midnight on New Year's Eve or over the next few days. Surviving the crush is proof that you're blessed by the gods! Yasaka-jinja also sponsors Kyoto's biggest festival, Gion Matsuri (p231).

Chion-in
Buddhist Temple

(知恩院; Map p214; 400 Rinka-chō, Higashiyama-ku; admission to inner buildings & garden ¥300, grounds free; ⏰9am-4.30pm; **S** Tōzai line to Higashiyama Station) Chion-in was established in 1234 on the site where Hōnen, one of the most famous figures in Japanese Buddhism, taught his brand of Buddhism (Jōdo, or Pure Land, Buddhism) and eventually fasted to death. Today, the temple serves as the headquarters of the Jōdo sect, the most popular sect of Buddhism in Japan. It's the most popular pilgrimage temple in Kyoto and it's always a hive of activity. For visitors with a taste for the grand, this temple is sure to satisfy.

The oldest of the present buildings date back to the 17th century. The two-storey *san-mon*, a Buddhist temple gate at the main entrance, is the largest temple gate in Japan and prepares you for the massive scale of the temple. The immense main hall contains an image of Hōnen. It's connected to another hall, the Dai Hōjō, by a 'nightingale' floor.

Up a flight of steps southeast of the main hall is the temple's giant bell, which was cast in 1633 and weighs 70 tonnes. It is the largest bell in Japan. The bell is rung by the temple's monks 108 times on New Year's Eve each year.

The temple is close to the northeastern corner of Maruyama-kōen.

Gion   Neighbourhood

祇園周辺; Map p214; Higashiyama-ku; Keihan line to Gion-Shijō Station, **S** Tōzai line to Sanjō-Keihan) Gion is Kyoto's famous entertainment and geisha district on the eastern bank of the Kamo-gawa. Modern architecture, congested traffic and contemporary nightlife establishments rob the area of some of its historical beauty, but there are still some lovely places left for a stroll and the district looks very attractive in the evening.

Gion falls roughly between Sanjō-dōri and Gojō-dōri (north and south, respectively) and Higashiōji-dōri and Kawabata-dōri (east and west, respectively). In case you're wondering, Gion rhymes with 'key on'.

Hanami-kōji is the main north–south avenue of Gion, and the section south of Shijō-dōri is lined with 17th-century restaurants and teahouses, many of which are exclusive establishments for geisha entertainment.

Another must-see spot in Gion is Shimbashi (sometimes called Shirakawa Minami-dōri), which is one of Kyoto's most beautiful streets, and, arguably, among the most beautiful streets in all of Asia, especially in the evening and during cherry-blossom season. To get there, start at the intersection of Shijō-dōri and Hanami-kōji and walk north, then take the third left.

217

Northern Higashiyama

The northern Higashiyama area at the base of the Higashiyama mountains is one of the city's richest areas for sightseeing. It includes such first-rate attractions as Nanzen-ji, Ginkaku-ji, Hōnen-in and Shūgaku-in Rikyū. You can spend a wonderful day walking from Keage Station on the Tōzai subway line all the way north to Ginkaku-ji via the Tetsugaku-no-Michi (the Path of Philosophy), stopping in the countless temples and shrines en route.

Tetsugaku-no-Michi (Path of Philosophy)   Neighbourhood

(哲学の道; Map p220; Sakyō-ku; S Tōzai line to Keage, ☐ Kyoto City Bus 5 to the Eikandō-michi or Ginkakuji-michi stops) The Tetsugaku-no-Michi is a pedestrian path that runs along a canal near the base of the Higashiyama. It's lined with cherry trees and a host of other blooming trees and flowers.

The path takes its name from one of its most famous strollers: 20th-century philosopher Nishida Kitarō, who is said to have meandered along the path lost in thought. It only takes 30 minutes to complete the walk, which starts just north of Eikan-dō and ends at Ginkaku-ji.

Hōnen-in   Buddhist Temple

(法然院; Map p220; 30 Goshonodan-chō, Shishigatani, Sakyō-ku; ☯6am-4pm; ☐ Kyoto City Bus 5 to the Eikandō-michi or Ginkakuji-michi stops) **FREE** This fine temple was established in 1680 to honour Hōnen, the charismatic founder of the Jōdo school. It's a lovely, secluded temple with carefully raked gardens set back in the woods.

Be sure to visit in November for the maple leaves. Normally, you cannot enter the main hall, but two special openings happen yearly (admission ¥500/800 autumn/spring; 1-17 April and 1-7 November).

The temple is a 10-minute walk from Ginkaku-ji, on a side street that is accessible from the Tetsugaku-no-Michi; heading south on the path, look for the English sign on your left, then cross the bridge over the canal and follow the road uphill.

Ginkaku-ji   Buddhist Temple

(銀閣寺; Map p220; 2 Ginkaku-ji-chō, Sakyō-ku; admission ¥500; ☯8.30am-5pm Mar-Nov, 9am-4.30pm Dec-Feb; ☐ Kyoto City Bus No 5 to the Ginkakuji-michi stop) In 1482 Shōgun Ashikaga Yoshimasa constructed a villa here as a genteel retreat from the turmoil of civil war. The villa's name translates as 'Silver Pavilion', but the shōgun's ambition to cover the building with silver was never realised. After Yoshimasa's death, the villa was converted into a temple.

Walkways lead through the gardens, which include meticulously raked cones of white sand (said to be symbolic of a mountain and a lake), tall pines and a pond in front of the temple. A path also leads up the mountainside through the trees.

Note that Ginkaku-ji is one of the city's most popular sites, and it is almost always crowded, especially during the spring and autumn. We strongly recommend visiting right after it opens or just before it closes.

From JR Kyoto or Keihan Sanjō Station, take bus 5 and get off at the Ginkakuji-michi stop. From Demachiyanagi Station or Shijō Station, take bus 203 to the same stop.

Okazaki-kōen Area   Neighbourhood

(岡崎公園; Okazaki, Sakyo-ku; S Tōzai Line to Higashiyama Station) Right in the heart of the northern Higashiyama area, you'll find Okazaki-kōen, which is Kyoto's museum district, and the home of one of Kyoto's most popular shrines, Heian-jingū.

Take bus 5 from Kyoto Station or Keihan Sanjō Station and get off at the Kyoto Kaikan Bijutsu-kan-mae stop and walk north, or walk up from Keihan Sanjō Station (15 minutes). From Higashiyama Station, walk roughly north for five minutes.

Kyoto Municipal Museum of Art   Museum

(京都市美術館; Map p220; 124 Enshōji-chō, Okazaki, Sakyō-ku; admission varies; ☯9am-5pm, closed Mon; S Tōzai line to Higashiyama)

CHRISTIAN KOBER / GETTY IMAGES ©

Don't Miss
Nanzen-ji

This is one of the finest temples in Kyoto, with its expansive grounds and numerous subtemples. It began as a retirement villa for Emperor Kameyama but was dedicated as a Zen temple on his death in 1291. Civil war in the 15th century destroyed most of the temple; the present buildings date from the 17th century. It operates now as headquarters for the Rinzai school of Zen.

At its entrance stands the massive *san-mon* (gate). Steps lead up to the 2nd storey, which has a fine view over the city. Beyond the gate is the main hall of the temple, above which you will find the Hōjō, where the Leaping Tiger Garden is a classic Zen garden well worth a look. (Try to ignore the annoying audio explanation of the garden.) While you're in the Hōjō, you can enjoy a cup of tea while gazing at a small waterfall (¥500; ask at the reception desk of the Hōjō).

Dotted around the grounds of Nanzen-ji are several subtemples that are often skipped by the crowds.

To get to Nanzen-ji from JR Kyoto or Keihan Sanjō Station, take bus 5 and get off at the Nanzen-ji Eikan-dō-michi stop. You can also take the Tōzai subway line from the city centre to Keage and walk for five minutes downhill. Turn right (east, towards the mountains) opposite the police box and walk slightly uphill (again toward the mountains) and you will arrive at the main gate of the temple.

NEED TO KNOW

南禅寺; Map p220; Fukuchi-chō, Nanzen-ji, Sakyō-ku; admission Hōjō garden ¥500, San-mon gate ¥300-400, grounds free; ⏰8.40am-5pm Mar-Nov, to 4.30pm Dec-Feb; Ⓢ Tōzai line to Keage, 🚌Kyoto City Bus 5 to the Eikandō-michi stop

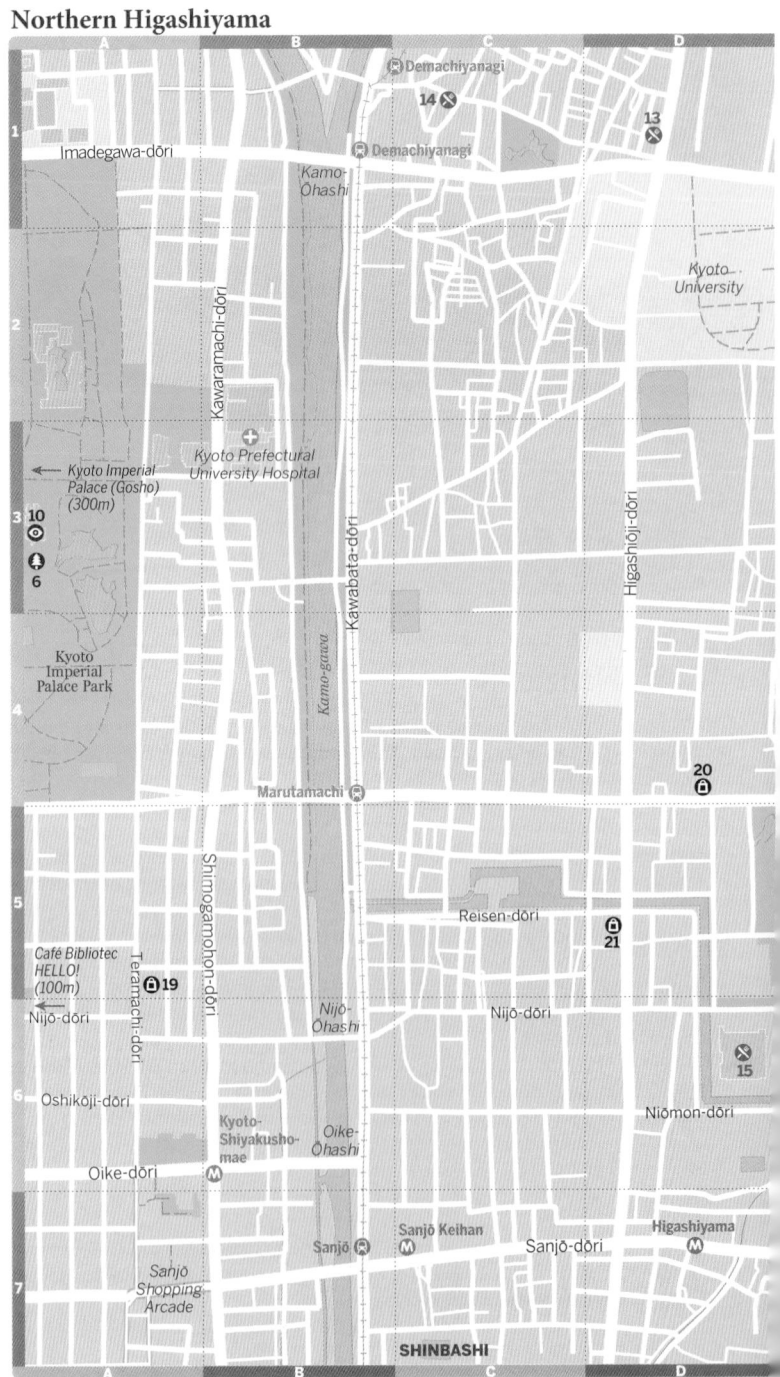

KYOTO

Demachiyanagi

14

13

Imadegawa-dōri

Kamo-
Ōhashi

Demachiyanagi

Kyoto
University

Kyoto Imperial
Palace (Gosho)
(300m)

10

6

Kyoto Prefectural
University Hospital

Kyoto
Imperial
Palace Park

20

Marutamachi

Reisen-dōri

21

Café Bibliotec
HELLO!
(100m)

19

Nijō-dōri

Nijō-
Ōhashi

Nijō-dōri

Oshikōji-dōri

15

Kyoto-
Shiyakusho-
mae

Oike-
Ōhashi

Niōmon-dōri

Oike-dōri

Sanjō

Sanjō Keihan

Sanjō-dōri

Higashiyama

Sanjō
Shopping
Arcade

SHINBASHI

0 400 m
0 0.25 miles

Shira-kawa

Imadegawa-dōri

Ginkaku-ji-Michi

17

3

SAKYŌ-KU

Yoshida-jinja

Takenaka
Inari-sha

Kaguraoka-dōri

11

5

Shirakawa-dōri

Munetada-jinja

Shinnyo-dō

Tetsugaku-no-Michi
(Path of Philosophy)

Kurodani
Temple

Kurodani
Pagoda

Marutamachi-dōri

Okazaki-jinja

4

16

Shira-kawa

Okazaki-kōen

9

2

Biwa-ko Sosui Canal

7

Nijō-dōri

Kyoto City
Zoo

8

Lake Biwa
Aqueduct
Museum

1 Nanzen-ji

Shirakawa-dōri

12

Keage

18

HIGASHIYAMA-KU

Northern Higashiyama

⊙ **Don't Miss Sights**
  1 Nanzen-ji G6

⊙ **Sights**
  2 Eikan-dō H5
  3 Ginkaku-ji H2
  4 Heian-jingū E5
  5 Hōnen-in H2
  6 Kyoto Imperial Palace Park A3
  7 Kyoto Municipal Museum of Art E6
  8 National Museum of Modern
     Art E6
  9 Okazaki-kōen Area E5
 10 Sentō Gosho Palace A3
 11 Tetsugaku-no-Michi (Path of
     Philosophy) H2

⊜ **Sleeping**
 12 Westin Miyako Kyoto F7

⊗ **Eating**
 13 Cafe Proverbs 15:17 .... D1
 14 Falafel Garden C1
 15 Goya D6
 16 Hinode Udon G5
 17 Omen H2

⊙ **Drinking & Nightlife**
 18 Kick Up G7

⊙ **Shopping**
 19 Ippōdō A5
 20 Kyoto Handicraft Center D4
 21 Zōhiko D5

The Kyoto Municipal Museum of Art organises several major exhibitions a year, including the excellent Kyoten exhibition, which showcases Japan's best living artists. It's held from late May until early June most years (check with the TIC for exact dates). Kyoto-related works form a significant portion of the permanent collection.

National Museum of Modern Art
Museum

(京都国立近代美術館; Map p220; www.momak. go.jp/english; Enshōji-chō, Okazaki, Sakyō-ku; admission ¥420; ⊙9.30am-5pm, closed Mon; **S** Tōzai line to Higashiyama) This museum is renowned for its compact collection of contemporary Japanese ceramics and paintings.

Heian-jingū
Shinto Shrine

(平安神宮; Map p220; Nishitennō-chō, Okazaki, Sakyō-ku; admission to garden ¥600; ⊙6am-5pm Nov-Feb, 6am-6pm Mar-Oct; **S** Tōzai line to Higashiyama, ☐Kyoto City Bus 5 to the Kyoto Kaikan/Bijyutsukan-mae stop) This impressive shrine complex was built in 1895 to commemorate the 1100th anniversary of the founding of Kyoto. The buildings are colourful replicas, reduced to two-thirds of the size of the Kyoto Gosho of the Heian period.

The spacious garden, with its large pond and Chinese-inspired bridge, is also meant to represent the kind of garden that was popular in the Heian period. About 500m in front of the shrine there is a massive orange torii (Shintō shrine gate). Although it appears to be entirely separate from the shrine, this is actually considered the main entrance to the shrine itself.

Two major events are held at the shrine: Jidai Matsuri (Festival of the Ages), on 22 October, and *takigi nō*, from 1 to 2 June.

Shūgaku-in Rikyū
Historical Building

(修学院離宮; Map p204; Yabusoe, Shūgakuin, Sakyō-ku; ☐Kyoto City Bus 5 to the Shūgaku-in Rikyū-michi stop) FREE This imperial villa was begun in the 1650s by the abdicated emperor Go-Mizunoo, and work was continued after his death in 1680 by his daughter Akenomiya. Designed as an imperial retreat, the villa grounds are divided into three large garden areas on a hillside: lower, middle and upper.

The gardens' reputation rests on their ponds, pathways and impressive use of 'borrowed scenery' in the form of the surrounding hills; the view from the Rinun-tei Teahouse in the upper garden is particularly impressive.

Tours, in Japanese, start at 9am, 10am, 11am, 1.30pm and 3pm (50 minutes). You must make advance reservations through the Imperial Household Agency. An audio guide is available for non-Japanese-speakers.

From Kyoto Station, take bus 5 and get off at the Shūgaku-in Rikyū-michi stop. The trip takes about an 45 minutes. From the bus stop it's a 15-minute walk (about

1km) to the villa. You can also take the Eiden Eizan line from Demachiyanagi Station to the Shūgaku-in stop and walk east about 25 minutes (about 1.5km) towards the mountains. Needless to say, a taxi is also a good option here.

Northwest Kyoto

Northwest Kyoto has many excellent sights spread over a large area. Highlights include Kinkaku-ji (the famed Golden Pavilion) and Ryōan-ji, with its mysterious stone garden. Note that three of the area's main sights, Kinkaku-ji, Ryōan-ji and Ninna-ji can easily be linked together to form a great half-day tour out of the city centre.

Kinkaku-ji   Buddhist Temple
(金閣寺; Map p204; 1 Kinkaku-ji-chō, Kita-ku; admission ¥400; ⊙9am-5pm; 🚌Kyoto City Bus 205 from Kyoto Station to the Kinkakuji-michi stop, Kyoto City Bus 59 from Sanjo-Keihan station to the Kinkakuji-mae stop) Kyoto's famed 'Golden Pavilion', Kinkaku-ji is one of Japan's best-known sights. The original building was built in 1397 as a retirement villa for Shōgun Ashikaga Yoshimitsu. His son converted it into a temple.

Note that this temple can be packed almost any day of the year. We recommend going early in the day or just before closing.

Ryōan-ji   Buddhist Temple
(龍安寺; Map p204; 13 Goryōnoshitamachi, Ryōan-ji, Ukyō-ku; admission ¥500; ⊙8am-5pm Mar-Nov, 8.30am-4.30pm Dec-Feb; 🚌Kyoto City Bus 59 from Sanjō-Keihan station to the Ryoanji-mae stop) This temple belongs to the Rinzai school of Zen and was founded in 1450. The main attraction is the garden arranged in the *kare-sansui* style. An austere collection of 15 rocks, apparently adrift in a sea of sand, is enclosed by an earthen wall. The designer, who remains unknown, provided no explanation.

The viewing platform for the garden can be packed solid but the other parts of the temple grounds are also interesting and less crowded. Among these, Kyoyo-chi pond is perhaps the most beautiful, particularly in autumn. If you want to enjoy the *kare-sansui* garden without the crowds, try to come right at opening time.

Note that you can walk to Ryōan-ji from Kinkaku-ji in about half an hour.

Kare-sansui-style garden at Ryōan-ji

Arashiyama & Sagano Area

Arashiyama and Sagano, at the base of Kyoto's western mountains (known as the Arashiyama), is Kyoto's second-most important sightseeing district after Higashiyama. On first sight, you may wonder what all the fuss is about: the main street and the area around the famous Tōgetsu-kyō bridge have all the makings of a classic Japanese tourist trap. But once you head up the hills to the temples hidden among the greenery, you will understand the appeal.

Bus 28 links Kyoto Station with Arashiyama. Bus 11 connects Keihan Sanjō Station with Arashiyama. The most convenient rail connection is the ride from Shijō-Ōmiya Station on the Keifuku-Arashiyama line to Arashiyama Station (take the Hankyū train from downtown to get to Shijō-Ōmiya). You can also take the JR San-in line from Kyoto Station or Nijō Station and get off at Saga Arashiyama Station (be careful to take only the local train, as the express does not stop in Arashiyama). Finally, a fast way to get there from the middle of Kyoto (downtown and central Kyoto) is to take the Tōzai subway line to the westernmost stop (Uzumasa-Tenjin-gawa) and take a taxi from there to Arashiyama (the taxi ride will take about 15 minutes and cost around ¥1600.

The sites in this section are all within walking distance of Arashiyama Station. We suggest walking from this station to Tenryū-ji, exiting the north gate, checking out the bamboo grove, visiting Ōkōchi Sansō, then walking north to Giō-jior Adashino Nembutsu-ji. If you have time for only one temple in the area, we recommend Tenryū-ji. If you have time for two, we suggest adding Giō-ji.

Tenryū-ji
Buddhist Temple

(天龍寺; Map p204; 68 Susukinobaba-chō, Saga Tenryū-ji, Ukyō-ku; admission ¥600; ◷8.30am-5.30pm, to 5pm 21 Oct-20 Mar; ⊡Kyoto City Bus 28 from Kyoto Station to the Arashiyama-Tenryuji-mae stop) One of the major temples of the Rinzai school of Zen, Tenryū-ji was built in 1339 on the former site of Emperor Go-Daigo's villa after a priest had dreamt of a dragon rising from the nearby river. The dream was interpreted as a sign that the emperor's spirit was uneasy and the temple was constructed as appeasement – hence the name *tenryū* (heavenly dragon).

Arashiyama Bamboo Grove

MARSER / GETTY IMAGE

The present buildings date from 1900, but the main attraction is the 14th-century Zen garden.

Arashiyama's famous **bamboo grove** lies just outside the north gate of the temple.

Arashiyama Bamboo Grove   Park

(嵐山竹林; ⊗ Map p204; Ogurayama, Saga, Ukyō-ku; ◷ dawn to dusk; ℞ Hankyū line to Arashiyama) FREE Arashiyama's famed Bamboo Grove is a magical place. The atmosphere is other-worldly and it's quite unlike any other forest we've ever experienced. The effect is quite hypnotic as the bamboo stalks seem to continue forever in all directions.

It's best accessed from the north gate of Tenryū-ji, which brings you right into the thick of it. From here, you can make a leisurely stroll up to the lovely Ōkōchi Sansō Villa.

Arashiyama Monkey Park Iwatayama   Park

(嵐山モンキーパークいわたやま; Map p204; 8 Genrokuzan-chō, Arashiyama, Ukyō-ku; adult/child ¥550/250; ◷ 9am-5pm 15 Mar-Oct, to 4pm Nov-14 Mar; ℞ Kyoto City Bus 28 from Kyoto Station to the Arashiyama-Tenryuji-mae stop) Home to some 200 Japanese monkeys of all sizes and ages, this park is fun for kids and animal lovers of all ages. Though it's common to spot wild monkeys in the nearby mountains, here you can see them close up. It makes for an excellent photo opportunity, not only for the monkeys but for the panoramic view over Kyoto.

Refreshingly, it is the animals who are free to roam while the humans who feed them are caged in a box! Just be warned: it's a steep climb up the hill to get to the monkeys. If it's a hot day, you're going to be drenched by the time you get to the spot where they gather.

The entrance to the park is up a flight of steps just upstream of the Tōgetsu-kyō bridge (near the orange torii of Ichitani-jinja). Buy your tickets from the machine to the left of the shrine at the top of the steps.

Arashiyama Area

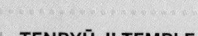

BY IJUIN KOKO, PROFESSIONAL GUIDE AND AUTHOR

1 TENRYŪ-JI TEMPLE

One of my favorite gardens in Kyoto is inside this temple. When you stroll around the main hall to the far side, your breath will be taken away by the sight waiting for you. Stop to savour the view from many vantage points, as the pond garden is designed to have a perfect view from any point. This artificial landscape matches the natural landscape of mountains in the distance as if they are also part of the garden. This is *shakkei* or 'borrowed landscape'.

2 BAMBOO GROVE

Going out from the north garden exit of Tenryu-ji, suddenly you will find yourself in a lane surrounded by towering bamboo trees. You'll probably feel the temperature is several degrees cooler here. Early in the morning, on weekdays or in the low season, you may have the place all to yourself.

3 ŌKŌCHI-SANSŌ

This magnificent villa and garden was the lifetime work of Ōkōchi Denjiro, a famous samurai movie actor. Ōkōchi's villa is now open to the public to enjoy the garden and the views over Kyoto. The garden gives you ideas as to what you can do with your own even if it is a small one, as each part is designed in a small scale.

4 GIŌ-JI

Out of the 1600 temples in Kyoto, this is one of my all-time favourites. It hardly looks like a temple at all, but more like a small three-room hut with an intimate garden. If you go expecting a grand temple, you'll be disappointed but if you slow down and soak up the calm stillness of the garden, you will emerge refreshed and alive.

GERARD WALKER / GETTY IMAGES ©

⭐ Don't Miss
Ōkōchi Sansō

This villa was the home of Ōkōchi Denjiro, an actor in samurai films. The superb gardens allow fine views over the city and are open to visitors; they are particularly lovely during the autumn foliage season. The admission fee is hefty but includes tea and a cake (save the tea/cake ticket that comes with your admission). The villa is a 10-minute walk through the bamboo grove north of Tenryū-ji. When you get to the top of the bamboo grove, the entrance will be diagonally in front of you to the right.

NEED TO KNOW

大河内山荘; Map p204; 8 Tabuchiyama-chō, Sagaogurayama, Ukyō-ku; admission ¥1000; ⊙9am-5pm; 🚌Kyoto City Bus No 28 from Kyoto Station to the Arashiyama-Tenryuji-mae stop

....

Southeast Kyoto

Southeast Kyoto contains some of Kyoto's most impressive sights, including Tōfuku-ji, with its lovely garden, and Fushi-Inari Taisha, with its hypnotically beautiful arcades of Shintō shrine gates.

Fushimi Inari-taisha   Shinto Shrine
(伏見稲荷大社; Map p204; 68 Yabunouchi-chō, Fukakusa, Fushimi-ku; ⊙dawn to dusk; 🚃JR Nara line to Inari) **FREE** This stunning shrine complex was dedicated to the gods of rice and sake by the Hata family in the 8th century. As the role of agriculture diminished, deities were enrolled to ensure prosperity in business. Nowadays, the shrine is one of Japan's most popular, and is the head shrine for some 30,000 Inari shrines scattered the length and breadth of Japan.

The entire complex sprawls across the wooded slopes of Inari-yama. A pathway wanders 4km up the mountain and is lined with thousands of red torii.

There are also dozens of stone foxes. The fox is considered the messenger of Inari, the god of the rice harvest (and, more recently, business). The Japanese traditionally see the fox as a sacred, somewhat mysterious figure capable of 'possessing' humans. The key often seen in the fox's mouth is for the rice granary.

To get to the shrine from Kyoto Station, take a JR Nara line train to Inari Station. From Keihan Sanjō Station take the Keihan line to Fushimi-Inari Station. The shrine is just east of both of these stations.

Southwest Kyoto

Southwest Kyoto is home to two notable sights, including the famous 'Moss Temple' (Saihō-ji) and Katsura-Rikyū.

Saihō-ji   Buddhist Temple

(西芳寺; 56 Jingatani-chō, Matsuo, Nishikyō-ku; admission ¥3000; 🚌 Kyoto City Bus No 28 from Kyoto Station to the Matsuo-taisha-mae stop) The main attraction at this temple is the heart-shaped garden designed in 1339 by Musō Kokushi. The garden is famous for its luxuriant moss, hence the temple's other name, Koke-dera (Moss Temple). While the reservation procedure is troublesome and the entry fee rather steep, a visit to the temple is highly recommended – the lush, shady garden is among the best in Kyoto.

Before you visit the garden, you will be asked to copy a sutra using a Japanese ink brush. It's not as hard as it sounds, as you can trace the faint letters on the page – and don't worry about finishing. Once in the garden, you're free to move about as you wish.

Take bus 28 from Kyoto Station to the Matsuo-taisha-mae stop and walk 15 minutes southwest. From Keihan Sanjō Station, take Kyoto bus 63 to Koke-dera, the last stop, and walk for two minutes.

Katsura Rikyū   Historic Building

桂離宮; Map p204; Katsura Detached Palace; Katsura Misono, Nishikyō-ku; 🚌 Kyoto City Bus 33 to the Katsura Rikyū-mae stop) FREE This palace is considered to be one of the finest examples of Japanese traditional architecture. It was built in 1624 for the emperor's brother, Prince Toshihito. Every conceivable detail of the villa, the teahouses, the large pond with islets and the surrounding garden has been given meticulous attention.

Tours (around 40 minutes), in Japanese, commence at 10am, 11am, 2pm and 3pm. You should be there 20 minutes beforehand. An explanatory video is shown in the waiting room and a leaflet is provided in English. You must make advance reservations with the Imperial Household Agency (p209). Visitors must be over 20 years of age.

To get to the villa from Kyoto Station, take bus 33 and get off at the Katsura Rikyū-mae stop, which is a five-minute walk from the villa. The easiest access from the city centre is to take a Hankyū line train from Hankyū Kawaramachi Station to Hankyū Katsura Station, which is a 15-minute walk from the villa. A taxi from Hankyū Katsura Station to the villa will cost about ¥700. Note that some *tokkyū* (express) trains don't stop in Katsura.

Visiting Saihō-ji

Entry to Saihō-ji is part of a tour only, and advance reservation is required. To visit, send a postcard at least one week before the date you wish to come and include your name, number of visitors, address in Japan, occupation, age (you must be over 18) and desired date (choice of alternative dates preferred). Enclose a stamped, self-addressed postcard for a reply to your Japanese address – eg buy an *ōfuku-hagaki* (send-and-return postcard set) at a Japanese post office. The address:

Saihō-ji
56 Jingatani-chō
Matsuo, Nishikyō-ku
Kyoto-shi 615-8286

If You Like...
Shintō Shrines

If you like Fushimi Inari-taisha, you'll like these two other Shintō shrines in Kyoto:

1 KAMIGAMO-JINJA
(上賀茂神社; Map p204; 339 Motoyama, Kamigamo; ⏰6am-5pm; 🚍Kyoto City Bus 9 to the Kamigamo-misonobashi stop) This shrine is one of Japan's oldest shrines and predates the founding of Kyoto. Established in 679, it is dedicated to Raijin, the god of thunder, and is one of Kyoto's 17 Unesco World Heritage Sites. The two large, conical white-sand mounds in front of Hosodono hall are said to represent mountains sculpted for gods to descend upon. The shrine is a five-minute walk from Kamigamo-misonobashi bus stop.

2 KITANO TENMAN-GŪ
(北野天満宮; Map p204; Bakuro-chō, Kamigyō-ku; ⏰5am-6pm Apr-Oct, 5.30am-5.30pm Nov-Mar; 🚍Kyoto City Bus 50 from Kyoto Station or bus 10 from Sanjo-Keihan to the Kitano-Tenmangū-mae stop) This is a fine, spacious shrine on Imadegawa-dōri. If you're in town on the 25th of any month, be sure to catch the **Tenjin-san market-fair** here. It's one of Kyoto's two biggest markets and is a great place to pick up some interesting souvenirs.

Kitayama Area

Starting on the north side of Kyoto city and stretching almost all the way to the Sea of Japan, the Kitayama (Northern Mountains) are a natural escape prized by Kyoto city dwellers. Attractions here include the village of Ōhara, with its pastoral beauty, the fine mountain temple at Kurama, and the river dining platforms at Kibune.

Ōhara   Neighbourhood
(大原; Ōhara; 🚍Kyoto Bus 17 or 18 from Kyoto Station to the Ōhara stop) Since ancient times Ōhara, a quiet farming town about 10km north of Kyoto, has been regarded as a holy site by followers of the Jōdo school of Buddhism. The region provides a charming glimpse of rural Japan, along with the picturesque Sanzen-in, Jakkō-in and several other fine temples.

It's most popular in autumn, when the maple leaves change colour and the mountain views are spectacular. During the peak foliage season of November, this area can get very crowded, especially on weekends.

It's most easily accessed by a Kyoto bus from Kyoto Station. Note, these are tan coloured, unlike Kyoto City buses, which are usually light green.

Sanzen-in   Temple
(三千院; 540 Raigōin-chō, Ōhara, Sakyō-ku; admission ¥700; ⏰8.30am-5pm Mar-Nov, to 4.30pm Dec-Feb; 🚍Kyoto Bus 17 or 18 from Kyoto Station to the Ōhara stop) Founded in 784 by the priest Saichō, Sanzen-in belongs to the Tendai sect of Buddhism. The temple's Yusei-en is one of the most photographed gardens in Japan, and rightly so. Take some time to sit and enjoy the garden.

After seeing Yusei-en, head off to the Ojo-gokuraku Hall (Temple of Rebirth in Paradise) to see the impressive Amitabha trinity, a large Amida image flanked by attendants Kannon, goddess of mercy, and Seishi, god of wisdom. After this, walk up to the hydrangea garden at the back of the temple, where in late spring and summer you can walk among hectares of blooming hydrangeas.

To get to Sanzen-in, follow the signs from Ōhara's main bus stop up the hill past a long arcade of souvenir stalls. The entrance is on your left as you crest the hill.

Jakkō-in   Temple
(寂光院; 676 Kusao-chō, Ōhara; admission ¥600; ⏰9am-5pm Mar-Nov, to 4.30pm Dec-Feb; 🚍Kyoto Bus 17 or 18 from Kyoto Station to the Ōhara stop) This fine little temple lies on the other side of the village from the more famous Sanzen-in. It's worth a visit both for its intimate atmosphere and the pleasant walk that takes you there.

Unfortunately the main building of the temple burned down in 2000 and

DAMIEN DOUXCHAMPS / GETTY IMAGES ©

Don't Miss
Tōfuku-ji

Founded in 1236 by the priest Enni, Tōfuku-ji belongs to the Rinzai sect of Zen Buddhism. The present temple complex includes 24 subtemples. The huge *san-mon* is the oldest Zen main gate in Japan. The Hōjō (abbot's hall) was reconstructed in 1890. The gardens, laid out in 1938, are well worth a visit.

Tōfuku-ji is a 20-minute walk (2km) southeast of Kyoto Station. You can also take a local train on the JR Nara line and get off at JR Tōfukuji Station, from which it's a 10-minute walk southeast. Alternatively, you can take the Keihan line to Keihan Tōfukuji Station, from which it's also a 10-minute walk.

NEED TO KNOW

東福寺; Map p204; 15-778 Honmahi, Higashiyama-ku; admission to garden ¥400, Tsūtenkyō bridge ¥400, grounds free; ⏰9am-4pm Apr-Oct, 8.30am-4pm Nov-early Dec, 9am-3.30pm early Dec-Mar; 🚃JR Nara line to Tōfukuji

---

he newly reconstructed main hall is acking some of the charm of the original. Nonetheless, it's a nice spot and the walk here is pleasant.

Jakkō-in lies to the west of Ōhara. Walk ut of the bus station up the road to the raffic lights, then follow the small road the left. It's easy to get lost on the way, ut any villager will be happy to point you the right direction.

Kurama & Kibune Neighbourhood
(鞍馬・貴船; Kurama, Sakyō-ku; 🚃Eiden Eizan line from Demachiyanagi Station to Kibune-guchi, for Kibune, or Kurama, for Kurama) Only 30 minutes north of Kyoto on the Eiden Eizan main line, Kurama and Kibune are a pair of tranquil valleys long favoured by Kyotoites as places to escape the crowds and stresses of the city below. Kurama's main attractions are its mountain temple

If You Like…
Temples

If you like Nanzen-ji, we think you'll like these other beautiful but slightly less commonly visited Kyoto temples:

1 EIKAN-DŌ

(永観堂; Map p220; 48 Eikandō-chō, Sakyō-ku; admission ¥600; ◷9am-5pm; S Tōzai line to Keage, 🚌Kyoto City Bus 5 to the Eikandō-michi stop) Just north of Nanzen-ji, this temple is famous for its autumn foliage. It's mobbed during November but quiet the rest of the year.

2 KENIN-JI TEMPLE

(建仁寺; Map p214; Komatsu-chō, Shijo sagaru, Yamatoōji-dōri, Higashiyama-ku; admission ¥500; ◷10am-4pm; 🚃Keihan line to Gion-Shijō) This Zen temple in the heart of Gion has a fantastic dry landscape garden and pleasant grounds that you can walk through at night.

3 MYŌSHIN-JI

(妙心寺; Map p204; 64 Myoshin-ji-chō, Hanazono, Ukyō-ku; admission to main temple free, other areas of the complex ¥500; ◷9.10-11.50am, 12.30pm, 1-3.40pm; closed irregularly; Bus Kyoto City Bus No 10 from Sanjo-Keihan to the Myōshin-ji Kita-mon-mae stop) In northwest Kyoto, this complex of Zen temples is like an enclosed world within the city.

and its onsen (hot springs). Kibune, over the ridge, is a cluster of ryokan (traditional Japanese inns) overlooking a mountain stream. It is best enjoyed in the summer, when the ryokan serve dinner on platforms built over the rushing waters of the Kibune-gawa, providing welcome relief from the summer heat.

The two valleys lend themselves to being explored together. In the winter one can start from Kibune, walk for an hour or so over the ridge, visit Kurama-dera and then soak in the onsen before heading back to Kyoto. In the summer the reverse is best; start from Kurama, walk up to the temple, then down the other side to Kibune to enjoy a

meal suspended above the cool river (unfortunately, restaurants in Kibune are known to refuse solo diners).

If you happen to be in Kyoto on the night of 22 October, be sure not to miss the Kurama-no-hi Matsuri (Kurama Fire Festival), one of the most exciting festivals in the Kyoto area.

To get to Kurama and Kibune, take the Eiden Eizan line from Kyoto's Demachiyanagi Station. For Kibune, get off at the second-to-last stop, Kibune Guchi, take a right out of the station and walk about 20 minutes up the hill. For Kurama, go to the last stop, Kurama, and walk straight out of the station. Both destinations are ¥410 and take about 30 minutes to reach.

Kurama-dera Buddhist Temple

(鞍馬寺; 1074 Kurama Honmachi, Sakyō-ku; admission ¥200; ◷9am-4.30pm; 🚃Eiden Eizan line from Demachiyanagi Station to Kurama) This temple was established in 770 by the monk Gantei from Nara's Tōshōdai-ji. After seeing a vision of the deity Bishamon-ten, guardian of the northern quarter of the Buddhist heaven, Gantei established Kurama-dera just below the peak of Kurama-yama. Originally under the Tendai sect, Kurama has been independent since 1949, describing its own brand of Buddhism as Kurama Kyō.

The entrance to the temple is just up the hill from the Eiden Eizan main line's Kurama Station. A tram goes to the top for ¥100; alternatively, hike up by following the main path past the tram station. The trail is worth taking if it's not too hot, as it winds through a forest of towering old-growth sugi (cryptomeria) trees. At the top there is a courtyard dominated by the honden (main hall). Behind the honden, a trail leads off to the mountain's peak.

At the top, you can take a brief detour across the ridge to Ōsugi-gongen, a quiet shrine in a grove of trees. Those who want to continue to Kibune can take the trail down the other side. It's a 1.2km, 30-minute hike from the honden to the valley floor of Kibune. On the way down are two pleasant mountain shrines, Sōjō-ga-dani Fudō-dō and Okuno-in Maō-den.

Kurama Onsen — Onsen

(鞍馬温泉; 520 Kurama Honmachi, Sakyō-ku; admission to outdoor/indoor bath ¥1000/2500; ⓧ10am-9pm; 🚉Eiden Eizan line from Demachi-yanagi Station to Kurama Station) One of the few onsen within easy reach of Kyoto, Kurama Onsen is a great place to relax after a hike. The outdoor bath has a fine view of Kurama-yama; the indoor bath includes use of sauna and relaxation areas. Buy tickets from the machine outside the door of the main building (instructions are in Japanese and English).

To get to Kurama Onsen, walk straight out of Kurama Station, turn left up the main road and follow it for about 10 minutes. You'll see the baths down on your right. There's also a free shuttle bus that runs between the station and the onsen, leaving approximately every 30 minutes.

✪ Festivals & Events

There are hundreds of festivals happening in Kyoto throughout the year. Listings of these can be found in the *Kyoto Visitor's Guide* or *Kansai Scene*. The following are some of the major and most spectacular festivals. These attract hordes of spectators from out of town, so you will need to book accommodation well in advance.

Setsubun Matsuri at Yoshida-jinja — Festival

This festival is held on the day of *setsubun* (2, 3 or 4 February; check with the TIC), which marks the last day of winter in the Japanese lunar calendar. In this festival, people climb up to Yoshida-jinja in the northern Higashiyama area to watch a huge

bonfire (in which old good-luck charms are burned). It's one of Kyoto's more dramatic festivals. The action starts at dusk.

Aoi Matsuri — Parade

The Hollyhock Festival dates back to the 6th century and commemorates the successful prayers of the people for the gods to stop calamitous weather. These days the procession involves imperial messengers carried in ox carts and a retinue of 600 people dressed in traditional costume. The procession leaves at around 10am on 15 May from the Kyoto Gosho and heads for Shimogamo-jinja.

Gion Matsuri — Parade

Perhaps the most renowned of all Japanese festivals, Gion Matsuri reaches a climax on 17 July with a parade of over 30 floats depicting ancient themes and decked out in incredible finery. On the three evenings preceding the main festival day, people gather on Shijō-dōri, many of them dressed in beautiful *yukata* (light summer kimonos), to look at the floats and carouse from one street stall to the next.

Aoi Matsuri procession
FRANK CARTER / GETTY IMAGES ©

Daimon-ji Gozan Okuribi   Festival

This festival, commonly known as Daimon-ji Yaki, is performed on 16 August as a means of bidding farewell to the souls of ancestors. Enormous fires in the form of Chinese characters or other shapes are lit on five mountains. The largest fire is always burned on Daimon-ji-yama, just above Ginkaku-ji, in northern Higashi-yama. The fires start at 8pm and the best position to watch from is the banks of the Kamo-gawa or, alternatively, pay for a rooftop view from a hotel.

Jidai Matsuri   Parade

The Festival of the Ages is of comparatively recent origin, only dating back to 1895. More than 2000 people, dressed in costumes ranging from the 8th century to the 19th century, parade from Kyoto Gosho to Heian-jingū on 22 October.

Kurama-no-hi Matsuri   Festival

In perhaps Kyoto's most dramatic festival, the Kurama Fire Festival, huge flaming torches are carried through the streets of Kurama by men in loincloths on 22 October (the same day as the Jidai Matsuri). Note that trains to and from Kurama will be completely packed with passengers on the evening of the festival (we suggest going early and returning late).

Sleeping

The most convenient areas in which to be based, in terms of easy access to shopping, dining and sightseeing attractions, are downtown Kyoto and the Higashi-yama area. The Kyoto Station area is also a good location, with excellent access to transport and plenty of shops and restaurants about. Transport information in the following listings is from Kyoto Station unless otherwise noted.

Kyoto Station Area

Capsule Ryokan Kyoto   Capsule Hotel ¥

(カプセル旅館京都; Map p208; ☎ 344-1510; www.capsule-ryokan-kyoto.com; capsule ¥3500, tw per person ¥3990; @ 🛜; 🚉 JR Tōkaidō Main line to Kyoto Station, 🅂 Karasuma line to Kyoto) This unique accommodation offers ryokan-style capsules (meaning tatami mats inside the capsules), as well as comfortable, cleverly designed private

Jidai Matsuri

FRANK CARTER / GETTY IMAGES

rooms. Each capsule also has its own TV and cable internet access point, while the private rooms have en suite bathrooms and all the amenities you might need. Free internet, wi-fi and other amenities are available in the comfortable lounge.

It's located a seven-minute walk from Kyoto Station, near the southeast corner of the Horikawa-Shichijo intersection.

Tour Club   Guesthouse ¥

(ツアークラブ; Map p208; ☏ 353-6968; www.kyotojp.com; 362 Momiji-chō, Higashinakasuji, Shōmen-sagaru, Shimogyō-ku; dm ¥2450, d per person ¥3490, tw per person ¥3490-3885, tr per person ¥2960-3240; ◉@?; ☒JR Tōkaidō main line, JR Tōkaidō shinkansen line, Ⓢ Karasuma line Kyoto, ☒Kintetsu Kyoto line) Run by a charming and friendly family, this clean, well-maintained guesthouse is a favourite of many foreign visitors. Facilities include wi-fi, a small Zen garden, laundry and free tea and coffee. The private rooms, which were recently refurbished, have en suite bathrooms.

It's a 10-minute walk from Kyoto Station; turn north off Shichijō-dōri at the Nagomikan coffee shop (looks like a bank) and keep an eye out for the English sign.

Budget Inn   Guesthouse ¥

(バジェットイン; Map p208; ☏ 0344-1510; www.budgetinnjp.com; 295 Aburanokōji-chō, Aburanokōji, Shichijō sagaru, Shimogyō-ku; tr/q/5-person r per person ¥3660/3245/2996; ◉@?; ☒JR Tōkaidō main line, JR Tōkaidō shinkansen line, Ⓢ Karasuma line, Kyoto, ☒Kintetsu Kyoto Line) This well-run guesthouse is an excellent choice. It's got eight Japanese-style private rooms, all of which are clean and well maintained. All rooms have their own bathroom and can accommodate up to five people, making this a good spot for families. The staff here is very helpful and friendly, and laundry and bicycle rental are available. All in all, this is a great choice in this price range. It's a seven-minute walk from Kyoto Station; from the station, walk west on Shiokōji-dōri, turn north one street before Horikawa and look for the English-language sign out front.

Detour:
Takao

A secluded mountain village tucked far away in the northwestern part of Kyoto, **Takao** (高雄; Takao; ☒JR Bus from Kyoto Station to the Yamashiro-Takao stop) is famed for autumn foliage and the temples of Jingo-ji, Saimyō-ji and Kōzan-ji.

There are two options for buses to Takao: an hourly JR bus that leaves from Kyoto Station, which takes about an hour to reach the Takao stop (get off at the Yamashiro-Takao stop); and Kyoto City bus 8 from Shijō-Karasuma (get off at the Takao stop). To get to Jingo-ji from these bus stops, walk down to the river, then look for the steps on the other side.

Ryokan Shimizu   Ryokan ¥

(Map p208; ☏ 371-5538; www.kyoto-shimizu.net; 644 Kagiya-chō, Shichijō-dōri, Wakamiya agaru, Shimogyō-ku; r per person from ¥5250; ◉@; ☒JR Tōkaidō main line, JR Tōkaidō shinkansen line, Ⓢ Karasuma line, Kyoto Station, ☒Kintetsu line) A short walk north of Kyoto Station, this travellers' ryokan is quickly building a loyal following of foreign guests, and for good reason: it's clean, well run and friendly. Rooms are standard ryokan style with one difference: all have bathrooms. Bicycle rental is available. Prices rise on Saturdays and nights before holidays.

Hotel Granvia Kyoto   Hotel ¥¥¥

(ホテルグランヴィア京都; Map p208; ☏ 344-8888; www.granvia-kyoto.co.jp; Shiokōji sagaru, Karasuma-dōri, Shimogyō-ku; tw/d from ¥32,340/28,875; ◉@≋; ☒JR Tōkaidō main line, JR Tōkaidō shinkansen line, Ⓢ Karasuma line, Kyoto Station, ☒Kintetsu Kyoto line) Imagine stepping straight out of bed and into the *shinkansen* (bullet train). This is almost possible when you stay at the Granvia,

Detour:
Manshu-in

Manshu-in (🎵 781 5010; Takenouchi-chō 42, Ichijōji; adult ¥500, child ¥300-400; 🕘 9am-4.30pm; underground rail 20min walk from Shūgakuin Station, Eizan line) About 30 minutes' walk north of **Shisen-dō** you'll reach the stately gate of Manshu-in, a popular retreat of former emperors and a great escape from the crowds. The temple was originally founded by Saichō on **Hiei-zan** but was relocated here at the beginning of the Edo period by Ryōshōhō, the son of Prince Hachijōnomiya Tomohito (who built **Katsura Rikyū**). The graceful temple architecture is often compared with Katsura Rikyū for its detailed woodwork and rare works of art, such as *fusuma-e* sliding doors painted by Kanō Eitoku, a famed artist of the Momoyama period. The *karesansui* garden by Kobori Enshū features a sea of gravel intended to symbolise the flow of a waterfall and stone islands representing cranes and turtles.

an excellent hotel located directly above Kyoto Station. Rooms are clean, spacious and well appointed, with deep bath tubs. This is a very professional operation with some good on-site restaurants, some of which have views over the city.

The hotel also has family rooms.

Dormy Inn Premium Kyoto Ekimae
Hotel ¥¥¥

(ドーミーイン PREMIUM 京都駅前; Map p208; 🎵 371-5489; www.hotespa.net/hotels/kyoto; Higashishiokōji-chō 558-8, Shimogyō-ku; tw/d from ¥26,000/22,000; @; 🚆 JR Tōkaidō main line to Kyoto Station, 🚇 Karasuma Subway line to Kyoto Station) Located almost directly across the street from Kyoto Station, this clean, efficient new hotel is a great choice for those who want to be near the station. Rooms are clean and well maintained and the on-site spa bath is a nice plus.

Downtown Kyoto

Hotel Unizo
Business Hotel ¥¥

(ホテルユニゾ京都; Map p210; 🎵 241-3351; www.hotelunizo.com/eng/kyoto; Kawaramachi-dōri-Sanjō sagaru, Nakagyō-ku; s/d/tw from ¥10,000/17,000/19,000; 😊 @ 🛜; 🚌 Kyoto City Bus 5 to the Kawaramachi-Sanjō stop, 🚇 Tōzai line to Kyoto Shiyakusho-mae) They don't get more central than this downtown business hotel: it's smack-dab in the middle of Kyoto's nightlife, shopping and dining district

and you can walk to hundreds of restaurants and shops within five minutes. It's a standard-issue business hotel, with small but adequate rooms and unit bathrooms. Considering the location and the condition of the rooms, it's great value.

Best Western Hotel Kyoto
Hotel ¥¥

(ベストウェスタンホテル京都; Map p210; 🎵 254-4055; http://kyoto.bwhotels. jp; Matsugae-chō 457, Kawaramachi-Rokkaku, Nakagyō-ku; s/tw from ¥18,000/33,000; @; 🚇 Tōzai line to Kyoto Shiyakusho-mae) ight in the middle of downtown Kyoto's main shopping district, the Best Western claims one of the most convenient locations in Kyoto. It's brand new and off to a good start. Rooms are small but spotless, with everything you might need, including helpful staff. You can get cheaper rates online.

Mitsui Garden Hotel Kyoto Sanjō
Hotel ¥¥

(三井ガーデンホテル 京都三条; Map p210; 🎵 256-3331; www.gardenhotels.co.jp/ eng/sanjo; 80 Mikura-chō, Nishiiru, Karasuma, Sanjō-dōri, Nakagyō-ku; s/d/tw from ¥10,500/17,600/18,800; @; 🚇 Tōzai & Karasuma lines to Karasuma-Oike, exit 6) Just west of the downtown dining and shopping district, this is a clean and efficient hotel that offers good value and reasonably comfortable rooms. It's just a minute or two to the nearest subway station.

Tawaraya
Ryokan ¥¥¥

(俵屋; Map p210; ☎211-5566; Fuyachō-Oike sagaru, Nakagyō-ku; r per person with 2 meals ¥42,263-84,525; ❄@; Ⓢ Tōzai Line to Kyoto Shiyakusho-mae, exit 8) Tawaraya has been operating for over three centuries and is one of the finest places to stay in Japan. Entering this ryokan is like entering another world, and you just might not want to leave. The ryokan has an intimate, private feeling and all rooms have bathrooms.

The gardens are sublime and the cosy study is the perfect place to linger with a book. A night here is sure to be memorable and is *highly* recommended.

Kyoto Hotel Ōkura
Hotel ¥¥¥

(京都ホテルオークラ; Map p210; ☎211-5111; http://okura.kyotohotel.co.jp; Kawaramachi-dōri, Oike, Nakagyō-ku; s/d/tw from ¥21,945/31,185/31,185; ❄@; Ⓢ Tōzai Line to Kyoto Shiyakusho-mae, exit 3) Located right in the midst of downtown, this is a well-run, comfortable hotel that claims the most convenient location of any luxury hotel in Kyoto. Rooms here are clean, spacious and comfortable and those on the upper floors have great views.

There are several excellent on-site restaurants and bars, along with hundreds within easy walking distance of the hotel. If you exhaust the possibilities in and around the hotel, you can walk downstairs and hop right onto the subway.

Hiiragiya Ryokan
Ryokan ¥¥¥

(柊屋; Map p210; ☎221-1136; www.hiiragiya.co.jp/en; Anekōji-agaru, Fuya-chō, Nakagyō-ku; r per person with 2 meals ¥36,750-86,900; ❄@; Ⓢ Tōzai line to Kyoto Shiyakusho-mae, exit 8) This classic ryokan has hosted celebrities and dignitaries from around the world. From the decorations to the service to the food, everything at the Hiiragiya is first class. Rooms in the old wing have great old Japan style, while those in the new wing are pristine and comfortable.

It's centrally located downtown within easy walk of two subway stations and lots of good restaurants.

Central Kyoto

Palace Side Hotel
Hotel ¥

(ザ・パレスサイドホテル; Map p204; ☎415-8887; www.palacesidehotel.co.jp; Karasuma-dōri, Shimotachiuri agaru, Kamigyō-ku; s/tw/d from ¥6000/9000/9800; ❄@; Ⓢ Karasuma Line to Marutamachi Station) Overlooking the Kyoto Imperial Palace Park, this excellent-value budget hotel has a lot going for it, starting with friendly English-speaking staff, great service, washing machines, an on-site restaurant, well-maintained rooms and free internet terminals. The rooms are small but serviceable. It's a three-minute walk from the subway.

Geisha wearing traditional wooden sandals
GALLO IMAGES / GETTY IMAGES ©

Below: Hiiragiya Ryokan (p235);
Right: Cherry blossom trees in the Gion district
(BELOW) GREG ELMS / GETTY IMAGES ©: (RIGHT) GUIZIOU FRANCK / HEMIS.FR / GETTY IMAGES ©

Tōyoko Inn
Kyoto Gojō Karasuma   Hotel ¥¥
(東横INN京都五条烏丸; Map p204; ☎344-1045; www.toyoko-inn.com; Karasuma-dōri, Matsubara sagaru, Gojō Karasuma-chō 393, Shimogyō-ku; s/tw incl breakfast from ¥6480/9480; @; S Karasuama line to Gojō) Those familiar with the Tōyoko Inn chain know that this hotel brand specialises in simple, clean, fully equipped but small rooms at the lowest price possible. There are all kinds of interesting extras: free breakfast, free telephone calls inside Japan and reduced rates on rental cars. They'll even lend you a laptop if you need to do some emailing.

It's a little south of the city centre, but easily accessed by the Karasuma subway line.

Citadines
Kyoto Karasuma Gojō   Hotel ¥¥¥
(シタディーン京都　烏丸五条; Map p204; ☎352-8900; www.citadines.jp/kyoto; Gojō-dōri, Karasuma Higashi iru, Matsuya-chō 432, Shimogyō-ku; tw/d from ¥23,100/23,100; @; S Karasuma line to Gojō) On Gojō-dōri, a bit south of the main downtown district, but within easy walking distance of the Karasuma subway line (as well as the Keihan line), this serviced apartment/hotel is a welcome addition to the Kyoto accommodation scene. The kitchens allow you to do your own cooking and other touches make you feel right at home.

Southern Higashiyama

Hyatt Regency Kyoto   Hotel ¥¥¥
(ハイアットリージェンシー京都; Map p214; ☎541-1234; www.kyoto.regency.hyatt.com; 644-2 Sanjūsangendō-mawari, Higashiyama-ku; r ¥19,000-49,000; ➌@☎; ☒Keihan Shichijō Station) The Hyatt Regency is an excellent, stylish, foreigner-friendly hotel at the southern end of Kyoto's southern Higashiyama sightseeing district. Many travellers consider this the best hotel in Kyoto. The staff here is extremely efficient

and helpful (there are even foreign staff members – something of a rarity in Japan).

The on-site restaurants and bar are excellent. The stylish rooms and bathrooms have lots of neat touches. The concierges are knowledgeable about the city and they'll even lend you a laptop to check your email if you don't have your own. It's a five-minute walk from the station.

Seikōrō Ryokan　　Ryokan ¥¥¥
(晴鴨楼; Map p214; ☏561-0771; http://ryokan. asia/seikoro; 467 Nishi Tachibana-chō, 3 chō-me, Gojō sagaru, Toiyamachi-dori, Higashiyama-ku; r per person with 2 meals from ¥26,250; ☺@☎; ☐Kyoto City Bus 17 or 205 to the Kawaramachi-Gojō stop) The Seikōrō is a classic ryokan with fine rooms and a grandly decorated lobby. It's fairly spacious, with excellent, comfortable rooms, attentive service and a fairly convenient midtown location. Several rooms look over gardens and all have private baths.

Ryokan Motonago　　Ryokan ¥¥¥
(旅館元奈古; Map p214; ☏phone 561-2087; www.motonago.com; 511 Washio-chō, Kōdaiji-michi, Higashiyama-ku; r per person with 2 meals from ¥17,850; ☺@☎; ☐Kyoto City Bus 206 to the Gion stop) This ryokan may have the best location of any ryokan in the city: right on Nene-no-Michi in the heart of the Higashiyama sightseeing district. It's got traditional decor, friendly service, nice bath tubs and a few small Japanese gardens.

Northern Higashiyama

Westin Miyako Kyoto　　Hotel ¥¥¥
(ウェスティン都ホテル京都; Map p220; ☏771-7111; www.miyakohotels.ne.jp/westin-kyoto; Keage, Sanjō-dōri, Higashiyama-ku; d & tw from ¥33,500, Japanese-style r from ¥41,500; ☺@☎☱; ☐Tōzai line to Keage, exit 2) The grande dame of Kyoto hotels occupies a commanding position overlooking the Higashiyama sightseeing district (making it one of the best locations for

237

sightseeing in Kyoto). Rooms are clean and well maintained, and the staff is at home with foreign guests.

Rooms on the north side have great views over the city to the Kitayama mountains. There is a fitness centre, as well as a private garden and walking trail. The hotel even has its own ryokan section for those who want to try staying in a ryokan without giving up the convenience of a hotel.

Arashiyama & Sagano

Hoshinoya   Hotel ¥¥¥
(星のや; Map p204; ☑871-0001; http://
global.hoshinoresort.com/hoshinoya_kyoto;
Genrokuzan-chō, Arashiyama 11-2, Nishikyō-ku; r
per person from ¥51,660; 🛜; 🚉Hankyū Line to
Arashiyama) Sitting in a secluded area on the south bank of the Oi-gawa in Arashi-yama (upstream from the main sightsee-ing district), this modern take on the classic Japanese inn is quickly becoming a favourite of well-heeled visitors to Kyoto in search of privacy and a unique experi-ence. Rooms feature incredible views of the river and the surrounding mountains.

The best part is the approach: you'll be chauffeured by a private boat from a dock near Togetsu-kyō bridge to the inn (note that on days following heavy rains, you'll have to go by car instead). This is easily one of the most unique places to stay in Kyoto.

Kansai Airport

**Hotel Nikkō
Kansai Airport**   Hotel ¥¥¥
(ホテル日航関西空港; ☑072-455-1111; www.
nikkokix.com; Senshū Kūkō Kita 1, Izumisano-shi,
Osaka-fu; s/tw/d from ¥21,945/32,340/30,030;
@🛜🏊; 🚉JR line Haruka Airport Express
to Kansai Airport) The only hotel at the airport is the excellent Hotel Nikkō Kansai Airport, just a five-minute walk from the international arrivals hall. The rooms here are spacious and comfortable. It's the perfect place to stay if you arrive late or have an early departure. There are several places to eat nearby. You can often get better rates by booking online.

🍴 Eating

Kyoto is a great place to explore Japanese cuisine and you'll find good restaurants regardless of your budget. If you tire of Japanese food, there are plenty of excellent international restaurants to choose from. You'll find the thickest concentration of eateries in downtown Kyoto, but also great choices in southern Higashiyama/ Gion and in and around Kyoto Station.

Because Kyoto gets a lot of foreign travellers, you'll find a surprising number of English menus and most places are quite comfortable with foreign guests.

'Flower garden' seafood dish

Kyoto Station Area

The new Kyoto Station building is chock-a-block with restaurants, and if you find yourself anywhere near the station around mealtime, this is probably your best bet in terms of variety and price.

There are several food courts scattered about the station building. The best of these can be found on the 11th floor on the west side of the building: the **Cube** (Map p208; 🕐11am-10pm) food court and Isetan department store's **Eat Paradise** (Map p208; 🕐11am-10pm) food court. In Eat Paradise, we like Tonkatsu Wako for *tonkatsu* (deep-fried breaded pork cutlet), Tenichi for sublime tempura, and Wakuden for approachable *kaiseki* (Japanese haute cuisine) fare. To get to these food courts, take the west escalators from the main concourse all the way up to the 11th floor and look for the Cube on your left and Eat Paradise straight in front of you.

Other options in the station include **Kyoto Rāmen Koji** (Map p208; 🕐11am-10pm), a collection of seven *rāmen* restaurants on the 10th floor (underneath the Cube). Buy tickets from the machines, which don't have English but have pictures on the buttons. In addition to *rāmen,* you can get green-tea ice cream and other Japanese desserts at Chasen, and *tako-yaki* (battered octopus pieces) at Miyako.

Downtown Kyoto

Downtown Kyoto has the best variety of approachable Japanese and international restaurants.

Ippūdō
Rāmen ¥

(一風堂; Map p210; 🕿213-8800; 653-1 Bantōya-chō, Nishikikōji higashiiru, Higashinotō-in, Nakagyō-ku; rāmen ¥750-950; 🕐11am-2am; 📷; Ⓢ Karasuma line to Shijō) There's a reason there's usually a line outside this joint at lunchtime: the *rāmen* is awesome and the bite-sized *gyōza* (dumplings) are to die for. We recommend the *gyōza* set meal, which costs ¥750 or ¥850, depending on your choice of *rāmen.*

Kerala
Indian ¥

(ケララ; Map p210; 🕿251-0141; 2F KUS Bldg, Kawaramachi, Sanjō agaru, Nakagyō-ku; lunch/dinner from ¥850/2600; 🕐11.30am-2pm & 5-9pm; 🖊📷; Ⓢ Tōzai Line to Kyoto Shiyakusho-mae Station) This is where we go for reliable Indian lunch sets – great *thalis* that include two curries, good naan bread, some rice, a small salad etc. Dinners are à la carte. It's on the 2nd floor; look for the display of food in the glass case at street level.

Warai
Okonomiyaki ¥

(わらい; Map p210; 🕿257-5966; 1F Mizukōto Bldg, 597 Nishiuoya-chō, Nishikikōji-dōri, Takakura Nishiiru, Nakagyō-ku; okonomiyaki from ¥600; 🕐11.30am-1am; 📷; Ⓢ Karasuma line to Shijō, Ⓡ Hankyū line to Karasuma) A great place to try *okonomiyaki* (savoury pancakes) in casual surroundings. It can get a little smoky, but it's a fun spot to eat. It's got sets from as little as ¥650 at lunch. It's about 20m west of the west end of Nishiki Market; look for the English sign in the window.

Café Bibliotec HELLO!
Cafe ¥

(カフェビブリオティックハロー！; 🕿231-8625; 650 Seimei-chō, Yanaginobanba higashi iru, Nijō, Nakagyō-ku; meals from ¥850; 🕐11.30am-midnight; 📷; Ⓢ Tōzai line to Kyoto Shiyakusho-mae) Like its name suggests, books line the walls of this cool cafe located in a converted *machiya.* You can get the usual range of coffee (¥450) and tea here, as well as light cafe lunches. This may be our favourite cafe in Kyoto, and it's worth the walk from the centre of town. Look for the plants out front.

Honke Tagoto
Noodles ¥

(本家田每; Map p210; 🕿221-3030; 12 Ishibashi-chō, Sanjō-dōri, Kawaramachi Nishi iru, Nakagyō-ku; noodle dishes from ¥840; 🕐11am-9pm; 📷; Ⓢ Tōzai line to Kyoto Shiyakusho-mae) One of Kyoto's oldest *soba* restaurants makes a good break for those who have overdosed on *rāmen.* It's in the Sanjō covered arcade and you can see inside to the tables.

Musashi Sushi
Sushi ¥

(寿しのむさし; 🕿222-0634; Kawaramachi-dōri, Sanjō agaru, Nakagyō-ku; all plates ¥137; 🕐11am-10pm; 📷; Ⓢ Tōzai line to Kyoto Shiya-kusho-mae, Ⓡ Keihan line to Sanjō) This is the

Department Store Dining

Yes, we know: the idea of dining in a department store sounds as appetising as dining in a gas station. However, Japanese department stores, especially those in large cities such as Tokyo and Kyoto, are loaded with good dining options. And, unlike many street-level shops, they're usually fairly comfortable with foreign diners (if there's any communication trouble, they can always call down to the bilingual staff at the information counter).

On their basement floors, you'll find *depachika* (from the English word 'department' and the Japanese word *chika,* which means 'underground'). A good *depachika* is like an Aladdin's cave of gustatory delights that rivals the best gourmet shops in any Western city. Meanwhile, on their upper floors, you'll usually find a *resutoran-gai* ('restaurant city') that includes restaurants serving all the Japanese standards – sushi, noodles, *tonkatsu* (deep-fried pork cutlets), tempura – along with a few international restaurants, usually French, Italian and Chinese.

If you find yourself feeling peckish in downtown Kyoto, here are some good department dining options:

Takashimaya (p246) At the corner of Shijō and Kawaramachi streets, this elegant department store has an incredible food floor (on the B1 level) and the best department store *resutoran-gai* in the city (on the 7th floor).

Daimaru (p246) On the north side of Shijō, between Kawaramachi and Karasuma streets, Daimaru has a food floor that rivals the one at Takashimaya (note the awesome Japanese sweet section) and a solid *resutoran-gai* on the 8th floor.

Fujii Daimaru (p246) On the south side of the Shijō-Teramachi intersection, the Tavelt food floor on the B1 level of this department store is the cheapest of the three. It usually has a great selection of take-away sushi/sashimi and fruit.

---

place to go to try *kaiten-zushi* (conveyor-belt sushi). Sure, it's not the best sushi in the world, but it's cheap, easy and fun. Look for the mini sushi conveyor belt in the window. It's just outside the entrance to the Sanjō covered arcade.

Kane-yo
Eel (unagi) ¥¥
(かねよ; Map p210; ☎221-0669; 456 Matsugaechō, Rokkaku, Shinkyōgoku, Nakagyō-ku; unagi over rice from ¥1200; ☻11.30am-8.30pm; 🖋; 🆂Tōzai line to Kyoto Shiyakusho-mae) This is a good place to try *unagi* (eel). You can sit downstairs with a nice view of the waterfall or upstairs on the tatami. The *kane-yo donburi* set (¥1200) is good value; it's served until 2pm. Look for the barrels of live eels outside and the wooden facade.

Ganko Zushi
Sushi ¥¥
(がんこ寿司; Map p210; ☎255-1128; 101 Nakajima-chō, Sanjō-dōri, Kawaramachi Higashi iru, Nakagyō-ku; lunch ¥1000-2000, dinner ¥3000; ☻11am-11pm; 🖋; 🆂Tōzai line to Kyoto Shiyakusho-mae or Sanjō Keihan, ᴿKeihan line to Sanjō) Near Sanjō-ōhashi bridge, this is a good place for sushi or just about anything else. There are plenty of sets to choose from, but we recommend ordering sushi à la carte. There's a full English menu, the kitchen is fast and they are used to foreigners. Look for the large display of plastic food models in the window.

Tsukiji Sushisei
Sushi ¥¥
(築地寿司清; Map p210; ☎252-1537; Takakura-dōri, Nishikikōji sagaru, Obiya-chō 581, Nakagyō; sushi sets ¥1260-3150; ☻11:30am-3pm & 5-10pm, 11:30am-10pm Sat, Sun & holidays; 🖋;

Ⓢ Karasuma Line to Shijō) On the basement floor, opposite Daimaru, this simple sushi restaurant serves excellent sushi at its counter and tables. You can order a set or just point at what looks good. You can see inside the restaurant from street level, so it should be easy to spot.

Kiyamachi Sakuragawa
Kaiseki ¥¥¥

(木屋町　櫻川; Map p210; ☎ 255-4477; Kiyamachi-dōri, Nijō sagaru, Kamikoriki-chō 491 1F, Nakagyō-ku; lunch/dinner sets from ¥5000/10,000; ⏱ 11.30am-2pm & 5-9pm, closed Sun; Ⓢ Tōzai line to Kyoto Shiyakusho-mae) This elegant restaurant, just north of downtown on Kiyamachi-dōri, is an excellent place to try *kaiseki*. The modest but fully satisfying food is beautifully presented and it's a joy to watch the chefs in action. Reservations are strongly recommended and smart-casual clothes are the way to go.

Yoshikawa
Tempura ¥¥¥

(吉川; Map p210; ☎ 221-5544; Oike sagaru, Tominokōji, Nakagyō-ku; lunch ¥3000-25,000, dinner ¥6000-25,000; ⏱ 11am-2pm & 5-8.30pm; 📖; Ⓢ Tōzai & Karasuma lines to Karasuma-Oike or Kyoto Shiyakusho-mae) This is the place to go for delectable tempura. It offers table

seating, but it's much more interesting to sit and eat around the small counter and observe the chefs at work. It's near Oike-dōri in a fine traditional Japanese-style building. Reservation required for tatami room; counter and table seating unavailable on Sunday.

Southern Higashiyama

Kasagi-ya
Teahouse ¥

(かさぎ屋; Map p214; ☎ 561-9562; 349 Masuya chō, Kōdai-ji, Higashiyama-ku; ⏱ 11am-6pm, closed Tue; 📖; 🚌 Kyoto City Bus 206 to the Higashiyama-Yasui stop) At Kasagi-ya, on the Ninen-zaka slope near Kiyomizu-dera, this funky old wooden shop has friendly staff and atmosphere to boot. It's a great place for a cup of green tea and a Japanese sweet to power you through a day of sightseeing in Higashiyama. *Matcha* (powdered green tea) with a sweet costs ¥700.

It's hard to spot; you may have to ask someone in the area to point it out.

Kagizen Yoshifusa
Teahouse ¥

(鍵善良房; Map p214; ☎ 561-1818; 264 Gion machi Kita gawa, Higashiyama-ku; kuzukiri ¥900; ⏱ 9.30am-6pm, closed Mon; 📖; 🚃 Hankyū

Ganko Zushi

241

SHAYNE HILL XTREME VISUALS / GETTY IMAGES ©

line to Kawaramachi, Keihan line to Gion-Shijō)
One of Kyoto's oldest and best-known
okashi-ya (sweet shops) sells a variety
of traditional sweets and has a peaceful
tearoom in back where you can sample
cold *kuzukiri* (transparent arrowroot
noodles), served with a *kuro-mitsu*
(sweet black sugar) dipping sauce. It's in
a traditional *machiya* up a flight of stone
steps.

Santōka
Rāmen ¥

(山頭火; Map p214; ☎532-1335; Sanjō kudaru
Higashi gawa, Higashiyama-ku; rāmen from ¥790;
🕙11am-2am Mon-Sat, 11am-midnight Sun &
national holidays; 📖; 🚆Keihan line to Sanjō,
🚇Tōzai line to Sanjō-Keihan) The young chefs
at this sleek restaurant dish out some
seriously good Hokkaidō-style *rāmen*.
You will be given a choice of three kinds
of soup when you order: *shio* (salt), *shōyu*
(soy sauce) or miso – we highly recommend you go for the miso soup.

For something totally decadent, try the
tokusen toroniku rāmen, which is made
from pork cheeks, of which only 200g can
be obtained from one animal. The pork
will come on a separate plate from the
rāmen – just shovel it all into your bowl.

The restaurant is located on the east
side and ground floor of the new Kyōen
restaurant and shopping complex.

Hisago
Noodles ¥

(ひさご; Map p214; ☎561-2109; 484
Shimokawara-chō, Higashiyama-ku; meals from
¥900; 🕙11.30am-7.30pm, closed Mon; 📖;
🚌Kyoto City Bus 206 to the Higashiyama-Yasui
stop) If you need a quick meal while in the
main southern Higashiyama sightseeing district, this simple noodle-and-rice
restaurant is a good bet. It's within easy
walking distance of Kiyomizu-dera and
Maruyama-kōen. *Oyako-donburi* (chicken
and egg over rice; ¥980) is the speciality
of the house.

There is no English sign; look for the
traditional front and the small collection
of food models on display. In the busy
seasons, there's almost always a queue
outside.

Omen Kodai-ji
Noodles ¥¥

(おめん 高台寺店; Map p214; ☎541-5007;
Kodaiji-dōri, Shimokawara Higashi iru, Masuya-
chō 358, Higashiyama-ku; noodles from ¥1100, set
menu ¥2980; 🕙11:30am-8:30pm; 🚌5min walk
from Higashiyama-Yasui bus stop) This branch
of Kyoto's famed Omen noodle chain is

the best place to stop while exploring the southern Higashiyama district. It's in a remodelled Japanese building with a light, airy feeling. The signature *udon* (thick white wheat) noodles are delicious and there are many other à la carte offerings.

Northern Higashiyama

Goya
Okinawan ¥

(ゴーヤ; Map p220; ✆752-1158; 114-6 Nishida-chō, Jōdo-ji, Sakyō-ku; ⏰11.30am-4pm & 5.30-11pm, closed Wed; 🚌Kyoto City Bus 5 to the Ginkakuji-michi stop) We love this Okinawan-themed restaurant for its tasty food, stylish interior and comfortable upstairs seating. It's the perfect place for lunch while exploring northern Higashiyama and it's just a short walk from Ginkaku-ji. At lunch it serves simple things like taco rice (¥880) and *gōya champurū* (bitter melon stir-fry; ¥680).

Dinners are more à la carte affairs with a wide range of *izakaya* (pub-eatery) fare, much of it with an Okinawan twist.

Falafel Garden
Israeli ¥

(ファラフェルガーデン; Map p220; ✆712 1856; 3-16 Tanaka Shimoyanagi-chō, Sakyō-ku; falafel from ¥380; ⏰11am-9.30pm, closed Wed; 🏧; 🚈Keihan line to Demachiyanagi, exit 7) Close to the Keihan and Eizan lines' Demachiyanagi Station, this funky Israeli-run place has excellent felafel and a range of other dishes, as well as offering a set menu (¥1150). We like the style of the open-plan converted Japanese house and the minigarden out the back, but the main draw is those tasty felafels!

Hinode Udon
Noodles ¥

(日の出うどん; Map p220; ✆751-9251; 36 Kitanobō-chō, Nanzenji, Sakyō-ku; noodle dishes from ¥450; ⏰11am-5pm, closed Sun (except for Apr & Nov); 🏧; 🚌Kyoto City Bus 5 to the Eikandō-michi stop) Filling noodle and rice dishes are served at this pleasant little shop. Plain *udon* here is only ¥450, but we recommend you spring for the *nabeyaki udon* (pot-baked *udon* in broth) for between ¥850 and ¥1000. This is a good spot for lunch when temple-hopping near Ginkaku-ji or Nanzen-ji.

Cafe Proverbs 15:17
Vegetarian ¥

(カフェプロバーブズ15:17; Map p220; ✆707-6856; Domus Hyakumanben 3F, 28-20 Tanakamonzen-chō, Sakyō-ku; food from ¥450; ⏰11.45am-10pm, to 6pm Wed, closed Mon; 🏧; 🚌Kyoto Bus 206 to the Hyakumamben stop) This is a pleasant spot for a cuppa (drinks ¥300) or a light vegetarian meal. Lunch sets include green curry, sandwiches and Japanese fare. It's on the 3rd floor but there's a small sign on street level.

Omen
Noodles ¥¥

(おめん; Map p220; ✆771-8994; 74 Jōdo-ji Ishibashi-chō, Sakyō-ku; noodles from ¥1100; ⏰11am-9pm; 🏧; 🚌Kyoto City Bus 5 to the Ginkakuji-michi stop) This noodle shop is named after the thick, white noodles served in a hot broth with a selection of seven fresh vegetables. Just say '*omen*' and you'll be given your choice of hot or cold noodles, a bowl of soup to dip them in and a plate of vegetables (you put these into the soup along with some sesame seeds).

It's a great bowl of noodles but don't stop there: the à la carte menu is also fantastic – ranging from excellent tempura to healthy vegetable dishes. It's about five minutes' walk from Ginkaku-ji in a traditional Japanese house with a lantern outside. Note that there's often a line during tourist high season.

Arashiyama & Sagano

Komichi
Cafe ¥

(こみち; Map p204; ✆872-5313; 23 Ōjōin-chō, Nison-in Monzen, Saga, Ukyō-ku; matcha ¥650; ⏰10am-5pm, closed Wed; 🚌Kyoto City Bus 28 from Kyoto Station to the Arashiyama-Tenryuji-mae stop) This friendly little teahouse is perfectly located along the Arashiyama tourist trail. In addition to hot and cold tea/coffee drinks, it serves *uji kintoki* (sweet *matcha* over shaved ice, sweetened milk and sweet beans – sort of a Japanese Italian ice) in summer and a variety of light noodle dishes year-round. The picture menu helps with ordering.

The sign is green and black on a white background.

Drinking

Kyoto has a great variety of bars, clubs and *izakayas*, all of which are good places to meet Japanese folks. And if you happen to be in Kyoto in the summer, many hotels and department stores operate rooftop beer gardens with all-you-can-eat-and-drink deals and good views of the city.

In addition to the places listed here, all the top-end hotels listed in the Sleeping section have at least one good bar on their premises. We particularly like the **Tōzan** (Sanjūsangendō-mawari, Hyatt Regency Kyoto; 5min walk from Shichijō Station, Keihan line) at the Hyatt.

McLoughlin's Irish Bar & Restaurant Bar
(マクラクランズ・アイリッシュバー＆レストラン; Map p210; 212-6339; 8F The Empire Bldg, Kiyamachi, Sanjō-agaru, Nakagyō-ku; 6pm-midnight, later on Fri & Sat, closed Tue; S Tōzai line to Kyoto Shiyakusho-mae) With a fine view over the city, free wi-fi and good food, this bar is a nice place to spend an evening in Kyoto. There's a great selection of local and international craft beers. It's also a good place to meet local expats and Japanese. It hosts music events as well.

Sama Sama Bar
(サマサマ; Map p210; 241-4100; 532 Kamiōsaka-chō, Kiyamachi, Sanjō agaru, , Nakagyō-ku; drinks from ¥600-700; 8pm-3am, closed Thu; S Tōzai line to Kyoto Shiyakusho-mae) This place seems like a very comfortable cave somewhere near the Mediterranean. Scoot up to the counter or make yourself at home on the cushions on the floor and enjoy a wide variety of drinks, some of them Indonesian (the owner is from Indonesia). It's down an alley just north of Sanjō; the alley has a sign for Sukiyaki Komai Tei.

Gion Finlandia Bar Bar
(ぎをん フィンランディアバー; Map p214; 541-3482; Gion-machi minamigawa (Hanamikōji Shijō sagaru hitosujime Nishi iru minamigawa), Higashiyama-ku; per drink about ¥900; 6pm-3am; Keihan line to Gion-Shijō)

This stylish Gion bar in an old geisha house is a great place for a civilised drink in southern Higashiyama. The 1st floor is decorated with Finnish touches, while the upstairs retains a Japanese feeling, with sunken floors and tatami mats. There's a wide selection of vodka on offer here. The cover charge is ¥500.

Kick Up Bar
(キックアップ; Map p220; 761-5604; Higashikomonoza-chō 331, Higashiyama-ku; drinks from ¥600, food from ¥500; 7pm-midnight, closed Wed; S Tōzai line to Keage, exit 1) Located just across the street from Keage Station this wonderful bar attracts a regular crowd of Kyoto expats, local Japanese and guests from nearby hotels. It's relaxing and friendly.

Entertainment

Most of Kyoto's cultural entertainment is of an occasional nature, and you'll need to check with the TIC or *Kansai Scene* to find out whether anything interesting coincides with your visit.

GEISHA DANCES

In the spring and autumn, Kyoto's geisha (or, properly speaking, *geiko* and *maiko*) perform fantastic dances, usually on seasonal themes. For a small additional fee, you can participate in a brief tea ceremony before the show. We *highly* recommend seeing one of these dances if you are in town when they are being held. Ask at the tourist information centre or at your lodgings for help with ticket purchase. Tour companies can also help with tickets.

Gion Odori Dance
(祇園をどり; 561-0224; Gion, Higashiyama-ku; admission/with tea ¥3500/4000; shows 1.30pm & 4pm) Held at **Gion Kaikan Theatre** (祇園会館; Map p214; Gion, Higashiyama-ku) near Yasaka-jinja; 1 to 10 November.

Miyako Odori Dance
(都をどり; 561-1115; Gion-chō South, Higashiyama-ku; seat nonreserved/reserved/reserved with tea ¥2000/4000/4500; shows 12.30pm, 2pm, 3.30pm & 4.50pm) At **Gion**

Kōbu Kaburen-jō Theatre (祇園甲部歌舞練場; Map p214; Gion-chō South, Higashiyama-ku), near Gion Corner; throughout April.

Kamogawa Odori
Dance
(鴨川をどり; ☎221-2025; Ponto-chō, Sanjō sagaru, Nakagyō-ku; normal/special seat/special seat with tea ¥2000/4000/4500; ◷shows 12.30pm, 2.20pm & 4.10pm) Held at **Ponto-chō Kaburen-jō Theatre** (Map p210; Ponto-chō, Sanjō sagaru, Nakagyō-ku), Ponto-chō; 1 to 24 May.

Kitano Odori
Dance
(北野をどり; ☎461-0148; Imadegawa-dōri, Nishihonmatsu nishi iru, Kamigyō-ku; admission/with tea ¥4000/4500; ◷shows 1.30pm & 4pm) At **Kamishichiken Kaburen-jō Theatre** (上七軒歌舞練場; Map p204; Imadegawa-dōri, Nishihonmatsu nishi iru, Kamigyō-ku), east of Kitano Tenman-gū; 25 March to 7 April.

Kyō Odori
Dance
(京をどり; ☎561-1151; Kawabata-dōri, Shijō sagaru; nonreserved/reserved seat ¥2000/4000, with tea plus ¥500; ◷shows 12.30pm, 2.30pm & 4.30pm) Held at **Miyagawa-chō Kaburen-jō Theatre** (宮川町歌舞練場; Map p214), east of the Kamo-gawa between Shijō-dōri and Gojō-dōri; from the first Saturday to the third Sunday in April.

GEISHA ENTERTAINMENT

If you want to see geisha perform and actually speak with them, one of the best ways is at **Gion Hatanaka** (祇園畑中; Map p214; ☎541-5315; www.thehatanaka.co.jp; Yasaka-jinja Minami-mon mae, Higashiyama-ku; r per person with 2 meals from ¥30,000; ☞☏; ☐Kyoto City Bus 206 to the Higashiyama-Yasui stop), a Gion ryokan that offers the **Kyoto Cuisine & Maiko Evening** (Map p214; ☎541-5315; www.kyoto-maiko.jp; 505 Minami-gawa, Gion-machi, Yasaka

Jinja Minamimon-mae; per person ¥18,000; ◷6-8pm Mon, Wed, Fri & Sat). Here, you can enjoy elegant Kyoto *kaiseki* food while being entertained by real Kyoto *geiko* and *maiko*.

KABUKI

Minami-za Theatre
Theatre
(南座; Map p210; ☎561-0160; Shijō-Ōhashi, Higashiyama-ku; performances ¥4200-27,000; ☐Keihan line to Gion-Shijō) This grand theatre in Gion is the oldest kabuki venue in Japan and it's a great place to get acquainted with this most beguiling of Japanese theatrical arts. The major event of the year is the **Kao-mise** (1 to 26 December), which features Japan's finest kabuki actors. Other performances take place on an irregular basis.

Ask at the tourist information centre or at your lodgings for help with ticket purchase. Tour companies can also help with tickets.

🔒 Shopping

The heart of Kyoto's shopping district is around the intersection of Shijō-dōri and Kawaramachi-dōri. The blocks to

Minami-za Theatre
JAMES MONTGOMERY / GETTY IMAGES ©

the north and west of here are packed with stores selling both traditional and modern goods. This is also home to Kyoto's largest department stores: **Marui,** (マルイ (OIOI); Map p210; 🕿 257-0101; 68 Shin-chō, Shijō-dōri Kawaramachi Higashi-iru, Shimogyō-ku; ⏰ 10.30am-8.30pm, restaurants 11am-10pm, supermarket 8am-10pm), **Takashimaya** (Map p210; 🕿 221 8811; Shijō Tominokōji kado; ⏰ 10am-8pm, restaurants 10am-10pm; S Hankyū Kyoto line to Kawaramachi), **Daimaru** (Map p210; 🕿 211 8111; Tachiuri Nishi-machi 79, Shijō-dōri Takakura Nishi iru; ⏰ 10am-8pm, restaurants 11am-9pm, closed 1 Jan; S Karasuma line to Shijō or Hankyū Kyoto line to Karasuma) and **Fujii Daimaru** (Map p210; 🕿 221-8181; Shijō-dōri Teramachi; ⏰ 10:30am to 8pm; S Hankyū line to Kawaramachi).

Some of the best shopping and people-watching can be had along Kyoto's three downtown shopping arcades: Shinkyōgoku shopping arcade, Teramachi shopping arcade and Nishiki Market (p206). Teramachi and Shinkyōgoku run parallel to each other in the heart of downtown. The former has a mix of tasteful and tacky shops; the latter specialises in tacky stuff for the hoards of schoolkids who visit Kyoto every year. Nishiki branches off Teramachi to the west, about 100m north of Shijō-dōri.

The place to look for antiques in Kyoto is Shinmonzen-dōri, in Gion. The street is lined with great old shops, many of them specialising in one thing or another (furniture, pottery, scrolls, prints etc). You can easily spend an afternoon strolling from shop to shop, but be warned: if something strikes your fancy you're going to have to break out the credit card – prices here are steep!

Teramachi-dōri, between Oike-dōri and Marutamachi-dōri, has a number of classic old Kyoto arts, crafts, antiques and tea shops. This is probably the best place for shopping if you're after 'old Kyoto' items.

Aritsugu
Knives

(有次; Map p210; 🕿 221-1091; 219 Kajiya-chō, Nishikikōji-dōri, Gokomachi nishi iru, Nakagyō-ku; ⏰ 9am-5.30pm; 🚃 Hankyū line to Kawaramachi) Located in Nishiki Market, this is one of the finest knife shops in Japan. There's usually someone on hand who can help you in English. If you purchase a knife, staff put a final edge on it with a giant stone sharpening wheel before packaging it.

Kyoto Handicraft Center

Markets

Markets are the best places to find antiques and bric-a-brac at reasonable prices and are the only places in Japan where you can actually bargain for a better price.

On the 21st of each month, **Kōbō-san Market** (弘法さん（東寺露天市）; Map p204; ☎691 3325; Kujō-chō 1, Tō-ji; ⏰dawn to dusk, 21st of each month) is held at Tō-ji to commemorate the death of Kōbō Daishi (Kūkai), who in 823 was appointed abbot of the temple. It's a ten-minute walk from Kyoto Station.

Another major market, **Tenjin-san Market** (天神さん（北野天満宮露天市）; Map p204; ☎461 0005; Bakuro-chō, Kitano Tenman-gū; ⏰dawn to dusk, 25th of each month; 🚌bus 50 or 101 from Kyoto Station to the Kitano Tenmangū-mae bus stop), is held on the 25th of each month at Kitano Tenman-gū, marking the day of the birth (and, coincidentally, the death) of the Heian-era statesman Sugawara Michizane (845–903).

Morita Washi
Handicrafts

(森田和紙; Map p204; ☎341-1419; 1F Kajinoha Bldg, 298 Ōgisakaya-chō, Higashinotōin-dōri, Bukkō-ji agaru , Shimogyō-ku; ⏰9.30am-5.30pm, to 4.30pm Sat, closed Sun; Ⓢ Karasuma line to Shijō) Not far from Shijo-Karasuma, this wonderful shop sells a fabulous variety of handmade *washi* (Japanese paper) for reasonable prices. It could be our favourite shop in Kyoto.

Zōhiko
Handicrafts

(象彦; Map p220; ☎752-7777; 10 Okazaki Saishōji-chō, Sakyō-ku; ⏰9.30am-6pm, closed Wed; 🚌Kyoto City Bus 206 from Kyoto Station to the Kumano-jinja-mae stop) This is our favourite lacquerware shop in Kyoto. While the outside is nondescript, the inside is a treasure trove of beautiful lacquerware and there's a fine gallery upstairs. It's very near Heian-jingū.

Bic Camera
Electronics

(ビックカメラ; Map p208; ☎353-1111; Kyoto Station Bldg, 927 Higashi Shiokōji-chō, Shimogyō-ku; ⏰10am-9pm; Ⓡ JR Tōkaidō main line to Kyoto Station, Ⓢ Karasuma line to Kyoto Station) Vast new electronics/camera shop, directly connected to Kyoto Station via the Nishinotōin gate; otherwise, it's accessed by leaving the north (Karasuma) gate and walking west. You will be amazed by the sheer amount of goods it has on display.

Just make sure that an English operating manual is available.

For computer parts, keep in mind that not all items on offer will work with English operating systems.

Kyoto Handicraft Center
Handicrafts, Souvenirs

(京都ハンディクラフトセンター; Map p220; ☎761-5080; 21 Entomi-chō, Shōgoin, Sakyō-ku; ⏰10am-6pm, closed 1-3 Jan; 🚌Kyoto City Bus 206 from Kyoto Station to the Kumano-jinja-mae stop) Just north of the Heian-jingū, this is a huge cooperative that sells, demonstrates and exhibits crafts (wood-block prints and *yukata* are a good buy here). It's the best spot in town for buying Japanese souvenirs and is highly recommended.

Ippōdō
Tea

(一保堂; Map p220; ☎211-3421; Teramachi-dōri, Nijō, Nakagyō-ku; ⏰9am-7pm Mon-Sat, to 6pm Sun & holidays, cafe 11am-5.30pm; Ⓢ Tōzai line to Kyoto Shiyakusho-mae) This is an old-fashioned tea shop selling all sorts of Japanese tea. You can ask to sample the tea before buying. There's an excellent adjoining cafe that sells a variety of green-tea drinks and Japanese sweets – it's a highly recommended spot to relax while shopping on Teramachi.

Junkudō
Bookshop

(ジュンク堂書店; Map p210; ☎253-6460; Kyoto BAL Bldg, 2-251 Yamazaki-chō, Kawaramachi-dōri, Sanjō sagaru, Nakagyō-ku; ⊙11am-8pm; ⑤Tōzai line to Sanjō-Keihan; ⊠Keihan line to Sanjō) In the BAL Building, this shop has a great selection of English-language books on the 7th floor. This is Kyoto's best bookshop now that the old Maruzen and Random Walk bookshops have closed (you may remember these shops if you visited in the past).

There is an excellent cafe on the top floor, which has a great view over Kyoto to the Higashiyama mountains. You can get light meals here as well as drinks.

ℹ Information

Money

Most of the major banks are near the Shijō-Karasuma intersection, two stops north of Kyoto Station on the Karasuma line subway.

International transactions (such as wire transfers) can be made at Bank of Tokyo-Mitsubishi UFJ (三菱東京UFJ銀行; ☎221-7161; ⊙9am-3pm Mon-Fri, 10am-5pm Sat, closed Sun, ATM 24hr), which is at the southeast corner of this intersection. There is another branch one block southwest of the intersection. Other international transactions can be made at Citibank (シティバンク; ☎212-5387; ⊙office 9am-3pm Mon-Fri, ATM 24hr), just west of this intersection.

Finally, you can change travellers cheques at most post offices around town, including the Kyoto Central Post Office, next to Kyoto Station. Post offices also have ATMs that accept foreign-issued cards. If your card doesn't work at postal ATMs, try the ATMs in 7-Eleven convenience stores. Failing that, try Citibank, which has a 24-hour ATM that accepts most foreign-issued cards.

Post

Kyoto Central Post Office (京都中央郵便局; ☎365-2471; 843-12 Higashishiokōji-chō, Shimogyō-ku; ⊙9am-9pm Mon-Fri, to 7pm Sat & Sun, ATMs 12.05am-11.55pm Mon-Sat, to 9pm Sun & holidays) Conveniently located next to Kyoto Station (take the Karasuma exit; the post office is on the northwestern side of the station). There's an after-hours service counter on the southern side of the post office, open 24 hours a day, 365 days a year. The ATMs here are open *almost* 24 hours a day.

Tourist Information

Kyoto Tourist Information Center (京都総合観光案内所; TIC; ☎343-0548; 2F Kyoto Station Bldg, Shimogyō-ku; ⊙8.30am-7pm) Located in the main concourse on the 2nd floor of the Kyoto Station building that runs between the *shinkansen* station and the front of the station (near Isetan department store), this is the main tourist information centre in Kyoto.

ℹ Getting There & Away

Travel between Kyoto and other parts of Japan is a breeze. In addition to air and train options, it is also possible to travel to/from Kyoto and other parts of Honshū, Shikoku and Kyūshū by long-distance highway buses.

Air

Kyoto is served by Osaka Itami Airport (ITM), which principally handles domestic traffic, and the Kansai International Airport (KIX), which principally handles international flights. There are frequent flights between Tokyo and Itami (around ¥24,600, 80 minutes), but unless you're very lucky with airport connections you'll probably find it as quick and more convenient to take the *shinkansen*. There are ample connections to/from both airports, though the trip to/from Kansai International Airport takes longer and costs more. Kyoto is also relatively close to Nagoya, in case you can only get a flight to Centrair airport.

Train

Kansai is served by the Tōkaidō and San-yō *shinkansen* lines, several JR main lines and a few private rail lines.

Shinkansen

Kyoto is on the Tōkaidō-San-yō *shinkansen* line, which runs between Tokyo and Kyūshū, with stops at places such as Nagoya, Osaka, Kōbe, Himeji and Hiroshima en route. The *shinkansen* operates to/from Kyoto Station. On the Tokyo end, it operates from Tokyo, Shinagawa and Shin-Yokohama stations. Fares and times for Hikari (the second-fastest type of *shinkansen*) between Kyoto and the following cities are as follows.

Hakata (¥15,210, three hours, 22 minutes)

Hiroshima (¥10,790, two hours)

Nagoya (¥5440, 40 minutes)

Shin-Osaka (¥2730, 15 minutes)

Tokyo (¥13,220, 2¾ hours)

WIBOWO RUSLI / GETTY IMAGES ©

Regular Trains

Nara The private Kintetsu line (sometimes written in English as the Kinki Nippon railway) links Kyoto (Kintetsu Kyoto Station, south side of the main Kyoto Station building) and Nara (Kintetsu Nara Station). There are fast direct *tokkyū* (¥1110, 33 minutes) and ordinary express trains (¥610, 40 minutes), which may require a change at Saidai-ji.

The JR Nara line also connects Kyoto Station with JR Nara Station (express, ¥690, 41 minutes), and this is a great option for Japan Rail Pass holders.

Osaka The fastest train other than the *shinkansen* between Kyoto Station and Osaka is the JR *shinkaisoku* (special rapid train), which takes 29 minutes (¥540). In Osaka, the train stops at both Shin-Osaka and Osaka Stations.

There is also the cheaper private Hankyū line, which runs between Hankyū Kawaramachi, Karasuma and Ōmiya Stations in Kyoto and Hankyū Umeda Station in Osaka (*tokkyū* or limited express Umeda–Kawaramachi, ¥390, 40 minutes). These trains are usually more comfortable than the JR trains, and if you board at Kawaramachi or Umeda, you can usually get a seat.

Alternatively, you can take the Keihan main line between Demachiyanagi, Sanjō, Shijō or Shichijō Stations in Kyoto and Keihan Yodoyabashi Station in Osaka (*tokkyū* to/from Sanjō ¥400, 51 minutes). Yodoyabashi is on the Midō-suji subway line. Again, these are more comfortable than JR trains and you can usually get a seat if you board in Demachiyanagi or Yodoyabashi.

Tokyo The *shinkansen* line has the fastest and most frequent rail links. The journey can also be undertaken by a series of regular JR express trains, but keep in mind that it takes around eight hours and involves at least two (often three or four) changes along the way. The fare is ¥7980. Get the staff at the ticket counter to write down the exact details of each transfer for you when you buy your ticket.

ℹ Getting Around

To/From the Airport

Osaka Itami Airport 大阪伊丹空港

There are frequent limousine buses between Osaka Itami Airport and Kyoto Station (the Kyoto Station airport bus stop is opposite the south side of the station, in front of Avanti department store). Buses also run between the airport and various hotels around town, but on a less regular basis (check with your hotel). The journey should take around 55 minutes and the cost is ¥1280. Be sure to allow extra time in case of traffic.

At Itami, the stand for these buses is outside the arrivals hall; buy your tickets from the machines and ask one of the attendants which stand is for Kyoto (hint: you've got a better chance of getting a seat if you board at the South Terminal).

MK Taxi (☏778-5489) offers limousine van service to/from the airport for ¥2300. Call at least two days in advance to reserve, or ask at the information counter in the arrivals hall on arrival in Osaka.

Kansai International Airport
関西国際空港

The fastest, most convenient way to travel between KIX and Kyoto is on the special Haruka airport express, which makes the trip in about 78 minutes. Most seats are reserved (¥3290, ¥3490, ¥3690 depending on season) but there are usually two cars on each train with unreserved seats (¥2980). Open seats are almost always available, so you don't have to purchase tickets in advance. First and last departures from Kyoto to KIX are 5.46am and 8.15pm; first and last departures from KIX to Kyoto are 6.33am Monday-Friday, 6.42am Saturday, Sunday and holidays and 10.16pm. Note that the Haruka is one of the few trains in Japan that is frequently late (although not usually by more than a few minutes). We suggest leaving a little extra time when heading from Kyoto to the airport to catch a flight.

It's also possible to travel by limousine bus between Kyoto and KIX (¥2500, about 90 minutes). In Kyoto, the bus departs from the same place as the Itami-bound bus.

A final option is the **MK Taxi Sky Gate Shuttle limousine van service** (☏778-5489), which will pick you up anywhere in Kyoto city and deliver you to KIX for ¥3500. Call at least two days in advance to reserve. The advantage of this method is that you are delivered from door to door and you don't have to lug your baggage through the train station. MK has a counter in the arrivals hall of KIX, and if there's room they'll put you on the next van to Kyoto. A similar service is offered by **Yasaka Taxi** (☏803-4800).

Bicycle

Kyoto is a great city to explore on a bicycle; with the exception of outlying areas it's mostly flat and there is a bike path running the length of the Kamo-gawa.

There are two bicycle-parking lots in town that are convenient for tourists: one in front of Kyoto Station and another off Kiyamachi-dōri, between Sanjō-dōri and Shijō-dōri. It costs ¥150 per day to park your bicycle here. Be sure to hang onto the ticket you pick up as you enter.

Kyoto Cycling Tour Project (京都サイクリングツアープロジェクト; **KCTP**; ☏354-3636; www.kctp.net; ☺9am-7pm) A great place to rent a bike. These folk rent bikes (¥1000 per day) that are perfect for getting around the city. KCTP also conducts a variety of excellent bicycle tours of Kyoto with English-speaking guides. These are a great way to see the city (check the website for details).

Public Transport

Bus

Kyoto has an extensive network of bus routes providing an efficient way of getting around at moderate

Kyoto Station
STEVE VIDLER / GETTY IMAGES ©

cost. Many of the routes used by visitors have announcements in English. The core timetable for buses is between 7am and 9pm, though a few run earlier or later.

The TIC stocks the *Bus Navi: Kyoto City Bus Sightseeing Map,* which is a good map of the city's main bus lines. This map is not exhaustive. If you can read a little Japanese, pick up a copy of the regular (and more detailed) Japanese bus map available at major bus terminals throughout the city.

Entry to the bus is usually through the back door and exit is via the front door. Inner-city buses charge a flat fare (¥220), which you drop into the clear plastic receptacle on top of the machine next to the driver on your way out. A separate machine gives change for ¥100 and ¥500 coins or ¥1000 notes.

On buses serving the outer areas, you take a numbered ticket *(seiri-ken)* when entering. When you leave, an electronic board above the driver displays the fare corresponding to your ticket number (drop the *seiri-ken* into the ticket box with your fare).

The main Kyoto Bus Information Centre (京都バス案内書) is located in front of Kyoto Station. Here you can pick up bus maps, purchase bus tickets and passes (on all lines, including highway buses), and get additional information. Nearby, there's a convenient English/Japanese bus-information computer terminal; just enter your intended destination and it will tell you the correct bus and bus stop.

When heading for locations outside the city centre, be careful which bus you board. Kyoto city buses are green, Kyoto buses are tan and Keihan buses are red and white.

Subway

Kyoto has two efficient subway lines, which operate from around 5.30am to around 11.30pm. The minimum fare is ¥210 (children ¥110).

The quickest way to travel between the north and south of the city is the Karasuma subway line. The line has 15 stops and runs from Takeda in the far south, via Kyoto Station, to the Kyoto International Conference Hall (Kokusaikaikan Station) in the north.

The east-west Tōzai subway line crosses Kyoto from Uzumasa-Tenjingawa in the west, meeting the Karasuma line at Karasuma-Oike Station, and continuing east to Sanjō Keihan, Yamashina and Rokujizō, in the east and southeast.

Taxi

Kyoto taxi fares start at ¥640 for the first 2km. The exception is MK Taxis (778-4141), the fares of which start at ¥580.

MK Taxis also provides tours of the city with English-speaking drivers. For a group of up to four, prices start at ¥21,800 for a three-hour tour. Another company offering a similar service is Kyōren Taxi Service (672-5111).

Most Kyoto taxis are equipped with satellite navigation systems. If you are going somewhere unusual, it will help the driver if you have the address or phone number of your destination, as both of these can be programmed into the system.

Kansai & Western Honshū

Kansai and western Honshū make the perfect add-ons to Kyoto.

Kyoto, which is actually part of Kansai, can serve as the base or jumping-off point for exploring the incredible wonders of these two regions.

Kansai is Japan's cultural heartland and it's the place where Japanese culture really came into its own. Less than an hour from Kyoto you'll find Nara, the first permanent capital of Japan. It's a compact and rich storehouse of cultural treasures, including some of its finest temples and Buddhist images. Even closer is the city of Osaka, which duplicates the urban experience of Tokyo but on a more manageable scale. Next along is Kōbe, one of Japan's more cosmopolitan cities.

Continuing west along the Inland Sea brings you to the fascinating region of western Honshū, where you'll find the island-turned-art museum of Naoshima, the city of Hiroshima and the island of Miyajima, home to an iconic Shintō shrine.

Itsukushima-jinja (p313), Miyajima

253

Kansai & Western Honshū

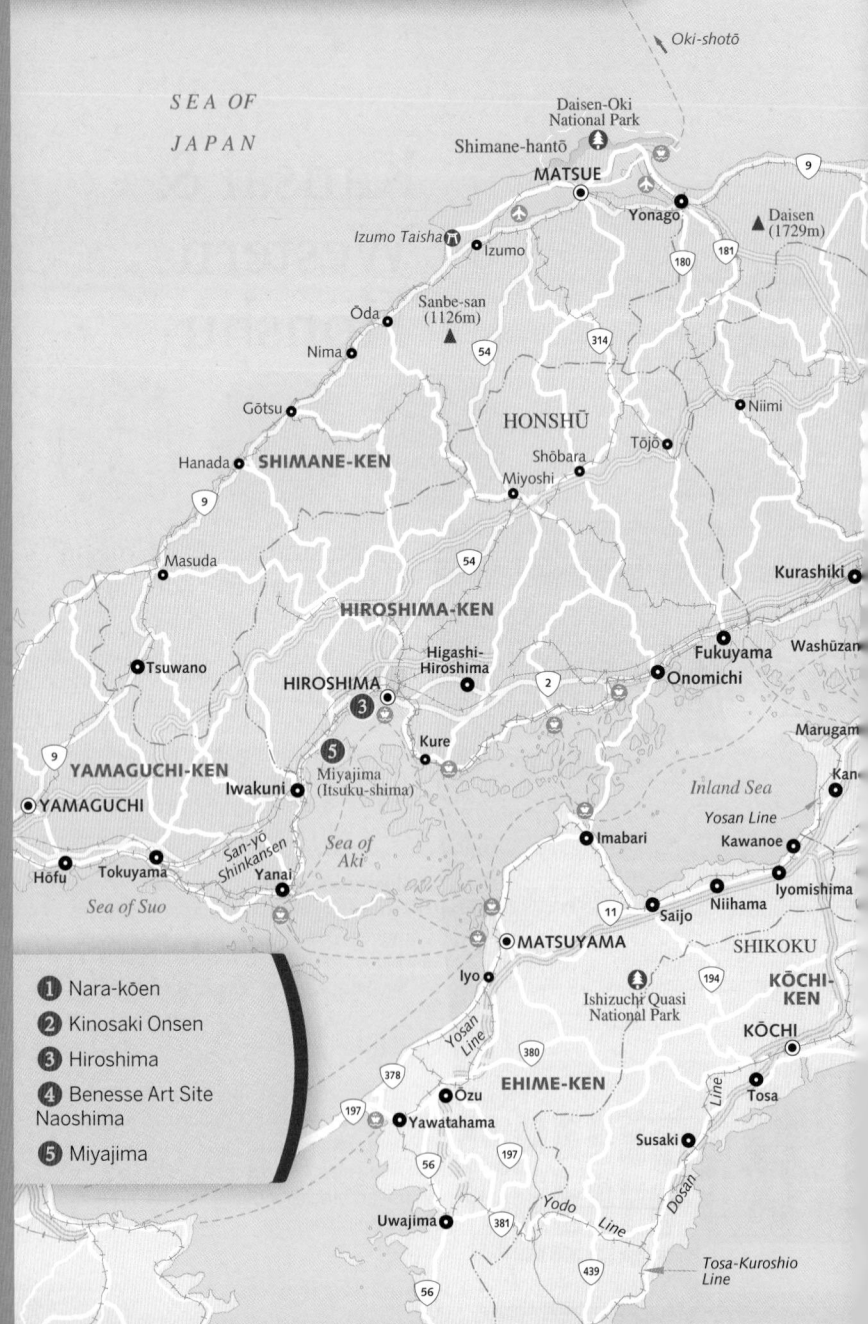

SEA OF JAPAN

Oki-shotō

Daisen-Oki National Park
Shimane-hantō
MATSUE
Yonago
Daisen (1729m)
Izumo Taisha
Izumo
Ōda
Sanbe-san (1126m)
Nima
Niimi
Gōtsu
HONSHŪ
Shōbara
Tōjō
Hanada
SHIMANE-KEN
Miyoshi
Masuda
Kurashiki
HIROSHIMA-KEN
Washūzan
Higashi-Hiroshima
Fukuyama
Tsuwano
HIROSHIMA
Onomichi
③
Kan
Kure
Marugam
⑤
YAMAGUCHI-KEN
Miyajima (Itsuku-shima)
Iwakuni
Inland Sea
Yosan Line
YAMAGUCHI
Kawanoe
Sea of Aki
Imabari
Iyomishima
Hōfu
Tokuyama
Niihama
Yanai
Saijo
Sea of Suo
MATSUYAMA
SHIKOKU
Iyo
KŌCHI-KEN
Ishizuchi Quasi National Park
KŌCHI
① Nara-kōen
② Kinosaki Onsen
③ Hiroshima
④ Benesse Art Site Naoshima
⑤ Miyajima
Ōzu
EHIME-KEN
Tosa
Yawatahama
Susaki
Uwajima
Yodo Line
Tosa-Kuroshio Line

Kansai & Western Honshū Highlights

Nara-kōen

A fine park within easy strolling distance of Kintetsu Nara Station, Nara-kōen (p277) contains some of Japan's most important cultural and historical treasures. It also contains some virgin forest, said to be the world's only such example inside a city. This park is lovely in any season.

Kinosaki Onsen

On the Sea of Japan coast in northern Kansai, the picturesque town of Kinos (p292) is the place for the classic Japanese onsen (hot springs) experience Put on your *yukata* (light cotton kimono) and a pair of sandals and spe the evening hopping from one fine h spring to the next, then head back to your ryokan (traditional Japanese inn and feast on locally caught king crabs

Guests entering an onsen in Kinosaki

ADAM HESTER / GETTY IMAGES ©

Hiroshima

3

Reborn from the ashes of the 1945
atomic blast, Hiroshima (p306) is not
a highlight in the traditional sense
of the word. Rather it is a chance to
learn about the horrors of nuclear
war and the power of the human
spirit to overcome adversity. While
the displays relating to the blast are
sobering in the extreme, they are
also enlightening and the vibrant
modern city of Hiroshima
inspires hope for the future.

Atomic Bomb Dome, Hiroshima

4

Benesse Art Site Naoshima

Benesse Art Site Naoshima (p302) represents the perfect interplay of art, architecture and nature. The island showcases
the architecture of Andō Tadao, who created a museum where art is illuminated
only by natural light. People who live on
Naoshima have a deep appreciation of art
and they welcome people from around
the world. Benesse House Museum

5

Miyajima

About an hour away from Hiroshima, the
island of Miyajima (p312) is home to one of
Japan's most iconic sights: the floating torii
(Shintō shrine gate) of Itsukushima-jinja.
After snapping the obligatory shot of the
gate, head up nearby Misen, a 530m peak
that offers sweeping views of the area. Miyajima is a great place to stay after visiting
Hiroshima and these two destinations make
a great overnight trip from Kansai.

Kansai & Western Honshū's Best...

Experiences

○ **Seeing the Daibutsu (Great Buddha)** This cosmic Buddha is truly awesome. (p280)

○ **Eating okonomiyaki in Hiroshima** Hiroshima's signature dish (savoury pancake; batter and cabbage cakes cooked on a griddle) is a savoury delight. (p310)

○ **Friday night in Osaka's Dōtombori area** Osakans know how to party and this is where they do it. (p270)

○ **Seeing the floating torii at Miyajima** This is the mother of all Shintō shrine gates. (p313)

Places for a Walk

○ **Nara-kōen** Spend a day with the deer at this temple-strewn park. (p277)

○ **Kōya-san's Oku-no-in cemetery** Towering trees and moss-covered monuments make this both spooky and spiritual. (p290)

○ **Miyajima's Mt Misen** Climb to the peak for beautiful Inland Sea views. (p314)

○ **Kinosaki** A stroll along the canal in the evening is magic in the moonlight. (p292)

Places to Stay

○ **Nishimuraya Honkan** One of the finest ryokan in Japan. (p294)

○ **Shukubō at Kōya-san** *Shukubō* (temple lodgings) are the only way to go here. (p288)

○ **Iwasō Ryokan** The perfect place for a night on the island of Miyajima. (p316)

○ **Benesse House** Where else can you spend the night in an art museum? (p304)

Temples & Shrines

○ **Tōdai-ji** One of Japan's most impressive temples. (p279)

○ **Kōfuku-ji** A towering pagoda with fine Buddhist images. (p279)

○ **Kasuga Taisha** An ancient Shintō shrine surrounded by lanterns and forest. (p281)

○ **Kōya-san's Garan** Home to a fantastic 'Great Pagoda'. (p288)

○ **Itsukushima-jinja** Japan's famous 'floating torii'. (p313)

ADVANCE PLANNING

○ **Three months before** Reserve accommodation well in advance, especially important if you plan to stay at Benesse House on Naoshima, or in the *shukubō* (temple lodgings) at Kōya-san.

○ **One month before** Consider getting an international driver's licence. This is recommended if you want to go off the beaten track and explore western Honshū or Kansai by car.

○ **One month before** Get a Japan Rail Pass. Good value if you plan to do extensive train travel around Kansai and western Honshū. Note that you must purchase an 'exchange order' outside Japan and then convert it into an actual pass once you arrive.

GETTING AROUND

○ **Walk or cycle** The best ways to get around Nara, Kōya-san, Osaka, Kōbe, Hiroshima, Naoshima and Nagasaki.

○ **Ferry** This is only way to access the islands of Naoshima and Miyajima (both in western Honshū).

○ **Train** Best for short trips between cities in Kansai and western Honshū.

○ **Shinkansen (bullet train)** Go high-speed for longer journeys between Kyoto and Hiroshima.

BE FOREWARNED

○ **Summer (July and August)** These months can be very hot and humid in Kansai and western Honshū. You can escape the heat by going up to a place like Kōya-san

○ **Seasonal festivals** Cherry-blossom season and autumn foliage season can bring huge crowds to Nara; escape them by going to lesser-known temples and shrines.

○ **Winter (November to March)** This season can be very cold up on Kōya-san.

Hiroshima's signature dish, *okonomiyaki*; **Above:** Kasuga Taisha (p281), Nara

(LEFT) MIXA / GETTY IMAGES ©;
(ABOVE) LISA ROMEREIN / GETTY IMAGES ©

Kansai & Western Honshū Itineraries

Using Kyoto as a base, it's possible to explore most of Kansai in a series of day trips. Once you've explored Kyoto and Kansai, consider heading west to Naoshima, Hiroshima and Miyajima.

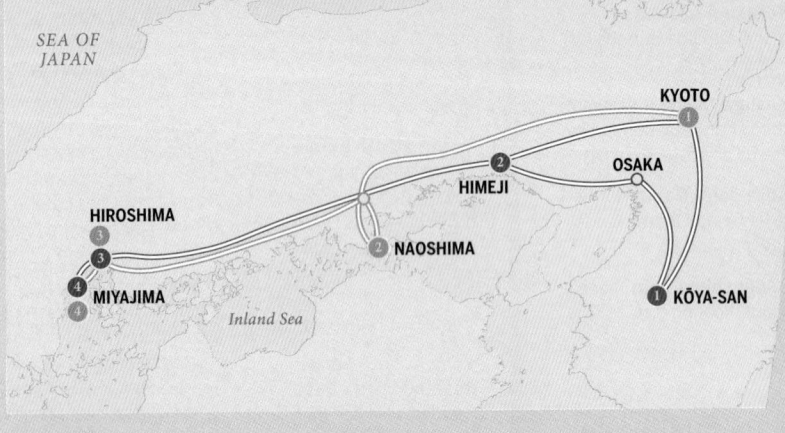

3 DAYS

KŌYA-SAN TO MIYAJIMA
Hiroshima & Miyajima

This itinerary assumes that you've already explored Kyoto and Kansai; it's particularly good for holders of a Japan Rail Pass.

First, in order to experience Japan's rich Buddhist traditions, head south to the ❶**Kōya-san** (p287) temple complex deep in the mountains of southern Kansai.

Return to Kyoto (or Osaka) and then grab a *shinkansen* (bullet train) and head west along the Inland Sea. If you are a real fan of Japanese castles, consider stopping at ❷**Himeji** (p299) to see the castle there, but keep in mind that it is presently undergoing renovation and the main keep of the castle will be under wraps until 2015.

Otherwise, head straight to ❸**Hiroshima** (p306). Visit the Peace Memorial Park to learn about the city's tragic history, then spend the evening sampling the delights of Hiroshima's famous oysters and *okonomiyaki*.

The next day, make the short journey to ❹**Miyajima** (p312), where you can see one of Japan's most famous sights, the 'floating torii'. If you have time, climb up Misen to savour the views over the Inland Sea. Consider spending a night on Miyajima, as the island is lovely after the crowds depart.

Finally, return to Hiroshima and catch a *shinkansen* east to Kyoto or Tokyo.

5 DAYS

KYOTO TO MIYAJIMA VIA NAOSHIMA

Along the Inland Sea

Start in ❶**Kyoto** and catch a *shinkansen* west to Okayama, where you can switch to a local train and then ferry to the wonderful island-turned-art museum of ❷**Naoshima** (p302). We recommend spending two nights on Naoshima to get the most out of all the museums and galleries there.

Then return to the mainland and continue west to ❸**Hiroshima** (p306). Allot at least half a day for the Peace Memorial Park to learn about the city's tragic history. Then, in the evening, gorge on Hiroshima's famous cuisine or catch a baseball game at the colourfully named

Mazda Zoom-Zoom Stadium Hiroshima, home of the Hiroshima Toyo Carp baseball team.

The following day, head to nearby ❹**Miyajima** (p312) to check out the famous 'floating torii' and climb up Mt Misen. Again, if you can afford the time, it's a good idea to spend one night on Miyajima, especially if you intend to trek all the way back to Tokyo the following day.

Finally, return to Hiroshima and catch a *shinkansen* east to Kyoto or Tokyo.

Itsukushima-jinja (p313), Miyajima
JUDY BELLAH / GETTY IMAGES ©

Discover Kansai & Western Honshū

At a Glance

○ **Osaka** All the urban madness of Tokyo in a more manageable package.

○ **Nara** (p276) One of the country's most rewarding destinations (especially for kids).

○ **Kōya-san** (p287) An Esoteric Buddhist complex high in the mountains of southern Kansai.

○ **Himeji** (p299) Home to Japan's finest castle (under renovation until 2015).

○ **Hiroshima** (p306) A city with a tragic past and an uplifting present.

OSAKA

♪06 / POP 2.8 MILLION

Osaka (大阪) is the working heart of Kansai. Famous for its down-to-earth citizens and the colourful *Kansai-ben* (Kansai dialect) they speak, it's a good counterpart to the refined atmosphere of Kyoto. First and foremost, Osaka is famous for its eating: the phrase *kuidaore* (eat till you drop) was coined to describe Osakans' love for good food. Osaka is also a good place to experience a modern Japanese city. It's only surpassed by Tokyo as a showcase of the Japanese urban phenomenon.

This isn't to say that Osaka is particularly attractive; it's an endless expanse of concrete boxes, pachinko (pinball) parlours and elevated highways. But the city somehow manages to rise above this and exert a peculiar charm, and a few architectural gems keep it interesting. At night, Osaka really comes into its own – this is when the streets come alive with flashing neon and beckoning residents with promises of tasty food and good times.

◉ **Sights & Activities**

Kita Area キタ

By day, Osaka's centre of gravity is the Kita area. There are few great attractions, but it does have the eye-catching Umeda Sky building, department stores, lots of eateries, and the activity of the big city. The past couple of years has seen a complete revamping of Osaka Station and there's more to come.

Osaka Aquarium (p265)
ANTONY GIBLIN / GETTY IMAGES ©

FRANK DEIM / GETTY IMAGES ©

Umeda
Sky Building
Notable Building

(梅田スカイビル; Map p264; www.kuchu-teien.com; 1-1-88 Ōyodonaka, Kita-ku; admission ¥700; ⏱ observation decks 10am-10.30pm, last entry 10pm; 🚇 JR line to Osaka) The Umeda Sky Building is Osaka's most dramatic piece of modern architecture, designed by Hara Hiroshi, who also designed Kyoto Station. Its twin-tower complex is like a space-age Arc de Triomphe, and from the top you can marvel at the incredible sprawl of humanity in all directions. Getting to the top is half the fun – for the final five storeys you take a glassed-in escalator across the open space between the two towers (definitely not one for vertigo sufferers). Tickets for the observation decks can be purchased once you get off the escalator.

Below the towers, you'll find **Takimi-kōji Alley** (滝見小路), a re-creation of an early Shōwa-era market street crammed with restaurants and *izakaya* (pub-eateries).

The building is reached via an underground passage that starts just north of both Osaka and Umeda Stations.

Central Osaka

Osaka-jō
Castle

(大阪城; www.osakacastle.net; 1-1 Osaka-jō; grounds/castle keep free/¥600, combined with Osaka Museum of History ¥900; ⏱ 9am-5pm, to 7pm Aug; 🚇 JR Osaka Loop line to Osaka-jō-kōen) This castle was built as a display of power by Toyotomi Hideyoshi after he achieved his goal of unifying Japan. One hundred thousand workers toiled for three years to construct an 'impregnable' granite castle, finishing the job in 1583. It was destroyed 32 years later by the armies of Tokugawa Ieyasu, rebuilt within 10 years, then suffered a further calamity when another generation of the Tokugawa clan razed it rather than let it fall to the forces of the Meiji Restoration in 1868.

The present structure is a 1931 concrete reconstruction of the original, which was refurbished in 1997. The interior houses an excellent collection of displays relating to the castle, Toyotomi Hideyoshi and the city of Osaka. On the 8th floor is an observation deck with 360-degree views. The castle and park are at their colourful best in the cherry-blossom and autumn-foliage seasons.

263

Osaka (Kita Area)

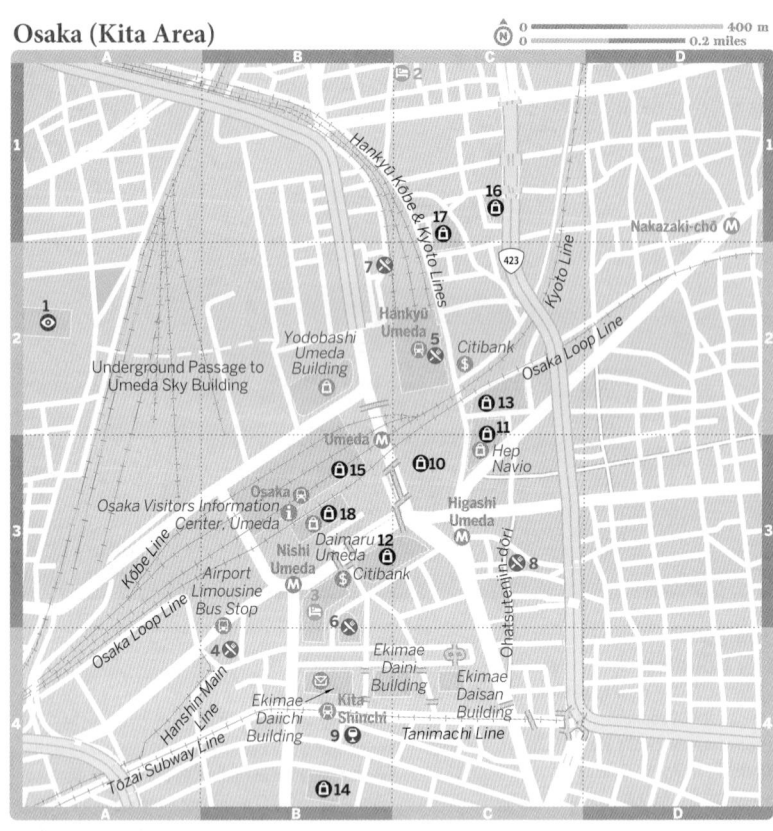

Osaka (Kita Area)

◎ Sights
1 Umeda Sky Building A2

◎ Sleeping
2 Hearton Hotel Kita Umeda C1
3 Hilton Osaka B3

◎ Eating
4 Gourmet Traveler B4
5 Hankyū Sanbangai C2
  Hilton Plaza ....(see 3)
6 Osaka Maru Building B3
7 Robatayaki Isaribi B2
  Shinkiraku ....(see 3)
8 Yukari C3

◎ Drinking & Nightlife
9 Karma B4
  Windows on the World .... (see 3)

◎ Shopping
10 Hankyū Department Store C3
11 Hankyū Men's C2
12 Hanshin Department Store B3
13 Hep Five C2
14 Junkudō B4
15 Lucua B3
16 Maruzen & Junkudō Umeda C1
17 NU Chayamachi C1
18 Tokyu Hands B3

The Ōte-mon gate, the main entrance to the park, is a 10-minute walk northeast of Tanimachi-yonchōme Station (Tanimachi 4-chome) on the Chūō and Tanimachi subway lines. You can also take the JR Osaka Loop line, get off at Osaka-jō-kōen and enter through the back of the castle.

Osaka Museum of History
Museum

(大阪歴史博物館; Osaka Rekishi Hakubu-tsukan; www.mus-his.city.osaka.jp; 4-1-32 Ōtemae; admission ¥600, combined with Osaka Castle Museum ¥900; ⊙9.30am-5pm, to 8pm Fri, closed Tue; [S] Tanimachi line to Tanimachi-yonchōme, exit 2) Just southwest of Osaka-jō, the Osaka Museum of History is housed in a sail-shaped building adjoining the NHK Broadcast Center. The museum is built where the Naniwa Palace (c 650) once stood, and you can see archaeological remains on the basement floor. There are also great views of Osaka-jō from the upper floors. There aren't full English explanations for everything so grab an audio guide. From the station exit, go right (east) about 300m.

Tempōzan 天保山

Trudging through the streets of Kita or Minami, you could easily forget that Osaka is actually a port city. A good remedy for this is a trip down to the Tempōzan seaside development, where there are several attractions, especially appealing for those with children. To get here, take the Chūō subway line to Osakakō Station, come down the stairs of exit 1 and walk towards the big wheel.

Osaka Aquarium
Aquarium

(海遊館; www.kaiyukan.com; 1-1-10 Kaigan-dōri; adult/child ¥2000/900; ⊙10am-8pm; [S] Chūō line to Osakakō) Osaka Aquarium is easily one of the best aquariums in the world and it's well worth a visit. A walkway winds its way past displays of life found on different ocean levels around the Pacific's 'ring of fire' region, from Antarctic penguins to coral-reef butterflyfish to unearthly jellyfish from the deep. Most impressive is the enormous central tank, which houses a whale shark and manta, among a huge variety of other fish and rays. There are good English explanations throughout. Not surprisingly, this is a very popular attraction, especially with families and school groups.

Festivals & Events

Kishiwada Danjiri Matsuri
Traditional Festival

Osaka's wildest festival, on 14 and 15 September, is a kind of running of the bulls except with *danjiri* (festival floats), many weighing over 3000kg. The *danjiri* are hauled through the streets by hundreds of people using ropes – take care and stand back. Most of the action takes place on the second day and the best place to see it is west of Kishiwada Station on the Nankai *honsen* line (main rail line, from Nankai Station).

Tenjin Matsuri
Traditional Festival

Held on 24 and 25 July, this is one of Japan's three biggest festivals. Try to make the second day, when processions of *mikoshi* (portable shrines) and people in traditional attire start at Osaka Temmangū and end up in hundreds of boats on the O-kawa. As night falls, there is a huge fireworks display.

Sleeping

There are plenty of places to stay in and around Kita and Minami. Minami, including Shinsaibashi, Dōtombori and Namba, has a bigger selection of restaurants and shops, but the Kita area is convenient if you want fast access to transport, with plenty of hotels around the stations. You can also explore Osaka from a base in Kyoto, and you'll find more budget accommodation in the old capital, which is only 40 minutes away by train. But keep in mind that the trains stop running a little before midnight (partygoers take note).

Kita Area

Hearton Hotel Kita Umeda
Hotel ¥¥

(ハートンホテル北梅田; Map p264; ☑6377-0810; www.heartonhotel.com/kit; 3-12-10 Toyosaki; s/tw ¥11,550/18,900; ⊝@; [S] Midō-suji line to Nakatsu) This is a good midrange option in a pleasant area a short walk north of Hankyū Umeda Station (even shorter from Nakatsu subway station), putting you right

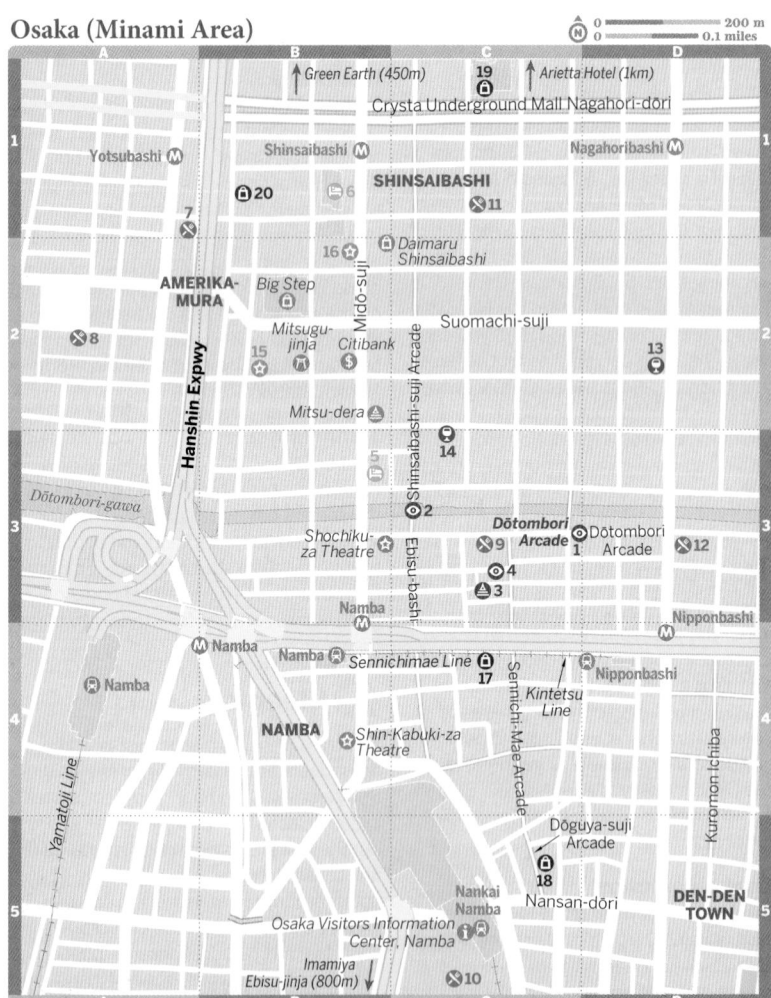

near transport and the restaurants and shops of Umeda. The clean, light rooms have a modern design and are slightly bigger than average for Japanese hotels. Staff are friendly and some English is spoken. Don't be put off by the rack-rate prices; you'll pay significantly less booking online.

Hilton Osaka   Hotel ¥¥¥
(ヒルトン大阪; Map p264; ☎6347-7111; www3.hilton.com; 1-8-8 Umeda; s from ¥18,000, tw ¥22,000-51,000; ❄@🛜🏊; 🚉JR line to Osaka) Just south of JR Osaka Station, this

is an excellent hotel at home with foreign guests. The rooms have a Japanese touch, there's a 15m pool in the fitness centre and the views from the 35th-floor Windows on the World bar are awesome. There are two floors of great restaurants below the hotel.

Minami Area

Arietta Hotel   Hotel ¥¥
(アリエッタホテル大阪; ☎6267-2787; www.thehotel.co.jp/en/arietta_osaka; 3-2-6 Azuchi-machi; s/tw incl breakfast from ¥7500/15,000;

Osaka (Minami Area)

◎ Don't Miss Sights
1 Dōtombori Arcade C3

◎ Sights
2 Ebisu-bashi C3
3 Hōzen-ji & Fudō-myōō statue C3
4 Hōzen-ji Yokochō C3

Sleeping
5 Cross Hotel Osaka B3
6 Hotel Nikkō Osaka B1

❽ Eating
7 Café Absinthe A1
8 Cuorerudino Pizzeria A2
9 Imai Honten C3
10 Namba Parks Mall C5

11 Nishiya C1
Sai-ji-ki .... (see 10)
12 Zauo D3

❻ Drinking & Nightlife
13 Cinquecento D2
14 Zerro C3

✪ Entertainment
15 Grand Café B2
16 Onzieme (11) B2

❻ Shopping
17 Bic Camera C4
18 Dōguya-suji Arcade C5
19 Tokyu Hands C1
20 Village Vanguard B1

😊 @ ; S Midō-suji line to Honmachi, exit 3)
Located in Honmachi, about 10 minutes' walk north of the Minami district (and served by the Midō-suji subway line), the Arietta has a warm, boutique-hotel feel. The good-sized rooms are minimalist, with wood floors and tiled bathrooms offering something different to the norm. Staff are welcoming and a breakfast of breads, coffee and juice is included. It's everything you need at a competitive price.

Cross Hotel Osaka　Hotel ¥¥¥
(クロスホテル大阪; Map p266; ☎ 6213-8281; www.crosshotel.com/osaka; 2-5-15 Shinsaibash-isuji; s/d/tw from ¥16,170/24,255/27,720; 😊 @; S Midō-suji line to Namba, exit 14) Cross Hotel is going for a trendy urban look, with black, white and dark red featuring in the stylish rooms and common areas. Rooms are average size, but they had us at the spacious Japanese-style bathrooms – a rare treat. Service is excellent and you'd have to sleep under Ebisu-bashi bridge to achieve a more central location. Online deals bump this down to upper-midrange territory.

Hotel Nikkō Osaka　Hotel ¥¥¥
(ホテル日航大阪; Map p266; ☎ 6244-1281; www.hno.co.jp; 1-3-3 Nishi-Shinsaibashi; s ¥11,000-24,000, d ¥13,000-30,000; 😊 @; S Midō-suji line to Shinsaibashi, exit 6) The Nikkō is a good central base in Minami and has direct access to Shinsaibashi subway station. Service is professional, rooms are modern and comfortable with spacious deluxe options, and there's even a 'ladies' floor, with special bathroom amenities. There are restaurants and bars on-site, and good views from the upper floors.

Eating

Kita Area

Robatayaki Isaribi　Izakaya, Yakitori ¥¥
(炉ばた焼き漁火; Map p264; ☎ 6373-2969; www.rikimaru-group.com/shop/isaribi.html; 1-5-12 Shibata; dishes ¥315; ⏰ 5-11.15pm; 🅿; 🚆 JR line to Osaka) Enjoy the lively atmosphere and Osakan friendliness here while you fill up on tasty meat, seafood and vegetable dishes served fresh off the grill. Individual items are all ¥315, or loosen the belt and make a night of it with the all-you-can-eat-and-drink option (from ¥3500). Find Isaribi in the basement, accessed via stairs in front of a liquor store. It's best to book for groups.

Yukari　Okonomiyaki ¥¥
(ゆかり; Map p264; ☎ 6311-0214; www.yukarichan.co.jp; Ohatsutenjin-dōri; okonomi-yaki ¥1000-2000; ⏰ 11am-1am; 🍴🅿; 🚆 JR line to Osaka) This popular restaurant in the Ohatsutenjin-dōri arcade serves up that great Osaka favourite, *okonomiyaki* (a mix of batter with shredded cabbage and various

Restaurant Halls

A lot of the dining action in Osaka can be found in the numerous food halls located on the upper floors of department stores, in underground shopping arcades and in basement floors of hotels. These typically have a variety of reasonably priced restaurants clustered together in one floor, all with food displays and prices in the windows, making it easy to browse and find something that takes your fancy.

Namba Parks Mall (Map p266)A huge variety of places under one roof just south of Namba Station. Try **Sai-ji-ki** (菜蒔季; Map p266; ☎6636-8123; 6th fl, Namba Parks, 2-10-70 Namba-naka; lunch/dinner from ¥1468/1888; ⏰11am-11pm, enter by 9pm; ⊖🖋♿; Ⓢ Midō-suji, Sennichimae, or Yotsubashi line to Namba), an organic all-you-can-eat restaurant.

Gourmet Traveler (グルメトラベラー; Map p264; B2 fl, Herbis Plaza complex) Gourmet Traveler at the Herbis Plaza complex is located west of JR Osaka Station between the Hilton and the Ritz Carlton hotels. It has everything from a Belgian beer restaurant to Indian curry, as well as a smattering of Japanese places.

Hankyū Sanbangai (阪急三番街; Map p264; www.h-sanbangai.com; 🚃Hankyū line to Umeda) Go down to the B2 floor of Hankyū Umeda Station for Japanese and international restaurants and a good collection of shops selling cakes, pastries and chocolates. You'll know you're in the right place when you see the canal.

Osaka Maru Building (大阪丸ビル; Map p264; www.marubiru.com/restaurant; 🚃JR line to Osaka) There is a good variety of restaurants on the B2 floor of the distinctive cylindrical Maru Building, including Korean, Indian, *yakitori* and an *omuraisu* (fried rice wrapped in a thin omelette topped with sauce) specialist.

Hilton Plaza (ヒルトンプラザ; Map p264; www.hiltonplaza.com; 🚃JR line to Osaka) On the B2 floor beneath the Hilton Osaka. Among the restaurants worth trying here is the tempura specialist, **Shinkiraku** (新喜楽; Map p264; ☎6345-3461; East B2 fl, Hilton Plaza, 1-8-16 Umeda; lunch/dinner from ¥780/2000; ⏰11am-2.30pm & 5-11pm Mon-Fri, 11am-2.30pm & 4-10pm Sat & Sun & holidays; 🗂; 🚃JR line to Osaka).

fillings, slathered in a Worcestershire-style sauce and mayonnaise), cooked on a griddle right in front of you. There's lots to choose from on the picture menu, including veg options, but you can't really go wrong with the *tokusen mikkusu yaki* (okonomiyaki with fried pork, shrimp and squid; ¥1080). Look for the red-and-white signage out front.

Shinsaibashi & Around

Green Earth   Vegetarian ¥
(4-2-2 Kita-kyūhōji-machi; ¥550-850; ⏰11.30am-5pm Mon-Sat; ⊖🖋🗂; Ⓢ Midō-suji line to Shinsaibashi, exit 3) A haven for vegetarians and vegans, this small cafe serves up hearty sandwiches, curries and

pastas, with a generous daily lunch set for ¥700 (with drink ¥850). From Shinsaibashi, walk north up Midō-suji, turn left immediately after Namba Shrine (難波神社), take the second right and look for the English sign on the right.

Café Absinthe   Mediterranean ¥¥
(カフェアブサン; Map p266; ☎6534-6635; www.absinthe-jp.com; 1-2-27 Kitahorie; meals ¥1000-3000; ⏰3pm-3am, to 5am Sat & Sun, closed Tue; 🗂; Ⓢ Midō-suji line to Shinsaibashi, exit 7) For fantastic cocktails, nonalcoholic drinks and juices and a diverse Mediterranean menu (something of a rarity in Kansai), this friendly restaurant near the western edge of Ame-Mura is a must. The drinks and food here cost a little more,

but it's good value when you factor in quality ingredients, stylish surrounds and a friendly, laid-back atmosphere. And, yes, it does serve the eponymous absinthe.

Nishiya
Noodles ¥¥

(にし家; Map p266; ☎ 6241-9221; 1-18-18 Higashi Shinsaibashi; noodle dishes from ¥630, dinner courses ¥3000-5000; ⏰ 11am-11pm Mon-Sat, to 9.30pm Sun; 📋; Ⓢ Midō-suji line to Shinsaibashi, exit 5 or 6) A peaceful spot on the busy streets of Shinsaibashi, this welcoming Osaka landmark serves *udon* (thick white wheat noodles), a variety of hearty *nabe* (cast-iron pot) dishes, and *shabu-shabu* (thin slices of meat and vegetables cooked in a broth and dipped in sauce) courses for reasonable prices. Look for the traditional wooden sliding-door entrance and the food models.

Cuorerudino Pizzeria
Italian ¥¥

(ピッツェリア・クオーレルディーノ; Map p266; ☎ 4390-1383; www.cuorerudino.com; 1-14-26 Minamihorie; meals ¥700-1400; ⏰ 11.30am-11pm; 🚭; Ⓢ Midō-suji line to Shinsaibashi or Yotsubashi line to Yotsubashi) This new, casual pizzeria has an open kitchen with a large brick oven, so you can see the delicious thin-crust pizzas being prepared. Staff are enthusiastic and there's an interesting menu (in Japanese and Italian) of mostly pizzas but also antipasto and desserts. Smoking only on the outdoor terrace.

Imai Honten
Noodles ¥¥

(今井本店; Map p266; ☎ 6211-0319; http://d-imai.com; 1-7-22 Dōtombori; dishes from ¥630; ⏰ 11am-10pm, closed Wed; 📋; Ⓢ Midō-suji line to Namba) Step into an oasis of calm amid the chaos to be welcomed by kimono-clad staff at one of the area's oldest and most revered *udon* specialists. Try the *kitsune udon* – noodles topped with soup-soaked slices of fried tofu. There's no English sign outside, but look for the traditional front and the tree.

Zauo
Seafood ¥¥

(ざうお難波本店; Map p266; ☎ 6212-5882; www.zauo.com; B1 fl, Washington Hotel Plaza, Nipponbashi 1-1-13; meals ¥680-6000; ⏰ 5pm-midnight Mon-Fri, 11.30am-midnight Sat & Sun; Ⓢ Sakai-suji line to Nipponbashi, exit 6, or Midō-suji line to Namba) In a country where seafood is sometimes eaten so fresh it's still moving, it makes sense to find a restaurant where fish swim around the tables and patrons try to catch them for dinner. If you're lucky enough to hook something, there's celebratory drumming and your fish is whisked away to be

Dōtombori & Around

Dōtombori Arcade is crammed with eateries. The dining isn't refined, but if you want heaping portions of tasty food in a very casual atmosphere, it can be a lot of fun. And because it sees a lot of tourists, most of the big restaurants here have English menus.

Tako-yaki (battered octopus pieces)
BRENT WINEBRENNER / GETTY IMAGES ©

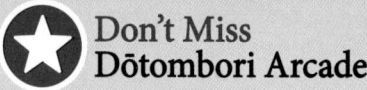

FRANK DEIM / GETTY IMAGES ©

★ Don't Miss
Dōtombori Arcade

Dōtombori, situated in Osaka's Minami area, is the city's liveliest night spot. Crammed with eateries and bars it is centred on Dōtombori-gawa and **Dōtombori Arcade** (道頓堀; Map p266), a strip of restaurants and theatres where a peculiar type of Darwinism is the rule for both people and shops: survival of the flashiest.

In the evening, head to **Ebisu-bashi** (戎橋; Map p266) to sample the glittering nightscape. Below, the banks of the Dōtombori-gawa have been turned into attractive pedestrian walkways.

Just south of Dōtombori Arcade is **Hōzen-ji** (法善寺; Map p266), a tiny temple hidden down a narrow paved alley off Senichi-mae arcade. The temple is built around a moss-covered **Fudō-myōō statue** (Map p266). In place of standard offerings, people show their respects at the temple by splashing water over the statue, hence its bushy appearance. Running parallel to this alley is atmospheric **Hōzen-ji Yokochō** (法善寺横丁; Hōzen-ji Alley; Map p266), dotted with traditional restaurants and bars.

To the south of Dōtombori, in the direction of Nankai Namba Station, is a maze of arcades with more restaurants, pachinko (Japanese pinball) parlours, strip clubs and who knows what else. To the north of Dōtombori, between Midō-suji and Sakai-suji, the streets are crowded with hostess bars, clubs and pubs.

Namba, on the Midō-suji line, or Nipponbashi, served by the Sakai-suji and Sennichimae lines, are the nearest stations for Dōtombori.

prepared how you like (you pay based on the type of fish). It's best to order from the menu in case nothing is biting – try an eight-piece sushi *omakase nigiri*, or a very tasty *shio-yaki* (salt-grilled) fish set. There's a ¥300-per-person table charge. Reserve to get a table on a 'boat'.

Drinking & Nightlife

Osaka is a hard-working city but when quitting time rolls around, Osakans know how to party. Take a stroll through Minami on a Friday night and you'd be excused for thinking there's one bar for every resident of the city. In summer head up to one of the city's rooftop beer gardens for all you can drink and eat in fun, casual surrounds – the one atop Hanshin Department Store is particularly good.

For up-to-date info on upcoming bar/ club/music events in Osaka, check **iflyer** (http://iflyer.tv).

Kita

Minami might be Osaka's real nightlife district, but there are bars, clubs and *izakaya* in the neighbourhoods to the south and east of Osaka Station, and around Hankyū Umeda Station.

Karma
Bar, Restaurant

(カーマ; Map p264; www.club-karma.com; B1 fl, Zero Bldg, 1-5-18 Sonezakishinchi; ⏰5pm-3am, to 11pm Sun; 🚃JR line to Osaka) Spacious and white-wall stylish, Karma is a fine bar-restaurant to kick back in if you enjoy a bit of pumping music with your evening drink. It also serves light meals (dishes ¥600 to ¥1200). On Saturdays there are sometimes techno events with cover charges averaging ¥2500.

Windows on the World
Bar

(ウィンドーズオンザワールド; Map p264; 1-8-8 Umeda; ⏰5.30pm-12.30am Mon-Thu & Sun, to 1am Fri & Sat; 🚃JR line to Osaka) An unbeatable spot for sophisticated drinks with a view, Windows on the World is on the 35th floor of the Hilton Osaka. There's a ¥1750-per-person table charge and drinks average ¥2000.

Minami Area

This is the place for a big night out in Osaka, with numerous bars, clubs and restaurants packed into the streets and alleys of Shinsaibashi and Namba.

Zerro
Bar

(ゼロ; Map p266; 2-3-2 Shinsaibashi-suji; ⏰7pm-5am; Ⓢ Midō-suji line to Namba or Shinsaibashi) Zerro has a good range of drinks and food, energetic bilingual bartenders, and a street-level location ideal for a spot of people-watching. Come early for relaxed drinks and conversation; come late on the weekend for DJs, dancing and a lively crowd.

Cinquecento
Bar

(チンクエチェント; Map p266; 2-1-10 Higashi-Shinsaibashi; ⏰7.30pm-5am Mon-Sat, 8pm-3am Sun; Ⓢ Midō-suji line to Namba or Shinsaibashi) Everything at this cosy, aptly named bar is ¥500, including a hearty selection of food and the impressively extensive martini menu. It's not far from the corner of Sakai-suji; look for the 5 in a red circle.

Onzieme (11)
Club

(オンジェム; Map p266; www.onzi-eme.com; 11th fl, Midō-suji Bldg, 1-4-5 Nishi-Shinsaibashi; Ⓢ Midō-suji line to Shinsaibashi, exit 7) Those eager for a taste of Osaka nightlife at its craziest should head to the city's largest and most lively club. An assortment of local and internationally acclaimed house, hip-hop and techno DJs showcase their talents nightly, with the posh interior reminiscent of some of the more famous London establishments. Cover charges average ¥2500.

Grand Café
Club

(グランドカフェ; Map p266; http://grand-cafeosaka.com; B1 fl, Spazio Bldg, 2-10-21 Nishi-Shinsaibashi; Ⓢ Midō-suji to Shinsaibashi) This hip underground club hosts a variety of electronica-DJ and hip-hop events. There's a comfy seating area and several dance floors. Look for the English sign at street level.

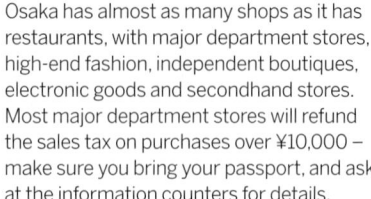 Shopping

Osaka has almost as many shops as it has restaurants, with major department stores, high-end fashion, independent boutiques, electronic goods and secondhand stores. Most major department stores will refund the sales tax on purchases over ¥10,000 – make sure you bring your passport, and ask at the information counters for details.

Kita Area

Kita is the place to come if you like browsing department stores. Many are clustered around the stations, including **Hankyū** (阪急; Map p264; www.hankyu-dept.co.jp/honten), **Hanshin** (阪神; Map p264; www.hanshin-dept.jp/hshonten), and the more youth-oriented **Hep Five** (Map p264; www.hepfive.jp), with the giant Ferris wheel on top; as well as recent additions to the Osaka retail scene **Lucua** (ルクア; Map p264; www.lucua.jp), in JR Osaka Station, and **NU Chayamachi** (NU 茶屋町; Map p264; http://nu-chayamachi.com). Fashion-savvy guys should also check out **Hankyū Men's** (阪急メンズ; Map p264; www.hankyu-dept.co.jp/mens) in the ship-shaped Hep Navio building. The department stores all have similar hours, opening 10am or 11am and closing 8.30pm or 9pm.

Maruzen & Junkudō Umeda Books (MARUZEN & ジュンク堂書店梅田店; Map p264; www.junkudo.co.jp/MJumeda.html; 7-20 Chaya-machi; ⏱10am-10pm; 🚆JR line to Osaka) This new behemoth bookshop, the largest in Osaka, is the result of two book specialists joining forces. There's a big range of English-language books on the 6th floor, with travel guides on the 3rd floor. It's in the new Andō Tadao–designed Chaska Chayamachi building.

Junkudō Books (ジュンク堂書店; Map p264; www.junkudo.co.jp; 1-6-20 Dōjima Avanza; ⏱10am-9pm; 🚆JR line to Osaka) This large bookshop has a great selection of foreign- and Japanese-language books. It's inside the Dōjima Avanza Building, about 10 minutes' walk from Osaka Station. Most English-language books are on the 3rd floor along with a cafe. English travel guides are on the 2nd floor.

Minami Area

Minami has a huge range of shops. International high-end brands have their outlets along Midō-suji, the main boulevard of Minami, between Shinsaibashi and Namba subway stations. Head to

Den Den Town

Taking its name from the Japanese word for electricity (*denki*), Den Den Town – Osaka's version of Tokyo's Akihabara – is looking a bit tired these days, no doubt suffering from the competition of flash electronic-goods megastores like Bic Camera. It consists of a long stretch of electronic-goods shops, but there are also manga stores, shops selling secondhand video games and CDs, and a couple of Cosplay outlets adding a touch of seediness. If you can ignore the rough edges, you'll find it's a good place to spot some bargains, and there are so many shops here you're bound to come across the gadget you need (though make sure it will work in your home country). To avoid sales tax, check if the store has a 'Tax Free' sign outside and bring your passport. Note that most stores are closed on Wednesday.

Den Den Town runs along Sakai-suji, starting southeast of Nankai Namba Station and continuing down to Ebisu-chō Station, which is on the Sakai-suji subway line (exit 1 or 2).

FRANK DEIM / GETTY IMAGES ©

the jam-packed Shinsaibashi-suji arcade (which connects to more arcades) for popular local and international chains, and Ame-Mura for out-there and vintage clothes, accessories and music.

Dōguya-suji Arcade   Market

(道具屋筋; Map p266; www.doguyasuji.or.jp/map_eng.html; Ⓢ Midō-suji line to Namba) Come here for all manner of pots, pans, knives, kitchen gadgets and just about anything related to the preparation, consumption and selling of food. There are even shopfront lanterns, bar signs and plastic food models (which make for interesting souvenirs). Start thinking about how to make room in the suitcase for that *rāmen* (egg noodle) strainer you never realised you needed.

Village Vanguard   Books, Homewares

ヴィレッジヴァンガード; Map p266; www.village-v.co.jp; 1-10-28 Nishi-Shinsaibashi; ◷11am-11pm; Ⓢ Midō-suji line to Shinsaibashi, exit 7) Village Vanguard bills itself as an 'exciting bookstore', but books are only half the story: between the cluttered racks of books and magazines are all sorts of odd items, amusing kitchen devices, homewares and more – prob-ably the stuff that Tokyu Hands rejected. It's a good spot to find a nontraditional memento of your time in Japan.

Tokyu Hands   Department Store

(東急ハンズ; Map p266; www.tokyu-hands.co.jp; 3-4-12 Minamisenba; ◷10.30am-8.30pm; Ⓢ Midō-suji line to Shinsaibashi) If you love gadgets, don't miss Tokyu Hands. From tools for jobs you didn't know existed to curios to please people with everything, this place is stocked to the rafters with things that you probably don't need but may very well want. Even if you don't buy anything, it's fun to browse. There's a smaller, new branch in **Umeda** (東急ハンズ; Map p264; www.tokyu-hands.co.jp; 10th-12th fl, Daimaru, 3-1-1 Umeda; ◷10am-9pm, to 8.30pm Sun; ℞JR line to Osaka).

Bic Camera   Electronics

(ビックカメラ; Map p266; www.biccamera.co.jp/shoplist/nanba.html; 2-10-1 Sennichimae; ◷10am-9pm; Ⓢ Midō-suji or Sennichimae line to Namba) Bic Camera is a one-stop shop for everything related to cameras, electronics and computers (but note that many computer-related items are designed for operation with a Japanese system). You are likely to find some of the best prices in the city at this vast shop.

ℹ Information

Money

ATMs at Citibank, large post offices and 7-Eleven stores take international cards. Major banks and post offices have currency exchange services. **Citibank** (シティバンク; http://citibank. co.jp; 2nd fl, Dai-ichi Semei Bldg, 1-8-17 Umeda; ⏰9am-8pm Mon-Fri, 10am-5pm Sat & Sun, ATM 24hr; ℝJR line to Osaka) Other branches at Shinsaibashi (Midō-suji Diamond Bldg, 2-1-2 Nishi Shinsaibashi; ⏰9am-3pm Mon-Fri, ATM 24hr; ⑤Midō-suji line to Shinsaibashi) and Umeda (7th fl, ABC-MART Umeda Bldg, 1-27 Chaya-machi, across from Hankyū Station; ⏰9am-3pm & 5-7pm Mon-Fri, 10am-4pm Sat, ATM 8am-10pm; ℝHankyū line to Umeda or JR line to Osaka); there's also a 24-hour ATM at Kansai International Airport.

Post

Osaka Central Post Office (大阪中央郵便局; Osaka Eki-mae Dai-ichi Bldg, Umeda 1-3-1; ⏰postal services 9am-9pm, ATM 24hr, closed 9pm-midnight Sun; ℝJR line to Osaka) Also has a postal-service window operating 7am to midnight daily. Currency exchange available 9am to 6pm weekdays. Near JR Osaka Station.

Tourist Information

Tourist offices can help book accommodation if you visit in person. There are offices in the main stations, and information counters at the airports. To get the low-down on upcoming events, pick up a copy of *Kansai Scene* magazine, available for free at major bookshops.

Osaka Visitors Information Center, Umeda (大阪市ビジターズインフォメーションセンター・梅田; ☎6345-2189; www.osaka-info. jp; ⏰8am-8pm) This is the main tourist office, inside JR Osaka Station at the north end of the central concourse. If you are coming out of the central gates, turn left (towards the North Gate Bldg and Lucua); it's on a corner on the left. There are other offices on the 1st floor of Nankai Namba Station (大阪市ビジターズインフォメーションセンター・なんば; ☎6631-9100; ⏰9am-8pm), the 3rd floor of Shin-Osaka Station (大阪市ビジターズインフォメーションセンター・新大阪; ☎6305-3311; ⏰9am-6pm) and at Tennō-ji Station (大阪市ビジターズインフォメーションセンター・天王寺; ☎6774-3077; ⏰9am-6pm).

ℹ Getting There & Away

Air

Osaka is served by two airports: **Kansai International Airport** (KIX; www.kansai-airport. or.jp/en), which handles all international and some domestic flights; and **Osaka Itami Airport** (ITM; http://osaka-airport.co.jp/), also called Osaka International Airport, which handles only domestic traffic. KIX is about 50km southwest of the city, on an artificial island in the bay. Itami is located in Osaka itself.

Train

Osaka is on the Tōkaidō–San-yō *shinkansen* line that runs between Tokyo and Hakata (in Kyūshū). Hikari *shinkansen* run from Shin-Osaka Station to Tokyo (¥13,750, three hours) and Hakata

---

Discount Passes

The **Kansai Thru Pass** (www.surutto.com) allows unlimited travel on most train, subway and bus lines throughout Kansai, except the JR line. That includes travel on the Nankai line, which serves Kansai International Airport. (The pass doesn't cover the Ise-shima region.) It also qualifies you for discounts at several attractions. Two-/three-day passes cost ¥3800/5000. It's possible to purchase multiple passes, and passes can be used on nonconsecutive days. Pick one up at the travel desk in the arrivals hall of Kansai International Airport, at Osaka's main tourist offices, or at the main bus information centre in front of Kyoto Station. Note that the Thru Pass is only available to travellers on temporary visitor visas (you'll have to show your passport).

Bottles of sake

JOHN BANAGAN / GETTY IMAGES ©

(¥14,590, three hours). Other cities on this line include Hiroshima (¥9950, 1½ hours), Kyoto, Kōbe and Okayama.

Kyoto

While *shinkansen* is the fastest way to travel between Kyoto and Shin-Osaka (from ¥1380, 15 minutes), the JR *shinkaisoku* (special rapid train) between JR Kyoto Station and the central JR Osaka Station (¥540, 28 minutes) may be more convenient if you want to avoid a change at Shin-Osaka.

The Hankyū line runs between Hankyū Umeda Station in Osaka and Hankyū Kawaramachi, Karasuma and Ōmiya Stations in Kyoto (*tokkyū* limited express train to Kawaramachi ¥390, 44 minutes). The Keihan line runs between Sanjō, Shijō or Shichijō Stations in Kyoto and Keihan Yodoyabashi Station in Osaka (*tokkyū* to Sanjō ¥400, 51 minutes). Yodoyabashi is on the Midō-suji subway line.

Kōbe

The *shinkansen* runs between Shin-Kōbe Station and Shin-Osaka Station (from ¥1450, 13 minutes). There is also a JR *shinkaisoku* train between JR Osaka Station and Kōbe's Sannomiya and Kōbe Stations (¥390, 24 minutes).

The Hankyū line is a little cheaper and usually less crowded. It runs from Osaka's Hankyū Umeda Station to Kōbe's Sannomiya Station (*tokkyū*, ¥310, 29 minutes).

Nara

The JR Kansai line links Osaka's Namba and Tennō-ji Stations to JR Nara Station via Hōryū-ji (*yamatoji kaisoku*, ¥540, 50 minutes). The Kintetsu Nara line runs from Namba (Kintetsu Namba Station) to Kintetsu Nara Station (¥540, 40 minutes).

ⓘ Getting Around

To/From the Airport

Kansai International Airport (KIX)

KIX is well connected to the city with a direct train line and regular buses.

The fastest way to travel between KIX and Osaka is the private Nankai Express Rapit, which runs to/from Nankai Namba Station (¥1390, 35 minutes). The JR Haruka limited airport express runs between KIX and Tennō-ji Station (unreserved seat ¥1760, 29 minutes) and Shin-Osaka Station (¥2470, 49 minutes). Regular JR express trains called *kankū kaisoku* also run between KIX and Osaka (¥1160, 70 minutes), Tennō-ji (¥1030, 52 minutes) and JR Namba (¥1030, 62 minutes) Stations. All these stations connect to the Midō-suji subway line.

There are a variety of bus routes between KIX and Osaka. Airport limousine buses run to/from Osaka Station, OCAT Namba, Uehonmachi and to the Tempōzan area. The fare is ¥1500 for most routes (¥1000 to OCAT) and it takes an average of 50 minutes, depending on traffic conditions (it can take up to 90 minutes to Umeda). See www.kate.co.jp for timetables.

Note that trains stop running from the airport at 11.30pm, and the last bus leaves just after midnight. If your flight arrives after this, your other option into Osaka is taxi. It takes about 50 minutes and there are standard fares to Osaka Umeda (¥14,000) and Namba (¥13,500). The late-night fare is an additional ¥2500. It's about ¥18,000 to Shin-Osaka.

Osaka Itami Airport

There are frequent limousine buses running between the airport and various parts of Osaka. Buses run to/from Shin-Osaka Station every 20 minutes from about 8am to 9pm (¥490, 25 minutes). Buses run at about the same frequency to/from Osaka and Namba stations (¥620, 25 minutes). At Itami, buy your tickets from the machine outside the arrivals hall. See www.okkbus.co.jp for timetables.

Train

Osaka has a good subway network and, like Tokyo, a JR loop line (known as the Kanjō-sen) that circles the city area, intersecting with the subways and other train lines. You're not likely to need any other form of transport unless you stay out late and miss the last train.

There are eight subway lines, but the one that short-term visitors will find most useful is the Midō-suji line (the red line), which runs north to south, stopping at Shin-Osaka, Umeda (next to Osaka Station), Shinsaibashi, Namba and Tennō-ji Stations. Most rides cost between ¥200 and ¥300.

There are a couple of good discount passes for train and subway travel.

NARA

☎0742 / POP 366,165

The first permanent capital of Japan, Nara (奈良) is one of the most rewarding destinations in the country. Indeed, with eight Unesco World Heritage Sites, Nara is second only to Kyoto as a repository of Japan's cultural legacy. The centrepiece is, of course, the Daibutsu (Great Buddha), which rivals Mt Fuji and Kyoto's Kinkaku-ji (Golden Pavilion) as Japan's single most impressive sight. The Great Buddha is housed in Tōdai-ji, a soaring temple that presides over Nara-kōen, a park filled with other fascinating sights that lends itself to relaxed strolling amid the greenery and tame deer.

Nara's best feature is its small size: it's quite possible to pack the most worthwhile sights into one full day. Many people visit Nara as a side trip from Kyoto, and comfortable express trains link the cities in about half an hour. Of course, it's preferable to spend two days here if you can. If your schedule allows for two days in Nara, you might spend one in Nara-kōen and the other seeing the sights to the west and southwest of Nara city (areas known as Nishinokyō and Ikaruga, respectively).

Deer at Nara-kōen

⊙ Sights

Nara retains the grid pattern of streets laid out in Chinese style during the 8th century. There are two main train stations: JR Nara and Kintetsu Nara. JR Nara Station is a little west of the city centre (but still within walking distance of the sights), while Kintetsu Nara is right in the centre of town. Nara-kōen, which contains most of the important sights, is on the eastern side, against the bare flank of Wakakusa-yama. Most of the other sights are west or southwest of the city and are best reached by bus or train. It's easy to cover the city centre and the major attractions in nearby Nara-kōen on foot, although buses and taxis do ply the city.

Nara tourist information offices stock the useful *Nara Sightseeing Map*. If you want something more detailed, ask if they have any copies of the excellent *Nara City Sightseeing Map*. If you read a bit of Japanese and want to explore Nara Prefecture, ask for a copy of *Nara-Yamatoji Kankō Mappu*.

Nara-kōen Area　奈良公園

Many of Nara's most important sights are located in Nara-kōen, a fine park that occupies much of the east side of the city. The park is home to about 1200 deer, which in pre-Buddhist times were considered messengers of the gods and today enjoy the status of National Treasures. They roam the park and surrounding areas in search of handouts from tourists, often descending on people who happen to be carrying food. You can buy *shika-sembei* (deer biscuits) from vendors for ¥150 to feed to the deer.

Nara National Museum　Museum
(奈良国立博物館; Nara Kokuritsu Hakubu-tsukan; ☏050-5542-8600; 50 Noboriōji-chō; admission ¥500; ◷9.30am-5pm) The Nara National Museum is devoted to Buddhist art and is divided into two sections, housed in different buildings. Built in 1894, the **Nara Buddhist Sculpture Hall & Ritual Bronzes Gallery** contains a fine

Local Knowledge

Nara-kōen

BY SHIBATA SUMIE, PROFESSIONAL NARA GUIDE

1 KŌFUKU-JI

This towering pagoda (p279) is a masterpiece of Japanese architecture. The treasure hall contains some impressive Buddhist statues and the grounds make for pleasant strolling.

2 ISUI-EN

A short walk from Kōfuku-ji brings you to Nara's finest garden: Isui-en (p279). This wonderful garden is beautiful in any season and you'll usually find something in bloom. The view over the pond takes in the roof of Tōdai-ji's Nandai-mon (gate) – it's a classic example of the *shakkei* (borrowed scenery) technique.

3 TŌDAI-JI

Dominating the east side of Nara-kōen, the Daibutsu-den (Great Buddha Hall; p280) is an arresting sight. Prepare to be blown away by the sight of the Daibutsu that it contains. This is one of the greatest sights in the Japanese archipelago.

4 FEEDING THE DEER

Buy some *shika-sembei* (deer biscuits) from a vendor in the park and get ready: the hungry deer of Nara-kōen will mob you and try everything they can to get those biscuits. The hundreds of sacred animals roam freely throughout the park and are said to be the divine messengers of Shintō deities at Kasuga Taisha. This is a must for those with kids in tow.

5 WALKING THE TRAILS NEAR KASUGA TAISHA

After exploring Tōdai-ji, explore the many walking trails around this shrine (p281). As you make your way through the tree-lined paths, you may find it hard to believe that you're still within Nara's city limits. The thousands of stone lanterns to be found here add a mysterious feeling to the area.

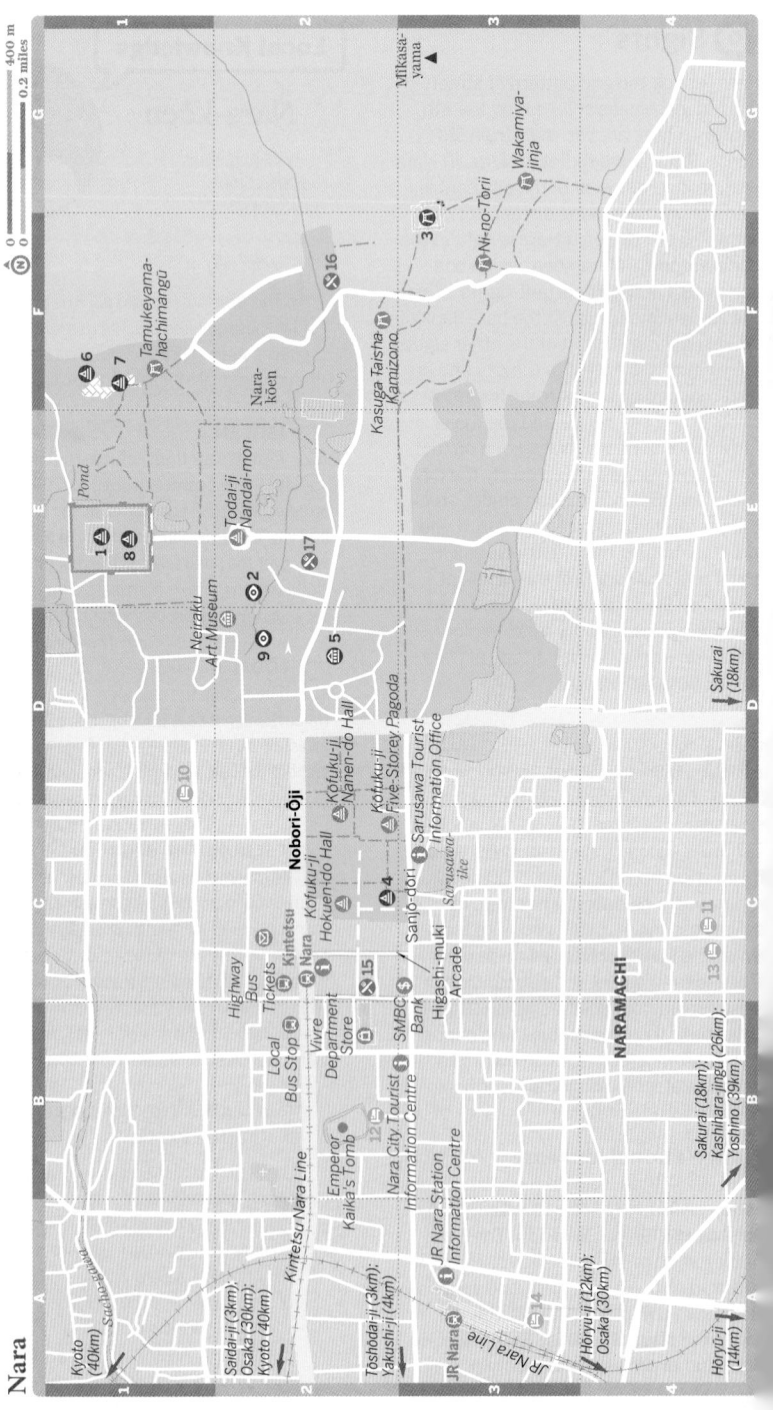

Nara

KANSAI & WESTERN HONSHŪ

400 m
0.2 miles

Kyoto (40km)
Suzhakumon
Saidai-ji (3km);
Osaka (30km);
Kyoto (40km)
Kintetsu Nara Line
Tōshōdai-ji (3km);
Yakushi-ji (4km)
JR Nara Station
Information Centre
JR Nara Line
Hōryū-ji (12km);
Osaka (30km)
Hōryū-ji (14km)
Sakurai (18km);
Kashihara-jingū (26km);
Yoshino (39km)

Highway Bus Stop
Local Bus Stop
Kintetsu Nara
Vivre Department Store
Nara City Tourist Information Centre
Emperor Kaika's Tomb
12

NARAMACHI
13
11

Noraku Art Museum
Neiraku Art Museum
9
2
5
1
8
10
Kōfuku-ji Hokuen-dō Hall
Kōfuku-ji Nanen-dō Hall
Kōfuku-ji Five-Storey Pagoda
Sarusawa Tourist Information Office
Sarusawa-ike
Sanjō-dōri
Higashi-muki Arcade
SMBC Bank
15

Tōdai-ji Nandai-mon
17
16
Nara-kōen
Tamukeyama-hachimangū
6
7
Pond

Kasuga Taisha Kamizono
Ni-no-Torii
Wakamiya-jinja
Mikasa-yama
3

Sakurai (18km)

Nara

◎ Sights
1	Daibutsu-den Hall	E1
2	Isui-en & Neiraku Art Museum	E2
3	Kasuga Taisha	F3
	Kōfuku-ji National Treasure Hall	(see 4)
4	Kōfuku-ji	C2
5	Nara National Museum	D2
6	Nigatsu-dō	F1
7	Sangatsu-dō	F1
8	Tōdai-ji	E1
9	Yoshiki-en	D2

⊜ Sleeping
10	Guesthouse Nara Backpackers	D1
11	Guesthouse Sakuraya	C4
12	Hotel Fujita Nara	B2
13	Ryokan Seikansō	C4
14	Super Hotel Lohas JR Nara-eki	A3

⊗ Eating
15	Mellow Café	C2
16	Mizutani-chaya	F2
17	Silk Road	E2

collection of *butsu-zō* (statues of Buddhas and bodhisattvas). The Buddhist images here are divided into categories, each with an excellent English explanation, making this a great introduction to Mahayana Buddhist iconography. The newer East and West wings, a short walk away, contain the permanent collections (sculptures, paintings and calligraphy) and are used for special exhibitions.

Kōfuku-ji   Buddhist Temple
(興福寺) This temple was transferred here from Kyoto in 710 as the main temple for the Fujiwara family. Although the original temple complex had 175 buildings, fires and destruction as a result of power struggles have left only a dozen standing. There are two pagodas – three storeys and five storeys – dating from 1143 and 1426, respectively. The taller of the two is the second tallest in Japan, outclassed by the one at Kyoto's Tō-ji by a few centimetres. Note that a new hall is being built in the centre of the temple grounds and construction isn't expected to be completed until 2018.

The **Kōfuku-ji National Treasure Hall** (興福寺国宝館; 48 Noboriōji-chō; admission ¥600; ☺9am-5pm) contains a variety of statues and art objects salvaged from previous structures. Enter by 4.45pm.

Isui-en & Neiraku Art Museum   Gardens
(依水園・寧楽美術館; 74 Suimon-chō; admission museum & garden ¥650; ☺9.30am-4.30pm, closed Tue Dec-Mar & Jun-Sep & New Year holidays) This garden, dating from the Meiji era, is beautifully laid out and features abundant greenery and a pond with ornamental carp. It's without a doubt the best garden in the city and well worth a visit. For ¥500 you can enjoy a cup of tea on tatami mats overlooking the garden. Note that you can also enjoy a cup without paying admission at the adjoining Sanshū restaurant (you still have to pay for the tea, though).

The adjoining Neiraku Art Museum, displays Chinese and Korean ceramics and bronzes (admission is included in garden entry). Enter by 4pm.

Yoshiki-en   Gardens
(吉城園; 68 Noboriōji-chō; ☺9.30am-5pm Mar–27 Dec) FREE This garden, located next door to Isui-en (to the right when you're facing the entrance of Isui-en), is a stunner. Originally a residence of the high priest of Tōdai-ji, it fell into private hands. The present garden was laid out in 1918 and contains a lovely thatched-roof cottage, a pond and several walking paths. It's particularly lovely in November and early December, when the maples turn a blazing crimson. Best of all, at the time of writing, entry was free for foreign tourists! Enter by 4.30pm. Look for the small English sign.

Tōdai-ji   Buddhist Temple
(東大寺) Nara's famous Daibutsu (Great Buddha) is housed in the Daibutsu-den Hall of this grand temple. It's Nara's star attraction and is often packed with tour groups and school children from across the country, but it's big enough to absorb huge crowds and it belongs at the top of any Nara itinerary.

Before you enter the temple be sure to check out the **Nandai-mon** (東大寺南大門), an enormous gate containing two fierce-looking **Niō guardians**. These recently restored wooden images, carved in the 13th century by the sculptor Unkei, are some of the finest wooden statues in all of Japan, if not the world. They are truly dramatic works of art and seem ready to spring to life at any moment. The gate is about 200m south of the temple enclosure.

Note that most of Tōdai-ji's grounds can be visited free of charge, with the exception of the main hall, the Daibutsu-den Hall.

Daibutsu-den Hall Buddhist Temple
(大仏殿; Hall of the Great Buddha; 406-1 Zōshi-chō; admission ¥500; ⏱7.30am-5.30pm Apr-Sep, to 5pm Oct, 8am-5pm Mar, to 4.30pm Nov-Feb) Tōdai-ji's Daibutsu-den is the largest wooden building in the world. Unbelievably, the present structure, rebuilt in 1709, is a mere two-thirds of the size of the original! The Daibutsu (Great Buddha) contained within is one of the largest bronze figures in the world and was originally cast in 746. The present statue, recast in the Edo period, stands just over 16m high and consists of 437 tonnes of bronze and 130kg of gold.

The Daibutsu is an image of Dainichi Buddha (also known as Vairocana Buddha), the cosmic Buddha believed to give rise to all worlds and their respective Buddhas. Historians believe that Emperor Shōmu ordered the building of the Buddha as a charm against smallpox, which ravaged Japan in preceding years. Over the centuries the statue took quite a beating from earthquakes and fires, losing its head a couple of times (note the slight difference in colour between the head and the body).

As you circle the statue towards the back, you'll see a wooden column with a hole through its base. Popular belief maintains that those who can squeeze through the hole, which is exactly the same size as one of the Great Buddha's nostrils, are ensured of enlightenment.

Left: Tōdai-ji (p279); **Below:** Feeding the deer in Nara-kōen

(LEFT) GUIZIOU FRANCK / HEMIS.FR / GETTY IMAGES ©; (BELOW) JASON MIN / TEAGOD / GETTY IMAGES ©

There's usually a line of children waiting to give it a try and parents waiting to snap their pictures. Adults sometimes try it, but it's really something for the kids. A hint for big kids: it's a lot easier to go through with both arms held above your head – and someone on either end to push and pull helps too.

Nigatsu-dō & Sangatsu-dō
Buddhist Temple

The Nigatsu-dō and Sangatsu-dō halls are almost subtemples of Tōdai-ji. They are an easy (uphill from the Daibutsu-den) walk east. You can walk straight east up the hill, but we recommend taking a hard left out of the Daibutsu-den exit, following the enclosure past the pond and turning up the hill. This pathway is among the most scenic walks in all of Nara.

As you reach the plaza at the top of the hill, the **Nigatsu-dō** (二月堂; ⏲7.30am-5.30pm Apr-Sep, to 5pm Oct, 8am-5pm Mar, to 5.30pm Nov-Feb) FREE is the temple hall with the verandah overlooking the plaza.

This is where Nara's Omizutori Matsuri is held. The verandah affords a great view over Nara, especially at dusk.

A short walk south of Nigatsu-dō is **Sangatsu-dō** (三月堂; admission ¥500; ⏲7.30am-5.30pm Apr-Sep, to 5pm Oct, 8am-5pm Mar, to 4.30pm Nov-Feb), which is the oldest building in the Tōdai-ji complex. This hall contains a small collection of fine statues from the Nara period.

Kasuga Taisha
Shintō Shrine

(春日大社; 160 Kasugano-chō; ⏲dawn-dusk) FREE This shrine was founded in the 8th century by the Fujiwara family and was completely rebuilt every 20 years, according to Shintō tradition, until the end of the 19th century. It lies at the foot of the hill in a pleasant, wooded setting with herds of sacred deer awaiting hand-outs. As with similar shrines in Japan, you will find several subshrines around the main hall.

Tōdai-ji

The Daibutsu (Great Buddha) at Nara's Tōdai-ji is one of the most arresting sights in Japan. The awe-inspiring physical presence of the vast image is striking. It's one of the largest bronze Buddha images in the world and it's contained in an equally huge building, the Daibutsu-den Hall, which is among the largest wooden buildings on earth.

Tōdai-ji was built by order of Emperor Shōmu during the Nara period (710–784) and the complex was finally completed in 798, after the capital had been moved from Nara to Kyoto. Most historians agree that the temple was built to consolidate the country and serve as its spiritual focus. Legend has it that over two million labourers worked on the temple, but this is probably apocryphal. What's certain is that its construction brought the country to the brink of bankruptcy.

The original Daibutsu was covered in gold leaf and cast in bronze in eight castings over a period of three years. The Daibutsu, or certain parts of it, has been recast several times over the centuries.

The temple belongs to the Kegon school of Buddhism, one of the six schools of Buddhism popular in Japan during the Nara period. Kegon Buddhism, which comes from the Chinese Huayan Buddhist sect, is based on the Flower Garland Sutra. This sutra expresses the idea of worlds within worlds, all manifested by the Cosmic Buddha (Vairocana or Dainichi Nyorai). The Great Buddha and the figures that surround him in the Daibutsu-den Hall are the perfect physical symbol of this cosmological map.

FACT FILE
The Daibutsu

Height: 14.98m

Weight: 500 tonnes

Nostril width: 50cm

The Daibutsu-den Hall

Height: 48.74m

Length: 57m

Number of roof tiles: 112,589

JEFFREY FRIEDL ©

Kokuzo Bosatsu
Seated to the left of the Daibutsu is Kokuzo Bosatsu, the bodhisattva of memory and wisdom, to whom students pray for help in their studies and the faithful pray for help on the path to enlightenment.

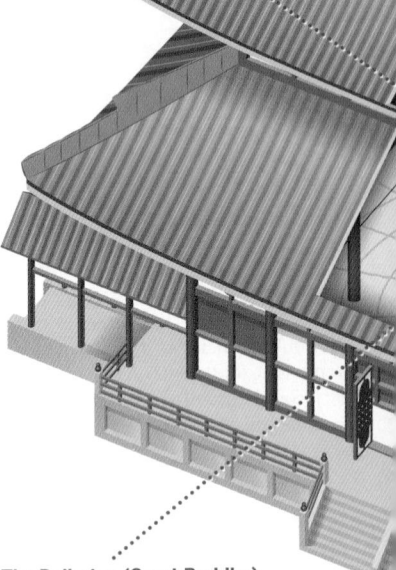

The Daibutsu (Great Buddha)
Known in Sanskrit as 'Vairocana' and in Japanese as the 'Daibutsu', this is the Cosmic Buddha that gives rise to all other Buddhas, according to Kegon doctrine. The Buddha's hands send the messages 'fear not' and 'welcome'.

JEFFREY FRIEDL ©

Komokuten
Standing to the left of the Daibutsu is Komokuten (Lord of Limitless Vision), who serves as a guardian of the Buddha. He stands upon a demon (*jaki*), which symbolises ignorance, and wields a brush and scroll, which symbolises wisdom.

Buddhas Around Dainichi
Sixteen smaller Buddhas are arranged in a halo around the Daibutsu's head, each of which symbolises one of the Daibutsu's different manifestations. They are graduated in size to appear the same size when viewed from the ground.

Tamonten
To the right of the Daibutsu stands Tamonten (Lord Who Hears All), another of the Buddha's guardians. He holds a pagoda, which is said to represent a divine storehouse of wisdom.

Hole in Pillar
Behind the Daibutsu you will find a pillar with a 50cm hole through its base (the size of one of the Daibutsu's nostrils). It's said that if you can crawl through this, you are assured of enlightenment.

Nyoirin Kannon
Seated to the right of the Daibutsu is Nyoirin Kannon, one of the esoteric forms of Kannon Bodhisattva. This is one of the bodhisattva that preside over the six different realms of karmic rebirth.

JEFFREY FRIEDL ©

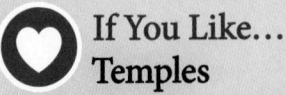

If You Like... Temples

If you like Tōdai-ji, we think you'll like these other beautiful temples in Nara Prefecture:

1 TŌSHŌDAI-JI
(唐招提寺; ☎33-7900; Gojō-chō 13-46; admission ¥600; ⏰8.30am-5pm, last entry by 4.30pm) A pleasant wooden temple, the main hall of which holds a wonderful thousand-armed Kannon (Buddhist god/goddess of mercy). It is located 22 minutes from downtown Nara by bus.

2 YAKUSHI-JI
(薬師寺; ☎33-6001; Nishinokyō-chō 457; admission ¥500; ⏰8.30am-5pm) A short walk from Tōshōdai-ji, this temple has a fine collection of ancient Buddhist images.

3 HŌRYŪ-JI
(法隆寺; admission ¥1000; ⏰8am-5pm 22 Feb-3 Nov, to 4.30pm 4 Nov-21 Feb) Arguably the oldest temple in Japan, the kondō (main hall) here is said to be the oldest wooden building in Japan (some would say the world). By bus, it takes one hour to get here from downtown Nara.

The approaches to the shrine are lined with hundreds of lanterns, and there are many hundreds more in the shrine itself. The lantern festivals held twice a year at the shrine are a major attraction.

While you're in the area, it's worth walking a few minutes south to the nearby shrine of Wakamiya-jinja.

Sleeping

Although Nara can be visited as a day trip from Kyoto, it is pleasant to spend the night here, allowing for a more relaxing pace.

Guesthouse Nara Backpackers   Guesthouse ¥
(ゲストハウス 奈良バックパッカーズ; ☎22-4557; www.nara-backpackers.com; 31 Yurugichō; dm ¥2400, r without bathroom from ¥3800 per person; 📶) In a lovely traditional Japanese building that used to be the home of a tea master, this gorgeous new guest house is an utterly charming place to stay for those who want to sample a night or two in a truly Japanese setting. You can choose from dorm rooms or three fine private tatami-mat rooms of varying sizes, some of which have garden views. Due to the presence of shoji (sliding paper doors) and traditional glass windows, it cannot accept children below the age of 10 (which is just as well, because parents of young children would spend their time on tenterhooks here), but for anyone else, it's highly recommended. Note that bathing facilities are shared and cooking facilities are available for those who want to self-cater.

Ryokan Seikansō   Ryokan ¥
(旅館静観荘; fax 22-2670; 29 Higashikitsuji-chō; per person without bathroom from ¥4200; 📶) This traditional ryokan has reasonable rates and a good Naramachi location. The rooms are clean and spacious with shared bathrooms and a large communal bath-tub. The management is used to foreign guests and there is a nice Japanese garden. It's a little long in the tooth, but the friendly reception makes up for it.

Guesthouse Sakuraya   Guesthouse ¥¥
(桜舎; www.guesthouse-sakuraya.com; 1 Narukawa-chō; per person incl breakfast ¥6000; 📶) This brand-new three-room guest house is a charming place to stay. It's described as a guest house, but it feels more like a ryokan – the rooms are traditional and the building is an atmospheric stunner. There's a lovely little central garden and a comfortable common room. The owner offers a Discovery of Japanese Culture course for ¥3000. Keep in mind that it's a traditional and relatively small place, so if you're looking for a party, head elsewhere.

Hotel Fujita Nara   Hotel ¥¥
(ホテルフジタ奈良; ☎23-8111; http://en.fujita-nara.com; 47-1 Shimosanjō-chō; s/tw

from ¥6500/8400; @ 📶) Right smack in downtown Nara and close to both main train stations, this efficient midrange hotel hits all the right notes: clean rooms, reasonable prices and some English-speaking staff. It's a good choice for those who want a conveniently located hotel.

Super Hotel Lohas JR Nara-eki
Hotel ¥¥

(スーパーホテルLohas・JR奈良駅; ☎27-9000; www.superhoteljapan.com/en/s-hotels/nara-lohas.html; 1-2 Sanjōhonmachi; s/tw incl breakfast ¥6980/12,800; @ 📶) Connected to JR Nara Station by an elevated walkway, this new Super Hotel has a lot going for it: clean compact rooms with en suite bathrooms, efficient service and a large communal 'onsen' (hot springs) bath. Free wi-fi in lobby and free LAN cable internet in guest rooms.

Eating

Nara is chock-a-block with good restaurants, most of which are near the train stations and in Naramachi. There aren't many good choices in Nara-kōen, but we

list one spot halfway between Tōdai-ji and Kasuga Taisha for those exploring that area.

Mellow Café
Cafe ¥

(メロー カフェ; ☎27-9099; 1-8 Konishi-chō; lunch from ¥980; ⏰11am-11.30pm; 📶 📱) Located down a narrow alley (look for the palm tree) not far from Kintetsu Nara Station, this open-plan cafe is a pleasant spot to fuel up for a day of sightseeing. The menu centres on pasta and pizza (there's a brick oven). There's an English sign and menu. Free wi-fi.

Mizutani-chaya
Teahouse ¥

(水谷茶屋; ☎22-0627; 30 Kasugano-chō; noodle dishes from ¥650; ⏰10am-4pm, closed Wed; 📱) Located in a small wooded grotto between Nigatsu-dō and Kasuga Taisha, this quaint thatched-roof teahouse is easily the most atmospheric spot for a cuppa (tea from ¥400) in Nara. It's perfectly located for a quick cup of *matcha* (powdered green tea) or some noodles to power your way through a day of sightseeing. In warm seasons, you can sit outside among the greenery. All in all, it's one of the more atmospheric places to eat in Nara.

Hōryū-ji

MUCHAN / GETTY IMAGES ©

Silk Road
Shokudō ¥¥

(シルクロードの終着駅; ☎25-0231; 16 Kasugano-chō; meals ¥1000; ⏰10am-7pm; 🈺) If you've got kids in tow, head into the Yume-Kaze Plaza (Yumekaze Hiroba in Japanese) dining/shopping complex across from the Nara National Museum to find this wonderful 'traincentric' restaurant. There are two huge model train layouts, which kids can actually control while eating bowls of standard Japanese curry rice and similar favourites.

ℹ️ Information

The main JR Nara Station information centre (☎22-9821; ⏰9am-5pm), in the old Nara Station building just outside the east exit of JR Nara Station, is the city's main tourist information centre and English-speakers are usually on hand. If you start from Kintetsu Nara Station, try the helpful Kintetsu Nara Station information office (☎24-4858; ⏰9am-9pm), which is near the top of the stairs above exit 3 from the station.

There are several other information offices in Nara, including the Nara City Tourist Information Centre (奈良市観光センター; ☎22-3900; ⏰9am-9pm) and the Sarusawa Tourist Information Office (猿沢観光案内所; ☎26-1991; ⏰9am-5pm).

All of the information offices stock the useful *Nara Sightseeing Map*.

The information centres can put you in touch with volunteer guides who speak English and other foreign languages, but you must book at least one day in advance. Two of these services are the YMCA Goodwill Guides (☎45-5920; http://eggnara.tripod.com/home.htm) and Nara Student Guides (☎26-4753; www.narastudentguide.org).

ℹ️ Getting There & Away

Bus

Buses to sights west (Yakushi-ji and Tōshōdai-ji) and southwest (Hōryū-ji) leave from stop 10, diagonally across from JR Nara Station, and stop 8 outside Kintetsu Nara Station.

Train

Kyoto

The JR Nara line connects JR Kyoto Station with JR Nara Station (JR *Miyakoji kaisoku*, ¥690, 45 minutes) and there are several departures an hour during the day. This is the best option for those with Japan Rail Passes.

The Kintetsu line, which runs between Kintetsu Kyoto Station (in Kyoto Station) and Kintetsu Nara Station, is the fastest and most convenient way to travel between Nara and Kyoto. There are *tokkyū* (¥1110, 33 minutes) and *kyūkō* (¥610, 40 minutes). The *tokkyū* trains run directly and are very comfortable; the *kyūkō* usually require a change at Yamato-Saidai-ji.

Osaka

The JR Kansai line links Osaka (Namba and Tennō-ji Stations) and Nara (JR Nara Station). A *kaisoku* (rapid) service connects Namba and JR Nara Station (¥540, 45 minutes) and Tennō-ji and JR Nara Station (¥450, 30 minutes).

The Kintetsu Nara line connects Osaka (Kintetsu Osaka Namba Station) with Nara (Kintetsu Nara Station). *Kaisoku* and *futsū* (local) services take about 36 minutes and cost ¥540. *Tokkyū* services do the journey in five minutes less but cost almost double, making them a poor option.

ℹ️ Getting Around

To/From the Airport

Nara is served by Kansai International Airport (KIX). There is a limousine bus service (Nara Kōtsū; www.narakotsu.co.jp/kousoku/limousine/nara_kanku.html) between Nara and the airport with departures roughly every hour in both directions (¥2000, 90 minutes). At Kansai International Airport, ask at the information counter in the arrivals hall, and in Nara visit the ticket office in the building across from Kintetsu Nara Station. Reservations are a good idea.

For domestic flights, there are limousine buses (Nara Kōtsū; www.narakotsu.co.jp/kousoku/limousine/nara_itami.html) to/from Osaka's Itami airport (¥1440, 60 minutes).

Limousine buses leave from stop 9 in front of JR Nara Station and stop 20 (Kansai International Airport) and 12 (Itami Airport) outside Kintetsu Nara Station.

KŌYA-SAN 高野山

☎0736 / POP 3797

Kōya-san is a raised tableland in northern Wakayama-ken covered with thick forests and surrounded by eight peaks. The major attraction here is the Kōya-san monastic complex, which is the headquarters of the Shingon school of Esoteric Buddhism. Though not quite the Shangri La to which it is occasionally compared, Kōya-san is one of the most rewarding places to visit in Kansai, not just for the natural setting of the area but also as an opportunity to stay in temples and get a glimpse of long-held traditions of Japanese religious life.

Although it is just possible to visit Kōya-san as a day trip from Nara, Kyoto or Osaka, it's *much* better to reduce the travel stress and stay overnight in one of the town's excellent *shukubō* (temple lodgings). Keep in mind that Kōya-san tends to be around 5°C colder than down on the plains, so bring warm clothes if you're visiting in winter, spring or autumn.

Whenever you go, you'll find that getting there is half the fun – near the end of its journey, the train winds through a series of tight valleys with mountains soaring on all sides, and the final vertiginous cable-car leg is not for the faint of heart.

History

The founder of the Shingon school of Esoteric Buddhism, Kūkai (known after his death as Kōbō Daishi), established a religious community here in 816. Kōbō Daishi travelled as a young priest to China and returned after two years to found the school. He is one of Japan's most famous religious figures and is revered as a bodhisattva, calligrapher, scholar and inventor of the Japanese *kana* syllabary.

Followers of Shingon believe that Kōbō Daishi is not dead, but rather that he is meditating in his tomb in Kōya-san's Oku-no-in cemetery, awaiting the arrival of Miroku (Maitreya, the future Buddha). Food is ritually offered in front of the tomb daily to sustain him during this meditation. When Miroku returns, it is thought that only Kōbō Daishi will be able to interpret his heavenly message for humanity. Thus, the vast cemetery here is like an amphitheatre crowded with souls gathered in expectation of this heavenly sermon.

Over the centuries, the temple complex grew in size and attracted many followers of the Jōdo (Pure Land) school of Buddhism. During the 11th century, it became popular with both nobles and commoners to leave hair or ashes from deceased relatives close to Kōbō Daishi's tomb.

Kōya-san is now a thriving centre for Japanese Buddhism, with more than 110 temples remaining and a large population. It is the headquarters of the Shingon school, which numbers 10 million members and presides over nearly 4000 temples all over Japan.

 Sights

The precincts of Kōya-san are divided into two main areas: the Garan (Sacred Precinct) in the west, where you will find interesting temples and pagodas, and the Oku-no-in, with its vast cemetery, in the east.

A *shodōkyōtsu-naihaiken* (joint ticket; ¥2000) that covers entry to Kongōbu-ji, the Kondō, Dai-tō, Treasure Museum and Tokugawa Mausoleum can be purchased at the Kōya-san Tourist Association (p291).

Kongōbu-ji Buddhist Temple
(金剛峯寺; admission ¥500; ◷8.30am-5pm) This is the headquarters of the Shingon school and the residence of Kōya-san's abbot. The present structure dates from the 19th century and is definitely worth a visit.

The main hall's **Ohiro-ma room** has ornate screens painted by Kanō Tanyu in the 16th century. The **rock garden** is interesting for the sheer number of rocks used in its composition, giving the effect of a throng of petrified worshippers eagerly listening to a monk's sermon.

Admission includes tea and rice cakes served beside the stone garden.

Garan Buddhist Temple
(伽藍; admission to each bldg ¥200; ◷8.30am-5pm) In this temple complex of several halls and pagodas, the most important buildings are the **Dai-tō** (大塔; Great Pagoda) and **Kondō** (金堂; Main Hall). The Dai-tō, rebuilt in 1934 after a fire, is said to be the centre of the lotus-flower mandala formed by the eight mountains around Kōya-san. It's well worth entering the Dai-tō to see the **Dainichi-nyōrai** (Cosmic

Buddha) and his four attendant Buddhas. It's been repainted and is an awesome sight. The nearby **Sai-tō** (西塔; Western Pagoda) was most recently rebuilt in 1834 and is more subdued.

Treasure Museum Museum
(霊宝館; Reihōkan; admission ¥600; ◷8.30am-5.30pm May-Oct, to 5pm Nov-Apr) The Treasure Museum has a compact display of Buddhist works of art, all collected in Kōya-san. There are some very fine statues, painted scrolls and mandalas. Enter 30 minutes before closing.

Tokugawa Mausoleum Monument
(徳川家霊台; Tokugawa-ke Reidai; admission without joint ticket ¥200; ◷8.30am-5pm) Built in 1643, the Tokugawa Mausoleum consists of two adjoining structures that serve as the mausoleums of Tokugawa Ieyasu (on the right) and Tokugawa Hidetada (on the left), the first and second Tokugawa shōguns, respectively. They are ornately decorated, as with most structures associated with the Tokugawa shōguns. The mausoleum is not far from the Namikirifudō-mae bus stop (波切不動前バス亭).

Sleeping

More than 50 temples in Kōya-san offer *shukubō* (temple lodgings). A stay at a *shukubō* is a good way to try *shōjin-ryōri* (Buddhist vegetarian cuisine – no meat, fish, onions or garlic). Most *shukubō* also hold morning prayer sessions, which guests are welcome to join.

Most lodgings *start* at ¥9500 per person including two meals. Note that most places add a supplemental charge for solo guests. There is a lot of variation in prices, not just between temples but also within them, depending upon room, meals and season (needless to say, the more you pay, the better the room and the meals will be). Most places ask that you check in by 5pm.

While we list phone numbers for the *shukubō* in this section, most places prefer that you reserve at least a week in advance by fax through the Kōya-san Tourist Association (p291); the home page has a form to be used for

Kōya-san

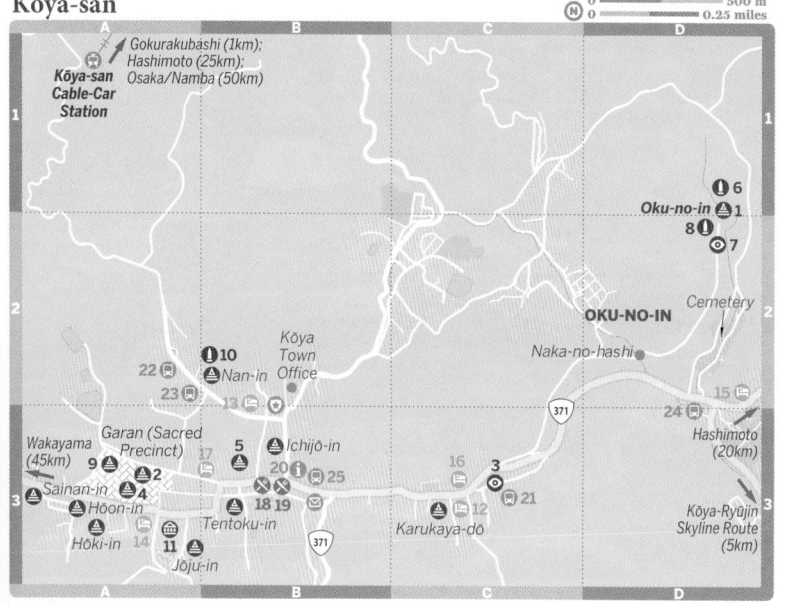

Kōya-san

◎ Don't Miss Sights
1 Oku-no-in D1

◎ Sights
2 Dai-tō A3
3 Ichi-no-hashi C3
4 Kondō A3
5 Kongōbu-ji B3
6 Kūkai Mausoleum D1
7 Mimyo-no-hashi D2
8 Miroku-ishi D2
9 Sai-tō A3
10 Tokugawa Mausoleum B2
Tōrō-dō ....(see 1)
11 Treasure Museum A3

🛏 Sleeping
12 Ekō-in C3
13 Fukuchi-in B2

14 Henjōson-in A3
15 Koyasan Guest House Kokuu D2
16 Shōjōshin-in C3
17 Sōji-in B3

⊗ Eating
18 Maruman B3
19 Nankai Shokudō B3

ℹ Information
20 Kōya-san Tourist Association............B3

ℹ Transport
21 Ichi-no-hashi-mae Bus Stop C3
22 Isshin-guchi-mae Bus Stop...............A2
23 Namikiri-fudō-mae Bus Stop A2
24 Oku-no-in-mae Bus Stop D3
25 Senjūin-bashi Bus Stop B3

ax reservations. Even if you contact
he temples directly, you will usually be
sked to go to the Tourist Association to
ick up a reservation slip-voucher. If you
refer to reserve by email, you can call
he Tourist Association and request their
mail address.

Koyasan Guest House Kokuu
Guesthouse ¥

(高野山ゲストハウスKokuu; ☎26-7216;
http://koyasanguesthouse.com; 49-43 Itogun
Kōyachō Kōyasan; capsules from ¥3500, s/d
from ¥6000/9000; @ 🛜) A capsule hotel
on Kōya-san? OK, this place is *not* your

289

WIBOWO RUSLI / GETTY IMAGES ©

★ Don't Miss
Oku-no-in

The Oku-no-in (奥の院) is a memorial hall/temple complex surrounded by a vast Buddhist cemetery. Any Buddhist worth their salt in Japan has had their remains, or a lock or two of hair, interred here just to ensure pole position when the Buddha of the Future (Miroku Buddha) comes to earth.

The best way to approach Oku-no-in is to walk or take the bus east to Ichi-no-hashi-mae bus stop. From here you cross the bridge, **Ichi-no-hashi** (一の橋), and enter the cemetery grounds along a winding, cobbled path lined by tall cedar trees and thousands of tombs. As the trees close in and the mist swirls, the atmosphere can be enchanting, especially as night falls.

At the northern end of the graveyard, you will find the **Tōrō-dō** (燈籠堂; Lantern Hall), which is the main building of the complex. It houses hundreds of lamps, including two believed to have been burning for more than 900 years. Behind the hall you can see the closed doors of the **Kūkai mausoleum** (空海の墓).

On the way to the Lantern Hall is the bridge **Mimyo-no-hashi** (御廟橋). Worshippers ladle water from the river and pour it over the nearby Jizō statues as an offering for the dead. The inscribed wooden plaques in the river are in memory of aborted babies and those who died by drowning.

Between the bridge and the Tōrō-dō is a small wooden building the size of a large phone booth, which contains the **Miroku-ishi** (みろく石). Pilgrims reach through the holes in the wall to try to lift a large, smooth boulder onto a shelf. The weight of the stone is supposed to change according to your weight of sin. We can only report that the thing was damn heavy!

Buses return to the centre of town from the Oku-no-mae bus stop or you can walk back in about 30 minutes.

typical capsule hotel. It's a clean, woodsy, light and airy spot, with a variety of nice private rooms in addition to the capsules. With the closure of the only other budget accommodations on Kōya-san, this is now the only inexpensive place to stay on the mountain.

It's a convivial place and it's now brought the Kōya-san experience within the range of even the most budget-conscious backpackers.

Fukuchi-in   Shukubo ¥¥
(福智院; ☎56-2021; fax 56-4736; r per person with meals from ¥12,600, single travellers ¥15,750; @ 🛜) This fine temple has outdoor baths with onsen water and a lovely garden designed by the famous designer Shigemori Mirei. Wi-fi is available for limited durations near the temple office.

Sōji-in   Shukubo ¥¥
(総持院; ☎56-2111; fax 56-4311; r per person with meals from ¥15,750, single travellers ¥18,900) At home with foreign guests, this temple has a lovely garden and some rooms with en suite bathrooms. There is one barrier-free room with Western-style beds. The top rooms here are among the best in Kōya-san.

Ekō-in   Shukubo ¥¥
(恵光院; ☎56-2514; ekoin@mbox.co.jp; r per person with meals from ¥10,000; @ 🛜) One of the nicer temples in town, Ekō-in is run by a friendly bunch of young monks and the rooms look onto beautiful gardens. This is also one of the two temples in town (the other is Kongōbu-ji; p288) where you can study zazen (seated meditation); call ahead to make arrangements for this. Unlike other shukubo, this temple does not charge extra for solo travellers.

Henjōson-in   Shukubo ¥¥
(遍照尊院; ☎56-2434; fax 56-3641; r per person with meals from ¥15,750, without bathroom ¥12,600) Nice rooms and communal baths make this a good choice.

Shōjōshin-in   Shukubo ¥¥
(清浄心院; ☎56-2006; fax 56-4770; r per person with meals from ¥9,600 or ¥11,100; 🛜)

Friendly spot with free in-room wi-fi and no extra charge for solo travellers.

 Eating

The culinary speciality of Kōya-san is shōjin-ryōri, which you can sample at your temple lodgings. If you're just in town for the day, you can try shōjin-ryōri at any of the temples that offer shukubo. Ask at the Kōya-san Tourist Association office and staff will call ahead to make reservations. Prices are fixed at ¥2700, ¥3700 and ¥5300, depending on how many courses you have. In addition, there are a few shokudō (all-round restaurants) in town but note that most close late in the afternoon.

Maruman   Shokudo ¥
(丸万; ☎56-2049; noodle dishes from ¥370; ⏰9am-5pm, closed irregularly, but usually on Tue or Wed) This simple shokudō is a good spot for lunch. All the standard lunch items are represented by plastic food models in the window; katsu-don (fried pork cutlet over rice) is ¥820. It's just west of the tourist office on the main street. If this is full or doesn't suit, Nankai Shokudō next door is similar.

ⓘ Information

Kōya-san Tourist Association (高野山観光協会; ☎56-2616; http://eng.shukubo.net/; ⏰Dec-Feb 8:30am-4:30pm, Mar-Jun 8:30am-5:00pm, Jul & Aug 8:30am-5:45pm, Sep-Nov 8:30am-5pm) In the centre of town in front of the Senjūin-bashi bus stop (千手院橋バス停), this tourist information centre stocks maps and brochures (such as the excellent English-language Koya San map/pamphlet), and English-speakers are usually on hand. While you're there, consider buying a shodōkyōtsū-naihaiken (joint ticket; ¥2000) to Kōya-san's biggest sights.

Kōyasan Interpreter Guide Club (☎090-1486-2588, 090-3263-5184; www.geocities.jp/koyasan_i_g_c) This club offers four-hour private tours of Kōya-san for ¥5000 per group with a volunteer guide. Professional guides cost from ¥10,000 per four-hour tour. It also offers regularly scheduled tours on Wednesday from

April to September for ¥1000 per person. The morning tour meets at Ichi-no-hashi at 8.30am, lasts three hours and covers Oku-no-in, Garan and Kongōbu-ji. The afternoon tour meets at Kongōbu-ji at 1pm, takes three hours, and covers the same sights.

 Getting There & Away

Unless you have a rental car, the best way to reach Kōya-san is by train on the Nankai-Dentetsu line from Osaka's Namba Station. The trains terminate at Gokurakubashi, at the base of the mountain, where you board a funicular railway (price included in train tickets) up to Kōya-san itself. From the cable-car station, you take a bus into the centre of town (walking is prohibited on the connecting road).

From Osaka (Namba Station) you can travel directly on a Nankai-Dentetsu line *kyūkō* to Kōya-san (¥1230, one hour and 40 minutes). For the slightly faster *tokkyū* service with reserved seats you need to pay a supplement (¥760). Nankai-Dentetsu offers the Kōya-san World Heritage ticket for ¥3310; this ticket covers entry to the main sites and round-trip *tokkyū* fare from Osaka's Nankai Namba Station (check at the Nankai office in Namba since conditions change all the time).

From Kyoto go via Namba in Osaka (taking the Nankai-Dentetsu line from Namba). Or, if you've got a Japan Rail Pass, take the JR line to Hashimoto, changing at Nara, Sakurai and Takada en route. From Hashimoto, you have no choice but to take the private Nankai-Dentetsu line to Kōya-san (¥810, 50 minutes).

Getting Around

Buses run on three routes from the top cable-car station via the centre of town to Ichi-no-hashi and Oku-no-in. The fare to the tourist office in the centre of town at Senjūin-bashi is ¥280. The fare to the final stop, Oku-no-in, is ¥400. An *ichi-nichi furee kippu* (all-day bus pass; ¥800) is available from the bus office outside the top cable-car station, but once you get into the centre of town you can reach most destinations quite easily on foot (including Oku-no-in, which takes about 30 minutes). Note that buses run infrequently, so you should make a note of the schedule before setting out to see the sights.

If you don't feel like walking, bicycles can be rented (per hour/day ¥400/1200) at the Kōya-san Tourist Association office.

KINOSAKI

☎0796 / POP 4134

Kinosaki is one of the best places in Japan to sample the classic Japanese onsen experience. A willow-lined canal runs through the centre of this town, and many of the houses, shops and restaurants retain something of their traditional charm. Add to this the delights of crab fresh from the Sea of Japan in winter, and you'll understand why this is one of our favourite overnight trips from the cities of Kansai.

Sights & Activities

Kinosaki's biggest attraction is its seven onsen. Guests staying in town stroll the canal from bath to bath wearing a *yukata* (light cotton kimono) and *geta* (wooden sandals). Most of the ryokan and hotels in town have their own *uchi-yu* (private baths), but also provide their guests with free tickets to the ones outside (*soto-yu*).

In addition to the town's great onsen, visitors might want to have a peek at the **Kinosaki Mugiwarazaikudenshokan** (城崎麦わら細工伝館; admission ¥300; ⏱9am-5pm, enter by 4.30pm, closed last Wed of every month), which has displays on one of the local handicrafts known as *mugiwarazaiku*, a decorative technique that employs barley straw cut into tiny pieces and applied to wood to form incredibly beautiful patterns. It's located off the canal, a short walk from Ichi-no-yu onsen.

The following is the full list of Kinosaki's onsen, in order of preference (you can get a map from the information office or your lodgings).

Gosho-no-yu   Onsen

(御所の湯; admission ¥800; ⏱7am-11pm, enter by 10.30pm, closed 1st & 3rd Thu) Lovely log construction, a nice two-level *rotemburo* (outdoor bath) and fine maple colours in autumn. The entry area is decorated like the Kyoto Gosho (Imperial Palace).

Sato-no-yu   Onsen

(さとの湯; admission ¥800; ⏱1-9pm, enter by 8.40pm, closed Mon) Fantastic variety of baths, including Arab-themed saunas, rooftop *rotemburo* and a 'Penguin Sauna (basically a walk-in freezer – the only one we've seen anywhere – good after a hot bath). Women's and men's baths shift floors daily, so you'll have to go two days in a row to sample all of the offerings.

Kou-no-yu
Onsen

(鴻の湯; admission ¥600; ⏰7am-11pm, enter by 10.30pm, closed Tue) Nothing fancy, but a good *rotemburo* and pleasant inside baths.

Ichi-no-yu
Onsen

(一の湯; admission ¥600; ⏰7am-11pm, enter by 10.30pm, closed Wed) Wonderful 'cave' bath.

Yanagi-yu
Onsen

(柳湯; admission ¥600; ⏰3-11pm, enter by 10.40pm, closed Thu) Worth a quick soak as you make your way around town. Nice wooden construction.

Mandara-yu
Onsen

(まんだら湯; admission ¥600; ⏰3-11pm, enter by 10.40pm, closed Wed) Small wooden *rotemburo*.

Jizo-yu
Onsen

(地蔵湯; admission ¥600; ⏰7am-11pm, enter by 10.40pm, closed Fri) Spacious main inside tub but no *rotemburo*. Good if others are crowded.

 Sleeping

Ryokan Yamamotoya
Ryokan ¥¥

(旅館山本屋; ☎32-2114; www.kinosaki.com/en; 835 Yushima, Kinosakichō; r per person with meals from ¥13,650; 🛜) This is a fine ryokan that is comfortable with foreign guests, has lovely rooms and serves excellent food. It's roughly in the middle of town, very close to Ichi-no-yu onsen. Solo travellers are only accepted in the spring and autumn and must pay a single supplement.

Suishōen
Ryokan ¥¥

(水翔苑; ☎32-4571; www.suisyou.com/en; per person with meals from ¥17,850, per person without meals Sun-Thu Japanese r ¥12,495, Western r ¥6,300, per person without meals Fri-Sat Japanese r ¥15,645, Western r ¥9,450; @🛜) This excellent ryokan is a short drive from the town centre, but they'll whisk you straight to the onsen of your choice in their own London taxi and pick you up when you're done. It's a strangely pleasant feeling to ride in the back wearing nothing but a *yukata*! The rooms are clean, and the private onsen is great, with indoor and outdoor baths. Solo travellers are charged extra.

Mikuniya
Ryokan ¥¥

(三国屋; ☎32-2414; www.kinosaki3928.com/english/index.htm; r per person with/without meals from ¥17,850/9,450; 🛜) About 150m on the right on the street heading into town from the station, this ryokan is a good choice. The rooms are clean, with nice Japanese decorations, and the onsen bath is soothing. There is an English sign. Wi-fi in main building only.

Kinosaki
ADAM HESTER / GETTY IMAGES ©

Tsuruya
Ryokan ¥¥

(つるや; ☏32-2924; www.kinosaki-tsuruya. com/english.html; r per person with/without meals from ¥10,330/5590) A few metres before Kou-no-yu onsen (as you approach from the station), this simple ryokan is comfortable with foreign guests. The rooms are plain but sufficient and the manager is helpful and speaks some English.

Nishimuraya Honkan
Ryokan ¥¥¥

(西村屋本館; ☏32-2211; www.nishimuraya. ne.jp/honkan/english; r per person incl 2 meals from ¥29,400, solo travellers from ¥44,100; 🛜) This classic is the ultimate inn here. If you would like to try the high-class ryokan experience, this is a good place. The two onsen baths are exquisite and most of the rooms look out over private gardens. The excellent food is the final touch.

🍴 Eating

Crab from the Sea of Japan is a speciality in Kinosaki during the winter months. It's called *kani* and the way to enjoy it is in *kani-suki,* cooked right at your table in a broth with vegetables. Note that most restaurants in Kinosaki shut down very early. This is because most people opt for the two-meal option at their accommodation. You should consider doing the same, at least during *kani* season.

Cafee Sorella
Cafe ¥

(カフェソレッラ; ☏32-2059; 84 Yushima, Kinosaki-chō; coffee from ¥320; ⏱9:30am-5:30pm, closed irregularly; 🛜) This simple coffee shop about 75m north of the Kinosaki Station on the main street is a good place for a cuppa and an internet fix (there's free wi-fi if you order a drink). There's an English sign and a picture menu.

Daikō Shōten
Shokudō ¥¥

(大幸商店; ☏32-3684; ⏱10am-9pm, to 11pm summer; 📖) This seafood shop/*izakaya* is a great place to try freshly caught local seafood in a casual atmosphere. From November until mid-April (the busy tourist season for Kinosaki), the restaurant section is upstairs, while downstairs is given over to selling vast quantities of crabs and other delights. For the rest of the year, the restaurant is on the ground floor. *Teishoku* (set-course meals) are available from ¥1480, but you'll never go wrong by just asking for

Kōbe

YOSHIKAZU ONISHI / GETTY IMAGES

the master's *osusume* (recommendations). It's diagonally across from Mikuniya, about 50m back towards the station.

Orizuru   Sushi ¥¥
(をり鶴; ☎32-2203; meals ¥3000; ◎lunch & dinner, closed Tue; 🗎) For decent sushi and crab dishes, try this popular local sushi restaurant on the main street. You can get a *jō-nigiri* (superior sushi set; ¥3700) or try the crab dishes in winter. It's between Ichi-no-yu and Gosho-no-yu, on the opposite side of the street. There is a small English sign.

ℹ Information

Accommodation information office (お宿案内所; ☎32-4141; ◎9am-6pm) Staff will gladly help you find a place to stay and make bookings, as well as provide maps of the town. The same office has rental bicycles available for ¥400/800 per two hours/day (return by 5pm). It is opposite the station.

ℹ Getting There & Away

Kinosaki is on the JR San-in line and there are a few daily *tokkyū* from Kyoto (¥4710, two hours and 22 minutes) and Osaka (¥5450, two hours and 42 minutes).

KŌBE

☎078 / POP 1.54 MILLION

Perched on a hillside overlooking the sea, Kōbe (神戸) is one of Japan's most attractive cities. It's also one of the country's most cosmopolitan places, having served as a maritime gateway to Kansai from the earliest days of trade with China. One of Kōbe's best features is its relatively small size – most of the sights can be reached on foot from the main train stations. And this is the main appeal of Kōbe: rather than a collection of sights, Kōbe is a city that is best enjoyed by casual wandering, enjoying the neighbourhoods and stopping in the many good restaurants and cafes as the whim strikes you. The most pleasant neighbourhoods to explore are Kitano, Chinatown and, after dark, the bustling area around Sannomiya Station.

 Sights

Kōbe's two main entry points are Sannomiya and Shin-Kōbe Stations. Shin-Kōbe Station, in the northeast of town, is where the *shinkansen* stops. A subway (Seishin-Yamate line, ¥200, two minutes) runs from here to the downtown Sannomiya Station, which has frequent rail connections with Osaka and Kyoto. It's possible to walk between the two stations in around 20 minutes. Sannomiya Station marks the city centre, although a spate of development in Kōbe Harbor Land is starting to swing the city's centre of gravity towards the southwest. Before starting your exploration of Kōbe, pick up a map of the city at one of the two information offices (one is inside Sannomiya Station and one is inside Shin-Kōbe Station).

Kitano   Neighbourhood
(北野; ®JR San-yō shinkansen to Shin-Kōbe or JR, Hankyū or Hanshin lines to Sannomiya) Twenty minutes' walk north of Sannomiya is the pleasant hillside neighbourhood of Kitano, where local tourists come to enjoy the feeling of foreign travel without leaving Japanese soil. A European–American atmosphere is created by the winding streets and *ijinkan* (literally 'foreigners' houses'), which housed some of Kōbe's early Western residents. Admission to some houses is free, for others it costs ¥300 to ¥700, and most are open from 9am to 5pm daily. Although these brick and weatherboard dwellings may not hold the same fascination for Western travellers that they hold for local tourists, the area itself is pleasant to stroll around and is dotted with good cafes and restaurants.

Kōbe Harbor Land
& Meriken Park   Neighbourhood
(神戸ハーバーランド・メリケンパーク; ⑤Kaigan line to Harbor Land, ®JR line to Kōbe) Five minutes' walk southeast of Kōbe Station, Kōbe Harbor Land is awash with megamall shopping and dining developments. This may not appeal to foreign

travellers the way it does to the local youth, but it's still a nice place for a stroll in the afternoon.

A five-minute walk to the east of Harbor Land you'll find Meriken Park, on a spit of reclaimed land jutting out into the bay. The main attraction here is the Kōbe Maritime Museum.

🛌 Sleeping

Hotel Trusty Boutique Hotel **¥¥**
(ホテルトラスティ神戸; 🕿 330-9111; www.trusty.jp/kobe; 63 Naniwamachi, Chūō-ku; s/d/tw from ¥6300/11,200/13,200; @; 🚊 JR, Hankyū or Hanshin lines to Sannomiya) The name of the place screams 'standard-issue business hotel', but this intimate little hotel in Kōbe's Kyūkyoryūchi district is actually a super-stylish boutique hotel. The rooms are on the small side, but they are very clean and have all the amenities that you might need. It's within relatively easy walking distance of the stations.

ANA Crowne Plaza Hotel Kōbe Hotel **¥¥¥**
(ANAクラウンプラザ神戸; 🕿 291-1121; www.anacrowneplaza-kobe.jp/en; 1-Chome, Kitano, Chūō-ku; s/d/tw from ¥8800/14,000/14,000; @ 🛜; S Seishin-Yamate subway to Shin-Kōbe, 🚊 JR San-yō shinkansen to Shin-Kōbe) You'll feel on top of the world as you survey the bright lights of Kōbe from this perch atop the city. Conveniently located near JR Shin-Kōbe Station, this first-class hotel offers clean and fairly spacious rooms and has an English-speaking staff. Downstairs in the **Oriental Avenue shopping centre** (アベニュー), you'll find several good restaurants to choose from.

B Kōbe Hotel **¥¥**
(ザ・ビー神戸; 🕿 333-4880; www.the-b-hotels.com/the-b-kobe/en; 2-11-5 Shimoyamate St, Chūō-ku; s/d/tw from ¥5500/8800/7600; @; S Seishin-Yamate line to Sannomiya) The centrally located B Kōbe is a good utilitarian choice if you've got business in Kōbe or just want a clean place to lay your head in the evening. Some of the

Left: Kōbe Harbor Land (p295); **Below:** Himeji-jō (p299)
(LEFT) HIRO / A.COLLECTIONRF / GETTY IMAGES ©; (BELOW) WIBOWO RUSLI / GETTY IMAGES ©

rooms are quite small, but if you're only there at night this shouldn't matter too much.

🍴 Eating

R Valentino
Italian ¥¥

(アール ヴァレンティーノ; ☎332-1268; 3rd fl, 4-5-13 Kanō-chō, Chūō-ku; pasta from ¥1500, lunch/dinner mains from ¥1600/3800; ☉lunch & dinner; 📖; 🚃JR, Hanshin or Hankyū lines to Sannomiya) Pizzas cooked in a brick oven are the draw at this Sannomiya Italian restaurant. It's very casual and comfortable and there's an English/Italian menu. The Italian owner can explain the specials and make recommendations.

Wakkoqu
Steakhouse ¥¥

(和黒; ☎262-2838; 3rd fl, Shin Kōbe Oriental Avenue shopping mall, 1-1 Kitano-chō; lunch/ dinner from ¥2940/7500; ☉lunch & dinner; 📖; 🚇Seishin-Yamate line to Shin-Kōbe, 🚃JR San-yō shinkansen to Shin-Kōbe) An elegant spot to try Kōbe beef, Wakkoqu is on the 3rd floor of the Oriental Avenue shopping centre at the base of the Crowne Plaza Kōbe hotel (just outside the elevator bank on the south side). The name 'Wakkoqu' is written in English on the menu displayed outside (and the menu is partially translated into English).

Azzuri
Pizzeria ¥¥

(アズーリ; ☎241-6036; 3-7-3 Yamamoto-dori, Chūō-ku; pizzas from ¥1155; ☉lunch & dinner; 🚃JR line to Motomachi) Said to be certified by the True Neapolitan Pizza Association (Associazione Verace Pizza Napoletana), this busy pizzeria is worth the walk to get there – just hope that there's a seat when you arrive (it's very popular with locals).

Arti
Indian ¥¥

(アールティ神戸北野ハンター坂本店; ☎222-8665; 2-14-13 Nakayamate-dori, Chuo-ku; dinner with 1 curry from ¥1120; ☉lunch & dinner; 📖; 🚃JR, Hanshin or Hankyū lines to Sannomiya) Kōbe is awash with Indian restaurants, but Arti stands head and shoulders above the crowd. There are two branches, but we like this one in Kitano for its pleasant surroundings. With an English menu and English-speaking staff, you'll have no trouble picking your favourite curries and breads to go with them.

ℹ️ Information

Citibank (シティバンク; ⊙9am-3pm Mon-Fri, ATM 24hr; 🚉JR, Hankyū or Hanshin lines to Sannomiya) South of Sogo Department Store; the ATM accepts international cards.

Tourist Information Office (神戸市総合インフォメーションセンター; ☎322-0220; ⊙9am-7pm; 🚉JR, Hankyū or Hanshin lines to Sannomiya) The city's main tourist information office is on the ground floor on the south side of JR Sannomiya Station's east gate. There's a smaller information counter on the 2nd floor of Shin-Kōbe Station, right outside the main *shinkansen* gate. Both information centres carry reasonably good free maps of the city, as well as a variety of pamphlets.

ℹ️ Getting There & Away

Train

Kōbe's JR Sannomiya Station is on the JR Tōkaidō line. A JR *shinkaisoku* train on this line is the fastest way between Kōbe and Osaka Station (¥390, 22 minutes) or Kyoto (¥1050, 54 minutes).

Two private lines, the Hankyū and Hanshin lines, also connect Kōbe and Osaka. The Hankyū line is the more convenient of the two, running between Kōbe's Hankyū Sannomiya Station and Osaka's Hankyū Umeda Station (*tokkyū*, ¥310, 27 minutes). The Hankyū line also has connections between Kyoto and Osaka, so you can travel between Kyoto and Kōbe (*tokkyū*, ¥600, 65 minutes, change at Jūsō or Umeda).

Shin-Kōbe Station is on the Tōkaidō/San-yō *shinkansen* line. The Hikari *shinkansen* goes to/from Fukuoka (¥14,270, two hours and 52 minutes) and to/from Tokyo (¥14,270, three hours and 10 minutes). Nozomi *shinkansen* are slightly faster. Other stations on this line include Osaka, Kyoto, Nagoya and Hiroshima.

ℹ️ Getting Around

To/From the Airport

Itami Osaka Airport

There are direct limousine buses to/from Osaka's Itami airport (¥1020, 40 minutes). In Kōbe, the buses stop on the southwestern side of Sannomiya Station.

Kansai International Airport (KIX)

There are a number of routes between Kōbe and KIX. By train, the fastest way is the JR *shinkaisoku* to/from Osaka Station, and the JR *kanku kaisoku* between Osaka Station and the airport (total cost ¥1660, total time 1¾ hours with good connections). There is also a direct limousine bus to/from the airport (¥2000, 1¼ hours), which is more convenient if you have a lot of luggage. The Kōbe airport bus stop is on the southwestern side of Sannomiya Station.

Cable cars, Kōbe

SHUKO YASUMI / A.COLLECTIONRF / GETTY IMAGES ©

Public Transport

Kōbe is small enough to travel around on foot. The JR, Hankyū and Hanshin railway lines run east to west across Kōbe, providing access to most of Kōbe's more distant sights. A subway line (the Seishin-Yamate line) also connects Shin-Kōbe Station with Sannomiya Station (¥200, two minutes). Another subway line (the Kaigan line) runs from just south of Sannomiya Station south towards the Harbor Land area. There is also a city-loop bus service that makes a grand-circle tour of most of the city's sightseeing spots (per ride/all-day pass ¥200/600). The bus stops at both Sannomiya and Shin-Kōbe stations; look for the retro-style green buses.

HIMEJI

📱079 / POP 536,300

Himeji-jō, the finest castle in all of Japan, towers over the small city of Himeji (姫路), a quiet city on the San-yō *shinkansen* route between Osaka and Okayama/Hiroshima. In addition to the castle, the city is home to the Hyōgo Prefectural Museum of History, and Kōko-en, a small garden alongside the castle. If you're a fan of castles, a visit to Himeji is a must. You can visit it as a day trip from Kyoto, Nara or Osaka, or as a stopover en route to Hiroshima.

 Sights

Himeji-jō   Castle
(姫路城; 68 Honmachi; adult/child ¥400/100; ⏰9am-5pm Sep-May, to 6pm Jun-Aug) The most magnificent castle in Japan, Himeji-jō is also one of only a handful of original castles in the country (most others are modern concrete reconstructions). In Japanese it is sometimes called *shirasagi* (white heron), a title that derives from the castle's stately white form.

Although there have been fortifications in Himeji since 1333, today's castle was built in 1580 by Toyotomi Hideyoshi and enlarged some 30 years later by Ikeda Terumasa. Ikeda was awarded the castle by Tokugawa Ieyasu when the latter's forces defeated the Toyotomi armies. In the following centuries it was home to 48 successive lords.

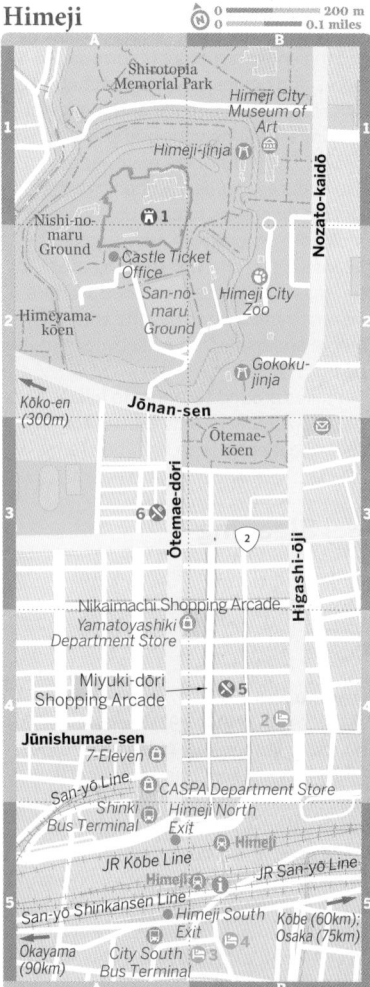

Himeji

◎ Sights
1 Himeji-jō...A1

⊜ Sleeping
2 APA Hotel Himejieki-kita..................B4
3 Hotel Nikkō Himeji............................B5
4 Tōyoko Inn...B5

⊗ Eating
5 Fukutei..B4
6 Me-n-Me..A3

The castle has a five-storey *tenshū* (main keep) and three smaller keeps, and the entire structure is surrounded by moats and defensive walls punctuated with rectangular, circular and triangular openings for firing guns and shooting arrows. The walls of the main keep also feature *ishiotoshi* – openings that allowed defenders to pour boiling water or oil onto anyone who made it past the defensive slits and was thinking of scaling the walls. All things considered, visitors are recommended to pay the admission charge and enter the castle by legitimate means.

It takes around 1½ hours to follow the arrow-marked route around the castle. Last entry is an hour before closing.

Sleeping

Himeji is best visited as a day trip from other parts of Kansai. If you'd like to stay, however, there are plenty of choices.

Tōyoko Inn　　　　　　　Hotel ¥
(東横イン; ☎284-1045; 97 Minamiekimae-chō; s/d/tw incl breakfast ¥5480/7980/8480; @ 🛜) This efficient business hotel is a good choice if you want to be close to the station. The rooms are serviceable, well maintained and, as usual in a business hotel, fairly small. As with other Tōyoko Inns, just about everything you need is supplied, including breakfast. Both wi-fi and LAN cable internet are available in each room for free.

APA Hotel Himejieki-kita　　　Hotel ¥¥¥
(APAホテル姫路駅北; ☎284-4111; 98 Higashiekimae-chō; s/d/tw from ¥7500/13,000/14,000; @ 🛜) This centrally located business hotel is pretty much everything a good hotel should be: well run and clean with reasonable-sized rooms (for a business hotel, that is). It's within easy walking distance of the castle and lots of restaurants. There's free wi-fi in the lobby and free LAN cable internet in each room.

Hotel Nikkō Himeji　　　Hotel ¥¥¥
(ホテル日航姫路; ☎222-2231; 100 Minamie-kimae-chō; s/d/tw ¥6800/13,000/12,000; @ 🛜) A stone's throw from the south side of the station, this hotel offers stylish and fairly spacious rooms and is the best choice for those who are looking for something nicer than a business hotel. The rooms here are larger and the bathtubs have almost enough room to stretch out in. Some of the upper rooms on the north side have views of the top of the castle. Free wi-fi is available in the lobby and restaurant; free LAN cable internet is available in guest rooms.

Eating

Most of the restaurants in Himeji are located in the shopping arcades north of the station (on the way to the castle).

Me-n-Me　　　　　　　Noodles ¥
(めんめ; ☎225-0118; 68 Honmachi; noodles from ¥550; ⏰11.30am-7pm, closed Wed; 📖) They make their own noodles at this

---

Himeji-jō Renovation

Himeji-jō is undergoing a massive renovation that is slated to finish in early 2015. Until it's completed, the *tenshū* (main keep) of the castle will be covered by a scaffoldlike structure that will obscure it from view. The rest of the castle will not be covered by any structure. It will be possible to enter the castle during the reconstruction period, although some areas (most notably, the castle keep) may be closed to the public from time to time. Call Himeji Tourist Information Office if you have any questions.

Detour:
Miho Museum

Located in the countryside of Shiga-ken near the village of Shigaraki, this IM Pei–designed **museum** (ミホミュージアム; ☎0748-82-3411; www.miho.or.jp; 300, Tashiro Momodani; adult/child ¥1000/300; ⊙10am-5pm Jan, Feb, mid Jun–mid Jul, mid-end Aug, mid–end Dec, closed Mon) is visually stunning. The museum houses the Shumei Family art collection, which includes examples of Japanese, Middle Eastern, Chinese and south Asian art.

A visit to the Miho Museum is something like a visit to the secret hideout of an archvillain in a James Bond film, and there is no doubt that the facility is at least as impressive as the collection it houses. Since a visit (including the journey from Kyoto or Osaka) can take the better part of a day, we highly recommend calling the museum to check what's on before making the trip.

To get there, take the JR Tōkaidō line from Kyoto or Osaka to Ishiyama Station, and change to a **Teisan Bus** (Teisan Konan Kōtsu; www.teisan-konan-kotsu.co.jp) bound for the museum (¥800, approximately 50 minutes).

homey little noodle joint a few minutes' walk from the castle. It's not fancy, but if you want an honest, tasty bowl of *udon* to power you through the day, this is the spot. There's no English sign: look for the white *noren* (curtains) in the doorway that show noodles being rolled out.

Fukutei Kaiseki ¥¥
(福亭; ☎222-8150; 75 Kamei-chō; lunch/dinner from ¥1500/3500; ⊙11.30am-2.30pm & 5-10pm Mon-Fri, 11.30am-2.30pm & 5-9pm Sat & Sun; 🗐) This stylish, approachable restaurant is a great lunch choice if you want something a little civilised. The fare here is casual *kaiseki* (Japanese haute cuisine): a little sashimi, some tempura and the usual nibbles on the side. At lunch try the excellent *omakese-zen* (tasting set; ¥1500). There's a small English sign. There's an English menu available at lunch, but not at dinner.

ⓘ Information

Himeji Tourist Information Office (姫路市観光案内所[姫路観光なびポート]; ☎287-0003; ⊙9am-7pm, closed 29 & 30 Dec) On the ground floor of Himeji Station, not far from the central gate (clearly marked with signs as you exit the turnstiles). While you're there, pick up a copy of the useful *Places of Interest Downtown Himeji* map or *Himeji Tourist Guide & Map*. The

castle is a 15-minute walk (1200m) straight up the main road from the north exit of the station. If you don't feel like walking, free rental cycles are available from an underground parking area halfway between the station and the castle; enquire at the information office.

ⓘ Getting There & Away

If you've got a Japan Rail Pass or are in a hurry, a *shinkansen* is the best way to reach Himeji from Kyoto (Hikari, ¥4930, 55 minutes), Hiroshima (Hikari, ¥7870, 61 minutes), and Shin-Osaka (Hikari, ¥3440, 28 minutes). Note that you cannot use the Nozomi *shinkansen* if you have a Japan Rail Pass, but you can use the Sakura *shinkansen*, which run fairly frequently between Himeji and Shin-Osaka stations. If you don't have a pass, a *shinkaisoku* on the JR Tōkaidō line is the best way to reach Himeji from Kyoto (¥2210, 94 minutes), Osaka (¥1450, 63 minutes) and Kōbe's Sannomiya Station (¥950, 37 minutes). From Okayama, to the west, a *tokkyū* JR train on the San-yō line takes approximately two hours including transit time and costs ¥1450.

NAOSHIMA

☎087 / POP 3300

Until not too long ago, the arty isle of Naoshima was no different from many others in the Inland Sea: home to a dwindling population subsisting on the joint proceeds of a dying fishing industry and the old-age pension. Today, as the location of the Benesse Art Site Naoshima, Naoshima is one of the area's biggest tourist attractions, offering a unique opportunity to see some of Japan's best contemporary art in gorgeous natural settings.

The project started in the early '90s, when the Benesse Corporation chose Naoshima as the setting for its growing collection of modern art. Naoshima now has a number of world-class art galleries and installations, and has attracted creative types from all over the country to set up home here.

In addition to the main sites, numerous works of outdoor art are situated around the coast, including the pumpkin sculpture by Kusama Yayoi that has become a symbol of the island.

⊙ Sights & Activities

During holiday seasons the museums can become quite crowded and you may find you have to queue. At peak times at Chichū Art Museum, a 'timed ticket' system may be in place, designating the time you are able to purchase a ticket and enter.

Art House Project   Art Installation
(家プロジェクト; www.benesse-artsite.jp/arthouse; combined ticket ¥1000; ⊙10am-4.30pm, closed Mon) In the old fishing village of Honmura (本村), half a dozen traditional buildings have been restored and turned over to contemporary artists to use as the setting for creative installations. Highlights include Ōtake Shinrō's shacklike **Haisha** house, its *Statue of Liberty* sculpture rising up through the levels; James Turrell's experiment with light in **Minami-dera**, where you enter in total darkness...and wait; and Sugimoto Hiroshi's play on the traditional **Go'o Shrine**, with a glass staircase, and underground 'Stone Chamber' (those who are claustrophobic or wide of hip will want to give this a miss).

The sites are within walking distance of each other. Take the Naoshima bus to the Nōkyō-mae stop, where you can buy your Art House Project ticket from the tobacco shop and start exploring. Or buy a ticket at the first site you visit.

Benesse House Museum   Gallery
(ベネッセハウス; www.benesse-artsite.jp/benessehouse-museum; admission ¥1000; ⊙8am-9pm) Award-winning architect Andō

Benesse House Museum

Tadao designed this stunning museum and hotel on the south coast of the island. Among the works here are pieces by Andy Warhol, David Hockney, Jasper Johns, and Japanese artists such as Ōtake Shinrō.

Chichū Art Museum
Gallery

(地中美術館; www.benesse-artsite.jp/chichu; admission ¥2000; ⊘10am-6pm, to 5pm Oct-Feb, closed Mon) A short walk from Benesse House is this Andō Tadao creation. The museum consists of a series of cool concrete-walled spaces sitting snugly underground. It provides a remarkable setting for several Monet water-lily paintings, some monumental sculptures by Walter de Maria and installations by James Turrell. Outside is the Chichū garden, created in the spirit of Monet's garden in Giverny.

Lee Ufan Museum
Gallery

(李禹煥美術館; www.benesse-artsite.jp/lee-ufan; admission ¥1000; ⊘10am-6pm, to 5pm Oct-Feb, closed Mon) The most recent addition to Benesse's suite of museums is yet another design from the irrepressible Andō. It houses works by the renowned Korean-born artist (and philosopher) Lee Ufan, who was a leading figure in the Mono-ha movement of the 1960s and 1970s.

Naoshima Bath – I Heart Yū
Bathhouse

(直島銭湯; www.naoshimasento.jp; admission ¥500; ⊘2-9pm Tue-Fri, 10am-9pm Sat & Sun, closed Mon) For a unique bathing experience, take a soak at this colourful fusion of Japanese bathing tradition and contemporary art, designed by Ōtake Shinrō. It's a couple of minutes' walk inland from Miyanoura port. Look for the building with the palm trees out front.

Sleeping

The accommodation scene is dominated by privately run *minshuku* (guest houses). Not a lot of English is spoken, but locals are becoming increasingly used to foreign guests. If you prefer hotel-style facilities, Benesse House hotel is your only real option. Alternatively, stay in Okayama or Uno port on the mainland, or Takamatsu

---

Local Knowledge

Benesse Art Site Naoshima

BY MARUYAMA CHIYUKI, BENESSE ART SITE STAFF

1 BENESSE HOUSE
Surely one of the world's most unusual art museums, Benesse House is a residential art museum – a hotel-cum-museum where the guests can peruse the galleries even after the museum has closed its doors to day visitors. This Andō Tadao–designed museum contains a variety of guest rooms, a spa, a cafe, two restaurants and artworks by Andy Warhol, David Hockney and Jasper Johns, among others.

2 ART HOUSE PROJECT
Taking the idea of residential art even further, the Benesse Art Site directors invited artists from several nations to transform a number of island structures into free-standing installations. These include a mesmerising local shrine with a glass staircase, a house with watery pools in place of tatami mats, and Minami-dera, where the artwork coalesces out of the darkness as your eyes adjust to the gloom.

3 CHICHŪ ART MUSEUM
Built into the earth (the name means 'in the middle of the earth'), this museum houses works by Monet, Walter de Maria and James Turrell. Andō's clever design allows natural light to enter and illuminate each work to its best advantage.

4 I HEART YŪ
One of Naoshima's newest attractions, this whimsical *sentō* (public bath) near the island's Miyanoura port may be the most unusual in the country. Designed by artist Ōtake Shinrō, the outside of the building is a riot of coloured tiles and posters, and inside, the bath-tubs are lined with a wild assortment of collages.

in Shikoku, and visit as a day trip. The Tourist Information Centre in Miyanoura has a complete list of lodgings. Rates increase during high season.

Tsutsuji-sō   Campground ¥
(つつじ荘; ☏892-2838; www.tsutsujiso.com; tents per person from ¥3675; 🚭) Perfectly placed on the beachfront not far from the Benesse Art Site area is this encampment of Mongolian-style *pao* tents. The cosy tents sleep up to four, have a small fridge and heater (but no air-con), and shared bathroom facilities. The tent-averse can opt instead for one of the caravans or cottages. Meals are available if reserved in advance. Cash only.

Minshuku Oyaji-no-Umi   Minshuku ¥
(民宿おやじの海; ☏090-5261-7670; http://yopopo.moo.jp; per person without bathroom incl breakfast ¥4200; @🛜) This is a good option for friendly, family-style lodgings, with tatami rooms (separated by sliding doors) and shared bathroom, in an old house close to the Art House Project in Honmura. Owners don't speak English; it's best to book via email if you don't speak Japanese. The entrance is next to the Cat Cafe.

Dormitory in Kūron   Hostel ¥
(ドミトリーin九龍; ☏892-2424; http://kawloon.gozaru.jp; dm ¥2800; @🛜) Basic dormitory accommodation just back from the ferry port in Miyanoura. Note that you'll pay ¥3500 if you show up without a reservation. Some English is spoken.

Benesse House   Boutique Hotel ¥¥¥
(☏892-3223; www.benesse-artsite.jp/en/benessehouse; tw/ste from ¥30,000/50,000; 🚭) A stay at this unique Andō-designed hotel-museum is a fabulous experience for art and architecture enthusiasts. Take the monorail to the hilltop 'Oval' wing, where rooms are arranged around a pool of water open to the sky, stay by the sea at a 'Beach' suite, or stick close to the art in the 'Museum' lodgings. Rooms have a clean, modern design and feature artworks from the Benesse collection. Best of all, you can roam around the Benesse House museum whenever the mood takes you.

Eating & Drinking

There are a few cafes in the Art House Project area and near the port at Miyanoura. Not many places open in the evenings and hours can be irregular.

Shioya Diner   Cafe ¥
(シオヤダイナー; dishes ¥400-1000; ⏰9am-9pm, closed Mon; 🛜📱) With rock-and-roll music, retro furniture and kitsch knick-knacks, Shioya is an odd mix of American diner and grandma's kitchen. The menu features tacos and chilli dogs, and they sometimes charcoal-grill Cajun chicken on the barbecue. It's a great place to relax over a coffee or a meal near Miyanoura port.

Cafe Salon Naka-Oku   Cafe, Restaurant ¥
(カフェサロン中奥; ☏892-3887; www.naka-oku.com; lunch from ¥650, dinner ¥380-750; ⏰11.30am-9pm, closed Tue; 📱) Up on a small hill at the rear of a farming plot, Naka-Oku is a good option in the Honmura area, and one of only a couple of places open in the evenings here. It's all wood-beamed warmth and cosiness, with homey specialities like *omuraisu* (fried rice wrapped in a thin omelette topped with sauce) at lunchtime, and small dishes with drinks in the evening.

Genmai-Shinshoku Aisunao   Cafe ¥
(玄米心食あいすなお; http://aisunao.jp; meals ¥600-900; ⏰11am-5.30pm; 🚭📱) 🌿 A tranquil rest stop within the Art House Project area, Aisunao has seating on raised tatami flooring, and a decidedly health-conscious menu – try the tasty Aisunao lunch set, with local brown rice, soup and vegies. Desserts (such as soy-milk ice cream), juices and fair-trade coffees are also on offer. It's around the corner from 'Gokaisho'. Look for the sign with a picture of a bowl of rice.

Cin.na.mon   Curry, Bar ¥
(シナモン; www.cin-na-mon.jp; meals ¥600-1000; ⏰11am-3pm & 5-10pm, closed Mon; 📱) The laid-back team here serve curries, cakes and smoothies by day, and open up the bar (with some light meals and snacks) at night. It's a short walk from the

Miyanoura port. It also has **accommodation** (シナモン; ☏840-8133; www.cin-na-mon. jp; per person incl breakfast ¥4000).

Museum Restaurant Issen
Kaiseki ¥¥¥

(日本料理一扇; ☏892-3223; www.benesse-artsite.jp/en/benessehouse/restaurant_cafe.html; breakfast & lunch from ¥2000, dinner courses from ¥6000; ⊙7.30-9.30am, 11.30am-2.30pm & 6-9.45pm; ⊖📖) The artfully displayed *kaiseki* dinners at this Benesse House basement restaurant are almost too pretty to eat. Courses feature seafood, but there is a veg-dominated option (request a couple of days ahead), and the menu changes with the seasons. Breakfast and lunch are also served. Reservations are recommended.

ⓘ Information

The ATMs at the post offices in Miyanoura and Honmura take international cards. Ask at the tourist office for directions.

Tourist Information Centre (☏892-2299; www.naoshima.net; ⊙8.30am-6pm) In the Marine Station at the Miyanoura ferry port. Has a comprehensive bilingual map of the island (also downloadable from the website), a walking map and a full list of accommodation options.

ⓘ Getting There & Away

Naoshima can be visited as a day trip from Okayama or Takamatsu, and it makes a good stopover if you're travelling between Honshū and Shikoku.

From Okayama, take the JR Uno line to Uno (¥570, about an hour); this usually involves a quick change of trains at Chayamachi. Ferries go to Naoshima's main port of Miyanoura from the port near Uno Station (¥280, 15 to 20 minutes, 13 daily). There are also ferries from Uno to the port of Honmura (¥280, 20 minutes, five daily).

From Takamatsu, ferries run to the port of Miyanoura (¥510, one hour, six to eight daily).

Ferry timetables are on the Naoshima map available on the tourist website, at www1.biz. biglobe.ne.jp/~shikoku (in Japanese), or at the tourist offices in Okayama and Takamatsu.

ⓘ Getting Around

It's possible to get around the main sights on foot. For example, it's just over 2km from Miyanoura port to Honmura and the Art House Project area.

Bicycle

Naoshima is great for cycling. **Cafe Ōgiya Rent-a-Cycle** (☏892-3642; per day ¥500; ⊙9am-7pm, to 6pm Dec-Feb) is inside the Marine Station at the Miyanoura ferry port. A few electric bikes are also available (per day ¥2000).

Chichū Art Museum (p303)

Bus

Minibuses run between Miyanoura, Honmura and Tsutsuji-sō once or twice an hour. It costs ¥100 per ride. From Tsutsuji-sō, there's a free Benesse shuttle, stopping at all the Benesse Art Site museums. In busy seasons buses can fill up quickly, especially towards the end of the day when people are returning to the port to catch ferries. Be sure to check the timetables and allow yourself enough time.

HIROSHIMA 広島

♪082 / POP 1,174,200

To most people, Hiroshima means just one thing. The city's name will forever evoke thoughts of 6 August 1945, when Hiroshima became the target of the world's first atomic-bomb attack. Hiroshima's Peace Memorial Park is a constant reminder of that day, and it attracts visitors from all over the world. But leafy Hiroshima, with its wide boulevards and laid-back friendliness, is a far from depressing place. Present-day Hiroshima is home to a thriving and internationally minded community, and it's worth spending a couple of nights here to experience the city at its vibrant best.

◉ Sights

Most sights can be reached either on foot or with a short tram ride. To catch a tram to the Atomic Bomb Dome and Peace Memorial Park area, hop on tram 2 or 6 at the terminal in front of the station (south exit) and get off at the Genbaku-dōmu-mae stop.

Atomic Bomb Dome　Historic Site
(原爆ドーム, Genbaku Dome; 🚃 Genbaku-dōmu-mae) Perhaps the starkest reminder of the destruction visited upon Hiroshima is the Atomic Bomb Dome, across the river from the Peace Memorial Park. Built by a Czech architect in 1915, the building served as the Industrial Promotion Hall until the bomb exploded almost directly above it. Everyone inside was killed, but the building itself was one of very few left standing anywhere near the epicentre. Despite local misgivings, a decision was taken after the war to preserve the shell of the building as a memorial. Declared a Unesco World Heritage Site in December 1996, the propped-up ruins are floodlit at night, and have become a grim symbol of the city's tragic past.

Peace Memorial Park　Park
(平和記念公園; Heiwa-kōen; 🚃 Genbaku-dōmu-mae) The large, leafy Peace Memorial Park is dotted with memorials, including the **cenotaph** (原爆死没者慰霊碑), which contains the names of all the known victims of the bomb. The cenotaph frames the **Flame of Peace** (平和の灯) at the other end of the pond, and the Atomic Bomb Dome across the river. The Flame of

Monument in the Peace Memorial Park

AME / A.COLLECTIONRF / GETTY IMAGES ©

Peace will only be extinguished once the last nuclear weapon on earth has been destroyed.

Just north of the road through the park is the **Children's Peace Monument** (原爆の子の像), inspired by Sadako Sasaki. When Sadako developed leukaemia at 11 years of age in 1955, she decided to fold 1000 paper cranes. In Japan, the crane is the symbol of longevity and happiness, and she was convinced that if she achieved that target she would recover. She died before reaching her goal, but her classmates folded the rest. The story inspired a nationwide spate of paper-crane folding that continues to this day.

Nearby is the **Korean Atomic Bomb Memorial** (韓国人原爆犠牲者慰霊碑). Many Koreans were shipped over to work as slave labourers during WWII, and Koreans accounted for more than one in 10 of those killed by the atomic bomb. Just north of this memorial is the **Atomic Bomb Memorial Mound** – the ashes of thousands of unclaimed or unidentified victims are interred in a vault below.

There are other monuments throughout the park, and plenty of benches, including along the riverside looking across to the Atomic Bomb Dome, making this a pleasant area to take a break and reflect.

Peace Memorial Museum   Museum

(平和記念資料館; www.pcf.city.hiroshima.jp; admission ¥50; ◷8.30am-5pm, to 6pm Mar-Nov, to 7pm Aug; ◉Genbaku-dōmu-mae or Chūden-mae) The lower floor of Hiroshima's peace museum presents the history of the city and, interestingly, explains the living conditions and sentiment during the war years. Upstairs is a depressing display showing the development of even more destructive weapons in the years since the dropping of the bomb, and rooms filled with items salvaged from the aftermath of the explosion. The displays are confronting and personal – ragged clothes, glasses, a child's melted lunch box – and there are

If You Like…
Historical Towns & Cities

If you like Hiroshima, we think you'll like these other less-visited but interesting towns and cities in western Honshū:

1 OKAYAMA
This western Honshū castle city is home to one of Japan's most famous gardens and a nice collection of art museums. From Hiroshima it's 40 minutes by *shinkansen*.

2 KURASHIKI
Not far from Okayama, this western Honshū city has a fine historic district with canals lined with old *kura* (storehouses). It's 15 minutes from Okayama by train.

3 ONOMICHI
Between Okayama and Hiroshima, this port town on the Inland Sea has a fine temple walk with great views. It's one hour from Hiroshima by train.

some gruesome photographs of victims. Some will find it upsetting, but it's a must-see in Hiroshima. In the corridor on the way out, it's worth taking time to watch the video testimonials of survivors. There are also English-speaking guides within the museum who can offer interesting insights.

Hiroshima National Peace Memorial Hall for the Atomic Bomb Victims   Memorial

(国立広島原爆死没者追悼平和祈念館; www.hiro-tsuitokinenkan.go.jp; 1-6 Nakajima-chō; ◷8.30am-6pm Mar-Nov, to 5pm Dec-Feb, to 7pm Aug; ◉Genbaku-dōmu-mae or Hon-dōri) FREE A walkway circles down into this peaceful, contemplative underground hall of remembrance, where there is a small central fountain. The shape of the fountain represents the time the bomb was dropped (8.15am), while the water

Hiroshima

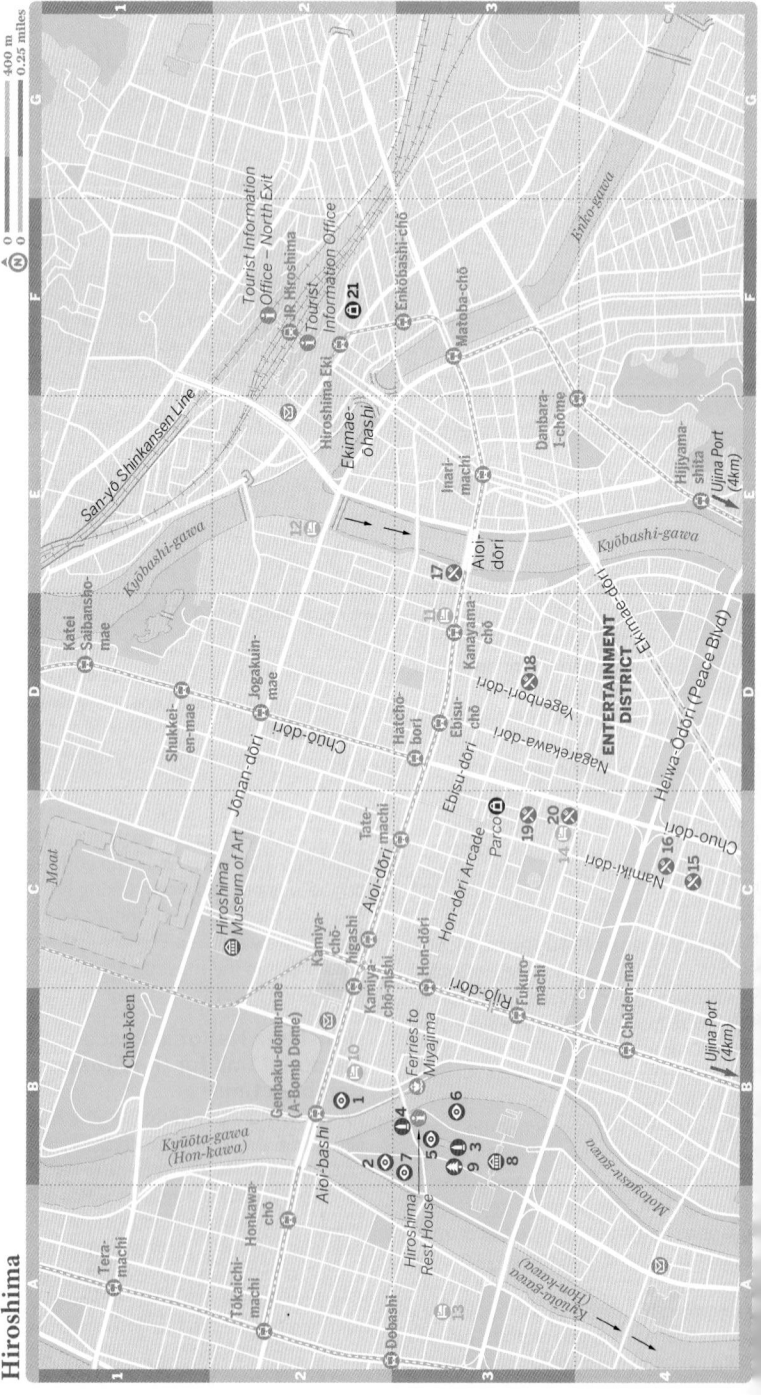

400 m
0.25 miles

Tourist Information
Office – North Exit
JR Hiroshima
Tourist
Information Office

San-yō Shinkansen Line

Hiroshima Eki

Ekimae-
ohashi

Kyōbashi-gawa

Enkō-gawa

Enkōbashi-chō

Matoba-chō

Inari-
machi

Dambara-
1-chōme

Kyōbashi-gawa

Hijiyama-
shita

Ujina Port
(4km)

Aioi-
dōri

Katei
Saibansho-
mae

Shukkei-
en-mae

Jogakuin-
mae

Chūō-dōri

Hiroshima
Museum of Art

Moat

Chūō-kōen

Jonan-dōri

Hatchō-
bori

Ebisu-
bori

Kanayama-
chō

ENTERTAINMENT
DISTRICT

Ebisu-chō

Yagenbori-dōri

Nagarekawa-dōri

Heiwa-Ōdori (Peace Blvd)

Ekimae-dōri

Tate-
machi

Aioi-dōri higashi

Ebisu-dōri

Hon-dōri Arcade

Parco

Hon-dōri

Rijo-dōri

Fukuro-
machi

Namiki-dōri

Chūō-dōri

Chūden-mae

Ujina Port
(4km)

Kamiya-
chō-
higashi

Kamiya-
chō-nishi

Kamiya-
chō

Ferries to
Miyajima

Gembaku-dōmu-mae
(A-Bomb Dome)

Aioi-bashi

Honkawa-
chō

Kyūōta-gawa
(Hon-kawa)

Hiroshima
Rest House

Tera-
machi

Tōkaichi-
machi

Dobashi

Kyūōta-gawa
(Hon-kawa)

Motoyasu-gawa

Hisroshima

◎ Sights
1	Atomic Bomb Dome	B2
2	Atomic Bomb Memorial Mound	B2
3	Cenotaph	B3
4	Children's Peace Monument	B3
5	Flame of Peace	B3
6	Hiroshima National Peace Memorial Hall for the Atomic Bomb Victims	B3
7	Korean Atomic Bomb Victims Memorial	B3
8	Peace Memorial Museum	B3
9	Peace Memorial Park	B3

🛌 Sleeping
10	Hiroshima Inn Aioi	B2
11	Hotel Active!	D3
12	Hotel Flex	E2
13	Ikawa Ryokan	A3
14	Sera Bekkan	C3

✪ Eating
15	Bakudanya	C4
16	Hassei	C4
17	Kaki-tei	E3
18	Nawanai	D3
19	Okonomi-mura	C3
20	Shanti Vegan Cafe	C3

⊚ Shopping
21	Aiyū-ichiba	F2

is an offering of relief to the victims. There is an adjoining room where the names and photographs of atomic-bomb victims are kept, along with evocative testimonies from survivors. The hall was built by architect Tange Kenzō, who also designed the Peace Museum, cenotaph and eternal flame.

🛌 Sleeping

Hiroshima has numerous places to stay in every price bracket. Most accommodation options also have their own bikes for rent (around ¥500 per day).

Ikawa Ryokan
Ryokan ¥
(いかわ旅館; 📞231-5058; www.ikawaryokan. net; 5-11 Dobashi-chō; s/tw from ¥4725/9450; @ 🛜; 🚋Dobashi) On a quiet side street, this is a large, family-run, hotel-style ryokan with three connected wings. There are Japanese- and Western-style rooms, all very clean, and most have private bathrooms (though there's also a large public bath). Wi-fi in the lobby.

Hotel Active!
Hotel ¥¥
(ホテルアクティブ！広島; 📞212-0001; www. hotel-active.com/hiroshima; 15-3 Nobori-chō; s/d incl breakfast from ¥5980/7875; ⊖ @; 🚋Kanayama-chō) This chic hotel has designer couches, satiny coverlets and extra-comfy desk chairs. It's right in the heart of things – within stumbling distance of bars and restaurants – and the bejewelled staff are pleasant. A buffet-style breakfast is included, making this a good-value option.

Sera Bekkan
Ryokan ¥¥
(世羅別館; 📞248-2251; www.yado.to; 4-20 Mikawa-chō; per person with/without meals from ¥12,600/8400; ⊖ @; 🚋Ebisu-chō) Off Namiki-dōri is this traditional ryokan with good-sized tatami rooms, large baths, a peaceful garden and great hospitality. Look for the dark-red-brick building on a corner across from a small car park.

Hotel Flex
Hotel ¥¥
(ホテルフレックス; 📞223-1000; www.hotel-flex.co.jp; 7-1 Kaminobori-chō; s/d incl breakfast from ¥6825/11,550; ⊖ @) Curves and concrete are the features at this designer hotel in a great spot on the river. Rooms are light with large windows; naturally, the ones on the river side of the building have the views. There's a bright, breezy cafe downstairs and a light breakfast.

Hiroshima Inn Aioi
Ryokan ¥¥¥
(広島の宿相生; 📞247-9331; www.galilei.ne.jp/ aioi; 1-3-14 Ōtemachi; per person with meals from ¥19,900; 🚋Genbaku-dōmu-mae) Kick back in your split-toe socks and *yukata* and enjoy city and park views from your room, or from the large bath on the 7th floor. The meals are an elaborate traditional spread of dishes, and you can opt for breakfast or dinner only. Friendly staff speak just a little English, but they do their best to manage.

Eating

Hiroshima is famous for oysters and *okonomiyaki* (savoury pancakes; batter and cabbage, with vegetables and sea-food or meat cooked on a griddle), served Hiroshima-style with individual layers and noodles. You'll come across plenty of places serving both. If you're looking for groceries and cheap eats, check out **Aiyū-ichiba marketplace** (愛友市場; I You Mart; www.iu-mart.jp).

Hassei
Okonomiyaki ¥

(八誠; 4-17 Fujimi-chō; dishes ¥450-1200; 🕐11.30am-2pm & 5.30-11pm, dinner only Sun, closed Mon; 🏧; 🚃Chūden-mae) The walls of this popular *okonomiyaki* specialist are covered with the signatures and messages of famous and not-so-famous visitors. Unless you're a sumō wrestler, you'll probably find a half-order more than enough to be getting on with at lunchtime. It's one block south of Heiwa-Ōdōri.

Okonomi-mura
Okonomiyaki ¥

(お好み村; 2nd-4th fl, 5-13 Shintenchi; dishes ¥700-1000; 🕐11am-2am; 🏧; 🚃Ebisu-chō) Twenty-five stalls spread over three floors, all of them serving up hearty variations of tasty *okonomiyaki* – this Hiroshima institution is a great place to get acquainted with the local speciality, and chat with the cooks over a hot griddle. It's in a building off Chūō-dōri, on the opposite side of the square to Parco.

Bakudanya
Noodles ¥

(ばくだん屋; www.bakudanya.net; 6-13 Fujimi-chō; noodles ¥680-1000; 🕐11.30am-midnight; 🏧; 🚃Chūden-mae) Come to this simple street-corner eatery to try another famous Hiroshima dish: *tsukemen,* a *rāmen*-like dish in which noodles and soup come separately. This is the original outlet; the chain has now spread across the country. A *nami* (medium-sized) serving of *tsukemen* is ¥780. Look for the green awning on the corner.

Left: Atomic Bomb Dome (p306);
Below: Paper cranes on display at the Peace Memorial Park (p306)
(LEFT) AME / A.COLLECTIONRF / GETTY IMAGES ©: (BELOW) LOU JONES / GETTY IMAGES ©

Shanti
Vegan Cafe   Vegan ¥

(ヴィーガンカフェ; www.shanti-yoga.
net; 2nd fl, Mondano Bldg, 2-20 Mikawa-chō;
lunch/dinner from ¥850/1500; ⊙11.30am-
9.30pm; ⊝🌱📵; 🚉Ebisu-chō) 🌿 Eat
hearty vegan and vegetarian meals
and cakes at this simple cafe beneath
a yoga studio. Locally sourced organic
vegetables go into tasty, thoughtfully
prepared dishes featuring pasta, brown
rice, burgers and salads. It's around the
corner from Sera Bekkan.

Nawanai   Izakaya ¥

(なわない; Fujimi Bldg, 12-10 Kanayama-chō;
⊙6pm-midnight; 🚉Kanayama-chō) In a basement and through a wooden door is this
welcoming izakaya, where you can mingle
with locals over fresh fish and a range of
local sakes. Try ko-iwashi (baby sardines),
available either as sashimi or delicious
tempura (¥600). There's a basic English
menu. From Aioi-dōri, go down Yagenbori-
dōri and take the fourth left; look up and
left for the sign in Japanese.

Kaki-tei   Seafood ¥¥

(牡蠣亭; 📞221-8990; www.kakitei.jp; 11
Hashimoto-chō; lunch/dinner from ¥1000/3800;
⊙11.30am-2.30pm & 5-10pm, closed Tue & 1st
& 3rd Wed of month; 📵; 🚉Kanayama-chō)
Come to this intimate bistro on the river-
bank for oysters prepared in a variety
of mouth-watering ways. There are also
oyster sets at lunch and dinner. Look for
the green noren and the words 'Oyster
Conclave'.

ⓘ Information

Money

Higashi Post Office has ATMs that accept
international cards and has currency-
exchange services. ATMs in 7-Elevens also take
international cards. Hiroshima Rest House
tourist information centre has a list of banks and
post offices that change money and travellers
cheques.

Post

Higashi Post Office (広島東郵便局; **2-62 Matsubara-chō;** ⏰9am-7pm Mon-Fri, to 5pm Sat, to 12.30pm Sun) The post office most convenient to the station.

Tourist Information

Tourist Information Office (観光案内所; ☎261-1877; ⏰9am-5.30pm) Inside the station near the south exit. There is another branch at the north exit (☎263-6822; ⏰9am-5.30pm).

Hiroshima Rest House (広島市平和記念公園レストハウス; ☎247-6738; www.mk-kousan. co.jp/rest-house; 1-1 Nakajima-machi; ⏰9.30am-6pm Apr-Jul & Sep, to 5pm Oct-Mar, to 7pm Aug; 🚊Genbaku-dōmu-mae) In Peace Memorial Park, next to Motoyasu-bashi. Offers the most comprehensive information about the city and the island of Miyajima.

ℹ️ Getting There & Away

Air

Hiroshima Airport (www.hij.airport.jp) is 40km east of the city, with limousine bus connections to/from Hiroshima Station (¥1300, 48 minutes), operating from 8.20am to 9.40pm.

Tram Passes

If you'll be taking at least four tram trips in a day, get a One-Day Trip Card, which allows unlimited travel for ¥600. A one-day card that covers trams plus return ferry to Miyajima is ¥840. The Two-Days Trip Card is a good deal at ¥2000, covering tram rides, ferry, and ticket for the ropeway on Miyajima (which normally costs ¥1800 return or ¥1000 one way). Buy passes from the tram terminal at the station, from the conductors on board (one-day cards only) or at various hotels and hostels.

Train

Hiroshima Station is on the JR San-yō line, which passes through and westwards to Shimonoseki. It's also a major stop on the Tokyo–Osaka–Hakata *shinkansen* line. Example *shinkansen* fares from Hiroshima:

Hakata ¥8190, 1¼ hours

Osaka ¥9440, 1½ hours

Tokyo ¥17,540, four hours

ℹ️ Getting Around

Tram

Hiroshima has an extensive tram service that will get you almost anywhere you want to go for a flat fare of ¥150. You pay by dropping the fare into the machine by the driver as you get off the tram. If you have to change trams to get to your destination, you should ask for a *norikae-ken* (transfer ticket). Daily tram passes are also available and convenient if you're taking a few tram rides.

MIYAJIMA 宮島

☎0829 / POP 1970

The small island of Miyajima is a Unesco World Heritage Site and one of Japan's most visited tourist spots. Its star attraction is the oft-photographed vermilion torii of Itsukushima-jinja, which seems to float on the waves at high tide – a scene that has traditionally been ranked as one of the three best views in Japan. Besides this feted view, Miyajima has some good hikes, temples, and cheeky deer that rove the streets and will snatch anything out of the hands of unsuspecting tourists.

Turn right as you emerge from the ferry terminal and follow the waterfront for 10 minutes to get to the shrine. The shopping street, packed with souvenir outlets and restaurants, as well as the world's largest *shakushi* (rice scoop), is a block back from the waterfront.

◎ Sights

Allow a few hours to wander around the sights; more if you plan on hiking Misen (p314). Ideally, try to stay overnight on

Miyajima

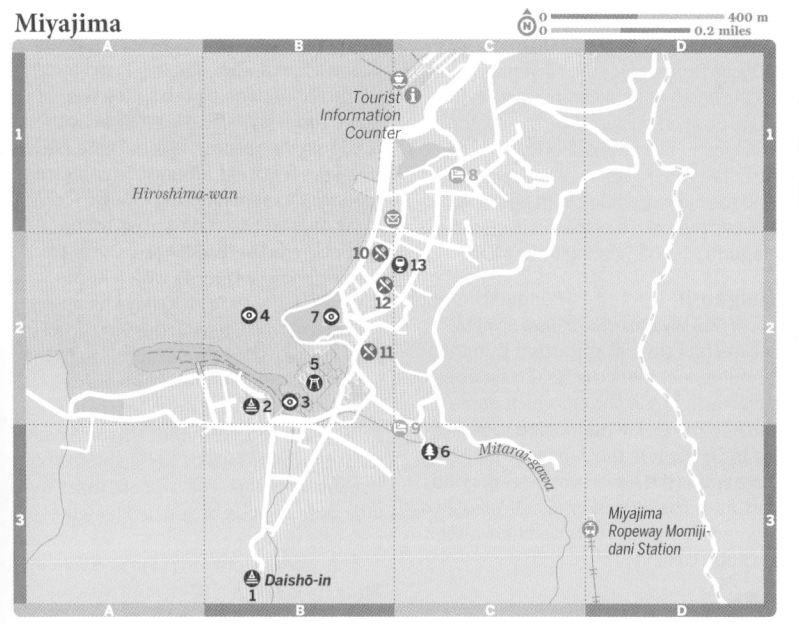

Miyajima

◎ Don't Miss Sights
1 Daishō-in B3

◎ Sights
2 Daigan-ji B2
3 Floating Nō Stage B2
4 Floating Torii B2
5 Itsukushima-jinja B2
6 Momiji-dani-kōen C3
7 Senjō-kaku B2

🛏 Sleeping
8 Guest House Kikugawa C1
9 Iwasō Ryokan C3

⊗ Eating
10 Mame-tanuki B2
11 Sarasvati B2
12 Yakigaki-no-hayashi B2

⊖ Drinking & Nightlife
13 Kaki-ya C2

the island to experience it in the quiet of the evening, and for photos of the 'floating torii' at sunset.

Itsukushima-jinja　Shinto Shrine

厳島神社; 1-1 Miyajima-chō; admission ¥300; ⊙6.30am-6pm Mar–mid-Oct, to 5.30pm mid-Oct–Nov, Jan & Feb, to 5pm Dec) Going back as far as the late 6th century, Itsukushima-jinja gives the island its real name. The shrine's present form dates from 1168, when it was rebuilt under the patronage of Taira no Kiyomori, head of the doomed Heike clan. Its pierlike construction is a result of the

island's holy status: commoners were not allowed to set foot on the island and had to approach the shrine by boat through the **floating torii** (大鳥居) out in the bay. Much of the time, however, the shrine and torii are surrounded by mud: to get the classic view of the torii that adorns the brochures, you'll need to come at high tide.

On one side of the floating shrine is a **floating nō stage** (能舞台), built by local lord Asano Tsunanaga in 1680 and still used for nō (stylised dance-drama) performances every year from 16 to 18 April.

313

Senjō-kaku
Pavilion

(1-1 Miyajima-chō; admission ¥100; ⏰8.30am-4.30pm) Dominating the hill immediately to the north of Itsukushima-jinja is this huge pavilion built in 1587 by Toyotomi Hideyoshi. The atmospheric hall is constructed with massive pillars and beams, and the ceiling is hung with paintings. It looks out onto a colourful five-storey **pagoda** (五重塔) dating from 1407.

Daigan-ji
Buddhist Temple

(大願寺; 3 Miyajima-chō; ⏰9am-5pm) Miyajima has several important Buddhist temples, including the 1201 Daigan-ji, just south of the shrine, which dates back to the Heian period and is dedicated to Benzaiten, the Japanese name for Saraswati (the Hindu goddess of good fortune). The seated image of Yakushi Nyorai here is said to have been carved by Kōbō Daishi.

 Activities

Misen
Walking, Ropeway

(弥山; http://miyajima-ropeway.info; ropeway 1-way/return ¥1000/1800; ⏰ropeway 9am-5pm) Covered with primeval forest, the sacred, peaceful Misen is Miyajima's highest mountain (530m), and its ascent is the island's finest walk. You can avoid most of the uphill climb by taking the two-stage **ropeway**, which leaves you with a 20-minute walk to the top. There are monkeys and deer around the cable-car station, and some fantastic views – on clear days you can see across to the mountain ranges of Shikoku. Close to the summit is a **temple** where Kōbō Daishi meditated for 100 days following his return from China in the 9th century. Next to the main temple hall close to the summit is a flame that's been burning continually since Kōbō Daishi lit it 1200 years ago. From the temple, a path leads down the hillside to Daishō-in and Itsukushima-jinja. The descent takes a little over an hour, or you can take the ropeway down.

The ropeway station (Momiji-dani Station), is about a 10-minute walk on from **Momiji-dani-kōen** (紅葉谷公園; **Momiji-dani Park**), or a few minutes on the free shuttle bus, which runs every 20 minutes from a stop near Iwasō Ryokan. A four-hour hike of Misen is detailed in Lonely Planet's *Hiking in Japan*.

View from Mt Misen

314

⭐ Don't Miss
Daishō-in

Just south of town at the foot of Misen, Daishō-in is a worthwhile stopping point on the way up or down the mountain. This Shingon temple is crowded with interesting things to look at: from Buddhist images and prayer wheels to sharp-beaked *tengu* (birdlike demons) and a cave containing images from each of the 88 Shikoku pilgrimage temples.

NEED TO KNOW
大聖院; 210 Miyajima-chō; ⏰8am-5pm

🛏 Sleeping

It's well worth staying on the island as you'll be able to enjoy the evening quiet after the day trippers have left. The **Miyajima Hotel Directory** (www4.ocn.ne.jp/~miyayado) has a list of the island's accommodation.

Guest House Kikugawa　Ryokan ¥¥
ゲストハウス菊がわ; ☏44-0039; www.kikugawa.ne.jp; 796 Miyajima-chō; s/tw from ¥6500/11,600; 🚭@🛜) This charming inn is built in traditional style and has lovely wooden interiors. There are Western- and

Japanese-style rooms, all with attached bathrooms. The tatami rooms are slightly larger and one has a loftlike bedroom. Meals are available. Heading inland from the ferry terminal, you'll walk through a tunnel; turn right after this and look for Kikugawa on the left opposite Zonkō-ji (存光寺) temple.

Iwasō Ryokan　Ryokan ¥¥¥
(岩惣; ☏44-2233; www.iwaso.com; Momiji-dani Miyajima-chō; per person with 2 meals ¥20,100-42,150; @) The Iwasō, open since 1854, offers the grand ryokan experience in exquisite gardens. It's especially stunning in

autumn when Momiji-dani (Maple Valley) explodes with colour. There are three wings: a stay in a lovely 'Hanare' cottage will set you back the most. Not all rooms have private bathrooms, but you can soak in the onsen in the main building. It's about 15 minutes to walk from the ferry port, or call and they will pick you up.

Eating & Drinking

There are plenty of places to eat along and around the main strip, where you can try the local oysters, as well as eel in various guises (on rice, or perhaps in a steamed bun). It's often very busy and at some places you may have to wait to get a seat. Just one street back from the main strip is the much quieter Machiya-dōri, with a few cafes and eateries. Most restaurants shut down after the crowds go home.

Sarasvati   Cafe ¥
(http://sarasvati.jp; 407 Miyajima-chō; lunch ¥1280; ☺8.30am-8pm; 🖥) The aroma of roasting coffee beans lures people into this cafe inside a former storehouse building from the early 1900s. Bare wooden floors and tables match a simple menu of traditional coffees (¥350-550; no frappuccinos here), cakes and the one pasta-set option for lunch.

Yakigaki-no-hayashi   Seafood ¥¥
(焼がきのはやし; 🕿44-0335; www.yakigaki-no-hayashi.co.jp; 505-1 Miyajima-chō; dishes ¥700-1400; ☺10.30am-5pm, closed Wed; 🖥) The oysters in the tank and on the barbecue outside are what everyone is eating here. Try a plate of nama-gaki (raw oysters) or kaki-furai (crumbed, fried oysters) for ¥1300. It's not all about the slimy shell-dwellers – there are other meals, such as udon sets, on offer too.

Mame-tanuki   Izakaya ¥¥
(まめたぬき; 🕿44-2131; 1113 Miyajima-chō; ☺11am-3.30pm & 5-11pm, closed dinner

Tue; 🖥) At this friendly place there's a floor-level wooden counter, with a space to dangle your legs underneath. By day there are lunch sets, such as anago meshi (steamed conger eel with rice; ¥1575) and fried oysters, and at night Mame-tanuki is one of the few places open late, serving drinks and izakaya-style dishes. There's no smoking in the evening. Look for the large blue sign with white writing.

Kaki-ya   Seafood
(牡蠣屋; 🕿44-2747; www.kaki-ya.jp; 539 Miyajima-chō; oysters ¥1000-2000; ☺10am-6pm) Kaki-ya is a sophisticated oyster bar on the main street. It serves delicious local oysters freshly grilled on the barbecue by the entrance, along with beers and wines by the glass.

ℹ️ Information

Tourist Information Counter (宮島観光案内所; 🕿44-2011; www.miyajima.or.jp; ☺9am-5pm) Inside the ferry terminal.

ℹ️ Getting There & Away

Miyajima is accessed by ferry, and is often visited as a day trip from Hiroshima.

The mainland ferry terminal is a short walk from Miyajima-guchi Station on the JR San-yō line, halfway between Hiroshima (¥400, 27 minutes) and Iwakuni (¥170, 10 minutes). The ferry terminal can also be reached by tram 2 from Hiroshima (¥270, 70 minutes), which runs from Hiroshima Station, passing Genbaku Dome on the way. Ferries shuttle regularly across to the island from Miyajima-guchi (¥170, 10 minutes). JR Pass holders should use the one operated by JR.

High-speed ferries (¥1800, 30 minutes, six to eight daily) operate direct to Miyajima from Hiroshima's Ujina port. Another option is to take a ferry directly from Peace Memorial Park in central Hiroshima (¥1900, 45 minutes, eight to 12 daily; the return trip costs ¥1500). These boats cruise under the bridges of Kyūōta-gawa before coming out into the bay towards Miyajima No reservation is required.

The Best of the Rest

Niseko (p318)
The roof of Hokkaidō offers some of the best hiking in Japan and plenty of onsen (hot spring) to soak in after your hikes.

Daisetsuzan National Park (p320)
Soaring mountains, active volcanoes, remote onsen, clear lakes and dense forest.

Iya Valley (p322)
Deep in the mountainous heart of Shikoku island, Iya Valley is a chance to step back in time to a simpler Japan and stay in a traditional rural house.

Nagasaki (p325)
Best known for its tragic fate in WWII, Nagasaki is a vibrant city that has played a major role in Japanese history for centuries.

Southwest Islands (p330)
The tropical south of Japan is pure cognitive dissonance: you'll often find yourself wondering, 'Is this Thailand or Japan?'

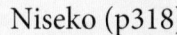

Top: Turtle in the shallows off Aka-jima;
Bottom: Pagoda in Naha, Okinawa-hontō

TOP: ROBERTMALLON.NET / GETTY IMAGES ©;
BOTTOM: CHRISTIAN KOBER / GETTY IMAGES ©

Niseko

♪0136 / POP 4650

HIGHLIGHTS

1. **Niseko United (p318)** Some of the most reliable lift-served powder skiing on earth.

2. **Hilton Niseko (p319)** Arguably the best accommodation in the area.

3. **Onsen (p318)** Nothing – and we mean nothing – beats a soak in a hot spring after a day on the slopes.

Niseko Annupuri
SHAYNE HILL XTREME VISUALS / GETTY IMAGES ©

Hokkaidō is dotted with world-class ski resorts, but the reigning prince of powder is unquestionably Niseko (ニセコ). There are four interconnected resorts with more than 800 skiable hectares along the eastern side of the mountain Niseko Annupuri. Soft and light powdery snow and an annual average snowfall of more than 15m make Niseko extremely popular with international skiers.

 Activities

Niseko United Skiing, Snowboarding
(ニセコユナイテッド; www.niseko.ne.jp/en; 8hr/1-day pass ¥4900/5900; ☺8.30am-9.30pm Nov-Apr) Niseko United is the umbrella name for four resorts, namely Niseko Annupuri, Niseko Village, Grand Hirafu and Hanazono. What makes Niseko United stand out from the competition is that you can ski or snowboard on all four slopes by purchasing a single all-mountain pass. This electronic tag gives you access to 18 lifts and gondolas, 60 runs, as well as free rides on the inter-mountain shuttle bus. If you're planning on skiing for several days, a week or even the season, you can also buy discounted multiday passes.

Onsen Options Onsen
Niseko has a brochure with 25 onsen options in the area, be they for use in winter or summer. Prices are generally around ¥500 to ¥700 per person. Winter visitors may like to opt for luxury at the Hilton Niseko Village (¥1000) or at the Niseko Grand Hotel (¥700), while those with their own wheels in summer will love Niimi Onsen (¥500) and Goshiki Onsen (¥600), both away in the mountains to the west of Niseko Annupuri and its skifields.

Sleeping

Niseko proper is spread out along the base of the four slopes. The closer you get to the slopes themselves, the more options you'll have. Hirafu and Annupuri host the vast majority of accommodation, while Niseko Village is centred on the upmarket Hilton. Most places will provide pick-up and drop-off for the slopes in winter, or you can take buses and shuttles to move about. It's strongly recommended that you book well in advance in winter.

Yumoto Niseko Prince Hotel
Hotel ¥¥¥

(湯元ニセコプリンスホテルひらふ亭; ☎23-2239; http://hirafutei.info/en; per person incl 2 meals from ¥11,760; P @ 🛜) If you're after comfort and convenience in the heart of Hirafu, this is it. You can virtually ski in the front door, there are both Western- and Japanese-style rooms and the onsen is tops. Excellent buffet meals will keep you more than happy.

Hilton Niseko
Resort ¥¥¥

(ニセコヒルトンヴィレジ; ☎44-1111; www.placeshilton.com/niseko-village; r from ¥20,000; P @ 🛜 🧍) There is no shortage of resort hotels in Niseko, though the Hilton enjoys the best location of all – it is quite literally attached to the Niseko Gondola. As you might expect from the name, spacious Western-style rooms at the Hilton are complemented by a whole slew of amenities spread out across a self-contained village. Check the website before arriving as special deals are usually available, which combine discounted room rates with breakfast and dinner buffets.

Annupuri Village
Chalet ¥¥¥

(アンヌプリ・ヴィレジ; ☎59-2111; www.annupurivillage.com; Niseko Annupuri; chalets for 2-10 people from ¥21,000-110,000; P @ 🛜) If you're travelling with a large group of friends, consider giving the resort hotels a pass and renting an immaculate ski chalet in Annupuri Village, located at the base of the Annupuri ski slopes. Natural hardwoods and picture windows are featured prominently from floor to ceiling, while rich stone fireplaces, spa-quality bathroom fixtures, professional kitchens and plasma TVs add a touch of modern class.

🍴 Eating & Drinking

Many of the lodges and ryokan offer great meals cooked to order, and the slopes have plenty of snacks, pizza, *rāmen* (egg noodles) and other goodies. After hours, things are tricky because lodging is spread out and buses are inconvenient, but there are plenty of watering holes in Hirafu.

Graubunden
Cafe ¥

(グラウビュンデン; ☎23-3371; www.graubunden.jp; ⏰8am-7pm Fri-Wed) Seriously good sandwiches, cakes, cookies and drinks in Hirafu East Village. A local favourite that has been open 20 years, Graubunden is the perfect spot to chill out with good service and a relaxed atmosphere.

Jojo's Café & Restaurant
Cafe ¥

(ジョジョズカフェ; ☎23-2220; www.nac-web.com/niseko/cafe.html; mains from ¥750; ⏰lunch & dinner; 🍴) Excellent casual dining to be had at the Niseko Adventure Centre (NAC). We're talking burgers, salads, pasta and tacos, and stupendous views of Yotei-zan from out on the terrace on a good day.

ℹ️ Information

At the base of the ski slopes lie several towns and villages that compose Niseko's population centre. Most of the restaurants and bars are clustered together in Hirafu (ひらふ), while Annupuri (アンヌプリ), Niseko Village (ニセコビレッジ) and Hanazono (花園) are much quieter and less developed. Further east are Kutchan (倶知安) and Niseko (ニセコ) proper, which are more permanent population centres that remain decidedly Japanese.

Niseko Tourist Information (ニセコ観光案内所; ☎44-2468; www.nisekotourism.com; ⏰9am-6pm) Has offices at JR Niseko Station and at the View Plaza Michi-no-Eki on Rte 66 heading into town. They have pamphlets, maps, bus timetables and help with bookings.

ℹ️ Getting There & Away

Bus

During the ski season, both **Chūō Bus** (☎011-231-0500; www.chuo-bus.co.jp) and **Dōnan Bus** (☎0123-46-5701; www.donanbus.co.jp) run regular highway uses from JR Sapporo Station and New Chitose Airport to Niseko. The trip takes around three hours depending on road conditions, costs ¥2300 (return ¥3850) and drops off at the welcome centre in Hirafu before continuing on to the Hilton and Annupuri. Reservations are necessary, and it's recommended that you book well ahead of your departure date. If you don't speak Japanese, ask the staff at the tourist information centres or your accommodation to make a reservation for you.

Car & Motorcycle

Scenic Rte 5 winds from Sapporo to Otaru around the coast, and then cuts inland through the mountains down to Niseko. Having a car will make it easier to move between the various ski slopes, though drive with extreme caution as fatalities have tragically occurred here in the past. In the summer (low season), public-transport services drop off, which provides more incentive to pick up a car in Sapporo or at New Chitose Airport.

Train

While there is a JR Hirafu Station, it is far from the town itself, and is not well serviced by local buses. From JR Niseko and JR Kutchan Stations, you will need to switch to local buses to access the villages at the base of the ski slopes. For these reasons, it's recommended that you travel to Niseko via highway bus or car. If, however, the bus lines are fully booked, trains run on the JR Hakodate line between Sapporo and Niseko (¥2400, two hours) via Kutchan (¥2090, 1¾ hours).

ℹ Getting Around

There are twice-hourly local buses linking JR Kutchan and JR Niseko Stations to Hirafu, Niseko Village, Annupuri and Hanazono. Pick up a schedule from the tourist information centres so that you don't miss your connection. Also, if you've purchased an all-mountain pass, you can ride the free hourly shuttle bus between the villages.

Daisetsuzan National Park

HIGHLIGHTS

1 **Hiking (p321)** Hike across the roof of Hokkaidō.

2 **Asahidake Onsen (p321)** A great entry to the park and some fantastic hot springs.

3 **Asahidake Ropeway (p321)** Get up into the mountains without breaking a sweat.

Asahi-dake, Daisetsuzan National Park
GAVIN HELLIER / GETTY IMAGES ©

Known as 'Nutakukamushupe' in Ainu, Daisetsuzan (大雪山国立公園; Big Snow Mountain) is Japan's largest national park, designated in 1934 and covering more than 2300 sq km. A vast wilderness area of soaring mountains, active volcanoes, remote onsen, clear lakes and dense forests, Daisetsuzan is the kind of place that stressed-out workers in Tokyo and Osaka dream about on their daily commute.

Virtually untouched by human hands, the park has minimal tourism, with most visitors basing themselves in the hot-spring villages on the periphery. The three main access points into the park are Asahidake Onsen in the northwest, Sōunkyō Onsen in the northeast and Tokachi-dake Onsen in the southwest.

Asahidake Onsen
旭岳温泉

☑ 0166

This forested hot-springs village, at 1100m above sea level, has a few small inns at the base of Asahi-dake, Hokkaidō's tallest peak. There are plenty of hiking options and healing onsen for afterwards.

Most onsen, even at the higher-end hotels, are open to the general public for day use. Prices range from ¥500 up to ¥1500.

Be prepared. There are no ATMs, shops or restaurants at Asahidake Onsen, so you'll need to have cash, and food sorted out if you are going camping or contemplating taking on the Grand Traverse. If you are staying, order meals at your accommodation house when you book.

Activities

Asahidake Ropeway
Ropeway

(旭岳 ロープウェイ; ☑ 68-9111; http://wakasaresort.com/eng/; 1 way/return 1 Jun–20 Oct ¥1600/2800, 21 Oct–31 May ¥1100/1800; ⏰ 6am-5.30pm Jul–mid-Oct, 9am-4pm mid-Oct–Jun) This ropeway runs from Asahidake Onsen (1100m) up to Sugatami (姿見) at 1600m, making **Asahi-dake** (旭岳; 2290m) a very feasible day hike. There are all sorts of hiking options. The ropeway runs year-round and the area is popular with backcountry types and with hard-core skiers and snowboarders through winter.

Sleeping

Lodge Nutapukaushipe Lodge ¥¥

(ロッジ・ヌタプカウシペ; ☑ 97-2150; r per person with 2 meals from ¥7500) 🍃 This log-cabin-style accommodation is an excellent choice, run by a real character who

Hiking in Daisetsuzan National Park

There are a lot of options for hiking in the national park, ranging from half-day trips to the Daisetsuzan Grand Traverse, a hard-core five- to seven-day, 55km hike the length of the park.

Get a copy of Shōbunsha's *Yama-to-Kōgen Chizu Map 3: Daisetsuzan* (昭文社 山と高原地図３大雪山), be prepared, and check the weather forecast. Visitor-centre staff will be more than happy to update you on conditions.

The season for this hike runs from early July to October. A tent and camping gear may be preferable to the extremely bare-bones huts. You'll need to carry in your own food and cooking supplies. This is also bear country, so be smart and tie a bell to your rucksack.

You could start at either Asahidake Onsen or Sōunkyō Onsen and you'll finish at Tokachi-dake Onsen. Pick up a copy of Lonely Planet's *Hiking in Japan*, do your homework before you go, and make the most of this adventure!

has handcrafted most of the furniture and fittings from local timber. The onsen is superb, as are the meals. You'll have to make a bit of an effort though as there isn't a website. Pick up the phone. You won't be disappointed.

Hotel Beamonte Hotel ¥¥¥
(ホテルベアモンテ; ☎ 97-2321; www.bearmonte.jp; r per person with 2 meals from ¥10,650; 🅿 @ 🛜) Across from the visitors centre, this is Asahidake's most upmarket accommodation. Modelled after an alpine chalet, the Beamonte combines elegant rooms (some with polished wooden floors) and a stunner of an onsen, offering a variety of indoor and outdoor rock tubs. Prices vary substantially depending on the season, and it can be quite full at times; calling ahead is a good plan. Visiting the bath only is possible for ¥1500.

ℹ️ Information

Asahidake Visitors Centre (旭岳ビジターセンター; ☎ 97-2153; www.town.higashikawa.hokkaido.jp/vc; ⊙ 9am-5pm Jun-Oct, to 4pm Nov-May) Hikers should pay a visit to this centre, which has excellent maps that the staff will mark with daily track conditions. If you're heading out on a long hike, inform them of your intentions. An onsen map is also available here, which lists the locations, prices and hours of the various baths.

ℹ️ Getting There & Away

There are three buses in both directions daily between bus stop 4 in front of JR Asahikawa Station and Asahidake Onsen (¥1320, 1½ hours). The first bus leaves Asahikawa at 9.25am, returning from Asahidake Onsen at 11am.

Iya Valley

HIGHLIGHTS

① **Staying in a traditional Japanese house (p324)** Sample the life of a rural Shikoku village

② **Iya Onsen (p324)** Take a cable car down to this impossibly scenic onsen.

③ **Chiiori (p324)** The original Chiiori Trust house is still the most spectacular.

Milling buckwheat grain, Iya Valley
ANTONY GIBLIN / GETTY IMAGES ©

The spectacular Iya Valley (祖谷渓) is a special place, its staggeringly steep gorges and thick mountain forests luring travellers to seek respite from the hectic 'mainland' lifestyle. Winding your way around narrow cliff-hanging roads as the icy blue water of the Yoshino-gawa shoots along the ancient valley floors is a blissful travel experience. The active soul can pick up some of the country's finest hiking trails around Tsurugi-san or try world-class whitewater rafting in the Ōboke and Koboke Gorges.

Ōboke & Koboke
大歩危・小歩危

Ōboke and Koboke are two scenic gorges on the Yoshino-gawa, which fluctuates from languid green waters to Class IV rapids. Driving through these rural river valleys provides the first verdant glimpse into the magic of Iya.

Spectacular scenery abounds in the deep canyons along Old Rte 32 – infrequent public buses (¥880, 55 minutes, 7:15am, 10:15am and 12:15pm) ply this narrow route between Awa-Ikeda and the Iya Valley.

To orient yourself in this maze of valleys, stop by **Lapis Ōboke** (ラピス大歩危; ☎0883-84-1489; www.yamashiro-info.jp/lapis; admission ¥500; ⏰9am-5pm Apr-Nov, to 5pm Dec-Mar) for basic tourist information. Its primary role is as a geology and local *yōkai* (ghost) museum – skip the rocks, but get acquainted with the folkloric apparitions, colourfully represented in a hall of delightful horrors (explained with some English signage).

South of Ikeda on Rte 32 between Koboke and Ōboke, around 20 companies run white-water rafting and kayaking trips from April to late November. **Happy Raft** (ハッピーラフト; ☎0887-75-0500; www.happyraft.com) steps from JR Tosa Iwahara Station, operates sensational daily trips with English-speaking guides (half day ¥5500 to ¥7500, full day ¥10,000 to ¥15,500).

Iya Onsen (祖谷温泉; ☎0883-75-2311; www.iyaonsen.co.jp; Matsuo Matsumoto 367-2; ¥1500; ⏰7am-9pm, to 7pm Jan-Feb) on Old Rte 32, is a great place to warm up after a chilling plunge through white water. A cable car descends a steep cliff face to some sulphurous open-air baths overlooking the river, and accommodation (per person with meals from ¥15,270) is available.

Stop by the tourist complex **River Station West-West** (☎0887-84-1117; www.west-west.com) for river gear at the Mont Bell shop, road snacks and pit stops at the *conbini* (convenience store) and excellent *soba* (buckwheat noodles) at the restaurant **Momiji-tei** (もみじ亭; ☎0883-84-1117; meals ¥900-2000; ⏰10am-5:30pm Thu-Tue) – try the *tempura soba* set (¥1400), either hot or cold.

Ōboke gorge
ISAO KURODA / GETTY IMAGES ©

Chiiori

High on a mountainside in the remote Iya Valley, looking out over forested hillsides and plunging gorges, is one of Japan's most unusual places to stay. **Chiiori** (📞0883-88-5290; www.chiiori.org; per person depending on group size ¥10,000-20,000) – 'The Cottage of the Flute' – is a once-abandoned 18th-century thatched-roof farmhouse that has been painstakingly restored towards its original brilliance. Unlike many such examples of cultural heritage in Japan, where concrete and plastic have wrecked the architectural aesthetic, here glistening red-pine floorboards surround open-floor hearths under soaring rafters.

Set amid steep hillsides dotted by thatched houses and forests strewn with narrow mountain paths, Iya was for centuries an example of an untouched coexistence of man and nature, albeit one that offered residents little hope of wealth and comfort.

In recent decades, however, the locals' traditional lifestyle and the balance with the environment have been rapidly upset; employment moved from agriculture to government-subsidised and frequently pointless construction, the effects of which – eg paved riverbeds – can be seen from almost any roadside. Lately, efforts have been made to promote sustainable, community-based tourism and realise the financial potential of traditional life – which until recently many locals saw as backward and valueless. It is a work in progress – many thatched roofs in the area are still hidden by corrugated-tin sheets – but by adding to the growing number of tourists visiting the area, largely because of the work of those involved in Chiiori, staying here helps to encourage those conservation efforts.

The house was bought as a ruin by the author and aesthete Alex Kerr in the early 1970s, and he went on to romanticise the Iya Valley in his award-winning book Lost Japan. Chiiori remains a beautiful and authentic destination for sensitive travellers, with its *shōji* (movable screens), antique furnishings and *irori* (traditional hearths) – all complemented by a gleaming, fully-equipped modern kitchen and gorgeous bathroom, complete with *hinoki* (Japanese cypress) tub. Since the establishment of the nonprofit **Chiiori Trust** (www.chiiori.org) in 2005, the local government has approached the trust to help restore smaller traditional houses in the area (called **Fusho**, **Seiko** and **Udoku**). These houses have been renovated to a similarly high standard and aesthetic as Chiiori and are also available as accommodation. All are outfitted with modern kitchens and bathrooms, and even washing machines.

To stay in these extraordinary environs, you must reserve in advance through Chiiori Trust. Because guests are required to check in at the **Ryugugake tourist information centre** (龍宮崖観光案内所; 📞0883-88-5120; 96-3 Wada, Higashi-Iya; ⏰9am-6pm) before heading to Chiiori (4.5km away), and because of the remote locations of Chiiori and the other houses, the Chiiori Trust strongly recommends that guests bring their own vehicles.

ⓘ Getting There & Away

Access to the area is via Ōboke Station, reached by train from Takamatsu (¥3000) or Tokushima (¥3170) with a change at Awa-Ikeda, or from Kōchi (¥2390). From Honshū, Nanpū limited express trains depart hourly from Okayama (¥4410, 1¾ hours); Okayama is on the Sanyō *shinkansen* line.

Getting around the valley itself involves some planning, because Iya's sights are widespread, and public transport is sporadic at the best of times. Four buses per day travel between Ōboke and Iya (¥640, 40 minutes). **Ikeda DK Taxi** (📞0883-76-0011) and **Ōboke Taxi** (📞0883-84-1225) are among several companies filling the gaps in the bus schedule.

The best way to explore the region is with your own wheels; you will thank the Daishi for the freedom and flexibility a car offers here. Rental cars are available in Shikoku's larger cities.

Nagasaki

☎095 / POP 443,400

HIGHLIGHTS

① **Nagasaki Atomic Bomb Museum (p325)** and **Peace Park (p326)** These sobering memorials to man's inhumanity still manage to inspire hope for a more peaceful future.

② **Dejima (p326)** This former Dutch trading outpost is a must for any fan of Japanese history.

③ **Glover Garden (p326)** Both historically significant and scenic, this is a must-see in Nagasaki.

Paper cranes on display, Nagasaki Peace Park (p326)
MARTIN MOOS / GETTY IMAGES ©

How ironic it is that the name Nagasaki (長崎) conjures up the tragic destruction of war, as for much of its history the city of Nagasaki was Japan's only link to the outside world; other parts of Nagasaki Prefecture (長崎県) served a similar role. A visit to the scenes of atomic devastation is a must, but beyond them you'll find that this one-of-a-kind, embracing city boasts a colourful trading history, alluring churches, shrines, temples and an East-meets-West culinary scene, prettily set within hills around a gracious harbour. Schedule a few days here to meet the people and get a sense of Nagasaki's spirit.

 Sights

URAKAMI (NORTHERN NAGASAKI)

Urakami, the hypocentre of the atomic explosion, is today a prosperous, peaceful suburb. While nuclear ruin seems comfortably far away seven decades later, many sights here keep the memory alive.

Nagasaki Atomic Bomb Museum
Museum

(長崎原爆資料館; www1.city.nagasaki.nagasaki.jp/peace/English.abm; 7-8 Hirano-machi; admission ¥200, audio guide ¥150; ⊙8.30am-6.30pm May-Aug, to 5.30pm Sep-Apr; ☒Matsuyama-machi) An essential Nagasaki experience, this sombre place recounts the city's destruction and loss of life through photos and artefacts, including mangled rocks, trees, furniture, pottery and clothing, a clock stopped at 11.02 (the hour of the bombing), first-hand accounts from survivors and stories of heroic relief efforts. Exhibits also include the postbombing struggle for nuclear disarmament, and conclude with a chilling illustration of which nations bear nuclear arms.

Nagasaki National Peace Memorial Hall for the Atomic Bomb Victims
Memorial

(国立長崎原爆死没者追悼平和祈念館; www.peace-nagasaki.go.jp; 7-8 Hirano-machi; ⊙8.30am-6.30pm May-Aug, to 5.30pm Sep-Apr; ☒Matsuyama-machi) **FREE** Adjacent to the

Atomic Bomb Museum and completed in 2003, this minimalist memorial by Kuryū Akira is a profoundly moving place. It is best approached by quietly reading the carved inscriptions and walking around the sculpted water basin. In the hall below, 12 glass pillars, containing shelves of books of the names of the deceased, reach skyward.

Peace Park   Park

(平和公園; Heiwa-kōen; 🚃 Ōhashi) FREE
North of the hypocentre, the Peace Park is presided over by the 10-tonne bronze Nagasaki Peace Statue (平和記念像), designed in 1955 by Kitamura Seibo. It also includes the dove-shaped Fountain of Peace (1969) and the Peace Symbol Zone, a sculpture garden with contributions on the theme of peace from around the world. On 9 August a rowdy antinuclear protest is held within earshot of the more respectful official memorial ceremony for those lost to the bomb.

Atomic Bomb Hypocentre Park   Park

(長崎爆心地公園; 🚃 Matsuyama-machi) FREE The park has a smooth, black stone column marking the point above which the bomb exploded. Nearby are bomb-blasted relics, including a section of the wall of the Urakami Cathedral.

CENTRAL NAGASAKI

Dejima   Historic Site

(出島) In 1641 the Tokugawa shōgunate banished all foreigners from Japan, with one exception: Dejima, a fan-shaped, man-made island 560m in circumference (15,000 sq metres) in Nagasaki harbour. From then until the 1850s, this small Dutch trading post was the sole sanctioned foreign presence in Japan; about the only local contact for the Dutch segregated here was with trading partners and courtesans, and an annual official visit to Edo, which took 90 days!

These days the city has filled in around the island and you might walk right past it. Don't. Seventeen buildings, walls and structures (plus a miniature Dejima) have been painstakingly reconstructed based on pictorial representations in the Dejima Museum (出島資料館; www1.city.nagasaki.nagasaki.jp/dejima; 6-1 Dejima-machi; admission ¥500; ⏰8am-7pm; 🚃Dejima). Restored and reopened in 2006 and constantly being upgraded, the buildings here are as instructive inside as they are good-looking outside, with exhibits covering the spread of trade, Western learning and culture, archaeological digs, and rooms combining Japanese tatami (woven floor matting) with Western wallpaper. There's excellent English signage. Allow at least two hours.

Nagasaki Museum of History & Culture   Museum

(長崎歴史文化博物館; www.nmhc.jp; 1-1-1 Tateyama; admission ¥600; ⏰8.30am-7pm, closed 3rd Tue of month; 🚃Sakura-machi) This large museum with attractive displays opened in 2005 to focus on Nagasaki's proud history of international exchange. The main gallery is a fabulous reconstruction of a section of the Edo-period Nagasaki Magistrate's Office, which controlled trade and diplomacy. Detailed English-language explanations were in the works at the time of writing.

SOUTHERN NAGASAKI

Glover Garden   Gardens

(グラバー園; 📞822-8223; www.glover-garden.jp; 8-1 Minami-yamate-machi; adult/student ¥600/300; ⏰8am-9.30pm 29 Apr–mid-Jul, to 6pm mid-Jul–28 Apr; 🚃Ōura Tenshudō-shita) Some former homes of the city's Meiji-period European residents have been reassembled in this hillside garden. Glover Garden is named after Thomas Glover (1838–1911), the Scottish merchant who built Japan's first railway, helped establish the shipbuilding industry and whose arms-importing operations influenced the course of the Meiji Restoration.

The best way to explore the garden is to take the moving walkways to the top of the hill then walk back down. The **Mitsubishi No 2 Dock building** (旧三菱第2ドックハウス; 📞822 8223; 8-1 Minami-yamatemachi; adult/student ¥600/300; ⏰8am-9:30pm 27 Apr–9 Oct, to 6pm 10 Oct–26 Apr) is highest, with panoramic views of the city and

The Atomic Explosion

When United States Air Force B-29 bomber *Bock's Car* set off from the Marianas on 9 August 1945 to drop a second atomic bomb on Japan, the target was Kokura on Kyūshū's northeastern coast. Due to poor visibility, the crew diverted to the secondary target, Nagasaki.

The B-29 arrived over Nagasaki at 10.58am amid heavy cloud. When a momentary gap appeared and the Mitsubishi Arms Factory was sighted, the 4.57-tonne 'Fat Man' bomb, with an explosive power equivalent to 21.3 kilotonnes of TNT (almost twice that of Hiroshima's 'Little Boy'), was released over Nagasaki.

The bomb missed the arms factory, its intended target, and exploded at 11.02am, at an altitude of 500m almost directly above the largest Catholic church in Asia (Urakami Cathedral). In an instant, it annihilated the suburb of Urakami and 74,000 of Nagasaki's 240,000 people. Ground temperatures at the hypocentre were estimated between 3000°C and 4000°C, and as high as 600°C 1.5km away. Everything within a 1km radius of the explosion was destroyed, and searing winds estimated at 1000km/h (typhoons generally top out at 150km/h) swept down the valley of the Urakami-gawa towards the city centre. With able-bodied men at work or at war, most victims were women, children and senior citizens, as well as 13,000 conscripted Korean labourers and 200 allied POWs. Another 75,000 people were horribly injured (and it is estimated that as many people died as a result of the after-effects). After the resulting fires burned out, a third of the city was gone.

Yet the damage might have been even worse had the targeted arms factory been hit. Unlike in the flatlands of Hiroshima or the Nagasaki port itself, the hills around the river valley protected outlying suburbs from greater damage.

harbour from the 2nd floor. Next highest is Walker House (旧ウォーカー住宅), filled with artefacts donated by the families, followed by Ringer House (旧リンガー住宅), Alt House (旧オルト住宅) and finally **Glover House** (旧グラバー住宅; ☑822 8223; 8-1 Minami-yamatemachi; admission adult/student ¥600/300; ☺8am-9.30pm 27 Apr-9 Oct, to 6pm 10 Oct-26 April). Halfway down is the Madame Butterfly statue of Japanese opera singer Miura Tamaki, inspiration of the famous opera by Puccini – the story took place here in Nagasaki. Exit the garden through the **Nagasaki Traditional Performing Arts Museum** (☑822 8223; 3-1 Minami-yamatemachi; admission adult/student ¥600/300; ☺8am-9.30pm 27 Apr-9 Oct, to 6pm 10 Oct-26 April), which has a display of dragons and floats used in Nagasaki's colourful Kunchi Matsuri.

 Sleeping

For ease of transport and access to restaurants and nightlife, we recommend staying near JR Nagasaki Station or Shianbashi.

Hotel Dormy Inn Nagasaki
Business Hotel ¥¥
(☑820-5489; www.hotespa.net/hotels/nagasaki; 7-24 Dōza-machi; s/d from ¥9500/13,000; ☺@; 🚃Tsuki-machi) Adjacent to Chinatown, this hotel would be worth it just for the location. Rooms are crisp and neat as a pin with quality mattresses. There are large gender-separated common baths and saunas in addition to in-room facilities. The breakfast buffet (¥1100) includes *sara udon*, and there's free soba served from 9.30pm to 11pm. Look for online discounts.

Richmond Hotel Nagasaki Shianbashi

Hotel ¥¥

(リッチモンドホテル長崎思案橋; ☎832-2525; www.richmondhotel.jp; 6-38 Motoshikkui-machi; s/d/tw from ¥8000/11,000/14,000; 😕@📶; 🚃Shianbashi) You can't be closer to the heart of Shianbashi than this travellers' favourite. Rooms are ultramodern with dark tones and flat-screen TVs. Deluxe rooms are large by Japanese standards. There's cheerful, English-speaking staff and a terrific breakfast buffet (¥1000) including Nagasaki specialities.

ANA Crowne Plaza Nagasaki Gloverhill

Hotel ¥¥

(ANAクラウンプラザ長崎グラバーヒル; ☎818-6601; www.anacrowneplaza-nagasaki.jp; 1-18 Minami-yamate-machi; s/d/tw from ¥8500/13,000/16,000; P😕@📶; 🚃Ōura-Tenshudō-shita) Near Glover Garden, Ōura Cathedral and the Dutch Slopes, this old-school hotel was getting a slick renovation as we went to press, with separate showers and baths, plush bedding and clean, contemporary lines. About the only downside: no view to speak of.

Garden Terrace Nagasaki

Hotel ¥¥¥

(ガーデンテラス長崎; ☎864-7777; www.gt-nagasaki.jp; 2-3 Akizuki-machi; r from ¥42,000; P😕@📶♨) If money is no object, this hillside hotel is a design masterpiece, clad in the unvarnished wood planks of architect Kuma Kengo. Generous rooms (50 sq metres plus) feature minimalist style, angular sofas and armchairs, fabulous baths and sweeping views. Nonstaying guests can visit for high-flying French or teppanyaki meals.

About the only disadvantage: distance, across the harbour from the city centre. If you miss the hotel shuttle from JR Nagasaki Station, a taxi costs about ¥1500.

Best Western Premier Hotel Nagasaki

Hotel ¥¥¥

(ベストウエスタンプレミアホテル長崎; ☎821-1111; www.bestwestern.co.jp/english/nagasaki; 2-26 Takara-machi; s/d incl breakfast from ¥15,000/23,000; P😕@📶; 🚃Takara-machi) The city centre's top hotel has a vast marble lobby, comfortably elegant rooms with marble-countered bathrooms and panoramic views from the top-floor steakhouse and buffet restaurant, where a Japanese–Western buffet breakfast is served (¥2000).

Eating

Nagasaki is a culinary crossroads and one of Japan's most interesting dining scenes.

Hōuntei

Izakaya ¥

(☎821-9333; 1-8 Motoshikkui-machi; dishes ¥360-520; ⏱5-11pm; 🚃Shianbashi) Patrons have been ordering the *hito-kuchi gyōza* (one-bite dumplings; ¥360 for 10) at this rustic hole in the wall since the 1970s. Also try *butanira-toji* (pork and shallots cooked omelette style;

Hirado Bridge, Nagasaki
MIXA / GETTY IMAGES ©

¥520). There's a picture menu. Look for the lantern and brown *noren* (door curtain) across from With Nagasaki.

Shippoku Hamakatsu   Kaiseki ¥¥
(卓袱浜勝; ☎826-8321; www.sippoku.jp; 6-50 Kajiya-machi; lunch/dinner menus from ¥1500/2940; ☺lunch & dinner; 📵; 🚃Shianbashi) Come here if you would like to experience *shippoku ryōri* and still afford your airfare home. Course menus are filling and varied (the Otakusa Shippoku is served on a dramatic round tray). In addition, there is a choice of either Japanese- or Western-style seating.

Yosso   Japanese ¥¥
(吉宗; ☎821-0001; 8-9 Hama-machi; set meals from ¥1260; ☺11am-8pm; 🚃Shianbashi) People have been coming to eat *chawanmushi* (Japanese egg custard) since 1866. Look for the traditional shopfront festooned with red lanterns. The Yosso *teishoku* (set-course meal ¥1260) adds fish, *soboro* (sweetened, ground chicken over rice), *kakuni* (stewed pork belly), dessert and more. There's no English menu, but a display case makes ordering easy.

The **Mirai Nagasaki Cocowalk** (みらい長崎ココウォーク; www.cocowalk. jp; 1-55 Morimachi; ☺10am-9pm; 🚃Mori-machi, 🚃JR Urakami) shopping mall features some 20 restaurants on its 4th and 5th floors. **Aletta** (☎801-5245; lunch/dinner ¥1580/1980; ☺lunch & dinner) is an airy buffet restaurant on the 4th floor, with a different national theme each month. On the 5th floor, **Big Man** (☎865-8600; sandwiches ¥350-850; ☺10am-9pm; 🚫📵🧑) serves burgers that are popular in nearby Sasebo, where a US naval base has brought yet another cultural influence. Some burgers have a Japanese twist, such as bacon-egg burgers or Kyūshū's own *kurobuta* (black pork) sandwiches.

ℹ Information

Tourist Information

In addition to tourist brochures available at information centres, look for the free English-language magazine *Nagazasshi*, published by local

expats, containing events, sightseeing tips and features. A new multilingual call centre (☎825-5175) caters to English-speaking visitors.

Nagasaki City Tourist Information Centre (長崎市総合観光案内所; ☎823-3631; www. at-nagasaki.jp/foreign/english; 1st fl, JR Nagasaki Station; ☺8am-8pm) Can assist with finding accommodation and has brochures and maps in English.

ℹ Getting There & Away

Air

There are flights between Nagasaki and Tokyo (Haneda; Japan Airlines & All Nippon Airways/Solaseed Air ¥39,070/33,670), Osaka (Itami; ¥25,700), Okinawa (¥25,500) and Nagoya (¥31,900).

Train

JR lines from Nagasaki head for Sasebo (for Hirado; *kaisoku*, ¥1600, 1¾ hours) or Fukuoka (Hakata Station; *tokkyū*, ¥4080, two hours). Most other destinations require a change of train. Nagasaki is not currently served by *shinkansen*.

ℹ Getting Around

To/From the Airport

Nagasaki's airport is located about 40km from the city. Airport buses (¥800, 45 minutes) operate from stand 4 of the Kenei bus terminal opposite JR Nagasaki Station and outside the Shinchi bus terminal. A taxi to the airport costs about ¥9000.

Tram

The best way of getting around Nagasaki is by tram. There are four colour-coded routes numbered 1, 3, 4 and 5 (route 2 is for special events) and stops are signposted in English. It costs ¥120 to travel anywhere in town, but you can transfer for free at the Tsuki-machi (築町) stop only (ask for a *noritsugi*, or transfer pass), unless you have a ¥500 all-day pass for unlimited travel, available from tourist information centres and many hotels. Most trams stop running around 11.30pm.

Southwest Islands

☏0997 / POP 13,700

HIGHLIGHTS

1 **Hiking on Yakushima (p331)**
From short strolls to an ascent
of Miya-no-ura-dake, Yakushima
offers some of Japan's best hiking.

2 **Shuri-jō (p333)** It may be a
modern reconstruction, but this
castle still captures the magic of
old Okinawa.

3 **Kerama Islands (p336)** World-
class beaches, whale-watching and
great diving make the Keramas
unmissable.

Yakushima
IPPEI NAOI / GETTY IMAGES ©

Yakushima 屋久島

Designated a Unesco World Heritage Site
in 1993, Yakushima is one of the most
rewarding islands in the Southwest Islands. The craggy mountain peaks of the
island's interior are home to the world-
famous *yakusugi* (屋久杉; *Cryptomeria
japonica*), ancient cedar trees that are
said to have been the inspiration for some
of the scenes in Miyazaki Hayao's animation classic *Princess Mononoke*.

Hiking among the high peaks and mossy
forests is the main activity on Yakushima,
but the island is also home to some
excellent coastal onsen and a few sandy
beaches.

Keep in mind that Yakushima is a place
of extremes: the mountains wring every
last drop of moisture from the passing
clouds and the interior of the island is one
of the wettest places in Japan. In the winter
the peaks may be covered in snow, while
the coast is still relatively balmy. Whatever
you do, come prepared and don't set off on
a hike without a good map and the proper
gear. An International Driving Permit will
also vastly increase your enjoyment here,
as buses are few and far between.

◉ Sights

Yakushima's main port is Miyanoura (宮之
浦), on the island's northeast coast. This
is the most convenient place to be based,
as most buses originate from here. From
Miyanoura, a road runs around the perimeter of the island, passing through the
secondary port of Anbō (安房) on the east
coast, and then through the hot-springs
town of Onoaida (尾の間) in the south.
Heading north from Miyanoura, the road
takes you to the town of Nagata (永田),
which has a brilliant stretch of white-sand
beach.

Nagata Inaka-hama   Beach
(永田いなか浜) On the island's northwest
coast in the village of Nagata is a beautiful
beach for sunsets, and it's where sea
turtles lay their eggs from May to July. It's
beside the Inaka-hama bus stop, served
by Nagata-bound buses from Miyanoura.

Issō-kaisuiyokujō   Beach

(一湊海水浴場) Another fine beach, located on the north coast of the island, about midway between Miyanoura and Nagata. It's a short walk from the Yahazu bus stop (served by any Nagata-bound bus from Miyanoura).

Activities

HIKING

Hiking is the best way to experience Yakushima's beauty. If you're planning anything more than a short stroll around Yakusugi Land, pick up a copy of the Japanese-language *Yama-to-Kougen-no-Chizu-Yakushima* (山と高原の地図屋久島; ¥840), available at major bookshops in Japan.

ONSEN

Yakushima has several onsen from beautifully desolate seaside pools to upmarket hotel facilities. The seaside onsen listed here are *konyoku* onsen (mixed-sex baths) where swimsuits are not allowed; women traditionally wrap themselves in a thin towel for modesty.

Hirauchi Kaichū Onsen   Onsen

(平内海中温泉; admission ¥100; ☾24hr) Onsen lovers will be in heaven here. The outdoor baths are in the rocks by the sea and can only be entered at or close to low tide. You can walk to the baths from the Kaichū Onsen bus stop, but the next stop, Nishikaikon, is actually closer. From Nishikaikon, walk downhill towards the sea for about 200m and take a right at the bottom of the hill.

Yudomari Onsen   Onsen

(湯泊温泉; admission ¥100; ☾24hr) This blissfully serene onsen can be entered at any tide. Get off at the Yudomari bus stop and take the road opposite the post office in the direction of the sea. Once you enter the village, the way is marked. It's a 800m walk and you pass a great banyan tree en route.

Sleeping

The most convenient place to be based is Miyanoura. You'll also find lodgings in larger villages and several bare-bones *yama-goya* (mountain huts) in the mountains. In July and August and the spring Golden Week holiday, it's best to reserve ahead, since places fill up early.

Sankara Hotel & Spa   Hotel ¥¥¥

(サンカラ; ☎47-3488; www.sankarahotel-spa.com; r per person with meals from ¥25,000; ⓟ@✿) 🌿 Overlooking Yakushima's southeast coast, this stunning collection of luxury villas blends ocean views with Balinese floral design elements. The main restaurant's French fusion cuisine is created by Chef Takei Chiharu who trained at several three-Michelin-star establishments in France; the menu utilises as much local and organic produce as possible, much of which is grown expressly for the hotel. All water used on the property comes directly from mountain run-off. Staff can pick you up, but if you have transport, look for the green signs in English along the road between Hirano and Hara. Guests 15 years and older only.

Lodge Yaedake-sansō   Lodge ¥¥

(ロッジ八重岳山荘; ☎42-1551; www17.ocn.ne.jp/~yakusima/lodge/index.html; r per person with meals ¥7800; ⓟ) This secluded accommodation features Japanese- and Western-style rooms in rustic riverside cabins connected by wooden walkways. You can soak up the beauty of your surroundings in the communal baths, and children will enjoy splashing in the river. Meals served in the tatami dining room are simple, balanced and exquisite. The lodge is located inland on the Miyanoura-gawa; staff can pick you up in Miyanoura. If it's full, it also runs the Minshuku Yaedake Honkan (民宿八重岳本館; ☎42-2552; 208 Miyanoura; r per person incl meals ¥6300; ⓟ) in town.

Sōyōtei   Ryokan ¥¥

(送陽邸; ☎45-2819; http://soyote.ftw.jp/u44579.html; r per person incl meals ¥13,650; ⓟ) On the northwest coast near Nagata

Inaka-hama, this gorgeous, family-run guest house has a collection of semidetached units that boast private verandahs and ocean views. The traditional structures feature rooftops unique to Yakushima, with stones serving as roof tiles – you'll recognise the place immediately. There is an outdoor bath overlooking the sea, but it's not always open. It's very close to the Inaka-hama bus stop.

Eating

There are a few restaurants in each of the island's villages, with the best selection in Miyanoura. If you're staying anywhere but Miyanoura, ask for the set two-meal plan at your lodgings. If you're going hiking, you can ask your lodging to prepare a *bentō* (boxed meal) the night before you set out.

If you need to stock up on supplies for camping or hiking, you'll find **Yakuden** (ヤクデン; 9am-10pm) supermarket on the main street in Miyanoura, just north of the entrance to the pier area.

Shiosai
Seafood ¥¥
(潮騒; ☏42-2721; dishes ¥1200; ⏰11.30am-2pm & 5.30-10pm Fri-Wed) Find a full range of Japanese standards such as *sashimi teishoku* (sashimi set; ¥1700) or the wonderful *ebi-furai teishoku* (fried shrimp set; ¥1400). Look for the blue and whitish building with automatic glass doors along the main road through Miyanoura.

Information

If you plan to get around the island by bus, we recommend buying a bus pass.

Tourist Information Centre (☏42-1019; ⏰8.30am-5pm) Miyanoura's ferry terminal has a useful information centre in the round white building as you emerge from the ferry offices. It can help you find lodgings and answer all questions about the island.

Getting There & Away

Air
JapanAir Commuter has flights between Kagoshima and Yakushima (¥13,900, 35 minutes, five daily). Yakushima's airport is on the northeastern coast between Miyanoura and Anbō. Hourly buses stop at the airport, though you can usually phone your accommodation for a pick-up or take a taxi.

Boat
Hydrofoil services operate between Kagoshima and Yakushima, some of which stop at Tanegashima en route. **Tane Yaku Jetfoil** (☏in Kagoshima 099-226-0128, in Miyanoura 42-2003) runs four Toppy and Rocket hydrofoils per day between Kagoshima (leaving from the high-speed ferry terminal just to the south of Minamifutō pier) and Miyanoura (¥7700, one hour 45 minutes for direct sailings, two hours 40 minutes with a stop in Tanegashima). There are also two hydrofoils per day between Kagoshima and Anbō Port (2½ hours) on Yakushima.

Getting Around

Local buses travel the coastal road part way around Yakushima roughly every hour or two, though only a few head up into the interior. Buses are expensive and you'll save a lot of money by purchasing a *furii jōsha kippu,* which is good for unlimited travel on Yakushima Kotsu buses. One-/two-day passes cost ¥2000/3000 and are available at the Tane Yaku Jetfoil office in Miyanoura.

Hitching is also possible, but the best way to get around the island is to rent a car. **Toyota Rent-a-Car** (☏42-2000; up to 12hr from ¥5250; ⏰8am-8pm) is located near the terminal in Miyanoura.

Okinawa-hontō　沖縄本島
☏098 / POP 1.39 MILLION

Okinawa-hontō is the largest island in the Southwest Islands, and the historical seat of power of the Ryūkyū dynasty. Although its cultural differences with mainland Japan were once evident in its architecture, almost all traces were completely obliterated in WWII. Fortunately, Allied bombing wasn't powerful enough to completely stamp out other remnants of Okinawan culture, and today the island is home to a unique culinary, artistic and musical tradition.

Prefectural capital Naha is a transportation hub for the other islands. War memorials are clustered in the south of the island, while there are some good beaches and other attractions on the Motobu peninsula. The north is relatively undeveloped.

NAHA 那覇

POP 315,000

Flattened during WWII, the prefectural capital of Naha is now a thriving urban centre. The city sports a convenient elevated monorail and a rapidly expanding skyline of modern high-rise apartments, as well as the inevitable traffic jams.

 Sights

Naha is fairly easy to navigate, especially since the main sights and attractions are located in the city centre. The main drag is Kokusai-dōri, while the Tsuboya pottery area is to the southeast via a series of covered arcades. The Shuri district is located about 3km to the east of the city centre.

The city's main artery, **Kokusai-dōri** (国際通り), is a riot of neon, noise, souvenir shops, bustling restaurants and Japanese young things out strutting their stuff. It's a festival of tat and tackiness, but it's a good time if you're in the mood for it.

Many people prefer the atmosphere of the three shopping arcades that run south off Kokusai-dōri roughly opposite Mitsukoshi Department Store: Ichibahon-dōri (市場本道り), Mutsumibashi-dōri (むつみ橋通り) and Heiwa-dōri (平和通り).

Tsuboya Pottery Street — Neighbourhood

(壺屋やちむん道り; Tsuboya Yachimun-dōri) One of the best parts of Naha is this neighbourhood, a centre of ceramic production from 1682, when Ryūkyū kilns were consolidated here by royal decree. Most shops along this atmospheric street sell all the popular Okinawan ceramics, including shiisā (lion-dog roof guardians) and containers for serving awamori, the local firewater. The lanes off the main street here contain some classic crumbling old Okinawan houses. To get here from Kokusai-dōri, walk south through the Heiwa-dōri arcade for about 350m.

Okinawa Prefectural Museum & Art Museum — Museum

(沖縄県立博物館・美術館; ☑941-8200; Omuromachi 3-1-1; admission ¥400; ☉9am-6pm Tue-Thu & Sun, to 8pm Fri & Sat) Opened in 2007, this museum of Okinawa's history, culture and natural history is easily one of the best museums in Japan. Displays are well laid out, attractively presented and easy to understand, with excellent bilingual interpretive signage. The art museum section holds interesting special exhibits with an emphasis on local artists. It's about 15 minutes' walk northwest of the Omoromachi monorail station.

Tsuboya Pottery Museum — Museum

(壺屋焼物博物館; ☑862-3761; 1-9-32 Tsuboya; admission ¥315; ☉10am-6pm Tue-Sun) In Tsuboya, you will find the excellent Tsuboya Pottery Museum, which contains some fine examples of traditional Okinawan pottery. Here you can also inspect potters' wheels and arayachi (unglazed) and jōyachi (glazed) pieces. There's even a cross-section of a nobori-gama (kiln built on a slope) set in its original location, where crushed pieces of pottery that date back to the 17th century lay suspended in earth.

Daichi Makishi Kōsetsu Ichiba — Market

(第一牧志公設市場; 2-10-1 Matsuo; ☉10am-8pm) Our favourite stop in the arcade area is the covered food market just off Ichibahon-dōri, about 200m south of Kokusai-dōri. The colourful variety of fish and produce on offer here is amazing, and don't miss the wonderful local restaurants upstairs. Keep in mind, however, that this is a working market, so please don't get in the way of shopkeepers and consider buying something as a souvenir.

Shuri District 首里

The original capital of Okinawa, Shuri's temples, shrines, tombs and castle were all destroyed in WWII, but the castle and surrounding structures were rebuilt in 1992.

Shuri-jō — Castle

(首里城; admission ¥800; ☉8.30am-8pm Jul-Sep, to 6pm Dec-Mar, to 7pm Apr-Jun & Oct-Nov)

The reconstructed castle sits atop a hill overlooking Naha's urban sprawl. It was originally built in the 14th century and served as the administrative centre and royal residence of the Ryūkyū kingdom until the 19th century.

Enter through the Kankai-mon (歓会門) and go up to the Hōshin-mon (奉神門), which forms the entryway to the inner sanctum of the castle, dominated by the impressive **Seiden** (正殿). Visitors can enter the Seiden, which has exhibits on the castle and the Okinawan royals. There is also a small collection of displays in the nearby **Hokuden**. To reach the complex, take the Yui-rail monorail to Shuri Station. Exit to the west, go down the steps, walk straight, cross one big street, then a smaller one and go right on the opposite side, then walk about 350m and look for the signs on the left.

Sleeping

Naha is the most convenient base for exploring Okinawa-hontō.

Hotel Sun Palace   Hotel ¥¥
(ホテルサンパレス球陽舘; ☎863-4181; www.palace-okinawa.com/sunpalace; 2-5-1 Kumoji; r per person incl breakfast from ¥6500; **P** ⊜ **@**) About three minutes' walk from Kokusai-dōri, the Sun Palace is a step up in warmth and quality from a standard business hotel. The fairly spacious rooms have interesting design touches and some have balconies; there's even a rooftop terrace, a refreshing bit of outdoor space laced with greenery.

Hotel JAL City Naha   Hotel ¥¥
(ホテルJALシティ那覇; ☎866-2580; http://naha.jalcity.co.jp; 1-3-70 Makishi; s/d from ¥8000/10,000; **P** ⊜ **@** 🛜) Right on Kokusai-dōri, the modern JAL City has 304 swish, modern rooms, in which even the single beds are wide enough to serve as cosy doubles. Staff here have very limited English, but service is excellent.

Eating & Drinking

Naha is the perfect spot to sample the full range of Okinawan cuisine.

Daichi Makishi
Kōsetsu Ichiba   Market ¥
(第一牧志公設市場; 2-10-1 Matsuo; meals from ¥800; ⏰10am-8pm) We highly recommend a meal at one of the eateries on the 2nd floor of this food market. Just have a look at what the locals are eating and grab a seat.

Ashibiunā   Okinawan ¥
(あしびうなぁ; ☎884-0035; 2-13 Shuri-jō; dishes ¥900; ⏰11.30am-3.30pm & 5.30-midnight; 📖) Perfect for lunch after touring Shuri-jō castle, Ashibiunā has a traditional ambience and serves staple set meals such as *goyā champurū* (bitter melon stir-fry; ¥840) and *okinawa-soba* (thick white noodles served in a pork broth; ¥840) around a picturesque garden. Facing the entrance to Kankai-mon, turn left and follow the road until just before the intersection. It's on your right with a black-and-white sign and plants over the gate.

Yūnangi   Okinawan ¥¥
(ゆうなんぎい; ☎867-3765; 3-3-3 Kumoji; dishes ¥1200; ⏰noon-3pm & 5.30-10.30pm Mon-Sat) You'll be lucky to get a seat here, but if you do, you'll be treated to some of the best Okinawan food around, served in traditional but bustling surroundings. Try the *okinawa-soba* set (¥1400), or choose among the appealing options in the picture menu. It's on a side street off Kokusai-dōri; look for the wooden sign above the doorway with white letters in Japanese.

Uchina Chaya Buku Buku   Teahouse
(うちなー茶屋ぶくぶく; ☎861-2950; 1-28-3 Tsuboya; tea ¥800; ⏰10am-4.30pm Mon-Wed, Fri & Sat) This incredibly atmospheric teahouse near the east end of the Tsuboya pottery area is worth a special trip. It takes its name from the traditional frothy Okinawan tea served here: *buku buku cha* (¥800), jasmine tea topped with toasty rice foam and crushed peanuts. It's up a small lane just north of Tsuboya-yachimun-dōri and overlooks a historic 160-year-old house.

Information

Post offices are scattered around town, including the **Miebashi post office** (美栄橋郵便局), on the ground floor of the Palette Kumoji building, the **Tomari-kō post office** (泊ふ頭郵便局; **Port building**), in the Tomari port building, and the **Kokusai-dōri post office** (国際通り郵便局), around the corner from Makishi Station.

Tourist Information Counter (☎857-6884; **1F Arrivals Terminal, Naha International Airport**; ☺9am-9pm) At this helpful prefectural counter, we suggest picking up a copy of the *Naha Guide Map* before heading into town. If you plan to explore outside Naha, also grab a copy of the *Okinawa Guide Map*.

Tourist Information Office (那覇市観光案内所; ☎868-4887; 2-1-4 Makishi; ☺8.30am-8pm Mon-Fri, 10am-8pm Sat & Sun) The city office has internet access and luggage storage for a small fee, and free maps and information. It's just off Kokusai-dōri (turn at Starbucks).

Getting There & Away

Air

Naha International Airport (OKA) has connections with Seoul, Taipei, Hong Kong and Shanghai. Connections with mainland Japan include Kagoshima (¥27,600, 1½ hours), Hiroshima (¥34,200, two hours), Osaka (¥36,400, 2¼ hours), Nagoya (¥41,100, 2½ hours) and Tokyo (¥43,070, 2¾ hours); significant discounts (*tabiwari* on All Nippon Airways and *sakitoku* on JAL) can sometimes be had if you purchase tickets a month in advance. Note that this is only a partial list; most large Japanese cities have flights.

Boat

Naha has regular ferry connections with ports in Honshū (Tokyo and Osaka/Kōbe) and Kyūshū (Kagoshima).

Marix (マリックスライン; ☎53-3112, **in Kagoshima 099-225-1551; www.marix-line. co.jp**) and **A Line** (☎**in Naha 861-1886, in Tokyo 03-5643-6170; www.aline-ferry.com**) operate four to six ferries a month running to/from Tokyo (¥24,500, 47 hours) and Osaka/Kobe (¥19,600, 42 hours), as well as daily ferries to/from Kagoshima (¥14,600, 25 hours). Note that if you ask for a *norihōdai kippu* you can sail from Kagoshima to Naha and get on and off the ferries freely within seven days.

There are three ports in Naha, and this can be confusing: Kagoshima/Amami Islands ferries operate from Naha Port (Naha-kō); Tokyo/Osaka/Kōbe ferries operate from Naha Shin Port (Naha Shin-kō); and Kume-jima and Kerama Islands ferries operate from Tomari Port (Tomari-kō).

Getting Around

The Yui-rail monorail runs from Naha International Airport in the south to Shuri in the north. Prices range from ¥200 to ¥290; day passes cost ¥600. Kenchō-mae Station is at the western end of Kokusai-dōri, while Makishi Station is at its eastern end.

Naha Port is a 10-minute walk southwest from Asahibashi Station, while Tomari Port is a similar distance north from Miebashi Station. Bus 101 from Naha bus terminal (那覇バスターミナル) heads further north to Naha Shin Port (20 minutes, hourly).

When riding on local town buses, simply dump ¥200 into the slot next to the driver as you enter. For longer trips, take a ticket showing your starting point as you board and pay the appropriate fare as you disembark. Buses run from Naha to destinations all over the island.

A rental car makes everything easier when exploring Okinawa-hontō. The rental-car counter in the arrivals hall of Naha International Airport offers information on the dozen or so rental companies in Naha, allowing you to comparison shop.

SOUTHERN OKINAWA-HONTŌ 沖縄本島の南部

During the closing days of the Battle of Okinawa, the southern part of Okinawa-hontō served as one of the last hold outs of the Japanese military and an evacuation point for wounded Japanese soldiers. A visit to the area, a day or half-day trip from Naha, is highly recommended for those with an interest in wartime history.

Okinawa's most important war memorials are clustered in the **Memorial Peace Park** (平和祈念公園; ☺dawn-dusk), located in the city of Itoman on the southern coast of the island. The centrepiece of the park is the **Okinawa Prefectural Peace Memorial Museum** (沖縄県平和祈念資料館; ☎997-3844; 614-1 Mabuni, Itoman-shi; admission ¥300; ☺9am-

5pm), which focuses on the suffering of the Okinawan people during the invasion of the island and under the subsequent American occupation. The main exhibits are on the 2nd floor. The museum strives to present a balanced picture of the Pacific War and the history that led to the invasion, but there is plenty here to stir debate. Outside the museum is the **Cornerstone of Peace** (☉dawn-dusk), which is inscribed with the names of everyone who died in the Battle of Okinawa.

To reach the park, take bus 89 from Naha bus terminal to the Itoman bus terminal (¥560, one hour, every 20 minutes), then transfer to bus 82, and get off at Heiwa Kinen-dō Iriguchi (¥460, 30 minutes, hourly).

An interesting stop en route to the Peace Park is the **Himeyuri no Tō** (ひめゆりの塔; Himeyuri Peace Museum; ☎997-2100; 671-1 Ihara; admission ¥300; ☉9am-5pm), located above a cave that served as an emergency field hospital during the closing days of the Battle of Okinawa. Here, 240 female high-school students were pressed into service as nurses for Japanese military wounded. As American forces closed in, the students were dismissed and the majority died. Bus 82 stops outside.

Directly south of Naha in Kaigungo-kōen is the **Former Japanese Navy Underground Headquarters** (旧海軍司令部壕; Kyūkaigun Shireibu-gō; ☎850-4055; 236 Tomigusuku; admission ¥420; ☉8:30am-5pm), where 4000 men committed suicide or were killed as the battle for Okinawa drew to its bloody conclusion. Only 250m of the tunnels are open, but you can wander through the maze of corridors, see the commander's final words on the wall of his room, and inspect the holes and scars in other walls from the grenade blasts that killed many of the men. To reach the site, take bus 33 or 46 from Naha bus terminal to the Tomigusuku-kōen-mae stop (¥230, 20 minutes, hourly). From there it's a 10-minute walk – follow the English signs (the entrance is near the top of the hill).

Kerama Islands
慶良間諸島

The islands of the Kerama group are a world away from the hustle and bustle of Okinawa-hontō, though even these islands can get crowded during the summer holiday season. The three main islands here are Zamami-jima, Aka-jima and Tokashiki-jima. You can easily visit any of these as a day trip from Naha, but we recommend a few days in a *minshuku* (Japanese guest house) on one of the islands to really savour the experience.

AKA-JIMA   阿嘉島

♪098 / POP 279

A mere 2km in diameter, tiny Aka-jima makes up for in beauty what it lacks in size. With some of the best beaches in the Keramas and an extremely peaceful atmosphere, it's easy to get stuck here for several days. There's also some great snorkelling and diving nearby.

There are great beaches on every side of the island, but for sheer postcard-perfect beauty, it's hard to beat the 1km stretch of white sand on the northeast coast known as **Nishibama Beach** (ニシバマビーチ). This beach can be crowded in summer; if you want privacy, there are quieter beaches on the other sides of the island.

Dive shop-hotel **Marine House Seasir** (ペンションシーサー; ☎0120-10-2737; www.seasir.com; r per person with meals ¥7350) at the west end of the main village, has good, clean Western- and Japanese-style rooms. Most of the guests are divers. It offers whale-watching tours (¥4800) from January to March.

Kawai Diving (☎987-2219; http://oki-zama mi.jp/~kawai/; 153 Aka; r per person incl meals from ¥6510; P @ 🛜), located along Maehama Beach on the south coast, has simple rooms and a family atmosphere. English-speaking staff are happy to tell guests about the island and take them diving (one/two dives ¥6300/10,500, equipment rental ¥1260 per piece).

Zamami Sonei Ferry (☎868-4567) has two or three fast ferries a day (¥3140, one hour, 10 minutes) and one regular ferry (¥2120, 1½ hours) to/from Naha's Tomari Port. A motorboat also makes four trips a day between Aka-jima and Zamami-jima (¥300, 15 minutes).

ZAMAMI-JIMA 座間味島

☎098 / POP 586

A stone's throw from Aka-jima, Zamami-jima is *slightly* more developed, but also has some great beaches and a few rocky vistas. It's got some brilliant offshore islands and great diving and snorkelling in the surrounding waters. There is a **tourist information office** (☎987-2277; ☺9am-5pm) at the port.

Furuzamami Beach (古座間味ビーチ), approximately 1km southeast from the port (over the hill), is a stunning 700m stretch of white sand that is fronted by clear, shallow water and a bit of coral. The beach is well developed for day trippers, and has toilets, showers and food stalls. You can also rent snorkelling gear here (¥1000).

If you fancy a little solitude, you'll find picturesque empty beaches in several of the coves on the other sides of the island. The best beaches, however, are on **Gahi-jima** (嘉比島) and **Agenashiku-jima** (安慶名敷島), which are located about a kilometre south of the port. Ringed by delightful white-sand beaches, they are perfect for a half-day *Robinson Crusoe* experience. One boat operator who can take you to these islands and arrange snorkelling trips is **Zamami**

Tour Operation (☎987-3586). The tourist information office can also help arrange boat tours (pick-up/drop-off ¥1500 per person round trip).

Zamami-jima makes a great day trip from Naha, but an overnight stay will be more relaxing. A good place to stay is **Joy Joy** (ジョイジョイ; ☎987-2445, 0120-10-2445; http://keramajoyjoy.com/index.html; 434-2 Zamami; r per person incl breakfast from ¥5250) in the northwest corner of the village. Accommodation is in a variety of rooms that surround a small garden. This pension also runs a dive shop, with beach and sea dive tours from ¥4730.

Minshuku Summer House Yū Yū (民宿サマーハウス遊遊; ☎987-3055; www.yuyu-okinawa.jp/index.html; 130 Zamami; r per person with/without meals from ¥6000/3500) is a friendly *minshuku* that is just up the street from Joy Joy in the main village. Both places are an easy walk from the pier.

Zamami Sonei (☎868-4567) has two or three fast ferries a day (¥3140, 50 minutes) and one regular ferry (¥2120, two hours) to/from Naha's Tomari Port. The ferries usually stop at Aka-jima en route from Naha to Zamami. A motorboat also makes four trips a day between Aka-jima and Zamami-jima (¥300, 15 minutes).

There are no buses or taxis on Zamami-jima, though nothing is too far away. Rental cars, scooters and bicycles are available near the pier.

Japan
In Focus

Japan Today 340
What's going on today in the Land of the Rising Sun?

History 342
A brief look at the events that made the country what it is today.

The People of Japan 350
Learn about the people you'll meet on your trip.

Food & Drink 354
Here's the scoop on what's on the menu in Japan (and how to order it).

Arts & Architecture 362
Delve deep into Japan's incredible artistic traditions.

Onsen 367
We'll help you get yourself into hot water.

Ryokan 369
Spend a night or three in a traditional Japanese inn – we show you how.

Family Travel 371
Here are some helpful hints for those travelling with the whole team.

Umbrellas, Kyoto Handicraft Center (p247)
LONELY PLANET / GETTY IMAGES ©

Japan Today

> *Japan appears to be entering a period of economic stagnation and inward-looking attitudes*

A *shinkansen* (bullet train) passes Mt Fuji (p121)

belief systems
(% of population)

| 84 | 71 | 8 | 2 |
| Shintoism | Buddhism | Other | Christianity |

if Japan were 100 people

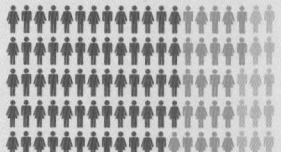

64 would be 15-64 years old
23 would be over 65 years old
13 would be 0-14 years old

population per sq km

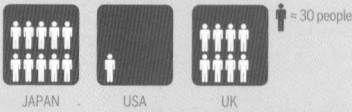

♟ ≈ 30 people

JAPAN   USA   UK

The Great East Japan Earthquake and the ensuing tsunami and nuclear accident were inflection points for Japan. Shortly after the quake, optimists predicted that the disaster would usher in long-needed changes and revive the nation. Now, more than two years on from that grim day, optimists are in short supply as Japan appears to be entering a period of economic stagnation, nationalist politics and inward-looking attitudes that hark back to days of *sakoku* (national seclusion).

Rebuilding the Northeast & the Future of Nuclear Power

The earthquake and following tsunami, which struck on 11 March 2011, took the lives of almost 16,000 people. The tsunami also caused the second-worst nuclear disaster in history at the Fukushima Dai-Ichi nuclear power plant. While government officials declared that cold shutdown had been achieved at the plant, concerns remain about radiation and the safety of food produced in local areas.

TAKESHI.K / GETTY IMAGES ©

Recovery

With the exception of the Fukushima Dai-Ichi nuclear plant, which will take years or even decades to decommission, most of Tōhoku has been cleaned up and the main infrastructure has been largely rebuilt. Needless to say, rebuilding a vast area of the country costs money. Sadly, this was money that Japan could hardly afford to spend, as the country was already in economic doldrums dating back to the Global Financial Crisis of 2008 and even further back to the 'lost decade' of the 1990s. In 2010, China surpassed Japan as the world's second-largest economy and countries like Korea and Malaysia are taking big bites out of industries that Japan used to dominate.

Neighbourhood Tensions

Given this backdrop of hard economic times, it's not surprising that nationalist politics have been enjoying something of a revival in recent years. Preaching the message that Japan can regain its former glory by returning to its 'Japanese roots', a number of politicians – like Ishihara Shintarō, the former governor of Tokyo, and Hashimoto Tōru, acting mayor of Osaka – formed nationalist political parties that garnered several seats in Japan's recent elections.

In 2012, Ishihara caused widespread outrage in China and Korea when he announced plans to purchase the disputed Senkaku Islands (known in China as the Daioyu Islands). The Japanese government intervened and purchased the islands and nationalised them, which further inflamed passions. While a direct confrontation was avoided, tensions were high at the time of writing. Meanwhile, as a result of the crisis initiated by Ishihara, the Japanese auto industry lost hundreds of millions of dollars as Chinese buyers avoided purchasing Japanese cars.

The nuclear disaster and the government's response to it caused a crisis of confidence in Japan. In a nation that otherwise prides itself on efficiency, technological expertise and clean government, questions were asked about the close ties between the nuclear industry and the ministries that regulate it.

The antinuclear movement in Japan, which had previously been a very small fringe group, grew to be a political force to be reckoned with. Anti-nuclear demonstrations, with protestors numbering in the tens and even hundreds of thousands, were held in several Japanese cities. Partially as a result of these demonstrations, nuclear power plants across the country were shut down one by one until, by May 2012, all of Japan's 54 nuclear plants were off line. However, less than two months later, the Oi nuclear plant in Fukui Prefecture was restarted and more restarts are scheduled.

341

History

Man in samurai costume at the Jidai Matsuri (p232), Kyoto

MASATOSHI AIDA / GETTY IMA

Japan's history is shaped by its distance from mainland Asia and the fact that China chose not to become an aggressive naval power. This allowed Japan to evolve into a truly unique culture. Japan's history can be divided into five main periods: prehistory, which comes to an end in about 400BC; preclassical, from 400BC until 710AD; classical, from 710 to 1185; medieval, from 1185 to 1600; and premodern to modern, from 1600 onward.

Prehistory

The origin of Japan's earliest inhabitants is obscure. There was certainly emigration via land bridges that once connected Japan with Siberia and Korea, but it is also thought that seafaring migrants from Polynesia may have landed on Kyūshū and Okinawa. It is likely that the Japanese people are a result of emigration from Siberia in the north, China and Korea to the west and, perhaps, Polynesian stock from the south.

c 10,000 BC
First evidence of the hunter-gatherer Jōmon people.

The first signs of civilisation in Japan are from the Neolithic period around 10,000 BC. This is called the Jōmon (Rope Mark) period after the discovery of pottery fragments with rope marks. The people at this time lived as fishers, hunters and food-gatherers.

This period was gradually superseded by the Yayoi era, which dates from around 300 BC and is named after the site near Tokyo where pottery fragments were found. The Yayoi people are considered to have had a strong connection with Korea and their most important developments were the wet cultivation of rice and the use of bronze and iron implements.

The period following the Yayoi era has been called the Kofun (Burial Mound) period by archaeologists who discovered thousands of grave mounds concentrated mostly in central and western Japan.

As more and more settlements banded together to defend their land, groups became larger until, by AD 300, the Yamato clan had loosely unified the nation through either conquest or alliance. With the ascendancy of the Yamato emperors, Japan for the first time became a true nation, stretching from the islands south of Kyūshū to the northern wilds of Honshū.

The Best... Places for Japanese History

1 Nara (p276)

2 Kyoto (p193)

3 Hiroshima (p306)

4 Okinawa-hontō (p332)

IN FOCUS HISTORY

Buddhism & Early Chinese Influence

In the mid-6th century, Buddhism was introduced from China via the Korean kingdom of Paekche. From the earliest days of the Yamato court, it was the custom to relocate the capital following the death of an emperor (presumably to free the capital from the taint of death). However, after the shift of the capital to Nara in 710, this long-held custom was altered as the capital remained there for the next 75 years.

Establishment of a Native Culture

By the end of the 8th century, the Buddhist clergy in Nara had become so politically meddlesome that Emperor Kammu decided to relocate the capital to insulate it against their growing influence. The site eventually chosen was Heian-kyō (modern-day Kyoto).

The Heian period (794–1185) saw a great flourishing in the arts and important developments in religious thinking as Chinese ideas and institutions were imported and adapted to the needs of the Japanese.

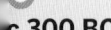

c 300 BC
The Yayoi people appear in southwest Japan (probably via Korea).

c 300
Suijin is the first verifiable emperor of Japan.

Mid-5th century
Writing, in the form of Chinese characters, is introduced into Japan.

343

Historical Periods

Jōmon 10,000–300 BC
Yayoi 300 BC–AD 300
Kofun 300–710
Nara 710–94
Heian 794–1185
Kamakura 1185–1333
Muromachi 1333–1576
Momoyama 1576–1600
Edo 1600–1868
Meiji 1868–1912
Taishō 1912–26
Shōwa 1926–89
Heisei 1989 to the present

During the late Heian period, emperors began to devote more time to leisure and scholarly pursuit and less time to government. This created an opening for the Fujiwara, a noble family, to capture important court posts and become the chief power brokers, a role the clan was able to maintain for several centuries.

The Heian period is considered the apogee of Japanese courtly elegance, but out in the provinces a new power was on the rise, that of the samurai (warrior class), which built up its own armed forces and readily turned to arms to defend its autonomy. Samurai families soon moved into the capital, where they muscled in on the court.

The Fujiwara were eventually eclipsed by the Taira clan, who ruled briefly before being ousted by the Minamoto family (also known as the Genji) at the battle of Dannoura (modern-day Shimonoseki) in 1185.

Domination through Military Rule

The Kamakura period (1185–1333) followed on from the Heian period. In 1192 Minamoto Yoritomo conquered the inhabitants of what is now Aomori-ken, thereby extending his rule to the tip of northern Honshū. For the first time in its history, all of Japan proper was now under unified rule. After assuming the title of shōgun (military leader), Minamoto set up his headquarters in Kamakura, while the emperor remained the nominal ruler in Kyoto. It was the beginning of a long period of feudal rule by successive samurai families. In fact, this feudal system was to linger on, in one form or another, until imperial power was restored in 1868.

The Kamakura government emerged victorious in battles with the Mongols (who attacked twice in the 13th century), but it was unable to pay its soldiers and lost the support of the samurai class. In an attempt to take advantage of popular discontent, Emperor Go-Daigo led an unsuccessful rebellion against the government and was exiled to Oki-shotō, the islands near Matsue in western Honshū, where he waited a year before trying again. The second attempt successfully toppled the government.

712 & 720
Writing of the *Kojiki* (Record of Old Things; 712) and *Nihon Shoki* (Record of Japan; 720).

1156
Two major provincial families, the Taira and the Minamoto, engage in bitter warfare.

1185
The Taira are toppled by Minamoto Yoritomo, who becomes the most powerful man in the land.

Kofun Burial Mounds

The origins of the Japanese imperial line and the Japanese people in general are shrouded in mystery. Much of what we do know comes from large, earthen burial mounds scattered around the islands of Honshū, Kyūshū and Shikoku. These burial mounds, called *kofun*, served as tombs for members of Japan's early nobility. The practice of building these mounds started quite suddenly in the 3rd century and died out gradually by the end of the 7th century. It was during this period that the forerunners of the present imperial family, the Yamato clan, were consolidating their power as rulers of Japan.

Country at War

This heralded the start of the Muromachi period (1333–1576). Emperor Go-Daigo refused to reward his warriors, favouring the aristocracy and priesthood instead. This led to the revolt of Ashikaga Takauji, who had previously changed sides to support Emperor Go-Daigo. Ashikaga defeated Go-Daigo at Kyoto, then installed a new emperor and appointed himself shōgun; the Ashikaga family later settled at Muromachi, an area of Kyoto.

The Ashikaga ruled with gradually diminishing effectiveness in a land slipping steadily into civil war and chaos. The Ōnin War, which broke out in 1467, developed into a full-scale civil war and marked the rapid decline of the Ashikaga family. *Daimyō* (domain lords) and local leaders fought for power in bitter territorial disputes that were to last for a century. This period, from 1467 to around the start of the Momoyama period in 1576, is known as the Warring States period (Sengoku-jigai).

Return to Unity

In 1568 Oda Nobunaga, the son of a *daimyō*, seized power from the imperial court in Kyoto and used his military genius to initiate a process of pacification and unification in central Japan. Oda was succeeded by his most able commander, Toyotomi Hide-yoshi, who extended unification so that by 1590 the whole country was under his rule.

The Christian Century

In the mid-16th century, when the Europeans first made their appearance, foreign trade was little regulated by Japan's central government. The first Europeans to arrive were the Portuguese, who were shipwrecked off southern Kyūshū in 1543. The Portuguese found an appreciative reception for their skills in firearm manufacture, skills which were soon adopted by the Japanese. The Jesuit missionary Francis Xavier arrived in Kagoshima in

13th century
Zen Buddhism becomes established in Japan.
Monk meditating

1400s & 1500s
Japan is in almost constant internal warfare, including the particularly fierce Ōnin War of 1467–77.

1549 and was followed by more missionaries, who quickly converted local lords keen to profit from foreign trade and assistance with military supplies. The new religion spread rapidly, gaining several hundred thousand converts, particularly in Nagasaki.

At first Oda Nobunaga saw the advantages of trading with Europeans and tolerated the arrival of Christianity as a counterbalance to Buddhism. Once Toyotomi Hideyoshi assumed power, however, this tolerance gradually gave way to a suspicion that an alien religion would subvert his rule. Edicts against Christianity were followed in 1597 by the crucifixion of 26 foreign priests and Japanese converts.

Peace & Seclusion

The supporters of Toyotomi Hideyoshi's young heir, Toyotomi Hideyori, were defeated in 1600 by Toyotomi's former ally, Tokugawa Ieyasu, at the Battle of Sekigahara. Tokugawa set up his field headquarters (*bakufu*) at Edo, now Tokyo, and assumed the title of shōgun. This marked the beginning of the Edo, or Tokugawa, period (1600–1868). The emperor and court continued to exercise purely nominal authority in Kyoto.

Under Tokugawa rule, Japan entered a period of *sakoku* (national seclusion). Japanese were forbidden on pain of death to travel abroad or engage in trade with foreign countries. Only the Dutch, Chinese and Koreans were allowed to remain in Japan, and they were placed under strict supervision. The Dutch were confined to the island of Dejima, near Nagasaki, and their contacts restricted to merchants and prostitutes.

By the turn of the 19th century, the Tokugawa government was falling into stagnation and corruption. Famines and poverty among the peasants and samurai further weakened the system. Foreign ships started to challenge Japan's isolation with increasing insistence, and the Japanese soon realised that their outmoded defences were ineffectual. Russian contacts in the north were followed by British and American visits. In 1853 Commodore Matthew Perry of the US Navy arrived with a squadron of Black Ships to demand the opening up of Japan to trade.

Samurai

The samurai were members of Japan's warrior class who were active in Japan from around the 12th century. The samurai's best-known weapon was the *katana* sword, though in earlier days the bow was also prominent. Arguably the world's finest swordsmen, samurai were formidable opponents in single combat. During modernisation in the late 19th century, the government, itself comprising samurai, realised that a conscript army was more efficient as a unified fighting force, and disestablished the samurai class. However, samurai ideals such as endurance and fighting to the death were revived through propaganda prior to WWII.

1543
The first Westerners, the Portuguese, arrive by chance, heralding the advent of firearms and Christianity.

1568
The warlord Oda Nobunaga seizes Kyoto and soon becomes the supreme power in the land.

1600
The warlord Tokugawa Ieyasu seizes power at the Battle of Sekigahara. Statue of Tokugawa Ieyasu at Tōshō-gū, Nikkō

A Narrow Escape for the Old Capitals

Historians have suggested that both Kyoto and Nara were on a list of some 180 cities earmarked for air raids by the US during WWII. Kyoto, with a population of more than one million people, had been a prime target for atomic annihilation; however, it escaped because it was not home to a significant number of munitions factories (although others have suggested it was merely a vagary of the weather that saved the city). Nara, it has been suggested, escaped merely due to having a population under 60,000, which kept it far enough down the list not to be reached before the unconditional surrender of Japan in September 1945.

The arrival of foreigners proved to be the decisive blow to an already shaky Tokugawa regime. Upset by the shōgunate's handling of the foreign incursion, two large *daimyō* areas in western Japan, the Satsuma and the Chōshū, allied themselves with disenchanted samurai. They succeeded in capturing the emperor in 1868, declaring a restoration of imperial rule and an end to the power of the shōgun. The ruling shōgun, Tokugawa Yoshinobu, resigned, and Emperor Meiji assumed control of state affairs.

Emergence from Isolation

The initial stages of the Meiji Restoration (1868–1912) were resisted in a state of virtual civil war. The abolition of the shōgunate was followed by the surrender of the *daimyō*, whose lands were divided into the prefectures that exist today. Edo became Japan's new capital and was renamed Tokyo (Eastern Capital).

Under the slogan *fukoku kyōhei* (rich country; strong military), the economy underwent a crash course in Westernisation and industrialisation. An influx of Western experts was encouraged and Japanese students were sent abroad to acquire expertise in modern technologies.

Japan's growing confidence was demonstrated by the abolition of foreign treaty rights and by the ease with which it trounced China in the Sino-Japanese War (1894–95). The subsequent treaty recognised Korean independence and ceded Taiwan to Japan. Friction with Russia eventually led to the Russo-Japanese War (1904–05), in which the Japanese army attacked the Russians in Manchuria and Korea. The Japanese Navy stunned the Russians by inflicting a crushing defeat on its Baltic fleet at the battle of Tsu-shima.

1853–54

US Commodore Matthew Perry uses 'gunboat diplomacy' to force Japan to open up for trade.

1902

Japan signs the Anglo-Japanese Alliance, the first equal alliance between a Western and non-Western nation.

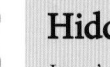

Hidden Christians

Japan's 'Christian Century' began in 1549 with the arrival of Portuguese missionaries on the island of Kyūshū. Within decades, hundreds of thousands of Japanese were converted.

The rapid rise of Christian belief, as well as its association with trade, new Western weaponry and control of Japanese territory, came to be viewed as a threat by the *bakufu* (military government) under Toyotomi Hideyoshi. The 1587 expulsion of missionaries began an era of suppression of Christians and thousands were estimated to have been executed during the next six decades. Many thousands of Christian peasants rebelled in the 1637–38 Shimabara Rebellion, after which Christianity was outlawed completely.

Other persecution took the form of *fumi-e*, where suspected Christians were forced to walk on images of Jesus. The Gregorian date on the front of the Dutch trading house on the island of Hirado was taken as proof of the Dutch traders' Christianity and used to justify their exile to Nagasaki's Dejima island, ushering in more than two centuries of *sakoku* (closure of the country).

Japanese Christians reacted by going under cover as *kakure Kirishitan* (hidden Christians). With no more priests, they worshiped in lay-led services in secret rooms inside private homes. On the surface, worship resembled other Japanese religions, including the use of Shintō *kamidana* altars and Buddhist *butsudan* ancestor, worship chests in homes, and ceremonial rice and sake. The sounds of worship, too, mimicked Buddhist incantations. Scholars put the numbers of hidden Christians at about 150,000.

It was not until 1865, 12 years after the arrival of the Black Ships (the first European ships), that Japan had its first large-scale church again, Oura Cathedral in Nagasaki, and missionaries began to return to Japan with its reopening in 1868. The Meiji government officially declared freedom of religion in 1871. Today, estimates put the number of Japanese Christians at between one and two million (about one percent of the population).

Industrialisation & Asian Dominance

On his death in 1912, Emperor Meiji was succeeded by his son, Yoshihito. His period of rule was named the Taishō era (1912–26). When WWI broke out, Japan sided against Germany but did not become deeply involved in the conflict. While the Allies were occupied with war, Japan took the opportunity, through shipping and trade, to expand its economy at top speed. At the same time, Japan gained a strong foothold in China.

1941
Japan enters WWII by striking Pearl Harbor on 7 December.

1945
On 6 August, Hiroshima becomes the first-ever victim of an atomic bombing.

1945–52
Japan experiences a US-led occupation.

Nationalism & the Pursuit of Empire

The Shōwa era (1926–89) commenced when Emperor Hirohito ascended the throne in 1926. He had toured extensively in Europe, mixed with European nobility and developed quite a liking for the British lifestyle.

A rising tide of nationalism was quickened by the world economic depression that began in 1930. Popular unrest was marked by plots to overthrow the government and political assassinations. This led to a strong increase in the power of the militarists who approved the invasion of Manchuria in 1931 and the installation there of a puppet regime controlled by the Japanese. In 1933 Japan withdrew from the League of Nations and in 1937 entered into full-scale hostilities against China.

As the leader of a new order for Asia, Japan signed a tripartite pact with Germany and Italy in 1940. The Japanese military leaders saw their main opponents to this new order for Asia, the so-called Greater East Asia Co-prosperity Sphere, in the United States.

World War II

When diplomatic attempts to gain US neutrality failed, Japan launched itself into WWII with a surprise attack on Pearl Harbor on 7 December 1941.

At first, Japan scored rapid successes, pushing its battle fronts across to India, down to the fringes of Australia and out into the mid-Pacific. The Battle of Midway opened the US counterattack, puncturing Japanese naval superiority and turning the tide of the war against Japan. By 1945, exhausted by submarine blockades and aerial bombing, Japan had been driven back on all fronts. In August of the same year, the declaration of war by the Soviet Union and the atomic bombs dropped by the US on Hiroshima and Nagasaki proved to be the final straw: Emperor Hirohito announced unconditional surrender.

Postwar Reconstruction

At the end of the war, the Japanese economy was in ruins and inflation was rampant. A program of recovery provided loans, restricted imports and encouraged capital investment and personal saving.

By the late 1950s, trade was again flourishing, and the economy continued to expand rapidly. From textiles and the manufacture of labour-intensive goods, such as cameras, the Japanese 'economic miracle' spread into virtually every sector of economic activity. Economic recession and inflation surfaced in 1974 and again in 1980, mostly as a result of steep increases in the price of imported oil, on which Japan is dependent. But despite these setbacks, Japan became the world's most successful export economy, generating massive trade surpluses and dominating such fields as electronics, robotics, computer technology, car manufacturing and banking.

1990s–early 2000s
After its 'bubble economy' bursts in the early 1990s, Japan enters a decade of recession.

1995
On 17 January an earthquake with a magnitude of 7.2 hits Kōbe, killing more than 5000 people.

2011
Japan is hit by an earthquake and tsunami on 11 March that kills more than 15,000 people.

The People of Japan

Senso-ji, Tokyo (p86)

CHRISTOPHER GROENHOUT / GETTY IMA

Japan is unusual among nations for the relative homogeneity of its population. This, combined with the distance of the Japanese islands from the Asian continent, has given rise to what some people – including some Japanese – refer to as 'Galápagos syndrome', namely, a truly peculiar culture. In point of fact, the Japanese are not as unique as outsiders and many Japanese like to believe. Rather, they exist within a continuum that contains Korean and Chinese cultures, with some notable differences.

Truly Unique?

The uniqueness and peculiarity of 'the Japanese' is a favourite topic of both Western observers and the Japanese themselves. It's worth starting any discussion of the people of Japan by noting that there is no such thing as 'the Japanese'. Rather, there are 127 million individuals in Japan with their own unique characters, interests and habits. And despite popular stereotypes to the contrary, the Japanese are as varied as any people on earth. Just as importantly, Japanese people have more in common with the rest of humanity than they have differences.

Why then the pervasive images of the Japanese as inscrutable or even bizarre? These stereotypes are largely rooted in language: few Japanese are able to speak English as well as, say, your average

Singaporean, Hong Kong Chinese or well-educated Indian, not to mention most Europeans. This difficulty with English is largely rooted in the country's appalling English education system, and is compounded by a natural shyness, a perfectionist streak and the nature of the Japanese language itself, which contains fewer sounds than any other major world language (making pronunciation of other languages difficult). Thus, what appears to the casual observer to be a maddening inscrutability is more likely just an inability to communicate effectively. Outsiders who become fluent in Japanese discover a people whose thoughts and feelings are surprisingly – almost boringly – similar to those of folks in other developed nations.

The Mongolian Spot

Almost all Japanese babies are born with a Mongolian spot, or *mōkohan*, on their bottoms or lower backs. This harmless bluish-grey birthmark is composed of melanin-containing cells. Mongolian spots are common in several Asian races including, as the name suggests, Mongolians, as well as in Native Americans. These birthmarks, which usually fade by the age of five, raise interesting questions about the origins of the Japanese people.

All this said, the Japanese do have certain characteristics that reflect its unique history and interaction with its environment. First, Japan is an island nation. Second, until WWII, Japan was never conquered by an outside power, nor was it heavily influenced by Christian missionaries. Third, until the beginning of last century, the majority of Japanese lived in close-knit rural farming communities. Fourth, most of Japan is covered in steep mountains, so the few flat areas of the country are quite crowded – people literally live on top of each other. Finally, for almost all of its history, Japan has been a strictly hierarchical place, with something approximating a caste system during the Edo period.

All of this has produced a people who highly value group identity and smooth social harmony – in a tightly packed city or small farming village, there simply isn't room for colourful individualism. One of the ways harmony is preserved is by forming consensus, and concealing personal opinions and true feelings. Thus, the free-flowing exchange of ideas, debates and even heated arguments that one expects in the West are far less common in Japan. This reticence about sharing innermost thoughts perhaps contributes to the Western image of the Japanese as mysterious.

Of course, there is a lot more to the typical Japanese character than just a tendency to prize social harmony. Any visitor to the country will soon discover a people who are remarkably conscientious, meticulous, industrious, honest and technically skilled. A touching shyness and sometimes almost painful self-consciousness are also undoubted features of many Japanese as well. These characteristics result in a society that is a joy for the traveller to experience.

And let us say that any visit to Japan is a good chance to explode the myths about Japan and the Japanese. While you may imagine a nation of suit-clad conformists or inscrutable automatons, a few rounds in a local *izakaya* (pub-eatery) will quickly put all of these notions to rest.

Population

Japan has a population of approximately 127 million people (the ninth-largest in the world) and, with 75% of it concentrated in urban centres, population density is extremely high. Areas such as the Tokyo–Kawasaki–Yokohama conurbation are so

351

densely populated that they have almost ceased to be separate cities, running into each other and forming a vast coalescence that, if considered as a whole, would constitute the world's largest city.

One notable feature of Japan's population is its relative ethnic and cultural homogeneity. This is particularly striking for visitors from the USA, Australia and other multicultural nations. The main reason for this ethnic homogeneity is Japan's strict immigration laws, which have ensured that only a small number of foreigners settle in the country.

The largest non-Japanese group in the country is made up of 650,000 *zai-nichi kankoku-jin* (resident Koreans). For most outsiders, Koreans are an invisible minority. Indeed, even the Japanese themselves have no way of knowing that someone is of Korean descent if he or she adopts a Japanese name. Nevertheless, Japanese-born Koreans, who in some cases speak no language other than Japanese, were only recently released from the obligation to carry ID cards with their fingerprints at all times, and some still face discrimination in the workplace and other aspects of their daily lives.

Aside from Koreans, most foreigners in Japan are temporary workers from China, Southeast Asia, South America and Western countries. Indigenous groups such as the Ainu have been reduced to very small numbers, due to intermarriage with non-Ainu and government attempts to hasten assimilation of Ainu into general Japanese society. At present, Ainu are concentrated mostly in Hokkaidō, the northernmost of Japan's main islands.

The most notable feature of Japan's population is the fact that it is shrinking. Japan's astonishingly low birth rate of 1.3 births per woman is among the lowest in the developed world and Japan is rapidly becoming a nation of elderly citizens. The population began declining in 2007, and will reach 100 million in 2050 and 67 million in 2100. Needless to say, such demographic change will have a major influence on the economy in coming decades.

Maiko (geisha in training), Kyo
PAUL CHESLEY / GETTY IMAGES

Places to Meet the Locals

o **Izakaya** The combination of sake and communal seating at these 'dining pubs' makes it easy to start chatting with your neighbours. More than likely, they'll break the ice by offering you a drink.

o **Sentō** The Japanese are fond of pointing out that getting naked is a good way of removing barriers of class and profession. It's also a good way of removing the barrier of nationality. If you're okay with a 'full monty' approach to socialising, then a visit to the local *sentō* (public bath) is a good way to meet the locals.

o **Hiring a volunteer guide** Volunteer guides are available in many sightseeing districts. Ask at the local tourist information centre.

o **In the mountains** The Japanese are keen hikers and the ones you meet on the trail seem to be extra friendly. A good opener is *Ii tenki desu ne* (Nice weather, isn't it?).

o **Doing a home visit/homestay** Many local tourist offices and community centres can arrange for you to visit a Japanese family for a meal or to stay the night.

Women in Japan

Traditional Japanese society restricted the woman's role to the home, where as housekeeper she wielded considerable power, overseeing all financial matters, monitoring the children's education and, in some ways, acting as the head of the household. Even in the early Meiji period (1868–1912), however, the ideal was rarely matched by reality: labour shortfalls often resulted in women taking on factory work, and even before that, women often worked side by side with men in the fields.

As might be expected, the contemporary situation is complex. There are, of course, those who stick to established roles. They tend to opt for shorter college courses, often at women's colleges, and see education as an asset in the marriage market. Once married, they leave the role of breadwinner to their husbands.

Increasingly, however, Japanese women are choosing to forgo or delay marriage in favour of pursuing their own career ambitions. Of course, changing aspirations do not necessarily translate into changing realities, and Japanese women are still significantly underrepresented in upper management and political positions, and there is a disproportionately high number of females employed as OLs (office ladies). This is, in part, due to the prevalence of gender discrimination in Japanese companies, as well as societal expectations. Japanese women are often forced to choose between having a career and having a family. Not only do many companies refuse to hire women for career-track positions, some Japanese men are not interested in having a career woman as a spouse.

Those women who do choose full-time work suffer from one of the worst gender wage gaps in the developed world: Japanese women earn only 66% of what Japanese men earn, compared to 76% in the USA, 83% in the UK and 85% in Australia according to figures released by respective governments). In politics, the situation is even worse: Japanese women hold only 10% of seats in the Diet, the nation's governing body.

Food & Drink

Sushi at the Tsukiji Fish Market (p68)

JAIME HOJJE LEE / GETTY IMA

Those familiar with Japanese cuisine know that eating is half the fun of travelling in Japan. Even if you've already tried some of Japan's better-known specialities in Japanese restaurants in your own country, you're likely to be surprised by how delicious the original is when served on its home turf. More importantly, the adventurous eater will be delighted to find that Japanese food is far more than just sushi, tempura or sukiyaki (sliced meat simmered with vegetables and sauce).

Eating in Japan

You may baulk at charging into a restaurant where both the language and the menu are likely to be incomprehensible. The best way to get over this fear is to familiarise yourself with the main types of Japanese restaurants so that you have some idea of what's on offer and how to order it. Those timid of heart should take solace in the fact that the Japanese will go to extraordinary lengths to understand what you want and will help you to order.

With the exception of *shokudō* (all-round restaurants) and *izakaya* (pub-style restaurants), most Japanese restaurants concentrate on a speciality cuisine. This naturally makes for delicious eating, but does limit your choice.

Restaurants: Here's the Drill

When you enter a restaurant in Japan, you'll be greeted with a hearty *irasshaimase!* (Welcome!). In all but the most casual places the waiter will next ask you *nan-mei sama* (How many people?). Answer with your fingers, which is what the Japanese do.

At this point you will be given an *oshibori* (a hot towel), a cup of tea and a menu. The *oshibori* is for wiping your hands and face. When you're done with it, just roll it up and leave it next to your place. Now comes the hard part: ordering. If you don't read Japanese, you can use the romanised translations to help you, or direct the waiter's attention to the Japanese script. If this doesn't work, there are two phrases that may help: *o-susume wa nan desu ka* (What do you recommend?) and *o-makase shimasu* (Please decide for me). If you're still having problems, you can try pointing at other diners' food or, if the restaurant has them, at the plastic food models in the window.

When you've finished eating, you can signal for the bill by crossing one index finger over the other to form the sign of an 'x'. This is the standard sign for 'bill please'. You can also say *o-kanjō kudasai*. Remember there is no tipping in Japan and tea is free of charge. Usually you will be given a bill to take to the cashier at the front of the restaurant. At more upmarket places, the host of the party will discreetly excuse themselves to pay before the group leaves. Unlike some places in the West, one doesn't usually leave cash on the table by way of payment. Only the bigger and more international places take credit cards, so cash is always the surer option.

When leaving, it is polite to say to the restaurant staff *gochisō-sama deshita* (it was a real feast).

The Best... Food Cities to

1 **Eat sushi** Tokyo (p97)

2 **Eat *kaiseki* (Japanese haute cuisine)** Kyoto (p238)

3 **Eat *okonomiyaki* (savoury Japanese pancakes)** Hiroshima (310)

4 **Eat *rāmen* (egg noodles)** Nagasaki (p328)

Types of Restaurants & Sample Menus

Shokudō

A *shokudō* is the most common type of restaurant in Japan. Easily distinguished by the presence of plastic food displays in the window, these inexpensive places usually serve a variety of *washoku* (Japanese dishes) and *yōshoku* (Western dishes).

At lunch, and sometimes dinner, the easiest meal to order at a *shokudō* is a *teishoku* (set-course meal), which is sometimes also called *ranchi setto* (lunch set) or *kōsu*. This usually includes a main dish of meat or fish, a bowl of rice, miso soup, shredded cabbage and some *tsukemono* (Japanese pickles). In addition, most *shokudō* serve a fairly standard selection of *donburi-mono* (rice dishes) and *menrui* (noodle dishes). When you order noodles, you can choose between *soba* (buckwheat noodles) and *udon* (thick white wheat noodles), both of which are served with a variety of toppings. If you're at a loss as to what to order, simply say *kyō-no-ranchi* (today's lunch), and they'll do the rest. Expect to spend from ¥800 to ¥1000 for a meal at a *shokudō*.

Rice Dishes

katsu-don	かつ丼	rice topped with a fried pork cutlet
niku-don	牛丼	rice topped with thin slices of cooked beef
oyako-don	親子丼	rice topped with egg and chicken
ten-don	天丼	rice topped with tempura shrimp and vegetables

355

Noodle Dishes

soba	そば	buckwheat noodles
udon	うどん	thick, white wheat noodles
kake soba/udon	かけそば/うどん	soba/udon noodles in broth
kitsune soba/udon	きつねそば/うどん	soba/udon noodles with fried tofu
tempura soba/udon	天ぷらそば/うどん	soba/udon noodles with tempura shrimp
tsukimi soba/udon	月見そば/うどん	soba/udon noodles with raw egg on top

Izakaya

An *izakaya* is the Japanese equivalent of a pub. It's a good place to visit when you want a casual meal, a wide selection of food, a hearty atmosphere and, of course, plenty of beer and sake. When you enter an *izakaya,* you are given the choice of sitting around the counter, at a table or on a tatami floor. You usually order a bite at a time, choosing from a selection of typical Japanese foods such as *yakitori,* sashimi and grilled fish, as well as Japanese interpretations of Western foods such as French fries and beef stew.

agedashi-dōfu	揚げだし豆腐	deep-fried tofu in a *dashi* broth
jaga-batā	ジャガバター	baked potatoes with butter
niku-jaga	肉ジャガ	beef and potato stew
shio-yaki-zakana	塩焼魚	whole fish grilled with salt
yaki-onigiri	焼きおにぎり	triangle of grilled rice with *yakitori* sauce
poteto furai	ポテトフライ	French fries
chiizu-age	チーズ揚げ	deep-fried cheese
hiya-yakko	冷奴	cold block of tofu with soy sauce and spring onions
sashimi mori-awase	刺身盛り合わせ	selection of sliced sashimi

Bowl of *rāmen*
KOKI IINO / GETTY IMAGES ©

Soba & Udon

Soba and *udon* are Japan's answer to Chinese-style *rāmen* (egg noodles). *Soba* are thin, brown buckwheat noodles; *udon* are thick, white wheat noodles. Most Japanese noodle shops serve both *soba* and *udon* in a variety of ways. Noodles are usually served in a bowl containing a light, bonito-flavoured broth, but you can also order them served cold and piled on a bamboo screen with a cold broth for dipping.

Sushi & Sashimi

Like *yakitori,* sushi is considered an accompaniment for beer and sake. Nonetheless, both Japanese and foreigners often make a meal of it, and it's one of the healthiest meals around. All proper sushi restaurants serve their fish over rice, in which case it's called sushi, or without rice, in which case it's called sashimi or *tsukuri* (or, politely, *o-tsukuri*). There are two main types of sushi: *nigiri-zushi* (served on a small bed of rice – the most common variety) and *maki-zushi* (served in a seaweed roll).

ama-ebi	甘海老	sweet shrimp
ebi	海老	prawn or shrimp
hamachi	はまち	yellowtail
ika	いか	squid
ikura	イクラ	salmon roe
kani	かに	crab
katsuo	かつお	bonito
maguro	まぐろ	tuna
tai	鯛	sea bream
tamago	たまご	sweetened egg
toro	とろ	choicest cut of fatty tuna belly
unagi	うなぎ	eel with a sweet sauce
uni	うに	sea urchin roe

Vegetarians & Vegans

Travellers who eat fish should have almost no trouble dining in Japan: almost all *shokudō* (all-round restaurants), *izakaya* (pub-style restaurants) and other common restaurants offer a set meal with fish as the main dish. Vegans and vegetarians who don't eat fish will have to get their protein from tofu and other bean products. Note that most *misoshiru* (miso soup) is made with *dashi* broth that contains fish, so if you want to avoid fish, you'll also have to avoid *misoshiru*.

Most big cities in Japan have vegetarian or organic restaurants which naturally serve a variety of choices that appeal to vegetarians and vegans. (See the Eating sections of the destination chapters for specific recommendations. Reviews that include the 🌱 symbol throughout this guide indicate places with a good vegetarian selection.)

In the countryside, you'll have to do your best to find suitable items on the menu, or try to convey your dietary preferences to the restaurant staff. Note that many temples in Japan serve *shōjin-ryōri* (Buddhist vegetarian cuisine), which is made without meat, fish or dairy products. A good place to try this is Kōya-san in Kansai.

Yakitori

Yakitori (skewers of grilled chicken and vegetables) is a popular after-work meal. *Yakitori* is not so much a full meal as an accompaniment for beer and sake. At a *yakitori-ya* (*yakitori* restaurant) you sit around a counter with the other patrons and watch the chef grill your selections over charcoal. The best way to eat here is to order several varieties, then order seconds of the ones you really like. Ordering can be a little confusing since one serving often means two or three skewers (be careful — the price listed on the menu is usually that of a single skewer).

yakitori	焼き鳥	plain, grilled white meat
hasami/negima	はさみ/ねぎま	pieces of white meat alternating with leek
sasami	ささみ	skinless chicken-breast pieces
kawa	皮	chicken skin
tsukune	つくね	chicken meatballs
gyū-niku	牛肉	pieces of beef
tebasaki	手羽先	chicken wings
shiitake	しいたけ	Japanese mushrooms
piiman	ピーマン	small green peppers
tama-negi	玉ねぎ	round, white onions
yaki-onigiri	焼きおにぎり	triangle of rice grilled with *yakitori* sauce

Rāmen

The Japanese imported this dish from China and put their own spin on it to make what is one of the world's most delicious fast foods. *Rāmen* dishes are big bowls of noodles in a meat broth, served with a variety of toppings, such as sliced pork, bean sprouts and leeks. In some restaurants, particularly in Kansai, you may be asked if you'd prefer *kotteri* (thick) or *assari* (thin) soup. Other than this, ordering is simple: just sidle up to the counter and say *rāmen,* or ask for any of the other choices usually on offer.

rāmen	ラーメン	soup and noodles with a sprinkling of meat and vegetables
chāshū-men	チャーシュー麺	*rāmen* topped with slices of roasted pork
wantan-men	ワンタン麺	*rāmen* with meat dumplings
miso-rāmen	みそラーメン	*rāmen* with miso-flavoured broth

Eating Etiquette

Chopsticks in rice Do not stick your *hashi* (chopsticks) upright in a bowl of rice.

Polite expressions When eating with other people, especially when you're a guest, it is polite to say *itadakimasu* (literally, I will receive) before digging in. At the end of the meal, you should thank your host by saying *gochisō-sama deshita* (it was a real feast).

Kampai It is bad form to fill your own glass with beer or sake.

Slurp When you eat noodles in Japan, it's perfectly OK, even expected, to slurp.

Okonomiyaki

The name means 'cook what you like', and an *okonomiyaki* restaurant provides you with an inexpensive opportunity to do just that. Sometimes described as Japanese pizza or pancake, the resemblance is in form only. At an *okonomiyaki* restaurant you sit around a *teppan* (iron hotplate), armed with a spatula and chopsticks to cook your choice of meat, seafood and vegetables in a cabbage and vegetable batter.

mikkusu	ミックス お好み焼き	mixed fillings of seafood, *okonomiyaki* meat and vegetables
modan-yaki	モダン焼き	*okonomiyaki* with *yaki soba* and a fried egg

Tonkatsu

Tonkatsu is a deep-fried breaded pork cutlet that is served with a special sauce, usually as part of a set meal *(tonkatsu teishoku)*. *Tonkatsu* is served both at speciality restaurants and at *shokudō*. Naturally, the best *tonkatsu* is to be found at the speciality places, where a full set will cost ¥1500 to ¥2500. When ordering *tonkatsu,* you are able to choose between *rōsu* (a fatter cut of pork) and *hire* (a leaner cut).

hire katsu	ヒレかつ	*tonkatsu* fillet
tonkatsu teishoku	とんかつ定食	set meal of *tonkatsu,* rice, *misoshiru* (miso soup) and shredded cabbage

Sweets

Although most restaurants don't serve dessert (plates of sliced fruit are sometimes served at the end of a meal), there is no lack of sweets in Japan. Most Japanese sweets (known generically as *wagashi*) are sold in speciality stores for you to eat at home. Many of the more delicate-looking ones are made to balance the strong, bitter taste of the special *matcha* (powdered green tea) served during the tea ceremony.

Okonomiyaki

Some Westerners find Japanese sweets a little challenging, due to the liberal use of a sweet, red *azuki*-bean paste called *anko*. This unusual filling turns up in even the most innocuous looking pastries. The next main ingredient is often pounded sticky rice *(mochi),* which has a consistency that is unfamiliar to many Westerners.

With such a wide variety of sweets, it's impossible to list all the names. However, you'll probably find many variations on the *anko*-covered-by-*mochi* theme.

Okashi-ya (sweet shops) are easy to spot; they usually have open fronts with their wares laid out in wooden trays to entice passers-by. Buying sweets is simple – just point at what you want and indicate with your fingers how many you'd like.

Japanese Tea & Coffee

o-cha	お茶	green tea
sencha	煎茶	medium-grade green tea
matcha	抹茶	powdered green tea used in the tea ceremony
bancha	番茶	ordinary-grade green tea, has a brownish colour
mugicha	麦茶	roasted barley tea
kōcha	紅茶	black, British-style tea
kōhii	コーヒー	regular coffee
burendo kōhii	ブレンドコーヒー	blended coffee, fairly strong
amerikan kōhii	アメリカンコーヒー	weak coffee
kafe ore	カフェオレ	café au lait, hot or cold

Sake barrels

CHRISTIAN KOBER / GETTY IMAGES ©

Sake

Brewed from rice, sake has been enjoyed for centuries in Japan, and although it's been overtaken in terms of consumption by beer and *shōchū* (distilled grain liquor) in recent years, it is still regarded by most Japanese people as the national drink. Indeed, what we call 'sake' in the West is more commonly known as *nihonshu* in Japan: the drink of Japan. Sake has traditionally been associated with Shintō and other traditional ceremonies, and you will still see huge barrels of sake (known as *o-miki*) on display at almost every shrine you visit.

Not surprisingly, sake makes the perfect accompaniment to traditional Japanese food, and sake pubs (*izakaya*) generally also serve excellent seasonal fish and other foods to go with the booze. Sake is drunk chilled *(reishu)*, at room temperature *(jō-on)*, warmed *(nuru-kan)* or piping hot *(atsu-kan)*, according to the season and personal preference. The top-drawer stuff is normally served well chilled. Sake is traditionally served in a ceramic jug known as a *tokkuri*, and poured into tiny cups known as *o-choko* or *sakazuki*. A traditional measure of sake is one *gō* (一合), a little more than 180ml, or 6 fluid oz. In speciality bars, you'll have the option of ordering by the glass, which will often be filled to overflowing and brought to you in a wooden container to catch the overspill. If you're in company, the tradition is to pour for your neighbour first, and then be waited on by them in turn.

Sake is brewed during the winter in the cold months that follow the rice harvest in September. The main ingredients are rice and yeast, together with a benign mould known as *kōji* that helps to convert the starch in the rice into fermentable sugars. Sake is categorised by law into two main classes: *futsū-shu* (ordinary sake), which makes up the bulk of what's produced, and premium sake known as *tokutei-meishōshu*, further classified by the extent to which the rice is refined before fermentation to remove proteins and oils that interfere with the flavour of the final product. This is generally shown on the label as the *seimai buai*, expressed as the percentage of the original size to which the grain is reduced by polishing before the brewing process starts. As a general rule, the lower this number, the better, or at least, the more expensive the sake will be. Sake made from rice polished to 60% or less of its original size is known as *ginjō*; rice polished to 50% or less of its original size produces the finest sake of all, known as *dai-ginjō*. Sake made only with rice and *kōji* (without the use of added alcohol) is known as *junmai-shu*, or 'pure rice' sake.

Arts & Architecture

Wood-block prints, Kyoto Handicraft Center (p247)

FRANK CARTER / GETTY IMA...

It's no secret that Japan has one of the world's richest artistic cultures. You can think of Japan as an oyster sitting at the end of the Silk Road: it absorbed all the artistic traditions of Asia and then polished them to produce the pearls you see before you today: sublime gardens, splendid decorative techniques, flamboyant textiles, ceramics to die for and the visual extravaganza known as kabuki, among many others.

Japanese Arts: Continental Roots with a Japanese Twist

Until the 19th century, the major influences on Japanese art came from China and Korea. While Japan was still living in the Stone Age, China had a well-developed technological culture. It's hardly surprising that when frequent contact was established Japan would be hungry for whatever skills and knowledge the Chinese had to give. In borrowing many aspects of Chinese culture, Japan also absorbed influences from distant cultures, such as Persia, Afghanistan and even ancient Rome, as China had maintained an active trade along the Silk Road. Perhaps the most important influence of all came from India, via China, in the form of Buddhism, which entered Japan in the 6th century.

Looking beyond these outside influences, the Japanese have always added something of their own to their arts. There is a fascination with the ephemeral, with the unadorned, with forms that echo the randomness of nature. A gift for caricature is also present, from early Zen ink paintings right up to the manga (comics) of contemporary Japan. There also exists a wildness and passion that is less evident in the arts of China. An interest in the grotesque or bizarre is also often visible, from Buddhist scrolls depicting the horrors of hell to the stylised depictions of body parts in the *ukiyo-e* (wood-block prints) of the Edo period.

The Best... Traditional Architecture

1 Katsura Rikyū (p227)

2 Tōdai-ji (p279)

3 Chion-in (p216)

4 Nishi Hongan-ji (p203)

Visual Art

Traditional Painting

From 794 to 1600, Japanese painting borrowed from Chinese and Western techniques and media, ultimately transforming them to its own aesthetic ends. By the beginning of the Edo period (Old Tokyo, 1600–1867), which was marked by the enthusiastic patronage of a wide range of painting styles, Japanese art had come completely into its own. The Kanō school, initiated more than a century before the beginning of the Edo era, continued to be in demand for its depiction of subjects connected with Confucianism, mythical Chinese creatures or scenes from nature. The Tosa school (1333–1576), which followed the *yamato-e* style of painting (considered the classical Japanese style, often used on scrolls during the Heian period, 794–1185), was also kept busy with commissions from the nobility, who were eager to see scenes re-created from classics of Japanese literature.

The Rimpa school (from 1600) not only absorbed the styles of painting that had preceded it, but progressed beyond well-worn conventions to produce a strikingly decorative and delicately shaded form of painting. The works of art produced by a trio of outstanding artists from this school – Tawaraya Sōtatsu, Hon'ami Kōetsu and Ogata Kōrin – rank among the finest of this period.

Ukiyo-e (Wood-Block Prints)

The term *ukiyo-e* means 'pictures of the floating world', and derives from a Buddhist metaphor for the transient world of fleeting pleasures. The subjects chosen by artists for these wood-block prints were characters and scenes from the tawdry, vivacious 'floating world' of the entertainment quarters in Edo, Kyoto and Osaka.

The floating world centred on pleasure districts such as Edo's Yoshiwara, and was a topsy-turvy kingdom, an inversion of the usual social hierarchies that were held in place by the power of the Tokugawa shōgunate. Here, money meant more than rank, actors and artists were the arbiters of style, and prostitutes elevated their art to such a level that their accomplishments matched the women of noble families.

The vivid colours, novel composition and flowing lines of *ukiyo-e* caused great excitement in the West, sparking a vogue that one French art critic dubbed Japonisme. *Ukiyo-e* became a key influence on Impressionists including Toulouse-Lautrec, Manet and Degas, and post-Impressionists. Among the Japanese the prints were hardly given more than passing consideration – millions were produced annually in Edo. They were often thrown away or used as wrapping paper for pottery. For many years, the Japanese continued to be perplexed by the keen interest foreigners took in this art form, which they considered of ephemeral value.

Ceramics

Ceramics are Japan's oldest art form: Jōmon-era (10,000–300 BC) pottery, with its distinctive cordlike decorative patterns, has been dated back some 15,000 years. When the Jōmon people were displaced by the Yayoi people around 300 BC, a more refined style of pottery appeared on the scene. While Jōmon pottery was an indigenous Japanese form, Yayoi pottery had clear Continental influences and techniques. Continental techniques and even artisans continued to dominate Japanese ceramic arts for the next millennium or more: around the 5th century AD, Sue ware pottery was introduced from Korea, and around the 7th century, Tang Chinese pottery became influential.

In the medieval period, Japan's great ceramic centre was Seto, in central Honshū. Here, starting in the 12th century, Japanese potters took Chinese forms and adapted them to Japanese tastes and needs to produce a truly distinctive pottery style known as Seto ware. One Japanese term for pottery and porcelain, *setomono* (literally 'things from Seto'), clearly derives from this still-thriving ceramics centre.

Today, there are more than 100 pottery centres in Japan, with scores of artisans producing everything from exclusive tea utensils to souvenir folklore creatures. Department stores regularly organise exhibitions of ceramics and offer the chance to see some of this fine work up close.

Shikki (Lacquerware)

The Japanese have been using lacquer to protect and enhance the beauty of wood since the Jōmon period. In the Meiji era (1868–1912), lacquerware became very popular abroad and it remains one of Japan's best-known products. Known in Japan as *shikki* or *nurimono*, lacquerware is made using the sap from the lacquer tree *(urushi)*, a close relative of poison oak. Raw lacquer is actually toxic and causes severe skin irritation in those who have not developed immunity. Once hardened, however, it becomes inert and extraordinarily durable.

Display of lacquerware

The most common colour of lacquer is an amber or brown colour, but additives have been used to produce black, violet, blue, yellow and even white lacquer. In the better pieces, multiple layers of lacquer are painstakingly applied and left to dry, and finally polished to a luxurious shine.

Traditional Theatre

Nō

Nō is a hypnotic dance-drama that reflects the minimalist aesthetics of Zen. The movement is glorious, the chorus and music sonorous, the expression subtle. A sparsely furnished cedar stage directs full attention to the performers, who include a chorus, drummers and a flautist. There are two principal characters: the *shite,* who is sometimes a living person but more often a demon or a ghost, whose soul cannot rest; and the *waki,* who leads the main character towards the play's climactic moment. Each nō school has its own repertoire, and the art form continues to evolve and develop.

Kabuki

The first performances of kabuki were staged early in the 17th century by an all-female troupe. The performances were highly erotic and attracted enthusiastic support from the merchant class. In true bureaucratic fashion, Tokugawa officials feared for the people's morality and banned women from the stage in 1629. Since that time, kabuki has been performed exclusively by men, giving rise to the institution of *onnagata* or *ōyama,* male actors who specialise in female roles.

Manga: Japanese Comics

The Japanese are insatiable readers of manga – a catch-all word covering cartoons, magazine and newspaper comic strips, and the ubiquitous comic book. Even high-art *ukiyo-e* (wood-block prints) were once a form of manga, evolving with the *kibyōshi* (yellow cover) wood blocks that were used to create adult story books. The great *ukiyo-e* artist Hokusai actually coined the word 'manga' by combining the characters for 'frivolous' and 'picture'.

The father of modern manga was Tezuka Osamu, who, in the late 1940s, began working cinematic effects based on European movies into his cartoons – pioneering multipanel movements, perspectives that brought the reader into the action, close-ups, curious angles and a host of movielike techniques. His adventurous stories quickly became movie-length comic strips – essentially films drawn on paper. What Tezuka started took off in a big way once weekly magazines realised that they could boost sales by including manga in their pages. As a result of Tezuka's innovations, Japanese comics are rarely slim affairs (weekly comics as thick as phone directories are not unusual).

You can find manga in any bookshop or convenience store in Japan, and these days, large bookshops in places such as Tokyo, Osaka and Kyoto will usually have a section devoted to English-language translations of popular manga. For real fans, we highly recommend a visit to the Kyoto International Manga Museum (p207).

During the course of several centuries, kabuki has developed a repertoire that draws on popular themes, such as famous historical accounts and stories of love-suicide, while also borrowing copiously from nō, *kyōgen* (comic vignettes) and *bunraku* (classical puppet theatre). Most kabuki plays border on melodrama, although they vary in mood.

Formalised beauty and stylisation are the central aesthetic principles of kabuki; the acting is a combination of dancing and speaking in conventionalised intonation patterns, and each actor prepares for a role by studying and emulating the style perfected by his predecessors. Kabuki actors are born into the art form, and training begins in childhood. Today, they enjoy great social prestige and their activities on and off the stage attract as much interest as those of popular film and TV stars.

Traditional Architecture

Upon glimpsing the visual chaos of Japan's urban centres, it's hard to believe that once upon a time, the local architectural aesthetic was governed by a preference for understated, back-to-nature design. Long before the Japanese borrowed and bested Western design motifs, the island nation honed its craft and style during two centuries of self-inflicted isolation when Tokugawa Ieyasu defeated the last of his enemies and secured total control for the Tokugawa shōgunate.

Japan's flamboyant temples are undoubtedly the best examples of the nation's early architectural abilities. Important religious complexes were usually quite large and featured a great hall surrounded by smaller buildings such as pagodas – the ancient version of the skyscraper – and structures that served as quarters for devotees.

Equally as impressive were the country's collection of feudal castles, although most of the bastions we see today are concrete replicas of the original wooden structures destroyed by war, fire or decay. Initially, the first feudal castles were simple mountain forts that relied more on natural terrain than structural innovation when defending the keep from invaders. Castle construction boomed during the 16th and 17th centuries, each one more impressive than the next; however, most were later razed by Edo and Meiji governments.

Principally simple and refined, the typical house was also constructed using post-and-beam timber, with sliding panels of wood or rice paper (for warmer weather) making up the exterior walls. *Shōji* (movable screens) would divide the interior rooms. In more densely populated areas, traditional housing took the form of *machiya* (traditional Japanese townhouse) and were usually built by merchants. Although most of the neat, narrow rows of these structures have been replaced with flashier modern dwellings, one can still stumble across *machiya* in Kyoto. The reasoning behind the gossamer construction of domestic dwellings was twofold: light materials were favourable during broiling summer months, and heavier building products were inadvisable due to the abundance of earthquakes.

Onsen

A *rotemburo* (outdoor onsen) in Nagano

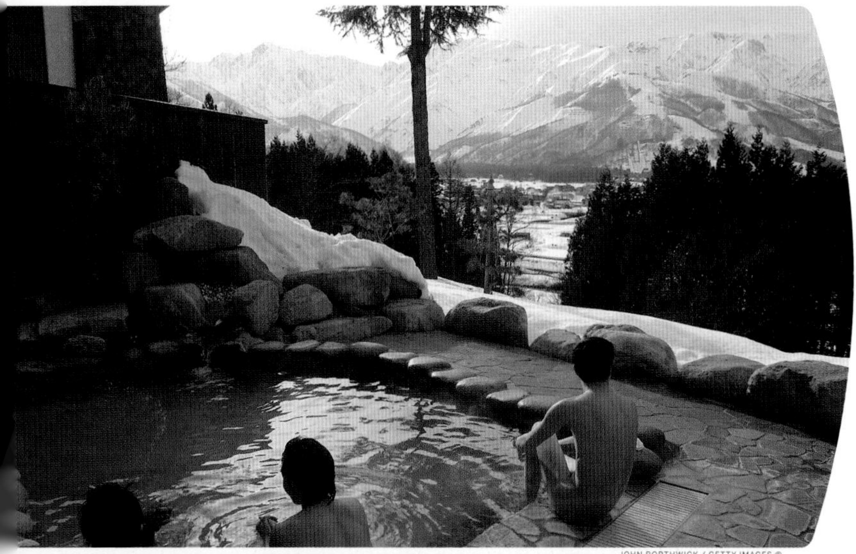

Japan is in hot water. Literally. The stuff percolates up out of the ground from one end of the country to the other. The Japanese word for a hot spring is onsen, and there are more than 3000 of them in the country. So if your idea of relaxation involves spending a few hours soaking your bones in a tub of bubbling hot water, then you've come to the right place.

Temples to Relaxation

Japanese onsen come in every size, shape and colour. And they are *everywhere*. There is an onsen on an artificial island in Tokyo Bay. There are onsen high up in the Japan Alps that you can only get to by walking for a full day over high mountain peaks. There are onsen bubbling up among the rocks on the coast that only exist when the tide is just right.

Over the millennia, the Japanese have turned the simple act of bathing in an onsen into something like a religion. Today, the ultimate way to experience an onsen is to visit an onsen ryokan, a traditional Japanese inn with its own private hot-spring bath on the premises. At an onsen ryokan you spend all day enjoying the bath, relaxing in your room and eating sumptuous Japanese food.

Etiquette

First: relax. That's what onsen are all about. You'll be relieved to hear that there really is nothing tricky about taking an onsen bath. If you remember just one basic point, you won't go too far wrong. This is the point: the water in the pools and tubs is for soaking in, not washing in, and it should only be entered after you've washed or rinsed your body.

This is the drill: pay your entry fee, if there is one. Rent a hand towel if you don't have one. Take off your shoes and put them in the lockers or shelves provided. Find the correct changing room/bath for your gender (man: 男; woman: 女). Grab a basket, strip down and put your clothes in the basket. Put the basket in a locker and bring the hand towel in with you.

Once in the bathing area, find a place around the wall (if there is one) to put down your toiletries (if you have them) and wash your body, or, at least, rinse your body. You'll note that some local men dispense with this step and just stride over to the tubs and grab a bucket (there are usually some around) and splash a few scoops over themselves.

Don't forget: the minerals in certain onsen can discolour jewellery, particularly anything made of silver. However, don't worry too much if you do forget to take off your silver wedding ring before jumping in the tub. After a few hours, the discoloration usually fades.

The Best...
Onsen

1 Kinosaki (p292)

2 Kayōtei (p191)

3 Takaragawa Onsen (p133)

4 Hirauchi Kaichū Onsen (p331)

Tattoo Warning

If you have any tattoos, you may not be allowed to enter Japanese onsen (hot springs) or *sentō* (public baths). The reason for this is that Japanese *yakuza* (mafia) members almost always sport tattoos. Banning people with tattoos is an indirect way of banning gangsters. If your tattoo is small enough to cover with some Band-Aids, then cover it up and you'll have no problem. Otherwise, ask the people at the front desk if you can go in despite your tattoos. The phrase to use is: '*Irezumi wa daijōbu desu ka*' (Are tattoos okay?).

Ryokan

Hiiragiya Ryokan (p235), Kyoto

LONELY PLANET / GETTY IMAGES ©

Let's face it: a hotel is a hotel wherever you go. And while some of Japan's hotels are very nice indeed, you're probably searching for something unique to the culture. If this is what you're after, you'll be pleased to learn that Japan is one of the last places in Asia where you can find truly authentic traditional accommodation: ryokan.

The Ryokan Experience

Simply put, ryokan are traditional Japanese inns. They are Japanese-style accommodations with tatami mat rooms and futons instead of beds. Most serve Japanese-style breakfast and dinner as well.

The service is what sets ryokan apart from even the best hotels. At a good ryokan, you will be assigned a personal maid who sees to your every need. These ladies seem to have a sixth sense: as soon as you finish one course of your dinner, you hear a knock on the door and she brings the next course. Then, when you stroll down the hall to take a bath, she dashes into your room and lays out your futon.

Many ryokan in Japan pride themselves on serving *kaiseki ryōri* (Japanese haute cuisine) that rivals that served in the best restaurants. Staying at one of these so-called *ryōri ryokan* (cuisine ryokan) is like staying at a three-star residential restaurant, where you sleep in your own private dining room.

Another wonderful variety is the onsen ryokan: a ryokan with its own private hot-spring bath. Some of the top places have rooms with private en suite onsen baths, usually built overlooking gardens. When you stay at an onsen ryokan, your day involves a grueling cycle of bathe-nap-eat-repeat.

Of course, it would be irresponsible to suggest that all ryokan fit this description. A lot of places that call themselves ryokan are really just hotels with Japanese-style rooms. Some places may not even serve dinner. That isn't to say they aren't comfortable: simple ryokan are often very friendly and relaxing and they may cost less than hotels in some places.

Note that ryokan may not have en suite bath-tubs or showers and at some simple places, even the toilet facilities are shared. If this is an issue, be sure to enquire when you make a reservation.

The Best... Ryokan in Japan

1 Tawaraya (p235)

2 Hiiragiya (p235)

3 Kayōtei (p191)

4 Nishimuraya Honkan (p294)

Architecture

A high-end ryokan is the last word in relaxation. The buildings themselves set the tone: they employ traditional Japanese architecture in which the whole structure is organic, made entirely of natural materials such as wood, earth, paper, grass, bamboo and stone. Indeed, a good ryokan is an extension of the natural world. And, nature comes into the ryokan in the form of the Japanese garden, which you can often see from the privacy of your room or even your bath-tub.

Ryokan Made Easy

Needless to say, staying in a ryokan (traditional Japanese inn) is not quite like staying at a hotel. Here are a few things to remember:

Shoes Remove your shoes in the entryway before stepping up onto the tatami mats or wooden flooring.

Bathing Rinse your body before getting in the bath-tub.

Luggage Should not be placed in the *tokonoma* (sacred alcove) in your room.

Yukata (light cotton robes) Can be worn in all areas of the ryokan and even outside (in places such as Kinosaki where people stroll to nearby onsen in *yukata*).

Family Travel

Yuki Matsuri (snow festival; p42), Sapporo

NAOMI PARKER ©

Japan is a great place to travel with kids. The usual worries that parents face when travelling with children – concerns about safety and food – are simply not concerns in ultra-safe and spotless Japan. Instead, your biggest challenge will probably be keeping your children entertained. The very things that many adults come to Japan to see – the temples, gardens and shrines – often bore kids silly. Luckily, there is no shortage of child-friendly attractions in Japan: you can't swing a cat without hitting an amuse-ment park, game centre, zoo or kitschy shopping centre.

Older Children

If your children are older, get them out and about: go on a hike (Kyoto is perfect for this), rent a bicycle, or take a stroll with them through a youth-oriented shopping area such as Harajuku or Shibuya in Tokyo or Shinkyōgoku in Kyoto. If that fails, head to one of Japan's many amusement parks like Tokyo Disneyland or Universal Studios Japan.

Kids & Food

Food can be an issue in Japan if your child is a picky or unadventurous eater. Let's face it: even adults can be put off by some of the weird things found in Japanese cuisine – asking a kid to eat sea urchin or squid might simply be too much. Choose your restaurants carefully. If you're going to a *kaiseki* (Japanese haute cuisine) place, have your lodgings call ahead to see if they can make some kid-friendly dishes. Ditto if you'll be dining at your ryokan (traditional Japanese inn).

Need to Know

- **Breastfeeding** Not usually done in public, but department stores have rooms for this.
- **Changing facilities** In department stores, airports, large train stations and some public buildings.
- **Cots** Available in many hotels (try to book in advance) but not usually ryokan (traditional Japanese inn).
- **Health** Neither food-borne nor infectious diseases are a big problem in Japan. Do bring any medicine you'll need from home.
- **High chairs** Available in many restaurants.
- **Kids' menus** Usually only in so-called family restaurants.
- **Nappies (diapers)** Widely available.
- **Strollers** Available in Japan, but consider bringing your own.
- **Transport** Comfortable and safe, but no child seats in taxis (but available for rental cars).

You'll find a lot of so-called family restaurants in Japan and these usually serve something that even finicky kids can stomach (pizza, fried chicken and French fries often feature on the menu). These places often serve special children's meals (sometimes called *o-ko-sama ranchii*).

Finally, if your child simply will not eat Japanese food, don't worry: the big cities are chock-a-block with international restaurants, while fast-food restaurants can be found even in smaller towns. In rural areas, however, you might find that Japanese food is the only thing available – you can always stock up on food your child likes at a supermarket before heading into the hinterland.

Most supermarkets stock a good selection of baby food. Organic baby food is hard to find, so if this is a concern, consider bringing a supply from home.

If your child has dietary restrictions or allergies, get them written down. If necessary, ask the proprietor of your first night's lodgings to write these for you in Japanese.

Getting Around

Most cities are fairly accessible to those with strollers. You'll find elevators in most train stations and many large buildings (departments stores etc). However, many attractions like temples and shrines do not have ramps, which makes it necessary to frequently pick up your stroller. One issue, particularly in Kyoto, is the relative lack of footpaths when you get away from the main streets – this can make walking with a stroller or a young child a little hair-raising. Luckily, Japanese tend to be safe drivers.

Child seats for taxis are generally not available, however, most rental-car agencies will provide a car seat if you request one in advance.

Finally, you will almost certainly find that Japanese love kids and will fawn over the young ones, declaring them to be *'kawaii'* (cute). Unfortunately, this love of children doesn't always extend to people giving up seats on trains or buses to those with children in tow. That said, most trains and buses do have *yūsen-zaseki* (priority seating for elderly, handicapped, pregnant women and those with young children). Standing near one and glaring at its able-bodied occupant is sometimes enough to free up a seat.

Survival
Guide

DIRECTORY   **374**

Accommodation   374

Customs Regulations   374

Electricity   375

Embassies &
Consulates   375

Gay & Lesbian Travellers   376

Health   377

Insurance   377

Internet Access   377

Climate   377

Left Luggage   379

Maps   379

Money   379

Opening Hours   381

Public Holidays   381

Solo Travellers   382

Telephone   382

Time   383

Toilets   383

Tourist Information   383

Travellers
with Disabilities   383

Visas   384

Women Travellers   384

TRANSPORT   **385**

Getting There & Away   385

Getting Around   386

LANGUAGE   **394**

Shinjuku Station, Tokyo
WILL ROBB / GETTY IMAGES ©

Directory

Accommodation

Japan offers a range of accommodation, from cheap guest houses to first-class hotels. In addition to the Western-style hotels, you'll also find distinctive Japanese-style places such as ryokan (traditional Japanese inns) and *minshuku* (Japanese guest houses).

Reservations

It can be hard to find accommodation during high-season holiday periods (cherry-blossom season, autumn foliage season, Golden Week holiday and the O-Bon holiday period). If you plan to be in Japan during these periods, you should make reservations as far in advance as possible.

Tourist information offices at main train stations can usually help with reservations, and are often open until about 6.30pm or later. Even if you are travelling by car, the train station is a good first stop in town for information, reservations and cheap car parking.

Making phone reservations in English is usually possible at larger hotels and foreigner-friendly ryokan. Providing you speak clearly and simply, there will usually be someone around who can get the gist of what you want.

Japanese Inn Group (http://japaneseinngroup. com/) is a collection of foreigner-friendly ryokan and guest houses. You can book member inns via its website or phone/fax. Pick up a copy of its excellent guide to member inns at major tourist information centres in Japan.

Hotels

You'll find a range of Western-style hotels in most Japanese cities and resort areas. So-called business hotels are efficient, utilitarian hotels that are geared to Japan's business travellers; while the rooms tend to be small, they are usually perfectly adequate for a night's stay. Luxury hotels are what you'd find anywhere else in the world. Sample hotel charges:

Single room in a business hotel ¥8000

Twin room in a business hotel ¥12,000

Single room in a luxury hotel ¥17,000

Twin room in a luxury hotel ¥23,000

In addition to the 5% consumption tax that is levied on all accommodation in Japan, you may have to pay an additional 10% or more as a service charge at luxury hotels.

Customs Regulations

Customs allowances:

Alcohol Up to three 760mL bottles.

Gifts/souvenirs Up to ¥200,000 in total value.

Perfume Up to 2oz.

Tobacco products Up to 100 cigars or 400 cigarettes or 500g.

You must be over the age of 20 to qualify for these allowances. Customs officers will confiscate any pornographic materials in which pubic hair is visible.

There are no limits on the importation of foreign or Japanese currency. The export of foreign currency is also unlimited but there is a ¥5 million export limit for Japanese currency.

Visit **Japan Customs** (www.customs.go.jp/ english/index.htm) for more information on Japan's customs regulations.

Book Your Stay Online

For more accommodation reviews by Lonely Planet authors, check out lonelyplanet.com/ hotels. You'll find independent reviews, as well as recommendations on the best places to stay. Best of all, you can book online.

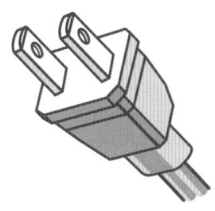

Electricity

100V/50Hz/60Hz

Embassies & Consulates

Australia Tokyo Embassy (Map p62; ☏ 03-5232-4111; www.australia.or.jp/en/; 2-1-14 Mita, Minato-ku, Tokyo); Fukuoka Consulate (☏ 092-734-5055; 7th fl, Tenjin Twin Bldg, 1-6-8 Tenjin, Chūō-ku, Fukuoka); Osaka Consulate (☏ 06-6941-9448; 16th fl, Twin 21 MID Tower, 2-1-61 Shiromi, Chūō-ku, Osaka)

Canada Tokyo Embassy ☏ 03-5412-6200; www.canadainternational.gc.ca/japan-japon/index.aspx; 7-3-38 Akasaka, Minato-ku, Tokyo); Nagoya Consulate (☏ 052-972-0450; Nakatō Marunouchi Bldg, 6F, 3-17-6 Marunouchi, Naka-ku, Nagoya); Sapporo Consulate (☏ 011-281-6565; Nikko Bldg, 5F, Kita 4 Nishi 4,

Chūō-ku, Sapporo); Hiroshima Consulate (☏ 082-246-0057; 4-33 Komachi, Naka-ku, Hiroshima)

France Tokyo Embassy (☏ 03-5798-6000; www.ambafrance-jp.org; 4-11-44 Minami Azabu, Minato-ku, Tokyo); Osaka Consulate (☏ 06-6131-5278; Manulife Place Dojima, 6F, Dojimahama 1-4-19, Kita-ku, Osaka)

Germany Tokyo Embassy (☏ 03-5791-7700; www.japan.diplo.de/Vertretung/japan/ja/Startseite.html.html; 4-5-10 Minami Azabu, Minato-ku, Tokyo); Osaka Consulate (☏ 06-6440-5070; 35th fl, Umeda Sky Bldg Tower East, 1-1-88-3501 Ōyodonaka, Kita-ku, Osaka)

Ireland Tokyo Embassy (☏ 03-3263-0695; www.irishembassy.jp; Ireland House, 2-10-7 Kōji-machi, Chiyoda-ku, Tokyo)

Netherlands Tokyo Embassy (☏ 03-5776-5400; http://japan.nlembassy.org/; 3-6-3 Shiba-kōen, Minato-ku, Tokyo); Osaka Consulate (☏ 06-6944-7272; 33rd fl, Twin 21 MID Tower, 2-1-61 Shiromi, Chūō-ku, Osaka)

New Zealand Tokyo Embassy (☏ 03-3467-2271; www.nzembassy.com/japan; 20-40 Kamiyama-chō, Shibuya-ku, Tokyo); Osaka Consulate (☏ 06-6373-4583; Umeda Centre Bldg, 2-4-12 Nakazaki-nishi, Kita-ku, Osaka)

Russia Tokyo Embassy (Map p72; ☏ 03-3583-4445; www.rusconsul.jp; 2-1-1, Azabudai, Tokyo; ☉ 9.30am-12.30pm Mon-Fri); Sapporo Consulate (☏ 011-561-3171~2; http://sapporo.rusembassy.org/; 2-5 12-chōme Nishi, Minami 14-jo, Chūō-ku, Sapporo)

Practicalities

o **Newspapers & Magazines** There are three main English-language daily newspapers in Japan: the *Japan Times, Daily Yomiuri* and *Asahi Shimbun/International Herald Tribune*. In the bigger cities, these are available at bookshops, convenience stores, train-station kiosks and some hotels. In the countryside, you may not be able to find them anywhere. Foreign magazines are available in major bookshops in the bigger cities.

o **Electricity** The Japanese electric current is 100V AC. Tokyo and eastern Japan are on 50Hz, and western Japan, including Nagoya, Kyoto and Osaka, is on 60Hz. Most electrical items from other parts of the world will function on Japanese current. Japanese plugs are the flat two-pin type.

o **Weights & Measures** Japan uses the international metric system.

Sleeping Price Ranges

For all of Japan, where more than one accommodation is listed within a particular budget category, entries are organised by preference (most appealing options are listed first).

Since air-conditioning is ubiquitous in Japan (due to its hot summers), we only mention air-con in reviews when a place does not have it.

The following price ranges refer to a double room for hotels, and per person double occupancy for ryokan (traditional Japanese inns; without meals). Unless otherwise stated, tax (ie the national 5% consumption tax) is included in the price, but note that some hotels quote exclusive of taxes.

○ **¥** less than ¥8000 (Tokyo), less than ¥6000 (elsewhere)

○ **¥¥** ¥8000–20,000 (Tokyo), ¥6000–15,000 (elsewhere)

○ **¥¥¥** more than ¥20,000 (Tokyo), more than ¥15,000 (elsewhere)

Accommodation tends to be more expensive in big cities than in rural areas. Likewise, in resort areas accommodation is more expensive during the warm months. In ski areas like Hakuba and Niseko, accommodation prices go up in winter and down in summer. Finally, accommodation should be booked months in advance in Kyoto during the cherry-blossom season (late March to early April) and the autumn foliage season (November).

South Korea Tokyo Embassy
(☎ 03-3455-2601; http://
jpn-tokyo.mofat.go.kr/jpn/
index.jsp; 1-7-32 Minami Azabu,
Minato-ku, Tokyo); Fukuoka
Consulate (☎ 092-771-0461;
1-1-3 Jigyohama, Chūō-ku,
Fukuoka)

UK Tokyo Embassy
(☎ 03-5211-1100; http://
ukinjapan.fco.gov.uk/en/; 1
Ichiban-chō, Chiyoda-ku, Tokyo);
Osaka Consulate (☎ 06-6120-
5600; 19th fl, Epson Osaka Bldg,
3-5-1 Bakurōmachi, Chūō-ku,
Osaka)

USA Tokyo Embassy
(Map p72; ☎ 03-3224-5000;
http://japan.usembassy.
gov/; 1-10-5 Akasaka, Minato-
ku, Tokyo); Osaka Consulate
(☎ 06-6315-5900; http://
osaka.usconsulate.gov/;
2-11-5 Nishitenma, Kita-ku,
Osaka)

Gay & Lesbian Travellers

With the possible exception of Thailand, Japan is Asia's most enlightened nation with regard to the sexual preferences of foreigners. Shinjuku-nichōme in Tokyo is an established scene where English is spoken and meeting men is fairly straightforward.

In provincial areas there may be one so-called 'snack' bar, where gay men meet. Snack bars can be found in the central entertainment districts of towns and cities. They are usually small places capable of seating only a dozen or fewer customers. They may appear like hole-in-the-wall bars. Note that most snack bars cater to heterosexual customers. Gay-friendly snack bars are extremely difficult to locate without an inside connection.

Eating Price Ranges

Price ranges in this book are for a main meal per person unless otherwise stated.

○ **¥** less than ¥2000 (Tokyo), less than ¥1000 (elsewhere)

○ **¥¥¥** 2000–5000 (Tokyo), ¥1000–4000 (elsewhere)

○ **¥¥¥** more than ¥5000 (Tokyo), more than ¥4000 (elsewhere)

The lesbian scene is growing but is still elusive for most non-Japanese-speaking foreigners. Outside Tokyo you may find it difficult to break into the local scene unless you spend considerable time in a place or have local contacts who can show you around.

Staying in hotels is simple as most have twin rooms, but love hotels are less accessible; if you know someone Japanese and can overcome the language barrier, a stay in a love hotel may be possible, but some are not particularly foreigner friendly.

Utopia (www.utopia-asia.com) is the site most commonly frequented by English-speaking gays and lesbians.

There are no legal restraints to same-sex sexual activities of either gender. Public displays of affection are not really done, whether the couple be same-sex or heterosexual, but they are not usually a problem in cities. In the countryside, they may raise some eyebrows, but that's probably all.

Health

Japan is an advanced country with high standards of hygiene and few endemic diseases. There are no special immunisations needed to visit and, other than bringing pre-scription medications from home, no special prepara-tions to make. Hospitals and clinics can be found all over the archipelago, and only the smallest outer islands lack medical facilities.

Insurance

A travel-insurance policy to cover theft, loss and medical problems is essential. Some policies will specifically exclude 'dangerous activities', which can include scuba diving, motorcycling and even trekking.

You may prefer a policy that pays doctors or hospitals directly rather than having you pay on the spot and claim later. If you have to claim later, make sure you keep all documentation. Some policies ask you to call (reverse charge) a centre in your home country where an immediate assessment of your problem is made. Check that the policy covers ambulances or an emergency flight home.

Be sure to bring your insurance card or other certificate of insurance to Japan; Japanese hospitals have been known to refuse treatment to foreign patients with no proof of medical insurance.

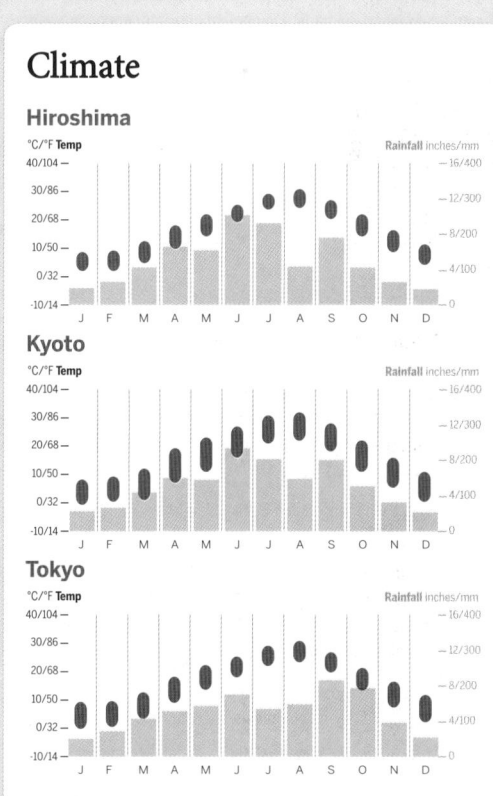

Internet Access

Internet access in a nutshell:

Current 100V AC; 50Hz in east Japan, 60Hz in west Japan.

Climate

Hiroshima

°C/°F **Temp**

Rainfall inches/mm

Kyoto

°C/°F **Temp**

Rainfall inches/mm

Tokyo

°C/°F **Temp**

Rainfall inches/mm

Connections LAN cable access more common than wi-fi.

Internet-cafe rates ¥200 to ¥700 per hour.

Plugs Flat two-pin type, identical to most ungrounded North American plugs.

If you plan on bringing your laptop to Japan, make sure that it is compatible with the current and check to see if your plug will fit the wall sockets. Transformers and plug adaptors are readily available in electronics districts, such as Tokyo's Akihabara, Osaka's Den Den Town or Kyoto's Teramachi-dōri.

In this book, an internet symbol @ indicates that the accommodation option has at least one computer with internet for guests' use and/or LAN cable internet access in guest rooms. We also note where wi-fi is available 📶. Note that wi-fi is far less common in Japanese hotels than in their Western counterparts. About a third of hotels in Japan have free wi-fi; another third charge for wi-fi; and a third have no wi-fi at all.

It is much more common to find LAN cable internet access points in hotel rooms (the hotels usually provide LAN cables, but you may want to bring your own to avoid having to ask for one everywhere you stay). These LAN connections usually work fine, but you may occasionally find it difficult to log on due to software or hardware compatibility issues or configuration problems – the front-desk staff *may* be able to help.

You'll find internet cafes and other access points in most major Japanese cities.

Getting Online in Japan

Japan is one of the world's most technologically advanced countries, but if you're expecting to find free internet hot spots wherever you go, you're in for a surprise. Sure, wi-fi or mobile internet is everywhere, but most of it is available only to subscribers of various Japanese services, many of which are not easy for travellers to join (especially those who don't speak and read Japanese). **Freespot Map** (www.freespot.com/users/map_e.html) has a list of internet hot spots, but it's not exhaustive and the maps are in Japanese, but it's quite useful. Failing that, here are some ways to get online:

○ **Starbucks** All Starbucks stores in Japan offer free wi-fi to customers. You must register online to use the service (go to https://service.wi2.ne.jp/wi2net/SbjReg/2/?locale=en).

○ **B-Mobile SIM cards** If you bring an internet device that takes a SIM card, you can buy B-Mobile Visitor SIM cards from major electronics shops in big cities such as Tokyo, Osaka and Kyoto. You can also order them online (go to www.bmobile.ne.jp/english/) and have them delivered to your first night's lodgings or even to the post office at your arrival airport to hold for you). These will usually allow internet use for a specific length of time (a month is common). Note that the amount of data you can download is limited and your device must be unlocked and you must be able to input the APN settings. These are data-only (ie no voice) but you can use Skype with them.

○ **Boingo** Subscribers to Boingo's global plan (www.boingo.com) can use BB Mobilepoint wi-fi at McDonald's restaurants and some other spots.

○ **Portable internet connections** You can rent data cards, USB dongles or pocket wi-fi devices from various phone-rental companies. The most user-friendly option with English service is provided by Rentafone Japan (p383), which offers two types of pocket wi-fi from ¥3900 per week with unlimited use.

○ **Free wi-fi in Kyoto** The city of Kyoto has recently launched a free wi-fi access program for foreign travellers, with hot spots across the city. You must email to get the access code. Go to http://kanko.city.kyoto.lg.jp/wifi/en/ to find a map of hot spots and to get started. Note that access is limited to three hours, but you can get another access code for additional hours.

As a rule, internet connections are fast (DSL, ADSL or optic fibre) and reliable.

Left Luggage

Only major train stations have left-luggage facilities, but almost all stations have coin-operated storage lockers (¥100 to ¥500 per day, depending on size). The lockers are rented until midnight (not for 24 hours). After that time you have to insert more money before your key will work. If your bag is simply too large to fit in the locker, ask someone '*tenimotsu azukai wa doko desu ka?*' (Where is the left-luggage office?).

Maps

If you'd like a map of Japan before arriving, both Nelles and Periplus produce reasonable ones. If you want something more detailed, wait until you get to Tokyo or Kyoto, where you'll find lots of detailed maps in both English and Japanese.

The Japan National Tourist Organization's free *Tourist Map of Japan,* available at JNTO-operated tourist information centres inside the country and JNTO offices abroad, is a reasonable English-language map that is suitable for general route planning.

The *Japan Road Atlas* (Shobunsha) is a good choice for those planning to drive around the country; unfortunately, it's out of print (you might be able to find a copy online, but it won't be cheap). Those looking for something less bulky should pick up a copy of the *Bilingual Atlas of Japan* (Kodansha). Of course, if you can read a little Japanese, you'll do much better with one of the excellent *Super Mapple* road atlases published by Shobunsha.

Medical Care in Japan

While the Japanese medical system is extensive and comprehensive, the level of care is very uneven. Here are some things to note if you need to seek medical attention:

o It is better to seek care at university hospitals or other large hospitals rather than clinics.

o Japanese doctors and hospitals are sometimes reluctant to treat foreigners. It helps to carry proof of insurance and be willing to show it. If a doctor or hospital seems reticent about giving care, you should insist on it (even though Japan has no Hippocratic oath, doctors can be told that they have to treat patients in need of care).

o Most hospitals and clinics have regular hours (usually in the mornings) when they will see patients.

o Hotels and ryokan (traditional Japanese inns) that cater to foreigners will usually know the best hospitals in a particular area and will also know hospitals with English-speaking doctors.

o Most doctors speak some English. However, it helps to bring along a Japanese speaker if possible to help you explain your condition and to navigate the hospital.

Money

The currency in Japan is the yen (¥). The Japanese pronounce yen as 'en', with no 'y' sound. The kanji for yen is 円.

Yen denominations:

¥1 Coin; lightweight, silver colour

¥5 Coin; bronze colour, hole in the middle, value in Chinese character only

¥10 Coin; copper colour

¥50 Coin; silver colour, hole in the middle

¥100 Coin; silver colour

¥500 Coin; large with silver colour

¥1000 Banknote

¥2000 Banknote (rare)

¥5000 Banknote

¥10,000 Banknote

The Japanese postal system has recently linked its ATMs to the international Cirrus and Plus networks, and 7-Eleven convenience stores have followed suit, so getting money is no longer the issue it once

Currency Warning

Exchange rates for the US dollar and euro are reasonable in Japan. All other currencies, including the Australian dollar and the currencies of nearby countries, fetch very poor exchange rates. If you want to bring cash to Japan, we suggest US dollars or euros. Or, if you must change other currencies into yen, we suggest doing so in your home country.

was for travellers to Japan. Of course, it always makes sense to carry some foreign cash and some credit cards just to be on the safe side.

ATMs

Automated teller machines are almost as common as vending machines in Japan. Unfortunately, most of these do not accept foreign-issued cards. Even if they display Visa and MasterCard logos, most accept only Japan-issued versions of these cards.

Fortunately, Japanese postal ATMs accept cards that belong to the following international networks: Visa, Plus, MasterCard, Maestro, Cirrus, American Express, Diners Club, Discover and China Unionpay cards. Check the sticker(s) on the back of your card to see which network(s) your card belongs to. You'll find postal ATMs in almost all post offices, and you'll find post offices in even the smallest Japanese village.

Note that postal ATMs work with bank or cash cards – you cannot use credit cards, even with a pin number, in postal ATMs. That is to say, you cannot use postal ATMs to perform a cash advance.

Most postal ATMs are open 9am to 5pm Monday to Friday, 9am to noon on Saturday, and are closed on Sunday and holidays. Some postal ATMs in very large central post offices are open longer hours. The central post offices in major cities are open *almost* 24 hours a day.

In addition, 7-Eleven convenience stores across Japan have linked their ATMs to international cash networks, and these often seem to accept cards that for one reason or other will not work with postal ATMs. They are also open 24 hours. So, if you can't find an open post office or your card won't work

with postal ATMs, don't give up: ask around for a 7-Eleven (pronounced like 'sebun erebun' in Japanese).

International cards also work in the ATMs at **Citibank Japan** (www.citibank.co.jp/en/banking/branch_atm/index.html). If you find that your card doesn't work in a postal or 7-Eleven ATM, this is a good last-ditch bet. Visit its site for a branch locator.

Finally, before leaving your home country, check that your ATM card can be used abroad and consider informing the issuing bank that you plan to use the card abroad.

Credit Cards

Cash and carry is still very much the rule in Japan. If you do decide to bring a credit card, you'll find Visa the most useful, followed by MasterCard, Amex and Diners Club. Note also that Visa cards can be used for cash advances at Sumitomo Mitsui banks in Japan, but you might have to go to a specific branch to do this.

Warning: Japan Is a Cash Society

Be warned that cold hard yen is the way to pay in Japan. While credit cards are becoming more common, cash is still much more widely used, and travellers cheques are rarely accepted. Never assume that you can pay for things with a credit card; always carry sufficient cash. The only places where you can count on paying by credit card are department stores, large hotels and at major JR ticket offices.

For those without credit cards, it would be a good idea to bring some travellers cheques as a backup. As in most other countries, the US dollar is still the currency of choice in terms of exchanging cash and cashing travellers cheques.

Exchanging Money

You can change cash or travellers cheques at most banks, major post offices, discount ticket shops, some travel agencies, some large hotels and most big department stores. Note that discount-ticket shops (known as *kakuyasu kippu uriba* in Japanese) often have the best rates. These can be found around major train stations. However, only US dollars and euros fetch decent exchange rates.

Taxes

Japan has a 5% consumption tax (*shōhizei*). If you eat at expensive restaurants and stay in top-end accommodation, you will also encounter a service charge that varies from 10% to 15%.

Tipping

There is little tipping in Japan. If you want to show your gratitude to someone, give them a gift rather than a tip.

Opening Hours

Business hours in Japan are fairly standard. Almost all museums, many other sights and many businesses close over the New Year period (30 or 31 December to 3 or 4 January). We do not list New Year closures in this guide in most instances because this is standard. Also, most museums in Japan are closed on Monday. Note that when a place is normally closed on a Monday, it will usually open on Monday if that Monday is a national holiday (in which case it will most likely be closed on the following Tuesday). The following is a list of typical business hours:

Banks Open 9am to 3pm Monday to Friday.

Bars Open 6pm to midnight or later, closed one day per week.

Department stores Open 10am to 7pm, closed one or two days per month. Often open for all or part of the New Year's holidays (making them good places to buy food during this time).

Museums Open 9am or 10am to 5pm, closed Monday.

Offices Open 9am to 5pm or 6pm Monday to Friday.

Post offices Local open 9am to 5pm Monday to Friday; central open 9am to 7pm Monday to Friday and 9am to 3pm Saturday (larger cities may have after-hours window open 24 hours a day, seven days a week).

Restaurants Open 11am to 2pm and 6pm to 11pm, closed one day per week.

Smaller shops Open 9am to 5pm, may be closed Sunday.

Using a Japanese Postal ATM

Postal ATMs are relatively easy to use. Here's the drill: press 'English Guide', select 'Withdrawal', then insert your card, press 'Visitor Withdrawal', input your PIN, then hit the button marked 'Kakunin' (確認), then enter the amount, hit 'Yen' and 'Confirm' and you should hear the delightful sound of bills being dispensed.

Public Holidays

Japan has 15 national holidays. When a public holiday falls on a Sunday, the following Monday is taken as a holiday. If that Monday is already a holiday, the following day becomes a holiday as well. And if two weekdays (say, Tuesday and Thursday) are holidays, the day in between also becomes a holiday.

Japan's national holidays:

Ganjitsu (New Year's Day) 1 January

Seijin-no-hi (Coming-of-Age Day) Second Monday in January

Kenkoku Kinem-bi (National Foundation Day) 11 February

Shumbun-no-hi (spring equinox) 20 or 21 March

Shōwa-no-hi (Shōwa Emperor's Day) 29 April

Kempō Kinem-bi (Constitution Day) 3 May

Midori-no-hi (Green Day) 4 May

Kodomo-no-hi (Children's Day) 5 May

Umi-no-hi (Marine Day) Third Monday in July

Keirō-no-hi (Respect-for-the-Aged Day) Second Monday in September

Shūbun-no-hi (autumn equinox) 22 or 23 September

Taiiku-no-hi (Health-Sports Day) Second Monday in October

Bunka-no-hi (Culture Day) 3 November

Kinrō Kansha-no-hi (Labour Thanksgiving Day) 23 November

Tennō Tanjōbi (Emperor's Birthday) 23 December

You will find transport crowded and accommodation bookings hard to come by during the following high-season travel periods:

Shōgatsu (New Year) 31 December to 3 January

Golden Week 29 April to 5 May

O-Bon mid-August

Solo Travellers

Japan is an excellent place for solo travellers: it's safe, convenient and friendly. Almost all hotels have single rooms, and business-hotel singles can cost as little as ¥4000. Ryokan usually charge by the person, not the room, which keeps the price down for the solo. The only hitch is that some ryokan owners baulk at renting a room to a single traveller, when they might be able to rent it to two people instead, especially during busy times.

Many restaurants have small tables or counters that are perfect perches for solo travellers. *Izakaya* (pub-eateries) are also generally welcoming to solo travellers, and you probably won't have to wait long before you're offered a drink and roped into a conversation, particularly if you sit at the counter. Finally, the 'gaijin bars' in the larger cities are generally friendly, convivial places; if you're after a travel partner or just an English-speaking conversation partner, you'll find these are good places to start.

Telephone

Japanese telephone codes consist of an area code plus the number. You do not dial the area code when making a call in that area. When dialling Japan from abroad, dial the country code, 81, followed by the area code (drop the '0') and the number. The most common toll-free prefixes are 0120, 0070, 0077, 0088 and 0800. Directory-assistance numbers:

Local directory assistance ☎104 (¥60 to ¥150 per call)

Local directory assistance in English ☎0120-36-4463 (from 9am to 5pm Monday to Friday)

International directory assistance ☎0057

International Calls

The following international numbers may be useful:

International operator-assisted calls ☎0051 (KDDI; operators speak English)

Direct-dial international numbers KDDI ☎001 010, SoftBank Telecom ☎0041 010, NTT ☎0033 010

Prepaid International Phonecards

Because of the lack of payphones from which you can make international phone calls in Japan, the easiest way to make a call is to buy a prepaid international phone card. Most convenience stores carry at least one of the following, which can be used with any regular payphone:

○ KDDI Superworld Card

○ NTT Communications World Card

○ SoftBank Telecom Comica Card

Local Calls

The Japanese telephone system is extremely reliable and efficient. Unfortunately, the number of payphones is decreasing fast as more and more Japanese buy mobile phones. Local calls from payphones cost ¥10 per minute; unused ¥10 coins are returned after the call is completed but no change is given on ¥100 coins.

In general it's much easier to buy a *terefon kādo* (telephone card) when you arrive rather than worry about always having coins on hand. Phone cards are sold in ¥500 and ¥1000 denominations (the latter earns you an extra ¥50 in calls) and can be used in most green or grey payphones. Cards are available from vending machines (some of which can be found in public phone booths) and convenience stores. They come in myriad designs and are also a collectable item.

Mobile Phones

Japan's mobile-phone networks use 3G (third generation) mobile-phone technology on a variety of frequencies. Thus, *non-3G mobile phones cannot be used in Japan,* which means that most foreign mobile phones *will not work* there. Furthermore, SIM cards are not commonly available. Thus, for most foreigners who want to use a mobile phone, the only solution is to rent one.

Several telecommunications companies specialise in short-term rentals including **Rentafone Japan** (090-9621-7318, toll free within Japan 0120-746-487; www. rentafonejapan.com). Rentals start at ¥3900 per week. Domestic calls cost ¥35 per minute.

Time

All of Japan is in the same time zone: nine hours ahead of Greenwich Mean Time (GMT). Sydney and Wellington are ahead of Japan by one and three hours respectively), and most of the world's other big cities are behind: New York by 14 hours, Los Angeles by 17 and London by nine. Japan does not have daylight savings time (also known as summer time).

Toilets

You will come across both Western-style toilets and Asian squat toilets. When you are compelled to squat, the correct position is facing the hood, away from the door. Take special care to ensure the contents of your pockets don't spill out! Toilet paper isn't always provided, so it is always a good idea to carry tissues with you. You may be given small packets of tissues on the street, which is a common form of advertising.

In many bathrooms, separate toilet slippers are provided – usually located just inside the toilet door. These are for use in the toilet only, so remember to change out of them when you leave.

It's quite common to see men urinating in public – the unspoken rule is that it's acceptable at night-time if you happen to be drunk. Public toilets are free. The katakana for 'toilet' is トイレ, and the kanji is お手洗い. You'll often also see the kanji signs:

o 女 (female)

o 男 (male)

Tourist Information

You will find tourist information offices (*kankō annai-sho;* 観光案内所) in most cities and towns and even in some small villages. They are almost always located inside or in front of the main train station. Staff members may speak some English, but don't

count on it. English-language materials are usually available. Naturally, places that get a lot of foreign visitors are more likely to have English-speaking staff and English-language materials. Nonetheless, with a little patience and a smile you will usually be able to get the information you need from even the smallest local tourist information office.

The **Japan National Tourism Organization** (JNTO; www.jnto.go.jp) is Japan's main English-language information service for foreign travellers. JNTO produces a great deal of useful literature, which is available from its overseas offices as well as its Tourist Information Center in Tokyo. Most of its publications are available in English and, in some cases, other European and Asian languages. The organisation's website is a very useful tool when planning your journey to Japan.

JNTO has overseas offices in Australia, Canada, France, Germany, the UK and the USA (see the JNTO website for exact locations and contact details).

Travellers with Disabilities

Japan gets mixed marks in terms of ease of travel for those with disabilities. On the plus side, many new buildings have access ramps, traffic lights have speakers playing melodies when it is safe to cross, train platforms have raised dots and lines to provide guidance for the visually impaired, and some ticket machines in Tokyo have Braille. Some attractions also offer free entry for disabled persons and one companion. On the negative side, many of Japan's cities are still rather difficult for disabled persons to negotiate, often due to the relative lack of normal footpaths on narrow streets.

Train cars on most lines have areas set aside for people in wheelchairs. Those with other physical disabilities can use the seats near the train exits, called *yūsen-zaseki*. You will also find these seats near the front of buses; usually they're a different colour from the regular seats.

Useful organisations and services for travellers with disabilities:

Japanese Red Cross Language Service Volunteers (Map p72; ☎ 3438-1311; http://accessible.jp.org/tokyo/en/index.html; 1-1-3 Shiba Daimon, Minato-ku, Tokyo) Has loads of useful information, and also produces an excellent guide, *Accessible Tokyo*, which can be requested by email, mail or telephone – or found on its website.

Accessible Japan (www.tesco-premium.co.jp/aj/index.htm) Details the accessibility of hundreds of sites in Tokyo, including hotels, sights and department stores, as well as general information about getting around Japan.

Visas

Generally, visitors who are not planning to engage in income-producing activities while in Japan are exempt from obtaining visas and will be issued a 90-day *tanki-taizai* (temporary-visitor) visa on arrival. Nationals of Australia, Canada, France, Ireland, Italy, the Netherlands, New Zealand, Spain, the UK and the USA are eligible for this visa.

Stays of up to six months are permitted for citizens of Austria, Germany, Ireland, Mexico, Switzerland and the UK. Citizens of these countries will almost always be given a 90-day temporary visitor visa upon arrival, which can usually be extended for another 90 days at immigration bureaux inside Japan.

Japanese law requires that visitors entering on a temporary-visitor visa possess an ongoing air or sea ticket or evidence thereof. In practice, few travellers are asked to produce such documents, but it pays to be on the safe side.

For additional information on visas and regulations, contact your nearest Japanese embassy or consulate, or visit the website of the **Ministry of Foreign Affairs of Japan** (www.mofa.go.jp).

Women Travellers

Japan is a relatively safe country for women travellers, though perhaps not quite as safe as some might think. Crimes against women are generally believed to be widely underreported, especially by Japanese women. Foreign women are occasionally subjected to some forms of verbal harassment or prying questions. Physical attacks are very rare, but have occurred.

The best advice is to avoid being lulled into a false sense of security by Japan's image as one of the world's safest countries and to take the normal precautions you would in your home country. If a neighbourhood or establishment looks unsafe, then treat it that way. As long as you use your common sense, you will most likely find that Japan is a pleasant and rewarding place to travel as a woman.

Several train companies have recently introduced women-only cars to protect female passengers from *chikan* (men who feel up women and girls on packed trains). These cars are usually available during rush-hour periods on weekdays on busy urban lines. There are signs (usually in pink) on the platform indicating where you can board these cars, and the cars themselves are usually labelled in both Japanese and English (again, these are often marked in pink).

If you have a problem and you find the local police unhelpful, you can call the **Japan Helpline** (☎0120-46-1997), a nationwide emergency number that operates 24 hours a day, seven days a week.

Transport

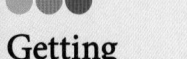

Getting There & Away

Entering the Country

While most travellers fly to Japan via Tokyo, there are several other ways of getting into and out of the country. For a start, there are many other airports that can make better entry points than Tokyo's somewhat inconvenient Narita International Airport. It's also possible to arrive by sea from South Korea, China and Russia.

Flights, tours and rail tickets can be booked online at lonelyplanet.com/bookings.

 ## Air

There are flights to Japan from all over the world, usually to Tokyo, but also to a number of other airports. Although Tokyo may seem the obvious arrival and departure point, for many visitors this may not be the case. For example, if you plan to explore western Japan or the Kansai region, it might be more convenient to fly into Kansai International Airport near Osaka.

Airports

There are international airports situated on the main island of Honshū (Nagoya, Niigata, Osaka/Kansai, Haneda and Tokyo Narita), as well as on Kyūshū (Fukuoka, Kagoshima, Kumamoto and Nagasaki), Okinawa (Naha) and Hokkaidō (Sapporo):

The majority of international flights to/from Tokyo use **Narita** (NRT; www.narita-airport.jp/en/), about an hour from Tokyo by express train (¥2940).

Some international flights now go via **Tokyo International Airport** (HND; www.tokyo-airport-bldg.co.jp/en/), better known as Haneda Airport, about 30 minutes from Tokyo by monorail and thus more convenient (and cheaper) than Narita. There's a new international terminal and runway; new international flights are being added all the time.

Domestic Airfares

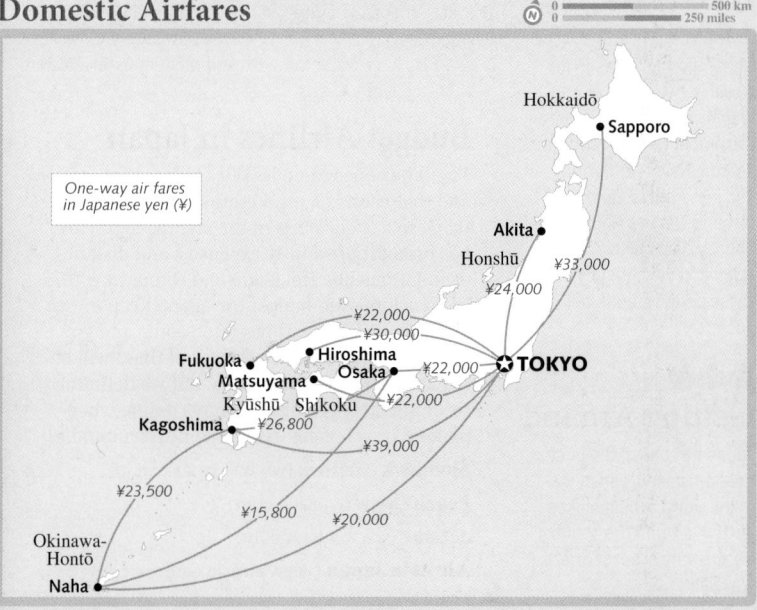

Baggage Forwarding

If you have too much luggage to carry comfortably or just can't be bothered, you can do what many Japanese travellers do: send it to your next stop by *takkyūbin* (express shipping companies). Prices are surprisingly reasonable and overnight service is the norm. Perhaps the most convenient service is Yamato Takkyūbin, which operates from most convenience stores. Simply pack your luggage and take it to the nearest convenience store; staff will help with the paperwork and arrange for pick-up. Note that you'll need the full address of your next destination in Japanese, along with the phone number of the place.

All of Osaka's international flights go via **Kansai International Airport** (KIX; www.kansai-airport.or.jp/en/index.asp), which serves the key Kansai cities of Kyoto, Osaka, Nara and Kōbe.

Near Nagoya, **Central Japan International Airport** (Centrair NGO; www.centrair.jp/en) has international connections with 12 countries.

Tickets

Generally, high season for travel between Japan and Western countries is in late December (around Christmas and the New Year period) and late April to early May (around Japan's Golden Week holiday), as well as July and August. If you must fly during these periods, book well in advance.

Getting Around

Japan has one of the best public-transport systems in the world, which makes getting around the country an absolute breeze for travellers.

 Air

Air services in Japan are extensive, reliable and safe. In many cases, flying is much faster than even *shinkansen* (bullet trains) and not that much more expensive. Flying is also an efficient way to travel from the main islands to the many small islands, particularly the Southwest Islands (the southern islands of Kagoshima and Okinawa Prefectures).

Airlines in Japan

Japan Airlines (JAL; ☎ 03-5460-0522, 0570-025-121; www.jal.co.jp/en) A major international carrier with an extensive domestic network.

All Nippon Airways (ANA; ☎ 0570-029-709, in Osaka 06-7637-6679, in Tokyo 03-6741-1120; www.ana.co.jp/eng) The other major Japanese international and domestic carrier.

Japan Trans Ocean Air (JTA; ☎ 03-5460-0522, 0570-025-071; www.jal.co.jp/jta) A smaller domestic carrier that mostly services routes in the Southwest Islands.

Tickets & Discounts

For domestic flights, return fares are usually around 10% cheaper than buying two one-way tickets. You can also get advance-purchase reductions: both ANA and JAL offer discounts of up to 50% if you purchase your ticket a month or more in advance,

Budget Airlines in Japan

Japan has opened up its skies to low-cost carriers and the result is a proliferation of budget airlines flying to various parts of the archipelago. This has brought previously expensive and distant destinations like Hokkaidō and Okinawa within the reach of even budget travellers. Keep in mind that budget airlines often come and go, so we cannot guarantee that all of these will be flying when you're in country, but we definitely recommend checking their fares online when making travel plans – you might save a bundle.

Skymark Airlines (www.skymark.co.jp)

Peach (www.flypeach.com)

Jetstar (www.jetstar.com)

Air Asia Japan (www.airasia.com)

with smaller discounts for purchases made one to three weeks in advance. Seniors over 65 also qualify for discounts on most Japanese airlines, but these are sometimes only available if you fly on weekdays.

ANA also offers the Star Alliance Japan Airpass for foreign travellers on ANA or Star Alliance network airlines. Provided you reside outside Japan, purchase your tickets outside Japan and carry a valid international ticket on any airline, you can fly up to five times within 60 days on any ANA domestic route for only ¥10,500 per flight (a huge saving on some routes). Visit www.ana.co.jp/wws/us/e/travelservice/reservations/special/airpass.html for more details.

🚗 Car & Motorcycle

Driving in Japan is quite feasible, even for just the mildly adventurous. The major roads are signposted in English; road rules are generally adhered to and driving is safer than in a lot of other Asian countries; and petrol, while expensive, is not prohibitively so. Indeed, in some areas of the country it can prove much more convenient than other forms of travel and, between a group of people, it can also prove quite economical.

In some parts of Japan (most notably Hokkaidō, the Noto Peninsula, some parts of Kyūshū and the Southwest Islands), driving is really the only efficient way to get around unless you have a good touring bicycle or fancy long waits for buses each time you need to make a move.

Driving Licence

Travellers from most nations are able to drive in Japan with an International Driving Permit backed up by their own regular licence. The International Driving Permit is issued by your national automobile association and costs around US$5 in most countries. Make sure it's endorsed for cars and motorcycles if you're licensed for both.

Travellers from Switzerland, France and Germany (and others whose countries are not signatories to the Geneva Convention of 1949 concerning international driving licences) are not allowed to drive in Japan on a regular International Driving Permit. Rather, travellers from these countries must have their own licence backed by an authorised translation of the same licence. These translations can be made by their embassy or consulate in Japan or by the Japan Automobile Federation. If you are unsure which category your country falls into, contact the nearest JNTO office for more information.

Foreign licences and International Driving Permits are only valid in Japan for six months. If you are staying longer, you will have to get a Japanese licence from the local department of motor vehicles.

Climate Change & Travel

Every form of transport that relies on carbon-based fuel generates CO_2, the main cause of human-induced climate change. Modern travel is dependent on aeroplanes, which might use less fuel per kilometre per person than most cars but travel much greater distances. The altitude at which aircraft emit gases (including CO_2) and particles also contributes to their climate change impact. Many websites offer 'carbon calculators' that allow people to estimate the carbon emissions generated by their journey and, for those who wish to do so, to offset the impact of the greenhouse gases emitted with contributions to portfolios of climate-friendly initiatives throughout the world. Lonely Planet offsets the carbon footprint of all staff and author travel.

Expressways

The expressway system is fast, efficient and growing all the time. Tolls cost about ¥24.6 per kilometre. Tokyo to Kyoto, for example, will cost ¥10,050 in tolls.

There are good rest stops and service centres at regular intervals. A prepaid highway card, available from tollbooths or at the service areas, saves you having to carry so much cash and gives you a 4% to 8% discount in the larger card denominations. You can also pay tolls with most major credit cards. Exits are usually fairly well signposted in English, but make sure you

Driving in Japan

Unless you plan on driving in central Tokyo or Osaka or forget that the Japanese drive on the left, you should have no major problems driving in Japan. In fact, driving here is remarkably sane compared to many countries (perhaps because it's so difficult to pass the test). Still, there are a few peculiarities that are worth keeping in mind.

Petrol stations While self-serve petrol stations are becoming popular, full-service stations are still the rule. And in Japan, when they say 'full service', they really mean it. They'll empty your ashtray, take any garbage you have, wipe your windshield and then wave you back into traffic. And if you're wondering how to say 'fill 'er up' in Japanese, it's '*mantan*' (full tank).

Chains If you drive in mountain areas in winter, you might be required to put chains on your car. If you rent a car in these areas, it will probably come equipped. Petrol stations in mountain areas will usually put the chains on for a charge (¥1000 to ¥2000). There may be police stops in these areas to make sure that cars have chains.

signposts follow international conventions. JAF has a *Rules of the Road* book available in English and five other languages for ¥1000.

Maps & Navigation

If you can find a used copy of the *Road Atlas Japan* (Shōbunsha), grab it. It's all in English (romaji) with enough names in kanji to make navigation possible even off the major roads. Unfortunately, it's out of print and hard to find these days. If you're really intent on making your way through the back blocks, a Japanese map will prove useful even if your knowledge of kanji is nil. The best Japanese road atlases by far are the *Super Mapple* series (Shōbunsha), which are available in bookshops and some convenience stores.

There is a reasonable amount of signposting in romaji, so getting around isn't all that difficult, especially in developed areas. If you are attempting tricky navigation, use your maps imaginatively – watch out for the railway line, the rivers, the landmarks. They're all useful ways of locating yourself when you can't read the signs. A compass will also come in handy when navigating.

These days, many rental cars come equipped with satellite navigation systems, making navigation a snap, provided you can figure out how to work the system. With most of these systems, you can input the phone number of your destination, which is easy, or its address, which is just about impossible if you don't read Japanese. Even

know the name of your exit as it may not necessarily be the same as the city you're heading towards.

Fuel

You'll find *gasoreen sutando* (petrol stations) in almost every town and in service stations along the expressways. The cost of petrol per litre ranges from ¥141 to ¥144 for regular and ¥152 to ¥155 for high octane.

Hire

You'll usually find car-rental agencies clustered around train stations and ferry piers. Typical rates for a small car are ¥5000 to ¥7000 per day, with reductions for rentals of more than one day. On top of the rental charge, there's about a ¥1000-per-day insurance cost.

Communication can sometimes be a major problem when hiring a car. Some of the offices will have a rent-a-car phrasebook, with questions you might need to ask in English. Otherwise, just speak as slowly as possible and hope for the best. A good way to open the conversation is to say '*kokusai menkyō wo motteimasu*' (I have an international licence).

Toyota Rent-a-Car (☎ in Japan 0800-7000-111, outside Japan 81-3-5954-8020; http://rent.toyota.co.jp/en/index.html) has the largest rental network and has a very informative website which allows reservations from overseas.

Road Rules

Driving is on the left. There are no unusual rules or interpretations of them and most without programming in your destination, with the device on the default '*genzai-chi*' (present location) setting, you will find it very useful.

Local Transport

All the major cities offer a wide variety of public transport. In many cities you can get day passes for unlimited travel on bus, tram or subway systems. Such passes are usually called an *ichi-nichi-jōsha-ken*. If you're staying for an extended period in one city, commuter passes are available for regular travel.

Bus

Almost every Japanese city has an extensive bus service, but it's usually the most difficult public-transport system for foreign travellers to use. Destinations and stops are often written only in Japanese.

Fares are usually paid when you get off. In Tokyo and some other cities, there's a flat fare regardless of distance. In the other cities, you take a ticket (known as a *seiri-ken*) as you board that indicates the zone number at your starting point. When you get off, an electric sign at the front of the bus indicates the fare charged at that point for each starting zone number. You simply pay the driver the fare that matches your zone number (you put both the *seiri-ken* and the fare into the fare box). There is often a change machine near the front of the bus that can exchange ¥100 and ¥500 coins and ¥1000 notes.

Taxi

Taxis are convenient and can be found even in very small cities and on tiny islands; the train station is the best place to look. Fares are fairly uniform throughout the country. Flagfall (posted on the taxi windows) is ¥600 to ¥710 for the first 2km, after which it's around ¥100 for each 350m (approximately). There's also a time charge if the speed drops below 10km/h. A red light in the lower right corner of the windshield indicates if a taxi is available (it says 'vacant' in Japanese) – this can be difficult to spot during the day. At night, taxis usually have the light on their roof on when they're vacant and off when they're occupied, but there are regional variations.

Don't open the door when you get into the taxi; the driver does that with a remote release. The driver will also shut the door when you leave.

Communication can be a problem with taxi drivers, but perhaps not as much as you fear. If you can't tell the driver where you want to go, it's useful to have the name written down in Japanese. At hotel front desks there will usually be business cards complete with name and location, which can be used for just this purpose.

Tipping is not necessary. A 20% surcharge is added after 11pm or for taxis summoned by radio. There may also be an added charge if you arrange the taxi by phone or reserve the taxi. Finally, taxis can usually take up to four adult passengers (one person can sit in the front). Drivers are sometimes willing to bend the rules for small children.

Train & Subway

Several cities, especially Osaka and Tokyo, have mass-transit rail systems

Train Terminology

PRONUNCIATION	SCRIPT	ENGLISH
futsū	普通	local
green-sha	グリーン車	1st-class car
jiyū-seki	自由席	unreserved seat
kaisoku	快速	JR rapid or express
kaku-eki-teisha	各駅停車	local
katamichi	片道	one way
kin'en-sha	禁煙車	nonsmoking car
kitsuen-sha	喫煙車	smoking car
kyūkō	急行	ordinary express
ōfuku	往復	round trip
shin-kaisoku	新快速	JR special rapid train
shinkansen	新幹線	bullet train
shitei-seki	指定席	reserved seat
tokkyū	特急	limited express

Passes & Discount Tickets

JAPAN RAIL PASS

The **Japan Rail Pass** (www.japanrailpass.net/eng/en001.html) is a must for anyone planning to do extensive train travel within Japan. Not only will it save you a lot of money, it will save you from having to fish for change each time you board a train.

The most important thing to note about the pass is this: the Japan Rail Pass must be purchased outside Japan. It is available to foreign tourists and Japanese overseas residents (but not foreign residents of Japan). The pass cannot be used for the super-express Nozomi *shinkansen* (bullet-train) service but is OK for everything else (including other *shinkansen* services). Children between the ages of six and 11 qualify for child passes, while those aged under six ride for free.

Since a one-way reserved-seat Tokyo–Kyoto *shinkansen* ticket costs ¥13,220, you only have to travel Tokyo–Kyoto–Tokyo to make a seven-day pass come close to paying off. Note that the pass is valid only on JR services; you will still have to pay for private train services.

In order to get a pass, you must first purchase an 'exchange order' outside Japan at a Japan Airlines or All Nippon Airways office or a major travel agency. Once you arrive in Japan, you must bring this order to a JR Travel Service Centre (in most major JR stations and at Narita and Kansai International Airports). When you validate your pass, you'll have to show your passport.

The clock starts to tick on the pass as soon as you validate it. So don't validate it if you're just going into Tokyo or Kyoto and intend to hang around for a few days. Instead, validate when you leave those cities to explore the rest of the country.

For more information on the pass and overseas purchase locations, visit the Japan Rail Pass website.

JR EAST PASS

The **JR East Pass** (www.jreast.co.jp/e/eastpass/index.html) is a great deal for those who only want to travel in eastern Japan. The passes are good on all JR lines in eastern Japan (including Tōhoku, Yamagata, Akita, Jōetsu and Nagano *shinkansen*, but not including the Tōkaidō *shinkansen*). This includes the area around Tokyo and everything north of Tokyo to the tip of Honshū but doesn't include Hokkaidō. In addition to the normal five- and 10-day passes, four-day 'flexible' passes allow travel on any four consecutive or nonconsecutive days within any one-month period.

For normal passes, 'adult' means anyone over 26, 'youth' means anyone between 12 and 25, and 'child' means anyone between six and 11. For the Green passes, there are only adult passes (anyone over 12) and child passes (anyone between six and 11).

As with the Japan Rail Pass, this can only be purchased outside Japan (in the same locations as the Japan Rail Pass) and can only be used by those with temporary visitor visas (you'll need to show your passport).

DURATION (DAYS)	REGULAR (ADULT/ CHILD)	GREEN (ADULT/ CHILD)
7	¥28,300/14,150	¥37,800/18,900
14	¥45,100/22,550	¥61,200/30,600
21	¥57,700/28,850	¥79,600/39,800

JR WEST KANSAI AREA PASS

A great deal for those who only want to explore the Kansai area, the **Kansai Area Pass** (www.westjr.co.jp/global/en/travel-information/pass/kansai/) covers unlimited travel on JR lines between most major Kansai cities, such as Himeji, Kōbe, Osaka, Kyoto and Nara. It also covers JR trains to/from Kansai International Airport but does not cover any *shinkansen* lines. The pass also entitles holders to reserved seats at no extra charge (you'll have to reserve each trip before boarding the train). Passes are only good on consecutive days.

For these passes, 'child' means anyone between six and 11 (children under six travel free). The pass can be purchased at the same places as the San-yō Area Pass (both inside and outside Japan) and also entitles you to discounts at station car-hire offices. This pass can only be used by those with a temporary visitor visa.

DURATION (DAYS)	REGULAR (ADULT/YOUTH/CHILD)	GREEN (ADULT/CHILD)
5	¥20,000/16,000/10,000	¥28,000/14,000
10	¥32,000/25,000/16,000	¥44,800/22,400
flexible 4	¥20,000/16,000/10,000	¥28,000/14,000

JR KANSAI WIDE AREA PASS

This is similar to the JR West Kansai Area Pass, but it also allows travel on the Sanyō *shinkansen* between Osaka and Okayama as well as trains going as far as Kinosaki in the north and Shingū in the south, including a variety of *tokkyū* (limited express trains). The pass is valid for four days and costs ¥7000/3500 per adult/child. For these passes, 'child' means anyone between six and 11 (children aged under six travel free). The pass can be purchased at the same places as the JR West Kansai Area Pass (both inside and outside Japan) and also entitles you to discounts at station car-hire offices. Like the JR West Kansai Area Pass, this pass can only be used by those with a temporary visitor visa.

DURATION (DAYS)	REGULAR (ADULT/CHILD)
1	¥2000/1000
2	¥4000/2000
3	¥5000/2500
4	¥6000/3000

JR WEST SAN-YŌ AREA PASS

Similar to the JR East Pass, the **San-yō Area Pass** (www.westjr.co.jp/global/en/travel-information/pass/sanyo/) allows unlimited travel on the San-yō *shinkansen* line (including the Nozomi super express) between Osaka and Hakata, as well as local trains running between the same cities. The pass is only good on consecutive days.

For this pass, 'child' means anyone between six and 11 (children aged under six travel free). The pass can be purchased both inside Japan (at major train stations, travel agencies and Kansai International Airport) and outside Japan (same locations as the Japan Rail Pass). Again, it can only be used by those with a temporary visitor visa. The pass also entitles you to discounts at station rental-car agencies.

DURATION (DAYS)	REGULAR (ADULT/CHILD)
4	¥20,000/10,000
8	¥30,000/15,000

Kansai Thru Pass

This pass allows unlimited travel on all non-JR private train lines and most bus lines in Kansai.

comprising a loop line around the city centre and radial lines into the central stations and the subway system. Subway systems operate in Fukuoka, Kōbe, Kyoto, Nagoya, Osaka, Sapporo, Tokyo and Yokohama. They are usually the fastest and most convenient way to get around the city.

🚆 Train

Japanese rail services are among the best in the world: they are fast, frequent, clean and comfortable. The 'national' railway is **Japan Railways**, commonly known as 'JR', which is actually a number of separate private rail systems providing one linked service.

The JR system covers the country from one end to the other and also provides local services around major cities such as Tokyo and Osaka. JR also operates buses and ferries, and convenient ticketing can combine more than one form of transport.

In addition to JR services, there is a huge network of private railways. Each large city usually has at least one private train line that services that city and the surrounding area, or connects that city to nearby cities. These are often a bit cheaper than equivalent JR services.

Types of Trains

The slowest trains stopping at all stations are called *futsū* or *kaku-eki-teisha*. A step up from this is the *kyūkō* (ordinary express), which stops at only a limited number of stations. A variation on the *kyūkō* trains is the *kaisoku* (rapid) service (usually operating on JR lines). Finally, the fastest regular (non-*shinkansen*) trains are the *tokkyū* (limited-express) services, which are sometimes known as *shin-kaisoku* (again, usually operating on JR lines).

SHINKANSEN

The fastest and best-known services are JR's *shinkansen*, Japan's famed 'bullet trains'. *Shinkansen* lines operate on separate tracks from regular trains, and, in some places, the *shinkansen* station is a fair distance from the main JR station (as is the case in Osaka).

On most *shinkansen* routes, there are two or three types of service: faster express services stopping at a limited number of stations, and slower local services stopping at more stations. There is no difference in fare, except for the Green Car (1st-class) carriages, which cost slightly more.

There are reserved and unreserved cars on all trains. If you're travelling outside peak travel periods, you can usually just show up and expect to get a seat in an unreserved car. If you're travelling during a peak period, it is a good idea to stop at a JR station to make a reservation a few days prior to your departure.

Classes

Most long-distance JR trains, including *shinkansen*, have regular and Green Car

---

Train Reservations from Abroad

First, keep in mind that you do not usually have to make reservations in advance for train travel in Japan. The only times you should consider reserving in advance are Golden Week (late April to early May), Obon (mid-August) and New Year.

Unfortunately, it is not possible to make reservations for JR trains online in English. However, most travel agents who handle the Japan Rail Pass can also make train reservations and sell you tickets in advance, but they will charge a fairly hefty surcharge to do this. A list of travel agents can be found at www.japanrailpass.net/eng/en001.html.

There's one more thing to keep in mind: if you've got a Japan Rail Pass, you will not be able to reserve travel through a travel agent outside Japan. The reason for this is that you must activate the pass in Japan and show the pass when you make reservations.

In all cases, if you're nervous about getting seats for your train travel in Japan, you can always walk into a JR office and book all your train travel immediately upon arrival or early in your stay (you can reserve travel up to a month in advance at JR ticket offices inside Japan).

Tickets & Reservations

Tickets for most journeys can be bought from train-station vending machines, ticket counters and reservation offices. For reservations of complicated tickets, larger train stations have *midori-no-madoguchi*. Major travel agencies in Japan also sell reserved-seat tickets, and you can buy *shinkansen* (bullet train) tickets through Japan Airlines (JAL) offices overseas if you will be flying JAL to Japan.

On *futsū* (local) services, there are no reserved seats. On the faster *tokkyū* (limited express) and *shinkansen* services you can choose to travel reserved or unreserved. However, if you travel unreserved, there's always the risk of not getting a seat and having to stand, possibly for the entire trip. This is a particular danger at weekends, peak travel seasons and on holidays. Reserved-seat tickets can be bought any time from a month in advance to the day of departure.

Information and tickets can be obtained from travel agencies, of which there are a great number in Japan. Nearly every train station of any size will have at least one travel agency in the station building to handle all sorts of bookings in addition to train services. Japan Travel Bureau (JTB) is the big daddy of Japanese travel agencies. However, for most train tickets and long-distance bus reservations, you don't need to go through a travel agency – just go to the ticket counters or *midori-no-madoguchi* of any major train station.

carriages. The seating is slightly more spacious in Green Car carriages (think of a typical business-class seat on an aircraft). The Green Car carriages also tend to be quieter and less crowded. However, all Green Car seats are reserved, so if you've got a Green Japan Rail Pass, you'll have to reserve every trip in advance (with a regular pass you just go through the turnstiles and get on the next available train).

Schedules & Information

The most complete timetables can be found in the *JR Jikokuhyō* (Book of Timeta-bles), which is available at all Japanese bookshops but is written in Japanese. JNTO, however, produces a handy English-language *Railway Timetable* booklet that explains a great deal about the services in Japan and gives timetables for the *shinkansen* services, JR *tokkyū* and major private lines. If your visit to Japan is a short one and you will not be straying far from the major tourist destinations, this booklet may well be all you need.

Major train stations all have information counters, and you can usually get your point across in simplified English.

If you need to know anything about JR, such as schedules, fares, fastest routes, lost baggage, discounts on rail travel, hotels and car hire, call the **JR East Infoline** (☎050-2016-1603; www.jreast.co.jp/e/customer_support/infoline.html; ☗10am-6pm). Information is available in English, Korean and Chinese. More information can be found on the website. The website **Hyperdia** (www.hyperdia.com) is also a useful online source for schedules and is probably the most user-friendly English-language site.

Language

Japanese pronunciation is not difficult as most of its sounds are also found in English. You can read our pronunciation guides as if they were English and you'll be understood just fine. Just remember to pronounce every vowel individually, make those with a macron (ie a line above them) longer than those without, and pause slightly between double consonants.

To enhance your trip with a phrasebook, visit **lonelyplanet.com**. Lonely Planet iPhone phrasebooks are available through the Apple App store.

Basics

Hello.
こんにちは。　　　　　konnichiwa
How are you?
お元気ですか?　　　　o-genki des ka
I'm fine, thanks.
はい、元気です。　　　hai, genki des
Excuse me.
すみません。　　　　　sumimasen
Yes./No.
はい。/いいえ。　　　　hai/ iie
Please. (when asking/offering)
ください。/どうぞ。　　kudasai/dōzo
Thank you.
どうもありがとう。　　dōmo arigatō
You're welcome.
どういたしまして。　　dō itashimashite
Do you speak English?
英語が話せますか?　　eigo ga hanasemas ka
I don't understand.
わかりません。　　　　wakarimasen
How much is this?
いくらですか?　　　　ikura des ka
Goodbye.
さようなら。　　　　　sayōnara

Accommodation

I'd like to make a booking.
部屋の予約を　　　　　heya no yoyaku o
お願いします。　　　　onegai shimas
How much is it per night?
1泊いくらですか?　　　ippaku ikura des ka

Eating & Drinking

I'd like ..., please.
…をください。　　　　... o kudasai
What do you recommend?
おすすめは何　　　　　o-susume wa nan
ですか?　　　　　　　des ka
That was delicious.
おいしかった。　　　　oyshikatta
Bring the bill/check, please.
お勘定をお願い　　　　o-kanjō o onegai
します。　　　　　　　shimas

I don't eat ...
…は食べません。　　　... wa tabemasen
   chicken　　鶏肉　　tori-niku
   fish　　　　魚　　　sakana
   meat　　　肉　　　niku
   pork　　　豚肉　　buta-niku

Emergencies

I'm ill.
気分が悪いです。　　　kibun ga warui des
Help!
たすけて!　　　　　　taskete
Call a doctor!
医者を呼んで!　　　　isha o yonde
Call the police!
警察を呼んで!　　　　keisatsu o yonde

Directions

I'm looking for (a/the) ...
…を探しています。　　... o sagashite imas
   bank
   銀行　　　　　　　ginkō
   ... embassy
   大使館　　　　　　taishikan
   market
   市場　　　　　　　ichiba
   museum
   美術館　　　　　　bijutsukan
   restaurant
   レストラン　　　　restoran
   toilet
   お手洗い/トイレ　　o-tearai/toire
   tourist office
   観光案内所　　　　kankō annaijo

Behind the Scenes

Author Thanks

Chris Rowthorn

I'd like to thank the fantastic author team on this edition of Japan: Craig McLachlan, Ben Walker, Rebecca Milner, Laura Crawford, Wendy Yanagihara, Trent Holden and Kate Morgan. I would also like to thank the brilliant inhouse team: Emily Wolman, Rebecca Chau, Martine Power, Anne Mason, Barbara Delissen, Diana Von Holdt and all the others who worked on this book. Thanks to Jeffrey Friedl for his excellent photographs of Tōdaiji, Kana Hattori for her Kōbe picks, Mie Ito for more Kōbe picks, and Michael Lambe for Kyoto bar recommendations. I'd also like to thank my wife Hiroe for her incredible support during this whole process. Thank you to all the readers who were kind enough to send in your advice for the book. Finally, I'd like to thank all the kind people of Japan who made my research trip such a joy.

Acknowledgments

Climate map data adapted from Peel MC, Finlayson BL & McMahon TA (2007) 'Updated World Map of the Köppen-Geiger Climate Classification', *Hydrology and Earth System Sciences*, 11, 1633¬44.

Illustrations p80-1 and p282-3 by Michael Weldon.

Cover photographs: Front: Pagoda and cherry blossoms at sunrise, Ocean, Corbis; Back: Sensō-ji, Tokyo, Gianni Iorio, 4Corners.

This Book

This 2nd edition of Lonely Planet's *Discover Japan* was coordinated by Chris Rowthorn, and researched and written by Chris Rowthorn, Laura Crawford, Trent Holden, Craig McLachlan, Rebecca Milner, Kate Morgan, Ben Walker and Wendy Yanagihara. This guidebook was commissioned in Lonely Planet's Oakland office, and produced by the following:

Commissioning Editors Emily K Wolman, Rebecca Chau

Coordinating Editor Anne Mason

Senior Cartographer Diana Von Holdt

Coordinating Layout Designer Frank Deim

Managing Editors Barbara Delissen, Martine Power, Angela Tinson

Managing Layout Designer Chris Girdler

Assisting Editors Briohny Hooper, Elizabeth Jones, Charlotte Orr, Amanda Williamson

Cover Research Naomi Parker

Internal Image Research Kylie McLaughlin

Language Content Branislava Vladisavljevic

Thanks to Laura Crawford, Petra Delsing, Ryan Evans, Larissa Frost, Jane Hart, Genesys India, Jouve India, Asha Ioculari, Alison Lyall, Annelies Mertens, Catherine Naghten, Takita Naoya, John Osman, Trent Paton, Michael Schaller, Julie Sheridan, Kerrianne Southway, Aude Vauconsant, Gerard Walker, Sawako Yoshioka

SEND US YOUR FEEDBACK

We love to hear from travellers – your comments keep us on our toes and help make our books better. Our well-travelled team reads every word on what you loved or loathed about this book. Although we cannot reply individually to postal submissions, we always guarantee that your feedback goes straight to the appropriate authors, in time for the next edition. Each person who sends us information is thanked in the next edition, the most useful submissions are rewarded with a selection of digital PDF chapters.

Visit **lonelyplanet.com/contact** to submit your updates and suggestions or to ask for help. Our award-winning website also features inspirational travel stories, news and discussions.

Note: We may edit, reproduce and incorporate your comments in Lonely Planet products such as guidebooks, websites and digital products, so let us know if you don't want your comments reproduced or your name acknowledged. For a copy of our privacy policy visit lonelyplanet.com/privacy.

Index

A

accommodation 49, 374, *see also individual locations*
costs 376
language 394
ryokan 369-70
activities 42-5, *see also individual activities*
air travel 385-7
airlines 386
domestic airfares **385**
airports 385-6
Haneda 119
Hiroshima 312
Kansai International (KIX) 275-6
Nagasaki 329
Narita 118
Osaka Itami 249
Aka-jima 336-7
amusement parks
Tokyo Disney Resort 89
Tokyo Joypolis 89
Anbō 330
Andō, Tadao 272, 302-3, 304
Aoi Matsuri 231
Aoyama Rei-en 75
Arashiyama 196, 224-5
Arashiyama Bamboo Grove 31, 225
architecture 363, 366
gasshō-zukuri 157
area codes 382
Art House Project 302

arts 362-6
Asahidake Onsen 321-2
Ashi-no-ko 138
ATMs 48, 380
Atomic Bomb Dome 306
Atomic Bomb Hypocentre Park 326
atomic bomb sites
Hiroshima 306-7
Nagasaki 327
atomic bombings 327, 349

B

bamboo grove 31, 225
bathrooms 383
Battle of Okinawa 336
beaches
Agenashiku-jima 337
Aka-jima 336-7
Furuzamami beach 337
Gahi-jima 337
Issō-kaisuiyokujō 331
Nagata Inaka-hama 330
Nishibama beach 336
Zamami-jima 337
Benesse Art Site 257, 303
Benesse House Museum 302-3
Bessho Onsen 158
books 47
budget 49
bullet trains, *see shinkansen*
burial mounds 345
bus travel 389
business hours 381

C

cable cars, *see ropeways*
cabs 389
Capsule Ryokan Kyoto 46
car travel 387-9
castles 23
Himeji-jō 23, 299-300
Matsumoto-jō 172

Nijō-jō 211
Shuri-jō 333-4
cell phones 48, 383
Central Honshū 143-91, **145**
getting around 149
highlights 146-7
hiking 148
itineraries 150-1
onsen 148
overnight getaways 148
planning 149
ceramics 364
cherry-blossom viewing 15, 22, 42-3, 75, 90
Chiiori 324
children, travel with 26, 87, 371-2
Chōkoku-no-mori 137-8
climate 42-5, 48, 377
climbing, *see hiking*
coffee 360
comics 365
consulates 375-6
credit cards 48, 380
cuisine, *see food*
culture 350-3
currency 48
customs regulations 374

D

Daibutsu (Kamakura) 140
Daibutsu (Nara) 17, 279
Daibutsu-den Hall 280
Daimon-ji Gozan Okuribi 232
Daisetsuzan National Park 320-2
Daishō-in 315
Dejima 326
Den Den Town 272
department store dining 240
dining, *see food*
disabilities, travellers with 383-4
diving
Kerama Islands 336-7
Dōtombori 28, 269-71

Dōtombori Arcade 270
drinks
  tea 360
  coffee 360
  sake 361
driving, *see* car travel
driving licence 387
D.T. Suzuki Museum 46, 184-5

E

earthquakes 340-1
eating, *see* food
economy 341
electricity 375
embassies 375-6
emergencies
  language 394
etiquette
  food 358
  onsen 368
  tipping 381
events 42-5, *see also* festivals
  & events
exchange rates 49
exchanging money 381

F

family travel 26, 87, 371-2
festivals & events 42-5
  Aoi Matsuri 231
  Daimon-ji Gozan Okuribi 232
  Gion Matsuri 231
  Jidai Matsuri 232
  Kurama-no-hi Matsuri 232
  Matsumoto Bonbon 174
  Setsubun Matsuri at
    Yoshida-jinja 231
  Takayama Matsuri 153
films 47
fish market, *see* Tsukiji Fish
  Market
floating torii 313
food 13, 17, 354-61
  costs 376
  department store dining 240

etiquette 358
izakaya 356
language 394
okonomiyaki 359
rāmen 358
restaurant halls (Osaka) 268
sashimi 357
shokudō 355
soba 357
sushi 357
sweets 359-60
tonkatsu 359
types of restaurants 355-8
udon 357
vegetarians & vegans 357
yakitori
Fuji Five Lakes 125
Fuji-Yoshida 125
Fushimi Inari-taisha 197

G

galleries, *see* museums
gardens & parks 11, 18, 90
  Arashiyama Bamboo Grove
    31, 225
  Arashiyama Monkey Park
    Iwatayama 225
  Glover Garden 326
  Gyokusen-en 185-6
  Hama-rikyū Onshi-teien 64
  Imperial Palace East Garden
    90
  Isui-en & Neiraku Art
    Museum 279
  Kenroku-en 18, 185
  Kitanomaru-kōen 90
  Kiyosumi-teien 86
  Koishikawa Kōrakuen 77
  Kyoto Imperial Palace Park
    209
  Maruyama-kōen 215-16
  Memorial Peace Park
    (Okinawa-hontō) 335
  Nara-kōen 256
  Ōkōchi-sansō 225
  Peace Memorial Park
    (Hiroshima) 306-7

Peace Park 326
Shinjuku-gyoen 90
Ueno-kōen 82
Yoshiki-en 279
Yoyogi-kōen 73
gasshō-zukuri 157
gay travellers 376-7
geiko, see geisha
geisha 22
  districts 77, 181, 207, 217
  dances 20, 244-5
Giō-ji 225
Gion 217
Gion Matsuri 42-5, 231
Gōra 137-8
Great East Japan earthquake
  340-1

H

Hakone 135-9
Hakone-machi 138-9
Hakuba 170-2
hanami 90
health 377
  medical care 379
Hida district 152-60
Hida Folk Village 156
Hida-Furukawa 158
Hida-no-Sato 156
Hiiragiya ryokan 14, 235
hiking 16, 21, 148
  Daisetsuzan National Park
    321
  Hakuba 171
  Kamikōchi 21, 161
  Kyoto 21, 202
  Magome to Tsumago 19,
    21, 176
  Northern Japan Alps 163
  Tateyama-Kurobe Alpen
    Route 21, 180
  Yakushima 331
Himeji 299-301, **299**
Himeji-jō 299-300
Himeyuri no Tō 336
Hiroshima 24, 257, 306-12, **308**

Hiroshima National Peace Memorial Hall for the Atomic Bomb Victims 307-9
history 25, 342-9
　Buddhism 343
　Chinese influence 343
　Christian century 345-6, 348
　Edo period 346
　Heian period 343-4
　Kamakura period 344
　Kofun burial mounds 345
　Meiji Restoration 347
　Muromachi period 345
　nationalism 349
　peace & seclusion 346-7
　periods 344
　postwar reconstruction 349
　samurai 346
　Shōwa era 349
　Taishō era 348
　unification 345
　WWII 349
Hokkaidō 29, 318, 321
holidays 381-2
Honshū, see Central Honshū, Kansai & Western Honshū
hot springs, see onsen

I

immigration 385
Imperial Household Agency 209
Imperial Palace 61
insurance 377
internet access 48, 377-9
　wi-fi (Kyoto) 46
Inuyama 158
Ishihara Shintarō 341
Ishikawa Prefecture 181-91
Issō-kaisuiyokujō 331
itineraries 32-41
Itoman 335
Iya Valley 322-4
izakaya 356

J

Japan Alps 160-5
Japanese language 394
Jidai Matsuri 232
JR SCmaglev and Railway Park 46

K

kabuki 28, 46, 245, 365
Kaga Onsen 191
Kaigungo-kōen 336
Kamakura 55, 139-41
Kamikōchi 25, 147, 161-3
Kanazawa 146, 181-90, 182-3
Kanazawa Castle Park 184
Kansai & Western Honshū 253-316, 254-5
　accommodation 258
　getting around 259
　highlights 256-7
　itineraries 260-1
　planning 259
　shrines 259
　temples 259
　walking 258
Kansai International Airport (KIX) 275-6
Kawaguchi-ko 126-8
Kayōtei 13, 15, 191
Kayōtei ryokan 14, 191
Kenroku-en 18, 185
Kerama Islands 336-7
Kibune 229-30
Kinkaku-ji 197
Kinosaki 13, 292-5
Kinosaki Onsen 256
Kishiwada Danjiri Matsuri 265
Kiso Valley Nakasendō 176-81
Kiso-Fukushima 179
Kitano 295
Kitayama 228-32
Kiyomizu-dera 197
Kōbe 295-9
Kōbe Harbor Land 295-6
Koboke 323

Kōya-san 19, 287-92, 289
Kurama 229-30
Kurama-no-hi Matsuri 232
Kurama onsen 13, 231
Kurashiki 307
Kyoto 193-251, 195
　accommodation 198, 232-8
　Arashiyama & Sagano 224-5, 238, 243
　central Kyoto 208-11, 235-6
　downtown Kyoto 206-7, 234-5, 239-41, 210
　drinking 244
　entertainment 244-5
　festivals & events 199, 231-2
　food 238-43
　getting around 199, 249-51
　greater Kyoto map 204
　highlights 196-7
　itineraries 200-1
　Kitayama 228-32
　Kyoto Station area 203-6, 232-4, 239, 208
　markets 247
　northern Higashiyama 218-23, 237-8, 243
　northwest Kyoto 223
　resources 199
　shopping 245-8
　sights 202-31
　southeast Kyoto 226-7
　southern Higashiyama 212-17, 236-7, 241-3, 214
　southwest Kyoto 227
　tourist information 248
　travel tips 213
　travel to/from 248-9
　travel within 249-51
　walking 198
　walking tour 200-1

L

lacquerware 364-5
language 48, 394
left luggage 379
lesbian travellers 376-7
luggage 386

M

magazines 375
Magome 19, 147, 176-7
maiko, see geisha
manga 365
Manshu-in 234
maps 379
markets
  Daichi Makishi Kōsetsu
    Ichiba 333
  Kyoto 247
  Nishiki Market 26, 206-7
  Ōmichō Market 186-7
  Tsukiji Fish Market 16, 55,
    68-70
Matsumoto 172-6
Matsumoto Bonbon 174
measures 375
Meguro-gawa 75
Meiji-jingū 54, 74
Meriken Park 295-6
Miho museum 301
Minakami 133-5
Misen 314
Miyajima 257, 312-16, **313**
Miyanoshita 137
Miyanoura 330-2
mobile phones 48, 383
money 48, 49, 379-81
Mongolian spot 351
Moto-Hakone 138-9
motorcycle travel 387-9
Mt Fuji 21, 22, 120-8
  tours 121
museums
  21st Century Museum of
    Contemporary Art 184
  Asakura Chōso Museum 83
  Benesse House Museum
    302-3
  Bridgestone Museum of
    Art 61
  Chichū Art Museum 303
  D.T. Suzuki Museum 184
  Edo-Tokyo Museum 84-5
  Fujii Folk Museum 153
  Ghibli Museum 71

Hakone Museum of Art 138
Hakone Open-Air Museum
  137-8
Hakone Sekisho 139
Hida Folk Archaeological
  Museum 153
Hirata Folk Art Museum 155
Idemitsu Museum of Arts 61
Ishikawa Prefectural Art
  Museum 185
Japan Folk Crafts Museum 61
Japan Ukiyo-e Museum 173
Japanese Sword Museum
  75-6
Kanazawa Noh Museum 184
Karakuri Museum 154
Kusakabe Folk Crafts
  Museum 153
Kutani Kosen Gama Kiln 186
Kutaniyaki Art Museum 191
Kyoto International Manga
  Museum 207
Kyoto Municipal Museum of
  Art 218
Kyoto National Museum 212
Lee Ufan Museum 303
Matsumoto City Museum of
  Art 173
Matsumoto Open-Air
  Architectural Museum 173
Miho museum 301
Mori Art Museum 65
Musée Tomo 67
Museum of Contemporary
  Art, Tokyo (MOT) 85
Nagamachi Yūzen-kan 184
Nagasaki Atomic Bomb
  Museum 325
Nagasaki Museum of History
  & Culture 326
Nara National Museum
  277-9
Narukawa Art Museum 139
National Art Center Tokyo 61
National Museum of
  Emerging Science &
  Innovation (Mirai-kan) 89
National Museum of Modern
  Art (Kyoto) 222

National Museum of Modern
  Art (MOMAT) 77
National Museum of Western
  Art 83
National Science Museum
  83
National Shōwa Memorial
  Museum 77
Nezu Museum 74-5
Ōhi Pottery Museum 186
Okinawa Prefectural Museum
  & Art Museum 333
Okinawa Prefectural Peace
  Memorial Museum 335-6
Orinasu-kan 211
Osaka Museum of History
  265
Peace Memorial Museum
  307
POLA Museum of Art
  138
Shitamachi Museum
  82
Sumō Museum 86
Takayama Festival Floats
  Exhibition Hall 153
Takayama Museum of
  History & Art 154-5
Takayama Shōwa-kan 154
Tokyo Metropolitan Museum
  of Art 83
Tokyo Metropolitan Museum
  of Photography 70
Tokyo Metropolitan Teien Art
  Museum 71
Tokyo National Museum
  79, 80-1
Treasure Museum 288
Tsuboya Pottery Museum
  333
Ukiyo-e Ōta Memorial
  Museum of Art 73-4
Umekōji Steam Locomotive
  Museum 206
Utsukushi-ga-hara Open Air
  Museum 174
Waki-honjin (Okuya) & Local
  History Museum 178
Yūshū-kan 77
music 47

N

Nagamachi District 184
Nagano Prefecture 165-81
Nagasaki 325-9
Nagasaki National Peace Memorial Hall for the Atomic Bomb Victims 325-6
Nagata 330
Nagata Inaka-hama 330
Naha 333-5
Nakamachi 173
Nakamura House 180
Nakasendō post road 19, 176
Nanzen-ji 196, 219
Naoshima 13, 301-6
Naoshima Bath - I Heart Yū 303
Nara 276-87, **278**
  accommodation 284-5
  food 285-6
  sights 277-84
Narai 180-91
Nara-kōen 256, 277
newspapers 375
Nigatsu-dō 281
Nikkō 55, 129-33
Ninen-zaka & Sannen-zaka 215
Niseko 318-20
Nishijin 211
Nishiki Market 26, 206-7
Nishimuraya Honkan 14, 294
Nō 365
Nomura Samurai House 184
Noto Peninsula (Noto-hantō) 189
Nozawa Onsen 167-70
nuclear power 340-1

O

Ōboke 323
Ōhara 228
Okayama 307

Okazaki-kōen 218
Okinawa-hontō 332-6
Ōkōchi sansō 225, 226
okonomiyaki 359
Oku-no-in 290
Onoaida 330
Onomichi 307
onsen 12-13, 167, 367-8
  Bokuden-no-yu 161
  Chūzen-ji Onsen 132
  Fukuchi Onsen 167
  Hakone-Yumoto Onsen 136-7
  Hirauchi Kaichū Onsen 331
  Hirayu Onsen 167
  Hōshi Onsen Chōjūkan 133
  Kamikōchi Onsen Hotel 161
  Kayōtei 13, 191
  Kinosaki 13, 256, 292-3
  Kisoji Resort 178
  Kurama onsen 13, 231
  Nakazaki Sansou Okuhida-no-yu 164
  Ōedo Onsen Monogatari 87
  onsen ryokan 367-8, 370
  Onsen-ji 127
  Shin-Hotaka Onsen 13, 163-6
  Shirahone Onsen 167
  Takaragawa Onsen 133
  tattoos 368
  Tensui Onsen 126
  Utsukushi-ga-hara Onsen & Asama Onsen 174
  Yakushima 331
  Yamanaka Onsen 191
  Yamashiro Onsen 191
  Yudomari Onsen 331
opening hours 381
Osaka 262-76
  accommodation 265-7
  central Osaka 263-5
  Dōtombori 28, 269-71
  drinking & nightlife 271
  festivals & events 265
  food 267-71
  Kita area 262-3, 265-6, 267-8, 271, 272, **264**

Minami area 266-7, 271, 272-3, **266**
  Shinsaibashi 268-9
  shopping 272-3
  sights & activities 262-5
  Tempōzan 265
  tourist information 274
  travel to/from 274-5
  travel within 275
Osaka Aquarium 265
Osaka Itami Airport 276
Osaka-jō 263-4
Ōwakudani 138

P

painting 363
palaces
  Imperial Palace 61
  Katsura Rikyū 227
  Kyoto Imperial Palace (Gosho) 208-9
  Sentō Gosho Palace 209
parks, *see* gardens & parks
passports 385
Peace Memorial Museum 307
Peace Memorial Park 306-7
Peace Park (Nagasaki) 326
people & society 350-3
planning
  basics 48-9
  budgeting 48-9
  calendar of events 42-5
  children, travel with 371-2
  highlights 8-31
  itineraries 32-41
  repeat visitors 46
  resources 47
  travel seasons 42-5, 48-9
politics 341
Ponto-chō 207
pop culture 29
population 340, 351-2
pottery 364
  Naha 333
public holidays 381-2

000 Map pages

R

rail travel, *see* train travel
rāmen 358
religion 340
restaurants, *see* food
ropeways
  Asahidake Ropeway 321
  Kachi Kachi Yama Ropeway 126
  Misen 314
  Shin-Hotaka Ropeway 163
  Tateyama-Kurobe Alpen Route 180
ryokan 14, 15, 369-70
Ryōgoku Kokugikan 112

S

sake 361
samurai 346
Sangatsu-dō 281
Sanja Matsuri 90
Sanmachi-suji 153
sashimi 357
Seison-kaku 184
Senjō-kaku 314
Sensō-ji 86
sentō 353
Setsubun Matsuri at Yoshida-jinja 231
Shibuya 54, 71-3
Shibuya Crossing 71-2
Shiga Kōgen 166-7
Shin-Hotaka-no-yu 165
Shin-Hotaka Onsen 13, 163-6
shinkansen 22, 46, 392
Shirakawa-gō 160
Shiroyama-kōen 154
Shōgatsu (New Year) 42
shokudō 355
shopping 30, 56, *see also* individual locations
shrines 18
  Fuji Sengen-jinja 125
  Fushimi Inari-taisha 197, 226
  Futarasan-jinja 131

  Hakone-jinja 139
  Heian-jingū 222
  Itsukushima-jinja 313
  Kamigamo-jinja 228
  Kasuga Taisha 281
  Kitano Tenman-gū 228
  Meiji-jingū 54, 74
  Taiyūin-byō 131
  Tōshō-gū 129
  Tsurugaoka Hachiman-gū 139-40
  Yasaka-jinja 216
  Yasukuni-jinja 76-7
Shūgaku-in Rikyū 222
skiing 29
  Hakuba 170-1
  Happō-One 170
  Niseko 318-19
snorkelling
  Kerama Islands 336-7
soba 357
solo travellers 382
Sōun-zan 138
Southwest Islands 330-7
Sumida-gawa fireworks 90
sumō 24, 112
sushi 357

T

Takao 233
Takayama 147, 152-60, **154**
  accommodation 155-8
  food 158-9
  sights & activities 153-5
Takayama Matsuri 42-3, 153
Takayama-jinya 153
Tateyama-Kurobe Alpen Route 146
tattoos 368
taxes 381
taxis 389
Tawaraya ryokan 14, 235
tea 360
telephone services 48, 382-3
temples 11, 18, 284, *see also* shrines

Chion-in 216
Daigan-ji 314
Daishō-in 315
Daitoku-ji 209-11
Eikan-dō 230
Engaku-ji 139
Garan 288
Ginkaku-ji 11, 218
Giō-ji 225
Hase-dera 140
Hida Kokubun-ji 154
Higashi Hongan-ji 203
Hōnen-in 11, 218
Hōryū-ji 284
Jakkō-in 228-9
Kenchō-ji 139
Kenin-ji 230
Kinkaku-ji 11, 197, 223
Kiyomizu-dera 197, 213
Kōdai-ji 215
Kōfuku-ji 279
Kongōbu-ji 288
Kurama-dera 230
Manshu-in 234
Myōryū-ji 186
Myōshin-ji 230
Nanzen-ji 196, 219
Nishi Hongan-ji 203
Rinnō-ji 130-1
Ryōan-ji 11, 223
Saihō-ji 227
Sanjūsangen-dō 212
Sanzen-in 228
Sensō-ji 86
Shōren-in 11, 212
Tenryū-ji 224-5
Tōdai-ji 17, 279-80, 282-3
Tōfuku-ji 11, 229
Tō-ji 203
Tōshōdai-ji 284
Yakushi-ji 284
Zenshō-ji 191
Zōjō-ji 70
Tenjin Matsuri 42-3, 265
Teramachi District 154, 186
Tetsugaku-no-Michi (Path of Philosophy) 218
theatre 365-6

theme parks 89
time 383
tipping 48, 381
Tōdai-ji 17, 279-80, 282-3
Tōfuku-ji 229
toilets 383
Tokugawa Mausoleum 288
Tokyo 51-141, **53**
  accommodation 56, 90-7
  Akihabara 78, 104, 117
  architecture 27
  Asakusa 84-7, 97, 105-6, **92**
  drinking & nightlife 105-9
  Ebisu 70-1, 93-4, 101, 107, 114, **76**
  entertainment 109-12
  festivals & events 90
  food 97-105
  getaways 57
  getting around 57, 118-19
  Ginza 64-5, 91-3, 99-100, 106, 113-14, **66**
  greater Tokyo map **62-3**
  Harajuku 73-5, 102-3, 108-9, 115-16, **82**
  highlights 54-5
  Iidabashi & Northwest Tokyo 76-7
  itineraries 58-9
  Kagurazaka 77
  Marunouchi (Tokyo Station area) 60-1, 90-1, 98-9, 112-13, **66**, **90-1**
  Meguro 70-1, 93-4, 101, 107, 114, **76**
  museums 61
  Odaiba 87-90, **98**
  resources 57
  riverboats 119
  Roppongi 65-70, 93, 100-1, 106, 114, **72**
  Shibuya 71-3, 94-5, 102, 107-8, 115, **84**
  Shinjuku & West Tokyo 75-6, 95-7, 103-4, 109-12, 116-17, **88**
  shopping 56, 112-20
  sights & activities 60-90
  Sumida-gawa 84-7, 97, 105-6, **92**
  Tokyo Bay 87-90, **98**
  tourist information 117-18
  train travel 119-20
  travel to/from 118
  travel within 118-19
  Tsukiji 64-5, 68-9, 91-3, 99-100, 106, **66**
  Tsukiji Fish Market 68-9
  Ueno 78-84, 97, 104-5, 117-20, **96**
  walking tour 58-9
Tokyo Metropolitan Government Offices 75
Tokyo National Museum 79, 80-1
Tokyo Sky Tree 46, 85
Tokyo Tower 67
tonkatsu 359
tourist information 383, *see also individual locations*
train travel 389-93, *see also individual locations*
  passes & discount tickets 390-1, 393
  reservations 392-3
  schedules & information 393
  shinkansen 46, 392-3
travel to/from Japan 385-6
travel within Japan 49, 386-93
trekking, *see* hiking
Tsukiji Fish Market 16, 55, 68-70
Tsumago 19, 147, 178-9
Tsumago-honjin 178
tsunami 340-1
Tsurugi-dake 163
tuna auction 70

U
udon 357
Ueno-kōen 82
Ueno Zoo 84

Umeda Sky Building 263
Utsukushi-ga-hara-kōgen 174

V
vacations 381-2
vegans 357
vegetarians 357
visas 48, 384

W
walking tours
  Tokyo 58-9
  Kyoto 200-1
war memorials
  Nagasaki 325-6
  Okinawa-hontō 335-6
weather 42-5, 48, 377
websites 47
weights 375
wi-fi 48, 378
women in Japan 353
women travellers 384
wood-block prints 363
World Heritage Sites
  Atomic Bomb Dome 306
  Kamigamo-jinja 228
  Miyajima 312-16
  Nara 276
  Nikkō 129
  Yakushima 330-2

Y
yakitori 358
Yakushima 330-2
Yanaka-reien 83
Yari-ga-take 163
Yoshijima Heritage House 153

Z
Zamami-jima 337

NOTES

How to Use This Book

These symbols give you the vital information for each listing:

⏩	Telephone Numbers	🛜	Wi-Fi Access	🚌	Bus
☺	Opening Hours	🏊	Swimming Pool	⛴	Ferry
Ⓟ	Parking	🍴	Vegetarian Selection	Ⓜ	Metro
⊝	Nonsmoking	📖	English-Language Menu	Ⓢ	Subway
✳	Air-Conditioning	🧒	Family-Friendly	⊖	London Tube
@	Internet Access	🐾	Pet-Friendly	🚋	Tram

All reviews are ordered in our authors' preference, starting with their most preferred option. Additionally:

Sights are arranged in the geographic order that we suggest you visit them, and within this order, by author preference.

Eating and Sleeping reviews are ordered by price range (budget, mid-range, top end) and within these ranges, by author preference.

Look out for these icons:

FREE No payment required

🌿 A green or sustainable option

Our authors have nominated these places as demonstrating a strong commitment to sustainability – for example by supporting local communities and producers, operating in an environmentally friendly way, or supporting conservation projects.

Map Legend

Note: Not all symbols displayed appear on the maps in this book

Sights
- 🏖 Beach
- 🐦 Bird Sanctuary
- 🛕 Buddhist
- 🏰 Castle/Palace
- ✝ Christian
- ☯ Confucian
- 🛕 Hindu
- ☪ Islamic
- 卐 Jain
- ✡ Jewish
- ❶ Monument
- 🏛 Museum/Gallery/Historic Building
- 🏚 Ruin
- ♨ Sento Hot Baths/Onsen
- ⛩ Shinto
- 🛕 Sikh
- ☯ Taoist
- 🍷 Winery/Vineyard
- 🐾 Zoo/Wildlife Sanctuary
- ● Other Sight

Activities, Courses & Tours
- 🏄 Bodysurfing
- 🤿 Diving/Snorkelling
- 🛶 Canoeing/Kayaking
- ● Course/Tour
- ⛷ Skiing
- 🤿 Snorkelling
- 🏄 Surfing
- 🏊 Swimming/Pool
- 🚶 Walking
- 🏄 Windsurfing
- ● Other Activity

Sleeping
- 🛏 Sleeping
- ⛺ Camping

Eating
- 🍴 Eating

Drinking & Nightlife
- ☕ Drinking & Nightlife
- ☕ Cafe

Entertainment
- 🎭 Entertainment

Shopping
- 🛍 Shopping

Transport
- ✈ Airport
- ⊗ Border crossing
- 🚌 Bus
- 🚠 Cable car/Funicular
- 🚲 Cycling
- ⛴ Ferry
- Ⓜ Metro station
- 🚝 Monorail
- Ⓟ Parking
- ⛽ Petrol station
- Ⓢ Subway station
- 🚕 Taxi
- 🚉 Train station/Railway
- 🚋 Tram
- Ⓤ Underground station
- ● Other Transport

Information
- 🏦 Bank
- 🏛 Embassy/Consulate
- ✚ Hospital/Medical
- @ Internet
- 👮 Police
- 📮 Post Office
- ☎ Telephone
- 🚻 Toilet
- ⓘ Tourist Information
- ● Other Information

Geographic
- 🏖 Beach
- 🗼 Lighthouse
- 👁 Lookout
- ▲ Mountain/Volcano
- 🌴 Oasis
- 🏞 Park
-)(Pass
- 🧺 Picnic Area
- 💧 Waterfall

Population
- ✪ Capital (National)
- ◉ Capital (State/Province)
- ● City/Large Town
- ● Town/Village

Boundaries
- International
- State/Province
- Disputed
- Regional/Suburb
- Marine Park
- Cliff; Wall

Routes
- Tollway
- Freeway
- Primary
- Secondary
- Tertiary
- Lane
- Unsealed road
- Plaza/Mall
- Steps
- Tunnel
- Pedestrian overpass
- Walking Tour
- Walking Tour detour
- Path/Walking Trail

Hydrography
- River, Creek
- Intermittent River
- Canal
- Water
- Dry/Salt Lake
- Reef

Areas
- Airport/Runway
- Beach/Desert
- Cemetery (Christian)
- Cemetery (Other)
- Glacier
- Mudflat
- Park/Forest
- Sight (Building)
- Sportsground
- Swamp

REBECCA MILNER

Tokyo Rebecca moved to Tokyo from California in 2002 for 'one year' that turned into 10. She's since lived west of Shinjuku, east of the Sumida-gawa and now calls Meguro home. Even when not on assignment, you can find her cycling around the city in search of new cafes or tracking down obscure onsen in the countryside. She also writes a dining column for the *Japan Times* and has written about travel in Japan for the *Guardian* and *CNN Travel*.

KATE MORGAN

Mt Fuji & Around Tokyo Kate's first encounter with Japan was back in 2005 when she moved to Osaka to teach English to kindergarten kids. Since returning to Australia, she manages to find her way back to her 'second home' every couple of years to eat *tako-yaki*, soak in onsen and watch punk bands in basement live houses. Kate lives in Melbourne, Australia, and works as a freelance writer and editor. She has written for other Lonely Planet books such as *Phuket* and *Southern Africa*.

BENEDICT WALKER

The Japan Alps & Central Honshū Inspired by a primary school teacher, or the memory of a past life, Ben's love of Japan blossomed early. At 17 he was runner-up in the Australian finals of the Japan Foundation Japanese Speech Contest, and had made two solo trips to Japan. In 1998, with a degree in communications under his belt, Ben hit the road in earnest. After long stints in Canada and Europe, he found himself teaching English in Osaka until his tattered Lonely Planet guide led him to the mountains of Matsumoto, where he found work as a translator and lived like a local. Dividing his time between Canada, Australia and Japan, Ben has also been known to manage the travel needs of rock stars and dabble in the arts. For the latest check out: www.wordsandjourneys.com.

WENDY YANAGIHARA

Okinawa & the Southwestern Islands As the daughter of an *Issei* (first generation Japanese-American) in California, Wendy grew up summering in Japan with her mother. It wasn't until this book, however, that she had the pleasure of exploring the 88-temple pilgrimage, the diversity of Ryukyuan dialects and an affinity for *jiimami-dōfu*. Previously, she has worked on several editions of the Japan, Tokyo and Tokyo Encounter guidebooks for Lonely Planet.

Our Story

A beat-up old car, a few dollars in the pocket and a sense of adventure. In 1972 that's all Tony and Maureen Wheeler needed for the trip of a lifetime – across Europe and Asia overland to Australia. It took several months, and at the end – broke but inspired – they sat at their kitchen table writing and stapling together their first travel guide, *Across Asia on the Cheap*. Within a week they'd sold 1500 copies. Lonely Planet was born.

Today, Lonely Planet has offices in Melbourne, London and Oakland, with more than 600 staff and writers. We share Tony's belief that 'a great guidebook should do three things: inform, educate and amuse'.

Our Writers

CHRIS ROWTHORN

Coordinating Author, Kyoto, Kansai Born in England and raised in the USA, Chris has lived in Kyoto since 1992. Soon after his arrival in Kyoto, Chris started studying the Japanese language and culture. In 1995 he became a regional correspondent for the *Japan Times*. He joined Lonely Planet in 1996 and has worked on guides to Kyoto, Tokyo, Japan and hiking in Japan. When not on the road, he spends his time seeking out Kyoto's best restaurants, temples, hiking trails and gardens. Chris wrote a book in Japanese with professional guide Koko Ijuin, called *Pro ga Oshieru: Genba no Eigo Tsuyaku Gaido Skiru* (Pro English Guide Skills), for Japanese guides who want to explain the country to Western tourists. He conducts walking tours of Kyoto, Nara and Tokyo. For more on Chris, check out his website at www.chrisrowthorn.com or his blog at www.insidekyoto.com.

Read more about Chris at:
lonelyplanet.com/members/chrisrowthorn

LAURA CRAWFORD

Osaka, Hiroshima & Western Honshū English born and Australian raised, Laura first arrived in Japan as an undergraduate studying Japanese at a university in Kansai. She later travelled up and down the country, set up home in Osaka for two years, returned to Oz to write a thesis on Japanese English, and eventually landed a job as an editor in Lonely Planet's Melbourne office. Her favourite on-the-road task: touring the Kuniga coast and seeing incredibly old trees on the Oki Islands.

TRENT HOLDEN

Mt Fuji & Around Tokyo After several trips to Japan, Trent jumped at the opportunity to head back to discover its coastal beaches and conquer Fuji. A champion of budget travel, he's a connoisseur of combini store *bentō* and vending-machine booze, and a lover of Japanese punk and *okonomiyaki*. Trent has co-authored more than a dozen books for Lonely Planet including guides to India, Nepal and the Philippines.

CRAIG MCLACHLAN

Hokkaidō Craig has walked the length of Japan (3200km in 99 days!), climbed Japan's 100 Famous Mountains, hiked the 88 Temples of Shikoku, cycled the 33 Temples of Saigoku, and walked from the Sea of Japan to the Pacific scaling all of Japan's 3000m peaks! Books on these adventures have been published in English and Japanese. A 'freelance anything', Craig has an MBA from the University of Hawaii and is also a pilot, hiking guide, karate instructor and Japanese interpreter. See www.craigmclachlan.com.

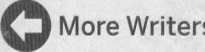 **More Writers** . . . .

Published by Lonely Planet Publications Pty Ltd
ABN 36 005 607 983
2nd edition – November 2013
ISBN 978 1 74220 116 0
© Lonely Planet 2013   Photographs © as indicated 2013
10 9 8 7 6 5 4 3 2 1
Printed in China